The Apples Of New York

S. A. Beach

Printing Statement:

Due to the very old age and scarcity of this book,
many of the pages may be hard to read due to the
blurring of the original text, possible missing pages,
missing text, dark backgrounds and other issues
beyond our control.

Because this is such an important and rare work, we
believe it is best to reproduce this book regardless of
its original condition.

Thank you for your understanding.

INDEX TO ILLUSTRATIONS.

HALF-TONE PLATES.

	FACING PAGE.
Admirable	2
Arctic	8
Blenheim	22
Cabashea	28
Cox Orange	42
Cranberry Pippin	44
Early Harvest	50
Early Joe	52
Early Ripe	54
Fall Orange	60
Gladstone	76
Golden Sweet	82
Haas	90
Hawley	94
Hoadley	100
Hook	102
Jefferis	108
Jersey Sweet	110
Judson	112
Landsberg	118
Late Strawberry	120
Longfield	122
Lowell	128
McMahon	136
Magog	138
Ohio Pippin	148
Parry White	156
Patten	158
Pomona	164
Porter	166
Pumpkin Russet	170
Sharp	198
Sops of Wine	202
Sour Bough	204
Tetofsky	220
Workaroe	246
Montreal Beauty (Crab)	262

COLOR PLATES.

Alexander	4
Benoni	16
Bismarck	20

iii

COLOR PLATES — Continued.

FACING PAGE.

Champlain	30
Chenango	34
Collamer	36
Constantine	40
Cranberry Pippin	44
Detroit Red	46
Dudley	48
Early Harvest	50
Early Strawberry	56
Fall Pippin	62
Fameuse	66
Fanny	68
Fishkill	70
Gravenstein	84
Keswick	116
Lee Sweet (section)	136
Lee Sweet (whole fruit), see Volume I	230
McIntosh	132
McLellan (Section)	136
McLellan (whole fruit)	134
Maiden Blush	140
Mother	144
Munson	146
Oldenburg	150
Pease	160
Primate	168
Pumpkin Sweet	172
Red Astrachan	178
Red June	180
Ribston	184
Shiawassee	200
Stump	208
Sweet Bough	216
Twenty Ounce	228
Victoria	232
Wealthy	236
Williams	242
Wolf River	244
Yellow Transparent	248
Excelsior (Crab)	254
Hyslop (Crab)	256
Large Red Siberian (Crab)	258
Martha (Crab)	260
Red Siberian (Crab)	264
Transcendent (Crab)	266

THE APPLES OF NEW YORK.

ADIRONDACK.

REFERENCE. 1. Taylor, *U. S. Pom. Rpt.*, 1893:285.
SYNONYMS. None.

This variety is said to have originated in Clinton county. We have received no reports of its being grown outside of the locality of its origin. Taylor gives the following description of it. (1). "Roundish, conical; regular, of medium size, with smooth surface, becoming glossy when rubbed; color rich yellow, washed and striped with red; dots small, straw color, slightly elevated; cavity large, round, deep, flaring; stem of medium length and thickness, slightly knobbed; basin small, nearly round, very shallow, with convex sides, slightly and regularly ribbed and downy; calyx segments rather small, meeting; eye small, closed. Skin thin, tough; core large, broad, heart-shaped, moderately open, clasping; seeds numerous, oval, plump, grayish brown; flesh yellowish white, granular, rather dry, tender; flavor mild subacid; quality good. Season, October to January in Clinton county, New York. Tree a good grower; resembles Baldwin in its bearing habit; hardy at its place of origin. This variety is said to have originated from seed of Westfield (Seek-No-Further) crossed with Hubbardston. It is a promising early winter apple for Northern New York and New England."

ADMIRABLE.

REFERENCES. 1. Downing, 1869:354. 2. Leroy, 1873:813. fig. 3. Hogg, 1884:214. 4. *N. Y. Sta. An. Rpt.*, 8:339, 348. 1889. 5. Beach, *Ib.*, 11:589, 595, 1892. 6. Beach and Clark, *N. Y. Sta. Bul.*, 248:110. 1904.

SYNONYMS. ADMIRABLE (6). SMALL'S ADMIRABLE (1, 2, 3, 4, 5). *Small Admirable* (6).

Fruit green or yellow, not particularly attractive. At its best it is very good for dessert use, but as grown at this Station it usually ranks but fair to good in quality and the fruit is very apt to show imperfect spots in the flesh which are evidently due to some physiological defect. In England it is regarded as an excellent kitchen and dessert apple and the tree is said to be an immense bearer and well adapted for dwarf culture (3). So far as tested at this Station the tree has been an annual cropper and very productive, often yielding full crops. A portion of the fruit may sometimes be kept through the winter, but ordinarily the season for this variety is November and December (6). Not recommended for cultivation in New York.

Historical. This variety originated in England (2, 3).

TREE.

Tree dwarfish with short, stout, slow-growing branches. *Form* rather flat, spreading and somewhat drooping. *Twigs* short, somewhat curved, stout to rather slender; internodes short to above medium. *Bark* dark brown tinged with olive-green, lightly streaked with scarf-skin; pubescent. *Lenticels* numerous, small to medium, oval, slightly raised. *Buds* deeply set in bark, medium to small, broad, plump, obtuse to somewhat acute, appressed or free, pubescent.

FRUIT.

Fruit quite uniform in size and shape for any particular crop but varies under different conditions from below medium to above. *Form* oblate conic to roundish conic, pretty regular but sometimes indistinctly ribbed. *Stem* medium to long, slender, pubescent. *Cavity* acute, moderately deep to deep, broad, smooth or thinly russeted. *Calyx* closed or open; lobes reflexed. *Basin* moderately shallow, rather narrow, sometimes abrupt, somewhat furrowed and wrinkled.

Skin varies from pale green to attractive lemon-yellow, sometimes with brownish blush. *Dots* numerous, small, light or russet.

Calyx tube rather narrow, elongated funnel-form. *Stamens* median.

Core rather large, somewhat abaxile; cells open; core lines clasping. *Carpels* long, obovate. *Seeds* rather large, long, plump, pointed, medium brown.

Flesh whitish, firm, moderately coarse, crisp, quite juicy, mild subacid, very aromatic, good to very good in quality in well grown fruit.

Season October to January.

ALBION.

Fruit intermediate in type between Fall Pippin and Lowell. In color it resembles Fall Pippin but in form it is more like Lowell. Season October to late fall or early winter. We have been unable to learn the origin of this variety. It is but little cultivated in this State.

FRUIT.

Fruit large to very large. *Form* roundish oblong, irregular. *Stem* short to medium, slender. *Cavity* acuminate, deep, medium to wide, russeted. *Calyx* small to medium, tightly closed; lobes short, narrow, acute. *Basin* shallow, medium to narrow in width, obtuse, furrowed and wrinkled.

Skin smooth, waxy, pale yellow mingled with green. *Dots* green or russet or submerged and whitish.

Calyx tube narrow, cone-shape to funnel-form. *Stamens* marginal.

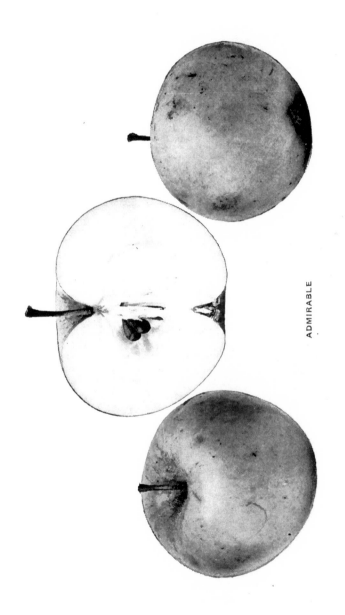

ADMIRABLE

Core large, abaxile; cells open or partly closed; core lines clasping. *Carpels* elongated, ovate, pointed, mucronate. *Seeds* few, medium to large, rather narrow, long, acute.

Flesh moderately coarse, very tender, juicy, mild subacid, good.

ALEXANDER.

REFERENCES. 1. Forsyth, **1824**:131. 2. *London Hort. Soc. Cat.*, **1831**: No. 10. 3. Kenrick, **1832**:65. 4. Floy-Lindley, **1833**:11. 5. *Mag. Hort.*, 1:395. 1835. 6. Downing, **1845**:79. fig. 7. Thomas, **1849**:146. 8. Cole, **1849**:118. 9. Emmons, *Nat. Hist. N. Y.*, 3:32. 1851. 10. Barry, **1851**:282. 11. Elliott, **1854**:120. 12. Gregg, **1857**:41. 13. Hooper, **1857**:11. 14. *Am. Pom. Soc. Cat.*, **1862**. 15. Warder, **1867**:510. 16. Fitz, **1872**:152. 17. Leroy, **1873**:333. fig. 18. *Ia. Hort. Soc. Rpt.*, **1879**:538. 19. Downing, **1881**:11 index, app. 20. Hogg, **1884**:72. 21. Roach, *Montreal Hort. Soc. Rpt.*, **1886-87**:27. 22. Wickson, **1889**:244. 23. Lyon, *Mich. Hort. Soc. Rpt.*, **1890**:288. 24. Bailey, *An. Hort.*, **1892**:234. 25. Hoskins, *Rural N. Y.*, 53:278. 1894. 26. Gaucher, **1894**: No. 14. col. pl. 27. Dempsey, *Ont. Stas. An. Rpt.*, 1:24. 1894. 28. Burrill and McCluer, *Ill. Sta. Bul.*, 45:312. 1896. 29. Stinson, *Ark. Sta. Bul.*, 43:102. 1896. 30. Waugh, *Vt. Sta. Bul.*, 61:29. 1897. 31. *Can. Hort.*, 20:283. 1897. 32. Woolverton, *Ont. Fr. Stas. An. Rpt.*, 5:5. 1898. figs. 33. Bunyard, *Jour. Roy. Hort. Soc.*, **1898**:354. 34. Craig, *Cyclopedia of Amer. Hort.*, 3:1404. 1901. 35. Hansen, *S. D. Sta. Bul.*, 76:22. 1902. 36. Munson, *Me. Sta. Rpt.*, **1902**:83, 85, 86. 37. Budd-Hansen, **1903**:36. fig. 38. Powell and Fulton, *U. S. B. P. I. Bul.*, 48:36. 1903. 39. Beach and Clark, *N. Y. Sta. Bul.*, 248:111. 1904. 40. Scriber, *Can. Hort.*, 28:248. 1905.

SYNONYMS. *Albertin* (17, 26). ALEXANDER (1, 2, 5, 6, 7, 8, 9, 10, 11, 12, 13, 14, 15, 16, 18, 19, 21, 22, 23, 24, 27, 28, 29, 30, 31, 32, 34, 35, 36, 37, 38, 39, 40). *Alexander*(34, 26). *Alexander the First*(31). *Alexandre*(17, 26). *Aporta* (3, 4, 6, 9, 13, 17, 20, 26, 31). *Aporta Nalivia* (26). *Aubertin* (17, 26). *Beauty of Queen* (17, 26). *Belle d'Orleans* (17, 26). *Comte Woronzoff* (17, 26). *Corail* (17, 26). *English King* (19, 26). *Empereur Alexandre I* (17, 26). *Empereur Alexandre de Russie* (17, 26). *Empereur de Russie* (17, 26). EMPEROR ALEXANDER (3, 4, 20, 33). *Emperor Alexander* (2, 6, 9, 10, 11, 13, 26, 32). *Fin d'Automne* (17, 26). *Grand Alexander* (26). GRAND-ALEXANDRE (17). *Grand Alexandre* (26). *Gros-Alexandre* (17, 26). *Jolly Gentleman* (26). KAISER ALEXANDER (26). *Korallen Apfel* (26). *Phœnix* (26). *Phönix* (17, 26). *Pomona Britannica* (17, 26). *Président Napoléon* (17, 26). *Russian Emperor* (2, 6, 9, 13, 20, 26). *Stoke Tulip* (26). *Wolf River* incorrectly (39). *Wunderapfel* (26).

Alexander is a typical representative of the class of Russian apples commonly known as the Aport group. Fruit very large, attractive red or striped, coarse in texture, medium to good in quality, suitable for culinary rather than for dessert use. The fruit is apt to crack and decay about the stem and calyx and often becomes discolored where it is chafed by constantly rubbing

against some twig or branch; there is also a considerable loss from
premature dropping of the fruit. Notwithstanding these faults
many fruit growers now regard Alexander favorably as a commercial variety as in some markets there is a strong demand for
the fruit at good prices. It is being used to some extent for export trade (40). Its season begins in September and extends
through October or into November. It may be held in cold
storage till November. It goes down quickly and as it does not
stand heat well before going into storage it should be shipped the
day it is picked and under ice (39). As it ripens continuously
during a period of from four to six weeks it should have more
than one picking. The tree is hardy, vigorous and moderately
productive. In some localities it is subject to blight. It can be
recommended for planting in commercial orchards to a limited
extent. In the West it is now largely supplanted by its Wisconsin
seedling Wolf River (34, 36).

Historical. Introduced into England from Russia in 1817 (20). The
exact date of the introduction of this variety into America is not known.
The Massachusetts Horticultural Society made several importations of
European varieties which were distributed among the members of the society.
Mr. Manning exhibited what was supposed to be Alexander before the
Massachusetts Horticultural Society at its meeting on September 18, 1830.
Whether this was Alexander or not, the shipment of varieties of which
Alexander was one had evidently been made prior to that date.[1]

It has been widely disseminated and is now pretty well known in the apple
growing districts from the Atlantic to the Pacific. Thus far it has not been
grown to any considerable extent in New York state but at the present time
its cultivation is on the increase.

TREE.

Tree large to medium, vigorous to moderately vigorous with long, stout
branches. *Form* upright spreading to roundish, open and somewhat inclined
to droop after bearing heavy crops. *Twigs* short, curved, stout with large
terminal buds; internodes medium. *Bark* brown mingled with olive-green,
lightly streaked with scarf-skin; slightly pubescent near tips. *Lenticels*
scattering, medium in size, oval, raised. *Buds* medium in size, plump, obtuse,
free, slightly pubescent.

FRUIT.

Fruit large, uniform in size and shape. *Form* roundish conic to slightly
oblate conic, regular or approaching broadly angular, symmetrical. *Stem*
medium to rather short, moderately thick. *Cavity* acute to acuminate, deep,
broad, symmetrical, occasionally lipped, russeted, often with broad, con-

1 *N. E. Farmer,* Sept. 24, 1830:78.

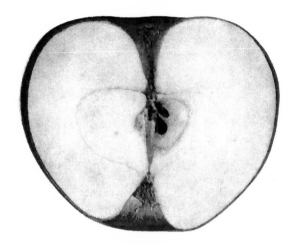

ALEXANDER   (Reduced Size)

spicuous, outspreading russet rays. *Calyx* medium to large, usually open; lobes medium to short, rather narrow, acute. *Basin* rather small, deep, narrow to nearly medium in width, abrupt, nearly smooth, symmetrical.

Skin moderately thick, tough, smooth, glossy, somewhat waxy, greenish or pale yellow deepening to orange-yellow in the sun, often entirely overspread with lively red or handsomely striped and splashed with bright carmine. *Dots* inconspicuous, small, scattering. *Prevailing effect* red or striped.

Calyx tube variable, long to short, wide to medium, conical to funnelshape. *Stamens* median to basal.

Core small, usually axile; cells often not uniformly developed, closed or very slightly open; core lines slightly clasping. *Carpels* elliptical to slightly ovate, emarginate. *Seeds* medium in size, wide, short, rather plump, obtuse to acute.

Flesh nearly white with faint yellow tinge, firm, coarse, moderately crisp, tender, juicy, mild subacid, fair to good.

Season September and October or early November.

AMSTERDAM.

REFERENCES. 1. Downing, 1876:43 app. 2. Ragan, *U. S. B. P. I. Bul.*, 56:20. 1905.

SYNONYMS. AMSTERDAM (2). AMSTERDAM SWEET (1). *Amsterdam Sweet* (2). *Hightop Sweet* incorrectly (1).

Downing describes this fruit as medium in size, pale greenish-yellow, striped and splashed with light and dark bright red; flesh white, half fine, tender, juicy, rather rich, sweet, slightly aromatic; season October and November. Origin Amsterdam, N. Y., on the farm of Joseph Britten (1). We find no account of Amsterdam except the one above mentioned, and have not seen the variety.

ANISIM.

REFERENCES. 1. Schroeder, *Montreal Hort. Soc. Rpt.*, 1886-87:71. 2. Hoskins, *Rural N. Y.*, 52:299. 1893. figs. 3. Greene, *Minn. Sta. Bul.*, 32:240. 1893. 4. Budd, *Ia. Sta. Bul.*, 31:334. 1895. 5. Thomas, 1897:626. 6. Budd, *Ia. Sta. Bul.*, 41:66, 69, 71. 1899. 7. *Am. Pom. Soc. Cat.*, 1899:15. 8. Munson, *Me. Sta. Rpt.*, 1902:83, 86, 95. 9. Hansen, *S. D. Sta. Bul.*, 76:23. 1902. fig. 10. Budd-Hansen, 1903:38. fig.

SYNONYMS. ANISIM (1, 2, 3, 4, 5, 6, 7, 8, 9, 10). *Anisim* of Peterson (9). *Borsdorfer* of Wragg (9). *13 M* (3, 8, of Budd 9). *14 M* of Budd (9). *Good Peasant* of Patten (9). *Jonathan* of the North (4). *Swedish Borsdorf* of Patten (9). *Zuzoff* of Tuttle (9).

Hansen (9) reports that this Russian apple is proving very valuable in Minnesota and other parts of the Northwest. It may be of some value in those portions of New York state where superior hardiness is a prime requisite. Hansen's description is given below. "Tree a strong grower in the nursery and orchard and a prodigious bearer; young trees upright, spreading with age; limbs long, slender with a very strong shoulder; leaves narrow, pointed, dark green. The beautiful color of the fruit attracts favorable attention — Fruit below medium, roundish conical, slightly angular; surface greenish-yellow, covered almost wholly with a beautiful dark crimson, with heavy blue bloom; dots white, minute; cavity regular, acute, usually slightly russeted; stem medium; basin narrow, very shallow, corrugated, sometimes flat; calyx closed. Core closed, clasping; tube short, broad; stamens median, flesh greenish white, with green veins, good. Early winter."

ANTONOVKA.

REFERENCES. 1. *Montreal Hort. Soc. Rpt.*, **8**:28, 70, 130. 1881–82. fig. 2. Budd, *Ia. Hort. Soc. Rpt.*, **1882**:76. 3. Gibb, *Ib.*, **1883**:432. 4. Budd, *Am. Pom. Soc. Rpt.*, **1883**:71. 5. Ib., *Ia. Agr. Coll. Bul.*, **1883**:22. 6. Ib., **1885**:8. 7. Van Deman, *U. S. Pom. Rpt.*, **1886**:272. fig. 8. Schroeder, *Montreal Hort. Soc. Rpt.*, **1886–87**:72. 9. Budd, *Ia. Agr. Coll. Bul.*, **1890**:24. 10. *Can. Hort.*, **13**:175, 216. 1890. 11. Budd, *Ia. Sta. Bul.*, **19**:537. 1892. 12. Taylor, *Mc. Pom. Soc. Rpt.*, **1892**:57, 58. 13. Bailey, *An. Hort.*, **1892**:234. 14. *Can. Hort.*, **16**:359. 1893. 15. *Ib.*, **17**:289, 290, 291. 1894. 16. Troop, *Ind. Sta. Bul.*, **53**:124. 1894. 17. *Nat. Nurseryman*, **3**:32. 1895. 18. Stinson, *Ark. Sta. Bul.*, **43**:104. 1896. 19. Hamilton, *Can. Hort.*, **20**:412. 1897. 20. *Am. Pom. Soc. Cat.*, **1897**:11. 21. Thomas, **1897**:286, 626. fig. 22. Budd, *Ia. Sta. Bul.*, **41**:66, 69, 70, 71, 73, 74. 1899. 23. Troop, *Ind. Sta. Rpt.*, **1899**:79. 24. Macoun, *Can. Dept. Agr. Rpt.*, **1899**:78. 25. Hansen, *S. D. Sta. Bul.*, **76**:25. 1902. fig. 26. Farrand, *Mich. Sta. Bul.*, **205**:43. 1903. 27. Budd-Hansen, **1903**:38. fig.

SYNONYMS. ANTENOVKA (23). ANTONOVKA (1, 2, 3, 4, 5, 6, 7, 8, 9, 10, 11, 12, 13, 14, 16, 18, 19, 20, 21, 22, 24, 25, 26, 27). ANTONOWKA (15, 17). *Antony* (3, 14). *Bergamot*, 424 (25). *Cinnamon* (24). *German Calville* (24). *German Calville*, *324* (spurious) (25). *No. 224* (25). *No. 236* (1, 2, 4, 5, 6, 9, 25). *Possarts Nalivia* (2, 4, 5). *Russian Gravenstein*, *105* (25). *26 M* (1, 2, 4, 5, 9, 25). *Vargul*, *277* (25).

A Russian fruit of no practical value for this state. Hansen (25) describes it as "large, roundish, irregular, obscurely angular; surface yellow; dots minute, raised, white, suffused; cavity deep, regular, with radiating, often large patch of russet, stem medium; basin abrupt, corrugated or wavy; calyx closed. Core closed; cells ovate, slit; tube funnel-shaped; stamens median; seeds ten to sixteen, small, pointed, plump, a few imperfect; flesh yellow, juicy, sprightly spicy subacid, good. October."

APORT.

REFERENCE. 1. Gibb, *Montreal Hort. Soc. Rpt.*, **8**:32. 1881–82. SYNONYMS. None.

This name is applied to a pretty well defined group of Russian apples. Alexander is the typical variety of this group.

The name Aport has also been applied to a particular Russian variety which resembles Alexander closely.[1]

1 Hansen, *S. D. Sta. Bul.*, **76**:26. 1902.

APORT ORIENT.

REFERENCES. **1.** *Montreal Hort. Soc. Rpt.*, **8**:73. 1881–82. **2.** *Ia. Hort. Soc. Rpt.*, **1882**:78. **3.** Budd, *Ia. Agr. Coll. Bul.*, **1883**:30. **4.** *Montreal Hort. Soc. Rpt.*, **9**:82. 1883. fig. **5.** Budd, *Ia. Agr. Coll. Bul.*, **1885**:9. **6.** Schroeder, *Montreal Hort. Soc. Rpt.*, **12**:72. 1886–87. **7.** Budd, *Ia. Agr. Coll. Bul.*, **1890**:24. **8.** ib., *Ia. Sta. Bul.*, **19**:538. 1892. **9.** (?) Beach, *N. Y. Sta. An. Rpt.*, **13**:579. 1894. **10.** Budd, *Ia. Sta. Bul.*, **41**:71. 1899. **11.** Munson, *Me. Sta. Rpt.*, **1902**:83. **12.** Hansen, *S. D. Sta. Bul.*, **76**:26. 1902. **13.** Budd-Hansen, **1903**:39.

SYNONYMS. APORT (1, 2, 3, 4, 5, 6, 7, 11, 12, 13). APORT ORIENT (8, 10). (APORT ORIENTAL, 9)? *No. 12 Orel* (7). *No. 252* (1, 2, 3, 4, 7, 11). *23 M* (1, 2, 3). *Oporto* (4).

A Russian apple, large, yellow, mostly covered with mixed red, striped and splashed with dark crimson, very attractive but coarse-grained and inferior in quality. It begins to ripen about the middle of August. The tree comes into bearing rather young and gives full crops in alternate years. Not recommended for New York state.

ARCTIC.

REFERENCES. **1.** *N. Y. Sta. An. Rpt.*, **8**:347. 1889. **2.** Munson, *Me. Sta Rpt.*, **1896**:70. **3.** Waugh, *Vt. Sta. Bul.*, **61**:29. 1897. **4.** *Am. Pom. Soc. Cat.*, **1899**:15. **5.** Beach, *W. N. Y. Hort. Soc. Rpt.*, **1900**:34. **6.** Waugh, *Vt. Sta. An. Rpt.*, **14**:286. 1901. **7.** *Me. Sta. Rpt.*, **1902**:83, 89, 95, 96. **8.** Budd-Hansen, **1903**:39. **9.** Powell and Fulton, *U. S. B. P. I. Bul.*, **48**:36. 1903.

SYNONYMS. None.

One of the most valuable characteristics of the Arctic is its ability to endure cold climates. It has probably been planted more extensively in Northern New York, New England and Canada than in any other regions. It is reported as being pretty hardy in Central Iowa where the climate is too severe for Baldwin, Rhode Island *Greening* and other varieties of a similar grade of hardiness. Munson (7) states that it is worthy of trial where Baldwin will not succeed. The tree is vigorous. In some districts it has the reputation of being productive, in others it is called a shy bearer. The fruit is very attractive, mild subacid, good but not high in quality. It somewhat resembles Baldwin in size and color, but is more oblate, and the skin is of a somewhat lighter and brighter red than that of Baldwin. The cavity is often marked with outspreading rays of reddish or green russet as in the Baldwin. The dots are round, scattering, whitish, often areolar and not elongated in the region of the cavity as they often are on the Baldwin. It does not keep so well as the Hubbardston. In Western New York its season may extend from October to February, but when grown farther north is later (6, 7). In some parts of Northern New York it is being grafted over to other sorts. Waugh (6) states that this is also being done in the Isle La Motte region of Vermont, nevertheless he believes it will be grown there in moderate quantities for years to come.

Historical. The Arctic was introduced by Mr. O. K. Gerrish, now of Lakeville, Mass. He states that it originated as a chance seedling in a garden near Cape Vincent, N. Y., about 1862. About 1887 he bought the tree from Mr. John H. Esseltyne on whose farm it was growing. After taking propagating wood from it, he destroyed the tree to prevent theft of scions.

TREE.

Tree a moderate grower with long, moderately stout branches. *Form* spreading and open somewhat like Tompkins King. *Twigs* short, stocky; internodes medium length; slightly pubescent near tips. *Bark* dark reddish-brown, streaked and mottled with thin scarf-skin. *Lenticels* scattering, conspicuous, medium to large, roundish to somewhat elongated, raised. *Buds* medium to large, broad, obtuse, flat, free, pubescent. *Leaves* large, dark green, broad and rather thick.

FRUIT.

Fruit above medium to large. *Form* oblate, sometimes roundish conic, often faintly ribbed; pretty uniform in size and shape. *Stem* short and rather thick to medium. *Cavity* moderately shallow to rather deep, broad, usually symmetrical or slightly furrowed, and having outspreading rays of red or green russet. *Calyx* medium to rather large; segments broad, obtuse, closed or partly open. *Basin* abrupt, medium to wide and deep, often compressed or slightly furrowed and corrugated.

Skin nearly smooth, slightly roughened by the light russet or whitish dots; deep yellow or greenish-yellow, often almost wholly covered with a bright red obscuring the stripes of deeper red.

Calyx tube short, conical varying to funnel-form. *Stamens* median.

Core medium, axile or nearly so; cells closed or partly open; core lines clasping the cylinder of the tube. *Carpels* broadly roundish to nearly obcordate, emarginate, slightly tufted. *Seeds* often abortive; when normally developed they are medium to rather large, flat, obtuse, sometimes slightly tufted, dark.

Flesh somewhat tinged with yellow, firm, moderately coarse, crisp, juicy, mild subacid, good in quality.

Uses. Adapted rather for market and culinary uses than for dessert.

Season October to February or later.

ARCTIC

AUGUST.

REFERENCES. 1. *N. Y. Sta. An. Rpt.*, **7**:89. 1888. **2.** *Me. Sta. Rpt.*, **1893**:132. **3.** *N. Y. Sta. An. Rpt.*, **13**:586. 1894. **4.** *Mich. Sta. Bul.*, **118**:59. 1895. **5.** *Ib.*, **129**:39. 1896. **6.** *N. Y. Sta. An. Rpt.*, **15**:270. 1896. **7.** *Mich. Sta. Bul.*, **143**:200. 1897. **8.** *Ib.*, **152**:219. 1898. **9.** *Ib.*, **205**:47. 1903.
SYNONYMS. None.

This hybrid is classed by some as an apple and by others as a crabapple. The tree is hardy, comes into bearing early and is reliably productive. The fruit is medium to small for an apple but very large for a crabapple. It has a slight crabapple flavor and is of fairly good quality for culinary use. Not recommended for planting in New York.

Historical. Originated from seed of Wealthy by Peter M. Gideon, Excelsior, Minn., from whom it was received in 1888 for testing at this Station. It has been tested at experiment stations in different States but it appears to be practically unknown to fruit growers.

TREE.

Tree moderately vigorous. *Form* upright spreading and somewhat drooping, open. *Twigs* short, curved, slender; internodes short. *Bark* clear brown, lightly streaked with scarf-skin; slightly pubescent. *Lenticels* scattering, medium in size, oblong, slightly raised. *Buds* medium in size, plump, acute, free, not pubescent.

FRUIT.

Fruit medium to small, occasionally above medium, uniform in size and shape. *Form* roundish oblate to roundish conic, nearly symmetrical, regular or somewhat ribbed. *Stem* rather short to medium in length, moderately slender. *Cavity* acute approaching acuminate, medium to deep, moderately broad, symmetrical, usually not russeted. *Calyx* rather large, closed; lobes long, acute, reflexed. *Basin* moderately shallow to rather deep, moderately wide, somewhat abrupt, slightly furrowed and wrinkled.

Skin pale yellow or greenish, sometimes almost entirely overspread and mottled with rather bright red, striped and splashed with carmine, covered with bloom. *Dots* whitish, small, scattering, inconspicuous. *Prevailing color* red in well colored specimens.

Calyx tube rather small, short, conical. *Stamens* median to nearly basal. *Core* medium in size to above, usually axile; cells often unsymmetrical, usually closed, sometimes wide open; core lines clasping. *Carpels* ovate. *Seeds* light brown, medium to above, moderately wide, plump, acute.

Flesh slightly tinged with yellow, half-fine, moderately juicy, breaking, mild subacid, with a slight crabapple flavor; quality fairly good for culinary use.

Season August and early September.

AUGUSTINE.

REFERENCES. **1.** *Horticulturist,* **1848** (cited by **5**). **2.** Downing, **1857**:207. **3.** Warder, **1867**:711. **4.** Thomas, **1885**:502. **5.** Ragan, *U. S. B. P. I. Bul.,* **56**:31. 1905.

SYNONYMS. None.

A pleasant flavored dessert apple formerly grown to a very limited extent in some portions of the state but now practically unknown. Fruit medium to rather large, roundish conic or slightly inclined to oblong, yellow splashed and striped with red; flesh moderately juicy to rather dry, not crisp, tender, sweet; season August.

AUTUMN BOUGH.

REFERENCES. **1.** *London Hort. Soc. Cat.,* **1831**:No. 36. **2.** Parsons, *Horticulturist,* **1**:209. 1846. **3.** *Am. Pom. Soc. Cat.,* **1852**. **4.** *Mag. Hort.,* **19**:68. 1853. **5.** Elliott, **1854**:66. fig. **6.** Downing, **1857**:71. **7.** *Mag. Hort.,* **25**:154. 1859. **8.** Warder, **1867**:712. **9.** Thomas, **1875**:198. **10.** Downing, **1881**:11 index, app. **11.** Lyon, *Mich. Hort. Soc. Rpt.,* **1890**:288. **12.** Bailey, *An. Hort.,* **1892**:234.

SYNONYMS. AUTUMN BOUGH (1, 2, 3, 4, 5, 7, 11, 12). *Autumn Bough* (9). AUTUMNAL BOUGH (8). AUTUMN SWEET BOUGH (6, 9, 10). *Autumn Sweet Bough* (5). *Fall Bough* (6, 9). *Late Bough* (6, 9). *Montgomery Sweet* (10). *Philadelphia Sweet* (6, 9). *Summer Bellflower* (6).

This is regarded by many as one of the best sweet apples of its season for dessert use and is esteemed also for culinary purposes. The tree is medium in size, upright or roundish, moderately vigorous to vigorous, healthy, long-lived, comes into bearing fairly young and is reliably productive. The fruit hangs well to the tree. It is suitable for local market but it does not ship well. So far as we can learn it is not grown commercially but it is occasionally cultivated for home use and is still listed by some nurserymen.

In 1846 Robert B. Parsons, of Flushing, N. Y., described it as "a very superior fruit, ranking indeed among our best sweet apples, and worthy of extensive cultivation. It is rather large, somewhat of a calville-shape, though with the ribs not quite so prominent as is usual with apples of that class; oblong, diminishing very much to the eye. Skin smooth, pale yellow, with a few scattered dots. Eye of medium size, and very deeply sunken. Stalk rather slender, set in a deep narrow cavity. Flesh white, very tender, and with a rich and sweet, yet sprightly flavor. Ripens from 25th of Eighth month to the 20th of Ninth month. The tree is exceedingly productive, and of very vigorous growth " (2).

AUTUMN STREAKED.

REFERENCES. **1.** Gibb, *Am. Pom. Soc. Rpt.,* **1887**:50. **2.** Lyon, *U. S. Pom. Bul.,* **2**:39. 1888. **3.** *N. Y. Sta. An. Rpt.,* **8**:349. 1889. **4.** *Ib.,* **13**:579. 1894.

SYNONYMS. AUTUMN STREAKED (1, 2, 3, 4). *Herbst Strefling* (1). *Herbst Streifling* (2). *No. 964* (1).

This fruit approaches the Oldenburg type in some respects. It is of good size and usually attractive in color, sprightly subacid, very good for culinary purposes; season September. The tree is hardy, comes into bearing young and is a good biennial bearer.

Historical. A Russian apple received from T. H. Hoskins, Newport, Vt., in 1888 for testing at this Station (3, 4).

Tree.

Tree moderately vigorous with short, stout branches. *Form* spreading, flat, rather dense. *Twigs* short, curved, stout with large terminal buds; internodes short. *Bark* dull brown, mingled with olive-green, heavily coated with gray scarf-skin; pubescent. *Lenticels* scattering, medium to large, oval, slightly raised. *Buds* prominent, large, broad, plump, obtuse, free, pubescent.

Fruit.

Fruit large. *Form* roundish to roundish oblate, somewhat inclined to conic, regular or obscurely ribbed; sides often unequal. *Stem* short to medium, rather slender. *Cavity* medium to rather large, acute to acuminate, moderately deep, rather wide, slightly furrowed, greenish-russet. *Calyx* large, closed or partly open. *Basin* uneven, wide, abrupt, wrinkled.

Skin yellow or pale yellow, shaded, striped and splashed with red and overspread with pinkish bloom. *Prevailing effect* striped red.

Core large, open.

Flesh yellowish, firm, a little coarse, rather crisp, moderately juicy, sprightly subacid, good.

AUTUMN SWAAR.

REFERENCES. 1. *Genesee Farmer*, 1838 (cited by 10). 2. Downing, 1857:115. 3. Hooper, 1857:14. 4. *Am. Pom. Soc. Cat.*, 1862. 5. Warder, 1867:572. fig. 6. Downing, 1869:82. 7. Lyon, *Mich. Hort. Soc. Rpt.*, 1890:288. 8. Bailey, *An. Hort.*, 1892:234. 9. Budd-Hansen, 1903:41. 10. Ragan, *U. S. B. P. I. Bul.*, 56:107. 1905.

SYNONYMS. AUTUMN SWAAR (4, 7, 8, 9). AUTUMNAL SWAAR (1, 2, 3, 6). *Autumnal Swaar* (10). FALL SWAAR (10, of the West 5). *Fall Swaar* of West (6, 9, 10).

This belongs to the Fall Orange group and the fruit resembles Fall Orange very closely. It is very good in quality for either dessert or culinary uses. The tree is hardy, vigorous and spreading; not satisfactorily productive (7). It is occasionally found in cultivation in this state but is now seldom or never planted. Its origin is unknown.

Fruit.

Fruit above medium to medium, sometimes large. *Form* oblate to roundish conic. *Stem* often short, thick and irregularly knobbed. *Cavity* acute, deep, broad, often lipped or irregular, with concentric russet marks and with outspreading russet rays. *Calyx* medium to small, closed or slightly open. *Basin* medium in depth, medium to narrow, abrupt, slightly ridged.

Skin orange-yellow or greenish, in some cases with a decided blush but not striped, roughened by almost invisible, capillary netted russet lines which become more distinct, larger and concentric about the base and apex. *Dots* conspicuous, irregular, russet or red areolar with russet center. *Prevailing effect* yellow.

Calyx tube funnel-form. *Stamens* median.

Core medium to rather small, nearly axile; cells partly open or closed; core lines clasp the funnel-cylinder. *Carpels* emarginate, somewhat elliptical, tufted. *Seeds* numerous, large to medium, plump, tufted, brown.

Flesh yellow, tender, breaking, juicy, agreeable, mild subacid, decidedly aromatic, sprightly, very good.

Season September.

AUTUMN SWAAR AND FALL ORANGE COMPARED.

The fruit of Fall Orange as compared with that of Autumn Swaar is larger, more inclined to conic, has smaller seeds and a fleshy pistil point projecting into the base of the calyx tube. The flesh is whiter, more acid, less aromatic and less tender. The flesh of well grown and well ripened Autumn Swaar is decidely yellower, more tender and milder with a very pleasant, peculiarly aromatic flavor.

AUTUMN SWEET SWAAR.

REFERENCES. 1. *Albany Cultivator*, 5:247. 1848. 2. Thomas, 1849:145. 3. Barry, 1851:282. 4. Elliott, 1854:121. 5. Downing, 1857:115. 6. Gregg, 1857:41. 7. Warder, 1867:471. fig. 8. Lyon, *Mich. Hort. Soc. Rpt.*, 1890:288. 9. Ragan, *U. S. B. P. I. Bul.*, 56:33. 1905.

SYNONYMS. AUTUMN SWAAR (3, 9). *Autumn Sweet* (9). AUTUMN SWEET SWAAR (8). AUTUMNAL SWAAR (1, 2, 4, 6). *Autumnal Sweet* (9). AUTUMNAL SWEET SWAAR (5, 7). *Autumnal Sweet Swaar* (9). *Sweet Golden Pippin* (5, 9). *Sweet Swaar* (2, 3, 5, 6, 7, 9).

In 1848 Thomas described this as one of the finest autumnal sweet apples (1). It is now seldom found in cultivation in this state. Its origin is unknown.

TREE.

Tree moderately vigorous to vigorous, productive. *Form* upright spreading.

FRUIT (1, 2, 4, 6).

Fruit large. *Form* roundish oblate, sometimes slightly ribbed. *Stem* varying from long and slender to thick and fleshy, yellow and red. *Cavity* acute, deep, wavy, green. *Calyx* medium in size, closed. *Basin* shallow, wide, slightly furrowed.

Skin smooth, waxen yellow, sometimes blushed. *Dots* rare, minute.

Core medium in size; cells somewhat open; core lines clasping. *Seeds* numerous, plump, pale.

Flesh whitish tinged with yellow, fine, moderately juicy, very sweet, spicy, agreeable, very good to best.

Season September and October.

BAILEY SPICE.

References. 1. *N. Y. Agr. Soc. Trans.,* **1849**:350. 2. Bailey, *Horticulturist,* **5**:286. 1850. fig. 3. Hovey, *Mag. Hort.,* **16**:542. 1850. fig. 4. Barry, **1851**:283. 5. Elliott, **1854**:121. 6. Downing, **1857**:116. 7. Hooper, **1857**:14. 8. Gregg, **1857**:41. 9. Warder, **1867**:712. 10. Thomas, **1875**:205.

Synonyms. Bailey Spice (2, 3, 4, 5, 7, 8). Bailey's Spice (1, 6, 9, 10).

A dessert apple of medium size, light yellow color and subacid, spicy flavor, in season in September and October.

Historical. In 1850 J. W. Bailey, of Plattsburgh, published the following account of the origin of this variety (2, 3). "The original tree is now growing in my grounds, and was planted there fifty years ago by my grandfather, Captain Nathaniel Platt. It is a great bearer, and I think I never knew an apple so invariably fair and perfect as this."

So far as we have learned this variety is no longer planted and is nearly obsolete in New York.

BAKER SWEET.

References. 1. Downing, **1857**:117. 2. Warder, **1867**:712. 3. Thomas, **1875**:492.

Synonyms. Baker Sweet (2. 3). Baker's Sweet (1). *Late Golden Sweet* (1). *Long Stem Sweet* (1). *Winter Golden Sweet* (1, 3).

A golden yellow apple of good size and attractive appearance. Because it is sweet, not a late keeper and drops readily from the tree it is of little commercial value except where it can be disposed of in local market, notwithstanding that the tree is very productive. It is a good variety for the home orchard where a sweet apple, ripening in late autumn, is desired.

Historical. This is an old variety, formerly much grown in parts of New England (1). It is but little grown in New York state.

Tree.

Tree medium size, only moderately vigorous or a slow grower; branches dark, rather slender, somewhat resembling Jonathan (1). *Form* spreading. *Twigs* rather stout.

Fruit.

Fruit large to medium, pretty uniform in size and shape. *Form* roundish to oblate, usually regular. *Stem* short to rather long, rather slender. *Cavity* large, acute to acuminate, deep, rather broad, sometimes partly russeted and with outspreading rays, symmetrical. *Calyx* pubescent, medium, closed; lobes broad at base, acute. *Basin* shallow to moderately deep, narrow to above medium in width, somewhat abrupt, a little furrowed.

Skin moderately thin, tough, nearly smooth except for some patches of russet and conspicuous russet dots, good yellow with shade of brownish-red blush on exposed cheek. *Prevailing effect* good yellow.

Calyx tube medium, somewhat funnel-shape. *Stamens* median.

Core above medium to large, abaxile; cells open, sometimes unsymmetrical; core lines meeting. *Carpels* very broadly ovate to roundish, tufted. *Seeds* dark, medium to rather small, plump, acute, tufted.

Flesh yellowish, firm, moderately fine, rather tender, rather juicy, very sweet, pleasant, good to very good.

Season October to December.

BANKS.

REFERENCES. **1.** Craig and Allen, *Can. Hort.*, **16**:420. 1893. fig. **2.** *Nova Scotia Fr. Gr. Assn. Rpt.*, **1894**:81, 129. **3.** Sears, *Can. Hort.*, **22**:476. 1899. **4.** Caston, *Ont. Fr. Stas. An. Rpt.*, **9**:55. 1902. **5.** *Am. Pom. Soc. Rpt.*, **1903**:166.

SYNONYMS. BANKS (2, 3, 4, 5). BANKS GRAVENSTEIN (2). BANKS RED GRAVENSTEIN (1). *Banks Red Gravenstein* (4). *Red Gravenstein* (3).

In 1903 R. W. Starr, Wolfville, Nova Scotia, presented to the American Pomological Society the following report concerning this variety (5). "A bud sport from Gravenstein, much the same in season and flavor, but bright red, less ribbed, more regular in shape, and generally a little smaller in size. First noticed and propagated by C. E. Banks, of Berwick, Kings Co., N. S. It is well liked and is being quite largely planted." It appears that this sport first came into bearing about 1880 (1). In 1899 Sears (3) remarked, "The Banks or Red Gravenstein is gaining in popularity because it combines with the superior quality of the ordinary Gravenstein the bright red color which people demand who judge the apple by its appearance alone."

Except in the points of difference above noted Banks appears to be identical with Gravenstein and the reader is referred to the description of that variety for a technical account of the tree and fruit. So far as we can learn this variety is not yet planted to any considerable extent in New York.

BEAUTIFUL ARCAD.

REFERENCES. **1.** *Montreal Hort. Soc. Rpt.*, **9**:104. 1883. **2.** *Ia. Hort. Soc. Rpt.*, **1883**:443. **3.** *Ia. Agr. Coll. Bul.*, **1885**:17. **4.** Gibb, *Montreal Hort. Soc. Rpt.*, **1886–87**:15. **5.** *Ib., Am. Pom. Soc. Rpt.*, **1887**:48. **6.** Budd, *Rural N. Y.*, **47**:692. 1888. **7.** Taylor, *Me. Pom. Soc. Rpt.*, **1892**:57. **8.** Harris, *U. S. Pom. Rpt.*, **1892**:274. **9.** Thomas, **1897**:248. fig. **10.** Hansen, *S. D. Sta. Bul.*, **76**:28. 1902. **11.** Budd-Hansen, **1903**:44. **12.** Ragan, *U. S. B. P. I. Bul.*, **56**:29, 39, 353. 1905.

SYNONYMS. *Arcad Krasivui* (3). *Arkad Krasivui* (5, 12). ARKAD KRASIWUI (1). *Arkad Krasivui* (2, 5, 12). BEAUTIFUL ARCAD (2, 3, 4, 5, 6, 7, 8, 9, 11). BEAUTIFUL ARCADE (10, 11). *Beautiful Arcade* (1, 5, 12). *No. 453* (5, 6, 10, 11, 12).

This is a Russian apple of good medium size, yellow, partly shaded and splashed with red, sweet, in season in August and September. It is considered a desirable variety in portions of the Upper Mississippi valley and in other districts where superior hardiness is a prime requisite.

BEAUTY OF KENT.

REFERENCES. **1.** Forsyth, **1803** :55. **2.** Ib., **1824** :93. **3.** *London Hort. Soc. Cat.*, **1831** :No. 59. **4.** Kenrick, **1832** :92. **5.** Floy-Lindley, **1833** :20. **6.** Downing, **1845** :81. **7.** Hovey, *Mag. Hort.*, **14** :250. 1848. fig. **8.** Kirtland, *Horticulturist*, **2** :544. 1848. **9.** Thomas, **1849** :146. **10.** Cole, **1849** :114. **11.** Emmons, *Nat. Hist. N. Y.*, **3** :34. 1851. **12.** Barry, **1851** :283. **13.** Elliott, **1854** :167. **14.** Hooper, **1857** :15. **15.** Gregg, **1857** :41. **16.** Downing, *Horticulturist*, **19** :364. 1864. figs. **17.** Warder, **1867** :584. **18.** Fitz, **1872** :152. **19.** Leroy, **1873** :97. fig. **20.** Hogg, **1884** :17. **21.** Lyon, *Mich. Hort. Soc. Rpt.*, **1890** :288. **22.** Wickson, **1889** :245. **23.** Bailey, *An. Hort.*, **1892** :234. **24.** Bunyard, *Jour. Roy. Hort. Soc.*, **1898** :354. **25.** Budd-Hansen, **1903** :109. **26.** Powell and Fulton, *U. S. B. P. I. Bul.*, **48** :46. 1903. **27.** Garden, **64** :239. 1903. fig. *bearing nursery trees.*

SYNONYMS. BEAUTE DE KENT (19). BEAUTY OF KENT (1, 2, 3, 4, 5, 6, 7, 8, 9, 10, 11, 12, 13, 14, 15, 16, 17, 18, 20, 21, 22, 23, 24, 27). *Beauty of Kent* (19, 26). KENT BEAUTY (25, 26). *Kentish Pippin* (19, of some 3). *Pepin de Kent* (19). *Pippin Kent* (19).

Fruit large, beautiful, showy, suitable for culinary use, in season from late September to November. The tree is large, vigorous, upright, comes into bearing rather young, is a reliable cropper and moderately productive. In England where it originated it is said to do best under garden culture in warm soil and on Paradise stock; grown in clay and other uncongenial soils it loses quality (27). It is but little known in New York.

BELBORODOOSKOE.

REFERENCES. **1.** Gibb, *Am. Pom. Soc. Rpt.*, **1887** :55. No. 37. **2.** *N. Y. Sta. An. Rpt.*, **8** :349. 1889. **3.** Beach, *Ib.*, **12** :599. 1893. **4.** Thomas, **1897** :265, fig. **5.** Hansen, *S. D. Sta. Bul.*, **76** :29. 1902.

SYNONYMS. BELBORODOOSKOE (2, 3). BELLERDOVSKOE (4, 5). *Bielborodovskæ* (1). WHITE BORODOVKA (1).

A Russian apple, medium to large, pale greenish-yellow, sometimes blushed, coarse, rather juicy, mild subacid to nearly sweet, good; season August. It does not appear to be worthy the attention of New York fruit growers.

BENNINGER.

REFERENCES. **1.** Churchill, *N. Y. Sta. An. Rpt.*, **8** :355. 1889. **2.** Bailey, *An. Hort.*, **1892** :235. **3.** Heiges, *U. S. Pom. Rpt.*, **1894** :17. **4.** Beach, *N. Y. Sta. An. Rpt.*, **15** :270. 1896. **5.** Taylor, *Am. Pom. Soc. Rpt.*, **1897** :36.

SYNONYMS. BENNIGER (2). BENNINGER (1, 3, 4, 5).

A pleasant-flavored dessert apple of good medium size and attractive appearance; in season during late August and September. It is too mild in flavor to be very desirable for culinary purposes. The tree is a pretty good grower, comes into bearing young and is productive.

Historical. Originated about 1830 on the farm of Uhlie Benninger near Slatington, Lehigh county, Pa. In that region it is said to be a good grower and a reliable and abundant cropper (4).

TREE.

Tree moderately vigorous with short stout branches. *Form* spreading, open. *Twigs* short, curved, stout with large . terminal buds; internodes medium. *Bark* clear brownish tinged with olive-green, lightly streaked with scarf-skin; pubescent. *Lenticels* conspicuous, quite numerous, medium in size, oblong, not raised. *Buds* deeply set in bark, medium in size, broad, obtuse, appressed, pubescent.

FRUIT.

Fruit medium or above. *Form* roundish oblate to roundish ovate, somewhat irregular; sides unequal. *Stem* short to medium, rather slender. *Cavity* acute or approaching acuminate, medium in width, moderately deep to deep, often somewhat russeted. *Calyx* medium in size, usually closed; lobes narrow, acuminate. *Basin* wide, moderately deep to shallow, smooth or slightly furrowed.

Skin rather thin, nearly smooth, yellow, blushed and streaked with red. *Dots* rather small, greenish.

Calyx tube usually short, wide, conical. *Stamens* marginal.

Core medium, abaxile; cells open; core lines slightly clasping or sometimes meeting.

Flesh whitish tinged with yellow, firm, moderately fine, crisp, rather juicy, mild subacid, good.

Season late August and September.

BENONI.

REFERENCES. **1.** *N. E. Farmer,* 9:46. 1830. **2.** Kenrick, **1832**:25. **3.** *Mag. Hort.,* 1:149, 363. 1835. **4.** Manning, **1838**:49. **5.** *Mag. Hort.,* 6:172. 1840. **6.** *Ib.,* 7:43. 1841. **7.** Downing, **1845**:70. **8.** Hovey, *Mag. Hort.,* 14:17. 1848. fig. **9.** Thomas, **1849**:136. **10.** Cole, **1849**:101. **11.** Emmons, *Nat. Hist. N. Y.,* 3:12. 1851. **12.** Hovey, 1:83. 1851. *col. pl.* and *fig.* **13.** Barry, **1851**:279. **14.** *Am. Pom. Soc. Cat.,* **1854. 15.** Elliott, **1854**:122. **16.** *Mag. Hort.,* 21:63. 1855. **17.** Gregg, **1857**:35. **18.** Hooper, **1857**:17, 106, 108. **19.** *Horticulturist,* 14:425. 1859. **20.** Warder, **1867**:650. fig. **21.** Fitz, **1872**:121, 148, 177. **22.** Hogg, **1884**:20. **23.** Lyon, *Mich. Hort. Soc. Rpt.,* **1890**:288. **24.** Bailey, *An. Hort.,* **1892**:235. **25.** Woolverton, *Ont. Fr. Stas. An. Rpt.,* 1:24. 1894. **26.** Burrill and McCluer, *Ill. Sta. Bul.,* 45:314. 1896. **27.** Dickens and Greene, *Kan. Sta. Bul.,* 106:51. 1902. **28.** Budd-Hansen, **1903**:47. fig.

SYNONYMS. None.

Benoni is a fine dessert apple, very attractive in appearance and excellent in quality but not large enough to be a good market variety. The tree comes into bearing moderately young and

BENONI

yields fair to good crops biennially. It begins to ripen early in August and its season extends into September.

Historical. Originated in Dedham, Massachusetts, where the original tree was still standing in 1848. It was introduced to notice by Mr. E. M. Richards shortly before 1832 (2). It is highly esteemed throughout the country and is generally listed by nurserymen throughout the middle and northern portions of the apple-growing regions of this continent (24).

TREE.

Tree rather large, vigorous. *Form* erect to somewhat roundish, dense. *Twigs* moderately long, straight, slender; internodes medium. *Bark* olive-green, shaded with light reddish-brown, lightly coated with scarf-skin, pubescent. *Lenticels* scattering, medium, oblong, slightly · raised. *Buds* deeply set in bark, medium size, plump, obtuse, appressed, slightly pubescent.

FRUIT.

Fruit medium to rather small. *Form* roundish inclined to conic, faintly ribbed toward the apex; sides unequal. *Stem* short to very short, slender. *Cavity* acute, rather narrow, moderately deep, wavy, greenish-russet. *Calyx* rather small to above medium, partly open, slightly pubescent. *Basin* medium in width and depth, abrupt, somewhat wrinkled.

Skin smooth, orange-yellow partly covered with lively red striped with deep carmine. *Dots* scattering, minute, whitish.

Stamens basal.

Core small to medium, axile; cells closed; core lines meeting. *Carpels* roundish, slightly elongated, emarginate. *Seeds* few, dark brown, medium in size, plump, obtuse.

Flesh yellow, firm, crisp, fine-grained, tender, juicy, pleasant subacid, good to very good.

Season August and early September.

BIETIGHEIMER.

REFERENCES. 1. Downing, **1881**:101 app. 2. Thomas, **1885**:521. 3. Hoskins, *Rural N. Y.*, 47:646. 1888. 4. Wickson, **1889**:243. 5. *Can. Hort.*, 13:239, 301. 1890. fig. 6. Bailey, *An. Hort.*, **1892**:234. 7. *Can. Hort.*, 16:14. 1893. 8. *Ib.*, 17:413. 1894. *col., pl.* 9. *Gard. and For.*, 8:390, 428. 1895. 10. *Am. Pom. Soc. Cat.*, **1897**:12. 11. Dickens and Greene, *Kan. Sta. Bul.*, 106:54. 1902. 12. Budd-Hansen, **1903**:48. fig. 13. Farrand, *Mich. Sta. Bul.*, 205:43. 1903.

SYNONYMS. BEITIGHEIMER (6). BIETIGHEIMER (7, 10, 12, 13). RED BEITIGHEIMER (9). *Red Beitigheimer* (6). RED BIETIGHEIMER (1, 2, 3, 4, 5, 8, 11).

Fruit remarkable only for its great size and beauty. It is a good cooking apple but coarse, subacid and not desirable for dessert use. The fruit being extremely large, drops badly before

the crop is ready to pick. In the nursery it is a rough grower
forming many badly shaped trees and for this reason it is best to
topwork it on some good straight stock. The tree comes into
bearing rather early and under favorable conditions is an annual
cropper but only moderately productive. It is a fine fruit for
exhibition but is not worthy of cultivation for either home use or
market.

Historical. Origin, Germany.

TREE.

Tree large, moderately vigorous to vigorous. *Form* upright spreading or
roundish, dense, with laterals inclined to droop. *Twigs* short, curved, stout,
with large terminal buds; internodes long. *Bark* dull brown tinged with
green, lightly streaked with scarf-skin; pubescent. *Lenticels* quite numerous,
conspicuous, medium in size, oval, raised. *Buds* prominent, large, broad,
plump, obtuse, free, pubescent.

FRUIT.

Fruit very large, pretty uniform in size and shape. *Form* roundish oblate
or inclined to conic, with broad, flat base, somewhat irregular. *Stem* medium
to short, thick. *Cavity* large, acute, or approaching acuminate, wide, moderately shallow to rather deep, sometimes furrowed, occasionally lipped,
often much russeted and with outspreading russet rays. *Calyx* medium to
small, closed; lobes rather narrow, acute. *Basin* varies from shallow and
obtuse to deep and abrupt, medium in width, somewhat wrinkled, often
marked with mammiform protuberances.

Skin thick, tough, smooth, bright pale yellow to greenish or whitish washed
with pinkish-red and sparingly and obscurely splashed with deeper red. *Dots*
numerous, small, inconspicuous, yellowish or russet.

Calyx tube broadly conical. *Stamens* usually basal or nearly so.

Core medium to large, axile to somewhat abaxile; cells partly open; core
lines clasping. *Carpels* cordate or broadly roundish, a little tufted. *Seeds*
numerous, large to medium, rather wide, broadly acute, rather light brown.

Flesh almost white, firm, very coarse, crisp, somewhat tough, juicy, subacid, fair to nearly good.

Season September and October.

BIRTH.

REFERENCES. 1. *Montreal Hort. Soc. Rpt.*, 8:42, 73. 1881-82. 2. Budd, *Ia.
Hort. Soc. Rpt.*, 1882:79. 3. *Ib.*, 1883:444, 685. fig. 4. *Montreal Hort.
Soc. Rpt.*, 1883:107. fig. 5. *N. Y. Sta. An. Rpt.*, 2:35. 1883. 6. *Ia. Agr.
Coll. Bul.*, 1885:18. 7. *Montreal Hort. Soc. Rpt.*, 1886-87:80. 8. *N. Y. Sta.
An. Rpt.*, 11:588. 1892. 9. *Ia. Sta. Bul.*, 41:70. 1899.

SYNONYMS. BIRTH (8, 9). CHRIST BIRTH (6). CHRIST BIRTH APPLE
(2, 3). *Christ Birth Apple* (4). CHRISTMAS (7). *No. 161* (7). *No. 477*

BIETIGHEIMER

(2, 6, 9). *161 M* (2). RESCHESTWENSKOE (5). *Roschdestvenskoe* (6).
ROSCHDESTWENSKOE (4). *Roschdestwenskoe* (3). ROSHDESTRENSKOE (1).

A Russian apple received in 1888 from Dr. T. H. Hoskins, Newport, Vt., for testing at this Station. Fruit above medium, roundish conic, slightly ribbed; skin greenish-yellow with a shade of brownish-red; flesh mild subacid, fair quality; ripens here in September. Not valuable.

BISMARCK.

REFERENCES. **1.** Hogg, **1884** :181. **2.** *Rural N. Y.,* **55** :275, 288, 321, 690, 1896. **3.** Van Deman, *Ib.,* **56** :241, 503, 534, 598, 662. 1897. *figs.* **4.** Green, *Am. Pom. Soc. Rpt.,* **1897** :32. **5.** *Rural N. Y.,* **57** :786. 1898. **6.** Bunyard, *Jour. Roy. Hort. Soc.,* **1898** :356. **7.** *Can. Hort.,* **22** :240. 1899. **8.** *Amer. Gard.,* **20** :124, 782. 1899. *figs.* **9.** Van Deman, *Rural N. Y.,* **58** :688. 1899. **10.** Beach, *W. N. Y. Hort. Soc. Rpt.,* **1900** :35. **11.** Waugh, *Vt. Sta. An. Rpt.,* **14** :288. 1901. **12.** *Can. Hort.,* **25** :47. 1902. **13.** *Rural N. Y.,* **61** :626. 1902. **14.** Budd-Hansen, **1903** :49. **15.** *Rural N. Y.,* **62** :809. 1903.

SYNONYMS. BISMARCK (2, 3, 4, 5, 6, 7, 8, 9, 11, 12, 13, 14, 15). BISMARK (10). PRINCE BISMARK (1). *Prince Bismark* (10).

Bismarck is evidently related to the Aport group of apples. In size and general appearance it somewhat resembles Alexander. Fruit large, attractive in color, suitable for kitchen and market purposes but inferior in dessert qualities. It ranks about with Alexander and Wolf River in quality. It begins to ripen in October and its season extends from October to early winter. It has not been tested enough in this country to demonstrate its market value. The tree is dwarfish, healthy, hardy, comes into bearing very young, is a reliable cropper and very productive. Even when grown as standards the trees may be planted much more closely together than ordinary commercial varieties.

Historical. Originated in the Province of Canterbury, New Zealand. Introduced into this country from England about ten years ago.

TREE.

Tree dwarfish with very short, stout, drooping branches. *Form* spreading, open. *Twigs* short, curved, moderately stout; internodes medium. *Bark* dull brownish, tinged with green, lightly coated with scarf-skin, pubescent. *Lenticels* scattering, medium to large, oval, slightly raised. *Buds* medium in size, plump, obtuse, free, pubescent.

FRUIT.

Fruit very large or large, rather uniform in size and shape. *Form* roundish oblate to roundish conic, flattened at the base, pretty regular; sides often

unequal. *Stem* short to medium, thick. *Cavity* usually rather large, acuminate, moderately wide to wide, deep, often compressed, greenish or russet
with outspreading russet rays. *Calyx* large, open; lobes short, rather broad,
nearly obtuse. *Basin* large to very large, usually symmetrical, deep, moderately wide to wide, very abrupt, sometimes broadly and irregularly furrowed
and wrinkled.

Skin rather thick, tough, smooth, greenish or yellow washed, mottled and
striped with two shades of red becoming solid dark red on the exposed
cheek, overspread with thin bloom and often marked with thin scarf-skin
about the base. *Dots* minute and russet or large and pale gray. *Prevailing
effect* attractive red with less of a striped appearance than Alexander.

Calyx tube wide, broadly conical to somewhat funnel-form. *Stamens*
basal.

Core medium to rather small, axile to somewhat abaxile; cells closed or
sometimes open; core lines meeting or slightly clasping. *Carpels* flat,
broadly ovate to nearly cordate, tufted. *Seeds* few, often abortive, medium
size, rather wide, short, plump, obtuse to acute, medium brown.

Flesh nearly white, moderately firm, coarse, rather tender, juicy, subacid,
sprightly, fair to good or nearly good.

Season October to early winter.

BLACK ANNETTE.

REFERENCES. 1. Elliott, 1854:167. 2. ? Warder, 1867:713. 3. Downing,
1869:99.

SYNONYMS. None.

A rather small dark red apple formerly grown to a limited extent in some
sections of New York and other Eastern states. Season November and December. It is now practically obsolete here. The Black Annette mentioned
by Hansen when grown in Central Iowa keeps through the winter which
indicates that it is distinct from the variety here described. See Vol. I.

BLENHEIM.

REFERENCES. 1. Turner, *London Hort. Soc. Trans.*, 3:322. 1819. 2. Forsyth, 1824:134. 3. *Pom. Mag.*, 1:No. 28. 1828. *col. pl.* 4. Ronalds, 1831:61.
fig. 5. *London Hort. Soc. Cat.*, 1831:No. 104. 6. Kenrick, 1832:72. 7. Floy-
Lindley, 1833:29. 8. Downing, 1845:81. 9. Horticulturist, 1:389. 1847.
10. Thomas, 1849:144. 11. Emmons, *Nat. Hist. N. Y.*, 3:29. 1851. 12. Elliott, 1854:167. 13. Hooper, 1857:19. 14. Lucas, Ed., *Ill. Handb. Obstk.*,
1:515. 1859. 15. Warder, 1867:713. 16. Regel, 1:461. 1868. 17. Berghuis,
1868:No. 61. *col. pl.* 18. *Tilt. Jour. Hort.*, 7:166. 1870. 19. Downing,
1872:3 app. 20. Leroy, 1873:139. fig. 21. *Am. Pom. Soc. Cat.*, 1875:6.
22. Lauche, 1882:No. 36. *col. pl.* 23. Bensel, *Rural N. Y.*, 42:65. 1883.
24. Hogg, 1884:24. 25. Lyon, *Mich. Hort. Soc. Rpt.*, 1890:288. 26. *Can.
Hort.*, 15:40, 72, 111, 124, 156, 188, 206. 1892. 27. Bailey, *An. Hort.*, 1892:
235. 28. *Can. Hort.*, 16:113, 299. 1893. 29. Bredsted, 2:157. 1893. 30. *Ont.
Fr. Stas. An. Rpt.*, 1:24. 1894. 31. Gaucher, 1894:No. 8. *col. pl.* 32. *Gard.
and For.*, 9:15. 1896. 33. Bunyard, *Jour. Roy. Hort. Soc.*, 1898:354. 34.

BISMARCK (Reduced Size)

Amer. Gard., 19:344. 1898. 35. Can. Hort., 24:353. 1901. figs. 36. Ont. Fr.
Stas. An. Rpt., 8:6. 1901. figs. 37. Eneroth-Smirnoff, 1901:197. 38. Macoun, Can. Dept. Agr. Bul., 37:40. 1901. 39. Budd-Hansen, 1903:51. 40.
Beach and Clark, N. Y. Sta. Bul., 248:113. 1904.

SYNONYMS. *Belle d' Angers* (31). BLENHEIM (20, 23, 34, 35, 36, 39, 40).
Blenheim (5, 18, 19). BLENHEIM ORANGE (1, 2, 4, 6, 13, 15, 26, 28, 32, 33).
Blenheim Orange (3, 5, 7, 8, 10, 11, 12, 18, 19, 20, 24, 31, 34, 35, 36, 39, 40).
BLENHEIM PIPPIN (3, 5, 7, 8, 9, 10, 11, 12, 16, 17, 18, 19, 21, 24, 25, 27, 29, 30,
38). *Blenheim Pippin* (6, 20, 26, 28, 31, 34, 35, 36, 39, 40). BLENHEIM SRENETT
(37). *Blooming Orange* (18, 19, 31). *Dredge's Fame* (31). *Dutch Mignonne*, err. (18, 19). *Gloucester Pippin* (31). GOLDREINETTE VON BLENHEIM
(14, 22, 31). *Goldreinette von Blenheim* (20). *Impératrice Eugénie* (31).
Kempster's Pippin (18, 19, 20, 24, 31, 32). LORD NELSON (incorrectly in some
nursery catalogues). *Lucius Apfel* (31). *Northampton* (31). *Northwick
Pippin* (5, 18, 19, 20, 24, 31). *Orange Blenheim* (31). *Orange Pippin* (31).
Perle d'Angleterre (31). *Prince of Wales* (31). *Pomme de Blenheim* (31).
Reinette de Blenheim (31). *Ward's Pippin* (31). *Woodstock* (2, 35, 36).
Woodstock Pippin (3, 5, 6, 7, 8, 10, 11, 12, 18, 19, 20, 24, 31, 34).

Fruit large to very large, yellow, more or less washed and striped with red, attractive in appearance and of excellent quality. The commercial season in the southeastern portions of the State is October. In Western New York it comes into season with the Twenty Ounce and keeps into early winter (31). Often specimens of it may be kept much later. Macoun gives its season in Ontario as November and December (28). The fruit is desirable both for home and market uses but the variety is usually unsatisfactory for commercial planting because it is not a good keeper, is variable in season and commonly suffers considerable loss in drops and culls. In some locations, however, it is considered a good profitable variety.

Origin Woodstock, Oxfordshire, England. It found its way into the London nurseries about the year 1818 (24). Although it has long been known in portions of New York and adjacent states and in Canada in no part of this region has it assumed very great commercial importance.

TREE.

Tree large, vigorous, productive, bearing its fruit singly and evenly distributed. *Form* upright spreading. *Twigs* very stout. *Bark* clear, light reddish-brown becoming dark.

FRUIT.

Fruit usually large or above medium. *Form* roundish oblate to roundish inclined to conic, usually pretty regular and symmetrical, sometimes a little furrowed at the apex. *Stem* short to medium. *Cavity* below medium to rather large, rather narrow to wide, moderately deep to deep, acute to acuminate, usually symmetrical, sometimes compressed or lipped, covered with russet which often extends beyond the cavity. *Calyx* large or very large; segments flat, separated at base plainly exposing the yellowish tube beneath; lobes obtuse. *Basin* large, broad, shallow and obtuse to deep and abrupt, somewhat furrowed and slightly wrinkled.

Skin moderately thin and tough, deep yellow overspread with a rather dull pinkish-red, in highly colored specimens developing a deep and rather bright red somewhat roughened in places with netted capillary russet lines. *Dots* numerous, small or conspicuously large and russet. *Prevailing effect* rather attractive red and yellow.

Calyx tube short, very wide, cone-shape. *Stamens* median to somewhat basal.

Core medium or below, axile or somewhat abaxile; cells often unequally developed, closed or partly open; core lines meeting. *Carpels* flat, tufted, emarginate. *Seeds* few and frequently abortive, irregular, often not plump, long, acute to acuminate, tufted.

Flesh tinged with yellow, rather firm, moderately juicy, crisp, moderately fine grained or a little coarse, somewhat aromatic, agreeable sprightly subacid, becoming rather mild subacid, good to very good; excellent either for dessert or culinary use.

Season. It is at its best from October to December but often may be kept until midwinter or later.

BLUSHED CALVILLE.

REFERENCES. 1. Budd, *Ia. Hort. Soc. Rpt.*, **1882**:80. 2. Schroeder, *Montreal Hort. Soc. Rpt.*, **1886** 87:72. 3. Budd, *Can. Hort.*, **11**:223, 246. 1888. 4. *Ib.*, *Rural N. Y.*, **47**:692. 1888. 5. *Ib.*, *Ia. Agr. Coll. Bull.*, **1890**:17. 6. *Ib.*, *Can. Hort.*, **13**:216. 1890. 7. Ib., *Ia. Sta. Bul.*, **19**:535. 1892. 8. Green, *Minn. Sta. Bul.*, **32**:241. 1893. 9. Munson, *Me. Sta. Rpt.* **1896**:73. 10. Thomas, **1897**:265. *fig.* 11. Hansen, *S. D. Sta. Bul.*, **76**:32. 1902. *fig.* 12. Budd-Hansen, **1903**:52.

SYNONYMS. BLUSHED CALVILLE (2, 3, 4, 5, 6, 7, 8, 9, 10, 11, 12). CALVILLE KRASMUI (1). *22* (2). *22 M* (1, 4, 5, 7, 8, 11, 12).

Blushed Calville is said to be hardy and desirable in northern apple-growing regions (11). As fruited at this Station the tree does not come into bearing very young and is not very productive. It is not recommended for planting in this state.

Historical. Origin Russia.

TREE.

Tree rather small, moderately vigorous with short, stout branches. *Form* upright spreading, open. *Twigs* medium in length, curved and stout with large terminal buds; internodes long. *Bark* brownish mingled with olive-green, lightly streaked with scarf-skin; slightly pubescent. *Lenticels* scattering, medium in size, round, slightly raised. *Buds* prominent, large, broad, plump, acute, free, slightly pubescent.

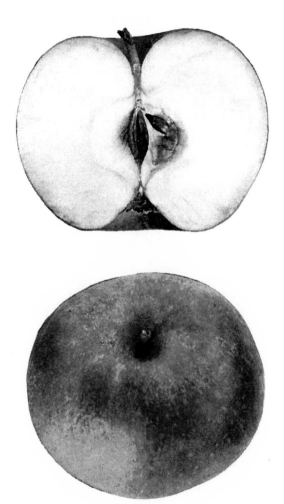

BLENHEIM

FRUIT.

Fruit medium to large, fairly uniform in shape and size. *Form* roundish conical, ribbed; sides unequal. *Stem* usually long and slender. *Cavity* acute to acuminate, rather narrow to moderately wide, moderately deep, sometimes russeted. *Calyx* large, closed or open. *Basin* medium in width and depth to wide and deep, a little abrupt, wrinkled.

Skin light green or yellowish, sometimes blushed.

Calyx tube broad, cone-shaped. *Stamens* median.

Core very large, abaxile; cells wide open; core lines clasping. *Seeds* medium in size, acute.

Flesh whitish, firm, rather coarse, crisp, tender, juicy, subacid, fair to good. *Season* early summer.

BONUM.

REFERENCES. 1. Robey, *Horticulturist*, 11:89. 1856. 2. Downing, 1857: 122. 3. *Am. Pom. Soc. Cat.*, 1860:240. 4. Warder, 1867:424. fig. 5. Leroy, 1873:147. fig. 6. Thomas, 1875:190. 7. Barry, 1883:343. 8. Bailey, *An. Hort.*, 1892:235. 9. Dempsey, *Ont. Fr. Stas. An. Rpt.*, 2:32. 1895. 10. Burrill and McCluer, *Ill. Sta. Bul.*, 45:315. 1896. 11. Alwood, *Va. Sta. Bul.*, 130:123. 1901. 12. Powell and Fulton, *U. S. B. P. I. Bul.*, 48:38. 1903. 13. Budd-Hansen, 1903:54. fig.

SYNONYMS. BONUM (1, 2, 3, 4, 5, 6, 7, 8, 9, 10, 11, 12, 13). *Magnum Bonum* (2, 4, 5, 7).

This is a southern variety of very good quality when grown under favorable conditions. It is in season during late fall and early winter. Probably it is not well adapted to regions as far north as New York, for although it has long been cultivated it is practically unknown among New York fruit growers.

Historical. Origin Davidson county, N. C. It was entered on the catalogue of the American Pomological Society in 1860, dropped from the list in 1862 and reëntered in 1869. According to Bailey's Inventory of North American Apples (8) it is now propagated but little by nurserymen.

TREE.

Tree moderately vigorous. *Form* upright spreading or roundish, open. *Twigs* moderately long, curved, moderately stout; internodes medium. *Bark* dull brown, lightly mottled with scarf-skin; slightly pubescent. *Lenticels* quite numerous, small, round, not raised. *Buds* medium in size, flat, acute, free, not pubescent.

FRUIT (2, 4, 6, 7, 13).

Fruit medium to large. *Form* oblate, regular. *Stem* long, slender to moderately thick, green. *Cavity* medium to large, deep, regular, often with a little green russet. *Calyx* large, closed. *Basin* medium in width, shallow, wrinkled.

Skin smooth, yellow, mostly covered with crimson and dark red, striped. *Dots* distinct, large, light with some having a dark center.

Calyx tube funnel-form. *Stamens* marginal.

Core small; cells closed; core lines scarcely meeting. *Carpels* ovate.
Seeds numerous, large, plump.

Flesh white, often stained next to the skin, firm, fine, tender, juicy, aromatic, mild subacid, very good for dessert.

Season September to November.

BOROVINKA.

REFERENCES.   1. *Montreal Hort. Soc. Rept.*, **8**:37.   1881–82.   **2.** *Ib.*, **8**:75.
1881–82.   **3.** Budd, *Ia. Hort. Soc. Rpt.*, **1882**:80.   **4.** Gibb, *Ib.*, **1883**:432.
5. *Montreal Hort. Soc. Rpt.*, **9**:80.   1883.   fig.   **6.** Budd, *Ia. Agr. Coll. Bul.*,
1885:9.   **7.** ? Schroeder, *Montreal Hort. Soc. Rpt.* **1886–87**:71.   **8.** *Ib.*,
1886–87:79.   **9.** Van Deman, *U. S. Pom. Rpt.*, **1888**:571.   **10.** Budd, *Ia. Agr.
Coll. Bul.*, **1890**:18.   **11.** *Can. Hort.*, **13**:216.   1890.   **12.** Budd, *Ia. Sta. Bul.*,
19:536.   1892.   **13.** Harris, *U. S. Pom. Rpt.*, **1892**:273, 278.   **14.** Taylor, *Me.
Pom. Soc. Rpt.*, **1892**:58.   **15.** Niemetz, *Can. Hort.*, **16**:113.   1893.   **16.**
Green, *Minn. Sta. Bul.*, **32**:240.   1893.   **17.** Stinson, *Ark. Sta. Bul.*, **43**:105.
1896.   **18.** Thomas, **1897**:629.   **19.** *Am. Pom. Soc. Cat.*, **1897**:12.   **20.** Hansen, *S. D. Sta. Bul.*, **76**:33.   1902.   **21.** Farrand, *Mich. Sta. Bul.*, **205**:43
1903.   **22.** Budd-Hansen, **1903**:54.   fig.

SYNONYMS. BOROVINKA (1, 5, 6, 8, 9, 10, 11, 12, 13, 14, 15, 16, 17, 19, 20,
21, 22). *Borovinka* (4). BOROVITSKY (18). BOROVINKA ANGLUSKAIA (2,
3). (ENGLISH BOROVINKA, 7)? MUSHROOM (4). *Mushroom* (5). *9 M* (2,
3). *No. 245* (6, 9, 10, 12, 17).

Borovinka resembles Oldenburg so closely that Hansen says the question
of their identity has not been settled (20). As fruited at this Station it is
distinct from Oldenburg; it is fully as attractive as Oldenburg in color but
it lacks uniformity in size and is not equal to that variety in flavor and
quality. The stock grown at this Station came from Professor J. L. Budd,
Ames, Ia., in 1890, and is doubtless the true Borovinka.

Historical. Origin Russia.

TREE.

Tree below medium size but moderately vigorous. *Form* upright spreading to rather flat, open. *Twigs* short, curved, stout; internodes short. *Bark*
dark brown, lightly mottled with scarf-skin; slightly pubescent. *Lenticels*
scattering, medium to large, oblong, slightly raised. *Buds* prominent, medium
in size, broad, plump, obtuse to acute, free, not pubescent.

FRUIT.

Fruit below medium to large, averaging medium; pretty uniform in shape
but not in size. *Form* roundish, slightly flattened at the ends, regular or
faintly ribbed. *Stem* medium in length, thick. *Cavity* acute, rather shallow
to moderately deep, moderately broad, slightly furrowed, sometimes with
faint radiating rays of russet. *Calyx* medium to rather large, closed; lobes
broad. *Basin* medium to rather deep, wide, somewhat abrupt, slightly furrowed, occasionally showing mammiform protuberances.

Skin thin, very tender, smooth, pale yellow, often entirely covered with broken stripes and irregular splashes of attractive bright red, overspread with thin bluish bloom. *Dots* numerous, conspicuous, very small, light colored.

Calyx tube large, rather wide, urn-shape to funnel-form widening in the lower part of the funnel cylinder. *Stamens* median to marginal.

Core small to medium, axile; cells closed or nearly so; core lines clasping. *Carpels* roundish, somewhat concave, mucronate, not emarginate. *Seeds* medium to rather large, moderately wide, plump, somewhat obtuse, dark brown.

Flesh tinged with yellow, medium in grain, crisp, tender, moderately juicy to juicy, agreeable subacid, slightly aromatic, good.

Season mid-August to mid-September.

BOSKOOP.

REFERENCES. **1.** Berghuis, **1868**: *col. pl.* No. 43. **2.** Oberdieck, *Monatshefte,* **1869**:193. **3.** Oberdieck, *Deutschlands beste Obstsorten,* 212. **4.** Lauche, *Ergänzungsband zum Ill. Handb.,* 265. **5.** *Montreal Hort. Soc. Rpt.,* **7**:56, 155. **1881. 6.** Downing, **1881**:77 app. fig. **7.** Budd, *Ia. Hort. Soc.,* **1882**: **8.** Barry, **1883**:342. **9.** Willard, *W. N. Y. Hort. Soc.,* **1889**:171 (reprint in *Mich. Hort. Soc. Rpt.,* **1889**:329). **10.** Palandt, *Gartenflora,* **38**:425. 1889. *col. pl.* **11.** Brodie, *Can. Hort.,* **12**:238. 1889. **12.** Bailey, *An. Hort.,* **1892**:234. **13.** Bailey, *Amer. Gard.,* **14**:501. 1893. **14.** Craig, *Can. Hort.,* **16**:138. 1893. fig. **15.** Bredsted, **1893**:233. **16.** Gaucher, *Pomologie,* **1894**:No. 20. *col. pl.* **17.** Beach and Clark, *N. Y. Sta. Bul.,* **248**:113. 1904.

SYNONYMS. BELLE DE BOSCOOP (11). BELLE OF BOSKOOP (9). BELLE DE BOSKOOP (6, 7, 8, 12, 13, 14, 15). *Belle de Boskoop* (16, 17). BOSKOOP (5, 17). *Reinette Belle de Boskoop* (16). *Reinette Monstrueuse* (16). *Reinette von Montfort* (16). SCHÖNER VON BOSKOOP (2, 3, 4, 10, 16). SCHOONE VON BOSKOOP (1). *Schoone van Boskoop* (16).

In some locations this fruit becomes highly colored with attractive bright red predominating, but more often the color is not good, being predominantly dull green or yellow and more or less russeted. It is more suitable for general market and culinary purposes than for dessert. It is of good size but does not rank high in quality; the texture is somewhat coarse, and the flavor rather too acid for an agreeable dessert apple, but late in the season its acidity becomes modified. It appears to be pretty hardy and a good bearer. When grown on warm soils in Southern New York it may be marketed in September, but in the more northern regions of the state it keeps into the winter. It is perhaps of sufficient merit to be worthy of testing but we are not yet ready to recommend it for general planting.

Historical. This variety is said to have originated from seed in 1856 in the nursery of the Ottolander family at Boskoop (1, 4). Palandt finds that it is identical with the variety described by Lauche and Oberdieck as "Reinette von Montfort" (4). It was imported into this country more than twenty-five years ago (5) and has gradually been disseminated to a limited extent in various portions of New York state.

TREE.

Tree rather large, moderately vigorous; branches long, moderately stout, crooked; lateral branches numerous and small. *Form* open, wide-spreading and drooping. *Twigs* rather short to long, straight, rather stout; internodes below medium to very long. *Bark* dark brownish-red, mingled with olive-green; somewhat pubescent. *Lenticels* numerous, conspicuous, small, oblong or roundish. *Buds* rather large, broad, plump, acute, free, slightly pubescent. *Leaves* large, broad.

FRUIT.

Fruit large. *Form* usually oblate, sometimes roundish oblate, obscurely ribbed, sometimes with oblique axis; pretty uniform in size and shape. *Stem* usually short and thick, sometimes rather long. *Cavity* rather large, acute to acuminate, somewhat furrowed, often irregular, deep, russeted. *Calyx* large; segments long or very long, acuminate, closed or somewhat open, sometimes separated at the base. *Basin* abrupt, rather narrow, moderately shallow to rather deep, sometimes slightly furrowed.

Skin dull green or yellowish, sometimes blushed and mottled with rather bright red, and striped with deeper red, roughened with russet flecks, often irregularly overspread with russet. *Dots* small and gray, mingled with others which are large, irregular and russet.

Calyx tube large, cone-shape. *Stamens* median to basal.

Core medium to small, somewhat abaxile; cells often unsymmetrical, closed or open; core lines slightly clasping. *Carpels* roundish or obcordate, a little tufted. *Seeds* apt to be abortive; when well developed they are long, irregular, obtuse to acute, somewhat tufted.

Flesh tinged with yellow, firm, somewhat coarse, tender, juicy, crisp, brisk subacid, good to very good.

Season. Commercial season September to November (17). As grown in Western New York generally some of the fruit may be kept till April.

BOUGH SWEET.

This variety is also known as Bough Apple, Large Yellow Bough, Sweet Bough and Summer Sweet Bough. It is listed in the late catalogues of the American Pomological Society[1] as Bough, *Sweet* but most nurserymen list it as Sweet Bough.[2] We prefer to recognize the name commonly accepted by nurserymen and accordingly have described the variety under the name Sweet Bough. See page 216.

BRESKOVKA.

REFERENCES. **1.** Schroeder, *Montreal Hort. Soc. Rpt.*, **1886–87**:80. **2.** Budd, *Can. Hort.*, **11**:246. 1888. **3.** *Ib.*, *Rural N. Y.*, **47**:692. 1888. **4.** *Ib.*, *Ia. Agr. Col. Bul.* **1890**:17. **5.** *Ib.*, *Ia. Sta. Bul.*, **19**:535. 1892. **6.** Green, *Minn.*

---

1 *Am. Pom. Soc. Cat.*, **1897**:12.
2 Bailey, *An. Hort.* **1892**:235, 250.

Sta. Bul., **32**:240. 1893. **7.** Thomas, **1897**:629. **8.** Hansen, *S. D. Sta. Bul.*, **76**:34. 1902. **9.** Budd-Hansen, **1903**:56.

SYNONYMS. BRESKOVKA (1, 2, 3, 4, 5, 6, 7, 8, 9). *152 M* (2, 3, 4, 5, 8, 9).

A hardy Russian variety of Yellow Transparent type, in season during late August and early September. The flesh quickly discolors as the ripening season advances. It is rather attractive in color for a yellow apple but does not average above medium size and it is not equal to Yellow Transparent in either flavor or quality. Not recommended for growing in New York.

BUNKER HILL.

REFERENCE. **1.** Downing, **1872**:4 app. *fig.*
SYNONYMS. None.

This variety has been planted to some extent in Central New York and is regarded by some fruit growers in that region as a profitable commercial sort. The tree is large, upright spreading, vigorous to moderately vigorous with long, spreading, moderately stout twigs. It is hardy, healthy, medium to long-lived and a reliable cropper, usually bearing heavy crops biennially. The fruit is subacid and good either for dessert or culinary uses. It is in season from mid-autumn to early winter.

Historical. Originated in the orchard of Dr. Paige, Dryden, Tompkins county, N. Y. (1).

FRUIT (1).

" Fruit medium, roundish conical, regular; skin pale whitish-yellow shaded, mottled, striped and splashed with two shades of red, rather thinly over two-thirds of the surface, and moderately sprinkled with light dots, a few being areole; stalk short, slender; cavity medium or large, a little greenish; calyx closed; basin medium, slightly corrugated; flesh quite white, sometimes a little stained next the skin, fine, tender, juicy, subacid, vinous, slight quince-like flavor; very good; core rather small."

BUTTER.

REFERENCES. **1.** Elliott, **1854**:125, 159, 174. **2.** Downing, **1857**:125. **3.** Warder, **1867**:392. **4.** Downing, **1869**:112. **5.** Fitz, **1872**:152. **6.** Thomas, **1875**:495. **7.** Ragan, *U. S. B. P. I. Bul.*, **56**:60. 1905.
SYNONYMS. None.

Downing describes a variety under this name which is above medium size, yellow, with whitish flesh, very sweet and rich, valuable for cooking and esteemed for making apple butter; season September and October (2, 4). Other varieties have been known under the name Butter which, as Downing remarks, " appears to be a favorite name with some to apply to any good sweet apple for sauce or cooking."

The references above cited do not all refer to the same variety.

CABASHEA.

REFERENCES. 1. *N. Y. Agr. Soc. Trans.*, 1849:350. 2. Emmons, *Nat. Hist. N. Y.*, 3:103. 1851. 3. Warder, 1867:714. 4. Thomas, 1875:495. 5. Beach, *Apples of New York*, 1:91. 1905.

SYNONYMS. CABASHEA (1, 3, 4, 5). *Cabashea* (2). CABASHIE (2).

The name Cabashea has been applied by many pomologists to the variety commonly known among fruit growers and fruit dealers as Twenty Ounce Pippin (5), an apple which comes in season about with Tompkins King. The variety which is generally known in Western New York as Cabashea comes in season about with the true Twenty Ounce but it is not so good a keeper. In 1851 Emmons published a cut of a section of this Cabashea showing well its characteristically oblate form. Emmons remarked, "This apple is more remarkable for its size than for its valuable qualities. . . . It is not, however, an inferior apple. For cooking it is certainly esteemed, as it has a pleasant and agreeable taste. It is, however, too large." The tree is hardy, healthy, medium to long-lived, and a pretty regular cropper, yielding moderate to rather light crops nearly annually. It is not considered a good commercial variety because it is not sufficiently productive and the fruit does not sell very well.

Historical. This variety appears to be a Western New York seedling (1). It is now seldom or never planted.

TREE.

Tree medium size, moderately vigorous. *Form* erect or somewhat spreading. *Twigs* medium to long, curved, spreading, stout to rather slender; internodes medium. *Bark* reddish-brown tinged with olive-green, streaked with scarf-skin, heavily pubescent near tips. *Lenticels* conspicuous, scattering, large, oval, raised. *Buds* large, broad, obtuse, free, pubescent; tips stout.

FRUIT.

Fruit large to very large, fairly uniform in size and shape. *Form* roundish oblate to decidely flat, obscurely ribbed; sides somewhat unequal. *Stem* usually short, moderately slender. *Cavity* acute, deep, very broad, often somewhat furrowed, much russeted with greenish russet often extending beyond the cavity. *Calyx* large or sometimes medium, usually closed; lobes long, medium in width, acute. *Basin* large, deep, wide, somewhat furrowed, unsymmetrical.

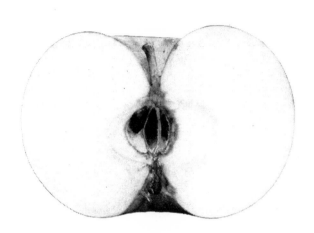

CABASHEA

Skin moderately tender, smooth, slightly unctuous, yellowish-green mottled and blushed with yellowish-red, with broad stripes and splashes of brighter and deeper red. *Dots* small, inconspicuous, often submerged. *Prevailing color* in many specimens yellowish-green with broad stripes of faint red; in more highly-colored specimens the red striping becomes quite distinct.

Calyx tube large, wide, conical. *Stamens* basal.

Core large, decidedly abaxile; cells wide open; core lines meeting. *Carpels* elongated ovate, distinctly concave, slightly tufted. *Seeds* few, medium size, irregular, plump, obtuse, dark.

Flesh greenish or tinged somewhat with yellow, rather firm, coarse, crisp, juicy, subacid or quite acid, fair for dessert, good for cooking.

Season September and October.

CATHEAD.

REFERENCES. 1. Forsyth, 1803:56. 2. Coxe. 1817:133. fig. 3. Thacher, 1822:122. 4. Floy-Lindley, 1833:48. 5. Downing, 1845:103. 6. Thomas, 1849:179. 7. Emmons, *Nat. Hist. N. Y.*, 3:86. 1851. 8. Elliott, 1854:168. 9. Warder, 1867:715. 10. Leroy, 1873:842. fig. 11. Hogg, 1884:41.

SYNONYMS. CATHEAD (2, 3, 8). *Cathead Greening* (5, 6, 8). CATSHEAD (1, 4, 5, 6, 7, 9, 11). *Catshead* (4, 10). *Catshead Greening* (10). *Costard* (4). *Costard Ray* (7). *Coustard* (4). *De Seigneur d'Automne* (10). *Grosse-Schafnasé* (10). *Round Catshead* (5, 8, 10). *Schafnasé* (10). *Tete d'Ange* (10). TETE DE CHAT (10).

Formerly grown in some of the home orchards of the state but now practically obsolete. Fruit very large, pale green, subacid. Used for cooking and evaporating. An old English variety. Ray described it as long ago as 1688 (4).

CELESTIA.

REFERENCES. 1. Warder, 1867:530. fig. 2. Downing, 1869:122. 3. Fitz. 1872:173. 4. Bailey, *An. Hort.*, 1892:236. 5. Dickens and Greene, *Kan. Sta. Bul.*, 106:52. 1902. 6. Beach and Clark, *N. Y. Sta. Bul.*, 248:114. 1904.

SYNONYMS. None.

Fruit not particularly attractive in color and as tested at this Station not superior to ordinary varieties in quality. Warder says (1) that it is essentially an amateur's fruit of very best quality but its texture and color disqualify it for market. The tree is a moderate grower and not very productive. Not recommended for cultivation in New York.

Historical. Originated from seed of Stillwater Sweet by L. S. Mote, Miami county, Ohio (1).

TREE.

Tree moderately vigorous with short, stout, curved branches. *Form* upright spreading, roundish, rather dense. *Twigs* short to moderately long, slightly curved, moderately slender; internodes medium to long. *Bark* clear brownish-red with some olive-green, lightly mottled with scarf-skin; pubescent. *Lenticels* numerous, small to medium, elongated or roundish, slightly raised. *Buds* medium size, plump, obtuse to somewhat acute, free, slightly pubescent.

FRUIT.

Fruit medium to large, usually above medium, uniform in size and shape. *Form* roundish inclined to conic, somewhat flattened at the base, markedly ribbed, irregular, somewhat angular. *Stem* medium to long, thick. *Cavity* obtuse to somewhat acute, moderately deep to deep, rather broad, somewhat furrowed, usually russeted. *Calyx* medium in size, usually closed; lobes medium in length, rather narrow, acute. *Basin* shallow, narrow, rather abrupt, much furrowed and wrinkled.

Skin thick, smooth, rather tender, yellow marbled with pale green, and occasionally having a thin brownish blush. *Dots* numerous, small, inconspicuous, submerged, light or russet.

Calyx tube very long to medium, deep, funnel-shape. *Stamens* median to somewhat marginal.

Core large, very abaxile to sometimes axile; cells open or closed; core lines clasping the funnel cylinder. *Carpels* elliptic to broadly obcordate, much concave, emarginate, much tufted. *Seeds* large, wide, long, obtuse, dark dull brown.

Flesh very strongly tinged with yellow, rather firm, moderately coarse, crisp, tender, juicy, pleasant, rather mild, subacid, good.

Season October to January.

CHAMPLAIN.

REFERENCES. **1.** *N. E. Farmer*, **1853** (cited by **14**). **2.** Downing, **1857**:128. **3.** Warder, **1867**:637. **4.** Downing, **1869**:368. fig. **5.** *Am. Pom. Soc. Cat.*, **1871**:10. **6.** Leroy, **1873**:828. fig. **7.** Thomas, **1875**:197, 496. **8.** Barry, **1883**:334. **9.** Bailey, *An. Hort.*, **1892**:245. **10.** *Ib.*, **1892**:250. **11.** *Am. Pom. Soc. Cat.*, **1897**:12. **12.** Waugh, *Vt. Sta. An. Rpt.*, **14**:290. 1901. **13.** Budd-Hansen, **1903**:61. **14.** Ragan, *U. S. B. P. I. Bul.*, **56**:300. 1905.

SYNONYMS. *Calkin's Pippin* (4, 14). CHAMPLAIN (1, 2, 3, 5, 11, 12, 13, 14). *Champlain* (4, 6, 7, 8, 14). *Geneva Pearmain* (4, 6, 14). *Haverstraw Pippin* (4, 14). *Large Golden Pippin* (4, 6, 14). *Nyack* (9, 13). NYACK PIPPIN (9). *Nyack Pippin* (4, 14). *Paper* (3, 4, 6, 14). *Paper-Skin* (3, 14). *Sourbough* (13). *Sour Bough* (4, 6, 7, 14). SUMMER PIPPIN (4, 6, 7, 8, 10, 14). *Summer Pippin* (13, 14). *Tart Bough* (4, 6, 14). *Underdunk* (4, 6, 14). *Vermont* (14). *Walworth* (4, 6, 14).

Nurserymen sometimes list this variety as Nyack, and sometimes as Summer Pippin, but seldom or never as Champlain (9, 10). Fruit of good size, smooth and attractive for a greenish-yellow apple. It is good for dessert and excellent for culinary use. Since it ripens in succession from late August till October, more than two pickings are required to secure the crop in good condition, neither too green nor too ripe. The tree is a good grower, hardy,

CHAMPLAIN

healthy, and moderately long-lived. It comes into bearing rather young and is a reliable cropper, yielding good crops biennially or almost annually. Some find Champlain a profitable commercial variety, but usually it is grown for home use rather than for market.

Historical. Origin unknown. In 1871 (5) it was included in the list of the American Pomological Society's Catalogue under the name Summer Pippin, but since 1897 it has been listed as Champlain (11). Old trees of it are frequently found in the home orchards throughout the state. It is now seldom planted.

TREE.

Tree medium to large, vigorous with long and moderately stout branches. *Form* upright spreading to roundish, open. *Twigs* long to medium, straight, moderately stout; internodes long. *Bark* dull brown tinged with olive-green, lightly streaked with scarf-skin, heavily pubescent. *Lenticels* scattering, medium size, oblong, slightly raised. *Buds* medium size, plump, obtuse, appressed, pubescent.

FRUIT.

Fruit medium to large, not very uniform in size or shape. *Form* roundish, rather conical to ovate or somewhat oblong, irregularly ribbed; sides somewhat unequal. *Stem* medium to long, medium to rather thick. *Cavity* acuminate to acute, moderately shallow to deep, rather narrow to medium in width, sometimes furrowed and usually lightly russeted. *Calyx* small to medium, closed or slightly open. *Basin* shallow to medium in depth, narrow, a little abrupt, nearly smooth.

Skin tender, greenish-yellow or pale yellow, often with a light crimson blush. *Dots* numerous, small, russet or submerged.

Calyx tube conical to funnel-form, usually rather short but sometimes elongated. *Stamens* median to marginal.

Core large, axile to somewhat abaxile; cells open; core lines clasp the funnel cylinder. *Carpels* smooth, elongated ovate, not emarginate. *Seeds* rather dark brown, medium size, rather narrow and short, plump, sharp pointed, almost acuminate.

Flesh white or with slight tinge of yellow, rather fine, very tender, juicy, sprightly, subacid, good to very good.

Season late August till October.

CHANDLER.

REFERENCES. **1.** Kenrick, **1835**:65. **2.** Floy-Lindley, **1846**:410, app. **3.** Thomas, **1849**:164. **4.** Cole, **1849**:122. **5.** Emmons, *Nat. Hist. N. Y.*, 3:67. 1851. **6.** Elliott, **1854**:168. **7.** Downing, **1857**:128. **8.** Hooper, **1857**:24. **9.** Warder, **1867**:715. **10.** Downing, **1869**:122. **11.** Fitz, **1872**:169.

SYNONYMS. CHANDLER (1, 2, 3, 4, 5, 6, 7, 8, 9, 10, 11). *Chandler's Red* (11). *General Chandler* (1). *Late Chandler* (10). *Winter Chandler* (6).

In 1854 Elliott included Chandler in a list of varieties unworthy of cultivation (6). It is a late fall apple, yellowish striped with red. Tree moderately vigorous but a great bearer (7, 10). An old variety supposedly of Connecticut origin though Kenrick (1) ascribes it to Chelmsford, Mass. There may be a confusion of two varieties. It is now but little cultivated.

Waugh describes another Chandler of sweet flavor which seems to be unknown in New York. He states that it is an old variety of Connecticut origin.

FRUIT (5, 6, 7, 10).

Fruit large. *Form* roundish, slightly oblate, irregular, unsymmetrical; sides unequal. *Stem* short.

Skin greenish-yellow, shaded and frequently striped with yellowish-red and with a few streaks of bright red. *Dots* light gray.

Core small. *Seeds* small.

Flesh greenish-yellow, tender, juicy, moderately rich, subacid.

Season mid-autumn to early winter.

CHARLAMOFF.

REFERENCES. 1. (?) Manning, *Till. Jour. Hort.*, 6:349. 1869. 2. Budd, *Ia. Hort. Soc. Rpt.*, 1880:525. 3. *Montreal Hort. Soc. Rpt.*, 1881:53, 156. 4. *Ib.*, 1881–82:38. 5. *Ib.*, 1883:83. 6. Gibb, *Ia. Hort. Soc. Rpt.*, 1883:434. 7. *Ia. Agr. Coll. Bul.*, 1885:10. 8. Schroeder, *Montreal Hort. Soc. Rpt.*, 1886–87:77. 9. Bailey, *An. Hort.*, 1892:236. 10. Taylor, *Me. Pom. Soc. Rpt.*, 1892:57, 58. 11. Butz, *Pa. Sta. Rpt.*, 1895:134. *col. pl.* 12. *Am. Pom. Soc. Cat.*, 1899:16. 13. Budd, *Ia. Sta. Bul.*, 41:66. 1899. 14. Macoun, *Can. Dept. Agr. Bul.*, 37:37. 1901. 15. Hansen, *S. D. Sta. Bul.*, 76:38. 1902. *fig.* 16. Budd-Hansen, 1903:61. *fig.*

SYNONYMS. *Arabka* (14). CHARLAMOFF (2, 3, 6, 8, 9, 10, 12, 13, 15). *Charlamoff* (3). (CHARLOMOSKI, 1)? CHARLAMOVSKOE (4). CHARLAMOWSKOE (3, 5). *Charlamowskoe* (6, 7). *No. 105* (8). *No. 262* (3, 5). *Peterson's Charlamoff* (16). POINTED PIPKA (11). *Pointed Pipka* (14, 16).

A Russian variety of the Oldenburg type imported for the Iowa Agricultural College by J. L. Budd. Macoun states that it has been grown under several different names in this country, the most common being Pointed Pipka and Arabka (14). Hansen declares that it is entirely distinct from the Charlamoff as grown by J. G. Mitchell and A. G. Tuttle which is a flat apple of upright habit of tree and not as valuable as many more of the same season.

It does very well at Ottawa, Canada, and further north. At its best it is a good dessert apple but it has the fault of remaining in prime condition for only a very short time (14). It ripens a little earlier than Oldenburg but as fruited at this Station is inferior to that variety in quality. It comes into bearing young and is a reliable cropper, yielding fair to heavy crops biennially. It is but little known among New York fruit growers. It may be found of some value in those sections of the state where superior hardiness is a prime requisite.

CHEESEBORO.

REFERENCES. **1.** *Mag. Hort.*, **17**:263. 1851. **2.** Emmons, *Nat. Hist. N. Y.*, **3**: *col. pl.* No. 20. 1851. **3.** Elliott, **1854**:168. **4.** Downing, **1857**:211. **5.** Hooper, **1857**:25. **6.** *Am. Pom. Soc. Rpt.*, **1860**:243. **7.** Warder, **1867**:522. **8.** Thomas, **1875**:496. **9.** Waugh, *Vt. Sta. An. Rpt.*, **14**:291. 1901. **10.** Ragan, *U. S. B. P. I. Bul.* **56**:70. 1905.

SYNONYMS. *Canada Reinette* (9). *Cathead* (9). CHEESEBORO (10). CHEESEBORO'S RUSSET (6). CHEESBOROUGH (7). CHEESEBOROUGH (2, 9). CHEESEBOROUGH RUSSET (1, 3, 4, 5, 8). *Cheeseborough Russet* (9, 10). *Forever Pippin* (10, of some West 3, 5). *Howard Russet* (3, 4, 5, 10). *Kingsbury Russet* (3, 4, 5, 10). *Oxheart* (9). *Pumpkin Sweet* of some (10). *Sweet Russet* (10). *York Russet* (10, of some 3, 5). *York Russeting* (10).

This is an old variety of unknown origin which is fast becoming obsolete. Tree large to very large, very vigorous, long-lived, a reliable cropper yielding good to heavy crops biennially or almost annually; form upright spreading or roundish. Fruit large to very large, conical, dull green overspread with thin russet, coarse, rather dry, subacid or becoming almost sweet, inferior in flavor and quality, suitable for kitchen use only; season October to early winter.

CHENANGO.

REFERENCES. **1.** *Horticulturist*, **9**:475. 1854. **2.** *Am. Pom. Soc. Cat.*, **1869**. **3.** Downing, **1869**:124. fig. **4.** Thomas, **1875**:190. **5.** *Ia. Hort. Soc. Rpt.*, **1879**:472. **6.** *Montreal Hort. Soc. Rpt.*, **1879**:24. **7.** Barry, **1883**:337. **8.** Wickson, **1889**:244. **9.** Lyon, *Mich. Hort. Soc. Rpt.*, **1890**:290. **10.** Bailey, *An. Hort.*, **1892**:236. **11.** *Ib.*, **1892**:249. **12.** *Munson, Me. Sta. Rpt.*, **1893**:132. **13.** Burrill and McCluer, *Ill. Sta. Bul.*, **45**:317. 1896. **14.** Waugh, *Vt. Sta. An. Rpt.*, **14**:291. 1901. **15.** Alwood, *Va. Sta. Bul.*, **130**:120. 1901. **16.** *W. N. Y. Hort. Soc. Rpt.*, **1901**:76. **17.** Hansen, *S. D. Sta. Bul.*, **76**:39. 1902. **18.** *Can. Hort.*, **26**:345. 1903. figs. **19.** Budd-Hansen, **1903**:62. **20.** Farrand, *Mich. Sta. Bul.*, **205**:44. 1903. **21.** Bruner, *N. C. Sta. Bul.*, **182**:20. 1903. **22.** Beach and Clark, *N. Y. Sta. Bul.*, **248**:115. 1904.

SYNONYMS. *Buckley* (3, 4). CHENANGO (2, 9, 10, 14, 16, 17, 18, 19, 20, 21, 22). CHENANGO STRAWBERRY (1, 3, 4, 5, 6, 7, 8, 13, 15). *Chenango Strawberry* (10, 11, 14, 17, 18, 19, 22). CHENANGO *Strawberry* (12). *Frank* (3, 4). *Jackson* (3, 4). SHERWOOD'S FAVORITE (11). *Sherwood's Favorite* (3, 4, 6, 7, 12, 14, 17, 18, 19, 22). *Smyrna* (3). *Strawberry* (1, 3, 4).

Fruit beautiful in appearance, yellowish-white striped with red, of excellent dessert quality and good also for culinary uses. The tree is an early and regular bearer, hardy, healthy, and pretty long-lived. Under favorable conditions it is an annual bearer, alternating rather light with heavy crops. The fruit begins to mature in September and ripens continuously during a period of several weeks. For this reason it should have more than one picking in order to secure the crop in the best condition. The latest ripening fruit may be kept in ordinary storage till November, but after that the color fades and it deteriorates much in quality, even though it may remain apparently sound (22). The fruit does not ship well because its flesh is too tender. Some find it a profitable variety to grow for local or special markets, but other varieties of its season are more desirable than Chenango for general commercial planting. It is recommended as an excellent variety for the home orchard.

Historical. Chenango, according to some accounts, originated in Lebanon, Madison county, N. Y.; others say that it was early brought into Chenango county by settlers from Connecticut. It has certainly been known in cultivation for more than fifty years (3). It is still propagated by nurserymen but the demand for the stock is quite limited.

TREE.

Tree medium size, vigorous with short, stout, curved branches. *Form* upright spreading to roundish, rather dense. *Twigs* long to medium, curved, moderately slender; internodes medium. *Bark* olive-green tinged with dull brown, lightly streaked with scarf-skin; pubescent. *Lenticels* scattering, small, round, not raised. *Buds* deeply set in bark, small, flat, obtuse, appressed, slightly pubescent.

FRUIT.

Fruit above medium to large, but under unfavorable conditions it may be small and poorly colored. *Form* elongated ovate or oblong conic, slightly ribbed. *Stem* short to medium, moderately thick. *Cavity* acute to acuminate, deep, narrow, often somewhat furrowed and compressed, usually not russeted. *Calyx* medium to large, partly open or closed; lobes often separated at the base, long, broad, obtuse. *Basin* usually small, medium to rather shallow, narrow to moderately wide, obtuse to somewhat abrupt, furrowed, sometimes wrinkled.

Skin rather tough, smooth, glossy, yellowish-white, often almost entirely overspread and mottled with attractive pinkish-red, conspicuously striped and splashed with bright carmine. *Dots* few, small, inconspicuous, light colored, often submerged.

Calyx tube long, funnel-shape or nearly so. *Stamens* median.

Core rather large, abaxile; cells often unsymmetrical, wide open or closed; core lines clasping. *Carpels* broadly ovate to oval, smooth. *Seeds* small, moderately wide, plump, obtuse, not tufted.

Flesh white, moderately firm, tender, juicy, mild subacid, very aromatic, good to very good.

Season latter part of August and through September.

CLAPPER FLAT.

REFERENCE. 1. Downing, 1869:127.
SYNONYMS. CLAPPER FLAT (1). *Flat* (1).

CHENANGO

Downing describes a variety under this name which originated in the town of Bethlehem, Albany county, N. Y. He states (1) that the tree is productive, the fruit above medium size, pale yellow mostly overspread with deep red, pleasant subacid and good in quality for culinary uses; season September and October. We do not know this variety and have found no account of it except that given by Downing.

CLARKE.

REFERENCES. 1. *Rural N. Y.*, **19**:375. 1868. 2. Downing, **1869**:127. 3. Leroy, **1873**:221. *fig.* 4. Burrill and McCluer, *Ill. Sta. Bul.*, **45**:317. 1896. 5. Powell and Fulton, *U. S. B. P. I. Bul.*, **48**:39. 1903. 6. Beach and Clark, *N. Y. Sta. Bul.*, **248**:115. 1904.

SYNONYMS. CLARKE (1, 2, 3, 4, 5, 6). *Clarke Beauty.*

This variety has been grown to a limited extent locally in some portions of Central New York. It is not a good commercial variety, being too tender and too easily bruised. It is very good for dessert. It is sometimes called Clarke Beauty. The tree is hardy, healthy and long-lived. It does not come into bearing very young but when mature is a reliable biennial cropper.

Historical. Originated with J. N. Clarke, Naples, Ontario county, N. Y. (1, 2). It is now rarely propagated.

TREE.

Tree large to medium, vigorous. *Form* upright spreading to roundish, rather dense. *Twigs* short, curved, stout; internodes medium. *Bark* brownish and olive-green, lightly mottled with scarf-skin; slightly pubescent. *Lenticels* scattering, medium size, oblong, slightly raised. *Buds* medium to large, broad, acute, free, slightly pubescent.

FRUIT.

Fruit medium to large, averaging above medium. *Form* roundish oblate to oblate conic or to oblong conic, usually faintly ribbed, unsymmetrical; not very uniform in shape. *Stem* short to medium in length, slender. *Cavity* acuminate, deep, rather narrow to moderately wide, usually partly russeted and often with narrow, broken, outspreading russet rays. *Calyx* small to rather large, closed or slightly open. *Basin* rather shallow to moderately deep, rather narrow, obtuse to moderately abrupt, slightly furrowed and wrinkled.

Skin thin, smooth, waxy, pale whitish-yellow or greenish, often faintly shaded with orange-red or sometimes blushed with crimson; under some conditions the fruit develops but a slight blush or none. *Dots* numerous, small, pale or russet, often submerged.

Calyx tube cone-shape.

Core medium to rather large, abaxile; cells open; core lines slightly clasping. *Carpels* broadly roundish, mucronate, slightly tufted. *Seeds* medium to rather large, moderately wide, plump, obtuse to acute, slightly tufted, rather light brown.

Flesh whitish, firm, moderately fine, crisp, tender, juicy, rather sprightly subacid, good to very good.

Season October to January; some portion of the fruit may keep till spring but by January it begins to deteriorate in flavor and quality.

CLYDE.

REFERENCES. 1. Barry, 1851:283. 2. Elliott, 1854:127. 3. Downing, 1857: 129. 4. Hoffy, *N. A. Pomol.*, 1860. *col. pl.* 5. Warder, 1867:694. fig. 6. *Am. Pom. Soc. Cat.*, 1875:6. 7. *Ia. Hort. Soc. Rpt.*, 1880:596. 8. *Mo. Hort. Soc. Rpt.*, 1884. 9. Lyon, *Mich. Hort. Soc. Rpt.*, 1890:290. 10. Bailey, *An. Hort.*, 1892:236. 11. Thomas, 1897:259. 12. Budd-Hansen, 1903:65.

SYNONYMS. CLYDE (3, 8, 9, 10). CLYDE BEAUTY (1, 2, 4, 5, 6, 7, 11). CLYDE Beauty (12). *Mackie's Clyde Beauty* (2, 3, 4, 11).

A large, late fall apple. So far as we can learn it is now but little grown in this state. Lyon reports that in Michigan the tree is vigorous, upright, very productive, and the fruit desirable for market (9).

Historical. This is a late autumn variety which originated with Mr. Mackie, of Clyde, Wayne county (3, 4).

TREE.

Tree vigorous, spreading. *Twigs* reddish-brown.

FRUIT.

Fruit large. *Form* roundish to oblong conic, more or less ribbed. *Stem* short, sometimes fleshy. *Cavity* acute, deep, rather wide, furrowed. *Calyx* small, closed. *Basin* medium in depth, somewhat abrupt, furrowed.

Skin waxy, green or yellow, washed and mottled with dull red and striped with carmine becoming bright red on the exposed side.

Core large and open. *Seeds* small, brown. *Flesh* white, often tender, juicy, sprightly, pleasant subacid, good to very good.

Season October to December.

COLLAMER.

The Collamer or Collamer Twenty Ounce is a sport of the Twenty Ounce, from which it differs in being more highly colored. As compared with Twenty Ounce, it is less mottled and striped but more completely covered with red, which often extends in an unbroken blush over a considerable portion of the fruit. In the Twenty Ounce this is seldom or never seen, but the red is mottled or appears in heavy stripes and splashes. So far as we have been able to determine, Collamer is more regular in shape and, if ribbed at all, is less distinctly ribbed than Twenty Ounce. The tree dif-

fers from Twenty Ounce in that the bark of the young twigs is more distinctly tinged with red. The fruit being more attractive than Twenty Ounce, Collamer is worthy of consideration for commercial planting where an apple of the Twenty Ounce type is desired.

Except in the points of difference above noted, Collamer appears to be identical with Twenty Ounce, and the reader is referred to the description of that variety for a technical account of the tree and fruit.

Historical. This variety originated as a sport of the Twenty Ounce tree in the orchard of J. B. Collamer, Hilton, N. Y. Mr. Collamer began propagating it about 1900.

COLTON.

REFERENCES. **1.** *Amer. Gard.*, **12**:573. 1891. figs. **2.** Bailey, *An. Hort.*, **1892**:237. **3.** Munson, *Me. Sta. Rpt.*, **1893**:132. **4.** Beach, *N. Y. Sta. An. Rpt.*, **15**:271. 1896. **5.** *Am. Pom. Soc. Cat.*, **1899**:16. **6.** Bruner, *N. C. Sta. Bul.*, **182**:20. 1903. **7.** Farrand, *Mich. Sta. Bul.*, **205**:44. 1903. **8.** Budd-Hansen, **1903**:67.

SYNONYMS. COLTON (1, 2, 3, 4, 7). COLTON *Early* (5, 6, 8). *Early Colton* (1).

Colton is a green or yellowish apple of fair to good quality, in season from the last of July to early September. The tree is a good grower, hardy, comes into bearing moderately young and yields good crops biennially.

Historical. Colton is said to have originated on the farm of Mr. Colton, Rowe, Franklin county, Mass., where it has been propagated since about 1840 under the name Early Colton (1).

TREE.

Tree large, vigorous with moderately long, stout, crooked branches. *Form* rather upright when young but eventually flat, spreading and open. *Twigs* moderately long, straight, moderately stout; internodes short. *Bark* dark brown, heavily mottled with scarf-skin; much pubescent. *Lenticels* quite numerous, rather conspicuous, medium to large, oblong, raised. *Buds* medium to large, broad, plump, acute, free, pubescent.

FRUIT.

Fruit medium in size. *Form* roundish, narrowing toward either end, slightly ribbed. *Stem* medium in length, stout. *Cavity* small, acute to slightly acuminate, shallow, narrow. *Calyx* medium in size, nearly closed; lobes long, rather recurved. *Basin* small, shallow, obtuse, wrinkled.

Skin pale greenish-yellow, sometimes with a shade of red. *Dots* numerous, large, greenish.

Calyx tube elongated funnel-form. *Stamens* median.

Core medium to rather large, somewhat abaxile; cells open; core lines clasping. *Carpels* broadly roundish.

Flesh whitish, rather coarse, crisp, juicy, mild subacid, fair to good.

Season last of July to early September.

COLVERT.

REFERENCES. 1. Warder, 1867:427. 2. Downing, 1869:131. 3. *Am. Pom. Soc. Cat.,* 1875:6. 4. Thomas, 1885:506. 5. Lyon, *Mich. Hort. Soc. Rpt.,* 1890:290. 6. Bailey, *An. Hort.,* 1892:237. 7. Powell and Fulton, *U. S. B. P. I. Bul.,* 48:39. 1903.

SYNONYMS. COLVERT (1, 2, 3, 4, 5, 6, 7). *Prussian* (2).

Ripens about with Twenty Ounce. It is inferior to that variety in size, color and quality, and is not as good a seller, but is more productive. The fruit is large, uniform in size, yellowish-green shaded and lightly striped with pinkish-red on the sunny side, smooth, showy and fairly attractive. It needs to be picked early to prevent loss from dropping. It is not a good keeper and is not much in demand among buyers, but sometimes it sells pretty well.

The tree is generally hardy, healthy and an excellent cropper. It generally succeeds well on any good apple land.

Historical. Origin uncertain (2). It has long been known and pretty widely disseminated but it is not much grown in New York. Even in those localities where it is best known the trees of this variety constitute less than one per cent of the orchards.

TREE.

Tree medium size to large, moderately vigorous to vigorous; branches long, medium stout, curved, crooked. *Form* upright spreading or roundish, open. *Twigs* above medium to long, usually nearly straight, moderately stout; internodes medium. *Bark* rather dark brownish-red, shaded with olive-green, lightly streaked with scarf-skin; pubescent. *Lenticels* scattering, medium, oblong, raised. *Buds* medium to large, broad, prominent, very plump, obtuse, free, pubescent. *Leaves* medium in size, broad.

FRUIT.

Fruit averages large, fairly uniform in size but rather variable in shape. *Form* oblate to oblate conic, obscurely ribbed, irregular and with sides sometimes unequal. *Stem* short, rather thick. *Cavity* acute to slightly acuminate, medium to nearly deep, medium in width to sometimes broad, usually very heavily russeted, sometimes compressed and frequently lipped. *Calyx* medium, closed or slightly open; lobes short, narrow, acuminate. *Basin* abrupt, medium in depth, narrow, slightly furrowed.

Skin very thick, rather tough, rather dull greenish-yellow, sometimes partly washed with red and striped and splashed with carmine. *Dots* inconspicuous, small, usually submerged; a few scattering ones are large and russet. *Prevailing color* greenish-yellow, not particularly attractive.

Calyx tube broadly conical to funnel-shape. *Stamens* median to basal.

Core axile, small; cells closed or partly open. *Carpels* broad-cordate, emarginate, tufted. *Seeds* large to above medium, wide, rather long, plump, acute; frequently they are abortive.

Flesh tinged with yellow, firm, nearly coarse, crisp, moderately tender, juicy, subacid, good.

Season October to January or February.

CONSTANTINE.

REFERENCES. 1. Leroy, **1873**:335. fig. 2. Budd, *Ia. Hort. Soc. Rpt.*, **1880**:524. 3. Gibb, *Montreal Hort. Soc. Rpt.*, **1881**:155. 4. Hogg, **1884**:95. 5. Gibb, *Montreal Hort. Soc. Rpt.*, **1886–87**:14. 6. *Ib.*, **14**:86. 1888. 7. Hoskins, *Rural N. Y.*, **51**:682. 1892. fig.

SYNONYMS. *Berry Apple* (7). CONSTANTINE (2, 3). GRAND DUC CONSTANTIN (1). GRAND DUKE CONSTANTINE (4, 5, 6, 7). *Grand Duke Constantine* (2, 3). *No. 457* (7). *Riabinouka* (7).

This fruit is of the Aport type and very closely resembles Alexander. The flesh is rather coarse, subacid and fair to good in quality. Some hold that it is rather better in flavor than Alexander. As grown at this Station, the fruit, as compared with that of Alexander, begins to ripen about a week later and continues longer in season. The trees are not so large and may be planted more closely together than those of Alexander. It is a reliable cropper, yielding good crops biennially or nearly annually. The percentage of marketable fruit is greater than that of Alexander because there are fewer drops, the apples are less apt to show cracks about the calyx and stem and the skin is less often discolored by chafing against the branches. We are not sure that it is as good a variety for commercial planting as Alexander, but it appears to be worthy of testing where a variety of the Alexander type is desired.

TREE.

Tree small to below medium size, at first moderately vigorous but with age it becomes a slow grower with short, stout, curved branches. *Form* spreading, open. *Twigs* moderately long, curved, slender; internodes long. *Bark* brown with some olive-green, lightly streaked with scarf-skin; pubescent near tips. *Lenticels* scattering, medium to small, oblong, not raised. *Buds* medium size, plump, obtuse, free, slightly pubescent.

FRUIT.

Fruit large or very large. *Form* roundish conic flat at the base, varying to oblate conic, regular or somewhat ribbed, symmetrical. *Stem* below medium to long, rather slender to moderately thick. *Cavity* large, acuminate or acute, very deep, broad, symmetrical, russeted and with outspreading rays of greenish-russet. *Calyx* medium to rather large, usually somewhat open; lobes medium in width and length, acute. *Basin* narrow to medium in width, moderately deep to deep, abrupt, smooth or slightly wrinkled.

Skin thick, tough, smooth, waxy, clear greenish-yellow or whitish, mottled, marbled and blushed with bright red over nearly the whole surface with wide broken stripes of carmine radiating from the cavity, overspread with thin bloom. *Dots* whitish or pale russet. *Prevailing effect* bright red.

Calyx tube long, wide, funnel-shape or conical. *Stamens* median or below.

Core medium size, somewhat abaxile; cells open or partly closed; core lines somewhat clasping. *Carpels* broadly ovate or approaching cordate, emarginate. *Seeds* medium or below, moderately wide, short, thick, plump, obtuse, dark brown.

Flesh whitish, moderately firm, coarse, tender, juicy, sprightly subacid, fair to good; suitable for culinary use and market.

Season late September to November.

COOPER.

REFERENCES. **1.** *Horticulturist,* 1:339,484. 1847. **2.** *Mag. Hort.,* 13:105, 200. 1847. **3.** Cole, **1849**:114. fig. **4.** Thomas, **1849**:147. **5.** Barry, **1851**:283. **6.** *Horticulturist,* 6:181. 1851. **7.** Emmons, *Nat. Hist. N. Y.,* 3:104. 1851. fig. **8.** Elliott, **1854**:127. **9.** Gregg, **1857**:41. **10.** Hooper, **1857**:26, 106, 109. **11.** Downing, **1857**:130. **12.** *Am. Pom. Soc. Cat.,* **1862.** **13.** Warder, **1867**:428. fig. **14.** Lyon, *Mich. Hort. Soc. Rpt.,* **1890**:290. **15.** Bailey, *An. Hort.,* **1892**:237. **16.** Budd-Hansen, **1903**:67.

SYNONYMS. *Beauty Red* (8, 11). COOPER (1, 2, 3, 4, 5, 6, 7, 8, 9, 10, 11, 12, 13, 14, 15, 16). *Lady Washington* (8, 11). *Seek-No-Further* of some, erroneously (8).

Fruit large, uniform, very attractive, rather light yellow indistinctly streaked with mixed red, mild subacid or nearly sweet, season October to December. The tree is very vigorous, upright spreading. Not recommended for planting in New York.

Historical. This is an old variety of unknown origin. In 1796 it was introduced from Connecticut into Ohio where it has been much esteemed (2). Evidently it has never been cultivated to any considerably extent in this State and is now practically unknown to New York fruit growers.

CORNELL.

REFERENCES. **1.** Downing, **1857**:131. **2.** *Am. Pom. Soc. Cat.,* **1862.** **3.** Warder, **1867**:716. **4.** Thomas, **1875**:200. **5.** Barry, **1883**:337. **6.** Lyon, *Mich. Hort. Soc. Rpt.,* **1890**:290. **7.** Bailey, *An. Hort.,* **1892**:237. **8.** Van

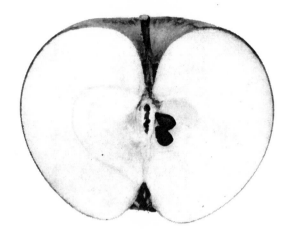

CONSTANTINE

Deman, *Rural N. Y.,* **61**:671. 1902. *fig.* **9.** Farrand, *Mich. Sta. Bul.,* **205**:44. 1903. **10.** Budd-Hansen, **1903**:67.

SYNONYMS. CORNELL (6, 8, 9). CORNELL FANCY (1, 2, 3, 4, 5, 7). *Cornell Fancy* (8). CORNELL *Fancy* (10). *Cornell's Favourite* (1).

Fruit usually of good medium size, sometimes large, waxen yellow and red, agreeable for dessert, in season from early September to November. The tree sometimes lacks vigor and productiveness (9).

Historical. Origin Pennsylvania (1). It is but little known in New York.

FRUIT.

Fruit above medium to large, uniform in size, somewhat variable in shape. *Form* roundish conic to oblate conic, often quite strongly ribbed, irregular; sides usually unequal. *Stem* medium to rather long and slender. *Cavity* moderately deep to deep, moderately wide, often compressed, sometimes lipped, sometimes russeted, with the russet extending beyond the cavity. *Calyx* below medium to rather large, closed or slightly open; lobes sometimes separated at the base, often upright, moderately acute. *Basin* deep, wide, rather abrupt, strongly furrowed, slightly wrinkled.

Skin moderately thick, tough, smooth, clear pale waxen yellow, partly overspread with thin attractive pinkish-red, often quite regularly splashed and striped with bright carmine. *Dots* conspicuous, variable, often large, irregular, russet or areolar with russet center, varying to small, light colored and submerged. *Prevailing effect* handsome red striped over clear yellow.

Calyx tube rather large, rather short, conical. *Stamens* median.

Core below medium, variable, nearly axile to decidedly abaxile; cells variable, open or closed; core lines meeting or slightly clasping. *Carpels* broadly ovate, slightly emarginate, sometimes tufted. *Seeds* numerous, rather large, dark brown, rather narrow, long, plump, acute to acuminate, sometimes tufted.

Flesh tinged with yellow, often affected with "Baldwin Spot," firm, moderately coarse, crisp, moderately tender, juicy, agreeable, mild subacid, aromatic, rich, sprightly, very good.

Season early September to November.

CORNER.

REFERENCE. **1.** Heiges, *U. S. Pom. Rpt.,* **1894**:18.
SYNONYMS. None.

We have neither seen Corner nor received any report concerning it. The following account of it was given in 1894 by S. B. Heiges, then United States Pomologist (1).

"Size above medium; oblate; cavity wide, deep, marked by russet netting; stem one-half inch, medium diameter; basin, medium, regular, marked by russet; calyx segments with mammiform bases, wide, long, converging or slightly reflexed; surface moderately smooth; color yellow, washed with red and striped with crimson; dots numerous, russet, some with dark centers, depressed; flesh yellowish, moderately fine grained, tender, moderately juicy; core large, wide, clasping, closed; flavor mild subacid; quality very good. Season early winter. Well known locally in Orange county, N. Y."

COX ORANGE.

REFERENCES. 1. *Horticulturist*, 13:168. 1858. 2. Downing, **1869**:135. 3. Leroy, **1873**:517. fig. 4. *Am. Pom. Soc. Cat.*, **1881**:8. 5. Hogg, **1884**:55. 6. Thomas, **1885**:507. 7. Bailey, *An. Hort.*, **1892**:237. 8. Bunyard, *Jour. Roy. Hort. Soc.*, **1898**:356. 9. Willard, *Rural N. Y.*, **58**:754. 1899. 10. Thomas, *Garden*, **59**:34. 1901. figs.

SYNONYMS. *Cos Orange* (3). COX ORANGE (8). *Cox's Orange* (3). COX'S ORANGE PIPPIN (1, 2, 4, 5. 6. 7, 9, 10). *Cox's Orange Pippin* (3). ORANGE DE COX (3). *Reinette Orange de Cox* (3).

One of the best in quality of the English dessert apples; in season from late September to early winter. The fruit is of medium size or above medium, red and yellow. When highly colored it is attractive, with the red predominant. The tree is a moderate grower and productive. It is well adapted for growing on dwarf stock, either Paradise or Doucin. It is not recommended for commercial planting, but it is a desirable variety for the home orchard.

Historical. Cox Orange is said to have originated in 1830 from seed of Ribston, at Colnbrook Lawn near Slough, Bucks, England (5). It is sometimes propagated by American nurserymen but it has never been extensively planted in this country and its cultivation is not increasing.

TREE.

Tree medium size or above, moderately vigorous with rather slender branches. *Form* upright, thickly branched, dense. *Twigs* long to medium, rather slender, irregularly crooked; internodes medium or below. *Bark* olive-green somewhat mottled with reddish-brown, slightly pubescent. *Lenticels* numerous, conspicuous, medium size, oblong, raised. *Buds* medium size to rather small, roundish, obtuse, appressed, pubescent. *Leaves* small to medium size and inclined to be narrow.

FRUIT.

Fruit medium or above, pretty uniform in size and shape. *Form* roundish oblate, sometimes slightly inclined to conic, regular or faintly ribbed, symmetrical, axis sometimes oblique. *Stem* usually obliquely inclined, short, thick, sometimes long. *Cavity* obtuse to somewhat acuminate, rather shallow to moderately deep, rather narrow, often somewhat russeted. *Calyx* rather small, closed or partly open. *Basin* rather shallow and obtuse to moderately deep and abrupt, rather narrow to moderately wide, smooth or slightly furrowed.

Skin rather thin, tough, smooth, attractive, washed with orange-red deepening to bright red and mottled and splashed with carmine, over a deep yellow background. *Dots* conspicuous, large, areolar with pale gray or russet center.

Calyx tube cone-shape or funnel-form. *Stamens* median to basal.

COX ORANGE

Core medium size, somewhat abaxile; cells usually symmetrical, open or closed; core lines clasping the funnel cylinder. *Carpels* thin, obovate to obcordate, emarginate, usually smooth. *Seeds* reddish-brown, above medium size, wide, obtuse to acute, often abortive.

Flesh yellow, firm, nearly fine, crisp, tender, very juicy, rich, sprightly subacid or becoming mild subacid, decidedly aromatic, very good to best.

Season late September to January.

CRANBERRY PIPPIN.

REFERENCES. **1.** Downing, **1845**:106. **2.** Thomas, **1849**:179. **3.** Emmons, *Nat. Hist. N. Y.*, **3**:88. 1851. **4.** Elliott, **1854**:169. **5.** Warder, **1867**:402. **6.** Lyon, *Mich. Hort. Soc. Rpt.*, **1890**:290. **7.** Bailey, *An. Hort.*, **1892**:237. **8.** *Amer. Gard.*, **16**:425. 1895. **9.** Woolverton, *Ont. Fr. Stas. An. Rpt.*, 2:9. 1895. fig. **10.** *Ib.*, 3:6. 1896. fig. **11.** Macoun, *Can. Dept. Agr. Bul.*, 37:43. 1901. **12.** Beach and Clark, *N. Y. Sta. Bul.*, **248**:116. 1904.
SYNONYMS. None.

In some sections this has proved a desirable apple, but in others it has not been successful. It is well known in some localities in the Hudson valley, in Northern and Western New York and in Ontario, where it is favorably regarded as a fall or early winter apple because of its good size, bright and attractive color and its uniform size and shape. It is a good storage apple, stands shipping well and brings good prices. It is suitable for market, cooking and evaporating, but not for dessert. It appears to be quite resistant to the attacks of scab. The trees are hardy and often very productive, but in some cases it is reported as undesirable because unproductive. It is said to be a shy bearer when young, but becomes productive with age.

Historical. Originated near Hudson, Columbia county (1).

TREE.

Tree large, very vigorous; branches stout, spreading. *Form* upright becoming somewhat spreading. *Twigs* long, moderately stout, light grayish-brown, quite pubescent; internodes short. *Bark* dull reddish-brown with some olive-green and thickly mottled with scarf-skin. *Lenticels* scattering medium to small, usually roundish. *Buds* medium or sometimes small, rather broad, deeply set, obtuse or sometimes acute, pubescent, appressed. *Leaves* dark green, broad, medium to large; foliage rather dense.

FRUIT.

Fruit large. *Form* roundish oblate, symmetrical. *Stem* short. *Cavity* broad, wavy. *Calyx* closed or somewhat open. *Basin* moderately deep, russeted. *Skin* smooth, shining, clear light yellow, handsomely blushed, striped and splashed with scarlet. *Dots* many, large, often red areolar with russet center. General appearance beautiful and attractive. *Flesh* white or with slight yellowish tinge, moderately juicy, mild subacid.

Season October to February. In the vicinity of its origin its season closes from a month to six weeks earlier than either Hubbardston or Tompkins King. In Northern New York and Ontario its season is late fall and early winter and often extends to midwinter.

CREAM.

REFERENCES. 1. *N. E. Farmer*, **1831** (cited by 3). **2.** Downing, **1869**:137. **3.** Ragan, *U. S. B. P. I. Bul.*, **56**:82. 1905.

SYNONYMS. None.

This variety originated in Queens county, N. Y. So far as we know it is no longer cultivated. Downing describes the tree as a vigorous grower and an early bearer and the fruit as medium or below, yellowish, fine-grained, pleasant, sweet, in season in September and October. Valued by some for dessert and culinary uses.

CROW EGG.

REFERENCES. 1. Kenrick, **1832**:43. **2.** Downing, **1857**:211. **3.** Warder, **1867**:716. **4.** Burrill and McCluer, *Ill. Sta. Bul.*, **45**:318. 1896.

SYNONYMS. CROW EGG (2). CROW'S EGG (1, 3, 4). *Egg Jop?* (2).

A sweet apple which is still occasionally found in very old orchards but is now practically obsolete. Some esteem it highly for dessert. Downing calls it not very good in quality (2). The old trees are productive.

TREE.

Tree moderately vigorous. *Form* upright spreading; top roundish, open; branches long, slender, crooked. *Twigs* medium in size, curved, slender; internodes very short. *Bark* reddish-brown, streaked with scarf-skin, slightly pubescent. *Lenticels* numerous, very small, oblong. *Buds* small, plump, obtuse, deeply set in the bark. *Leaves* medium in size, narrow.

FRUIT.

Fruit about medium in size. *Form* roundish to oblong or ovate. *Stem* long, slender. *Cavity* obtuse to sometimes acute, shallow, medium in width, symmetrical or obscurely furrowed, bright green or sometimes with outspreading russet. *Calyx* small to medium, closed. *Basin* small, shallow, narrow, somewhat abrupt, furrowed and wrinkled.

Skin tough, nearly smooth, bright pale yellow or greenish sometimes with faint bronze blush. *Dots* numerous, very small but conspicuous, russet.

Calyx tube rather small, funnel-shape or cone-shape. *Stamens* median.

Core large, abaxile; cells usually symmetrical and open; core lines clasping the funnel cylinder or meeting when the tube is conical. *Carpels* ovate, nearly smooth. *Seeds* numerous, rather light brown, flat, acute to acuminate.

Flesh whitish, firm, crisp, tender, rather juicy, sweet, agreeably flavored, good to very good.

Season October and November.

CRANBERRY PIPPIN

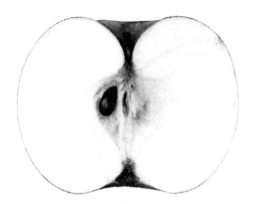

CRANBERRY PIPPIN

CZAR THORN.

REFERENCES. **1.** *Montreal Hort. Soc. Rept.*, **1881**:53. **2.** *Ib.*, **1883**:75. **3.** *Ia. Hort. Soc. Rpt.*, **1883**:430. **4.** Budd, *Ia. Agr. Coll. Bul.*, **1885**:7. **5.** Gibb, *Am. Pom. Soc. Rpt.*, **1887**:44. **6.** Taylor, *Me. Pom. Soc. Rpt.*, **1892**:57. **7.** Beach, *W. N. Y. Hort. Soc. Rept.*, **1896**:50. **8.** Hansen, *S. D. Sta. Bul.*, **76**:43. 1902. fig.

SYNONYMS. CZAR THORN (3, 4, 5, 6, 7, 8). *Czar Thorn* (2). *Czarskui Schip* (4). *No. 140 M* (8). *No. 206* (4, 5, 8). *Tars Thorn* (1). *Tsarskui Schip* (5). *Zarskischip* (7). ZARSKI SCHIP (2). *Zarski Schip* (3). ZARSKI ZARS (1).

A Russian apple of medium size, roundish conic, green and yellow usually shaded and striped with crimson; flesh rather coarse, sweet, hardly fair in quality; season September; not valuable.

DEADERICK.

REFERENCES. **1.** *U. S. Pom. Rpt.*, **1895**:22. **2.** Watts, *Tenn. Sta. Bul.*, **1**:11. 1896. fig. **3.** Taylor, *Am. Pom. Soc. Rpt.*, **1897**:37.

SYNONYMS. *Ben Ford* (2). DEADERICK (1, 2, 3). *Ozark Pippin* (2).

A good-sized green apple, of somewhat better color than Rhode Island *Greening*, but it does not keep as well, and is inferior to that variety in quality. The tree is a strong grower, healthy, and so far as tested here comes into bearing young and gives promise of being very productive. It has not been on trial long enough to indicate whether or not it has sufficient merit to be considered a promising variety for this state. In Tennessee it is considered a very valuable early winter apple (2).

Historical. Originated with Benjamin Ford, Washington county, Tenn. It was first disseminated as Ozark Pippin (2).

TREE.

Tree rather vigorous. *Form* spreading and somewhat upright. *Twigs* moderately stout, nearly straight; internodes short. *Bark* bright brownish-red. *Lenticels* roundish, often conspicuous, scattering, small. *Buds* medium size, appressed, obtuse, short, pubescent. *Leaves* medium size, somewhat narrow; often the base of the petioles is conspicuously streaked with red.

FRUIT.

Fruit large. *Form* broadly roundish, often rather conical, sometimes broadly ribbed, pretty regular, uniform. *Stem* medium to rather long, slender. *Cavity* large, acute to acuminate, deep, broad, usually smooth and symmetrical, sometimes slightly furrowed, occasionally prominently lipped. *Calyx* small, partly open or closed; lobes rather narrow, acute. *Basin* small, shallow, obtuse to somewhat abrupt, nearly smooth, a little wrinkled.

Skin moderately thick, tough, smooth, rather bright green becoming yellow, usually partly covered with a thin pinkish-red blush upon which there are often seen red, areolar dots with russet or whitish center; commonly the dots are whitish and often submerged. *Prevailing color* green or yellowish.

Calyx tube long, funnel-form. *Stamens* median to nearly marginal..

Core a little abaxile, medium to small; cells symmetrical, open or nearly so; core lines clasp the base of the cylinder. *Carpels* thin, generally smooth, broadly roundish, narrowing toward the base, slightly emarginate. *Seeds* numerous, medium or above, rather wide, obtuse.

Flesh yellowish, firm, moderately coarse, tender, rather juicy, pleasant sub-acid, good.

Season October to January.

DETROIT RED.

REFERENCES. **1.** *Mag. Hort.*, **10**:167. 1844. **2.** Downing, **1845**:106. **3.** *Horticulturist*, **1**:361. 1846. **4.** *N. Y. Agr. Soc. Trans.*, **1846**:192. **5.** Thomas, **1849**:164. **6.** Cole, **1849**:115. **7.** Emmons, *Nat. Hist. N. Y.*, **3**:65. 1851. fig., col. pl. **8.** Elliott, **1854**:130. **9.** Downing, **1857**:134. **10.** Warder, **1867**:532. fig. **11.** *Am. Pom. Soc. Cat.*, **1873**. **12.** Wickson, **1889**:245. **13.** Lyon, *Mich. Hort. Soc. Rpt.*, **1890**:290. **14.** Bailey, *An. Hort.*, **1892**:237. **15.** Waugh, *Vt. Sta. An. Rpt.*, **14**:291. 1901.

SYNONYMS. *Black Apple* of some (2, 9). BLACK DETROIT (5, 7). *Black Detroit* (2, 8). *Crimson Pippin* (6, 8, of some 2). DETROIT (1, 2, 4, 6, 8). *Detroit* (9). DETROIT BLACK (10). DETROIT RED (3, 9, 11, 12, 13, 14, 15). *Detroit Red?* (10).

Fruit growers in Western New York have commonly used the names Detroit Red and Detroit Black interchangeably for the remarkably variable variety which we are here describing as Detroit Red. We have been unable to determine whether there are in fact two distinct varieties of this type, or whether the differences which have been observed in the habit of growth and productiveness of the tree and in the form, size, general appearance, season and quality of the fruit, are altogether due to differences in the conditions under which the fruit has been produced. Speaking of these two names, Warder, in 1867, wrote, " I have put these two names together because the fruits presented as Black and as Red Detroit are so very much alike in all respects that it is not worth while to consider them distinct. * * * The Red variety may be distinct, as it keeps later."

Lyon (13) recognized two or more varieties of this type and distinguished them by the names Detroit Black and Detroit Red. Speaking of Detroit Red, he remarks : " There are probably several

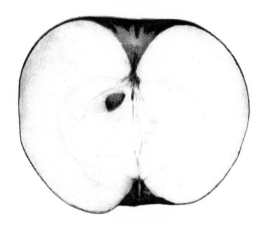

DETROIT RED

varieties grown under this name, none of them valuable;" and of The Detroit Black he says: " Unproductive, showy, valueless; it is probably the Detroit Red of Downing."

D. D. Stone, of Oswego, writes:[1] ' It seems to me that the two are not the same. Detroit Black seems to be more of a scrubby grower, the shape, size, firmness and color seem to be more constant and it does not crack so badly as the one we know as Detroit Red, but the season appears to be the same."

Detroit Red, or as it is often called, Detroit Black, as usually grown in Western New York, varies from medium to very large, commonly averaging about medium size. It is flattened at the ends, very dark crimson or purplish, becoming almost black, with snow-white flesh occasionally streaked with rose-pink. It is esteemed by many for dessert use because of its mild, pleasant flavor. There is considerable loss from premature dropping of the fruit and from fruit that is too small or too ill-shapen for market. It is quite variable in keeping qualities, being commonly in season about with Maiden Blush. The tree is a moderate grower, comes into bearing rather young, and is not a very reliable cropper. Some report that it is a shy bearer; others that it yields moderate to full crops biennially.

Historical. This is supposed to have been brought into the neighborhood of Detroit by the early French settlers and thence disseminated (1, 2, 4, 8). It was introduced into Ohio and Western New York before the middle of the last century. The variety is still sometimes listed by nurserymen (14). Its cultivation in New York state is declining and it is now seldom planted.

TREE.

Tree medium or eventually large, moderately vigorous to vigorous. *Form* upright spreading or roundish. *Twigs* medium to long, moderately slender, dark brown.

FRUIT.

Fruit very large to medium. *Form* oblate conic varying to roundish oblate, often strongly ribbed, irregular. *Stem* short, usually rather slender. *Cavity* often very large, acute to nearly acuminate, deep, moderately broad to very broad, frequently compressed, usually thinly russeted. *Calyx* variable, usually large, closed or somewhat open; lobes short, broad, rather obtuse. *Basin* medium in width and depth, obtuse to somewhat abrupt, irregularly furrowed and wrinkled and often with mammiform protuberances.

1 Letter, 1904.

Skin thick, rather tough, dark crimson, largely striped and splashed with purplish-carmine eventually becoming almost black, sometimes having a portion of the greenish-yellow ground color exposed. *Dots* numerous, conspicuous, very small, pale or russet.

Calyx tube rather short, wide, broadly conical. *Stamens* median to basal.

Core medium to large, axile; cells closed; core lines meeting or clasping. *Carpels* roundish to elliptical, rather flat, usually tufted. *Seeds* rather large, plump, obtuse to acute, moderately light brown.

Flesh white, sometimes streaked or stained with red, rather coarse, tender, juicy, agreeable mild subacid, very aromatic, good to very good.

Season last of September to December.

DUCHESS OF OLDENBURG.

This variety is often called Duchess or Duchess of Oldenburg, but the name now accepted for it by pomologists is Oldenburg, under which name it is described on page 150.

DUDLEY.

REFERENCES. **1.** *Me. Sta. Rpt.*, **1891** :97. **2.** *U. S. Pom. Ppt.*, **1891** :390. **3.** Bailey, *An. Hort.*, **1892** :245. **4.** Munson, *Me. Sta. Rpt.*, **1893** :132. **5.** Hoskins, *Amer. Gard.*, **14** :299. 1893. **6.** Munson, *Me. Sta. Rpt.*, **1902** :83, 91. **7.** Budd-Hansen, **1903** :71. **8.** Macoun, *Can. Dept. Agr. Rpt.*, **1903** :95.

SYNONYMS. DUDLEY (2, 6, 8). DUDLEY WINTER (1, 4). DUDLEY *Winter* (7). *Dudley's Winter* (6). NORTH STAR (3, 5). *North Star* (6, 7, 8).

A very hardy and productive variety which is being planted to a considerable extent in Northern New England. The fruit is pretty large, bright greenish-yellow washed and splashed with red, quite attractive in appearance and good in quality. Munson says that it is perhaps now more widely grown than any other of the newer sorts that have originated in New England. He considers it a valuable acquisition as a winter fruit for northern localities (6). As fruited at Geneva it is in season in September and October, although it may sometimes be kept into the winter. It is recommended for trial particularly where a very hardy apple of its season is desired.

Historical. A seedling of the Oldenburg, which originated with J. W. Dudley, Castle Hill, Aroostook county, Me. (1, 6). A few years ago it was introduced by a Rochester nursery under the name North Star but it was afterward found that this name had already been given to another variety and therefore the name Dudley Winter was retained for it, which, according to the accepted rules of nomenclature is shortened to Dudley.

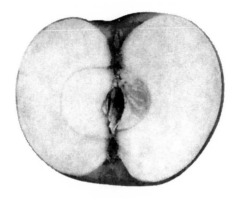

DUDLEY (Reduced Size)

TREE.

Tree small, moderately vigorous to vigorous; branches short, moderately stout. *Form* very spreading and drooping, rather dense. *Twigs* below medium length to short, almost straight, moderately stout to rather slender; internodes short to medium. *Bark* brown tinged with clear bright red, with but little or no scarf-skin and but slightly pubescent. *Lenticels* rather conspicuous, clear in color, scattering, medium in size, oblong, raised. *Buds* medium or above, rather prominent, plump, obtuse to acute, free or nearly so, somewhat pubescent.

FRUIT.

Fruit medium to large, uniform. *Form* roundish conic to roundish oblate, symmetrical. *Stem* long, rather thick. *Cavity* acute to almost acuminate, rather deep, broad, sometimes lightly russeted, obscurely furrowed. *Calyx* medium to large, open or partly closed. *Basin* decidedly abrupt, moderately deep to deep, moderately broad, obscurely furrowed, wrinkled.

Skin thin, tender, smooth, bright pale yellow or whitish mostly covered with a bright pinkish-red blush striped and splashed with bright carmine and covered with light bloom. *Dots* scattering, light, small. *General appearance* red or red striped over contrasting yellow, attractive.

Calyx tube long, moderately wide, funnel-shape or sometimes conical. *Stamens* median to marginal.

Core almost axile, medium or below; cells closed or partly open; core lines clasping or nearly so. *Carpels* broadly elliptical, not emarginate, slightly tufted. *Seeds* large, wide, long, somewhat flat, obtuse to acute, dull dark brown.

Flesh tinged with yellow, firm, crisp, nearly fine-grained, tender, very juicy, aromatic, brisk subacid eventually becoming mild, very good.

Season September and October or sometimes later.

DYER.

REFERENCES. **1.** Kenrick, **1835** :60. **2.** *Mag. Hort.*, 3 :37. 1837. **3.** Downing, **1845** :83. **4.** *Horticulturist*, 2 :289. 1847. **5.** Cole, **1849** :111. **6.** Thomas, **1849** :153. fig. **7.** Barry, **1851** :283, 286. **8.** Emmons, *Nat. Hist. N. Y.*, 3 :39. 1851. **9.** Elliott, **1854** :75. **10.** Hooper, **1857** :30. **11.** Hovey, *Mag. Hort.*, 27 :70. 1861. fig. **12.** *Am. Pom. Soc. Cat.*, **1862.** **13.** Warder, **1867** :639. fig. **14.** Lyon, *Mich. Hort. Soc. Rpt.*, **1890** :290. **15.** Bailey, *An. Hort.*, **1892** :238. **16.** Hansen, *S. D. Sta. Bul.*, 76 :47. 1902. **17.** Budd-Hansen, **1903** :72. fig.

SYNONYMS. *Bard Apple* (9, 11). *Beard Burden* (9, 11). *Bullripe* (9, 11). *Coe's Spice* (11). DYER (1, 3, 6, 8, 9, 10, 11, 12, 13, 14, 15, 16, 17). *Dyer* (4, 5, 7). *Golden Spice* (9, 11). *Mygatt's Bergamot* (9, 11). POMME ROYAL (2). *Pomme Royal* (6, 8, 9, 10, 11, 14, 16, 17). POMME ROYALE (4, 5, 7). *Pomme Royale* (3, 13). *Pomme Roye* (4). *Pomme Water* (9, 11). *Pommewater* in Ill. (13). *Smithfield Spice* (3, 5, 10, 11). *Tompkins* (9, 11). *White Spice* (9, 11). *Woodstock* (1).

One of the very finest dessert apples but not a good commercial variety (14). The fruit is of medium size, greenish-yellow with a shade of red. The crop does not ripen evenly and it requires more than one picking. It comes in

season late in August or early in September and ripens continuously until
midautumn. The tree is vigorous in the nursery but does not grow to be a
large tree in the orchard. It succeeds better when topworked upon some
hardier vigorous stock such as Tolman *Sweet* or Northern Spy. It is not
long-lived but comes into bearing rather young and yields good crops
biennially.

Historical. This variety has been supposed by some to be of French origin
and was formerly known as Pomme Royale, but Hovey believed it to be an
American apple (11). It was known in cultivation in Rhode Island during
the Revolutionary War (4). It was named Dyer by the Massachusetts Horticultural Society more than fifty years ago and has retained that name. It
is still occasionally listed by nurserymen (15). It is but little cultivated in
New York and is now seldom, if ever, planted in this state.

FRUIT (3, 9, 11, 13).

Fruit medium or sometimes large. *Form* roundish, slightly oblate, regular
or obscurely ribbed. *Stem* medium to long, slender. *Cavity* rather small,
acute, moderately deep to deep, sometimes lipped. *Calyx* small, closed; lobes
short to rather long, recurved. *Basin* medium to small, shallow to moderately
deep, furrowed.

Skin smooth, clear pale yellow or greenish, more or less flecked and marbled with thin russet with a brownish blush on one cheek. *Dots* dark or
russet.

Core medium size; cells open or closed; core lines clasping. *Seeds* numerous, plump, short, medium to small, pale.

Flesh yellowish-white, fine, very crisp, tender, aromatic, sprightly, mild
subacid, highly flavored, very good to best.

Season September and October.

EARLY HARVEST.

REFERENCES. 1. *Amer. Gard. Cal.*, 1806:584. 2. Coxe, 1817:101. fig. 3.
Thacher, 1822:129. 4. Buel, *N. Y. Bd. Agr. Mem.*, 1826:476. 5. Wilson,
1828:136. 6. Fessenden, 1828:131. 7. *London Hort. Soc. Cat.*, 1831:No. 355.
8. Kenrick, 1832:26. 9. Floy-Lindley, 1833:84. 10. *Mag. Hort.*, 1:362.
1835. 11. Manning, 1838:45. 12. *Ib.*, *Mag. Hort.*, 7:51. 1841. 13. Downing, 1845:72. fig. 14. French, *Horticulturist*, 1:256. 1846. 15. Hovey,
Mag. Hort., 14:115. 1848. fig. 16. Cole, 1849:97. fig. 17. Walker, *Mag.
Hort.*, 15:165. 1849. 18. Thomas, 1849:142. 19. Emmons, *Nat. Hist. N. Y.*,
3:16. 1851. 20. Barry, 1851:280. 21. Hovey, 1:75. 1851. *col. pl.* and fig.
22. *Am. Pom. Soc. Cat.*, 1852. 23. Elliott, 1854:84. fig. 24. Hooper, 1857:
31, 107, 111. 25. Gregg, 1857:36. fig. 26. Warder, 1867:403. fig. 27. Fitz,
1872:143, 160, 172. 28. Downing, 1872:10 index, app. 29. *Ib.*, 1881:11
index, app. 30. Hogg, 1884:67. 31. Wickson, 1889:243. 32. Lyon, *Mich.
Hort. Soc. Rpt.*, 1890:290. 33. Bailey, *An. Hort.*, 1892:238. 34. Stinson,
Ark. Sta. An. Rpt., 7:44. 1894. 35. Burrill and McCluer, *Ill. Sta. Bul.*, 45:
320. 1896. 36. Woolverton, *Ont. Fr. Stas. An. Rpt.*, 3:7. 1896. figs. 37.
Can. Hort., 20:328. 1897. figs. 38. Alwood, *Va. Sta. Bul.*, 130:121. 1901.
39. Waugh, *Vt. Sta. An. Rpt.*, 14:292. 1901. 40. Budd-Hansen, 1903:73. fig.

EARLY HARVEST

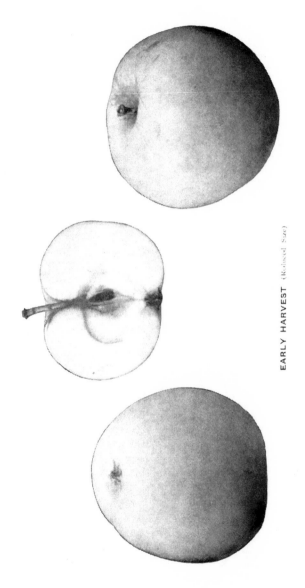

EARLY HARVEST (Reduced Size)

SYNONYMS. *Early French Reinette* (2, 8, 13, 15, 18, 19, 21, 23, 30, 34).
EARLY HARVEST (1, 7, 8, 10, 11, 12, 14, 15, 16, 17, 18, 19, 20, 21, 22, 24, 25,
26, 27, 28, 29, 30, 31, 32, 33, 34, 35, 36, 37, 38, 39, 40). *Early Harvest* (9,
23). *Early July Pippin* (24). *Early June* (23). HARVEST (23). *Harvest*
(21). *July Early Pippin* (15, 21, 30). JULY PIPPIN (9). *July Pippin* (13,
15, 18, 19, 21, 23, 30, 34). *Large Early* (15, 21, 30). *Large Early Harvest*
(15, 21). LARGE EARLY HARVEST (3). *Large White Juneating* (13, 15, 19,
21, 23, 30). *Maralandica* (29). *Oats* incorrectly (29). *Pomme d'Ete* of
Canada (30). *Prince's Early Harvest* (8, 30). PRINCE'S HARVEST (2, 4,
5, 6). *Prince's Harvest* (8, 13, 15, 18, 19, 21, 23, 24, 30, 34). *Prince's
Yellow Harvest* (30). *Tart Bough* (13, 15, 19, 21, 30). *Yellow Harvest*
(13, 15, 16, 18, 19, 21, 23, 24, 30, 34). *Yellow Juneating* (23).

Fruit medium, pale yellow, sometimes with a faint blush, tender,
sprightly subacid, and very good in quality. It is a desirable variety
for the home orchard because it is one of the earliest of the summer apples, and is excellent for either dessert or culinary uses.
It is not a desirable commercial variety because there is a comparatively large percentage of undersized or otherwise unmarketable
fruit, the color is such that it shows bruises very readily and it
keeps but a short time. The tree is a fairly good grower, moderately long-lived, comes into bearing rather early, is a biennial or
almost annual cropper and moderately productive.

Historical. Early Harvest has been known in cultivation for more than a
hundred years. Its origin is unknown but it is supposed to have originated
in America. At one time it was quite extensively cultivated for local market
in some localities but it is now seldom or never planted except for home use.

TREE.

Tree medium size, moderately vigorous. *Form* upright spreading or
roundish, open. *Twigs* moderately long, curved, rather stout; internodes
short. *Bark* dark brown with some olive-green, lightly streaked with scarf-
skin; slightly pubescent. *Lenticels* scattering, round, not raised. *Buds*
medium size, plump, obtuse, free, slightly pubescent.

FRUIT.

Fruit usually medium or below but sometimes rather large, uniform in
size and shape. *Form* oblate to nearly round, regular or slightly angular;
sides slightly unequal. *Stem* medium in length, moderately thick. *Cavity*
nearly acuminate, shallow, rather narrow to moderately broad, russeted and
with outspreading, broken russet rays. *Calyx* small to medium, closed;
lobes long, narrow. *Basin* shallow, moderately wide, obtuse, slightly
wrinkled.

Skin thin, tender, very smooth, clear pale waxen yellow, occasionally with deeper yellow on exposed check, sometimes slightly blushed. *Dots* numerous, large and small, submerged or russet.

Calyx tube short, funnel-shape. *Stamens* medium.

Core medium size, somewhat abaxile; cells closed or slightly open; core lines clasping. *Carpels* slightly obovate. *Seeds* small to rather large, narrow, long, plump, acute.

Flesh white, not firm, rather fine, crisp, tender, juicy, at first briskly subacid but eventually becoming milder, and more agreeable for dessert. Good to very good.

Season late July and August.

EARLY JOE.

REFERENCES. 1. *N. Y. Agr. Soc. Trans.*, 1843:52. 2. *Mag. Hort.*, 9:469. 1843. 3. *N. Y. Agr. Soc. Trans.*, 1846:187. fig. 4. Hovey, *Mag. Hort.*, 12:474. 1846. 5. *Ib.*, 13:159. 1847. fig. 6. Smith, *Horticulturist*, 1:386. 1847. fig. 7. *Cultivator*, 4:310. 1847. fig. 8. *Mag. Hort.*, 14:539. 1848. 9. Cole, 1849:105. fig. 10. Thomas, 1849:137. fig. 11. Emmons, *Nat. Hist. N. Y.*, 3:19. 1851. 12. Barry, 1851:280. 13. Elliott, 1854:75. fig. 14. Gregg, 1857:36. 15. Downing, 1857:76. 16. Hooper, 1857:32. 17. *Am. Pom. Soc. Rpt.*, 1860:240. 18. Warder, 1867:513. 19. Fitz, 1872:152, 172. 20. Leroy, 1873:404. figs. 21. *Ill. Hort. Soc. Rpt.*, 1877:124. 22. Hogg, 1884: 68. 23. Wickson, 1889:243. 24. Lyon, *Mich. Hort. Soc. Rpt.*, 1890:290. 25. Bailey, *An. Hort.*, 1892:238. 26. Macoun, *Can. Dept. Agr. Rpt.*, 1901: 96. 27. Waugh, *Vt. Sta. An. Rpt.*, 14:292. 1901. 28. Budd-Hansen, 1903: 74. fig.

SYNONYMS. EARLY JOE (1, 2, 3, 4, 5, 6, 7, 8, 9, 10, 11, 12, 13, 14, 15, 16, 17, 18, 19, 21, 22, 23, 24, 25, 26, 27, 28). JOE PRÉCOCE (20).

Fruit medium to small, red striped, excellent in flavor and quality for dessert use; season, August and early September. The tree is small to medium in size, slow growing, moderately long-lived, comes into bearing rather young and is a reliable biennial cropper. The fruit hangs pretty well to the tree until it is quite ripe. The crop contains a large percentage of undersized or otherwise unmarketable fruit. Recommended for the home orchard, but not for commercial planting.

Historical. Originated with Northern Spy and Melon in the orchard of Heman Chapin, East Bloomfield, Ontario Co., N. Y. This orchard was planted with seedling trees grown from seeds brought from Salisbury, Conn. about the year 1800. In October, 1843, Early Joe was exhibited at the fair of the New York State Agricultural Society, Rochester, N. Y., by Jonathan Buel of East Bloomfield (1). It has been widely disseminated and is still listed by nurserymen (25) but it is not cultivated extensively in any locality.

EARLY JOE

TREE.

Tree moderately vigorous, dwarfish with short, moderately stout, crooked branches. *Form* rather flat, spreading. *Twigs* short, straight, stout, with large terminal buds; internodes short. *Bark* dark brown, lightly streaked with scarf-skin; pubescent. *Lenticels* scattering, medium size, oblong, slightly raised. *Buds* medium size, plump, acute, free, slightly pubescent.

FRUIT.

Fruit small to medium, uniform in size and shape. *Form* oblate conic to conic, somewhat ribbed, rather symmetrical. *Stem* medium to long, rather slender to moderately thick. *Cavity* acute, shallow to medium in depth, rather broad, symmetrical, sometimes thinly russeted. *Calyx* medium size, closed or slightly open. *Basin* small to medium, usually shallow, medium in width or rather narrow, somewhat abrupt, smooth or slightly wrinkled.

Skin thin, tender, smooth, pale greenish-yellow, irregularly and obscurely striped and splashed with dull, dark red, in highly colored specimens becoming deeply blushed on the exposed cheek. *Dots* russet and greenish or nearly white.

Calyx tube medium in length, rather wide, broadly conical. *Stamens* median or basal.

Core medium to rather small, axile; cells slightly open or closed; core lines clasping. *Carpels* broadly obcordate to elliptical, decidedly concave. *Seeds* small to medium, rather wide, short, obtuse to acute.

Flesh tinged with yellow, fine, crisp, very tender, very juicy, mild subacid, very good to best.

Season August and September.

EARLY PENNOCK.

REFERENCES. 1. Humrickhouse, *Mag. Hort.*, 12:472. 1846. fig. 2. Cole, 1849:104. 3. Emmons, *Nat. Hist. N. Y.*, 3:14. 1851. 4. Barry, 1851:332. 5. Hooper, 1857:33, 106, 110. 6. Gregg, 1857:36. 7. Downing, 1857:137. 8. *Am. Pom. Soc. Cat.*, 1862. 9. Warder, 1867:594. fig. 10. Fitz, 1872:145. 11. *Ill. Hort. Soc. Rpt.*, 1875:49. 12. Thomas, 1875:191. 13. Downing, 1881:11 index, app. 14. Bailey, *An. Hort.*, 1892:238. 15. Budd-Hansen, 1903:74.

SYNONYMS. *August Apple* (7). EARLY PENNOCK (1, 2, 3, 4, 5, 6, 7, 8, 9, 10, 11, 12, 13, 14, 15). *Heicke's Summer Queen* (13). *Harmony* (7, ? of the south, 9). *Indian Queen* (7). *N. J. Red Streak* (7). *Shaker's Yellow* (7, 9). *Sleeper's Yellow* (5). *Warren Pennock* (5, 7).

Fruit large, showy, yellow covered with mixed striped red, but often the yellow predominates. Flesh yellow, moderately juicy, subacid, coarse, suitable for culinary use but not esteemed for dessert; season August. *Tree* hardy, a biennial cropper and moderately productive. Not recommended for planting in New York.

Historical. Origin unknown. It was first brought to notice in Ohio more than fifty years ago (1) where it was widely disseminated from some of the nurseries of that state. At one time it was being planted to a limited extent in New York but it has been almost wholly discarded.

EARLY RIPE.

REFERENCES. 1. Warder, 1867:717. 2. Downing, 1869:156. 3. Fitz, 1872: 151. 4. *Am. Pom. Soc. Cat.*, 1873. 5. Bailey, *An. Hort.*, 1892:238. 6. *Ill. Sta. Bul.*, 45:320. 1896. 7. *Mich. Sta. Bul.*, 143:200. 1897. 8. Thomas, 1897:634. 9. Alwood, *Va. Sta. Bul.*, 130:121. 1901. 10. *Kan. Sta. Bul.*, 106:52. 1902. 11. Budd-Hansen, 1903:74.

SYNONYMS. None.

Fruit of good medium size, yellowish-green, subacid, good for culinary use. The tree is a good grower, comes into bearing young, and yields full crops in alternate years.

Historical. The locality of its origin is unknown but it is supposed to have originated in Pennsylvania (2).

TREE.

Tree large, vigorous with moderately long, stout branches. *Form* upright spreading, rather dense, top roundish. *Twigs* long, stout, curved; internodes medium. *Bark* brown tinged with olive-green, lightly streaked with scarf-skin; heavily pubescent. *Lenticels* scattering, small to medium, oblong, slightly raised. *Buds* medium size, broad, plump, obtuse, appressed, pubescent.

FRUIT.

Fruit medium to above, fairly uniform in size but not in shape. *Form* roundish oblate somewhat inclined to conic, irregular, broadly ribbed. *Stem* often bracted, medium in length or short, thick. *Cavity* acute or approaching acuminate, usually shallow, rather broad, sometimes russeted. *Calyx* rather small, closed. *Basin* obtuse, usually very shallow, moderately wide, somewhat wrinkled.

Skin light yellowish-green. *Dots* numerous, small, pale gray or russet. *Calyx tube* rather narrow, funnel-form. *Stamens* median.

Core medium to rather large, abaxile; cells closed or partly open; core lines clasping. *Carpels* broadly roundish, emarginate. *Seeds* medium size, plump, obtuse.

Flesh white, quite firm, moderately coarse, crisp, tender, juicy, briskly sub-acid, becoming rather mild subacid when fully ripe, fair to good.

Season August.

EARLY STRAWBERRY.

REFERENCES. 1. Manning, 1838:46. 2. Downing, 1845:73. *fig.* 3. *Horti-culturist*, 1:145. 1846. 4. *Mag. Hort.*, 14:488. 1848. *fig.* 5. Thomas, 1849:139. *fig.* 6. Cole, 1849:101. *fig.* 7. Barry, 1851:280. 8. *Am. Pom. Soc. Cat.*, 1852. 9. Elliott, 1854:76. 10. Hooper, 1857:31, 106, 109. 11. Gregg, 1857:36. 12. *Horticulturist*, 14:425. 1859. 13. Warder, 1867:514. *fig.* 14. Downing, 1869:157. 15. Fitz, 1872:143, 151, 160. 16. Leroy, 1873: 310. *figs.* 17. Downing, 1881:12 index, app. 18. Wickson, 1889:243. 19. Watts, *Tenn. Sta. Bul.*, 5:78. 1890. 20. Lyon, *Mich. Hort. Soc. Rpt.*, 1890: 290. 21. Bailey, *An. Hort.*, 1892:238. 22. Budd-Hansen, 1903:75. *fig.*

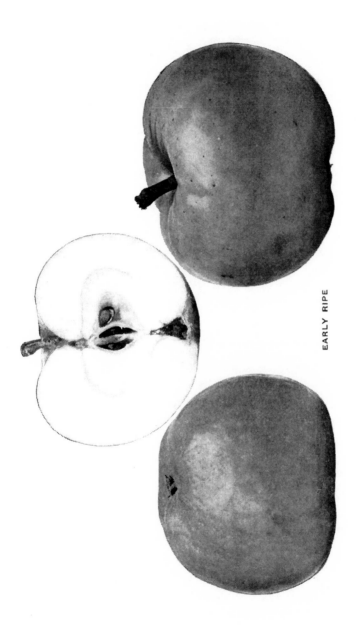

EARLY RIPE

SYNONYMS. AMERICAN RED JUNEATING (1). *American Red Juneating* (4, 5, 9, 13, 14, err. 5, ? 2). *De La Madeleine Rouge* (16). EARLY STRAW- BERRY (2, 3, 4, 5, 6, 7, 8, 9, 10, 11, 12, 13, 14, 15, 17, 18, 19, 20, 21, 22). *Early Strawberry* (16). FRAISE (16). *Louis XVIII* (16). *Red Juneating* (3, 6, 9, 10, 14, 15, 16, err. 4, err. of some American gardens, 2). *St. John Straw- berry* (17). *Striped Shropshire* (17). *Tennesee Early Red* (17).

Fruit of a very attractive bright deep red color, very desirable for dessert and good also for culinary uses. The tree is medium in size, a moderate grower, upright when young, but eventually be- coming roundish and somewhat spreading. It is hardy, healthy, comes into bearing young and yields moderate to good crops biennially or almost annually. It is not a very satisfactory variety for commercial planting because the demand for it is mostly lim- ited to local markets, a relatively high percentage of the apples are undersized or otherwise unmarketable and the fruit does not keep well. On account of its productiveness and high quality it is a desirable variety for the home orchard.

Historical. Early Strawberry is an American fruit which is said to have originated in the vicinity of New York (2, 3). It was formerly known to some under the name Red Juneating or American Red Juneating. The name Red Juneating has been applied also to the Margaret. In 1846 Downing published the following observations concerning these two varieties (3). " The Early Strawberry has a long stalk, and is a high colored fruit, striped with dark red. The Early Red Margaret has a short stalk and is a dull colored fruit, with faint red stripes. We have had both fruits in bearing this year, and have compared them for several years past. The Early Red Margaret is correctly shown in the beatiful colored plates of Ronald's *Pyrus Malus Brentifordensis*, and in the *Pomological Magazine*. Our Early Straw- berry apple is not described in any European work that we have seen. It is greatly superior to the Early Red Margaret in productiveness, and especially in *long keeping* and *ripening gradually*, qualities that are rare in early apples and for which the market dealers in New York rate the Strawberry very highly."

Early Strawberry has been extensively disseminated and is generally cata- logued by nurserymen throughout the apple-growing regions of America (21).

FRUIT.

Fruit below medium to medium, pretty uniform in shape and size. *Form* roundish conic or roundish, regular or somewhat ribbed; sides often unequal. *Stem* long and rather slender, often clubbed. *Cavity* acute or approaching acuminate, deep, broad, symmetrical, sometimes with faint radiating rays of russet. *Calyx* rather small, closed or sometimes open; lobes long, narrow. *Basin* small, shallow to moderately deep, narrow, obtuse, slightly furrowed.

Skin rather thick, tough, smooth, waxy, entirely red or yellow nearly covered with a rich dark red, mottled and irregularly striped and splashed with deeper red. *Dots* minute, grayish.

Calyx tube short, moderately wide, conical or approaching funnel-shape, with fleshy pistil point projecting into the base. *Stamens* median.

Core large, axile or somewhat abaxile; cells usually open, sometimes partly closed; core lines nearly meeting. *Carpels* broadly roundish to elliptical, much concave, emarginate. *Seeds* medium or above, wide, plump, obtuse, dark brown.

Flesh whitish-yellow often with streaks of red, moderately coarse, crisp, moderately tender, juicy, subacid, aromatic, sprightly, very good.

Season August.

EGG TOP.

REFERENCES. 1. *Mag. Hort.*, 10:210. 1844. 2. Elliott, 1854:169. 3. Hooper, 1857:34. 4. Warder, 1867:717. 5. Downing, 1869:159. 6. Thomas, 1875:498.

SYNONYMS. *Early June* (3). EGG TOP (1, 2, 4, 5, 6). *Eggtop* (3). EVE APPLE (3). *Eve* (2, 5). *Round Top* (2, 5). *Sheepnose* (2, 5). *Wine* of some (2, 5).

Fruit similar in shape to Black Gilliflower but not so large, somewhat streaked and shaded with red, pleasant flavored but not high in quality; good for dessert but not for cooking. Tree large, moderately vigorous and a regular and abundant bearer. In season from late fall to midwinter.

Historical. An old variety of uncertain origin. A few trees of it are occasionally found in the oldest orchards but it is now nearly obsolete.

ELGIN PIPPIN.

REFERENCES. 1. Bailey, *An. Hort.*, 1892:238. 2. Clayton, *Ala. Sta. Bul.*, 47:6. 1893. 3. Thomas, 1897:634. 4. Beach and Clark, *N. Y. Sta. Bul.*, 248:118. 1904.

SYNONYMS. None.

Fruit of good size and attractive appearance for a yellow apple. It evidently belongs to the Fall Pippin class but it does not closely resemble that variety and is not superior to it. Although it has much merit it does not excel other varieties of its season and is not recommended for planting in New York. The tree is a strong grower and productive.

Historical. Origin Alabama (2, 3). Downing questions whether it is identical with the White Spanish Reinette but it appears to be distinct from that variety.[1] Warder describes another variety under the name Elgin Pippin which we have not seen.[2]

TREE.

Tree vigorous, upright; branches long, moderately stout. *Form* very much spreading and somewhat drooping, rather dense. *Twigs* medium in

1 Downing, 1869:404.
2 Warder, 1867:717.

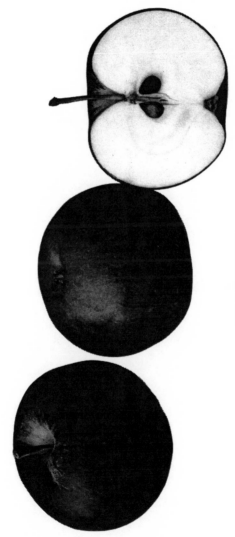

EARLY STRAWBERRY

size, curved, stout; internodes long. *Bark* brown, tinged with olive-green, mottled with scarf-skin, slightly pubescent. *Lenticels* scattering, large, oblong, raised. *Buds* large, broad, plump, obtuse, free, slightly pubescent.

FRUIT.

Fruit above medium to large, averages nearly large. *Form* oblate to roundish conic, distinctly ribbed, irregular; sides often unequal, sometimes elliptical, not uniform. *Stem* medium to very long, slender. *Cavity* acute to acuminate, medium in depth to deep, rather broad to narrow, usually with outspreading russet rays, sometimes decidedly compressed, sometimes lipped. *Calyx* medium to large, closed; lobes often leafy, long, acuminate. *Basin* sometimes oblique, shallow to moderately deep, moderately wide to rather narrow, obtuse to rather abrupt, often prominently and irregularly ribbed.

Skin thin, moderately tender, greenish yellow becoming deep yellow, sometimes with a faint bronze blush in the sun. *Dots* scattering, russet, or submerged and whitish.

Calyx tube rather large, moderately wide, conical or approaching funnelform. *Stamens* median to basal.

Core abaxile, medium to large; cells unsymmetrical, usually wide open; core lines meeting or slightly clasping. *Carpels* irregular, often somewhat ovate, much concave, tufted. *Seeds* often abortive, dark, rather large, long, flat, acute to acuminate.

Flesh whitish tinged with yellow, firm, moderately fine, crisp, tender, juicy, subacid, good.

Season September to December. Commercial limit, October.

ENGLISH PIPPIN.

REFERENCES. **1.** Gibb, *Am. Pom. Soc. Rpt.*, **1887**:50. **2.** Troop, *Ind. Sta. Bul.*, **53**:123. 1894. **3.** Budd, *Ia. Sta. Bul.*, **31**:328. 1895. **4.** Beach, *W. N. Y. Hort. Soc. Rpt.*, **1896**:51. **5.** Troop, *Ind. Sta. An. Rpt.*, **12**:79. 1899. **6.** Budd, *Ia. Sta. Bul.*, **41**:85. 1899. **7.** Beach and Clark, *N. Y. Sta. Bul.*, **248**:118. 1904.

SYNONYMS. ENGLISH PIPPIN (1, 2, 3, 4, 5, 6, 7). *Englischer Pepping* (1). *No. 587* (1). *Pepping Englischer* (1).

A Russian apple inferior in quality to standard varieties of its season. Not recommended for planting in New York.

FRUIT.

Fruit large. *Form* variable, roundish oblate to oblate conic or inclined to oblong truncate, ribbed; sides sometimes unequal. *Stem* short, usually not exserted. *Cavity* acuminate, rather wide, moderately deep, russeted and with outspreading russet. *Calyx* medium size, closed; lobes usually erect or connivent. *Basin* medium in width to rather narrow, deep, abrupt, irregularly furrowed.

Skin yellow or greenish, sometimes with shade of brownish-red overspread with thin white bloom. *Dots* minute, pale or russet.

Calyx tube cone-shape or approaching funnel-form. *Stamens* median.

Core large, somewhat abaxile; cells partly open; core lines meeting. *Seeds* medium size, obtuse.

Flesh tinged with yellow, moderately juicy, fine-grained, sprightly subacid, fair to good in quality.
Season late September to November.

ENGLISH SWEET.

Ramsdell or Ramsdell Sweet has been described by some leading
pomologists under the name English Sweet. Ramsdell *Sweet* is the
name accepted for this variety in the catalogue of the American
Pomological Society, and it is generally known among nurserymen and fruit growers as Ramsdell or Ramsdell Sweet. For a
description of this variety, the reader is referred to Ramsdell
Sweet, page 175.

FALL GREENING.

REFERENCES. **1.** Warder, **1867**:718.   **2.** Downing, **1869**:167.
SYNONYMS. None.

This variety originated at Claverack, Columbia county, N. Y. (1). According to Downing the tree is moderately vigorous and very productive. The
fruit medium size, greenish-yellow, subacid, good to very good. In season
from December to February.

Downing also mentions another Fall Greening of similar color, sprightly
subacid, in season from September to November; tree a poor grower.

We have not seen either of these varieties.

FALL HARVEY.

REFERENCES. **1.** Manning, **1838**:48.   **2.** Downing, **1845**:84.   **3.** Cole, **1849**:
117.   **4.** Hovey, *Mag. Hort.*, **15**:537.   1849.   fig.   **5.** Thomas, **1849**:155.   **6.**
Emmons, *Nat. Hist. N. Y.*, **3**:47.   1851.   *col. pl.* No. 74 and fig.   **7.** Barry,
1851:284.   **8.** Elliott, **1854**:132.   **9.** Gregg, **1857**:42.   **10.** Warder, **1867**:482.
11. *Am. Pom. Soc. Cat.*, **1869**.   **12.** Hoskins, *Amer. Gard.*, **15**:272.   1894.
13. Waugh, *Vt. Sta. An. Rpt.*, **14**:296.   1901.   **14.** Budd-Hansen, **1903**:79.
SYNONYMS.   FALL HARVEY (**1, 2, 3, 4, 5, 6, 7, 8, 9, 10, 11, 12, 14**).   *Fall
Harvey* (13).   *Fall Pippin* erroneously (13).   HARVEY (13).

Fruit large, yellow, showy, similar in general appearance to Fall Pippin
but less desirable where that variety can be grown. According to Hoskins (12) it is hardy in Northern Vermont and has there proved an excellent annual bearer. He considers it valuable for all Northern New England
and Canada. Cole (3) observes that the fruit is "fine and fair but not
first-rate, and rather apt to fall, or to rot on the tree." Elliott (8) says that
it is not productive but Hovey (4) and Cole (3) call it a vigorous grower
and a good bearer. In the nursery it may be easily known from Fall Pippin
by its yellow and more slender shoots (4).

FRUIT (2, 3, 4, 10).

Fruit large. *Form* roundish, slightly oblate, regular or somewhat ribbed
at the base; crown large, slightly oblique. *Stem* short, stout or rather slen-

der. *Cavity* rather shallow to deep, wide, uneven. *Calyx* small to large, closed. *Basin* narrow to rather wide, shallow, wrinkled.

Skin smooth, pale yellow to deep yellow, sometimes blushed. *Dots* small, gray or russet.

Core large, abaxile. *Seeds* medium size, acute, short, plump.

Flesh whitish or tinged with yellow, a little coarse, crisp, juicy, rich subacid, with high flavor, very good quality.

Season October to December.

FALL JENNETING.

REFERENCES. 1. *Mag. Hort.*, 12:474. 1846. 2. Hovey, *Ib.*, 13:161. 1847. fig. 3. Elliott, 1854:132. 4. Downing, 1857:213. 5. *Am. Pom. Soc. Cat.*, 1862. 6. Warder, 1867:533. fig. 7. Thomas, 1875:498. 8. Lyon, *Mich. Hort. Soc. Rpt.*, 1890:290. 9. Bailey, *An. Hort.*, 1892:239. 10. Budd-Hansen, 1903:80.

SYNONYMS. FALL GENETING (6). *Fall Gennetting* (3). FALL JENETTING (8). FALL JENNETING (1, 2, 4, 5, 7, 10). FALL JENNETTING (3, 9).

Fruit often large but variable in size, a considerable portion of the crop being undersized or otherwise unmarketable. It is of a green or yellowish color, shows bruises quite readily, does not stand shipping very well and is not a good keeper. It is very good for culinary uses and acceptable for dessert; being of light weight, it is less desirable than some other varieties for evaporating. The tree is an exceedingly strong grower and long-lived, eventually becoming very large, tall and spreading. It is hardy, healthy, comes into bearing rather young and is a reliable cropper, yielding moderately good to heavy crops biennially or nearly annually. There is apt to be considerable loss from premature dropping of the fruit. Not recommended for planting in New York.

Historical. It appears that this variety was brought into Western New York from Athens on the Hudson, about 1827 (1, 2). Elliott (3) in 1854 called it an old Connecticut variety. It has been grown more largely in portions of the Hudson valley and of Western New York than it has in other sections of the state but it has not been cultivated extensively in any locality. It is still listed by nurserymen (9) but in New York it is now seldom planted and is gradually going out of cultivation.

TREE.

Tree large, vigorous or very vigorous. *Form* spreading or somewhat roundish. *Twigs* moderately long, curved, moderately stout; internodes medium. *Bark* dark brown lightly streaked with gray scarf-skin; slightly pubescent. *Lenticels* scattering, medium size, oblong, slightly raised. *Buds* medium size, broad, plump, obtuse, free, pubescent.

Fruit above medium to large. *Form* roundish oblate inclined to conic, slightly ribbed at the base; sides unequal. *Stem* medium to short, moderately thick. *Cavity* acuminate, deep, wide, rather symmetrical, with outspreading rays of russet. *Calyx* below medium to rather large, closed or somewhat open; lobes long, narrow, acute, reflexed. *Basin* rather small, shallow, narrow, somewhat furrowed and wrinkled.

Skin thin, tough, smooth, pale greenish-yellow with faint brownish-red or bronze blush. *Dots* moderately numerous, rather inconspicuous, sometimes russet but more often whitish and submerged. *Prevailing effect* yellow.

Calyx tube rather long, narrow funnel-shape. *Stamens* median to basal.

Core small, axile to somewhat abaxile; cells symmetrical, closed; core lines clasping. *Carpels* somewhat roundish to broadly ovate. *Seeds* light brown, rather small, moderately narrow, plump, acute.

Flesh tinged with yellow, moderately firm, fine, crisp, tender, juicy, sprightly, subacid, good.

Season late September to December.

FALL ORANGE.

REFERENCES. 1. Thomas, *Cultivator*, 5:246. 1848. 2. *Ib.*, 1849:155. 3. Elliott, 1854:149. 4. Gregg, 1857:42. 5. Downing, 1857:143. 6. *Am. Pom. Soc. Cat.*, 1862. 7. Warder, 1867:718. 8. Downing, 1869:168. 9. *Ib.*, 1872:10 index, app. 10. Bailey, *An. Hort.*, 1892:239. 11. Burrill and McCluer, *Ill. Sta. Bul.*, 45:321. 1896. 12. Budd-Hansen, 1903:80. fig.

SYNONYMS. FALL ORANGE (1, 2, 4, 5, 6, 7, 8, 9, 10, 11, 12). *Fall Orange* (3). *Hogpen* (8). *Holden* (5, 8). *Holden Pippin* (8). *Hoypen* (5). *Jones' Pippin* (5, 8). *Long Island* (8). *Long Island Graft* (9). *N. Y. Bellflower* (9). ORANGE (3). *Orange* (8). *Red Check* (8). *Speckled* (9). *Westbrook* (9). *White Graft* of Wis. (8). *White Newell* (9).

When well grown Fall Orange is of good size, yellow or greenish, with occasionally a shade of red, agreeable subacid, and very good in quality for culinary use. When it becomes fully ripe so that its acidity is subdued it is an excellent dessert apple. The tree is thrifty, hardy, long-lived and a regular biennial cropper, often yielding pretty heavy crops. It is not generally regarded as a good commercial variety because its color is yellow, the fruit is rather tender and a poor shipper, and with heavy crops there is apt to be a comparatively large percentage of fruit that is undersized or otherwise unmarketable. It is in season from late September to early winter; sometimes a portion of the fruit is kept till spring.

FALL ORANGE

It resembles Autumn Swaar considerably in general appearance; for a comparison of the two varieties the reader is referred to the description of Autumn Swaar, pages 11, 12.

Historical. Fall Orange was described by Thomas in 1848 as a new or newly-introduced variety of unknown origin (1). In 1857 Downing gave its origin as Holden, Mass. (5). Since its introduction it has been sparingly disseminated in various parts of the state. Although it is still listed by some nurserymen (10) it is now seldom planted in New York.

FRUIT.

Fruit above medium to large; fairly uniform in size but not in shape. *Form* roundish conic, irregular. *Stem* medium to rather short, slender. *Cavity* acute to acuminate, deep, medium in width, regular or slightly compressed, often russeted and with outspreading russet rays. *Calyx* medium to large, open or sometimes nearly closed. *Basin* uneven, one side projecting higher than the other, moderately deep to deep, narrow to moderately wide, abrupt, furrowed.

Skin pale yellow or greenish, sometimes with brownish blush. *Dots* numerous, large and small, russet or sometimes reddish, areolar.

Calyx tube rather large, usually long, conical to funnel-form with fleshy pistil point projecting into the base; the lower part of the funnel cylinder is sometimes enlarged. *Stamens* median or below.

Core medium to rather small, axile; cells symmetrical; core lines meeting when the tube is short, clasping when it is long. *Carpels* elliptical to nearly cordate. *Seeds* not numerous, rather dark brown, medium to below, plump, obtuse.

Flesh white, moderately fine, crisp, rather tender, juicy, subacid, aromatic, very good.

Season late September to early winter.

* FALL PIPPIN.

REFERENCES. **1.** *Amer. Gard. Cal.,* **1806**:585. **2.** Coxe, **1817**:109. *fig.* **3.** Cobbett, **1821**:par. 300. **4.** Thacher, **1822**:120. **5.** Buel, *N. Y. Bd. Agr. Mem.,* **1826**:476. **6.** Fessenden, **1828**:131. **7.** Kenrick, **1832**:32. **8.** Floy-Lindley, **1833**:85. **9.** *Mag. Hort.,* 1:326, 364. 1835. **10.** Downing, **1845**:84. **11.** Floy-Lindley, **1846**:412 app. **12.** Phœnix, *Horticulturist,* 1:361. 1847. **13.** Downing, *Ib.,* 3:345. 1849. Cole, **1849**:117. *fig.* **15.** Thomas, **1849**: 155. *fig.* **16.** Phœnix, *Horticulturist,* 4:472. 1850. **17.** Barry, **1851**:283. **18.** Emmons, *Nat. Hist. N. Y.,* 3:44. 1851. *fig., col. pl.* No. 18. **19.** *Am. Pom. Soc. Cat.,* **1852**. **20.** Elliott, **1854**:78. *fig.* **21.** Gregg, **1857**:42. **22.** Hooper, **1857**:34, 106, 110. **23.** Warder, **1867**:571. *fig.* **24.** Downing, **1869**: 169. *fig.* **25.** Todd, **1871**:311. *fig.* **26.** Fitz, **1872**:143, 149, 162. **27.** Hogg, **1884**:74. **28.** Wickson, **1889**:244. **29.** Lyon, *Mich. Hort. Soc. Rpt.,* **1890**: 290. **30.** Bailey, *An. Hort.,* **1892**:239. **31.** Woolverton, *Ont. Fr. Stas. An. Rpt.,* 8:7. 1901. *figs.* **32.** Budd-Hansen, **1903**:80. *fig.* **33.** Beach and Clark, *N. Y. Sta. Bul.,* **248**:119. 1904.

SYNONYMS. *American Fall* (7). AUTUMN PIPPIN (4). *Cathead* incorrectly (24). *Cat Head* (25). *Cobbett's Fall* (7). *Cobbett's Fall Pippin* (27). *Concombre Ancien* (7). *De Rateau* (7). *D'Espange* (7). *Episcopal* (24, 25). FALL PIPPIN (1, 2, 3, 5, 6, 7, 8, 9, 10, 11, 12, 13, 14, 15, 16, 17, 18, 19, 20, 21, 22, 23, 24, 25, 26, 27, 28, 29, 30, 31, 32, 33). *Fall Pippin* (4). *Golden Pippin* (22, 25, erroneously 2, 24). *Holland Pippin* (2, 5, err. 15). *Philadelphia Pippin* (20, 24, 25). *Pound Pippin* (24, 25). *Pound Royal* (25, of some 24). *Prince's large Pippin of N. Y.* (2). *Reinnete Blanche d'Espagne* (7). *Summer Pippin* (2). *Van Duym's Pippin* (2). *Van Dyn's Pippin* (5). *York Pippin* (24, 25).

Fruit large, and, when fully ripe, of an attractive yellow color. The flesh is tender, rich and very good in quality, being excellent for dessert but especially desirable for culinary uses. The tree is a strong grower, hardy and very long-lived, eventually becoming large or very large. Since the foliage and fruit are both quite subject to the attacks of the apple-scab fungus, thorough preventive treatment for this disease is necessary in order to grow Fall Pippin successfully for commercial purposes.[1] The crop does not ripen uniformly, some of the fruit being ripe, well colored and ready for immediate use in September, while at the same time a considerable portion of the crop is still hard and green. When grown under favorable conditions and properly handled some portion of the crop may keep till midwinter or later, but even carefully selected fruit cannot be relied upon to hold in common storage till December 1st without considerable loss. In cold storage it may be held till January or February (33). Fall Pippin is generally in pretty good demand in local markets, and in portions of Eastern New York it is being used to a limited extent for the early export trade. It is one of the most desirable varieties of its season for the home orchard.

HOLLAND PIPPIN AND FALL PIPPIN COMPARED.

From the time of Coxe (2), Fall Pippin has by some been called Holland Pippin. The Holland Pippin indeed much resembles Fall Pippin, but it differs from it in being in season from mid-August

---

[1] Directions for treating apple scab are given in the reports of this Station for 1899:399-418, and for 1903:321-386.

FALL PIPPIN (Reduced Size)

to midautumn and in being more roundish and less flattened, and in having a short, thick stem which is not exserted.

Historical. Origin unknown. Downing (10) held the opinion that Fall Pippin is an American variety and probably a seedling raised in this country from either the White Spanish Reinette or the Holland Pippin, both of which it resembles. It has been widely disseminated from the Atlantic to the Pacific in most of the important apple-growing regions of the continent and is still listed by many nurserymen (30). We are unable to determine how long this variety has been in cultivation. In some New York orchards trees of it are found which are more than one hundred years old. It is quite generally grown for home use throughout New York, and also to a limited extent for market, but it is now seldom planted.

TREE.

Tree large, moderately vigorous to very vigorous, with large, long branches which eventually become somewhat drooping. *Form* spreading or roundish and rather dense. *Twigs* moderately long, curved, stout and with large terminal buds; internodes medium. *Bark* dark reddish-brown, somewhat tinged with green, heavily coated with gray scarf-skin; much pubescent. *Lenticels* scattering, medium size, oval, raised. *Buds* medium size, broad, plump, obtuse, free, pubescent.

FRUIT.

Fruit large or very large, pretty uniform in size and shape. *Form* roundish to roundish oblate, sometimes a little inclined to conic, or sometimes slightly oblong and truncate, often obscurely ribbed. *Stem* medium to rather long, thick. *Cavity* acute or approaching acuminate, moderately deep, moderately narrow to rather wide, symmetrical or sometimes compressed, russeted. *Calyx* medium to large, open; lobes separated at the base, moderately long, rather narrow, acuminate. *Basin* medium in depth to deep, moderately narrow to rather wide, abrupt, wavy, slightly wrinkled.

Skin thin, smooth, at first greenish-yellow but becoming clear yellow, sometimes faintly blushed. *Dots* numerous, small, pale and submerged or russet.

Calyx tube large, wide, long, conical to nearly funnel-form. *Stamens* median to basal.

Core medium size, somewhat abaxile; cells symmetrical, closed or partly open; core lines meeting or clasping. *Carpels* roundish, emarginate, tufted. *Seeds* rather dark brown, medium size, somewhat acute, plump.

Flesh whitish or tinged with yellow, moderately firm, rather fine, tender, very juicy, agreeable subacid, somewhat aromatic, very good.

Season late September to January.

FALL WINE.

REFERENCES. 1. *Mag. Hort.*, **14**:114. 1848. **2.** Cole, **1849**:108. **3.** *Ib.*, **1849**:109. **4.** Elliott, **1854**:77. **5.** *Horticulturist*, **10**:87. 1855. **6.** Hooper,

1857:36.   7. Downing, 1857:78.   8. *Am. Pom. Soc. Rpt.*, 1860:50, 240.   9.
Warder, 1867:434.   fig.   10. Downing, 1869:170.   fig.   11. Fitz, 1872:153.
12. Thomas, 1875:200.   13. Barry, 1883:338.   14. Wickson, 1889:244.   15.
Lyon, *Mich. Hort. Soc. Rpt.*, 1890:290.   16. Bailey, *An. Hort.*, 1892:239.
17. Budd-Hansen, 1903:81.   fig.

SYNONYMS. FALL WINE (1, 3, 4, 5, 6, 7, 8, 9, 10, 11, 12, 13. 14, 15, 16, 17).
House (10). *Hower* (10). *Musk Spice* (10). *Ohio Wine* (7, 10, 13).
Sharpe's Spice (7, 10). *Sweet Wine* (7, 10). *Uncle Sam's Best* (7, 10).
WINE (2). *Wine* of Cole (4).

Fruit medium or above, bright red, attractive; in season from September
to early winter. The tree is of medium size with rather drooping branches,
moderately vigorous, healthy, moderately long-lived and yields good to heavy
crops biennially. The fruit is apt to drop to a considerable extent before it
is fully mature. It is very tender, not a good shipper and not a desirable
commercial variety. It is not much valued for culinary use but it is generally
esteemed wherever it is known on account of its excellent dessert qualities.
It is not recommended for commercial planting in New York.

Fall Wine should not be confused with Twenty Ounce which in some sections of New York is known under the name of Wine apple.[1] It is also quite
distinct from the true Wine which is a large, showy apple that ripens in
midautumn and often keeps well through the winter.[2]

Historical. The origin of this variety is unknown. Elliott (4) says that
it was introduced into the West from the garden of Judge Jonathan Buel,
Albany, N. Y., about 1832. It has been a favorite variety in many parts of
the Middle West but has not been extensively cultivated in New York and
is now seldom or never planted in this state.

FRUIT.

Fruit medium or above. *Form* roundish oblate, somewhat ribbed; sides
often unequal. *Stem* medium to rather long. *Cavity* obtuse to somewhat
acute, wide, shallow to moderately deep, sometimes lipped. *Calyx* small to
medium, closed or partly open; lobes long, narrow, reflexed. *Basin* deep,
wide or medium in width, rather abrupt, furrowed.

Skin clear yellow washed with red which on the exposed cheek deepens to
a beautiful bright blush, indistinctly striped with carmine. *Dots* yellowish-
brown or russet.

Calyx tube long, narrow, funnel-form. *Stamens* median.

Core medium, axile; cells symmetrical, closed or slightly open; core lines
clasping. *Carpels* broadly roundish, tufted. *Seeds* medium size, rather wide,
acute.

Flesh tinged with yellow, tender, juicy, aromatic, very mild subacid or
almost sweet; very good for dessert but only fair for culinary use.

Season September to January.

---

1 See description of Twenty Ounce, page 227.
2 See description of Wine apple in Volume I of this Report, page 373.

FAMEUSE.

References. 1. Forsyth, 1824:101. 2. Buel, *N. Y. Bd. Agr. Mem.*, 1826: 476. 3. *London Hort. Soc. Cat.*, 1831:No. 757. 4. Kenrick, 1832:33. 5. Floy-Lindley, 1833:16. 6. Manning, 1838:55. 7. *Ib., Mag. Hort.*, 7:45. 1841. 8. Downing, 1845:91. 9. *Horticulturist*, 1:257. 1846. 10. Thomas, *Cultivator*, 5:306. 1848. fig. 11. *Ib.*, 1849:147. fig. 12. Cole, 1849:118. 13. Emmons, *Nat. Hist. N. Y.*, 3:36. 1851. col. pl. No. 48. 14. Hovey, 2:7. 1851. col. pl. and fig. 15. *Mag. Hort.*, 17:15. 1851. fig. 16. Goodrich, *Ib.*, 17:122. 1851. 17. *Am. Pom. Soc. Cat.*, 1852. 18. Elliott, 1854:77 19. Gregg, 1857:42. 20. Hooper, 1857:36, 107, 110. 21. Lothrop, *Mag. Hort.*, 32:363. 1866. 22. Warder, 1867:595. 23. Todd, 1871:25. fig. 24. Fitz, 1872:145. 25. Leroy, 1873:483. 26. *Montreal Hort. Soc. Rpt.*, 1876:12. 27. Jack, *Ib.*, 6:61. 1880. 28. Ib., 8:140. 1881-82. 29. Hogg, 1884:58. 30. Hoskins, *Rural N. Y.*, 47:249. 1888. 31. Wickson, 1889:245. 32. *Montreal Hort. Soc. Rpt.*, 14:88, 89. 1889. 33. Lyon, *Mich. Hort. Soc. Rpt.*, 1890: 290. 34. *Montreal Hort. Soc. Rpt.*, 15:19, 26. 1890. 35. Bailey, *An. Hort.*, 1892:239. 36. *Ib.*, 1892:249. 37. Taylor, *Me. Pom. Soc. Rpt.*, 1892:57. 38. *Amer. Gard.*, 14:425. 1893. 39. Burrill and McCluer, *Ill. Sta. Bul.*, 45:321. 1896. 40. *Can. Hort.*, 20:304. 1897. figs. 41. Woolverton, *Ont. Fr. Stas. An. Rpt.*, 5:12. 1898. figs. 42. *Can. Hort.*, 22:226. 1899. 43. Craig, *Amer. Gard.*, 20:27. 1899. 44. *Vt. Sta. Bul.*, 83:83-92. 1900. 45. *Can. Hort.*, 24:236. 1901. 46. Waugh, *Vt. Sta. An. Rpt.*, 14:293. 1901. 47. Budd-Hansen, 1903:82. fig. 48. Beach and Clark, *N. Y. Sta. Bul.*, 248:120. 1904. 49. Scriber, *Can. Hort.*, 28:277. 1905.

Synonyms. *Chimney Apple* (14, 16, 22, 25). De Neige (3, 25, 29). *De Neige* (14, 15). *du Marechal* (25). Fameuse (1, 2, 4, 6, 7, 9, 10, 11, 12, 13, 14, 15, 16, 17, 18, 19, 20, 21, 22, 23, 24, 26, 27, 28, 30, 31, 32, 34, 35, 37, 38, 39, 40, 41, 42, 43, 44, 45, 46, 47, 48). *Fameuse* (5, 8, 25, 29, 36). *La Belle Fameuse* (43). *La Fameuse* (29). *Neige* (2). *Neige-Framboise de Gielen* (25). Pomme de Neige (5, 8). *Pomme de Neige* (4, 9, 10, 11, 13, 14, 15, 16, 18, 20, 22, 23, 41). *Pomme de Niège* (1, 7, 12). *Pomme Fameuse* (3). *Pomme de Fameuse* (14, 15). *Sanguineus* (8, 14, 15, 18, 23, 25). Snow (36). *Snow* (2, 10, 12, 14, 16, 18, 20, 21, 22, 23, 25, 31, 33, 41, 43, 46, 47, 48).

Fameuse is one of the most desirable dessert apples of its season. It is very beautiful in appearance and the flesh is white, tender and excellent in flavor and quality for dessert. It is decidedly inferior to other varieties of its season for culinary purposes. It is well known in market, and during its season, which extends from October to the holidays, it usually sells above average market prices, particularly if well colored and free from scab or other imperfections. The fruit is often badly injured by the apple-scab fungus, but this may readily be controlled by proper preventive treatment.[1] It keeps well in cold storage. Some report that if free

---

[1] *N. Y. Sta. An. Rpt.*, 18:399-418. 1899. *Ib.*, 22:321-386. 1903.

from scab it may be held as long as Rhode Island *Greening* (48). In the Champlain district and in portions of the St. Lawrence valley it is one of the most important varieties found in commercial orchards. Generally speaking, it grows to a higher degree of perfection in those districts than it does in other apple-growing regions of New York. In the more southern sections of the state it appears to succeed best in the high elevations and on light well drained soil with clay subsoil. The tree is of medium size, a moderate grower, hardy, healthy, rather long-lived, and a reliable cropper yielding good to heavy crops biennially or sometimes nearly annually. The fruit hangs pretty well to the tree. Fruit of marketable grades is fairly uniform in size, but there is a considerable amount of it that is too small for market. In those portions of New York south of Lake Champlain and the St. Lawrence valley the fruit does not usually develop its best color, and in some seasons, and particularly in unfavorable localities, it is so poorly colored as to be quite unsatisfactory. In such locations it is better for the fruit grower to plant McIntosh instead of Fameuse if he desires to grow a variety of the Fameuse group.

Historical. Waugh (44) gives the following historical account of the Fameuse. " The history of Fameuse is obscure, probably beyond clearing up satisfactorily, but extremely interesting as far as we know or can guess at it. The turning point of speculation for years has been as to whether the variety is of American or European origin. One of the most interesting contributions to this discussion was made by Mr. Chauncey Goodrich, (16) of Burlington, Vt., in 1851. We quote the following extracts from this article :

' It is here one of the most common as well as oldest varieties; hundreds of barrels are sold in a single season in this town alone. . . . All American writers call it a Canadian apple; of this I think there is no proof. One hundred and twenty years since, the French planted this variety on the eastern shore of Lake Champlain, opposite Fort Frederick on Crown Point, at a place called ' Chimney Point ' — more than fifty years before any other permanent settlement. From these old trees cions have been scattered through Vermont, and called the Chimney apple. A very intelligent and highly educated French seigneur residing on an old seignory eighty miles below Quebec informed me that this was one of the first varieties of apples planted on the place; that the trees were very old and were brought from France. The early French settlers planted the same variety at Ogdensburg, Detroit, and other places on Lakes Erie and Ontario, where it is still known as the ' Snow Apple'; also at Kaskaskia, Illinois, more than one hundred

FAMEUSE

and fifty years since, where the old trees are still productive, and apples from them are sent to St. Louis, &c. The same apple may be found in France, and in London of the growth of France.'

" It is hardly to be supposed that a seedling apple was produced in Canada at so early a day as to be distributed more than a thousand miles in every settlement made by the French, one hundred and fifty years since.

" Another fact tending to suggest a European origin for Fameuse is that it is usually found in the old gardens, in company with well known European varieties of pears, apples and other fruits.

" On the other hand the testimony of European pomologists is mostly against the theory of a European origin. The variety is known in the larger collections of all the countries of Europe, just as Ben Davis is, and has been known there for many years. But most European authors unhesitatingly assign a Canadian origin to the variety; and the variety seems too little known, too little appreciated, and too little at home with European surroundings for us to believe it originated there. Those who call it a European apple usually assign its nativity to France; but Leroy (25) the greatest of all French, and perhaps of all European authorities, did not know the variety. He says that Le Lectier cultivated the Pomme de Neige (synonym of Fameuse) at Orleans (France) before 1628; but Leroy did not know whether or not this was the same Pomme de Neige grown in Canada. In fact he says, ' I have never, up to the present time, met this apple Pomme de Neige on our soil. In place of it they have always sent me Calvill de Neige, ripening from January to March.' Most of the so-called Snow apples of Europe, in fact, are white skinned and totally different from the Snow, or Fameuse, of America.

" It is agreed that, whether the Fameuse came from Europe or not, it was distributed by the earliest of the French missionaries and planted by the first settlers. Quebec was founded shortly before 1600 and Montreal in 1641. The *seigniory du Cote de Beaupre*, said to be the oldest seignory in Quebec, was granted in 1636 and promptly colonized. Thus we have almost a hundred years of French settlement and missionary activity prior to 1700, the approximate date at which, according to Mr. Goodrich, the Fameuse was brought to Vermont. This seems to allow ample time for a Canadian origin for the variety and for its wide distribution in Quebec, Ontario and the Northern states.

" The early distribution of apples, either from Europe to Canada, or from place to place on this continent, was accomplished chiefly, almost exclusively, by seeds. Some of the missionaries knew the art of grafting, but there was small encouragement to practice it. From these considerations, and others which cannot be fully argued here, the writer is firmly convinced that the Fameuse originated in Canada from seed brought from France."

Tree.

Tree vigorous, with long, moderately stout branches. *Form* upright spreading or roundish, rather dense. *Twigs* medium size, curved, stout; internodes short. *Bark* dark brown tinged with red, lightly coated with scarf-skin; pubescent. *Lenticels* scattering, small, round or somewhat oval, slightly raised. *Buds* medium size, flat, obtuse, free, pubescent.

FRUIT.

Fruit hardly averages medium but sometimes is above medium size. *Form* roundish inclined to conic, sometimes a little oblate, regular, uniform, symmetrical. *Stem* medium to short but sometimes long, rather slender. *Cavity* acute to somewhat acuminate, moderately deep to deep, rather wide, often gently furrowed, sometimes partly russeted but generally smooth and red or greenish. *Calyx* rather small, usually closed. *Basin* medium in width and depth, rather small, somewhat abrupt, obscurely furrowed or wrinkled, often having mammiform protuberances.

Skin thin, tender, smooth, light bright red deepening to almost purplish black in highly colored specimens with a somewhat striped appearance toward the apex. In less highly colored specimens the striped effect is more noticeable. *Dots* few, scattering, light.

Calyx tube narrow, funnel-form. *Stamens* median or somewhat basal.

Core medium to rather small, axile; cells closed; core lines clasping. *Carpels* symmetrical, roundish or inclined to elliptical, somewhat emarginate, mucronate. *Seeds* dark, long, rather narrow, acute to acuminate.

Flesh white, sometimes streaked or stained with red, very tender, juicy, subacid becoming very mild subacid or sweetish, aromatic, very good for dessert.

Season October to midwinter.

STRIPED FAMEUSE. A variety has sometimes been propagated and disseminated under the name Fameuse which is recognized as Striped Fameuse. The tree is a thriftier grower in the nursery than the true Fameuse, but the fruit is less desirable, being inferior in color but similar in all other respects to Fameuse. It is mottled or thinly washed with bright red over a pale yellow background, striped and splashed with carmine.

OTHER VARIETIES OF THE FAMEUSE GROUP.

Waugh (44) remarks that one of the striking things about the Fameuse type is that it has the strong tendency to reproduce itself from seed. This has been taken advantage of in the last fifty years, and apples of the Fameuse type have been grown from seed by the hundred and planted in the orchard. This practice has prevailed largely in Quebec in neighborhoods where nurseries were scarce and grafted nursery trees expensive or unknown. He concludes, therefore, that the modern Fameuse apples are most certainly not all from the same original seed, the conspicuous variations among them being thus accounted for at least in part. He further observes that seedlings of the Fameuse often show so much

FANNY

departure from the common characters of Fameuse as to be readily recognized as something different. Such seedlings are generally accepted as new varieties, and in cases where they show conspicuous merit they are separately propagated by grafting, and eventually receive special names of their own. He then lists several named varieties of the Fameuse group, including Bloom, Brilliant, Canada Baldwin, Fameuse Green, Fameuse Noire, Fameuse Sucre, La Victoire, Louise, McIntosh, Hilaire and Shiawassee. The more important of these are described under their respective names in this volume.

FANNY.

REFERENCES. 1. Downing, 1869:173. fig. 2. Thomas, 1875:499. 3. *Am. Pom. Soc. Cat.*, 1877:8. 4. Barry, 1883:333. 5. *Am. Pom. Soc. Rpt.*, 1887: 93. 6. Bailey, *An. Hort.*, 1892:239. 7. *Rural N. Y.*, 55:642, 706, 707. 1896. fig. 8. *Ib.*, 56:292. 9. Budd-Hansen, 1903:83. fig.

SYNONYMS. None.

This is an attractive bright red fruit of good dessert quality. It begins to ripen about the first of September, and continues in season till late fall. The tree is quite vigorous, comes into bearing moderately early and is a reliable annual cropper. Some regard it as desirable for commercial planting (7, 8), but it has not proved so at this Station because it is somewhat deficient in size. On account of its beauty and excellent dessert quality it is worthy of being classed among the varieties desirable for the home orchard.

Historical. Originated with Dr. John K. Eshelman, Lancaster Co., Pa. (7). It has been as yet but little disseminated in New York.

TREE.

Tree moderately vigorous with moderately long, stout branches. *Form* flat, spreading, open. *Twigs* long, curved, moderately stout; internodes long. *Bark* brown tingled with olive-green, heavily streaked with scarf-skin; much pubescent. *Lenticels* quite numerous, medium size, round, not raised. *Buds* medium size, plump, obtuse, free, heavily pubescent.

FRUIT.

Fruit above medium to below medium size, pretty uniform in size and shape. *Form* roundish, slightly oblate varying to somewhat oblong or ovate, regular or slightly ribbed. *Stem* short to medium, slender. *Cavity* acute to nearly obtuse, medium in width and depth, sometimes russeted. *Calyx* small to medium, closed or partly open; lobes rather short, narrow, acute. *Basin* shallow to medium in depth, moderately wide, rather abrupt, usually furrowed.

Skin thin, tender, smooth, clear yellow mostly overlaid with bright red indistinctly striped with carmine. *Dots* small, yellowish.

Calyx tube rather wide, slightly funnel-form to conical with pistil point projecting into the base. *Stamens* median to marginal.

Core below medium, somewhat abaxile; cells open; core lines clasping. *Carpels* broadly ovate to elliptical, slightly emarginate. *Seeds* medium to large, moderately wide, flat, plump, acute.

Flesh whitish slightly tinged with yellow, moderately firm, fine, very tender, juicy, mild subacid, good to very good.

Season September to November or later.

FISHKILL.

REFERENCES. **1.** Downing, **1869**:176. **2.** *N. Y. Sta. An. Rpt.*, **11**:222. 1892. **3.** Waugh, *Vt. Sta. An. Rpt.*, **14**:294. 1901.

SYNONYMS. FISHKILL (*2*, *3*). FISHKILL BEAUTY (*1*). *Fishkill Beauty* (*2*).

Fruit large, rather attractive in appearance, but not good enough in quality to displace standard sorts of its season either for culinary or dessert uses. Downing remarks that it is apt to decay on the tree (1), but this has not proved true in our experience with the variety. The tree comes into bearing rather early and is almost an annual bearer, yielding fair to good crops of uniformly large fruit. Should it possess superior hardiness it may be worthy of trial in those regions where this character is a prime requisite.

Historical. Origin Fishkill, N. Y.

TREE.

Tree vigorous with long, slender, curved branches; laterals willowy, long, slender. *Form* upright spreading or roundish, rather dense. *Twigs* short to medium, straight, moderately slender, rather geniculate; internodes medium to long. *Bark* brown tinged with clear reddish brown, mottled with scarf-skin; slightly pubescent. *Lenticels* numerous, small or below medium, generally elongated and narrow, usually not raised. *Buds* small to above medium, plump, obtuse to somewhat acute, usually free or nearly so.

FRUIT.

Fruit very large to large, uniform in size and shape. *Form* nearly round varying to somewhat oblate or oblate conic, regular, obscurely ribbed. *Stem*

FISHKILL

medium to long, thick to slender. *Cavity* varying from somewhat obtuse to slightly acuminate, moderately deep to deep, rather broad, usually symmetrical, sometimes lipped, sometimes lightly russeted. *Calyx* rather small, closed or slightly open. *Basin* shallow, usually moderately wide, obtuse, angularly furrowed and wrinkled, with some tendency to develop mammiform protuberances.

Skin a little rough, thick, tough, dull yellow washed with dull or brownish-red, in highly colored specimens deepening to a bright red blush, mottled, striped and splashed with deep carmine, often overspread with thin whitish bloom. *Dots* numerous, conspicuous, medium size, russet. *Prevailing effect* attractive although rather dull red.

Calyx tube rather long, wide, varying from elongated conical to funnel-shape. *Stamens* median to marginal.

Core below medium to rather large, abaxile; cells usually symmetrical, open; core lines clasping. *Carpels* roundish to broadly obcordate, somewhat emarginate, slightly tufted. *Seeds* light brown, below medium to rather large, narrow, rather long, plump, varying from obtuse to acuminate.

Flesh whitish or tinged with yellow, firm, coarse, moderately crisp, moderately tender, juicy, mild subacid, fair to good in flavor and quality.

Season November to February.

FORD.

REFERENCES. **1.** Downing, **1857** :144. **2.** Warder, **1867** :719. **3.** Thomas, **1875** :499.

SYNONYMS. None.

The fruit of Ford is described as large, roundish, yellow; flesh solid, rather acid but of high flavor and good quality. Season October to January (1, 3). We do not know this variety and so far as we can discover it is no longer propagated. According to Downing it originated in Canaan, Columbia county, N. Y. (1).

FRANCHOT.

REFERENCE. **1.** Downing, **1869** :182.

SYNONYMS. None.

According to Downing this variety originated in Otsego county, N. Y. The tree is productive, the fruit medium size, yellow, shaded and splashed with red; flesh pleasant, aromatic, good. Season October to January (1). So far as we can learn it is not now being propagated.

FULLERTON SWEET.

REFERENCE. **1.** Downing, **1869** :185.

SYNONYMS. None.

A variety of unknown origin which has been fruited in Orange county (1). The fruit much resembles Autumn Bough. It is below medium, pale yellow; flesh tender, sweet, very good; season October and November. We do not know this variety and so far as we can learn it is not being propagated.

GARDEN ROYAL.

REFERENCES. 1. Manning, *Mag. Hort.*, **13**:438. 1847. 2. Hovey, *Ib.*, **14**: 18. 1848. fig. 3. Thomas, *Cultivator*, **5**:212. 1848. 4. Cole, **1849**:106. fig. 5. Thomas, **1849**:139. fig. 6. Barry, **1851**:284. 7. *Am. Pom. Soc. Cat.*, **1854**. 8. Elliott, **1854**:81. 9. *Mag. Hort.*, **21**:63. 1855. 10. Downing, **1857**:79. 11. Warder, **1867**:719. 12. Lyon, *Mich. Hort. Soc. Rpt.*, **1890**:292. 13. Bailey, *An. Hort.*, **1892**:239. 14. *Rural N. Y.*, **60**:247. 1901. 15. Budd-Hansen, **1903**:88. fig. 16. Farrand, *Mich. Sta. Bul.*, **205**:44. 1903.
SYNONYMS. None.

Garden Royal is not a good variety for commercial planting because the fruit is too small and its season early and short, but by many it is considered one of the very best dessert apples of late summer and early autumn. The fruit is of regular form, very handsome deep yellow striped with orange-red and dark crimson. The flesh is very tender, aromatic and with a delicate, pleasant acid flavor; season, August and September. The tree when full grown is of medium size, moderately vigorous, with roundish head. It appears to be hardy, healthy and long-lived, comes into bearing young and is a reliable biennial cropper.

Historical. Origin Sudbury, Mass. (2). It is occasionally found in this state in home orchards. It is now little propagated by nurserymen and seldom planted.

FRUIT.

Fruit medium or below. *Form* round, slightly oblate, often a little inclined to conic, regular or obscurely ribbed. *Stem* short to medium, straight, rather slender. *Cavity* acute sometimes approaching acuminate, rather deep and broad, slightly furrowed, often faintly russeted. *Calyx* small to above medium, open or partly closed; lobes often separated at base, rather short, acute. *Basin* moderately shallow, rather wide, obtuse to somewhat abrupt, slightly wrinkled.

Skin thin, greenish-yellow, sometimes entirely overspread with red, irregularly striped and splashed with carmine. *Dots* numerous, rather conspicuous, medium or above, often irregular, russet or yellowish.

Calyx tube medium size, funnel-shape. *Stamens* median to nearly marginal. *Core* small, axile; cells closed or slightly open; core lines clasping. *Carpels* small, elliptical, emarginate.

Flesh tinged with yellow, fine, tender, juicy, agreeable mild subacid, aromatic, very good.

Season late August and September.

GARDNER SWEET PEARMAIN.

REFERENCE. 1. Downing, 1869:188.
SYNONYMS. None.

A Long Island variety, the fruit of which, according to Downing (1), is medium in size, nearly covered with red; flesh whitish, sweet, good; season September. This variety is unknown to us; so far as we have been able to learn it is no longer propagated.

GENESEE FLOWER.

REFERENCE. 1. Lyon, *Mich. Hort. Soc. Rpt.*, 1890:290.
SYNONYMS. *Demary*. FLOWER (OF GENESEE) (1). *Flower of Genesee. Hawkins Pippin. Pride of Genesee.*

Fruit large, remarkably uniform in size and shape, with very few culls. In color and general appearance it resembles Pumpkin Sweet, commonly called Pound Sweet. It is not an apple of high dessert quality, but is very good for culinary uses, having a pleasant mild subacid flavor. It does not always sell well because the color is green and the variety is not generally well known. With some growers the tree is not a satisfactory cropper, but others find it a regular and abundant bearer, yielding good to heavy crops almost annually, and regard the variety as desirable for commercial planting.

Historical. This variety appears to be known by the name Genesee Flower more than by any other, but Mr. Nelson Bogue of Batavia informs us that it is also known locally under the various names Flower of Genesee, Pride of Genesee, Hawkins Pippin, and Demary. He states that the original tree, now about sixty years old, is still standing on the old Demary farm, in the town of Alexander, Genesee county, N. Y. The cultivation of this variety appears to be confined principally to the counties of Genesee, Wyoming and Orleans, and it does not appear to be increasing.

FRUIT.

Fruit large. *Form* roundish, somewhat oblate. *Stem* short, rather slender. *Cavity* broad, moderately deep, russeted. *Calyx* medium size, partly open. *Basin* shallow, irregular, often distinctly ridged.

Skin light green mingled with light yellow. *Dots* numerous, pale, with a few that are large and russet.

Flesh nearly white, mild subacid, good for culinary use but not much esteemed for dessert.

Season late September to November.

GIDEON.

REFERENCES. **1.** Gideon, *Am. Pom. Soc. Rpt.*, **1885**:26. **2.** *Mo. Hort. Soc. Rpt.*, **1886**:233. **3.** *Am. Pom. Soc. Cat.*, **1889**:6. **4.** Bailey, *An. Hort.*, **1892**: 239. **5.** Beach, *N. Y. Sta. An. Rpt.*, **13**:580. 1894. **6.** Woolverton, *Ont. Fr. Stas. An. Rpt.*, **4**:2. 1897. *figs.* **7.** Waugh, *Vt. Sta. Bul.*, **61**:30. 1897. *figs.* **8.** *Am. Gard.*, **22**:132. 1901. *figs.* **9.** *Me. Sta. An. Rpt.*, **18**:83. 1902. **10.** Hansen, *S. D. Sta. Bul.*, **76**:51. 1902. *fig.* **11.** Budd-Hansen, **1903**:88. *fig.* **12.** Powell and Fulton, *U. S. B. P. I. Bul.*, **48**:42. 1903. **13.** Farrand, *Mich. Sta. Bul.*, **205**:44. 1903. **14.** Beach and Clark, *N. Y. Sta. Bul.*, **248**: 121. 1904.

SYNONYMS. GIDEON (1, 2, 3, 4, 5, 6, 7, 8, 9, 10, 11, 12, 13, 14). *Gideon White* (14).

Fruit decidedly attractive in general appearance being of good size, clear waxen yellow often with a bright pinkish blush but it is deficient in quality and apt to be defective in that the flesh becomes withered and discolored about the core as soon as the fruit reaches maturity. It is not a good variety for holding in cold storage as it stands heat poorly before going into storage and when in storage goes down quickly. In ordinary storage it is inferior to Hubbardston in keeping qualities, being in season from October to December or possibly later (14). The tree is of an exceptionally fine habit in the nursery, and in the orchard it is an upright vigorous grower, very hardy and healthy, comes into bearing young and yields full crops biennially or nearly annually. It is not recommended for planting in New York except it be as a stock upon which to topwork less hardy varieties.

Historical. Originated by Peter M. Gideon, Excelsior, Minn., from crab seed. The following is his statement of its parentage. "The Gideon is a seedling of the small crab; the seed came from Boston, where the tree was surrounded in the orchard by Blue Pearmain. I consider the tree a cross between those two. The tree resembles Blue Pearmain; seed was taken from the crab" (1).

TREE.

Tree medium to large, vigorous or moderately vigorous. *Form* at first upright but becoming spreading and open. *Twigs* short, curved, stout with large terminal buds; internodes medium. *Bark* brown mingled with some olive-green, lightly streaked with scarf-skin; heavily pubescent. *Lenticels* quite numerous, medium to small, oblong, slightly raised. *Buds* prominent, large, broad, plump, obtuse, free, pubescent.

FRUIT.

Fruit usually above medium to large, uniform in size. *Form* roundish conical or somewhat ovate, sometimes inclined to oblong, angular. *Stem* long to below medium, slender. *Cavity* acute or somewhat acuminate, deep, broad to medium in width, sometimes lightly russeted. *Calyx* small, closed; lobes medium in length, rather narrow, acute, reflexed. *Basin* small to medium, sometimes oblique, shallow or very shallow, narrow to medium in width, rather obtuse, somewhat wrinkled, usually with narrow but not prominent ridges.

Skin rather thin, glossy, clear pale waxen yellow, sometimes with beautiful pink blush on exposed cheek. *Dots* light, submerged, inconspicuous, except where the skin is blushed.

Calyx tube short, narrow, often funnel-shape with very short, truncate cylinder. *Stamens* marginal to median.

Core medium size, axile or abaxile; cells closed or open; core lines meeting the limb or clasping the cylinder. *Carpels* round to broadly ovate or elliptical, emarginate, tufted. *Seeds* rather large, irregular, medium in width, rather long, not very plump, acute to acuminate, tufted, light brown.

Flesh whitish or tinged with yellow, of rather soft loose texture, a little coarse, crisp, juicy, brisk subacid to mild subacid, fair to good.

Season October.

GINNIE.

REFERENCES. **1.** *N. Y. Sta. An. Rpt.*, **2**:35. 1883. **2.** Beach and Paddock, *N. Y. Sta. An. Rpt.*, **14**:252, 257. 1895. **3.** Beach and Clark, *N. Y. Sta. Bul.*, **248**:121. 1904.

SYNONYMS. AUNT GINNIE (1, 2). *Aunt Ginnie* (3). GINNIE (3).

An autumn apple of good color and good quality. Tree rather upright, moderately vigorous, moderately productive. It comes into bearing early and yields some fruit nearly every year. Not recommended for planting in New York.

Historical. Received from Ellwanger and Barry, Rochester, N. Y., in 1883 for testing at this Station. We do not know its origin. So far as we have learned it is practically unknown among New York fruit growers.

FRUIT.

Fruit medium to large. *Form* oblate conic, broad and flattened at the base, obscurely ribbed. *Stem* medium, usually not exserted. *Cavity* large, acuminate, broad, deep, with conspicuous, broad, irregular, outspreading russet rays. *Calyx* small, nearly closed. *Basin* shallow to medium in depth, rather narrow to moderately wide, furrowed and wrinkled.

Skin yellow nearly covered with bright red and marked with broad stripes and splashes of bright carmine. *Dots* minute, russet. *Prevailing effect* red striped.

Calyx tube funnel-form. *Stamens* basal or nearly so.

Core very large, abaxile; cells pretty symmetrical, open; core lines clasp the funnel cylinder. *Carpels* broadly roundish, emarginate, tufted. *Seeds* medium in size, rather wide, obtuse to somewhat acute.

Flesh whitish, rather coarse, moderately juicy, aromatic, subacid, good to very good.

Season late September to early winter; commercial limit November in common storage (3).

GLADSTONE.

REFERENCES. **1.** Hogg, 1884:150. **2.** *N. Y. Sta. An. Rpt.*, **11**:224. 1892. **3.** Hansen, *S. D. Sta. Bul.*, **76**:52. 1902.

SYNONYMS. GLADSTONE (2, 3). MR. GLADSTONE (1).

Fruit of good size, and when highly colored rather attractive. In general appearance it is intermediate between Oldenburg and Gravenstein, perhaps resembling Gravenstein in color more than Oldenburg. It is not equal to either of these varieties in quality. The tree comes into bearing young, is an annual cropper and productive. Not recommended for planting in New York.

Historical. This is a comparatively recent introduction from England. It has not been extensively disseminated and so far as we can learn its cultivation is not increasing in this country.

TREE.

Tree rather small, moderately vigorous with short, stout branches. *Form* spreading and inclined to droop. *Twigs* moderately long, curved, stout, with large terminal buds; internodes medium in size. *Bark* brown, tinged with olive-green, lightly streaked with scarf-skin; pubescent. *Lenticels* numerous, conspicuous, medium size, round, slightly raised. *Buds* medium size, broad, flat, obtuse, appressed, slightly pubescent.

FRUIT.

Fruit medium to large, uniform. *Form* roundish oblate, slightly conic, obscurely ribbed; sides usually unequal. *Stem* medium in length, moderately slender. *Cavity* acuminate to acute, rather wide, moderately deep to deep, sometimes with outspreading russet. *Calyx* below medium to rather large, closed or somewhat open. *Basin* rather small, shallow to medium in depth, medium in width to rather wide, a little abrupt, slightly furrowed and wrinkled.

Skin thin, smooth, greenish-yellow or pale yellow, more or less thinly overspread with red, irregularly mottled, splashed and distinctly striped with pinkish carmine. *Dots* rather numerous, inconspicuous, light colored, submerged.

Calyx tube rather short, cone-shape to funnel-form. *Stamens* median.

Core medium to rather large, usually axile; cells symmetrical, closed or slightly open; core lines clasping. *Carpels* broadly roundish, very slightly emarginate. *Seeds* rather dark brown, very wide, flat, obtuse to acute.

Flesh slightly tinged with yellow, moderately firm, a little coarse, crisp, tender, juicy, mild subacid, fair in quality.

Season September and October.

GLORIA MUNDI.

REFERENCES. **1.** *Dom. Encyc.,* **1804** (cited by **4**). **2.** *Am. Gard. Cal.,* **1806** :585. **3.** Coxe, **1817** :117. fig. **4.** Thacher, **1822** :131. **5.** Buel, *N. Y. Bd. Agr. Mem.,* **1826** :476. **6.** Fessenden, **1828** :129. **7.** *London Hort. Soc. Cat.,* **1831** :No. 447. **8.** Kenrick, **1832** :49. **9.** Floy-Lindley, **1833** :86. **10.** Downing, **1845** :110. fig. **11.** Cole, **1849** :122. **12.** Thomas, **1849** :182. **13.** Phœnix. *Horticulturist,* **4** :470. **1850.** **14.** Emmons, *Nat. Hist. N. Y.,* **3** :41. **1851.** *col. pl.* No. 35 and fig. **15.** Elliott, **1854** :174. **16.** *Mag. Hort.,* **23** :83. **1857.** **17.**

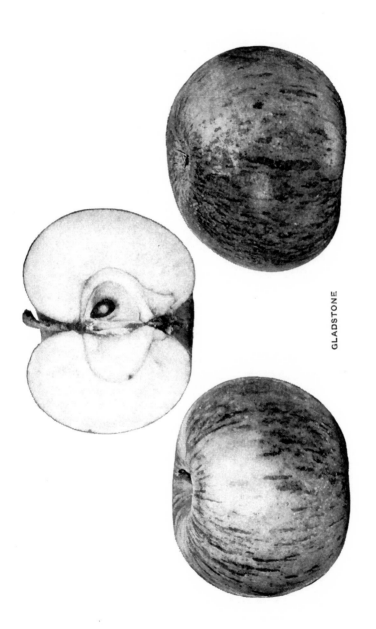

GLADSTONE

Hooper, 1857:39. **18.** Warder, 1867:719, 725. **19.** Downing, 1869:191. **20.** Fitz, 1872:168. **21.** Leroy, 1873:407. *fig.* **22.** Downing, 1881:11 index, app. **23.** Hogg, 1884:85. **24.** Wickson, 1889:245. **25.** Lyon, *Mich. Hort. Soc. Rpt.,* 1890:292. **26.** Green, *Rural N. Y.,* 49:604. 1890. **27.** Bailey, *An. Hort.,* 1892:240. **28.** Bunyard, *Jour. Roy. Hort. Soc.,* 1898:354. **29.** *Can. Hort.,* 23:75. 1900. **30.** Bruner, *N. C. Sta. Bul.,* 182:20. 1903.

SYNONYMS. *American Gloria Mundi* (4, 7, 21). *American Mammoth* (7, 10, 15, 17, 19, 21). *Baltimore* (10, 12, 14, 21, 23, 26, of some 19). *Baltimore Pippin* (15, 17, 19). *Belle Dubois* (23). *Belle Josephine* (19, 21). *Copp's Mammoth* (22). *Glazenwood* (10). *Glazenwood Gloria Mundi* (19, 21, 23). GLORIA MUNDI (1, 7, 10, 11, 14, 16, 17, 19, 22, 23, 24, 25, 27, 28, 29, 30). *Gloria Mundi* (5, 10, 12, 13, 15, 18, 20, 21, 26). *Impératrice Joséphine* (21). JOSÉPHINE (21). *Kinderhook Pippin* (14). *Mammoth* (21, 23). MAMMOTH PIPPIN (2, 3, 4, 5, 6, 8, 9, 12, 13, 15, 18, 20, 26). *Mammoth Pippin* (7, 10, 11, 14, 16, 17, 19, 21). *Melon* (21). *Mississippi?* (19). *Monstreuse Pippin* (21). *Monstrous Pippin* (23). *Mountain Flora* (22). *N. Y. Gloria Mundi* (3, 7, 8, 9, 10, 15, 19, 21). *Ox Apple* (10, 12, 14, 15, 19, 23, 26). *Pound* (17). *Vandyne Apple* (9).

Fruit of largest size; seldom cultivated except for exhibition; suitable only for culinary purposes. The tree is large, vigorous, spreading, hardy and long-lived. It has been commonly held to be unproductive, but a few fruit growers in Southeastern New York report that it is a good bearer and a profitable commercial variety. Season October to January.

Historical. The exact place of origin of this apple seems doubtful. In 1804 Mease stated, "It originated on the farm of Mr. Crooks, near Red Hook in New York" (1). Thirteen years later Coxe credited it with a Long Island origin (3). All that can be stated with certainty is that it is an old variety known in parts of Eastern New York, New Jersey and Pennsylvania in the beginning of the last century.

FRUIT.

Fruit very large or large, uniform. *Form* roundish with truncate ends, slightly conical, ribbed; sides usually unequal. *Stem* medium to short, moderately thick. *Cavity* large, acuminate, moderately deep to deep, broad, furrowed and compressed, sometimes slightly russeted. *Calyx* medium to large, open or partly closed; lobes separated at base, short, narrow. *Basin* large, moderately deep to deep, rather wide, somewhat abrupt, sometimes compressed, furrowed and wrinkled.

Skin greenish-yellow sometimes with faint bronze blush. *Dots* small to medium, often areolar with russet center, or light colored and submerged. *Prevailing effect* yellow or greenish.

Calyx tube very large, long, wide, broadly conical extending to core or approaching cylindrical below. *Stamens* median.

Core medium to rather large, usually decidedly abaxile; cells symmetrical, open; core lines usually clasping. *Carpels* broadly roundish to somewhat elliptical, slightly tufted. *Seeds* moderately dark brown, medium to rather small, rather narrow, short, plump, obtuse to acute, sometimes tufted.

Flesh slightly tinged with greenish-yellow, coarse, moderately crisp, rather tender, juicy, rather mild subacid, fair or nearly good in quality.

Season October to January.

THE GOLDEN PIPPINS.

The name Golden Pippin has been applied to several distinct varieties, the most important of which are mentioned below.

The Golden Pippin of England is a small, yellowish apple with shade of red, which is in season from November to March. This has already been described in Volume I, page 141.

The Golden Pippin of Westchester County, also known under the name of American Golden Pippin and by various other synonyms, is described as Golding, page 82, which is the name now accepted for this variety by pomologists. In addition to the varieties described below under the name Golden Pippin there are several other sorts which have been known under this name.

(I) GOLDEN PIPPIN.

REFERENCES. 1. Downing, 1869:195. 2. Thomas, 1875:500. 3. Bailey, *An. Hort.*, 1892:240...4. Ragan, *U. S. B. P. I. Bul.*, 56:123. 1905. 5. *Ib.*, 56:347. 1905.

SYNONYMS. *Butter Pippin* (1). GOLDEN PIPPIN (1, 2, 3, 4, 5). *Large Golden Pippin* (1). *Mammoth* (1, 2). *Pound Royal* (2, of some 1). *York Pippin* (1, 5).

This variety belongs in the Fall Pippin group of apples. In Central and Western New York it is often called York Pippin. The fruit is large, coarse-grained, with a very pleasant flavor, and is suitable for either dessert or culinary uses. As compared with Fall Pippin the fruit is harder, keeps longer and stands shipping better in hot weather. In Western New York its season in ordinary storage extends from about September 20 to January 1. It holds its flavor and quality well for a late fall and early winter sort. It frequently brings better prices than Fall Pippin, and we are informed it is sometimes exported. The tree is more spreading than that of Fall Pippin, and is perhaps somewhat hardier. It is generally healthy, vigorous, quite long-lived, and when full grown becomes a pretty large tree. It is a reliable cropper, bearing good to heavy crops biennially or sometimes annually. There is apt to be considerable loss by premature dropping of the fruit, and unless proper preventive measures are taken the crop may be seriously injured by apple scab and codling moth, but with proper treatment these pests may be kept under good control. Golden Pippin is grown to a considerable extent in various parts of New York state and in New England. In some sections it is regarded as one of the most desirable of the fall varieties for commercial planting.

Historical. The origin of this variety is unknown. It has long been in cultivation. In New York it is now found mostly in old orchards and, generally speaking, its cultivation is not increasing.

FRUIT.

Fruit very large or large, pretty uniform in size and shape. *Form* roundish to roundish oblate, sometimes slightly conic, often with a broad flat base and broadly ribbed toward the apex. *Stem* long to medium, thick, sometimes swollen. *Cavity* acute to acuminate, medium in depth, broad, usually rather symmetrical, sometimes lipped, russeted and often with heavy, outspreading russet rays. *Calyx* rather large, closed. *Basin* deep, moderately wide to wide, abrupt, slightly furrowed, sometimes irregularly compressed.

Skin rather tender, green or yellowish changing to a deeper and rather attractive yellow when fully mature, sometimes with bronze blush and russet flecks. *Dots* small to rather large and conspicuous, greenish and submerged or with russet point.

Calyx tube wide, conical. *Stamens* median to somewhat basal.

Core rather small, somewhat abaxile; cells open; core lines meeting or slightly clasping. *Carpels* roundish or approaching elliptical, sometimes obovate, heavily tufted. *Seeds* few, often not perfectly developed, medium size, irregular, rather dark brown, rather plump, acute.

Flesh yellowish, coarse, rather tender, juicy, agreeable mild subacid, somewhat aromatic, good to very good.

Season late September to December or January.

(II) GOLDEN PIPPIN.

REFERENCES. 1. Downing, 1869:194. 2. Bailey, *An. Hort.*, 1892:240.
SYNONYMS. GOLDEN PIPPIN (1, 2). *Pittstown Pippin* (1).

Downing states that this is an old apple grown many years ago in Adams, Mass. Tree upright and vigorous; fruit rather large, roundish oblate, sometimes conic, greenish-yellow with blush; flesh yellowish, sprightly subacid, good for cooking; season September and October (1).

It appears that this variety is no longer propagated in New York.

GOLDEN REINETTE.

REFERENCES. 1. Budd, *Ia. Agr. Coll. Bul.*, 1885:32, 35, 38. 2. *Ib.*, 1890:25 3. *Ib., Ia. Sta. Bul.*, 19:538. 1892. 4. Munson, *Me. Sta. An. Rpt.*, 1896:74, 80. 5. Lyon, *Mich. Sta. Bul.*, 152:221. 1898. 6. Munson, *Me. Sta. An. Rpt.*, 18:83. 1902. 7. Ragan, *U. S. B. P. I. Bul.*, 56:124. 1905.
SYNONYMS. *No. 51 Vor.* (1, 2). *No. 10* (7). *Solotoc renet* (1). *Zolotoi renet* (7).

In addition to the old English variety known as Golden Reinette which has been described in Volume I, page 142, there are at least two Russian apples that have been disseminated in this country under this name. One is a variety described by Munson as a promising autumn apple for Northern Maine, in season from September to December; fruit small, golden yellow washed and splashed with carmine (4, 6). What appears to be the same variety was received by this Station from Professor Budd, Ames, Ia., in 1890. It is decidedly inferior to the standard varieties of its season, which are in general cultivation throughout New York. Possibly on account of superior hardiness it may have some value in the more northern or elevated regions of the state.

TREE.

Tree moderately vigorous with short, moderately stout, curved branches. *Form* upright spreading or roundish, rather dense. *Twigs* long, curved, stout; internodes medium. *Bark* brown, mingled with reddish-brown, mottled with scarf-skin, slightly pubescent. *Lenticels* numerous, conspicuous, large, oblong, raised. *Buds* prominent, large, broad, long, plump, acute, free, slightly pubescent.

FRUIT.

Fruit medium to below. *Form* oblate conic to strongly roundish conic, flattened at the base, ribbed, rather irregular; sides unequal. *Stem* short, thick. *Cavity* acuminate, medium in depth to rather deep, moderately broad, often compressed, usually not russeted. *Calyx* large, open or partly closed, leafy; lobes usually separated at base, long, acute to acuminate. *Basin* shallow to moderately deep, medium in width to narrow, usually abrupt, slightly furrowed and wrinkled.

Skin pale greenish-yellow with faint splashes and stripes of red.

Calyx tube large, wide, broadly conical. *Stamens* basal to median.

Core medium size, often abaxile; cells usually unsymmetrical, closed or open; core lines clasping or nearly meeting. *Carpels* broadly roundish to elliptical. *Seeds* medium brown, medium to below, plump, rather obtuse.

Flesh yellowish, crisp, juicy, mild subacid.

Season September to December.

The other Russian apple, above referred to, was disseminated some years ago by Professor Budd. In 1885 he remarked that he was sending out, under the name Golden Reinette (51 Vor.), a variety having fruit medium to large, golden in color, fine-grained, juicy, subacid, almost best in quality (1). In 1890 he stated: "This has proven a fine tree on a great variety of soils where the air had free circulation. Its northern limit is not yet known, but I have not known its wood colored at Ames when the Wealthy by its side in nursery was nearly killed. Fruit medium to large, golden yellow, fine-grained, subacid, and nearly best in quality. Season here, December to February, depending on time of picking and mode of storage" (2). In 1892 Budd further reported: "This has not proven true to name as received from the Bogdanoff estates in Russia. It is a member of the Anis family, of fine size and excellent quality. Season late fall, and early winter north" (3).

GOLDEN SWEET.

REFERENCES. 1. Kenrick, 1832:37. 2. Downing, 1845:84. 3. Phœnix, *Horticulturist*, 1:361. 1846. 4. *N. Y. Agr. Soc. Trans.*, 1846:189. 5. Thomas, 1849:136. 6. Cole, 1849:102. fig. 7. Barry, 1851:280. 8. Emmons, *Nat. Hist. N. Y.*, 3:40. 1851. fig. 9. Elliott, 1854:81. fig. 10. Gregg, 1857:37. fig. 11. Hooper, 1857:41. 12. *Am. Pom. Soc. Cat.*, 1862. 13. Warder, 1867:551. fig. 14. Downing, 1869:196. fig. 15. Wickson, 1889:244. 16. Lyon, *Mich. Hort. Soc. Rpt.*, 1890:292. 17. Bailey, *An. Hort.*, 1892:240. 18. Waugh, *Vt. Sta. An. Rpt.*, 14:295. 1901. 19. Budd-Hansen, 1903:90. fig.

SYNONYMS. *Early Golden Sweet* (14). GOLDEN SWEET (2, 3, 4, 5, 6, 8, 9, 11, 12, 13, 14, 15, 16, 17, 18, 19). GOLDEN SWEETING (7, 10). *Orange Sweet* (6, 9). ORANGE SWEETING (1). *Orange Sweeting* (2, 13, 14). *Trenton Early* (9). *Yellow Sweeting* ? (1).

Fruit of good medium size, attractive clear yellow when fully mature, rich, sweet, very good in flavor and quality. Cultivated principally for home use. Of no commercial value except that it is sold in limited quantities in local markets. In season from the middle of August to the last of September. The tree is a good grower, healthy, hardy, moderately long-lived, comes into bearing rather young and yields moderate to heavy crops biennially.

Historical. An old Connecticut variety (2). Its exact origin is unknown. It has been pretty generally disseminated throughout the state but is nowhere grown extensively. It is listed by nearly all nurserymen (17).

TREE.

Tree large, vigorous. *Form* roundish spreading, inclined to droop, dense. *Twigs* long, curved, slender; internodes long. *Bark* brown, lightly mottled with scarf-skin; pubescent. *Lenticels* quite numerous, medium size, oval, slightly raised. *Buds* medium size, broad, plump, obtuse, free, slightly pubescent.

FRUIT.

Fruit below medium to nearly large, uniform in size and shape. *Form* roundish to roundish oblate or somewhat ovate, regular or faintly ribbed. *Stem* very long, moderately thick. *Cavity* acute, of medium depth, medium in width to rather narrow, symmetrical, usually partly russeted, often with outspreading russet rays. *Calyx* medium to small, closed; lobes medium in length, narrow, acute. *Basin* shallow to moderately deep, narrow to medium in width, somewhat obtuse, smooth, symmetrical, furrowed.

Skin thin, tender, smooth, waxy, yellowish-green becoming clear pale yellow when fully mature.

Calyx tube medium in width, cone-shape to truncate funnel-form. *Stamens* median.

Core medium to rather small, abaxile; cells often unsymmetrical, open; core lines clasping the funnel cylinder. *Carpels* ovate. *Seeds* medium to rather small, rather narrow, angular, acute, medium brown.

Flesh yellowish-white, firm, fine-grained, moderately tender, juicy, very sweet, aromatic, good to very good.

Season mid-August to late September.

GOLDEN WHITE.

REFERENCES. 1. Gibb, *Ia. Hort. Soc. Rpt.*, 1883:447. 2. Brodie, *Montreal Hort. Soc. Rpt.*, 1885:72. 3. Hoskins, *Mich. Hort. Soc. Rpt.*, 1886:221. 4. *Montreal Hort. Soc. Rpt.*, 1886-7:16. 5. *Can. Hort.*, 13:157, 332. 1890. 6. Beach and Paddock, *N. Y. Sta. An. Rpt.*, 14:252. 1895. 7. Beach, *W. N. Y. Hort. Soc. Rpt.*, 1896:50. 8. Budd-Hansen, 1903:91.

SYNONYMS. *Beel Solotofskaja* (1). GOLDEN WHITE (1, 2, 3, 4, 5, 6, 7, 8). *No. 978* (3, 5, 8). *No. 979* (8). *No. 981* (8).

Fruit of medium size, greenish-yellow, streaked with bright red in the sun, subacid, fair quality; season September. The tree comes into bearing rather young, and yields full crops biennially. Evidently not desirable for planting in New York.

Historical. A Russian apple received for testing at this Station from T. H. Hoskins, Newport, Vt., in 1888.

TREE.

Tree rather small, a slow grower with short, stout branches. *Form* spreading, open. *Twigs* short, curved, stout, with large terminal buds; internodes short. *Bark* dull brown mingled with olive-green, coated with gray scarf-skin; heavily pubescent. *Lenticels* scattering, large, oval or elongated, raised. *Buds* large, prominent, broad, plump, obtuse, free, much pubescent.

FRUIT.

Fruit medium size. *Form* oblate inclined to conic, flattened at the base, ribbed. *Stem* small to medium. *Cavity* small, acuminate, narrow, moderately shallow, russeted. *Calyx* open or partly open. *Basin* large, irregular, moderately deep, wrinkled.

Skin greenish-yellow nearly overlaid with red and striped with carmine. *Dots* numerous, large, light. *Prevailing effect* red or striped red.

Calyx tube large, cone-shape to funnel-form.

Core medium size, somewhat abaxile; cells usually symmetrical, closed or partly open; core lines clasping. *Carpels* roundish, emarginate, tufted. *Seeds* above medium, plump, wide, obtuse.

Flesh white with faint salmon tinge, fine-grained, moderately juicy, subacid, fair or sometimes good in quality.

Season September and October.

GOLDING.

REFERENCES. 1. *London Hort. Soc. Cat.*, 1831:No. 479. 2. Kenrick, 1835: 64. 3. Downing, 1857:79. fig. 4. *Mag. Hort.*, 30:162. 1864. 5. Warder, 1867:636. fig. 6. Thomas, 1875:226. 7. *Am. Pom. Soc. Cat.*, 1877:6.

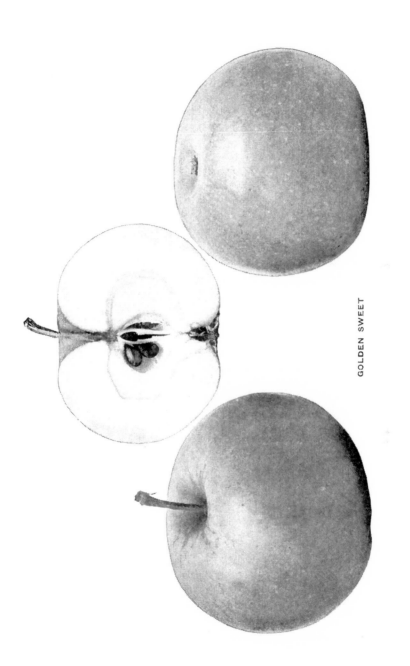

GOLDEN SWEET

8. Barry, 1883:342. **9.** Lyon, *Mich. Sta. Bul.*, 105:108. 1894. **10.** *Am. Pom. Soc. Cat.*, 1897:13. **11.** Budd-Hansen, 1903:92. *fig.* **12.** Ragan, *U. S. B. P. I. Bul.*, 56:125. 1905.

SYNONYMS. *American Golden* (12). AMERICAN GOLDEN PIPPIN (2, 4, 5, 7, 8). *American Golden Pippin* (3, 6, 10, 11, 12). *Golden Apple* (12). GOLDEN PIPPIN (3, of Westchester Co., 6). *Golden Pippin* (5, of Westchester Co., 8 and 12). GOLDING (1, 9, 10, 11, 12). *Newtown Greening* (3, 12). *N. Y. Greening* (3, 5, 6, 12). *Ribbed Pippin* (3, 12).

Fruit medium or above, yellow, sometimes with shade of brownish-red; flesh rather coarse, aromatic, subacid and excellent in quality for either dessert or culinary uses. It is much subject to scab and a comparatively large percentage of the crop is apt to be unmarketable unless thorough treatment is given to prevent injury from insects and fungus diseases. The tree is rather large, vigorous, hardy, long-lived and moderately productive yielding moderate to heavy crops biennially. In some sections it is regarded as a pretty good commercial variety particularly in portions of Eastern New York.

Historical. In 1857 Downing wrote (3) regarding this variety, that although it was one of the finest American fruits and an old variety, it was not generally known. It was said to have been cultivated in Westchester and adjoining counties for more than fifty years where it was considered profitable for market and superior for family use. So far as we can learn Golding is now seldom or never planted in New York.

GRANDMOTHER.

REFERENCES. **1.** *Montreal Hort. Soc. Rpt.*, 1881–82:39, 73. **2.** Budd, *Ia. Hort. Soc. Rpt.*, 1882:78. **3.** *Montreal Hort. Soc. Rpt.*, 1883:105. *fig.* **4.** Gibb, *Ia. Hort. Soc. Rpt.*, 1883:443. **5.** *Am. Pom. Soc. Rpt.*, 1883:72. **6.** Budd, *Ia. Agr. Coll. Bul.*, 1883:27. **7.** *Ib.*, 1885:18. **8.** Schroeder, *Montreal Hort. Soc. Rpt.*, 12:71. 1886–7. **9.** *Ia. Agr. Coll. Bul.*, 1890:24. **10.** Bailey, *An. Hort.*, 1892:240. **11.** Budd, *Ia. Sta. Bul.*, 19:542. 1892. **12.** Munson, *Me. Sta. An. Rpt.*, 12:74, 80. 1896. **13.** Thomas, 1897:277. *fig.* **14.** Macoun, *Can. Dept. Agr. Rpt.*, 1899:79. **15.** Troop, *Ind. Sta. An. Rpt.*, 12:80. 1899. **16.** Hansen, *S. D. Sta. Bul.*, 76:54. 1902. *fig.* **17.** Budd-Hansen, 1903:92.

SYNONYMS. *Baboushkino* (1). *Babuscheno* (16, 17). BABUSCHKINO (3). *Babushkino* (4, 7). *Bogdanoff* (14). *Bogdanoff Steklianka* (14). GRANDMOTHER (2, 4, 5, 6, 7, 8, 9, 11, 12, 13, 14, 15, 16, 17). *Grandmother* (3). GRAND MOTHER (1, 10). *No. 6 M* (1, 2, 6, 9, 11). *No. 6* (8). *No. 469* (1, 2, 3. 6, 7, 11, 12, 16, 17). *No. 84 Vor.* (9, 11). *Red Reinette* (14).

Fruit of good medium size, greenish-yellow, sometimes with slight blush. It shows the marks of handling readily, is not very uniform in size nor does it excel in quality. Season late fall and early winter. The tree is a good thrifty grower, comes into bearing young, is reliably productive and is almost an annual bearer, yielding moderate to good crops. It does not appear to be valuable for planting in New York.

Historical. A Russian variety which has been disseminated for trial in various sections of the country. It has been thus far but little planted in this state.

TREE.

Tree large, rather vigorous with long, stout branches. *Form* spreading, rather flat, open. *Twigs* medium length, curved, moderately stout; internodes short. *Bark* dark brown or reddish-brown, lightly streaked with scarf-skin; pubescent. *Lenticels* quite numerous, medium size, roundish, raised. *Buds* medium to large, broad, plump, obtuse, free, pubescent.

FRUIT.

Fruit medium to rather large. *Form* ovate to roundish conic, quite flat at base, a little angular; sides unequal; fairly uniform. *Stem* short or very short, rather thick. *Cavity* acute to acuminate, narrow, moderately deep to shallow or scarcely depressed, much russeted and often with outspreading russet. *Calyx* large to medium, closed or somewhat open; lobes medium in length, broad, acute. *Basin* deep to medium in depth, medium in width to rather wide, abrupt, usually furrowed and wrinkled.

Skin smooth, light greenish-yellow, sometimes with faint blush. *Dots* numerous, inconspicuous, light and submerged, or sometimes areolar with dark center.

Calyx tube medium in length, wide, broadly conical. *Stamens* basal.

Core medium to small or abortive, axile or abaxile; cells symmetrical, usually closed; core lines meeting *Carpels* variable, irregular, broadly ovate or obovate, emarginate, slightly tufted. *Seeds* below medium to rather large, rather dark brown, plump, obtuse to acute.

Flesh with slight green or yellow tinge, moderately firm, coarse, neither crisp nor tender, very juicy, subacid to briskly subacid, slightly aromatic, fair to good in flavor and quality.

Season November to January.

GRAVENSTEIN.

REFERENCES. 1. Forsyth, 1824:105. 2. *Pom. Mag.*, 3:No. 98. 1830. *col. pl.* 3. *London Hort. Soc. Cat.*, 1831:No. 489. 4. Kenrick, 1832:34. 5. Floy-Lindley, 1833:52. 6. Manning, 1838:53. 7. *Ib.*, *Mag. Hort.*, 7:45. 1841. 8. Downing, 1845:85. *fig.* 9. *Horticulturist*, 1:196. 1846. 10. Cole, 1849:110. *fig.* 11. Thomas, 1849:149. *fig.* 12. *Horticulturist*, 5:200. 1850. 13. Barry, 1851:284. 14. Emmons, *Nat. Hist. N. Y.*, 3:32, 104. 1851. *fig., col. pl.* No. 28. 15. Hovey, 2:15. 1851. *col. pl.* 16. *Am. Pom. Soc. Cat.*, 1852. 17. Elliott, 1854:83. 18. Gregg, 1857:43. *fig.* 19. Hooper, 1857:41, 107, 111. 20. De Wolf and Hovey, *Mag. Hort.*, 23:444. 1857. 21. Warder, 1867:487. *fig.* 22. Fitz, 1872:143, 149, 152. 23. Leroy, 1873:338. *fig.* 24. *Horticulturist*, 30:32. 1875. 25. Downing, 1881:11 index, app. 26. Hogg, 1884:96. 27. Wickson, 1889:243. 28. Lyon, *Mich. Hort. Soc. Rpt.*, 1890:292. 29. Bailey, *An. Hort.*, 1892:240. 30. Stinson, *Ark. Sta. An. Rpt.*, 6:55. 1893. 31. Gaucher, 1894:No. 10. *col. pl.* 32. Saunders, *Ont. Fr. Gr. Assn. An. Rpt.*, 27:51. 1895. 33. *Amer. Gard.*, 16:381. 1895. *fig.* 34. Burrill and McCluer, *Ill. Sta. Bul.*, 45:303. 1896. 35. Bunyard, *Jour. Roy. Hort. Soc.*, 1898:354. 36. *Can. Hort.*, 22:133. 1899. 37. Van Deman, *Rural N. Y.*, 59:20. 1900. 38. Woolverton, *Ont. Fr. Stas. An. Rpt.*, 8:8. 1901. *figs.* 39. Waugh, *Vt. Sta. An. Rpt.*, 14:295. 1901. 40. *Can. Hort.*, 25:167. 1902. *fig.* 41. Budd-

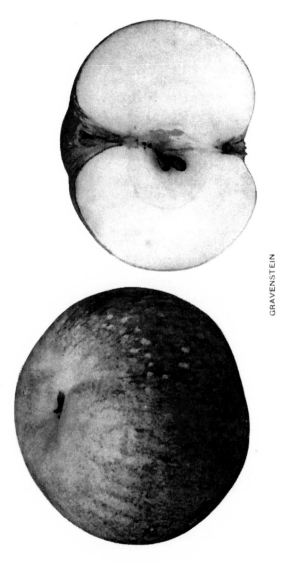

GRAVENSTEIN

Hansen, **1903**:93. fig. **42.** Bruner, *N. C. Sta. Bul.*, **182**:20. 1903. **43.** Powell and Fulton, *U. S. B. P. I. Bul.*, **48**:43. 1903. **44.** Beach and Clark, *N. Y. Sta. Bul.*, **248**:122. 1904.

SYNONYMS. *Blumen-Calvill* (31). *Calville de Gravenstein* (31). *Calville Grafensteiner* (23, 31). *Diel's Sommerkönig* (31). *Early Congress* (25). *Grafen-Apfel* (31). *Grafensteiner* (15, 23, 31). *Grave Slige* (23). *Grave Slije* (8, 15, 17, 31). GRAVENSTEIN (1, 2, 3, 4, 5, 6, 7, 8, 9, 10, 11, 12, 13, 14, 15, 16, 17, 18, 19, 20, 21, 22, 23, 24, 25, 26, 27, 28, 29, 30, 32, 33, 34, 35, 36, 37, 38, 39, 40, 41, 43, 44). *Gravenstein* (31). GRAVENSTEINER (31). *Gravensteiner* (23). *Gravenstine* (31). *Ohio Nonpareil* (17, 23, 31). *Paradies Apfel* (31). *Pomme Graefenstein* (31). *Prinzessin-Apfel* (31). *Ripp Apfel* (31). *Sabine* (31). *Sabine of the Flemings* (15, 23). *Strohmer* (31). *Stromling* (31). *Tom Harryman* (31).

Gravenstein is an apple of good size, attractive appearance and excellent quality. For culinary purposes it is perhaps unexcelled by any variety of its season. It often sells at comparatively high prices. In many sections of the state the tree is regarded as not quite hardy, being somewhat subject to sunscald and canker. It comes into bearing moderately early, is quite productive and a pretty reliable cropper. The crop ripens continuously during a period of several weeks and should have two or three pickings. Beginning in the latter half of September it continues in season till early November. When properly handled a considerable portion of the fruit may remain apparently sound much later than this but the color fades and the quality and flavor deteriorate. As compared with other varieties of its class it stands up well in good dry cold storage (44). There is apt to be considerable loss from the dropping of the fruit before it is properly colored and there is also a rather high percentage of low grade or unmarketable fruit. In spite of these serious faults its cultivation in commercial orchards is gradually increasing in some sections of the state, particularly in portions of the Hudson valley where fruit growers find it a desirable apple for both domestic and foreign markets.

Historical. The following excellent account of the history of this variety was given by Hovey in 1851 (15). "The origin of the Gravenstein remains in some doubt. It is said to have been originally found in the Duke of Augustinberg's garden at Gravenstein, in Holstein, and that the original tree was growing there in the middle of the last century; another statement is, that it derived its name from being found in the garden of the castle of Gräfenstein, in Sleswick; and Diel says, that it was supposed by some to have been introduced from Italy. Be this as it may, it is a common apple throughout Germany and Sweden, and was received from thence into the English collections. It is undoubtedly of similar origin with the Red Astrachan and Duchess of Oldenburg, possessing the peculiar habit of growth, form of foliage, and texture of the fruit, which distinguish the German apples.

"At what time it was first introduced into our gardens we are not aware. But as neither Coxe or Thacher describe or name it, we suppose it was some time subsequent to the account given of it in the Transactions of the London Horticultural Society in 1822. It is at the present time considerably cultivated, though not to the extent its merits deserve."

In 1857 Captain DeWolfe stated that the Gravenstein was imported by him from Denmark in May, 1826 (20). In a letter dated October 11, 1829, published in the New England Farmer, Judge Buel, of Albany, called attention to the importation of Gravenstein and other German apples, trees of which he had presented to the members of the Massachusetts Horticultural Society. Hovey states that in view of this it appears that Gravenstein was imported to the vicinity of Albany probably prior to 1826 (20). After these early importations Gravenstein gradually found its way into cultivation in various portions of the country. For many years it has been pretty generally disseminated through New York state, but in most localities it is grown to a limited extent only.

TREE.

Tree large, vigorous. *Form* upright spreading to roundish, open. *Twigs* medium to long, curved, moderately stout; internodes long. *Bark* brownish-red, mingled with olive-green, lightly streaked with scarf-skin; pubescent. *Lenticels* very scattering, medium to small, oblong, not raised. *Buds* medium in size, plump, acute, free, pubescent.

FRUIT.

Fruit large to above medium, fairly uniform in size but not in shape. *Form* oblate to roundish, somewhat irregular, broad at the base, slightly angular about the basin. *Stem* short to medium, thick. *Cavity* rather large, acute to acuminate, moderately deep to deep, rather narrow to broad, irregularly russeted. *Calyx* large, open or sometimes closed; lobes large, long, very broad, acute. *Basin* irregular, medium in depth to deep, medium to wide, obtuse to somewhat abrupt, wrinkled.

Skin thin, tender, slightly rough, greenish-yellow to orange-yellow overlaid with broken stripes of light and dark red. *Dots* few, small, light. *Prevailing effect* yellow striped.

Calyx tube large, conical to funnel-shape. *Stamens* median.

Core medium in size, strongly abaxile; cells open; core lines clasping the funnel cylinder. *Carpels* broadly ovate, emarginate. *Seeds* medium to large, medium in width, rather long, plump, acute to acuminate, medium brown.

Flesh yellowish, firm, moderately fine, crisp, moderately tender, juicy, sprightly subacid, aromatic, very good to best.

Season late September till early November.

RED TYPES OF THE GRAVENSTEIN.

Several instances are known where bud sports of the Gravenstein have originated which bear highly colored red fruit, but in other respects are quite like the typical Gravenstein. Some of these sports have neither been described nor propagated but others of them have been introduced into cultivation under distinct names. Gaucher and Leroy each describe a Red Gravenstein.[1] A Red Gravenstein which originated in Nova Scotia is now cultivated under the name Banks. For an account of this variety the reader is referred to Banks, page 14.

GREAT MOGUL.

REFERENCES. 1. Regel, 1 :453. 1868. 2. Budd, *Ia. Agr. Coll. Bul.*, **1885** :24, 35, 36, 37. 3. Lyon, *U. S. Pom. Bul.*, 2 :41. 1888. 4. Budd, *Ia. Sta. Bul.*, 18 :519. 1892. 5. Troop, *Ind. Sta. Bul.*, **53** :124. 1894. 6. Stinson, *Ark. Sta. An. Rpt.*, 9 :105. 1896. 7. Troop, *Ind. Sta. Rpt.*, **12** :80. 1899. 8. *Ib., Ia. Sta. Bul.*, **41** :85. 1899. 9. Ragan, *U. S. B. P. I. Bul.*, **56** :128. 1905.

SYNONYMS. GREAT MOGUL (1, 2, 3, 4, 5, 6, 7, 8, 9). *54 M* (3). *Grosser Mogul* (2, 9). *Vilikui Mogul* (2, 9).

Fruit large, greenish, blushed and striped with red, somewhat resembling Alexander in type but tending to be more oblong, less broadly striped with carmine, and on the whole less attractive in color and form. Tree a fine grower, comes into bearing rather young, is an annual bearer and productive. It is not recommended for growing in New York.

Historical. An apple of Russian origin which was introduced into the United States about twenty-five years ago (1, 2, 3).

TREE.

Tree a good grower when young but when full grown is rather below medium size. *Form* open, spreading, rather drooping with rather short stout branches and drooping laterals. *Twigs* below medium to short, stout, irregularly geniculate. *Bark* clear brownish-red to very dark brown almost black, mottled lightly with gray scarf-skin, slightly pubescent. *Lenticels* very conspicuous, medium to large, oblong, generally elongated and russeted. *Buds* very prominent, large, broad, plump, acute, free, lightly attached to the bark, scales not well united, pubescent.

FRUIT.

Fruit large to very large. *Form* roundish ovate, sometimes varying to oblong conic or to oblate conic, slightly angular. Usually the fruit is pretty regular in form, shape and size. *Stem* medium to nearly long, rather thick, often clubbed or swollen. *Cavity* usually very acuminate, sometimes acute, moderately deep, moderately wide, sometimes with outspreading russet rays, smooth, symmetrical, often lipped. *Calyx* medium to rather large, closed or

---

1 Leroy, **1873** :339. Gaucher, **1894** :No. 11.

slightly open, lobes long, broad, acute. *Basin* rather small, often oblique, narrow to medium in width, shallow to moderately deep, somewhat abrupt, smooth or slightly wrinkled, symmetrical.

Skin rather thick, tough, smooth, somewhat waxy, pale greenish-yellow more or less overspread with rather bright pinkish-red, often indistinctly striped with carmine. *Dots* inconspicuous, numerous, small, scattering, gray.

Calyx tube medium, elongated, conical or somewhat funnel-form with wide limb and fleshy pistil point projecting into the base. *Stamens* marginal to median.

Core somewhat abaxile; cells often unsymmetrical, varying from wide open to nearly closed; core lines slightly clasping. *Carpels* broadly ovate, elongated, slightly emarginate. *Seeds* numerous, compactly filling the cells, medium to large, variable in shape, rather short, very wide, plump, obtuse or sometimes acute, light brown.

Flesh nearly white, slightly tinged with yellow, not very firm, moderately fine, not crisp, tender, juicy, subacid mingled with sweet, fair to good in quality.

Season October to December.

GREEN SEEK-NO-FURTHER.

REFERENCES. **1.** Coxe, **1817**:131. fig. **2.** Kenrick, **1832**:53. **3.** Thomas, **1849**:181. fig. **4.** Emmons, *Nat. Hist. N. Y.*, 3:38. 1851. fig. **5.** Elliott, **1854**:137. **6.** Warder, **1867**:720. **7.** Downing, **1869**:202.

SYNONYMS. *Autumn Secknofurther* (4). *Bracy's Seek-no-further* (5). *Flushing Seek-no-further* (7). GREEN SEEK-NO-FURTHER (3, 5, 6, 7). SEEKNOFURTHER (4). *Seeknofurther* (5, 7, of Coxe 3). SEEK-NO-FURTHER (1). *White Seek-no-further* (7). WINTER SEEK-NO-FURTHER (2).

A large yellowish-green apple with faint blush of orange-red, very good in quality; season early winter. The tree is a rather slow grower, but eventually forms a regular, compact head and is quite productive. Desirable for the home orchard (1, 7.)

Historical. The earliest description of this variety which we find is that given by Coxe (1) who remarks that it is a native of one of the eastern states. Downing states that it originated in the garden of William Prince, Flushing, N. Y. (7). It is now seldom found in cultivation in New York.

FRUIT.

Fruit large. *Form* roundish conic or a little inclined to oblate conic, ribbed. *Stem* short to medium, thick. *Cavity* large, acute to somewhat acuminate, deep, broad, more or less marked with faint greenish-russet. *Calyx* moderately large, closed or slightly open. *Basin* deep, rather wide, abrupt, furrowed and wrinkled.

Skin moderately thick, tough, greenish-yellow or yellow with faint orange-red blush. *Dots* variable, large and small, often irregular, areolar with russet center or whitish and submerged.

Calyx tube large, moderately long, wide, conical. *Stamens* median.

Core small, axile; cells symmetrical, closed; core lines meeting or slightly clasping. *Carpels* roundish to broadly ovate, tufted. *Seeds* rather numerous, above medium, narrow, long, acute to acuminate, tufted.

Flesh yellowish-white, moderately coarse, crisp, tender, very juicy, sprightly, rich subacid, very good.

Season October to January.

GROSH.

REFERENCES. **1.** *Western Horticultural Review*, **1853** (cited by **4**). **2.** *Gard. Monthly*, **1861**:124 (cited by **3**). **3.** Kenrick, *Mag. Hort.*, **29**:73. 1863. fig. **4.** Warder, **1867**:464, 735. fig. **5.** Warder, **1867**:720. **6.** Downing, **1869**:205. **7.** *Ib.*, **1869**:89. **8.** *Ib.*, **1872**:37 app. **9.** *Am. Pom. Soc. Cat.*, **1877**:16. **10.** Barry, **1883**:356. **11.** Thomas, **1885**:528. **12.** Bailey, *An. Hort.*, **1892**:252. **13.** *Ill. Sta. Bul.*, **45**:345. 1896. **14.** *Am. Pom. Soc. Cat.*, **1897**:13. **15.** Lyon, *Mich. Sta. Bul.*, **143**:200. 1897. **16.** Van Deman, *Rural N. Y.*, **58**:722. 1899. fig. **17.** Ragan, *U. S. B. P. I. Bul.*, **56**:132. 1905.

SYNONYMS. BEAUTY OF THE WEST (7, 13). *Beauty of the West* (17). *Big Rambo* (4, 8, 16, 17). *Cummings Rambo* (17). *English Rambo* (16). *French Rambo* of some (17). GROSH (5, 6, 14, 15, 16, 17). *Grosh* (9). *Grosh's Mammoth* (17). *Large Rambo* (17). *Large Summer Rambo* (17). *Lothringer Rambour* (17). *Mammoth Rambo* (17). *Monstrous Rambo* (17). *Musgrove* (16). *Musgrove's Cooper* (4, 7, 8, 17). *Naylor Rambo* (17). OHIO BEAUTY (2). *Ohio Beauty* (4, 7, 8, 16, 17). *Pickaway Rambo* (17). *Rambour Lorraine* (17). *Summer Rambo* (9, 17). *Sweet Rambo* incorrectly (17). WESTERN BEAUTY (3, 4, 8, 9, 10, 12). *Western Beauty* (7, 13, 16, 17, ? 14).

Fruit large, uniform and when well colored rather attractive, being mottled and striped with red. The flesh is tender, sprightly, pleasant subacid, in season from September till early winter. The tree is a strong grower, comes into bearing early and is a reliable cropper, yielding moderate to good crops almost annually. There is apt to be considerable loss from premature dropping of the fruit. So far as we can learn this variety has been as yet but little grown in New York. It appears to be worthy of further testing.

Summer Rambo much resembles this variety in general appearance but ripens about a month earlier.

Historical. Origin unknown. It was first brought to notice in Ohio, where it has been much grown under the name of Western Beauty.

TREE.

Tree vigorous with very long, moderately stout, curved branches. *Form* upright spreading to roundish, open. *Twigs* long to below medium, somewhat curved, moderately stout; internodes medium or below. *Bark* clear reddish-brown mingled with olive-green, lightly streaked with scarf-skin; pubescent near tips. *Lenticels* clear brownish, conspicuous, quite numerous, medium or above, roundish, raised. *Buds* medium to large, prominent, broad, plump, obtuse, free or nearly so, slightly pubescent.

FRUIT.

Fruit large or very large, very uniform in size and shape. *Form* roundish oblate to somewhat conical, regular or sometimes elliptical. *Stem* short to above medium, moderately thick. *Cavity* acuminate to acute, deep, wide, often somewhat compressed, smooth and green or sometimes russeted, symmetrical or gently furrowed, sometimes lipped. *Calyx* above medium to very large, usually somewhat open disclosing the yellow calyx tube; lobes separated at the base, rather long, often leafy, acute to acuminate. *Basin* often oblique, large, medium in depth and width to deep and rather wide, abrupt, usually somewhat furrowed.

Skin thick, tough, waxy, greenish-yellow becoming clear bright yellow when fully mature, washed and mottled with bright red and striped and splashed with carmine, except in highly-colored specimens the yellow predominates. *Dots* numerous, small to rather large, pale gray or russet, often areolar or whitish and submerged.

Calyx tube rather large, wide at the top, conical or approaching funnelform. *Stamens* nearly basal to above median.

Core small to medium, axile or somewhat abaxile with hollow cylinder in the axis; cells symmetrical, closed or partly open; core lines clasping. *Carpels* broadly roundish to ovate, emarginate, often tufted. *Seeds* moderately numerous, moderately dark brown, often abortive, medium size, moderately wide, obtuse to acute.

Flesh whitish, slightly tinged with yellow, rather firm, medium to rather coarse, crisp, tender, juicy, sprightly subacid, a little aromatic, good or sometimes very good.

Season September to January.

GRUNDY.

REFERENCES. **1.** Hansen, *S. D. Sta. Bul.*, **76**:56. 1902. **2.** Budd-Hansen, **1903**:95. **3.** *Jewell Nursery Co. Cat.*, **1903**:7. **4.** Ragan, *U. S. B. P. I. Bul.*, **56**:133. 1905.

SYNONYMS. GRUNDY (1, 2, 3, 4). *Thompson Seedling No. 38* (1, 2, 3, 4).

Fruit large, regular, subacid, yellow marbled with red. Season September and October. Tree vigorous, spreading, productive. Originated from seed taken from New York to Grundy county, Iowa, by Mrs. J. S. B. Thompson in 1861. It has received favorable notice as a hardy variety in that region, but has not been sufficiently tested in this state to determine its value here (2).

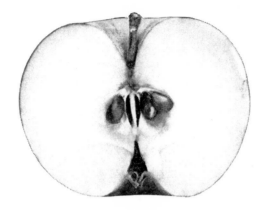

HAAS

HAAS.

REFERENCES. **1.** *Horticulturist,* **25** :55. 1870. **2.** Downing, **1872** :10 app. *fig.* **3.** Barry, **1883** :345. **4.** Thomas, **1885** :512. **5.** *Can. Hort.,* **11** :69, 73. 1888. **6.** Bailey, *An. Hort.,* **1892** :240. **7.** Woolverton, *Ont. Fr. Stas. An. Rpt.,* **1** :24. 1894. **8.** Stinson, *Ark. Sta. Bul.,* **43** :103. 1896. **9.** Munson, *Me. Sta. Rpt.,* **1896** :70. **10.** Waugh, *Vt. Sta. An. Rpt.,* **14** :296. 1901. **11.** Munson, *Me. Sta. Bul.,* **82** :95. 1902. **12.** Dickens and Greene, *Kan. Sta. Bul.,* **105** :53. 1902. **13.** Hansen, *S. D. Sta. Bul.,* **76** :56. 1902. **14.** Budd-Hansen, **1903** :96. *fig.* **15.** Farrand, *Mich. Sta. Bul.,* **205** :44. 1903. **16.** Beach and Clark, *N. Y. Sta. Bul.,* **248** :123. 1904.

SYNONYMS. FALL QUEEN (2, 3, 7). *Fall Queen* (4, 5, 14, 16). *Gros Pomier* (2, 14). *Gros Pommier* (2). HAAS (5, 6, 9, 10, 11, 12, 13, 14, 15, 16). *Haas* (2, 3, 7). HASS (8). *Horse,* of some (2). HOSS (1). *Hoss* (2).

Fruit of good medium size and very attractive bright red color but only fair in quality. With some growers it has proved profitable because the tree comes into bearing young and is very thrifty, hardy and productive, but on account of the inferior quality of its fruit doubtless it will be eventually wholly supplanted by better kinds.

Historical. Originated on the grounds of Gabriel Cerré, St. Louis, Mo. (2). It has been widely disseminated throughout the Middle West and Southwest where it is recognized as one of the hardiest of American apples. In New York it has been planted to a limited extent only and its cultivation is not increasing.

TREE.

Tree large, very vigorous with long, slender branches. *Form* at first comparatively tall and upright but becoming spreading or roundish. *Twigs* long, curved, slender with large terminal buds; internodes long. *Bark* brown or reddish-brown, lightly streaked with scarf-skin; pubescent. *Lenticels* quite numerous, medium size, oval, not raised. *Buds* medium to large, broad, plump, obtuse, free, pubescent.

FRUIT.

Fruit medium to above. *Form* oblate a little inclined to conic, somewhat ribbed; sides usually unequal. *Stem* medium to short, thick, often partly red. *Cavity* acute to acuminate, deep, broad, usually symmetrical, more or less covered with thin greenish-russet. *Calyx* small to medium, closed or nearly so; lobes separated at base, short, narrow, acuminate. *Basin* moderately narrow, rather deep, abrupt, smooth or slightly furrowed and wrinkled.

Skin thin, tough, smooth, yellow, mottled, washed and nearly covered with deep bright red or brownish-red, striped and splashed with deep carmine. *Dots* small to rather large, inconspicuous, numerous, pale or russet. *Prevailing effect* red striped with carmine.

Calyx tube very variable, rather long and wide, conical or approaching funnel-form. *Stamens* median or below.

Core below medium to above, somewhat abaxile; cells symmetrical, open or sometimes closed; core lines clasping. *Carpels* broadly roundish to elliptical. *Seeds* dark brown, medium to large, of medium width, plump, acute.

Flesh white, often stained with red, firm, moderately fine, a little tough, moderately juicy to juicy, sprightly subacid, aromatic, a little astringent, poor to fair or sometimes nearly good.

Season October to early winter. In common storage the ordinary commercial limit is November (16).

HAGLOE.

REFERENCES. 1. Coxe, 1817:107. fig. 2. Thacher, 1822:126. 3. Fessenden, 1828:131. 4. Downing, *Horticulturist*, 3:249. 1848. 5. Thomas, 1849: 141. 6. Downing, 1854:146. 7. Elliott, 1854:137. 8. Hooper, 1857:42. 9. *Horticulturist*, 14:425. 1859. 10. *Am. Pom. Soc. Cat.*, 1862. 11. Warder, 1867:596. 12. Barry, 1883:334. 13. Bailey, *An. Hort.*, 1892:240. 14. *Am. Pom. Soc. Cat.*, 1899:17. 15. Budd-Hansen, 1903:96.

SYNONYMS. HAGLOE (7, 8, 11, 12, 13, 14, 15). HAGLOE CRAB (1, 2, 3), but incorrectly. SUMMER HAGLOE (4, 5, 6, 9, 10). *Summer Hagloe* (7).

In 1817 Coxe gave the following description of this variety (1). " The fruit, when fully ripe, has a yellow ground streaked with bright red — the size about middling, the form round, flat at the ends; the stalk large — the flesh remarkably soft and woolly, but not dry — the taste acid, but highly flavoured. * * * It ripens in August and September; keeps a long time without rotting — it bears abundantly and early: the growth of the tree is very uncommon; thick strong shoots; buds, particularly at the extremity of the branches, very large; the colour of the wood dark — the size of the tree small: the Hagloe is an uncommonly fine cooking apple; and from its great beauty and large size, added to its abundant bearing, is a valuable market fruit."

The tree is not a very good grower but comes into bearing rather young and yields moderate to good crops annually or nearly annually. The quality of the fruit is such that it is valued chiefly for culinary use and market. It is of good size and pretty uniform but the color is predominantly pale yellow rather faintly striped with red. It is not sufficiently attractive for a good market sort.

Historical. It is now held that Hagloe originated in America (14, 15). Coxe and some later writers confused this variety with the English cider fruit known as Hagloe Crab but eventually this error was discovered (4) and the name Summer Hagloe came to be commonly accepted among pomologists for this variety, under which name it was listed by the American Pomological Society in 1862 (10). In 1899 the name was changed to Hagloe (14) in the catalogue of the American Pomological Society. This variety is but little known in New York.

TREE.

Tree rather small, a slow grower with moderately long, crooked branches. *Form* flat, spreading, rather dense. *Twigs* short, straight, stout with large terminal buds; internodes medium. *Bark* brown with some olive-green, lightly mottled with scarf-skin; pubescent near tips. *Lenticels* scattering, large to medium, oblong, raised. *Buds* medium to large, broad, plump, obtuse, free, pubescent.

FRUIT.

Fruit medium to large, pretty uniform. *Form* roundish truncate to roundish conic, ribbed; sides often unequal. *Stem* short to medium, rather thick. *Cavity* acute, medium in width and depth, symmetrical, russeted and with rather irregular, outspreading russet. *Calyx* below medium to above, closed or open; lobes often separated at the base, narrow, acuminate. *Basin* moderately deep, narrow to medium in width, abrupt, nearly smooth.

Skin rather tender, smooth, somewhat glossy, pale greenish-yellow washed and mottled with pinkish-red marked with splashes and narrow stripes of bright carmine. *Dots* light, inconspicuous. *Prevailing effect* yellow, faintly striped.

Calyx tube moderately long, wide, conical. *Stamens* basal.

Core usually small, axile to abaxile; cells usually open; core lines clasping. *Carpels* broadly ovate, emarginate, tufted. *Seeds* rather light brown, small to medium, roundish, very plump, obtuse.

Flesh white, moderately fine, tender, rather juicy, sprightly subacid, good for culinary purposes.

Season late August and September.

HARVEST REDSTREAK.

REFERENCES. 1. Downing, 1857:214. 2. Warder, 1867:436. 3. Downing, 1869:211. 4. Thomas, 1875:501. 5. Ragan, *U. S. B. P. I. Bul.,* 56:138. 1905.

SYNONYMS. *Early Red Pippin* (5). *Early Redstreak* (2). *Early Red Streak* (3). HARVEST REDSTREAK (2, 5). HARVEST RED STREAK (1, 3, 4). *Striped Harvest* (3, 5).

Fruit of medium size, smooth, greenish-yellow or whitish striped and splashed with red. Flesh whitish, coarse, subacid, good for culinary use; season August and September. It is not sufficiently attractive in color for a good market variety. The tree is medium to large, with round head, moderately vigorous to very vigorous and yields good to heavy crops biennially.

Historical. This is an old variety of unknown origin. It is rarely found in New York and is now seldom or never planted.

HASKELL.

REFERENCES. 1. Manning, *Mag. Hort.,* 6:172. 1840. 2. *Ib.,* 7:45. 1841. 3. *Thomas,* 1849:145. *fig.* 4. Cole, 1849:108. *fig.* 5. *Cultivator,* 6:342. 1849. 6. Barry, 1851:284. 7. Elliott, 1854:137. 8. Gregg, 1857:43. 9. Downing, 1857:82. 10. Warder, 1867:385. 11. Lyon, *Mich. Hort. Soc. Rpt.,* 1890:292. 12. Bailey, *An. Hort.,* 1892:240. 13. Hoskins, *Rural N. Y.,* 53: 278. 1894. 14. Powell and Fulton, *U. S. B. P. I. Bul.,* 48:44. 1903. 15. Beach and Clark, *N. Y. Sta. Bul.,* 248:124. 1904.

SYNONYMS. HASKELL (14, 15). HASKELL SWEET (1, 2, 3, 5, 6, 7, 8, 9, 10, 11, 12, 13). *Haskell Sweet* (4, 14, 15). SASSAFRAS SWEET (4). *Sassafras Sweet* (6, 7, 8, 9).

Fruit large, of good appearance for a greenish-yellow apple, sweet, excellent for culinary use, in season from September to late fall or early winter. The crop does not ripen uniformly. The earliest ripening fruit becomes fully mature in September while at the same time others are green and hard. In ordinary storage the commercial limit appears to be early November and in cold storage the middle of January (15). The tree is a thrifty grower, comes into bearing moderately young and yields full crops biennially. Desirable for the home orchard.

Historical. Origin, Ipswich, Mass. (2, 5). It is not commonly known in New York. It is occasionally listed by nurserymen (12) but is now seldom planted.

TREE.

Tree large, vigorous; branches long, moderately stout with numerous small spurs. *Form* upright spreading or roundish, rather open. *Twigs* moderately long, curved, moderately stout; internodes long. *Bark* brown, heavily mottled with scarf-skin; pubescent. *Lenticels* quite numerous, small, round, not raised. *Buds* medium size, plump, obtuse, free, pubescent.

FRUIT.

Fruit large or above medium, uniform in size and shape. *Form* roundish or oblate, regular. *Stem* short, usually not exserted. *Cavity* acute to acuminate, deep or moderately deep, moderately narrow to rather wide, somewhat furrowed, russeted and with some outspreading russet rays. *Calyx* large, closed. *Basin* wide, moderately deep, rather abrupt, smooth or somewhat wrinkled.

Skin greenish-yellow, more or less dotted and flecked with russet, occasionally with a bronze blush. *Dots* numerous, large, dark.

Calyx tube large, cone-shape to funnel-form. *Stamens* median.

Core rather small, axile; cells symmetrical, closed; core lines clasping. *Carpels* broad at the middle narrowing toward base and apex, emarginate. *Seeds* medium size, short, plump, obtuse.

Flesh yellowish, a little coarse, moderately crisp, tender, very sweet, aromatic, very good in flavor and quality.

Season September to late fall or early winter.

HAWLEY.

REFERENCES. 1. Hovey, *Mag. Hort.*, 13:112, 535. 1847. *fig.* 2. *Cultivator*, 4:114. 1847. *fig.* 3. Leavenworth, *Horticulturist*, 2:27. 1847. *fig.* 4. *Cultivator*, 5:246. 1848. 5. Cole, **1849**:112. *fig.* 6. Thomas, **1849**:156.

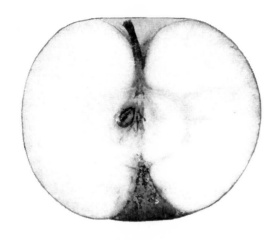

HAWLEY

fig. **7.** Emmons, *Nat. Hist. N. Y.,* **3**:48. 1851. *col. pl.* No. 24, *fig.* **8.**
Hovey, **2**:39. 1851. *col. pl.* and *fig.* **9.** Barry, **1851**:284. **10.** *Horticulturist,*
7:484. 1852. **11.** *Am. Pom. Soc. Cat.,* **1852.** **12.** *Mag. Hort.,* **19**:68. 1853.
13. Elliott, **1854**:137. **14.** *Mag. Hort.,* **20**:241. 1854. **15.** Downing, **1857**:82.
16. Gregg, **1857**:44. *fig.* **17.** Hooper, **1857**:43. **18.** *Horticulturist,* **13**:481.
1858. **19.** Warder, **1867**:410. *fig.* **20.** Leroy, **1873**:375. *fig.* **21.** Bailey,
An. Hort., **1892**:240. **22.** Waugh, *Vt. Sta. An. Rpt.,* **14**:296. 1901.

SYNONYMS. *Douse* (3, 5, 8, 10, 13, 20). *Dows* (1, 3, 8, 13, 20). *Dowse*
(2, 4, 6, 9, 10, 16, 20, 22). HAWLEY (1, 2, 3, 4, 5, 6, 7, 8, 9, 10, 11, 12, 13, 14,
15, 16, 17, 18, 19, 20, 21, 22). *Howley* (20).

Hawley is a very large apple of the Fall Pippin type in color,
size and form. When the color is fully developed it is a handsome
yellow. Season September and October. It is of delicious dessert
quality and desirable for the home orchard but not well adapted
for market because the tree is not very productive and the fruit
often is scabby and sometimes it water-cores and rots at the core.
The tree is a moderate grower in the nursery but in the orchard
it is rather vigorous, medium in size to large, hardy and rather long-
lived. It does not come into bearing very young. When mature
it bears quite regularly but is usually a light or moderate cropper.

Historical. Originated on the farm of Mr. Mathew Hawley, New Canaan,
N. Y., about 1750, from seeds which Mr. Hawley obtained from Milford,
Conn. (1, 3). The original tree lived nearly a century. The variety
gradually became disseminated throughout New York state. It has long
been known in cultivation in different parts of the state, particularly in
Columbia, Onondaga, Cayuga, Tompkins, Seneca and Monroe counties. It
is now rarely listed by nurserymen and is seldom planted.

FRUIT.

Fruit large or very large, pretty uniform in size and shape. *Form* nearly
globular to somewhat oblate or slightly conic, sometimes inclined to elliptical,
more or less distinctly ribbed. *Stem* medium in length, rather slender.
Cavity acute to nearly obtuse, deep, wide and with outspreading russet rays.
Calyx below medium to rather large, partly closed; lobes often separated at
base, reflexed, wide, acute. *Basin* moderately deep to deep, medium to wide,
very abrupt, often decidedly furrowed.

Skin fair, smooth, waxy, rather thin, pale green deepening to yellow as it
matures, sometimes showing a faint brownish blush, with scattering russet
dots and flecks especially toward the cavity.

Calyx tube large, wide, cone-shape, yellow or brownish.

Core below medium to above; cells closed; core lines meeting. *Carpels*
rather flat, tufted, roundish, emarginate. *Seeds* few, obtuse. When well
developed they are medium in size, but often some are abortive.

Flesh tinged with yellow, soft, very tender, rather fine-grained, juicy, rich, mild subacid, very good especially for dessert.

Season September to November or later.

HAWTHORNDEN.

REFERENCES. 1. Hooker, *Pom. Lond.*, 1813:T. 44 (cited by 2). 2. Forsyth, 1824:106. 3. *Pom. Mag.*, 1828:No. 34. *col. pl.* 4. *London Hort. Soc. Cat.*, 1831:No. 530. 5. *Mag. Hort.*, 1:326. 1835. 6. Manning, 1838:48. 7. *Ib.*, *Mag. Hort.*, 7:45. 1841. 8. Downing, 1845:86. 9. Cole, 1849:113. 10. Hovey, *Mag. Hort.*, 17:18. 1851. fig. 11. Barry, 1851:284. 12. Emmons, *Nat. Hist. N. Y.*, 3:40. 1851. 13. *Mag. Hort.*, 19:174. 1853. 14. Elliott, 1854:171. 15. Gregg, 1857:43. 16. Hooper, 1857:43. 17. *Am. Pom. Soc. Cat.*, 1862. 18. Warder, 1867:410. fig. 19. Leroy, 1873:376. fig. 20. Thomas, 1875:501. 21. *Montreal Hort. Soc. Rpt.*, 1:10. 1876. 22. *Ib.*, 5:24. 1879. 23. Hogg, 1884:105. 24. *Rural N. Y.*, 45:233. 1886. figs. 25. Lyon, *Mich. Hort. Soc. Rpt.*, 1890:292. 26. Bailey, *An. Hort.*, 1892:241. 27. Gaucher, 1894:No. 13. *col. pl.* 28. Dempsey, *Ont. Fr. Stas. An. Rpt.*, 1:24. 1894. fig. 29. Bunyard, *Jour. Roy. Hort. Soc.*, 1898:354.

SYNONYMS. *Hawley (27)* but erroneously. HAWTHORNDEAN (2, 6, 7). *Hawthorndean (23)*. HAWTHORNDEN (1, 3, 4, 5, 8, 9, 10, 11, 12, 13, 14, 15, 16, 17, 18, 19, 20, 21, 22, 23, 24, 25, 26, 27, 28, 29). *Lincolnshire Pippin (27)*. *Lord Kingston (27)*. *Maiden's Blush* erroneously (10). *Old Hawthorndean (23, 27)*. *Pomme de Hawthornden (27)*. *Red Hawthornden (10)*. *Shoreditch White (27)*. *Weisser Hawthornden (27)*. *Wheeler's Kernel (27)*. *White Apple (27)*. *White Hawthorndean (23, 27)*. *White Hawthornden (3, 4, 8, 10, 12, 14)*.

A Scotch variety which has done fairly well in various parts of this country from New England to California. Warder (18) says of it: "This famous Scotch fruit appears to do very well in this country, but it must yield the palm to its American cousin and representative, the Maiden's Blush, which possesses all its good qualities as a market and kitchen fruit, with attractive appearance."

The tree is said to be a vigorous grower and a biennial cropper, and the fruit is above medium to large, regular, fair, white sometimes nearly overspread with faint blush that deepens to bright red in the sun. Flesh mild subacid, not of high flavor, pleasant, good. Season September and October.

We are not acquainted with this variety. It appears to be but little known among New York fruit growers. It is still occasionally listed by nurserymen (26).

HIBERNAL.

REFERENCES. 1. Budd, *Ia. Hort. Soc. Rpt.*, 1880:525. 2. Gibb, *Montreal Hort. Soc. Rpt.*, 1881:156. 3. Tuttle, *Ib.*, 8:136. 1881–82. 4. *Ib.*, 1883:98. 5. Gibb, *Ia. Hort. Soc. Rpt.*, 1883:440. 6. Budd, *Ia. Agr. Coll. Bul.*, 1885:15. 7. Gibb, *Montreal Hort. Soc. Rpt.*, 1886–87:15. 8. Schroeder, *Ib.*, 1886–87:71. 9. Craig, *Ib.*, 1886–87:103. 10. Budd, *Ia. Agr. Coll. Bul.*, 1890:20. 11. *Can. Hort.*, 13:216. 1890. 12. Budd, *Ia. Sta. Bul.*, 19:537. 1892. 13. Bailey, *An. Hort.*, 1892:241. 14. Taylor, *Me. Pom. Soc. Rpt.*, 1892:57, 58. 15.

Freeborn, *Nat. Nurseryman,* **1894**:132. **16.** Can. Hort., **17**:7. 1894. **17.**
Gard. and For., **8**:340. 1895. **18.** Munson, *Me. Sta. Rpt.,* **1896**:74. **19.** Waugh,
Vt. Sta. Bul., **61**:30. 1897. **20.** *Am. Pom. Soc. Cat.,* **1897**:13. **21.** Troop, *Ind.
Sta. An. Rpt.,* **12**:80. 1899. **22.** Waugh, *Vt. Sta. An. Rpt.,* **14**:296. 1901.
23. Macoun, *Can. Dept. Agr. Bul.,* **37**:39. 1901. **24.** Hansen, *S. D. Sta. Bul.,*
76:57. 1902. fig. **25.** Munson, *Me. Sta. An. Rpt.,* **1902**:83, 87. **26.** Budd-
Hansen, **1903**:98. fig.

SYNONYMS. HIBERNAL (1, 2, 3, 4, 5, 6, 7, 9, 10, 11, 12, 13, 14, 15, 16, 17, 18,
19, 20, 21, 22, 23, 24, 25, 26). *Hibernal* (8). *No. 378* (1, 2, 4, 5, 6, 10, 12, 15,
18, 25, 26). *Orsimui* (4, 5, 6). OSIMOE (8). *Romna* (23).

A Russian variety which is proving valuable in portions of the Upper Mississippi valley and the Northwest because of its ability to withstand the rigor-
ous climatic conditions of those regions. Hansen says of it: "This variety
represents what is probably the hardiest type of the Russian race of apples; there
are several sorts closely resembling, or identical with, Hibernal. Tree vigorous, very spreading, productive. The strong spreading growth makes it
especially desirable as a stock for top-grafting, probably the best we have
at the present time. Fruit large, irregular, oblate to roundish oblate conical; skin thick; surface greenish-yellow, with a dull bronze mixed red on
sunny side, with a few dull crimson splashes; dots white, minute, obscure,
often some large russet dots; cavity regular, medium deep, with a large patch
of russet radiating out irregularly over nearly the entire base, this is a
marked characteristic; stem medium, often short; basin narrow, rather
shallow, wrinkled; calyx half open or open. Core closed, meeting; tube
funnel-shaped; stamens median; seeds few; flesh acid, with some astrin-
gency, juicy, good for cooking. Early winter" (24, 26).

Macoun reports "Flesh yellowish, crisp, tender, juicy, acid; core small;
quality above medium; season September to November. Tree very hardy, a
strong, spreading grower, and very productive. Although not a good dessert
fruit this is a fine cooking apple and on account of its great hardiness and
productiveness is one of the best of the Russian apples" (23).

HICKS.

REFERENCES. **1.** Hicks, *Horticulturist,* **21**:333. 1866. fig. **2.** Downing,
1869:215. **3.** Burrill and McCluer, *Ill. Sta. Bul.,* **45**:308, 316, 324. 1896.
4. Thomas, **1897**:639.

SYNONYMS. *Buckram* (2, 3). HICKS (1, 2, 3, 4).

A sweet apple of medium size, yellowish striped and splashed with crimson; season middle of August. It is but little known except in certain localities on Long Island. Not recommended for general planting in this state.

Historical. Hicks originated as a chance seedling and was brought to
notice by Isaac Hicks, North Hempstead, L. I. (1, 2).

HIGHTOP SWEET.

REFERENCES. **1.** Thacher, **1822**:128. **2.** Hovey, *Mag. Hort.,* **14**:390. 1848.
3. Cole, **1849**:97. **4.** Phoenix, *Horticulturist,* **4**:472. 1850. **5.** Emmons,
Nat. Hist. N. Y., **3**:16. 1851. fig. **6.** Elliott, **1854**:139. **7.** *Am. Pom. Soc.*

Cat., **1856.** **8.** *Mag. Hort.*, **22** :181. 1856. **9.** Downing, **1857** :151. **10.** Gregg, **1857** :40. **11.** Warder, **1867** :553. **12.** *Ill. Hort. Soc. Rpt.*, **1869** :33. **13.** Fitz, **1872** :145. **14.** Thomas, **1875** :189. **15.** Downing, **1881** :11 index, app. **16.** Barry, **1883** :333. **17.** Lyon, *Mich. Hort. Soc. Rpt.*, **1890** :292. **18.** Bailey, *An. Hort.*, **1892** :250. **19.** Munson, *Me. Sta. Rpt.*, **1893** :132. **20.** Hoskins, *Rural N. Y.*, **1894** :248. **21.** Budd-Hansen, **1903** :99. fig.

Synonyms. *Early Sweet* (15). High Top Sweet (19). *High Top Sweet* (13). Hightop *Sweet* (21). High Top Sweeting (1, 5, 6, 8, 12, 15). *High Top Sweeting?* (2, 3). Summer Sweet (3). *Summer Sweet* (5, 6, 9, 14). Summer Sweeting (2). Sweet June (4, 10, 13, 18). *Sweet June* (6, 9, 11, 14, 16, 19, 20, 21).

Fruit of medium size; flesh yellowish, very sweet, rich and of very good quality; season July and August. Tree upright, vigorous, very productive.

Historical. In 1822 Thacher (1) remarked: "This tree, it is believed, is peculiar to the old Plymouth colony. The first settlers, either from choice, or for want of other varieties, cultivated it more generally than any other apple. It is now much on the decline. The fruit is under the middle size; of a yellowish colour, pleasant taste; but chiefly used for baking, and for drying. It is ripe in August, and is not long preserved. The tree is remarkable for its long upright stem."

It appears that this variety was introduced into Ohio from Connecticut and Massachusetts and afterward disseminated westward under the name of Sweet June. In 1892 Bailey (18) found that although various nurserymen were offering Sweet June for sale none of them mentioned Hightop Sweet. Some have held that the Sweet June of the West is not identical with the Hightop Sweet of Massachusetts (12). We have not had the opportunity of determining whether this is true, but if they are identical it appears strange that the name Hightop Sweet should be entirely dropped by those who are propagating it in the West. This variety is but little known in New York.

HILAIRE.

References. **1.** *Ia. Hort. Soc. Rpt.*, **1879** :453. **2.** *Montreal Hort. Soc. Rpt.*, **1886–87** :95. **3.** Bailey, *Mich. Sta. Bul.*, **31** :54. 1887. **4.** Downing, **1881** :102 app. fig. **5.** Waugh, *Vt. Sta. Bul.*, **83** :87. 1900.

Synonyms. *Cabane du Chien* (3, 5, 6). *Fameuse Baldwin*, of some (5). St. Hilaire (1, 2, 3, 4, 5, 6).

An apple which resembles Fameuse in the color of its skin and in the color and texture of its flesh, but the flesh has more of a sprightly acid flavor and the fruit keeps better than that of Fameuse. Waugh reports (5) that it is not now grown in the vicinity of its origin. Professor U. P. Hedrick of the Michigan Agricultural College, who supplied the fruit for the following description, states that as grown in Michigan the variety is hardy, productive and gives promise of being a valuable acquisition.

Historical. This is said to have originated in the orchard of Alexis Dery, Quebec (4). Probably a seedling of Fameuse (2). So far as we know it is not grown in New York.

TREE.

Tree large, vigorous; a heavy alternate bearer (2). *Twigs* short, curved, slender; internodes short. *Bark* dark brown, with light coat of streaked scarf-skin, slightly pubescent. *Lenticels* scattering, small, oblong, raised. *Buds* small, plump, acute, free, slightly pubescent.

FRUIT.

Fruit medium to above, uniform in size. *Form* oblate to roundish-oblate, rather irregular. *Stem* medium, moderately slender. *Cavity* acuminate or acute, moderately deep and broad, not russeted, symmetrical. *Calyx* medium, usually closed; lobes broad, obtuse. *Basin* medium in depth to shallow, moderately wide to rather narrow, rather abrupt, slightly wrinkled, symmetrical.

Skin thin, tender, smooth, pale yellow or whitish almost completely overspread with attractive red of the Fameuse hue becoming as highly colored as the Fameuse or McIntosh and covered with faint bloom; stripes obscure if any. *Dots* very numerous, small, red, sometimes gray or russet. *Prevailing effect* brilliant deep pinkish-red deepening to purplish-red.

Calyx tube long, rather narrow, funnel-shape. *Stamens* median to basal.

Core nearly axile, small to medium; cells closed or partly open; core lines clasping the funnel cylinder. *Carpels* round, slightly emarginate. *Seeds* dark, numerous, medium to large, wide, obtuse to acute.

Flesh whitish sometimes tinged with red, fine, crisp, tender, juicy, sprightly subacid, good to very good.

Season November to January. A better keeper than Fameuse.

HILTON.

REFERENCES. 1. Downing, 1857:151. 2. Warder, 1867:721. 3. Thomas, 1875:502.

SYNONYMS. None.

This variety originated in Columbia county, N. Y. According to Downing (1) the tree is vigorous and productive; the fruit large, yellowish-green, subacid, excellent for culinary purposes. Season September and October.

So far as we can discover this variety is not now known in cultivation.

HOADLEY.

REFERENCES. 1. Goff, *Wis. Sta. An. Rpt.*, 11:347. 1894. 2 *Ib., Am. Pom. Soc. Rpt.*, 1899:236.

SYNONYMS. None.

A variety of the Oldenburg type which much resembles Oldenburg except that its season is about a month later. It is decidedly attractive in general appearance and of good quality for culinary purposes. The tree is a moderate grower, comes into bearing early and so far as tested here is very productive. It appears to be worthy of testing where an apple of this type is desired.

Historical. Received from the Wisconsin Experiment Station in 1896 for testing at this Station.

TREE.

Tree moderately vigorous. *Form* upright spreading when young. *Twigs* short, straight, stout; internodes medium. *Bark* brown and reddish-brown, lightly streaked with scarf-skin, slightly pubescent. *Lenticels* scattering, medium size, round, not raised. *Buds* medium to large, broad, plump, obtuse, free, pubescent.

FRUIT.

Fruit above medium to large, sometimes very large. *Form* roundish oblate inclined to conic, a little angular; sides unequal. *Stem* short, thick to slender. *Cavity* acute to obtuse, deep, broad, pretty symmetrical, thinly and irregularly russeted. *Calyx* rather large, closed or partly open; lobes long, broad, acute to obtuse. *Basin* deep to medium in depth, rather narrow to moderately wide, abrupt, slightly furrowed.

Skin moderately thick, tough, attractive yellow or greenish-yellow largely overspread with rather light bright red, mottled and irregularly striped and splashed with carmine. *Dots* inconspicuous, small, submerged, pale.

Calyx tube variable, short, rather wide, funnel-shape, sometimes broadly conical with core lines meeting. *Stamens* median to nearly marginal.

Core medium size, abaxile; cells open; core lines meeting or slightly clasping. *Carpels* broadly cordate or elliptical, slightly tufted. *Seeds* medium or below, wide, moderately long, usually plump, rather obtuse, dark colored.

Flesh tinged with yellow, pretty firm, a little coarse, crisp, tender, very juicy, brisk subacid, good.

Season late September to November.

HOG ISLAND SWEET.

REFERENCES. 1. Downing, 1857:152. 2. Warder, 1867:721. 3. Downing, 1872:10 index, app. 4. Thomas, 1875:502. 5. Lyon, *Mich. Hort. Soc. Rpt.*, 1890:292.

SYNONYMS. HOG ISLAND SWEET (1, 2, 3, 4, 5). *Sweet Pippin* (1). *Van Kleek's Sweet* (3).

A beautiful and excellent sweet apple in season from September to early winter. It is an old variety which had its origin on Hog Island, near Long Island, N. Y. (1). It is but little known. The tree is vigorous and productive.

FRUIT.

Fruit medium to large, pretty uniform. *Form* roundish conical to oblate, broad at the base, regular or obscurely ribbed. *Stem* short to medium, moderately thick. *Cavity* acute, deep, rather broad, heavily russeted and with outspreading russet rays. *Calyx* medium to large, closed or partly open; lobes short, broad, acute. *Basin* shallow to medium in depth, narrow to moderately wide, abrupt, broadly furrowed.

Skin thick, rather tough, somewhat roughened with flecks and patches of russet, pale yellow or greenish washed and mottled with red overlaid with

HOADLEY

broad and narrow stripes and splashes of carmine. *Dots* numerous, small, russet. *Prevailing effect* bright striped red over a yellow background.

Calyx tube long, wide, conical to funnel-shape. *Stamens* basal to median.

Core small to medium, abaxile to nearly axile; cells somewhat unsymmetrical, open; core lines slightly clasping the funnel cylinder or meeting. *Carpels* roundish obovate to elliptical, emarginate. *Seeds* medium or below, sometimes tufted, rather wide, rather short, plump, acute to somewhat obtuse.

Flesh tinged with yellow, moderately coarse, crisp, tender, juicy, very sweet, somewhat aromatic, good to very good.

Season September to early winter.

HOLLAND PIPPIN.

REFERENCES. 1. Coxe, 1817:109. fig. 2. Downing, 1845:86. 3. *Ib., Horticulturist*, 3:345. 1848. 4. Thomas, 1849:156. fig. 5. Cole, 1849:110. 6. Downing, Chas., *Horticulturist*, 8:196. 1853. 7. Elliott, 1854:138. 8. Hovey, *Mag. Hort.*, 22:555. 1856. fig. 9. Hooper, 1857:45. 10. Gregg, 1857:37. 11. *Am. Pom. Soc. Cat.*, 1862. 12. Warder, 1867:506. 13. Wickson, 1889:244. 14. Lyon, *Mich. Hort. Soc. Rpt.*, 1890:292. 15. Bailey, *An. Hort.*, 1892:241. 16. Beach and Clark, *N. Y. Sta. Bul.*, 248:124. 1904.

SYNONYMS. FALL PIPPIN (1). *French Pippin* (7). HOLLAND PIPPIN (1, 2, 3, 4, 5, 6, 7, 8, 9, 10, 11, 12, 13, 14, 15, 16). *Pie Apple* (2, 7, 8). *Reinette d'Hollande* (2). *Reinette d'Holland* (7). *Summer Pippin* (2, 7, 8).

There are two varieties in cultivation in New York under the name Holland Pippin. One is a winter apple in season from late autumn to April or May which has already been described under the name Holland Winter, Vol. I., page 159. The other begins to ripen earlier than Fall Pippin and is in season during September and October. This variety was formerly confused by some with the Fall Pippin. The following comparison of the two varieties was given by Downing in 1848 (3).

"The Holland Pippin, though considerably resembling this apple in the growth of the tree, and size and shape of the fruit, is a totally distinct apple from the Fall Pippin. In fact, while the Fall Pippin is one of the best autumn table apples (at least in this district), the Holland Pippin is of very inferior quality for dessert, and is, in fact, only a *cooking* apple. As a kitchen fruit, however, it is one of the most valuable *summer* fruits we know — for it bears regularly and well, comes into use at the beginning of August, and continues fit for pies, tarts, and sauce, *until* October, when the Fall Pippin *begins* to ripen. The Holland Pippin is fit for use while the skin is quite green, but the Fall Pippin, not until it turns quite yellow. Finally, the stalk of the Holland Pippin is short, and set in a wide cavity, while that of the Fall Pippin is large, and set in a cavity often narrow, and comparatively shallow. With these points of difference, these two apples ought not to be confounded."

Holland Pippin is grown to a limited extent for market. It appears to be more valued for this purpose in certain portions of the Hudson valley than in other sections of the state. The fruit is large and when kept free from scab its general appearance is good for a green apple. The crop ripens unevenly. Some of the apples ripen early and are correspondingly short-lived while others ripen later and keep correspondingly later. It varies greatly in keeping qualities in different seasons, some years keeping well till late fall or early winter (16). The tree is a good grower, hardy or nearly so, healthy, pretty long-lived and generally quite productive yielding moderate to heavy crops biennially or sometimes annually.

Historical. Origin unknown. It is an old variety which has long been in cultivation in this and adjoining states. It is still listed by nurserymen but it is not being planted to any considerable extent.

TREE.

Tree large or moderately large, vigorous. *Form* spreading or roundish. *Twigs* medium to long, curved, stout; internodes medium. *Bark* dark brown, heavily coated with gray scarf-skin; pubescent. *Lenticels* scattering, small to medium, oval, not raised. *Buds* medium size, plump, obtuse, free, pubescent.

FRUIT.

Fruit usually large or very large, sometimes medium, pretty uniform in size and shape. *Form* roundish often decidedly flattened at the end varying to oblate conic, obscurely ribbed. *Stem* medium to short, usually rather slender. *Cavity* acute or sometimes acuminate, medium in width to broad, moderately shallow to deep, usually covered with thick outspreading russet. *Calyx* pubescent, medium to small, closed or partly open; lobes rather long, acute. *Basin* usually rather shallow but varying to moderately deep, medium in width to rather narrow, abrupt to somewhat obtuse, ridged and wrinkled.

Skin thin, tough, nearly smooth, rather pale yellow or greenish with more or less of a brownish-red blush which is conspicuously marked with large, irregular, areolar dots. *Dots* numerous, large and small, often submerged and greenish.

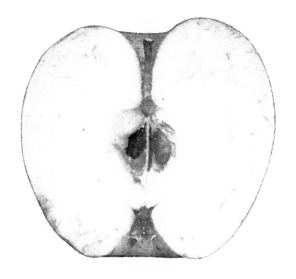

HOOK

Calyx tube wide, broadly conical to truncate funnel-form. *Stamens* below median to basal.

Core medium to large, abaxile; cells unsymmetrical, open; core lines meeting or somewhat clasping. *Carpels* broad, narrowing toward base and apex, slightly emarginate, a little tufted. *Seeds* medium size, rather narrow, acute to somewhat acuminate.

Flesh nearly white, medium to slightly coarse-grained, moderately crisp, rather tender, very juicy, brisk subacid, good for culinary uses.

Season September and October.

HOOK.

REFERENCE. 1. (?) *Mich. Pom. Soc. Rpt.*, **1880**:183.
SYNONYMS. None.

Fruit of good medium size, rather attractive pale yellow with tender flesh of mild subacid flavor. It is in season during October and November. It is especially esteemed for dessert use.

Historical. This variety was received from Schoharie county, N. Y., where it is well known and has the reputation of being one of the most desirable dessert apples of its season. We have not yet been able to determine its origin, nor the extent of its distribution.

FRUIT.

Fruit medium size, pretty uniform in shape and size. *Form* roundish ovate or inclined to oblong conic, sometimes roundish truncate. *Stem* short, rather slender. *Cavity* acuminate, moderately shallow to deep, broad, often lipped, smooth or with some outspreading russet rays. *Calyx* medium size, usually somewhat open; lobes rather narrow to wide, acute to acuminate. *Basin* medium in width and depth, obscurely furrowed and wrinkled.

Skin smooth, clear yellow or greenish-yellow. *Dots* inconspicuous, minute, usually submerged.

Calyx tube large, conical or approaching funnel-form. *Stamens* median or below.

Core rather small, axile; cells symmetrical, closed or a little open; core lines meeting or somewhat clasping. *Carpels* smooth, flat, obcordate to elliptical, emarginate. *Seeds* medium brown, rather large, wide, flat, obtuse.

Flesh whitish with slight tinge of yellow, very tender, fine-grained, juicy, mild subacid, somewhat aromatic, very good.

Season October and November.

HOWARD BEST.

REFERENCES. 1. Bailey, *Mich. Sta. Bul.*, **31**:52. 1887. 2. *N. Y. Sta. An. Rpt.*, **11**:223. 1892.
SYNONYMS. HOWARD'S BEST (2). HOWARD'S BEST RUSSIAN (1).

This is an attractive apple which bears a decided resemblance to Alexander in form, color and quality. The tree is a moderate grower, comes into bearing rather young and yields moderate to good crops almost annually. We have not yet determined whether or not it is superior to Alexander.

Historical. Received in 1892 for testing at this Station from C. G. Patten, Charles City, Ia. (2).

TREE.

Tree moderately vigorous with short, moderately stout, crooked branches. *Form* rather flat and spreading, inclined to droop. *Twigs* short, straight, slender with large terminal buds; internodes short to medium. *Bark* dull brown tinged with olive-green, lightly streaked with scarf-skin; pubescent. *Lenticels* scattering, small, oblong, not raised. *Buds* small, plump, obtuse, free, slightly pubescent.

FRUIT.

Fruit above medium, usually large to very large. *Form* oblate conic, rather flat at the base, somewhat ribbed, symmetrical. *Stem* medium to long, thick. *Cavity* acute, deep, medium in width to wide, symmetrical, sometimes compressed, heavily russeted. *Calyx* large, open; lobes separated at base, short, narrow, acute. *Basin* moderately shallow to rather deep, rather narrow, abrupt, distinctly furrowed to nearly smooth.

Skin rather tough, smooth, waxy, light yellowish-green, mottled, striped and splashed with bright, dark red over a large part of the surface. *Dots* indistinct, medium size, gray, scattering.

Calyx tube short, wide, conical or approaching funnel-form. *Stamens* basal to median.

Core medium size, nearly axile; cells closed or slightly open; core lines clasping or nearly meeting. *Carpels* very broadly ovate or inclined to elliptical, slightly emarginate, tufted. *Seeds* medium to small, wide, short, rather flat, obtuse.

Flesh slightly tinged with yellow, firm, rather coarse, tender, very juicy, sprightly subacid, fair to good.

Season September and October.

HUNTER PIPPIN.

REFERENCE. 1. Downing, 1876:54 app.
SYNONYMS. None.

A chance seedling which originated in Westport, N. Y. Downing describes the tree as moderately vigorous and a good annual bearer; fruit medium size, whitish-yellow; flesh brisk subacid; season August (1).

So far as we can learn this variety is not being propagated.

HURLBUT.

REFERENCES. 1. Cole, 1849:118. *fig.* 2. Emmons, *Nat. Hist. N. Y.*, 3:31. 1851. *col. pl.* and *fig.* 3. Downing, 1857:155. 4. *Am. Pom. Soc. Cat.*, 1862. 5. Warder, 1867:722. 6. Thomas, 1875:201. 7. Barry, 1883:347. 8. Lyon, *Mich. Hort. Soc. Rpt.*, 1890:292. 9. Bailey, *An. Hort.*, 1892:241. 10. Mun-

son, *Me. Sta. Rpt.*, **1893**:133. **11.** Dempsey, *Ont. Fr. Stas. An. Rpt.*, 1:24.
1894. **12.** Burrill and McCluer, *Ill. Sta. Bul.*, **45**:326. 1896. **13.** Munson,
Me. Sta. An. Rpt., **18**:89. 1902. **14.** Powell and Fulton, *U. S. B. P. I. Bul.*,
48:45. 1903. **15.** Beach and Clark, *N. Y. Sta. Bul.*, **248**:126. 1904.

SYNONYMS. HURLBURT (2). HURLBUT (1, 3, 4, 6, 7, 8, 9, 10, 11, 12, 13, 14,
15). *Hurlbut Stripe* (3). HURLBUTT (5).

The general appearance of Hurlbut is good yet it is not particularly attractive either in size or color nor does it take first rank for
either home use or market. The tree is a strong grower, comes
into bearing moderately young and yields heavy crops biennially.
Because of the tendency of the tree to overproduction in bearing
years the size of the fruit is in many cases reduced and a considerable portion of it is too small to be marketable. Hurlbut has
proved to be a profitable variety with some fruit growers but
although it has long been known in cultivation and has been quite
widely disseminated it has nowhere gained prominence as a commercial variety.

Historical. In 1849 Cole (1) wrote: " The original tree is still flourishing
on the farm of General Leonard Hurlbut, Winchester, Conn." It is still quite
frequently listed by nurserymen (9) but is not being planted to any considerable extent.

TREE.

Tree rather large, vigorous or moderately vigorous. *Form* spreading or
roundish and somewhat inclined to droop. *Twigs* moderately long, slightly
curved, moderately stout to rather slender; internodes below medium to
short. *Bark* dark brown to clear brownish-red, heavily mottled with scarf-
skin; slightly pubescent. *Lenticels* scattering, small, round, slightly raised.
Buds medium size, broad, plump, obtuse, free, slightly pubescent.

FRUIT.

Fruit below medium to above, fairly uniform in size and shape. *Form*
roundish, slightly oblate or inclined to oblate conic, somewhat angular, rather
symmetrical. *Stem* medium to short, rather slender. *Cavity* acute, shallow
to medium in depth, medium in width, symmetrical or compressed, usually
covered with heavy outspreading russet. *Calyx* medium or below, usually
closed; lobes medium to long, narrow, acute. *Basin* shallow to medium in
depth, narrow to nearly medium in width, somewhat abrupt, smooth or
slightly wrinkled.

Skin thick, tough, smooth, greenish-yellow largely overspread with brownish-red or dull red, splashed and striped with carmine. *Dots* scattering, inconspicuous, usually submerged, sometimes russet.

Calyx tube very short, wide, truncate conical with fleshy pistil point projecting into the base. *Stamens* marginal.

Core medium size, abaxile; cells wide open to nearly closed; core lines meeting or slightly clasping. *Carpels* nearly round. *Seeds* numerous, rather large, moderately wide, long, rather plump, acute.

Flesh white or yellowish, moderately firm, rather fine, tender, crisp, very juicy, aromatic, mildly subacid, good to very good.

Season variable; October to December or January (15).

ISHAM.

REFERENCES. **1.** Bailey, *An. Hort.*, **1892**:242. **2.** Hoskins, *Rural N. Y.*, 53:310. 1894. **3.** *Am. Pom. Soc. Cat.*, **1899**:17. **4.** Hansen, *S. D. Sta. Bul.*, **76**:60. 1902. fig. **5.** *Kan. Sta. Bul.*, **106**:53. 1902. **6.** Budd-Hansen, 1903: 105.

SYNONYMS. ISHAM SWEET (1, 2, 3, 4, 5). ISHAM *Sweet* (6).

A red sweet apple of medium size, in season in late fall and early winter. It has been grown to some extent in some of the Western states but it has not been much tested in New York and it is doubtful whether it is desirable for planting in any portion of this state.

Historical. Isham originated from seed of Bailey *Sweet*. It was introduced about 1864 by F. K. Phœnix, Delavan, Wis. (2).

TREE.

Tree moderately vigorous. *Form* upright spreading. *Twigs* medium to long, rather stout, in some cases quite blunt at the tips, straight or nearly so; internodes rather long. *Bark* reddish-brown overlaid with heavy grayish scarf-skin, not pubescent or very sparingly so. *Lenticels* rather inconspicuous, rather scattering, irregular in size and shape, not raised. *Buds* large, prominent, fleshy, heavily pubescent, adhering to bark.

FRUIT (4, 6).

Fruit medium. *Form* roundish, slightly tapering. *Stem* short. *Cavity* regular, acute, with much radiating russet. *Calyx* open; segments flat, convergent. *Basin* very shallow, minutely wrinkled.

Skin yellowish-green mostly covered with brownish-red, solid and mixed on sunny side, striped and broadly splashed on the shady side. *Dots* distinct, russet, numerous, minute; a few large russet dots.

Calyx tube funnel-shape. *Stamens* median.

Core closed; cells round, entire. *Seeds* long, large, flat.

Flesh very yellow with yellow veinings, firm, very sweet, very good.

JACK.

REFERENCES. **1.** (?) Hooper, **1857**:46. **2.** (?) Downing, **1869**:206. **3.** (?) *Ill. Sta. Bul.*, **45**:334. 1896.

SYNONYMS. (*Early Jack* 1)? (JACK APPLE 1)? (OSKALOOSA 2, 3)?

Fruit of good medium size, yellow; flesh very tender, rich, mild subacid. It is highly esteemed for its excellent dessert quality but it is too tender to stand shipping very well and on account of its irregular shape and yellow color it is not sufficiently attractive for market purposes. The tree is not a vigorous grower and has rather slender twigs.

Possibly this is identical with Oskaloosa which has Jack as a synonym, (2, 3) but we have been unable to obtain fruit of Oskaloosa and the available descriptions of that variety are so meager that it is impossible to determine whether or not it is identical with the variety described above.

Historical. Jack is grown to a very limited extent in East Bloomfield, Ontario county, N. Y. We have not obtained it from any other locality. We have been unable to learn where it originated, or whether it is the Jack mentioned by Hooper (1).

TREE.

Tree not very vigorous with moderately long, slender, crooked branches. *Form* at first upright spreading but becoming roundish and rather dense. *Twigs* long, straight, slender; internodes short. *Bark* brown or reddish-brown, lightly streaked with scarf-skin; slightly pubescent near tips. *Lenticels* quite numerous, rather conspicuous, medium size, oblong, slightly raised. *Buds* small, plump, obtuse, appressed, slightly pubescent.

FRUIT.

Fruit medium or above, sometimes rather large, not uniform in shape or size. *Form* oblate varying to roundish oblate or to oblate conic, very irregular, obscurely ribbed, often with the sides somewhat furrowed and unequal. *Stem* short to medium, slender. *Cavity* acuminate, usually deep, medium in width, russeted, with concentric russet lines often extending beyond the cavity, sometimes lipped. *Calyx* medium size, usually open. *Basin* small to medium, rather shallow to moderately deep, narrow to medium in width, unsymmetrical, irregularly furrowed or nearly smooth.

Skin rather thin, waxy, glossy, attractive yellow with shades of green, sometimes faintly tinged with red and marbled with whitish scarf-skin over the base somewhat after the manner of Yellow Newtown. *Dots* mostly small and depressed mingled with a few that are larger, scattering and irregular with russet center.

Calyx tube medium in width and length, conical to somewhat funnel-form. *Stamens* median or below.

Core medium in size, somewhat abaxile; cells usually symmetrical, somewhat open; core lines clasping. *Carpels* elliptical, deeply emarginate. *Seeds* medium or below, wide, short, rather flat, obtuse, mingled with light and dark brown.

Flesh tinged with yellow, moderately firm, moderately crisp or breaking, very tender, moderately juicy, very mild subacid, very good for dessert. *Season* October and November.

JARVIS.

REFERENCE. 1. *N. Y. Sta. An. Rpt.*, 11 :223. 1892.
SYNONYMS. *Crandall Seedling* (1). JARVIS (1). *No. 25* (1).

Fruit large and when well colored partly overspread and striped with red; flesh tender, juicy, subacid, pleasant but not superior in flavor or quality; season late September to early winter. It is possibly desirable for local market but it is not recommended for general cultivation.

Historical. The original tree is standing near Ithaca, N. Y., on land once owned by a Mr. Jarvis from whom the variety takes its name. It is grown to a limited extent in the vicinity of Ithaca but so far as we know is not cultivated in any other portion of the state. Received for testing at this Station in 1892 from C. B. Crandall.

JEFFERIS.

REFERENCES. 1. Thomas, 1849:149. 2. *Mag. Hort.*, 18:491. 1852. 3. *Am. Pom. Soc. Cat.*, 1854. 4. Elliott, 1854:139. 5. *Mag. Hort.*, 21:62. 1855. 6. Gregg, 1857:44. 7. Downing, 1857:83. fig. 8. Hooper, 1857:47. 9. *Mag. Hort.*, 24:109. 1858. 10. Hoffy, *N. A. Pom.*, 1860. col. pl. 11. *Horticulturist*, 17:104, 150. 1862. 12. Warder, 1867:440. fig. 13. Barry, 1883:338. 14. Van Deman, *U. S. Pom. Rpt.*, 1888:570. 15. Lyon, *Mich. Hort. Soc. Rpt.*, 1890:292. 16. Bailey, *An. Hort.*, 1892:242. 17. Burrill and McCluer, *Ill. Sta. Bul.*, 45:309, 323. 1896. 18. Powell, *Del. Sta. Bul.*, 38:18. 1898. 19. Macoun, *Can. Dept. Agr. Rpt.*, 1901:96. 20. Beach, *Western N. Y. Hort. Soc. Rpt.*, 1901:76. 21. Budd-Hansen, 1903:105. 22. Bruner, *N. C. Sta. Bul.*, 182:21. 1903. 23. Farrand, *Mich. Sta. Bul.*, 205:45. 1903. 24. Powell and Fulton, *U. S. B. P. I. Bul.*, 48:45. 1903. 25. Beach and Clark, *N. Y. Sta. Bul.*, 248:126. 1904.

SYNONYMS. *Everbearing* (20). *Grantham* (17). JEFFERIES (10, 12, 14, 17, 20). JEFFERIS (3, 4, 7, 13, 15, 16, 18, 19, 21, 22, 23, 24, 25). JEFFRIES (1, 2, 5, 6, 8, 9, 11).

Fruit of medium size, yellow, blushed and splashed with red; flesh tender, mild subacid, delicious. It begins to ripen in September and continues in season till early winter. Commercial limit October (25). It is an excellent variety for the home orchard but not for commercial planting because it ripens unevenly, is apt to be deficient in size and is not especially attractive in color. The tree is a moderately vigorous grower, hardy, healthy, comes into bearing moderately early and is a reliable cropper yielding full crops biennially.

Historical. Originated with Isaac Jefferies, Newlin township, Chester county, Pa. It was named after the originator by the Committee of the Pennsylvania Horticultural Society which awarded this variety the premium for the best seedling apple exhibited in 1848 (10).

TREE.

Tree medium size, moderately vigorous. *Form* upright to roundish, open. *Twigs* short, straight, slender; internodes long. *Bark* brown mingled with olive-green, lightly streaked with scarf-skin; slightly pubescent. *Lenticels*

JEFFERIS

scattering, small, oblong, not raised. *Buds* small, plump, obtuse, free, pubescent.

FRUIT.

Fruit small to medium, very uniform in size and shape. *Form* roundish oblate often inclined to conic, regular or obscurely ribbed. *Stem* medium length, thick to moderately slender. *Cavity* acute to acuminate, medium in depth to deep, medium to broad, symmetrical, russeted but slightly if at all. *Calyx* small to medium, closed or partly open; lobes short, rather broad, acute. *Basin* moderately shallow to rather deep, moderately wide, somewhat abrupt, smooth or nearly so, symmetrical.

Skin thin, tough, greenish-yellow or pale yellow more or less blushed and mottled with moderately dull red overlaid with narrow splashes and stripes of carmine. *Dots* small, scattering, inconspicuous, submerged or russet.

Calyx tube narrow, conical to funnel-shape. *Stamens* marginal to median. *Core* small, axile, or nearly so; cells slightly open; core lines somewhat clasping or meeting. *Carpels* elliptical to somewhat obovate, emarginate, sometimes tufted. *Seeds* numerous, medium to rather large, wide, long, flat, very irregular, obtuse.

Flesh yellowish-white, firm, fine, crisp, tender, very juicy, mild subacid, very good.

Season September to January.

JEFFERSON COUNTY.

REFERENCES. 1. *Horticulturist,* 10:254. 1855. fig. 2. Downing, 1857:156. 3. Warder, 1867:723. 4. *Am. Pom. Soc. Cat.,* 1873. 5. Thomas, 1875:201. 6. Lyon, *Mich. Hort. Soc. Rpt.,* 1890:292.

SYNONYMS. None.

This variety originated in Jefferson county, N. Y., hence its name (2). The tree is of medium size, moderately vigorous; form somewhat drooping; twigs rather slender. It comes into bearing young and is a reliable bearer producing some fruit nearly every year, alternating heavy with lighter crops. The fruit is yellow shaded and splashed with red, not very bright in color, in season during October and November. It is particularly suitable for dessert, the flesh being tender, rather firm, crisp, of good flavor and excellent quality but it is not regarded as a good market variety for there is apt to be a rather large amount of small, imperfect or otherwise unmarketable fruit and when the fruit does not color properly, as happens in many cases, it is of poor flavor. It was listed by the American Pomological Society in 1873. It has been sparingly disseminated in various parts of the country but is as yet little known. So far as we can learn it is not being planted in New York.

JENNETTING or JUNEATING.

This name has been applied by some to White Juneating. For a description of this variety together with Hogg's account of the derivation of the name the reader is referred to White Juneating, page 240.

JERSEY SWEET.

REFERENCES. 1. Downing, 1845:87. 2. *N. Y. Agr. Soc. Trans.*, 1846:190.
3. Cole, 1849:110. 4. Thomas, 1849:145. fig. 5. Barry, 1851:284. 6. Emmons, *Nat. Hist. N. Y.*, 3:25. 1851. 7. Waring, 1851:26. 8. Elliott, 1854:
86. fig. 9. Hooper, 1857:48. 10. *Ib.*, 1857:107, 111. 11. *Am. Pom. Soc.
Cat.*, 1862. 12. *Horticulturist*, 17:104, 150. 1862. 13. Warder, 1867:395.
14. Fitz, 1872:153. 15. Lyon, *Mich. Hort. Soc. Rpt.*, 1890:292. 16. Bailey,
An. Hort., 1892:242. 17. Hoskins, *Rural N. Y.*, 53:278. 1894. 18. *Mich.
Sta. Bul.*, 118:60. 1895. 19. *Ib.*, 143:200. 1897. 20. *Ib.*, 205:45. 1903.
21. Budd-Hansen, 1903:105. 22. Beach and Clark, *N. Y. Sta. Bul.*, 248:126.
1904.

SYNONYMS. *American* (13). JERSEY SWEET (5, 7, 10, 12, 13, 16, 18, 21).
JERSEY SWEETING (1, 2, 3, 4, 6, 8, 9, 14, 17).

An early autumn apple of medium size. It does not always
color well but under favorable conditions it is highly colored, rich
in flavor, tender and excellent in quality for either dessert or culinary uses. It is one of the best of the sweet apples of its season
for planting for home use in New York but it has proved unsatisfactory as a commercial sort because it ripens at a time when there
is little demand for fruit of this kind, is not a good keeper, is apt
to be scabby and does not always color well. The tree is hardy,
moderately long-lived, comes into bearing young and bears nearly
every year, yielding moderate to good or sometimes heavy crops.
The fruit comes in season late in August or early in September
and ripens in succession during a period of several weeks; often
some portion may be kept till early winter, but its commercial limit
in ordinary storage is September or early October (22).

Historical. Origin unknown. Elliott calls it an American variety (8).
It is pretty well known in different parts of New York state, but is now
rarely found except in old orchards. It is commonly listed by nurserymen
(16) but is now seldom or never planted except occasionally for home use.

TREE.

Tree rather large, moderately vigorous to vigorous; branches long, moderately stout, filled with spurs. *Form* upright to roundish, open. *Twigs* moderately long, straight, slender; internodes long. *Bark* brown, lightly streaked
with scarf-skin; pubescent near tips. *Lenticels* scattering, medium to small,
oblong, not raised. *Buds* medium size, plump, obtuse, appressed, pubescent.

JERSEY SWEET

FRUIT.

Fruit medium size. *Form* roundish ovate inclined to conic or to oblate conic; sides unequal. *Stem* long to medium length, rather slender. *Cavity* acute, usually rather deep, varying to shallow, medium in width, occasionally lipped, sometimes slightly russeted. *Calyx* small, closed; lobes medium to long, narrow, acute to acuminate. *Basin* rather small, moderately shallow to rather deep, narrow to medium in width, somewhat abrupt, ribbed and wrinkled.

Skin thin, tender, at first greenish-yellow but becoming clear yellow washed and mottled with brownish-red and overlaid with narrow stripes of bright carmine. *Dots* inconspicuous, greenish, submerged.

Calyx tube narrow, conical to funnel-form, often with fleshy pistil point projecting into the base. *Stamens* median.

Core medium size or above, axile or nearly so; cells symmetrical, usually closed; core lines clasping the funnel cylinder. *Carpels* elongated ovate, tufted. *Seeds* medium to large, variable in length and width, acute to acuminate.

Flesh yellowish, moderately firm, fine, crisp, tender, juicy, sweet, good to very good.

Season September to December.

JUDSON.

REFERENCES. 1. *Am. Pom. Soc. Cat.*, **1899**:17. 2. *Ib.*, *Rpt.*, **1901**:49. 3. Hansen, *S. D. Sta. Bul.*, **76**:62. 1902. *fig.* 4. Budd-Hansen, **1903**:108. *fig.*

SYNONYMS. JUDSON (1, 2, 3, 4). *Thompson's Seedling No. 29* (3, 4).

Fruit large, green or yellowish, more or less covered with red, not especially attractive in appearance and only fair to good in quality. Season October to December. Not valuable enough to be worthy of trial in New York except perhaps in those districts where superior hardiness is particularly desirable.

Historical. Originated in Grundy county, Iowa, by J. S. B. Thompson.

TREE.

Tree moderately vigorous with short, moderately stout, somewhat drooping branches. *Form* open, roundish to spreading. *Twigs* above medium to short, somewhat curved, medium to stout, rather pubescent with large terminal buds; internodes medium or below. *Bark* brown or reddish-brown tinged with olive-green, heavily coated with gray scarf-skin; pubescent. *Lenticels* quite numerous, rather conspicuous, medium or below, round or irregularly elongated, not raised. *Buds* prominent, large to medium, broad, plump, obtuse, free or nearly so, pubescent.

FRUIT.

Fruit large or very large, fairly uniform in size but not in shape. *Form* roundish conical or a little inclined to oblong, indistinctly ribbed, irregular;

sides often unequal. *Stem* short to medium, thick. *Cavity* very acuminate, deep, moderately narrow to rather broad, somewhat furrowed, irregularly russeted, frequently compressed. *Calyx* large, usually somewhat open. *Basin* moderately deep to deep, medium in width, very abrupt, furrowed and wrinkled.

Skin smooth, rather tough, clear bright yellow washed with red which sometimes deepens to a pinkish blush, striped and splashed with carmine and mottled over the base with dull scarf-skin. *Dots* scattering, small to large, pale gray, conspicuous. *Prevailing effect* greenish-yellow; not particularly attractive.

Calyx tube long, wide, funnel-shape. *Stamens* variable but usually median. *Core* rather small, usually abaxile; cells sometimes unsymmetrical, wide open; core lines clasping. *Carpels* broadly ovate to elliptical, emarginate, sometimes tufted. *Seeds* rather dark brown, small to medium, rather numerous, very short, very plump, obtuse.

Flesh nearly white, firm, rather coarse, crisp, juicy, brisk subacid, fair to good.

Season October to December.

JULY.

REFERENCES.   1. *Rural N. Y.,* **1861** (cited by 15).   2. Hovey, *Mag. Hort.,* **29**:112, 1863.   3. Hanford, *Horticulturist,* **19**:273. 1864. fig.   4. Warder, **1867**:719.   5. Downing, **1869**:181. fig.   6. Thomas, **1875**:499.   7. *Ill. Hort. Soc. Rpt.,* **1876**:252.   8. *Ia. Hort. Soc. Rpt.,* **1879**:471.   9. Hoskins, *Rural N. Y.,* **47**:646. 1888.   10. Lyon, *Mich. Hort. Soc. Rpt.,* **1890**:292.   11. *Amer. Gard.,* **12**:570. 1891. figs.   12. Bailey, *An. Hort.,* **1892**:239.   13. Burrill and McCluer, *Ill. Sta. Bul.,* **45**:321. 1896.   14. Budd-Hansen, **1903**:108.   15. Ragan, *U. S. B. P. I. Bul.,* **56**:160. 1905.

SYNONYMS. *August* (4, 15, ot Cassel, Germany, 3). FOURTH OF JULY (2, 4, 6, 8, 9, 10, 11, 12, 13). *Fourth of July* (15, ? 5). JULY (1, 3, 7, 15). JULY, *Fourth of* (14). *McAdow's June* (4, 15). *Siberian August* (4, 15, of Germany 2). *Stewart's Nonpareil* (15, ? 4). TETOFSKI (5). *Tetofsky,* erroneously (4, 15).

This fruit closely resembles Tetofsky and some have considered the two varieties identical (4) but they are quite distinct in tree. It is not recommended for planting in New York because it is not equal to standard varieties of its season.

Historical. Hovey states that "The Fourth of July apple, in Germany called the Siberian August apple, was sent from the Russian province Liefland, in the year 1807, to the celebrated pomologist, Dr. Diel, and is celebrated, like all our summer apples which originated in Russia, for its great productiveness and hardiness" (2). It was introduced into Columbus, O., from Cassel, Germany (3). It has been disseminated to a considerable extent in various parts of this country and is still listed by a considerable number of nurserymen (12).

TREE.

Tree vigorous. *Form* upright, roundish and rather dense. *Twigs* short, straight, stout with large terminal buds; internodes medium. *Bark* dull

JUDSON

brown tinged with green, lightly streaked with scarf-skin; slightly pubescent. *Lenticels* scattering, small, oblong, not raised. *Buds* medium size, plump, obtuse, free, slightly pubescent.

FRUIT.

Fruit below medium to above, pretty uniform in shape but not in size. *Form* usually roundish conical, irregularly ribbed; sides often unequal. *Stem* medium to long, moderately slender, often bracted. *Cavity* acuminate to acute, moderately deep, medium to narrow, slightly furrowed, thinly russeted. *Calyx* medium to large, usually closed; lobes medium in length, moderately narrow, acuminate. *Basin* rather shallow to medium in depth, narrow, somewhat abrupt, furrowed and wrinkled.

Skin thin, tough, smooth, rather glossy, pale yellow washed and mottled with red striped and splashed with carmine and overspread with whitish bloom. *Dots* small, numerous, submerged, inconspicuous, light, areolar.

Calyx tube variable in length, funnel-shape. *Stamens* median to marginal. *Core* medium or below, axile; cells closed; core lines slightly clasping or meeting. *Carpels* roundish ovate or elongated ovate. *Seeds* very dark dull brown, medium size, moderately wide, short, plump, obtuse.

Flesh yellowish, a little coarse, crisp, tender, moderately juicy, sprightly subacid, fair to good.

Season last of July to September.

KAIGHN.

REFERENCES. **1.** Coxe, **1817**:128. *fig.* **2.** Downing, *Horticulturist,* **1**:341. **1847.** **3.** Cole, **1849**:125. **4.** Thomas, **1849**:173. **5.** Emmons, *Nat. Hist. N. Y.,* **3**:60. 1851. **6.** Elliott, **1854**:141. *fig.* **7.** Hooper, **1857**:49. **8.** Downing, **1857**:158. **9.** Warder, **1867**:681. *fig.* **10.** Downing, **1876**:55 app. **11.** Lyon, *Mich. Hort. Soc. Rpt.,* **1890**:294. **12.** Bailey, *An. Hort.,* **1892**:242.

SYNONYMS. KAIGHN (11). KAIGHN'S SPITZEMBURG (1). KAIGHN'S SPIT-ZENBERG (3, 6, 9). KAIGHN'S SPITZENBERGH (2). KAIGHN'S SPITZENBURG (7, 12). KAIGHN'S SPITZENBURGH (4, 5, 8). KAIGN'S SPITZENBURG (10). *Lady Finger* (erroneously 6, 7). *Long John* (6, 7). *Long Pearmain* (6, 7). *Ohio Wine* (6). *Red Pearmain* (6, 7, 8). *Red Phoenix* (6). *Red Pippin* (6). *Red Spitzenberg* (6). *Red Spitzenburg* (8). *Red Winter Pearmain* (6). *Russam* (6). *Scarlet Pearmain,* erroneously (6). Downing states that Kaign's Spitzenberg and Long Red Permain, for many years considered identical, are in reality distinct varieties in both tree and fruit. He gives a long list of synonyms for Long Red Pearmain including all of the synonyms cited above and adds, " The true Kaign's Spitzenburg, so far as I know, has no synonyms " (10).

This is an old variety of New Jersey origin which has been disseminated through various parts of the West even to the Pacific Coast. The fruit is showy and the tree productive. The tree makes a spreading, straggling growth (1, 11). According to Coxe (1) the fruit bears " a faint resemblance to the Esopus Spitzemberg but is more pointed toward the crown; the color is a lively but pale red, faintly streaked and full of white spots; the

skin is smooth, the stem long and deeply planted, the crown very hollow —
the flesh finely flavored, yellow, juicy and tender." It is now practically
obsolete in New York.

KALKIDON.

REFERENCES. 1. Budd, *Ia. Agr. Coll. Bul.*, 1885:25. 2. Schroeder, *Montreal Hort. Soc. Rpt.*, 1886-7:76. 3. Gibb, *Am. Pom. Soc. Rpt.*, 1887:56.
4. Lyon, *U. S. Pom. Bul.*, 2:41. 1888. 5. Beach, *N. Y. Sta. An. Rpt.*, 11:593.
1892. 6 *Ib.*, 13:589. 1894. 7. *Ib.*, 14:261. 1895. 8. Beach, Paddock and
Close, *Ib.*, 15:272, 281. 1896. 9. Beach and Clark, *N. Y. Sta. Bul.*, 248:127.
1904. 10. Ragan, *U. S. B. P. I. Bul.*, 56:161. 1905.

SYNONYMS. KALKIDON (3, 4, 9, incorrectly 10). KALKIDONSKOE (1).
KALKIDOUSKOE (5, 6, 7, 8). KALKIDOVSKOE (2). *Khalkidonskoe* (4, 9).
Khalkidouskoe (3, 10). *No. 540* (10). *No. 94* (1, 2, 3, 10).

A Russian variety which was received from Ellwanger and Barry, Rochester, N. Y., in 1884 for testing at this Station. It is an apple of moderately
attractive appearance and fair to good quality, in season in September and
October. The tree comes into bearing moderately young and is a reliable
biennial cropper. It is not recommended for planting in New York because
it is inferior to standard varieties of its season.

FRUIT.

Fruit large to medium, fairly uniform in size and shape. *Form* oblate
conical to ovate, regular or faintly ribbed. *Stem* medium to very short,
moderately thick. *Cavity* acute to almost acuminate, moderately shallow to
deep, medium in width, furrowed and compressed, russeted and with outspreading greenish-russet rays. *Calyx* medium to large, closed or partly
open; lobes medium in length, broad, acute. *Basin* shallow to medium in
depth, narrow to medium in width, rather abrupt, slightly furrowed.

Skin thick, rather tough, smooth, greenish or pale yellow, largely washed
and mottled with dull red, splashed and striped with carmine. *Dots* variable
in size, numerous, inconspicuous, submerged.

Calyx tube rather long, moderately wide, conical or funnel-shape. *Stamens*
median to marginal.

Core small, axile or sometimes abaxile; cells symmetrical, closed or open;
core lines clasping. *Carpels* ovate to elliptical, slightly emarginate, slightly
tufted. *Seeds* medium to large, wide, plump, acute to obtuse, dark brown.

Flesh tinged with yellowish-green, moderately fine-grained, tender, rather
juicy, mild subacid, fair to good.

Season September to midwinter (9).

KARABOVKA.

REFERENCES. 1. Gibb, *Montreal Hort. Soc. Rpt.*, 1883:74. 2. Budd, *Ia.
Agr. Coll. Bul.*, 1885:7. 3. Gibb, *Ia. Hort. Soc. Rpt.*, 1885:274. 4. *N. Y.
Sta. An. Rpt.*, 13:582. 1894. 5. Ragan, *U. S. B. P. I. Bul.*, 56:161. 1905.

SYNONYMS. *Kajabowka* (5). KARABOFF (2, 3, 4). *Karaboff* (1, 5).

KARABOVKA (5).   *Karabovka* (3, 4).   KARABOWKA (1).   *Karabowka* (2, 4).   *No. 21 M* (3, 4).   *No. 205* (2, 3, 4, 5).   Shro. to Ia. *No. 21* (5).

A Russian variety received from Ellwanger and Barry, Rochester, N. Y., in 1884 for testing at this Station. As grown here the tree does not come into bearing very early but when mature yields full crops biennially. The fruit is medium to rather small, not specially attractive in appearance, fair to possibly good in quality being inferior to standard sorts of its season. Season late August and September. It does not agree with the description of Karabovka given by Budd (2).

TREE.

Tree moderately vigorous with moderately long, stout, curved branches. *Form* rather open, flat, spreading. *Twigs* long, curved, stout, with large terminal buds; internodes medium. *Bark* dark brown, heavily streaked with scarf-skin; slightly pubescent near tips. *Lenticels* quite numerous, small to medium, round, slightly raised. *Buds* large, prominent, plump, obtuse, free, slightly pubescent.

FRUIT.

Fruit small to medium, uniform. *Form* oblate, regular, symmetrical. *Stem* medium in length, moderately thick to rather slender. *Cavity* acute to nearly acuminate, moderately deep to deep, narrow to medium in width, occasionally lipped, usually russeted. *Calyx* large, open or nearly closed; lobes short, rather broad, acute. *Basin* medium in depth, wide, furrowed or wrinkled and with mammiform protuberances.

Skin thin, tender, smooth, rather dull pale greenish-yellow, with scattering narrow stripes of dull dark red, or when highly colored it is largely striped, splashed and shaded with red, and overspread with pinkish bloom. *Dots* rather numerous, small, light, obscure, submerged.

Calyx tube large, medium in length, rather wide, broadly conical to funnel-shape. *Stamens* median to marginal.

Core medium size, axile; cells closed; core lines clasping. *Carpels* elliptical, emarginate. *Seeds* very dark dull brown, medium size, wide, rather short, flat, plump, obtuse.

Flesh nearly white, moderately fine, tender, moderately juicy, mild subacid with peculiar flavor, fair to good in quality.

Season late August and September.

KENTISH FILLBASKET.

REFERENCES. 1. Kenrick, 1832:95. 2. Downing, 1845:114. 3. Thomas, 1849:168. 4. Emmons, *Nat. Hist. N. Y.*, 3:62. 1851. 5. Elliott, 1854:172. 6. Hooper. 1857:49. 7. Warder, 1867:723. 8. Hogg, 1884:120. 9. Green, *Country Gentleman*, 1885:840. 10 *Ib.*, *Can. Hort.*, 11:8. 1888. 11. Bailey, *An. Hort.*, 1892:242. 12. Woolverton, *Ont. Fr. Stas. An. Rpt.*, 4:3. 1897. figs. 13. Bunyard, *Jour. Roy. Hort. Soc.*, 1898:354.

SYNONYMS. KENT FILLBASKET (13). KENTISH FILLBASKET (3). KENTISH FILLBASKET (1, 2, 4, 5, 6, 7, 8, 9, 10, 11, 12). *Lady de Grey's* (2, 5, 8).

Potter's Large (8). *Potter's Large Grey Seedling* (5). *Potter's Large Seedling* (2).

A very large, handsome, late autumn apple, desirable for cooking but not for dessert use. Tree a strong grower and a fair cropper. Not recommended for planting in New York.

According to Hogg (8) the Kentish Fillbasket of Miller, Forsyth and Rogers is a different variety being evidently the Kentish Codlin or common old English Codlin, a lemon-yellow apple which is in season from August to October.

The Kentish Fillbasket of Buel[1] appears to be the same as that of Forsyth.[2]

Historical. This is an old English variety. It has been sparingly cultivated in portions of New York state for many years and has been grown to some extent also in Ontario (12).

FRUIT.

Fruit very large. *Form* oblate or roundish, ribbed broadly and obscurely if at all, irregular, fairly uniform. *Stem* not exserted, short, medium in thickness. *Cavity* acute to somewhat acuminate, deep, broad, symmetrical or somewhat furrowed, green or more often with outspreading russet. *Calyx* small to rather large, closed or partly open; lobes broad, obtuse to acute. *Basin* pretty abrupt, moderately deep to deep, medium in width to wide, sometimes a little furrowed or wrinkled.

Skin thin, tough, smooth, somewhat waxy, pale yellow with thin brownish blush often deepening to red, somewhat mottled and splashed with carmine. *Dots* small usually not conspicuous, dark brown or grayish or submerged and whitish. *Prevailing effect* yellow somewhat striped with red.

Calyx tube wide, conical. *Stamens* basal to nearly median.

Core abaxile, medium to large; cells often unsymmetrical and open, sometimes closed; core lines nearly meeting. *Carpels* broadly ovate, mucronate, not emarginate, somewhat tufted. *Seeds* medium or below, plump, acute.

Flesh whitish, firm, moderately coarse, crisp, rather tender, juicy, brisk subacid, good.

Season October to December.

KESWICK.

REFERENCES. 1. Forsyth, **1824**:132. 2. *London Hort. Soc. Cat.*, **1831**:No. 225. 3. Kenrick, **1832**:89. 4. Floy-Lindley, **1833**:23. 5. Downing, **1845**:87. 6. Thomas, **1849**:156. 7. Emmons, *Nat. Hist. N. Y.* 3:37. 1851. 8. Barry, **1851**:280. 9. Elliott, **1854**:141. 10. Barry, *Horticulturist*, 10:87. 1855. 11. Gregg, **1857**:37. 12. Hooper, **1857**:25, 49, 107, 111. 13. *Am. Pom. Soc. Cat.*, **1860**. 14. Mead, *Horticulturist*, 17:150. 1862. 15. Warder, **1867**:688. fig. 16. Fitz, **1872**:160. 17. Hogg, **1884**:122. 18. Wickson, **1889**:243. 19. Lyon, *Mich. Hort. Soc. Rpt.*, **1890**:294. 20. Bailey, *An. Hort.*, **1892**:242. 21. Taft, *Mich. Sta. Bul.*, 105:108. 1894. 22. Lyon, *Ib.*, 118:60. 1895. 23 *Ib.*, 143:200. 1897. 24. Bunyard, *Jour. Roy. Hort. Soc.*, **1898**:354. 25. Dickens and

1 Buel, *N. Y. Bd. Agr. Mem.*, **1826**:477.
2 Forsyth, **1803**:50.

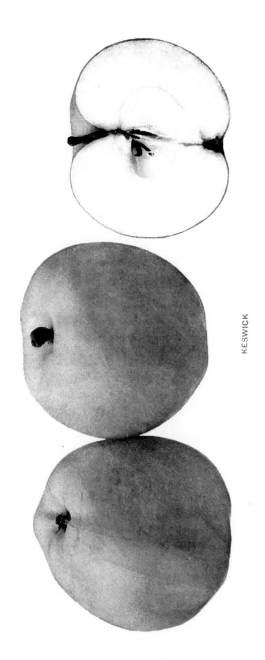

KESWICK

Greene, *Kan. Sta. Bul.*, **106**:53. 1902. **26.** Farrand, *Mich. Sta. Bul.*, **205**:45. 1903. **27.** Budd-Hansen, 1903:110. **28.** Beach and Clark, *N. Y. Sta. Bul.*, **248**:128. 1904.

SYNONYMS. CODLIN, KESWICK (1, 2, 24). KESWICK (19, 21, 22, 23, 26, 27, 28). KESWICK CODLIN (3, 4, 5, 6, 7, 8, 9, 10, 11, 12, 13, 14, 16, 17, 18, 19, 20, 24, 25). *Keswick Codlin* (27, 28). KESWICK CODLING (15). *No. 225* (2).

This variety is particularly esteemed on account of its excellence for culinary use. It is not adapted for storage, its commercial limit in ordinary storage being September and early October. It comes into season late in August or early in September and ripens continuously during a period of several weeks. It does not stand heat well before going into storage and goes down quickly (28). The fruit is of good medium size to rather large, greenish-yellow, sometimes with faint blush; flesh brisk subacid. It is grown chiefly for home use and only to a very limited extent for local market. The tree is a good grower, hardy, healthy, long-lived, comes into bearing quite young and yields good to very good crops almost annually.

This is distinct from the Codling or English Codling described by Coxe, Thacher, Forsyth and others.

Historical. Hogg (17) states that: "This excellent apple was first discovered growing among a quantity of rubbish behind a wall at Gleaston Castle, near Ulverstone, and was first brought into notice by one John Sander, a nurseryman at Keswick, who, having propagated it, sent it out under the name of Keswick Codlin.

"In the Memoirs of the Caledonian Horticultural Society, 1813, Sir John Sinclair says: 'The Keswick Codlin tree has never failed to bear a crop since it was planted in the episcopal garden at Rose Castle, Carlisle, twenty years ago.'"

It has long been known in this country and very old trees of it are found in some orchards but it is nowhere extensively cultivated being grown chiefly for home use. It is quite commonly listed by nurserymen (20).

TREE.

Tree medium to large, moderately vigorous. *Form* upright spreading to roundish. *Twigs* moderately long, curved, stout; internodes short. *Bark* dull brown, heavily coated with gray scarf-skin; pubescent. *Lenticels* numerous, rather conspicuous, medium to small, round, not raised. *Buds* medium to large, prominent, broad, plump, obtuse, free, pubescent.

FRUIT.

Fruit above medium to nearly large, not very uniform. *Form* roundish conic or inclined to oblong conic, rather broad at the base, distinctly ribbed;

sides frequently a little unequal. *Stem* medium to short, slender to rather thick. *Cavity* variably acute, medium in depth, to shallow, rather narrow to moderately broad, more or less russeted. *Calyx* medium size, closed; lobes long, medium in width, nearly acuminate. *Basin* shallow, moderately narrow, furrowed or angular, often with fleshy protuberances alternating with the calyx lobes.

Skin thin, tough, smooth, waxy, pale greenish or yellow, sometimes with a faint blush and often with a suture line extending out from the cavity. *Dots* submerged, inconspicuous or russet.

Calyx tube medium in length, rather wide, bluntly cone-shape. *Stamens* median.

Core variable, large, abaxile; cells wide open; core lines meeting. *Carpels* variable, roundish ovate. *Seeds* very light brown, very small, medium in width, short, very plump, acute.

Flesh nearly white, fine, tender, very juicy, brisk subacid, good for culinary use, too acid for dessert unless very ripe.

Season August and September.

KIRKBRIDGE.

REFERENCES. **1.** Downing, **1857**:160. **2.** *Mag. Hort.*, **24**:108. 1858. **3.** Warder, **1867**:671. **4.** *Am. Pom. Soc. Cat.*, **1871**:8. **5.** Downing, **1872**:10 index, app. **6.** Thomas, **1875**:195. **7.** Downing, **1881**:11 index, app. **8.** *Ib.*, **1881**:12 index, app. **9.** Budd-Hansen, **1903**:111.

SYNONYMS. *Bohannon* (2). *Conic June* (7). KIRKBRIDGE (2, 3, 7, 8, 9). KIRKBRIDGE WHITE (1, 4, 5, 6). *White June* (5). *Yellow Flat* (8). *Yellow June* (6, erroneously 3, of some 5).

Fruit small to medium, oblong conic, pale yellow or whitish; flesh white, fine, tender, juicy, pleasant subacid, good to very good. The tree is a moderate grower, comes into bearing young and is productive. Season August and September. Not recommended for planting in New York.

Historical. In 1867 Warder (3) wrote concerning Kirkbridge White: "This fruit has been pretty extensively cultivated in some parts of the Western states and sometimes it is mistaken for the Yellow June." It is said to be of American origin. It is but little known in New York.

LADY FINGER.

REFERENCE. **1.** Downing, **1869**:245.
SYNONYMS. None.

Under this name Downing (1) describes an apple which he received from Maryland, the fruit of which is of medium size, yellowish, nearly overspread with deep crimson; flesh white, tender, pleasant subacid, good to very good; season August.

Other varieties have been known under the name Lady Finger several of which have already been mentioned in the discussion of the winter apples. See Vol. I, page 183.

LANDSBERG

LANDSBERG.

REFERENCES. 1. Berghuis, 1868:No. 8. *col. pl.* 2. Downing, 1872:20 app. 3. Leroy, 1873:701. *fig.* 4. Lauche, 1:No. 38. 1882. *col. pl.* 5. Hogg, 1884:128. 6. Budd, *Ia. Agr. Coll. Bul.*, 1885:34, 41. 7. Lyon, *U. S. Pom. Bul.*, 2:42. 1888. 8. Gaucher, 1894:No. 17. *col. pl.* 9. Beach and Paddock, *N. Y. Sta. An. Rpt.*, 14:253, 261. 1895. 10. Powell and Fulton, *U. S. B. P. I. Bul.*, 48:47. 1903. 11. Beach and Clark, *N. Y. Sta. Bul.*, 248:129. 1904.

SYNONYMS. LANDSBERG (7, 11). LANDSBERGER REINETTE (2, 4, 5, 6, 8, 9). *Landsberger Reinette* (11). LANDSBURG (6). *Landsburger Reinette* (6, 7). LANSBERGER REINETTE (10). REINETTE DE LANDSBERG (3). *Reinette de Landsberg* (2, 8). REINETTE LANDSBERGER (1).

An attractive late autumn and early winter apple of good size and pleasant subacid flavor. The tree is thrifty, comes into bearing rather early and is reliably productive yielding good crops biennially. The fruit has a clear, pale waxen yellow or greenish skin which readily shows bruises. It is a good dessert apple but less desirable for culinary uses because when it is cooked it lacks character in texture, color and flavor. It is easily excelled for any purpose by standard sorts of its season and is not recommended for planting in New York.

Historical. Raised from seed about 1840 by Mr. Burkhardt, justice of the peace in Landsberg, Germany (2, 4). Imported from Silesia, Germany, in 1883 by Professor Budd for the Iowa State College (6).

TREE.

Tree vigorous. *Form* roundish or spreading, rather open. *Twigs* short to medium, nearly straight, rather stout; internodes medium. *Bark* olive-green tinged with brownish-red, mottled with scarf-skin; pubescent. *Lenticels* quite numerous, small, round, not raised. *Buds* large to below medium, broad, plump, generally obtuse, free, quite pubescent.

FRUIT.

Fruit medium to large, pretty uniform in shape and size. *Form* roundish conic to roundish oblate, obscurely angular, pretty regular; sides sometimes unequal. *Stem* short to medium. *Cavity* acute to acuminate, deep, rather wide, sometimes obscurely furrowed, usually smooth but sometimes russeted. *Calyx* segments long, acute, reflexed, sometimes closed. *Basin* medium in width and depth, often somewhat furrowed, wrinkled.

Skin thin, tough, smooth or slightly roughened by russet dots, waxen yellow or pale green, sometimes with attractive crimson blush. *Dots* numerous, submerged and whitish, sometimes russet. *Prevailing color* pale yellow, rather attractive.

Calyx tube large, wide, cone-shape. *Stamens* median.

Core abaxile, medium; cells usually symmetrical and wide open; core lines slightly clasping. *Carpels* broadly ovate, much concave, narrow toward the apex, nearly smooth. *Seeds* numerous, medium in size, broad, obtuse, medium brown, smooth or nearly so.

Flesh nearly white, very tender, crisp, rather fine-grained, mild subacid, agreeable in flavor, good to very good for dessert.

Season mid-October to January (8, 9). Some of the fruit keeps apparently sound till March or later but after January it loses in quality.

LATE STRAWBERRY.

REFERENCES. 1. Thomas, *Cultivator*, 5:246. 1848. 2. Thomas, **1849**:150. fig. 3. Cole, **1849**:111. 4. Waring, **1851**:21. 5. Emmons, *Nat. Hist. N. Y.*, 3:27. 1851. fig. 6. Barry, **1851**:282. 7. Elliott, **1854**:65. 8. Downing, **1857**:163. 9. Hooper, **1857**:54. 10. Gregg, **1857**:41. 11. *Am. Pom. Soc. Cat.*, **1862**. 12. Warder, **1867**:540. 13. Downing, **1869**:250. fig. 14. Todd, **1871**:154. fig. 15. *Ia. Hort. Soc. Rpt.*, **1879**:538. 16. Roach, *Montreal Hort. Soc. Rpt.*, **1886**–7:27. 17. Wickson, **1889**:245. 18. Lyon, *Mich. Hort. Soc. Rpt.*, **1890**:294. 19. Bailey, *An. Hort.*, **1892**:243. 20. Burrill and McCluer, *Ill. Sta. Bul.*, 45:329. 1896. 21. Budd-Hansen, **1903**:113. fig.

SYNONYMS. AUTUMN STRAWBERRY (1, 4, 6, 7, 10, 14, 15). *Autumn Strawberry* (2, 5, 8, 12, 13, 17, 21). FALL STRAWBERRY (3). LATE STRAWBERRY (2, 5, 8, 9, 11, 12, 13, 16, 17, 18, 19, 20, 21). *Late Strawberry* (1, 3, 6, 7). *Strawberry* (2, 7).

Different varieties have been called Late Strawberry but the name is now almost exclusively applied to the variety described below. This is an attractive apple, pale yellow overspread or striped and splashed with light and dark red, very good in quality especially for dessert use. Many esteem it one of the best dessert apples of its season. It comes into use in September and ripens in succession during a period of several weeks continuing in season till December. While this habit of successive ripening makes the variety more desirable for the home orchard it renders it less valuable for commercial purposes, since several pickings are required to secure the crop in prime condition. The fruit is hardly as large as is desirable for a good market variety but its attractive appearance and excellent quality render it suitable for local and fancy trade. The tree is medium to rather large, vigorous; form upright spreading to roundish. It is hardy, healthy, long-lived and a regular cropper-yielding moderate to heavy crops biennially or nearly annually.

Historical. Late Strawberry originated at Aurora, Cayuga county, N. Y. (13). In 1848 Thomas described it as a new and newly introduced apple (1).

FRUIT.

Fruit below medium to above, uniform in size and fairly uniform in shape. *Form* roundish to slightly oblong conic, sometimes quite strongly ribbed,

LATE STRAWBERRY

rather irregular. *Stem* long, rather slender, often curved. *Cavity* acuminate, deep, usually broad, furrowed, sometimes with thin radiating streaks of light russet mingled with carmine. *Calyx* large, open or partly open; lobes often separated at base, rather short, acute, erect or reflexed. *Basin* deep, moderately narrow to rather wide, abrupt, furrowed and wrinkled.

Skin attractive pale yellow often almost entirely overspread with bright pinkish-red, dotted and streaked with purplish-carmine. *Dots* small, not very numerous, inconspicuous, light colored. *Prevailing effect* bright striped red.

Calyx tube rather wide, conical to slightly funnel-shape. *Stamens* basal. *Core* rather small, nearly axile to somewhat abaxile; cells closed or somewhat open; core lines meeting or slightly clasping. *Carpels* obovate. *Seeds* rather large, flat, obtuse.

Flesh yellowish-white, fine, crisp, tender, juicy, somewhat sprightly aromatic, subacid, very good.

Season September to December.

LATHAM.

REFERENCE. 1. Downing, 1869:251.
SYNONYMS. None.

This is a variety which we have not seen; so far as we can learn it is no longer cultivated. According to Downing it originated in Sag Harbor, Suffolk county, N. Y.; tree very productive; fruit medium size, yellow mostly covered with light and dark red; flesh white, juicy, mild subacid, good; season November and December (1).

LEAD.

REFERENCES. 1. *Montreal Hort. Soc. Rpt.*, 8:40. 1881–82. 2. *Ia. Hort. Soc. Rpt.*, 1882:78. 3. *Montreal Hort. Soc. Rpt.*, 1883:102. 4. *Ia. Agr. Coll. Bul.*, 1883:28. 5 *Ib.*, 1885:11. 6. Schroeder, *Montreal Hort. Soc. Rpt.*, 1886–7:71. 7. *Ia. Agr. Coll. Bul.*, 1890:23. 8. Budd, *Ia. Sta. Bul.*, 19:540. 1892. 9. Bailey, *An. Hort.*, 1892:243. 10. Munson, *Me. Sta. Rpt.*, 1896:74, 79. 11. Stinson, *Ark. Sta. Bul.*, 43:105. 1896. 12. Thomas, 1897:291. fig. 13. Troop, *Ind. Sta. Rpt.*, 1899:80. 14. Hansen, *S. D. Sta. Bul.*, 76:64. 1902. 15. Munson, *Me. Sta. An. Rpt.*, 18:84. 1902.

SYNONYMS. LEAD (1, 2, 4, 5, 6, 7, 8, 9, 10, 11, 12, 13, 14, 15). *Lead Apple* (3). *No. 3 M* (2, 4, 7, 8, 10, 14, 15). *No. 277* (2, 4, 5, 10). *Svinsovka* (1). SWINEZ (3). *Swinzovska* (5).

As noted below two distinct Russian varieties have been disseminated under the name Lead. Some of the references cited above refer to one of these varieties and some to the other.

A Russian variety was received from the Iowa Agricultural College in 1890 for testing at this Station, the fruit of which is pale greenish-yellow with a blushed cheek and carmine splashes, medium size or above; flesh tender, rather juicy, subacid, fair quality; season late August and September. The tree does not come into bearing very young. It is an annual cropper but only moderately productive. It is not worthy of further testing for this region.

This appears to be the same variety as that described by Hansen under the name Lead with the synonym No. 362 (14). This he says is not the true Lead. He describes the true Lead with synonym No. 3 M as a Russian variety, large, heavy, roundish, greenish-yellow with dull blush; flesh greenish-white, sharp subacid, good in quality; season early winter.

LINCOLN PIPPIN.

REFERENCE. 1. Downing, 1881 :93 app. fig.
SYNONYMS. None.

Fruit medium to large, yellow with no blush, subacid, excellent for either dessert or culinary uses; season November and December. Under favorable conditions some portion of the fruit may be kept through the winter. The tree is large, spreading, somewhat open, moderately vigorous with rather short, stout twigs, hardy, long-lived. It does not come into bearing very young but when mature is a pretty reliable annual bearer, ripening the crop evenly. The fruit is fair, averages pretty uniform in size and shape and is reliable and satisfactory in color and quality. Downing describes it as "medium to large, roundish oblate, slightly conical, slightly angular, sides sometimes a little unequal; skin pale greenish-yellow, moderately sprinkled with grayish dots; stalk short to long, slender; cavity large, deep, calyx small, closed; basin small or medium, slightly corrugated; flesh half fine, pale whitish-yellow, tender, juicy, subacid, slightly aromatic; very good; core rather large. October, December " (1).

Historical. So far as we can learn this variety is cultivated only in the vicinity of Syracuse. Downing states that it is an old variety, said to have been brought to Syracuse from Connecticut; the original name having been lost it was named Lincoln after Reuben Lincoln who brought it into notice (1).

LINDENWALD.

REFERENCES. 1. Downing, 1869 :254. 2. Burrill and McCluer, *Ill. Sta. Bul.*, 45 :330. 1896.
SYNONYMS. None.

A variety which originated with J. G. Sickles, Stuyvesant, Columbia county, N. Y. Downing describes the fruit as of medium size, yellow with light shades of red; flesh crisp, juicy, pleasant subacid, good to very good; season September (1).

We have received no report of this being grown outside of the locality of its origin.

LONGFIELD.

REFERENCES. 1. Webster, *Montreal Hort. Soc. Rpt.*, 7 :52. 1881. 2. *Ib.*, 8 :71. 1881–82. 3. Budd, *Ia. Hort. Soc. Rpt.*, 1882 :77. 4. Gibb, *Ib.*, 1883 :425. 5. Webster, *Am. Pom. Soc. Rpt.*, 1883 :113. 6. Budd, *Ia. Agr. Coll. Bul.*, 1883 :28. 7. Gibb, *Montreal Hort. Soc. Rpt.*, 1883 :66. fig. 8. Budd, *Ia. Agr. Coll. Bul.*, 1885 :5. 9. Gibb, *Montreal Hort. Soc. Rpt.*, 1886–87 :15. 10. Schroeder, *Ib.*, 1886–87 :74. 11. Craig, *Ib.*, 1886–87 :103. 12. Hoskins, *Rural*

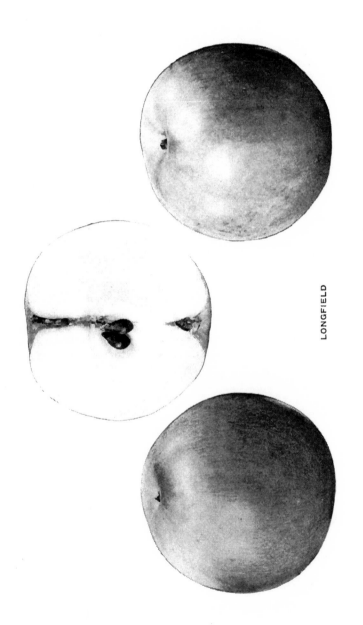

LONGFIELD

N. Y. **47**:558. 1888. **13.** *Am. Pom. Soc. Cat.*, **1889**:8. **14.** Gibb, *Can. Hort.*, **12**:27. 1889. **15.** *Ib.*, **13**:207, 216, 301. 1890. **16.** Budd, *Ia. Agr. Coll. Bul.*, **1890**:19. **17.** *Ia. Sta. Bul.*, **19**:536. 1892. **18.** *Can. Hort.*, **15**:29. 1892. **19.** Taylor, *Me. Pom. Soc. Rpt.*, **1892**:57, 58. **20.** Bailey, *An. Hort.*, **1892**:243. **21.** *Amer. Gard.*, **14**:50, 177, 305. 1893. **22.** *Can. Hort.*, **16**:204, 360. 1893. **23.** Craig, *Ont. Fr. Gr. Assn. An. Rpt.*, **26**:16. 1894. **24.** Beach, *N. Y. Sta. An. Rpt.*, **13**:582. 1894. **25.** Troop, *Ind. Sta. Bul.*, **53**:123. 1894. **26.** Craig, *Can. Dept. Agr. Rpt.*, **1894**:126. figs. **27.** Freeborn, *Nat. Nurseryman*, **2**:133. 1894. **28.** Van Deman, *Rural N. Y.*, **55**:848. 1896. **29.** Munson, *Me. Sta. Rpt.*, **1896**:75. **30.** Stinson, *Ark. Sta. Bul.*, **43**:105. 1896. **31.** Buckman, *Rural N. Y.*, **56**:39. 1897. **32.** Waugh, *Vt. Sta. Bul.*, **61**:31. 1897. **33.** Thomas, **1897**:291. fig. **34.** *Am. Gard.*, **19**:650, 682. 1898. **35.** *Rural N. Y.*, **57**:736, 819. 1898. **36.** Troop, *Ind. Sta. Rpt.*, **1899**:80. **37.** Hansen, *S. D. Sta. Bul.*, **76**:67. 1902. fig. **38.** Munson, *Me. Sta. An. Rpt.*, **18**:84, 85, 87, 95. 1902. **39.** Powell and Fulton, *U. S. B. P. I. Bul.*, **48**:47. 1903. **40.** Farrand, *Mich. Sta. Bul.*, **205**:45. 1903. **41.** Budd-Hansen, **1903**:116. **42.** Beach and Clark, *N. Y. Sta. Bul.*, **248**:129. 1904.

SYNONYMS. *English Pippin* (26). *587* (26). *57 M* (16). *56 M* (2, 3, 6, 10). *Good Peasant* (9). LANGERFELDSKOE (1, 4, 5, 7, 13). *Langerfeldskoe* (8). LONGFIELD (2, 3, 6, 8, 9, 10, 11, 12, 14, 15, 16, 17, 18, 19, 20, 21, 22, 23, 24, 25, 26, 27, 28, 29, 30, 31, 32, 33, 34, 35, 36, 37, 38, 39, 40, 41, 42). *Longfield* (4, 7). *Longfield's Apple* (1, 5). *No. 161* (2, 3, 6, 8, 16, 24, 29, 37).

The fruit of Longfield is usually below medium size but decidedly attractive in appearance for a yellow apple, being clear waxen yellow, lightly blushed with bright red. Its flesh is white, crisp, fine, very tender and of pleasant quality. It may well be classed among the fancy dessert apples; it is good also for culinary uses. In marketing this fruit it is necessary to handle it with great care because ordinarily its texture is so very tender and its color so delicate that it shows bruises very readily. It is not well adapted for holding outside of cold storage. In ordinary storage its commercial limit at Geneva is late September or early October (42) and in cold storage it may be kept till December (42); but as grown further north it may be kept through the winter (26). The tree is a moderate grower, very hardy and very productive; in fact it bears such heavy crops that the fruit is liable to be deficient in size. On account of the hardiness and productiveness of the tree and the beauty and good quality of the fruit Longfield is recommended for planting for home use and for local and special markets.

Historical. Longfield was first imported from Russia by the United States Department of Agriculture in 1870; later it was imported from various European sources for the Iowa Agricultural College by Professor Budd.

It is now frequently listed by nurserymen (20) and is being planted to a limited extent in various parts of the state, but it has not yet come to be commonly known among New York fruit growers.

TREE.

Tree medium in size with short, moderately stout, crooked branches and drooping laterals filled with small spurs. *Form* roundish or spreading, dense, rather low. *Twigs* medium in length, curved, moderately stout; terminal buds large; internodes short. *Bark* dark brown, lightly streaked with scarf-skin; pubescent. *Lenticels* scattering, medium size, oval, not raised. *Buds* medium size, broad, plump, obtuse, free, slightly pubescent.

FRUIT.

Fruit medium to small, usually below medium; uniform in size and shape. *Form* roundish conic, slightly ribbed. *Stem* medium to short, rather slender. *Cavity* acuminate to acute, medium to rather deep, narrow, quite symmetrical, usually slightly russeted. *Calyx* small, leafy, closed or partly open; lobes long, rather narrow, acute to acuminate. *Basin* small, shallow to medium in depth, narrow, somewhat abrupt, slightly furrowed and wrinkled.

Skin thin, tender, smooth, glossy, pale waxen yellow or whitish usually with a lively pinkish blush but not striped. *Dots* few, small, inconspicuous, whitish, usually submerged. *Prevailing* effect attractive bright pale yellow partly blushed with lively red.

Calyx tube narrow and elongated, often extending to the core. *Stamens* basal to median.

Core medium to above, axile or nearly so; cells symmetrical, not uniformly developed, closed or partly open; core lines clasping the funnel cylinder. *Carpels* roundish, slightly emarginate. *Seeds* rather large, moderately dark brown, long, acute approaching acuminate.

Flesh nearly white, fine, crisp, very tender, juicy, subacid, sprightly, aromatic, good to very good.

Season September to October or later.

LONG ISLAND PEARMAIN.

REFERENCES. **1.** Coxe, **1817** :144. *fig.* **2.** Warder, **1867** :682. **3.** Downing, **1869** :255.

SYNONYMS. *Autumn Pearmain* (2). *Hollow Crown Pearmain* (3). LONG ISLAND PEARMAIN (1, 2, 3). *Winter Pearmain* (2).

This is an old variety which Coxe (1) thus describes: "A handsome large apple, of an oblong form, about the size of a Priestly — the stem is short, not deeply planted; the crown large and hollow; the skin streaked with large blotches of red on a rich yellow ground, with faint russet spots — the flesh is tender, coarse and pleasant, partaking of that dryness characteristic of all the varieties of the pearmain — it ripens in October and keeps till March." Downing (3) states that it has sometimes been confused with Winter Pearmain which is an entirely different fruit. So far as we can discover, Long Island Pearmain is now obsolete in New York.

LONG RED PEARMAIN.

REFERENCE. 1. Downing, 1876:55 app.

SYNONYMS. *English Pearmain* incorrectly (1). *Hudson Red Streak* (1). *Kentucky Bellflower* (1). *Kentucky Gillflower* (1). *Kaighn's Spitzenburg* incorrectly (1). *Lady Finger* incorrectly (1). *Long John* (1). *Long Pearmain* (1). LONG RED PEARMAIN (1). *Mudhole* (1). *Park* (not of Kansas) (1). *Pearmain* (1). *Pound Royal* incorrectly (1). *Red Bellflower* incorrectly (1). *Red Pearmain* (1). *Red Phœnix* (1). *Red Pippin* (1). *Red Spitzenberg* (1). *Red Winter Pearmain* incorrectly (1). *Russam* (1). *Scarlet Pearmain* (1). *Sheepnose* of some (1). *Striped Pearmain* (1). *Wabash Bellflower* (1). *Winter Pearmain* (1).

This variety was for many years considered identical with Kaighn. See page 113. In 1876 Downing (1) stated that it was distinct from Kaighn in tree and fruit and gave the list of synonyms for it which is cited above.

The fruit is medium to large, oblong approaching conic, yellowish, shaded and striped with red; flesh coarse, pleasant subacid, good; season late fall and early winter.

LONG STEM.

REFERENCES. 1. Cole, 1849:106. 2. Hooper, 1857:55. 3. Warder, 1867: 725. 4. Downing, 1869:256. 5. Ragan, *U. S. B. P. I. Bul.*, 56:183. 1905.

SYNONYMS. None.

Several varieties of the apple have been known in cultivation under the name Long Stem. One of these has already been described (Volume I, page 196) as Long Stem of Pennsylvania; others are noticed below. The references cited above do not all refer to the same variety.

LONG STEM OF MASSACHUSETTS. The following is Cole's description of this variety (1): "Large medial; flattish-round; pale yellow, brown full in the sun; dark specks and patches; stem extremely long, slender, in a broad, deep cavity; calyx large, rather open, in a broad, shallow basin; flesh white, rather tender, juicy, of a rich, mild, delicious, sprightly, aromatic flavor. First-rate for the dessert or cooking. Sept. 1st, to the last of Oct. Good and constant bearer. Origin, East Bridgewater, Ms."

LONG STEM OF CONNECTICUT. Downing (4) describes this variety as having young shoots of dull reddish-brown, somewhat downy, with prominent, flattened buds. Fruit medium, roundish oblate, yellow; flesh fine-grained, sweet, rich, good. Season September to January.

LONGWORTH.

REFERENCES. 1. Downing, 1881:94 app. 2. Beach and Clark, *N. Y. Sta. Bul.*, 248:129. 1904.

SYNONYMS. LONGWORTH (2). LONGWORTH RED WINTER (1).

Fruit of fairly good color but not very large; inferior in quality to standard varieties of its season. It is variable in season (2); some years it keeps fairly well till midwinter, but generally speaking, as grown at this Station, its commercial limit in ordinary storage is November. The tree comes into bearing rather young and is a reliable cropper, yielding moderate to rather heavy crops biennially or sometimes annually. Not recommended for planting in New York.

Historical. Originated at Dubuque, Ia. (1). It was received for testing here in 1889 from Benjamin Buckman, Farmingdale, Ill.

LORD SUFFIELD.

REFERENCES. 1. Downing, 1869:257. 2. Ib., *Tilt. Jour. Hort.*, 7:303. 1870. 3. Hogg, 1884:136. 4. Goff, *Rural N. Y.*, 46:685. 1887. figs. 5. *Can. Hort.*, 15:347. 1892. 6. Bailey, *An. Hort.*, 1892:243. 7. Gaucher, 1894:No. 18. *col. pl.* 8. Dempsey, *Ont. Fr. Stas. An. Rpt.*, 1:24. 1894. 9. *Jour. Roy. Hort. Soc.*, 1898:356.

SYNONYMS. *Lady Suffield* (7). *Lady Sutherland* (7). *Livesley's Imperial* (7). LORD SUFFIELD (1, 2, 3, 4, 5, 6, 7, 8, 9).

This variety of the Keswick Codlin group is considered by some one of the best apples of the group. The fruit is suitable for cooking as early as the middle of July and remains in use till September. It is large, roundish, varying from oblate to somewhat oblong; green, marked with clear light russet flecks and dots; calyx closed; basin ridged, shallow; stem short; cavity moderately wide, shallow; core large, abaxile; cells open; flesh white, rather fine, moderately juicy, subacid, good for culinary use. The tree is very productive, which perhaps accounts in part for its being short-lived. As grown at this Station it has blighted so badly as to make it an undesirable variety for the orchard.

LOU.

REFERENCES. 1. *Am. Pom. Soc. Rpt.*, 1885:28. 2. *Mo. Hort. Soc. Rpt.*, 1886:233. 3. *Mich. Sta. Bul.*, 118:60. 1895. 4. Beach, Paddock and Close, *N. Y. Sta. An. Rpt.*, 15:272. 1896. 5. *Mich. Sta. Bul.*, 143:200. 1897. SYNONYMS. None.

A striped red apple of fairly good quality in season in early August. The tree is a good grower, comes into bearing rather young and is a reliable biennial cropper. It was originated from seed of Oldenburg by Peter M. Gideon, Excelsior, Minn., from whom it was received in 1888 for testing at this Station. It is not valuable for planting in New York.

LOUISE.

REFERENCES. 1. Woolverton, *Am. Pom. Soc. Rpt.*, 1889:155. 2. *Can. Hort.*, 15:19, 28. 1892. 3. Bailey, *An. Hort.*, 1892:247. 4. *Can. Hort.*, 16:401. 1893. 5. Beach, *N. Y. Sta. An. Rpt.*, 12:601. 1893. 6. Hoskins, *Rural N. Y.*, 53:278. 1894. 7. Smith, *Can. Hort.*, 18:349. 1895. 8. Lyon, *Mich. Sta. Bul.*, 143:200. 1897. 9. *Am. Pom. Soc. Cat.*, 1899:18. 10. Waugh, *Vt. Sta. Bul.*, 83:91. 1900. 11. Woolverton, *Can. Hort.*, 23:46. 1900. fig. 12. Ib., *Ont. Fr. Stas. An. Rpt.*, 7:8. 1900. figs. 13. Hansen, *S. D. Sta. Bul.*, 76:69. 1902. 14. Budd-Hansen, 1903:117. fig. 15. Farrand, *Mich. Sta. Bul.*, 205:45. 1903.

SYNONYMS. LOUISE (8, 10, 13, 15). LOUISE, *Princess* (9, 14). PRINCESS LOUISE (1, 2, 3, 4, 5, 6, 11, 12). *Princess Louise* (7, 10, 13). WOOLVERTON (7). *Woolverton* (4, 11, 12).

Louise is an apple of the Fameuse group. It is larger than Fameuse but not as large as McIntosh and has less red color and is less attractive than either of these apples. It is very desirable for dessert use but for culinaary purposes it is decidedly inferior to other varieties of its season. It is of a clear pale yellow color with lively blush and delicate bloom. It shows bruises readily and requires very careful handling. The tree is hardy, healthy, comes into bearing rather young and yields fair to moderately good crops almost annually. It is doubtful whether it will ever prove a desirable commercial variety.

Historical. Originated with L. Woolverton, Grimsby, Ontario, who states that it was a chance seedling that sprung up among a half dozen old Fameuse trees.[1] It was first exhibited before the Ontario Fruit Growers' Association in 1879 under the name of "Woolverton." It has been disseminated to a limited extent only in New York. The McIntosh has sometimes been mistakenly disseminated for this variety.

TREE.

Tree medium size, moderately vigorous to vigorous with long, slender branches and willowy laterals. *Form* upright spreading to roundish, rather dense. *Twigs* moderately long, straight or somewhat irregularly curved, rather geniculate, slender; internodes medium. *Bark* reddish-brown with some pale olive-green, lightly mottled with scarf-skin; somewhat pubescent toward the tips. *Lenticels* scattering, small to medium, roundish to oblong. *Buds* small to medium, deep-set, plump, acute, free or nearly so, somewhat pubescent.

FRUIT.

Fruit of good medium size; fairly uniform in size and shape. *Form* usually roundish, sometimes roundish oblate, often somewhat elliptical or obscurely angular; sides often unequal. *Stem* red, medium to rather long, usually slender. *Cavity* obtuse to acute or sometimes approaching acuminate, shallow to medium in depth, moderately broad, frequently furrowed. *Calyx* medium size, closed or sometimes slightly open. *Basin* usually shallow to medium in depth, narrow to moderately wide, rather obtuse, lightly furrowed and wrinkled.

Skin thin, rather tough, clear pale yellow or greenish, with lively red or pinkish blush, striped obscurely if at all, overspread with thin bloom. *Dots* inconspicuous, pale, usually submerged.

Calyx tube short, wide, conical to funnel-form. *Stamens* median to basal.

1 L. Woolverton, Letter, 1894.

Core medium to rather large, somewhat abaxile; cells symmetrical, partly open; core lines meeting. *Carpels* elongated ovate, sometimes emarginate. *Seeds* medium or below, moderately long, acute to acuminate.

Flesh whitish, not very firm, fine, crisp, very tender, very juicy, mild subacid, aromatic, with some of the perfume and texture of McIntosh, very good for dessert.

Season October to February or later.

LOWELL.

REFERENCES. 1. *Cultivator*, 5:246. 1848. 2. Cole, 1849:109. 3. Thomas, 1849:157. 4. Waring, 1851:27. 5. Barry, 1851:285. 6. Elliott, 1854:88. fig. 7. Hooper, 1857:55. 8. Gregg, 1857:46. fig. 9. Downing, 1857:166. 10. *Am. Pom. Soc. Cat.*, 1862. 11. Warder, 1867:576. 12. Fitz, 1872:145. 13. Lyon, *Mich. Hort. Soc. Rpt.*, 1890:294. 14. Bailey, *An. Hort.*, 1892:243. 15. *Mich. Sta. Bul.*, 105:108. 1894. 16. Lyon, *Ib.*, 118:60. 1895. 17. Burrill and Mc-Cluer, *Ill. Sta. Bul.*, 45:330. 1896. 18. *N. C. Bd. Agr. Bul.*, 1900:7. 19. *Kan. Sta. Bul.*, 106:53. 1902. 20. *Mo. Fr. Sta. Bul.*, 3:27. 1902. 21. Powell and Fulton, *U. S. B. P. I. Bul.*, 48:48. 1903. 22. Farrand, *Mich. Sta. Bul.*, 205:45. 1903. 23. Budd-Hansen, 1903:117. 24. Beach and Clark, *N. Y. Sta. Bul.*, 248:130. 1904.

SYNONYMS. *Greasy Pippin* (6, 9, 16, 22, 24, of some 23). LOWELL (2, 3, 4, 5, 6, 7, 8, 9, 10, 11, 12, 13, 15, 16, 17, 18, 19, 20, 21, 22, 23, 24). *Lowell* (1). LOWELL (Pippin) (14). *Orange* (1, 2, 3, 5, 7, 8, 9, of some 6). *Pound Royal* (2, 7, erroneously 6). *Queen Anne* (1, 2, 6, 7, 9, 11, of Northern Ohio 3, of Ohio 5). *Tallow* (2, 7). TALLOW APPLE (1). *Tallow Apple* (3, 6, 9, of some 23). *Tallow Pippin* (3, 5, 6, 11, 15, 24).

Fruit rather large; clear yellow with waxy surface. Flesh a little coarse, very juicy, sprightly subacid and desirable for either dessert or culinary uses. It ripens in succession through a period of several weeks and is apt to drop as it ripens. Its season extends from late August to October and under favorable conditions a portion of the fruit may be kept till winter (24). The tree is a good grower, hardy, long-lived and a reliable cropper giving good crops biennially and sometimes annually. This fruit is grown for home use and to a limited extent for local market.

Historical. Lowell is an old variety of American origin (6) which is quite generally known in many parts of the state, especially in Western New York. It is still commonly listed by nurserymen, but is being planted but little and its cultivation appears to be on the decline.

TREE.

Tree rather large, vigorous. *Form* upright spreading, rather open. *Twigs* long, curved, moderately stout; internodes medium. *Bark* dark brown,

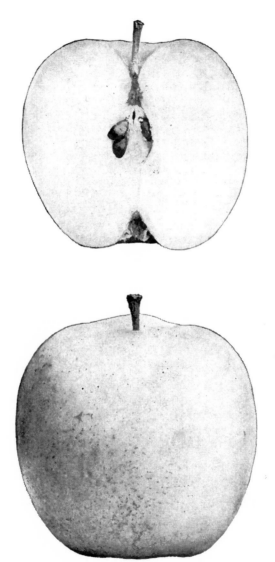

LOWELL

mottled with scarf-skin; heavily pubescent. *Lenticels* numerous, small to medium size, not raised. *Buds* prominent, medium to large, broad, plump, obtuse, pubescent.

FRUIT.

Fruit large, fairly uniform in size but somewhat variable in shape. *Form* roundish oblong inclined to conic, unsymmetrical, irregular. *Stem* medium to rather long, moderately thick, deflected to one side. *Cavity* acute or approaching acuminate, rather shallow to moderately deep, medium to rather broad, sometimes furrowed, occasionally compressed, often lightly russeted. *Calyx* medium to large, closed or partly open. *Basin* rather shallow to moderately deep, medium in width, somewhat abrupt, often slightly furrowed and wrinkled.

Skin thin, tender, smooth or with occasional russet dots and flecks, waxy, at first green but eventually becoming rich yellow. *Dots* very numerous, small, inconspicuous, brown or russet or submerged.

Calyx tube usually rather long, rather wide, conical approaching funnel-form. *Stamens* median or nearly so.

Core rather large, axile to somewhat abaxile; cells closed; core lines meeting or somewhat clasping. *Carpels* roundish to pointed obovate, emarginate. *Seeds* dark brown, not uniform in shape, medium size, obtuse to somewhat acute.

Flesh greenish or tinged with yellow, rather firm, medium to rather fine-grained, crisp, tender, very juicy, sprightly subacid, good to very good.

Season August to October.

LOWLAND RASPBERRY.

REFERENCES. 1. Gibb, *Ia. Hort. Soc. Rpt.*, 1883:438. 2. *Ib., Montreal Hort. Soc. Rpt.*, 1883:94. 3. *Ib., Am. Pom. Soc. Rpt.*, 1887:46. 4. Thomas, 1897:254. fig. 5. *U. S. Pom. Bul.*, 8:18. 1899. 6. Hansen, *S. D. Sta. Bul.*, 76:69. 1902. fig. 7. Budd-Hansen, 1903:117. fig.

SYNONYMS. HIMBEERAPFEL LIEVLANDER (1, 2). *Himbeerapfel Lievlander* (3). *Himbeerapfel Livlander* (3). *Lievland Raspberry* (7). LIVELAND RASPBERRY (4). LIVLAND RASPBERRY (3). LOWLAND RASPBERRY (6). LOW-LAND *Raspberry* (5, 7). *Lowland Raspberry* (1, 2, 3). *No. 340* (1, 2, 6, 7).

A Russian apple which, according to Hansen (6, 7), is medium to large, clear waxen-white, striped, shaded and marbled with light crimson; flesh white, often stained with red, fine, very tender, pleasant mild subacid, almost sweet; season August; as early as Yellow Transparent.

We do not know that this variety has been tested in New York.

LUBSK QUEEN.

REFERENCES. 1. Tuttle, *Montreal Hort. Soc. Rpt.*, 8:136. 1881-82. 2. Gibb, *Ia. Hort. Soc. Rpt.*, 1883:442. 3. Budd, *Ia. Agr. Coll. Bul.*, 1885:17. 4. *Am. Pom. Soc. Cat.*, 1889:8. 5. Budd, *Ia. Agr. Coll. Bul.*, 1890:19. 6. *Ia. Sta. Bul.*, 19:536. 1892. 7. *Can. Hort.*, 16:361. 1893. 8. Freeborn, *Nat. Nursery-*

man, **2**:132. 1894. **9.** Thomas, **1897**:291. *fig.* **10.** Hansen, *S. D. Sta. Bul.,*
76:70. 1902. *fig.* **11.** Budd-Hansen, **1903**:119. **12.** Ragan, *U. S. B. P. I.
Bul.,* **56**:185. 1905.

SYNONYMS. LUBSK QUEEN (1, 2, 4, 5, 6, 7, 8, 9, 10, 11). *Lubsk Queen* (12).
LUBSK REINETTE (3, 12). *Lubsk Reinette* (10, 11). *No. 444* (3, 5, 6, 8, 10,
11, 12). *Reinette Liubski* (2, 12). *Renet Liubskui* (3, 12).

A Russian variety which has attracted attention because of the beauty of
the fruit and superior hardiness and productiveness of the tree. In other
respects it does not rank high. It is fairly good in quality. Season August
and September.

Historical. Imported from Russia by the United States Department of
Agriculture in 1870 under No. 444. It was entered on the list of the
American Pomological Society in 1889 and dropped from the list at the
following meeting in 1891 (4). It has been planted but little in New York,
and so far as we have been able to learn its cultivation in this state is not
increasing.

TREE.

Tree moderately vigorous with long, slender, curved branches. *Form*
upright spreading or roundish, rather open. *Twigs* short, curved, slender;
internodes medium. *Bark* dull brown, roughly mottled with scarf-skin;
slightly pubescent near tips. *Lenticels* scattering, medium size, round, not
raised. *Buds* medium size, plump, obtuse, free, not pubescent.

FRUIT (10).

Fruit medium to large. *Form* regular, nearly round, truncated. *Stem*
medium to long. *Cavity* acute, rather small, slightly russeted. *Calyx* closed;
segments long, pointed. *Basin* shallow, wide, regular, with generally five
fine corrugations around the eye.

Skin very smooth, polished and waxlike, a brilliant white, more or less
covered with solid light rosy red, with delicate white bloom; a self-colored
apple, but sometimes with short red splashes on lighter ground. *Dots*
white, minute, numerous.

Calyx tube long, funnel-shape. *Stamens* marginal.

Core closed; cells ovate, slit. *Seeds* nine, plump.

Flesh snow white, firm, juicy, fine-grained, subacid, good.

Season August, September.

LYSCOM.

REFERENCES. **1.** *N. E. Farmer,* **1830** (cited by 17). **2.** Kenrick, **1832**:36.
3. *Mag. Hort.,* **1**:364, 395. 1835. **4.** Hovey, *Ib.,* **4**:48. 1838. **5.** Manning,
1838:51. **6.** Ib., *Mag. Hort.,* **7**:46. 1841. **7.** Downing, **1845**:89. **8.** Cole,
1849:111. **9.** Thomas, **1849**:151. **10.** Emmons, *Nat. Hist. N. Y.,* **3**:32.
1851. **11.** Elliott, **1854**:145. **12.** *Mag. Hort.,* **20**:241. 1854. **13.** Hooper,
1857:56. **14.** *Am. Pom. Soc. Cat.,* **1862.** **15.** Warder, **1867**:605. **16.** Lyon,
Mich. Hort. Soc. Rpt., **1890**:294. **17.** Ragan, *U. S. P. B. I. Bul.,* **56**:186.
1905.

SYNONYMS. LYSCOM (1, 2, 3, 4, 5, 6, 7, 8, 9, 10, 11, 12, 13, 14, 15, 16, 17).
Matthew's Stripe (3, 8, 17). *Osgood's Favourite* (3, 7, 8, 9, 17).

A very large apple somewhat resembling Twenty Ounce in general appearance but less attractive; flesh tender, mild, not high in flavor but acceptable for either dessert or culinary uses. The tree is a moderate grower and yields moderate to good crops. It is in season from late September or October to November or December. Not recommended for planting in New York because it is not superior to other varieties of its season.

Historical. Origin Southborough, Worcester county, Mass. (2). It is an old variety which has been quite widely disseminated. It is now nearly obsolete in New York.

FRUIT.

Fruit large or very large. *Form* roundish varying from a little oblate to slightly oblong conic, often broadly ribbed especially toward the apex. *Stem* deep set, short, moderately thick. *Cavity* acuminate, very deep, broad, symmetrical, russeted and with outspreading russet rays. *Calyx* medium to large, usually closed, pubescent. *Basin* often oblique, deep, moderately narrow to rather wide with broad, deep furrows.

Skin thick, tough, rather dull green or somewhat yellowish, striped, splashed and somewhat blushed with red.

Calyx tube wide, elongated cone-shape. *Stamens* median to basal.

Core rather large, axile; cells closed; core lines meeting or slightly clasping. *Carpels* ovate, slightly emarginate, somewhat tufted. *Seeds* short, often nearly round, plump, obtuse.

Flesh somewhat tinged with yellow, rather fine, tender, juicy, subacid becoming very mild subacid, good.

Season late September or October to November or December.

MABIE.

A red sweet apple of very good general appearance. It belongs in the same group as Victoria Sweet. Season late fall and early winter. A desirable variety of its class.

Historical. This is a local variety which has been grown to a limited extent in southern Rockland county. The following account of its origin is given by M. L. Bell, Sparkill, N. Y.:[1] "Mabie has been grown in Southern Rockland county, N. Y., and the adjacent portion of New Jersey for about forty-five years. About fifty years ago the original tree stood in an old stone fence row on the farm of Wm. Mabie. It was propagated in a local nursery and disseminated through the surrounding region where it is generally highly esteemed by those who have tested it."

FRUIT.

Fruit above medium to nearly large. *Form* roundish or somewhat inclined to oblong, a little irregular, unsymmetrical, not very uniform. *Stem* medium

---

[1] Letter, 1904.

to, rather long, moderately thick. *Cavity* large, acute to acuminate, moderately deep, wide, often obscurely furrowed, sometimes completely covered with russet which extends over the base of the fruit in broken rays. *Calyx* medium to rather large, closed or partly open. *Basin* medium size or below, pubescent, saucer-shape, medium in width and depth, a little obtuse to rather abrupt, smooth or slightly furrowed.

Skin very thick, tough, smooth or slightly roughened with russet dots, bright yellow mottled or deeply blushed with bright red, in highly colored specimens rather deep, dark red, obscurely striped with carmine and marked over the base with whitish scarf-skin. *Dots* often very small, gray, mingled with others that are large, whitish and areolar with russet center.

Calyx tube short, moderately wide, conical to funnel-form. *Stamens* median.

Core medium to rather large, axile to somewhat abaxile; cells closed or somewhat open; core lines clasping. *Carpels* roundish to broadly obovate, slightly tufted. *Seeds* dark brown, medium to small, plump, broadly acute.

Flesh slightly tinged with yellow, firm, medium grained, somewhat crisp, tender, juicy, sweet, good.

Season late fall and early winter.

McCARTY.

This appears to be a distinct strain or sport of Pumpkin Sweet. It is discussed under Pumpkin Sweet, page 173.

MAC DONOUGH.

REFERENCE. 1. Waugh, *Vt. Sta. An. Rpt.*, 14:299. 1901.
SYNONYMS. None.

A medium sized yellow apple of mild flavor, in season in August and September. We are unacquainted with this variety. Waugh (1) gave the following account of it in 1901: "A local variety, said to have originated on Cumberland Head, Clinton county, N. Y., opposite Grand Isle. A fairly good apple in many ways, but not common and not likely ever to become popular.

"Fruit roundish oblate, size medium, cavity medium deep and broad, waxy, slightly russetted, stem medium straight, basin shallow, corrugated, calyx nearly closed, color greenish-yellow, fine yellow when ripe, dots many, light greenish, bloom waxy, skin smooth, flesh greenish-white, mealy, core medium, closed, flavor neutral, nearly sweet, quality fair to good, season August-September. Tree hardy, rough dark bark, irregular in form, productive."

McINTOSH.

REFERENCES. 1. Downing, 1876:55 app. fig. 2. *Montreal Hort. Soc. Rpt.*, 5:17. 1879. 3. *Am. Pom. Soc. Cat.*, 1883:12. 4. Thomas, 1885:517. 5. Hoskins, *Mich. Hort. Soc. Rpt.*, 1886:220. 6. Ib., *Rural N. Y.*, 47:558. 1888. 7. Budd, *Can. Hort.*, 13:24. 1890. 8. *Ib.*, 15:19, 92, 124. 1892. 9. Bailey,

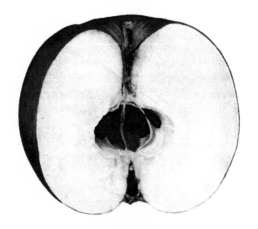

McINTOSH

An. Hort., **1892**:244. **10.** *Can. Hort.*, **16**:369. 1893. *col. pl.* **11.** Hoskins, *Am. Gard.*, **15**:288. 1894. **12.** Craig, *Can. Dept. Agr. Rpt.*, **1894**:125. **13.** Hoskins, *Rural N. Y.*, **53**:279. 1894. **14.** *Ib.*, **54**:238. 1895. **15.** *Ib.*, **55**:656. 691. 1896. **16.** *Ib.*, **55**:738, 819. 1896. **17.** *Ib.*, **56**:839. 1897. **18.** Can. *Hort.*, **22**:506. 1899. **19.** Whitney, *Ont. Fr. Gr. Assn. An. Rpt.*, **31**:12. 1899. **20.** *Ib., Can. Hort.*, **23**:24. 1900. *fig. of tree.* **21.** *Ib.*, **23**:45. 1900. *figs.* **22.** *Vt. Sta. Bul.*, **83**:91. 1900. *figs.* **23.** Taylor, *U. S. Dept. Agr. Yr. Bk.*, **1901**:383. *col. pl.* **24.** Waugh, *Vt. Sta. An. Rpt.*, **14**:299. 1901. **25.** *Ib., Rural N. Y.*, **61**:781. 1902. *figs.* **26.** *Kan. Sta. Bul.*, **106**:54. 1902 **27.** Hansen, *S. D. Sta. Bul.*, **76**:72. 1902. **28.** Budd-Hansen, **1903**:119 **29.** Farrand, *Mich. Sta. Bul.*, **205**:45. 1903. **30.** Powell and Fulton, *U. S. B. P. I. Bul.*, **48**:48. 1903. **31.** Beach and Clark, *N. Y. Sta. Bul.*, **248**:130. 1904. **32.** Scriber, *Can. Hort.*, **28**:277. 1905.

SYNONYMS. MACINTOSH RED (18). MCINTOSH (14, 16, 17, 19, 21, 25, 29). MCINTOSH RED (1, 2, 3, 4, 5, 6, 7, 8, 9, 10, 11, 12, 13, 15, 20, 26, 32). *McIntosh Red* (22, 23, 24, 27, 28, 30, 31).

This variety belongs in the Fameuse group. It is adapted to a wider range of localities than is the Fameuse. The fruit is very attractive in appearance, of bright deep red color and good size. The flesh is very tender, perfumed and delicious. It is desirable for local markets and special trade but because of its lack of firmness it is less suitable for general handling. As grown at this Station it begins to ripen in late September or early October. In Western New York it cannot be expected to keep much later than October in ordinary storage without considerable loss but in cold storage it may be held until December or January (31). When grown in more northern or elevated regions it is often held in good condition till midwinter or later. It is susceptible to scab but this may readily be controlled with proper treatment.[1] The crop ripens unevenly and a considerable portion of the fruit is liable to drop before it is ready to pick. On this account it is best to make two or three pickings. In some localities the tree is said to be a somewhat slow grower and not satisfactorily productive, but more often it is found to be a rather strong grower, hardy and healthy. It comes into bearing rather young and is a reliable cropper yielding good crops biennially and sometimes annually. It has not been sufficiently tested to demonstrate fully its value for commercial purposes but it is regarded by many as one of the most promising varieties of its class for general cultivation in New York.

---

[1] *N. Y. Sta. An. Rpt.*, **18**:399-418 1899. *Ib.*, **22**:321-386. 1903.

Historical. Originated as a chance seedling on the McIntosh homestead, Matilda township, Dundas county, Ontario, where Allan McIntosh began the propagation of this variety in the nursery about 1870 (20). It has been widely disseminated. It is now commonly propagated by nurserymen and its cultivation is on the increase in New York.

TREE.

Tree vigorous with numerous, small, slender laterals. *Form* roundish or spreading. *Twigs* above medium to short, straight or nearly so, rather slender; internodes long to below medium. *Bark* bright reddish-brown, lightly streaked with scarf-skin; slightly pubescent. *Lenticels* quite numerous, small, oval or elongated, raised. *Buds* deeply set in bark, medium to below, plump, obtuse to acute, free, slightly pubescent.

FRUIT.

Fruit above medium, sometimes large, pretty uniform in shape and size. *Form* roundish to somewhat oblate, regular or faintly ribbed, obscurely angular. *Stem* short, stout or moderately slender, usually not exserted, often with irregular protuberances. *Cavity* large, acuminate or somewhat acute, wide, medium in depth, somewhat broadly furrowed, often partly russeted. *Calyx* small, closed or partly open; lobes short to long, narrow, acute. *Basin* pubescent, rather small, medium in depth, narrow, abrupt, smooth or obscurely furrowed.

Skin thin, moderately tender, smooth, readily separating from the flesh, clear whitish-yellow or greenish washed and deeply blushed with bright red and striped with carmine; highly colored specimens become dark, almost purplish-red with the carmine stripes obscure or obliterated, overspread with thin, lilac bloom. Often the effect of the deep red is heightened by lively contrast with one or more spots of the clear pale yellow ground color where some twig or leaf pressed closely against the growing fruit. *Dots* whitish or yellow, usually very small.

Calyx tube short, conical or funnel-shape with broad limb. *Stamens* median to basal.

Core medium size, usually abaxile; cells usually wide open; core lines nearly meeting. *Carpels* roundish to elliptical, narrowing toward base and apex, smooth, much concave. *Seeds* medium brown, rather large, acute.

Flesh white or slightly tinged with yellow, sometimes veined with red, firm, fine, crisp, tender, very juicy, characteristically and agreeably aromatic, perfumed, sprightly, subacid, becoming mild and nearly sweet when very ripe, very good to best for dessert.

Season October to December or later.

McLELLAN.

REFERENCES. 1. Leavenworth, *Horticulturist*, 2:26. 1847. fig. 2. Thomas, 1849:169. 3. Cole, 1849:125. 4. Emmons, *Nat. Hist. N. Y.*, 3:67. 1851. 5. Hovey, *Mag. Hort.*, 20:508. 1854. fig. 6. Elliott, 1854:147. 7. Downing, 1857:87. 8. Hooper, 1857:57. 9. Warder, 1867:726. 10. *Am. Pom. Soc.*

Mc LELLAN ·

Cat., **1871** :8.   **11.** Lyon, *Mich. Hort. Soc. Rpt.*, **1890** :294.   **12.** Taylor, *Am. Pom. Soc. Rpt.*, **1895** :193.   **13.** Burrill and McCluer, *Ill. Sta. Bul.*, **45** :309, 330. 1896.   **14.** Farrand, *Mich. Sta. Bul.*, **205** :42. 1903.   **15.** Budd-Hansen, **1903** :120. fig.

Synonyms. *Martin* (1, 2, 6, 7).   McClellan (1, 5).   McLelan (8, 9).
McLellan (2, 3, 4, 6, 7, 10, 11, 12, 13, 14, 15).

A very choice dessert apple, handsome, fragrant, tender and excellent in quality. It comes into season a little later than Maiden Blush and may keep till January or February. When properly colored it is well adapted for fancy market and fruit-stand trade but when the color remains greenish, as it often does, the flavor is inferior. The fruit shows bruises readily and must be handled with extra care. It drops easily from the tree and on this account should be picked as soon as colored. In some cases it may pay to make two pickings. The tree comes into bearing young and is a reliable biennial bearer yielding good crops. It is only a moderately vigorous grower and probably it would be an advantage to topwork it upon some more vigorous and longer-lived stock, such as Northern Spy or Baldwin. It is not recommended for extensive commercial planting but in some cases it may be grown to a limited extent with profit.

Historical. The original tree was planted in a seedling orchard in Woodstock, Conn., about 1780 (1, 5). It has been sparingly disseminated and is known locally in various parts of New York state, but it is now seldom offered by nurserymen (12) and is little propagated.

Tree.

Tree medium in size, moderately vigorous with long and moderately stout branches. *Form* erect, roundish, open. *Twigs* medium to long, erect, stout, generally somewhat curved; internodes short to medium. *Bark* dull, very dark reddish-brown, sometimes tinged with green and overlaid with rather heavy scarf-skin; rather heavily pubescent. *Lenticels* quite numerous, not very conspicuous, medium to small, roundish, sometimes a little raised. *Buds* above medium to large, rather deeply set in the bark, broad, flat, obtuse to somewhat acute, free, very pubescent.

Fruit.

Fruit above medium to large; uniform in size and shape. *Form* roundish oblate to roundish conic, rather broad and flat at the base, symmetrical or nearly so, regular to elliptical. *Stem* short to medium, slender. *Cavity* acute to acuminate, rather wide, deep, symmetrical, sometimes a little furrowed, smooth. *Calyx* small to medium, partly open or closed; lobes long, acuminate *Basin* medium to rather small, abrupt, moderately shallow to deep, rather narrow to moderately wide, nearly round or sometimes angular, sometimes distinctly furrowed and wrinkled.

Skin tough, waxen, pale yellow or greenish, blushed and mottled with bright light red splashed and striped with bright carmine. Highly colored specimens are almost entirely red and very attractive. *Dots* numerous but mostly inconspicuous, whitish or russet.

Calyx tube funnel-form with wide limb or sometimes elongated. *Stamens* basal to median.

Core below medium to small, axile or nearly so; cells not uniformly developed, usually pretty symmetrical, closed or partly open; core lines clasping the funnel cylinder. *Carpels* smooth, roundish to elliptical narrowing toward the base and apex, slightly emarginate. *Seeds* rather small, obtuse, smooth, dark.

Flesh tinged with yellow, moderately firm, very tender, moderately fine-grained, juicy, moderately crisp, almost sweet, excellent in flavor, very good for dessert.

Season October to January or February or sometimes to March.

McMAHON.

REFERENCES. 1. *Am. Pom. Soc. Rpt.*, **1885**:27. 2. *Mich. Hort. Soc. Rpt.*, **1886**:221. 3. *Am. Pom. Soc. Rpt.*, **1887**:93. 4. *Rural N. Y.*, **46**:751. 1887. 5. *Can. Hort.*, **11**:220. 1888. fig. 6. *Am. Pom. Soc. Cat.*, **1889**:10. 7. *Am. Gard.*, **11**:243. 1890. 8. *Can. Hort.*, **13**:174, 216. 1890. 9. Van Deman, *U. S. Pom. Rpt.*, **1890**:413. 10. *Can. Hort.*, **14**:339. 1891. 11. Taylor, *Me. Pom. Soc. Rpt.*, **1892**:57, 50. 12. Bailey, *An. Hort.*, **1892**:244. 13. *Can. Hort.*, **15**:393. 1892. 14. *Ib.*, **16**:77, 134. 1893. col. *pl.* 15. Craig, *Ib.*, **16**:137. 1893. fig. 16. Ib., *Ont. Fr. Gr. Assn. An. Rpt.*, **26**:16. 1894. 17. Ib., *Can. Dept. Agr. Rpt.*, **1894**:125. 18. Ib., **1895**:93. fig. 19. Beach, *N. Y. Sta. An. Rpt.*, **15**:273. 1896. figs. 20. Thomas, 1897:643. 21. Waugh, *Vt. Sta. An. Rpt.*, **14**:300. 1901. 22. Hansen, *S. D. Sta. Bul.*, **76**:72. 1902. fig. 23. Powell and Fulton, *U. S. B. P. I. Bul.*, **48**:48. 1903. 24. Farrand, *Mich. Sta. Bul.*, **205**:42. 1903. 25. Budd-Hansen, **1903**:121. fig. 26. Beach and Clark, *N. Y. Sta. Bul.*, **248**:130. 1904. 27. Ragan, *U. S. B. P. I. Bul.*, **56**:188. 1905.

SYNONYMS. McMAHAN (14, 20). *McMahan* (27). McMAHAN WHITE (6, **7**, 15, 16, 17, 18). McMAHON (11, 19, 21, 22, 23, 25, 26, 27). McMAHON WHITE (1, 2, 3, 4, 5, 8, 9, 10, 12, 13, 24). *McMahon White* (19, 21, 22, 23, **25, 26,** 27).

A large apple of the Aport group, pale yellow or almost white, often with a delicate pink blush. The flesh is juicy, brisk subacid, fair to good in quality, excellent for culinary use. As grown at this Station it ripens unevenly and does not appear well adapted for storage (26). Season October to January or February. The

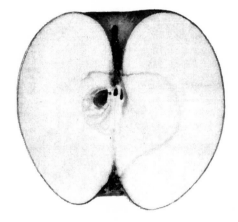

LEE

Mc LELLAN

McMAHON

tree comes into bearing rather young and yields good crops biennially. In 1895 Craig wrote concerning McMahon: "Attention is again drawn to some of its merits as an apple of value for regions where Northern Spy, Ribston Pippin and Rhode Island Greening cannot be grown profitably on account of their inability to withstand the severity of the climate. It has proved so far a remarkably vigorous and healthy grower, making probably more well matured wood growth than any other variety in the orchard, and is free from many of the defects characteristic to varieties unadapted to this climate. It has borne moderately heavy crops for the last two years. The fruit is of the largest size, smooth and handsome, though lacking in color as grown in this vicinity and somewhat soft in texture" (18). It is less desirable than standard kinds of its season for growing commercially in New York because it is only moderately attractive in general appearance, its color is such that it readily shows bruises and it does not rank high either in flavor or quality.

Historical. This variety originated about 1860 in Richland county, Wis., and is supposed to be a seedling of the Alexander. It is frequently listed by nurserymen, but it has thus far been but little planted in New York.

TREE.

Tree medium size, vigorous. *Form* rather spreading. *Twigs* medium size, slender, straight or nearly so; internodes above medium. *Bark* dull dark reddish-brown; slightly pubescent. *Lenticels* numerous, below medium or sometimes medium, elongated, somewhat raised, dull. *Buds* medium or below, rather acute, thin, often appressed, slightly pubescent.

FRUIT.

Fruit large or very large. *Form* roundish inclined to conic, faintly ribbed. *Stem* medium in length, moderately thick. *Cavity* remarkably acuminate, very deep, broad, compressed, slightly russeted and with outspreading rays. *Calyx* rather small, slightly open; lobes separated at base, short. *Basin* moderately deep, rather narrow to moderately wide, abrupt, compressed, slightly furrowed and wrinkled.

Skin pale greenish-yellow or nearly white with irregular stripes and patches of whitish scarf-skin extending out from the cavity over the base, and often having the cheek overspread with a thin blush which sometimes is faintly splashed and striped with carmine. *Dots* few, inconspicuous, small, greenish or russet.

Calyx tube rather long, wide, broadly conical inclined to funnel-form or cylindrical. *Stamens* median to basal.

Core medium to small, slightly abaxile to axile; cells pretty symmetrical, closed or slightly open; core lines nearly meeting or clasping. *Carpels* roundish or inclined to elliptical, slightly emarginate. *Seeds* rather dark brown, medium or below, moderately plump, obtuse to acute.

Flesh nearly white, nearly fine, tender, juicy, sprightly subacid, fair to good.

Season October to January or February.

MAGOG.

REFERENCES. 1. Downing, 1876:56 app. 2. Thomas, 1885:516. 3. *Can. Hort.,* 13:174. 1890. 4. Bailey, *An. Hort.,* 1892:243. 5. Hoskins, *Am. Gard.,* 15:256. 1894. 6. Beach, *N. Y. Sta. An. Rpt.,* 15:273. 1896. 7. *Am. Pom. Soc. Cat.,* 1899:18. 8. Powell and Fulton, *U. S. B. P. I. Bul.,* 48:48. 1903. 9. Budd-Hansen, 1903:122. 10. Farrand, *Mich. Sta. Bul.,* 205:45. 1903. 11. Beach and Clark, *N. Y. Sta. Bul.,* 248:130. 1904.

SYNONYMS. MAGOG (4, 8, 10). MAGOG *Red Streak* (7, 9). MAGOG RED STREAK (1, 2, 3, 5, 6). *Magog Red Streak* (4, 11).

Fruit of good size, rather attractive appearance and good to very good quality, especially for culinary uses.   Dr. Hoskins, who propagated it for several years, said in 1894: " It is a fair but uneven keeper, and might be well described as not quite valuable enough to retain, yet hardly deserving to be cast aside." It is reported as being very hardy in Northern New York, a good grower and a good bearer. As fruited at this Station the tree is a moderately good grower, comes into bearing rather young and yields moderate to good crops nearly annually. The keeping quality of the fruit varies in different seasons but its commercial limit in ordinary storage appears to be October. It remains in season to January or possibly later (11). It is not recommended for planting except perhaps for home use in localities where its superior hardiness gives it an advantage over ordinary varieties of its season.

Historical. Originated by Wm. Warren, Newport, Vt. (1). It has been planted to a considerable extent in portions of Northern New England, Northern New York and the parts of Canada adjoining. It is still propagated in a few nurseries (4).

TREE.

Tree moderately vigorous. *Form* upright spreading or roundish. *Twigs* short to medium, straight or nearly so, rather slender; internodes short to medium. *Bark* dark brown or brownish-red, lightly streaked with scarfskin, pubescent. *Lenticels* scattering, small, oval, not raised. *Buds* small to above medium, plump, obtuse, free, slightly pubescent.

MAGOG

FRUIT.

Fruit medium to large, averaging above medium, rather uniform in size but variable in shape. *Form* roundish to oblong, inclined to conic or some-what ovate, regular or faintly ribbed; sides often unequal. *Stem* medium to short, moderately thick to rather slender. *Cavity* acute or approaching acuminate, medium in depth, medium to rather narrow, usually smooth, occasionally lipped, often irregularly russeted. *Calyx* medium to small, closed; lobes medium length, rather narrow, acute to acuminate. *Basin* usually medium in width and depth, sometimes rather abrupt, coarsely wrinkled.

Skin thin, tough, smooth, waxy, pale greenish or yellow, lightly washed and mottled with thin brownish-red, sparingly striped and splashed with deeper red. *Dots* numerous, light, submerged, areolar, brown and russet. *Prevailing effect* yellow.

Calyx tube medium in width, long, conical to funnel-shape with long cylinder. *Stamens* nearly marginal.

Core large to medium, abaxile; cells open; core lines clasping the funnel cylinder. *Carpels* long ovate to broadly obcordate, sometimes tufted. *Seeds* light brown, small to medium, rather wide, short, very plump, obtuse to broadly acute.

Flesh tinged with yellow, rather firm, medium to rather fine-grained, tender, very juicy, sprightly, pleasant subacid, aromatic, good.

Season October to January or later.

MAIDEN BLUSH.

REFERENCES. 1. Coxe, 1817:106. fig. 2. Buel, *N. Y. Bd. Agr. Mem.,* 1826:476. 3. Wilson, 1828:136. 4. Fessenden, 1828:131. 5. *London Hort. Soc. Cat.,* 1831:No. 704. 6. Kenrick, 1832:27. 7. Thacher, 1822:130. 8. *Mag. Hort.,* 1:363, 396. 1835. 9. Downing, 1845:90. fig. 10. Thomas, 1849:157. fig. 11. Cole, 1849:113. fig. 12. Emmons, *Nat. Hist. N. Y.,* 3:40. 1851. col. pl. No. 30 and fig. 13. Barry, 1851:285. 14. Hovey, *Mag. Hort.,* 18:544. 1852. fig. 15. Elliott, 1854:469 app. 16. Hooper, 1857:57. 17. *Am. Pom. Soc. Rpt.,* 1860:240. 18. Warder, 1867:412. fig. 19. Fitz, 1872:143, 164. 20. Hogg, 1884:138. 21. *Rural N. Y.,* 47:713. 1888. 22. Wickson, 1889:244. 23. Lyon, *Mich. Hort. Soc. Rpt.,* 1890:294. 24. Bailey, *An. Hort.,* 1892:243. 25. *Can. Hort.,* 15:65. 1892. 26. *Ark. Sta. An. Rpt.,* 6:55. 1893. 27. *Ib.,* 7:44. 1894. 28. Hoskins, *Rural N. Y.,* 53:279. 1894. 29. *Ib.,* 55:7. 1896. 30. *Ill. Sta. Bul.,* 45:331. 1896. 31. Waugh, *Vt. Sta. An. Rpt.,* 14:299. 1901. 32. *Va. Sta. Bul.,* 130:124. 1901. 33. *Am. Pom. Soc. Cat.,* 1901:18. 34. Powell and Fulton, *U. S. B. P. I. Bul.,* 48:48. 1903. 35. Budd-Hansen, 1903:122. fig. 36. Beach and Clark, *N. Y. Sta. Bul.,* 248:130. 1904.

SYNONYMS. *Lady Blush* (36). MAIDEN BLUSH (1, 2, 3, 4, 5, 6, 7, 8, 9, 10, 11, 12, 13, 14, 15, 16, 17, 18, 19, 20, 21, 22, 23, 24, 25, 26, 27, 28, 29, 30, 31, 32, 33, 34, 35, 36). *Red Cheek* (11).

This is a beautiful apple of pale lemon-yellow color with crimson cheek. The flesh is white, sprightly, not superior in flavor but good in quality. It is valued especially for market and culinary uses. It makes very white evaporated stock. As grown in Western New York it is in season from September to November or December. Later than this although the fruit may appear sound it is deficient in quality. In cold storage its commercial limit appears to be about December 15th. It does not stand heat well before going into storage. It varies greatly in the time of maturing in different seasons. The earlier it matures the less satisfactory is it as a keeper (36). It is recognized as a standard market variety and usually sells above the average prices for varieties of its class. In many localities it has proven a very satisfactory variety for the commercial orchard, because the tree is a fine grower, hardy, pretty long-lived, comes into bearing rather young and is a reliable cropper, yielding good to heavy crops biennially or almost annually. In many cases the fruit does not mature uniformly and there is considerable loss from drops unless more than one picking is made in gathering the crop. Usually the fruit is pretty uniform in size but on unthrifty, old trees or under unfavorable circumstances a considerable amount of the fruit may be too small for market. It is sometimes badly injured by scab but this may readily be prevented by proper treatment.

Historical. Coxe described this variety in 1817 as very popular in the Philadelphia market and the best variety of its season for evaporating. He stated that it was named by Samuel Allinson, of Burlington, N. J., who first brought it to notice. In the American Pomological Society's Catalogue of fruits it is reported as either " wholly successful or successful" in nearly all the important apple-growing districts of the United States (33). It has long been well and favorably known in New York and it is still being planted both for commercial purposes and for home use.

TREE.

Tree medium size, moderately vigorous to vigorous. *Form* spreading, open. *Twigs* long, curved, slender; internodes short. *Bark* brown or reddish-brown, lightly mottled with scarf-skin; slightly pubescent. *Lenticels* quite numerous, small, round, not raised. *Buds* medium size, plump, obtuse, free, slightly pubescent.

FRUIT.

Fruit medium or above, sometimes large, uniform in size and shape. *Form* oblate a little inclined to conic, regular, symmetrical. *Stem* short to

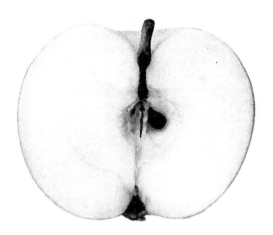

MAIDEN BLUSH

medium, rather slender. *Cavity* rather large, acute to obtuse, medium to wide, moderately deep to shallow, usually symmetrical, sometimes russeted. *Calyx* medium size, closed; lobes separated at base, medium length, moderately broad, acute. *Basin* moderately shallow, medium to wide, obtuse, regular, smooth or slightly furrowed, symmetrical.

Skin thin, tough, smooth, pale waxen yellow with crimson blush. *Dots* numerous, whitish and submerged or areolar.

Calyx tube small, narrow, conical to funnel-shape. *Stamens* median to marginal.

Core medium size, axile or somewhat abaxile, broadly elliptical; cells closed or slightly open; core lines meeting or slightly clasping. *Carpels* very broadly ovate. *Seeds* medium brown, moderately wide, moderately long, plump, acute.

Flesh white or with slight yellow tinge, fine, moderately crisp, tender, very juicy, subacid, good in quality especially for culinary uses.

Season September to November or December.

MAIDEN FAVORITE.

REFERENCES. 1. Downing, 1857:167. 2. Warder, 1867:725. 3. Thomas, 1875:505.

SYNONYMS. *Maiden's Apple* (1). MAIDEN FAVORITE (1, 2, 3).

A late fall and early winter variety which originated in Stuyvesant, Columbia county, N. Y. According to Downing it is a desirable amateur variety of delicacy and beauty, medium size or below, whitish or pale waxen yellow sometimes mottled with crimson. Flesh tender, crisp, very delicate, vinous, sweet, good to very good. Tree a rather slow grower with upright, slender branches, and a good bearer. We are not acquainted with this variety. So far as we have been able to learn it is not cultivated outside of the vicinity of its origin and is no longer propagated.

MARGARET.

REFERENCES. 1. Forsyth, 1803:50. 2. *Am. Gard. Cal.*, 1806:584. 3. Forsyth, 1824:114. 4. *Pom. Mag.*, 1:No.46. 1828. *col. pl.* 5. *London Hort. Soc. Cat.*, 1831:No. 708. 6. Kenrick, 1832:26. 7. Floy-Lindley, 1833:7. 8. Manning, 1838:46. 9. Downing, 1845:73. fig. 10. Cole, 1849:98. 11. Thomas, 1849:137. fig. 12. Emmons, *Nat. Hist. N. Y.*, 3:11. 1851. 13. Elliott, 1854:145. 14. Hooper, 1857:31. 15. Warder, 1867:717. 16. Fitz, 1872:160. 17. Downing, 1872:10 index, app. 18. Leroy, 1873:454. fig. 19. Barry, 1883:332. 20. Hogg, 1884:141. 21. Bailey, *An. Hort.*, 1892:238. 22. *Jour. Roy. Hort. Soc.*, 1898:354. 23. Waugh, *Vt. Sta. An. Rpt.*, 14:299. 1901. 24. Budd-Hansen, 1903:124.

SYNONYMS. *D'Eve* (18). *Duverson's June* (17). Early June of South (13). EARLY MARGARET (16). *Early Margaret* (4, 20). *Early Red* (24). EARLY RED JUNEATING (6). *Early Red Juneating* (7, 9, 11, 12, 13, 20). EARLY RED MARGARET (4, 7, 8, 9, 10, 11, 12, 14, 15, 17, 19, 21). *Early Red Margaret* (6, 13, 18, 20, 23). *Early Striped Juneating* (4, 5, 6, 7, 20). *Eve Apple* (7, of Ireland 4, 5, 6, 9, 12, 13, 20). *Herr's June* (17). *June of* some in Ohio (13). *Lammas* (3, 20). *Magdalene* (20). MARGARET (1, 2, 3, 13, 20, 22, 23, 24). *Margaret* (4, 5, 6, 7, 9, 12, 18). *Margaret, Early* (5). MARGARET, EARLY RED (5). *Margaretha Apfel* (4, 7, 9, 12, 13). *Marget Apple* (20). MARGUERITE (18). *Marguerite* (5, 20). *Maudlin* (18, 20). *Red Joaneting* (22). *Red June* of South (13). *Red Juneating* (4, 5, 6, 7, 9, 10, 11, 12, 13, 20). *Red Juneting* (3). *Reinette Quarrendon* (18). *Rother Jacobs* (18). *Rother Jacobs Apfel* (4, 7). *Striped Juneating* (5, 9, 11, 12, 13, 18, 20). *Striped Quarendon* (17). *Striped Quarrenden* (5, 18, 20). *Summer Traveller* (5, 17, 20). *Virginia June* (17).

An early summer apple, small to nearly medium, roundish ovate, yellowish striped and marbled with dull red. Flesh pleasant subacid, good; season late July and early August. It is a dessert apple suitable for the home orchard only. The tree is of medium size, moderately vigorous, upright, hardy, long-lived, comes into bearing fairly young and is a pretty reliable biennial cropper.

Historical. This is a very old English variety. Hogg (20) states that "It is without doubt the Margaret of Rea, Worlidge, Ray, and all our early pomologists except Miller." It has long been cultivated in this country, but only to a very limited extent. It is now rarely propagated by our nurserymen and seldom planted.

MILLER.

REFERENCES. **1.** Downing, **1857** :172. **2.** *Horticulturist,* **13** :530. 1858. **3.** Warder, **1867** :726. **4.** Downing, **1869** :275. **5.** Leroy, **1873** :469. fig. **6.** Thomas, **1875** :506. **7.** Lyon, *Mich. Hort. Soc. Rpt.,* **1890** :294.

SYNONYMS. MILLER (1, 3, 4, 5, 6, 7). MILLER SEEDLING (2).

This apple was brought to notice by James O. Miller, Montgomery, Orange county, N. Y. (1). Downing (4) describes the fruit as rather large, roundish oblate inclined to conic, yellow shaded, striped and splashed with light red. Flesh yellowish, crisp, pleasant subacid, good to very good. Season October and November (3). Lyon refers to it as a promising fruit for market and general purposes (7). We are unacquainted with this variety and have received no report concerning it from any of our correspondents.

MILLIGEN.

REFERENCES. **1.** *N. Y. Sta. An. Rpt.,* **8** :348. 1889. **2.** *U. S. B. P. I. Bul.,* **48** :49. 1903. **3.** Beach and Clark, *N. Y. Sta. Bul.,* **248** :132. 1904.

SYNONYMS. None.

Fruit of good size, rather attractive in general appearance, yellow striped with red, good to very good. It comes into season in October and some portion of the fruit may be kept in good condition till spring. In common storage there is apt to be a rather high rate of loss during late autumn, so that its commercial limit is October or early November, but it may be held in cold storage till midwinter (3). The tree is a vigorous grower, almost an annual bearer and usually produces good crops. It does not excel standard varieties of its season for any purpose. Not recommended for planting in New York.

Historical. This variety was originated by Mrs. Milligen, near Claysville, Washington county, Pa. It was received for testing at this Station from J. R. and R. A. Murdock, Pittsburg, Pa., in 1888.

MOSHER.

REFERENCES. 1. Downing, **1881**:97 app. 2. Waugh, *Vt. Sta. An. Rpt.*, **14**:300. 1901.

SYNONYMS. MOSHER (2). MOSHER SWEET (1). *Mosher Sweet* (2).

A good variety for the home orchard but not attractive enough for market (1). Originated in the orchard of Ephraim Mosher, Washington, N. Y., many years since. So far as we can learn this variety is not now being propagated by nurserymen and its cultivation appears to be declining. The tree is large, rather vigorous, upright spreading or roundish, a good grower, comes into bearing rather young and yields pretty good crops annually or nearly annually. Fruit medium, oblate conic, ribbed pale yellow or greenish; flesh white, moderately juicy, sweet, aromatic, good; season September and October.

MOTHER.

REFERENCES. 1. *Mag. Hort.*, **10**:210. 1844. 2. Thomas, *Cultivator*, **5**:306. 1848. fig. 3. *Horticulturist*, **3**:581. 1848. 4. Cole, **1849**:115. fig. 5. Hovey, *Mag. Hort.*, **15**:65. 1849. fig. 6. Thomas, **1849**:169. fig. 7. Waring, **1851**:27. 8. Emmons, *Nat. Hist. N. Y.*, **3**:58. 1851. 9. *Am. Pom. Soc. Cat.*, **1852**. 10. *Mag. Hort.*, **20**:241. 1854. 11. Elliott, **1854**:147. 12. Downing, **1857**:87. 13. Hooper, **1857**:62. 14. Gregg, **1857**:55. 15. *Mag. Hort.*, **28**:281. 1862. 16. Lothrop, *Mag. Hort.*, **32**:363. 1866. 17. Warder, **1867**:663. fig. 18. Fitz, **1872**:141. 19. Barry, **1883**:350. 20. Hogg, **1884**:7. 21. Lyon, *Mich. Hort. Soc. Rpt.*, **1890**:294. 22. Bailey, *An. Hort.*, **1892**:245. 23. Bunyard, *Jour. Roy. Hort. Soc.*, **1898**:356. 24. Alwood, *Va. Sta. Bul.*, **130**:124. 1901. 25. Dickens and Greene, *Kan. Sta. Bul.*, **106**:54. 1902. 26. *Rural N. Y.*, **61**:829. 1902. figs. 27. Budd-Hansen, **1903**:132. figs. 28. *Rural N. Y.*, **62**:7, 380. 1903. 29. Bruner, *N. C. Sta. Bul.*, **182**:21. 1903. 30. Powell and Fulton, *U. S. B. P. I. Bul.*, **48**:50. 1903. 31. Beach and Clark, *N. Y. Sta. Bul.*, **248**:133. 1904.

SYNONYMS. AMERICAN MOTHER (20). *Gardener's Apple* (20). *Mother Apple* (20). MOTHER (1, 2, 3, 4, 5, 6, 7, 8, 9, 10, 11, 12, 13, 14, 15, 16, 17, 18, 19, 21, 22, 24, 25, 26, 27, 28, 29, 30, 31). MOTHER OF AMERICA (23). *Queene Anne* (12, 20).

A beautiful red apple of good size, with tender, rich, aromatic flesh of best dessert quality. It is less desirable for culinary uses, being somewhat lacking in acidity. It resembles Esopus *Spitzenburg* to a marked degree but ripens earlier and is not so good a keeper. In ordinary storage it does not keep well and November

is its safe commercial limit, but in cold storage it may be held till
March or later (31). The tree is below medium size and but a
moderate grower. In many localities it is rather tender and liable
to scald or canker on the trunk and larger branches. On this
account it is desirable to topwork it upon Northern Spy or some
other hardy, vigorous stock. It does not come into bearing very
young and commonly is a biennial cropper yielding moderate to
good crops. It cannot be recommended for general commercial
planting but it is desirable for the home orchard.

Historical. Thomas described it in 1848 as "a new, handsome late autumn
and early winter apple, of the highest quality," and stated that it originated
at Bolton, Worcester county, Mass. (2). It is still listed by some nurserymen (22) but it is nowhere being extensively planted. It is but seldom found
in cultivation in New York.

TREE.

Tree below medium size, moderately vigorous or a rather slow grower.
Form upright spreading to roundish, rather open. *Twigs* long, curved, moderately stout; internodes long. *Bark* brown, mingled with olive-green, lightly
mottled with scarf-skin; slightly pubescent near tips. *Lenticels* numerous,
rather conspicuous, medium size, oval, raised. *Buds* rather prominent,
medium size, broad, plump, obtuse, free, pubescent.

FRUIT.

Fruit below medium to above, sometimes large, pretty uniform in size and
shape. *Form* roundish or roundish conic to oblong ovate, obscurely and
broadly ribbed. *Stem* long to medium, moderately slender to rather thick.
Cavity acute or approaching acuminate, rather shallow to moderately deep,
rather narrow to moderately broad, often russeted, sometimes furrowed or
compressed or lipped. *Calyx* small, closed or nearly so; lobes medium,
narrow, acute. *Basin* shallow, narrow, a little abrupt, somewhat furrowed
and wrinkled.

Skin thin, smooth, golden yellow nearly covered with bright deep red,
marbled and striped with carmine. *Dots* rather small, inconspicuous, yellowish or pale and submerged.

Calyx tube rather long, funnel-form with wide limb and narrow cylinder.
Stamens marginal.

Core medium to rather small, abaxile; cells nearly symmetrical, open or
partly open; core lines clasping. *Carpels* broadly ovate to roundish,
emarginate, mucronate. *Seeds* rather dark, medium or below, plump, acute
to acuminate.

Flesh fine, tender, juicy, very mild subacid, aromatic, very good to best in
flavor and quality.

Season late September to January; it is in its prime in November.

MOTHER

MOUNTAIN SWEET.

REFERENCES. 1. Warder, 1867:388. 2. Downing, 1869:282.
SYNONYMS. MOUNTAIN SWEET (1, 2). *Mountaineer* (1, 2).

Fruit of medium size, fairly good appearance and moderate to good quality, not superior to other varieties of its season and not recommended for planting in this state.

Historical. Origin Pennsylvania (1). It is but little known in New York and its cultivation in this state is not being extended.

TREE.

Tree medium or below, not a strong grower, with short, stout, curved branches. *Form* spreading or roundish, rather dense. *Twigs* short, straight, moderately stout; internodes short. *Bark* clear brown mingled with green, lightly streaked with scarf-skin; pubescent. *Lenticels* quite numerous, small, oblong, slightly raised. *Buds* medium size, plump, acute, free, slightly pubescent.

FRUIT.

Fruit variable, usually medium or above. *Form* roundish or roundish oblate, pretty regular, somewhat angular; sides unequal. *Stem* short to rather long, rather slender. *Cavity* nearly acuminate to somewhat obtuse, medium in depth, rather broad, russeted and with outspreading russet rays. *Calyx* small to rather large, closed or open; lobes separated at base, medium to long, rather narrow, acuminate. *Basin* moderately shallow to shallow, narrow to moderately wide, wavy.

Skin thick, rather tough, somewhat rough, clear pale yellow overlaid with faint pinkish blush and scattering stripes of deeper red. *Dots* numerous, inconspicuous, small, russet. *Prevailing effect* striped.

Calyx tube medium in length, rather wide, conical to somewhat funnelform. *Stamens* median to basal.

Core medium size, abaxile; cells open; core lines meeting or slightly clasping. *Carpels* broadly ovate to elliptical, emarginate. *Seeds* very small, rather wide, plump, acute, rather light brown.

Flesh white, moderately fine, very tender, juicy, sweet, good.

Season September to December.

MOUSE.

REFERENCES. 1. Downing, 1845:117. 2. Thomas, 1849:182. 3. Emmons, *Nat. Hist. N. Y.*, 3:82. 1851. 4. Elliott, 1854:147. 5. Hooper, 1857:62. 6. Warder, 1867:727.
SYNONYMS. *Moose* (1, 2, 3, 4, 5). MOUSE (1, 2, 3, 4, 5, 6).

An old variety which originated in Ulster county, N. Y., where it was formerly popular (1). According to Downing the fruit is large, roundish conical, pale greenish-yellow with brownish blush; flesh very white, fine-grained, delicate, mild subacid; good; season October to November.

This variety is unknown to us and we have received no reports concerning it from any of our correspondents.

MUNSON.

REFERENCES. 1. *Genesee Farmer*, 10:288. 1849. 2. Barry, 1851:285. 3. Humrickhouse, *Mag. Hort.*, 19:163. 1853. 4. Elliott, 1854:148. 5. Downing, 1857:174. 6. Gregg, 1857:44. 7. *Horticulturist*, 17:104, 150. 1862. 8. *Am. Pom. Soc. Cat.*, 1862. 9. Warder, 1867:388. fig. 10. Thomas, 1875:198. 11. Lyon, *Mich. Hort. Soc. Rpt.*, 1890:294. 12. Bailey, *An. Hort.*, 1892:245. 13. Hoskins, *Rural N. Y.*, 53:278. 1894. 14. Burrill and McCluer, *Ill. Sta. Bul.*, 45:333. 1896. 15. Munson, *Me. Sta. Rpt.*, 1896:71. 16. Ib., 18:89. 1902. 17. Budd-Hansen, 1903:133. fig. 18. Farrand, *Mich. Sta. Bul.*, 205:45. 1903. 19. Powell and Fulton, *U. S. B. P. I. Bul.*, 48:50. 1903. 20. Beach and Clark, *N. Y. Sta. Bul.*, 248:133. 1904.

SYNONYMS. *Meachem Sweet* (5). MUNSON (17, 18, 19, 20). MUNSON SWEET (2, 3, 5, 8, 9, 10, 11, 12, 13, 14, 15, 16). *Munson Sweet* (17, 19, 20). MUNSON SWEETING (4, 6). *Munson Sweeting* (1). NORTHERN SWEETING (1). *Orange Sweet* (5, 9). *Ray Apple* (5).

In some parts of New York this variety is better known under either the names Meachem Sweet or Rag Apple than it is under the correct name of Munson.

The fruit commonly averages about medium size. It is attractive in appearance for a yellow apple, being pale yellow often somewhat blushed; skin characteristically tough separating readily from the tender flesh; season late September to December. It is a desirable variety for home use but is not very satisfactory for growing commercially because there is little demand for a sweet apple of its season except in certain local markets. The tree is a good grower, comes into bearing rather early and is a pretty reliable cropper commonly yielding good crops biennially.

Historical. Origin uncertain. Supposed to have originated in Massachusetts. It is still propagated by nurserymen (12) but it is not being planted in New York now as much as it was a generation ago.

TREE.

Tree large, moderately vigorous to vigorous. *Form* spreading or roundish, rather dense. *Twigs* short to rather long, curved, stout to moderately slender with large terminal buds; internodes short. *Bark* dark brown, heavily streaked with scarf-skin; pubescent near tips. *Lenticels* quite numerous, rather conspicuous, medium size, roundish, raised. *Buds* large, prominent, broad, plump, obtuse, free, pubescent.

FRUIT.

Fruit below medium to rather large, averaging about medium size. *Form* roundish oblate, often somewhat elliptical, ribbed. *Stem* rather short, mod-

MUNSON

erately thick. *Cavity* medium to rather large, acuminate, narrow to medium width, rather unsymmetrical, lightly russeted. *Calyx* medium to small, closed; lobes rather narrow, acute. *Basin* shallow to very shallow, narrow, obtuse or a little abrupt, furrowed, often unsymmetrical.

Skin rather thick and tough separating readily from the flesh, smooth, greenish-yellow often somewhat blushed.

Calyx tube funnel-shape with long cylinder. *Stamens* marginal to median.

Core medium to large, axile or sometimes abaxile; cells often unsymmetrical, closed or somewhat open; core lines clasping the cylinder. *Carpels* roundish to elliptical, emarginate, tufted. *Seeds* medium size, rather short, flat, obtuse, dark brown.

Flesh tinged with yellow, moderately fine-grained, tender, moderately juicy, sweet, good to very good.

Season late September to December.

NORTHERN SWEET.

REFERENCES. 1. *Cultivator*, 6:353. 1849. 2. Battey, *Horticulturist*, 4:316. 1850. fig. 3. Jeffreys, *Ib.*, 4:413. 1850. 4. Barry, 1851:285. 5. Emmons, *Nat. Hist. N. Y.*, 3:42. 1851. col. pl. No. 50 and fig. 6. *Mag. Hort.*, 20:241. 1854. 7. Elliott, 1854:149. 8. Downing, 1857:177. 9. Gregg, 1857:45. 10. Hoffy, *N. A. Pom.*, 1860. col. pl. 11. *Am. Pom. Soc. Cat.*, 1862. 12. Warder, 1867:632. 13. Leroy, 1873:502. fig. 14. Thomas, 1875:508. 15. Lyon, *Mich. Hort. Soc. Rpt.*, 1881:316. 16. Bailey, *An. Hort.*, 1892:245. 17. Waugh, *Vt. Sta. An. Rpt.*, 14:302. 1901. 18. Budd-Hansen, 1903:138.

SYNONYMS. *Golden Sweet* (8, 10, 13). NORTHERN GOLDEN SWEET (5). *Northern Golden Sweet* (2, 7, 8, 13). *Northern Golden Sweeting* (10). NORTHERN SWEET (1, 2, 3, 4, 6, 7, 8, 10, 11, 12, 13, 14, 15, 16, 17, 18). NORTHERN SWEETING (9).

Fruit yellow or sometimes with a crimson cheek. Flesh whitish, fine, tender, juicy, sweet, very good; season midautumn. It is a good apple for the home orchard but not desirable for commercial purposes.

Historical. Supposed to be a native of Chittenden county, Vermont. Brought to notice by Jonathan Battey, Keeseville, Clinton county, N. Y., about 1849, who stated that it had then been cultivated in the vicinity of its origin for about fifty years (2). It has probably been grown more in the Champlain valley than in any other section of the state. It is still occasionally listed by nurserymen (16) but is now seldom planted.

OGDENSBURGH.

REFERENCE. 1. Downing, 1869:291.
SYNONYMS. None.

Originated with A. B. James, Ogdensburg, N. Y. According to Elliott's description cited by Downing (1) the fruit is medium size, whitish-yellow with brownish-blush; flesh tender, very mild subacid, very good; season November and December. We are unacquainted with this variety and have received no report concerning it from any of our correspondents.

OHIO NONPAREIL.

REFERENCES. **1.** *Mag. Hort.,* **14**:114. 1848. **2.** Emmons, *Nat. Hist. N. Y.,* **3**:77. 1851. fig. **3.** Elliott, **1854**:148. fig. **4.** *Mag. Hort.,* **22**:85, 506. 1856. **5.** Hooper, **1857**:15. **6.** Downing, C., *Mag. Hort.,* **27**:59. 1861. **7.** *Am. Pom. Soc. Cat.,* **1862.** **8.** Elliott, *Mag. Hort.,* **32**:51. 1866. **9.** Warder, **1867**:447. fig. **10.** Downing, **1869**:29. fig. **11.** *Am. Pom. Soc. Cat.,* **1869.** **12.** Fitz, **1872**:171. **13.** Thomas, **1875**:203. **14.** Barry, **1883**:340. **15.** Lyon, *Mich. Hort. Soc. Rpt.,* **1890**:294. **16.** Bailey, *An. Hort.,* **1892**:245. **17.** Budd-Hansen, **1903**:141. fig.

SYNONYMS. BELLFLOWER OF THE WEST (5). *Cattell Apple* (10, of Pennsylvania 6). MYERS NONPAREIL (3, 7, 8, 13). *Myers Nonpareil* (6, 9, 10, 12, 14). *Nonpareil* (6). OHIO NONPAREIL (1, 4, 6, 9, 10, 11, 12, 14, 15, 17). *Ohio Nonpareil* (5, 13). OHIO NONPAREIL (2, 16). *Red Bellflower* of some (5). *Rusty Core* (6, 10). *Wells* (5). *Western Beauty* (9, erroneously 10).

A fine fall apple of good color and good quality for either dessert or culinary purposes. The tree is a moderate grower and appears to be hardy and moderately long-lived. It does not come into bearing very young and is not always a reliable cropper. It is regarded as a good variety for home use and some recommend it for commercial planting. Season October and November.

Historical. Originated near Massillon, Ohio. Although this is an old variety having first been described in 1848 (1) we do not find that it has been much disseminated in New York. It is more popular in the Middle West and is still offered by nurserymen in that region (16).

TREE.

Tree medium size, moderately vigorous. *Form* rather spreading, not dense. *Twigs* medium length, curved, rather stout. *Bark* olive-green with some reddish-brown, thinly streaked and mottled with gray scarf-skin. *Lenticels* scattering, conspicuous, large, usually round, becoming laterally compressed. *Buds* medium to small, obtuse, appressed, pubescent.

FRUIT.

Fruit medium to large. *Form* roundish oblate, often obscurely ribbed. *Stem* medium to rather short, rather thick. *Cavity* rather large, acute, deep, pretty symmetrical, more or less russeted, the russet sometimes outspreading over the base. *Calyx* medium or above, closed or slightly open; lobes medium in length, narrow, acute. *Basin* rather small, medium in depth, narrow to moderately wide, somewhat abrupt, rather symmetrical.

Skin pale yellow to deep yellow almost entirely overspread with bright red, mottled and irregularly striped and splashed with carmine. *Dots* moderately numerous, small to medium, areolar with russet center or grayish.

Calyx tube moderately short, conical. *Stamens* basal to nearly median.

Core small, somewhat abaxile; cells symmetrical, not uniformly developed, nearly closed to somewhat open; core lines meeting or slightly clasping. *Carpels* roundish, rather flat, tufted. *Seeds* medium size, moderately long, plump, acute, tufted.

Flesh tinged with yellow, firm, moderately fine, crisp, tender, juicy, agreeable subacid, aromatic, good to very good.

Season October and November.

OHIO PIPPIN.

REFERENCES. 1. Warder, 1867:484. fig. 2. Downing, 1869:292. 3. *Am. Pom. Soc. Cat.*, 1881:12. 4. Thomas, 1885:223. 5. Taylor, *Am. Pom. Soc. Rpt.*, 1895:193. 6. Budd-Hansen, 1903:141. 7. Beach and Clark, *N. Y. Sta. Bul.*, 248:135. 1904.

SYNONYMS. *Buchanan* (1). *Ernst's Apple* (1). ERNST'S PIPPIN (4). *Ernst's Pippin* (2). OHIO PIPPIN (1, 2, 3, 5, 6, 7). *Ohio Pippin* (4). *Shannon* (1, 2, 3, 6).

Fruit of good medium size, quite attractive for a yellow apple, mild in flavor and of good quality. Season late September or October to January; October appears to be its commercial limit in this latitude (7). The tree attains good size, is rather vigorous and healthy, comes into bearing rather young and is a reliable cropper, being almost an annual bearer and often yielding full crops.

Historical. This variety is supposed to have originated in Dayton, Ohio (1, 2). It has been disseminated pretty widely in the Middle West but it is scarcely known among New York fruit growers.

TREE.

Tree rather vigorous. *Form* open, somewhat roundish or spreading and inclined to droop. *Twigs* short, straight, stout; internodes short. *Bark* dark dull brown, lightly streaked with scarf-skin, slightly pubescent near tips. *Lenticels* scattering, medium to below, oblong, not raised. *Buds* very deeply set in the bark, medium size, flat, obtuse, appressed, slightly pubescent.

FRUIT.

Fruit above medium to medium. *Form* oblate conic to roundish oblate, rather irregular in shape being often somewhat elliptical or obscurely ribbed. *Stem* short, slender, usually not exserted. *Cavity* rather large, acute or slightly acuminate, varying sometimes to rather obtuse, deep, broad, often furrowed, sometimes lipped, sometimes russeted and with outspreading russet rays. *Calyx* medium to large, open; lobes reflexed, rather broad, obtuse, separated at the base. *Basin* small and shallow to rather broad, deep and abrupt, sometimes compressed, wrinkled.

Skin smooth, somewhat glossy, attractive bright yellow often with a faint orange or pinkish blush. *Dots* whitish, submerged, sometimes russet or areolar with russet point.

Calyx tube short, rather wide above, cone-shape or approaching truncate funnel-form. *Stamens* basal or nearly so.

Core small, usually axile; cells symmetrical, closed or partly open; core lines clasping. *Carpels* broadly roundish, approaching elliptical, but slightly emarginate if at all, mucronate, slightly tufted. *Seeds* numerous, light colored, rather small, very plump, obtuse.

Flesh whitish or tinged with yellow, firm, fine, tender, crisp, moderately juicy, mild subacid becoming mildly sweet, good.

OKABENA.

REFERENCES. 1. *Am. Pom. Soc. Rpt.*, 1887:132. 2. *Ib., Cat.*, 1899:19. 3. Macoun, *Can. Dept. Agr. Rpt.*, 1901:97. 4. Hansen, *S. D. Sta. Bul.*, 76:78. 1902. fig. 5. Dickens and Greene, *Kan. Sta. Bul.*, 106:54. 1902. 6. Munson, *Me. Sta. An. Rpt.*, 18:84. 1902. 7. Budd-Hansen, 1903:141. fig.

SYNONYMS. OKABENA (1, 2, 3, 4, 5, 7). OKOBENA (6).

An autumn apple not particularly attractive in appearance, nor more than moderately good in quality. Not recommended for planting in New York.

Historical. Originated in 1871 near Worthington, Minn., from seed of Oldenburg said to be fertilized by Wealthy (7). Received for testing at this Station in 1892, from the Jewel Nursery Company which introduced this variety. In 1899 it was given a place on the list of the American Pomological Society as a variety of value in the Upper Mississippi valley (2). So far as we can learn it has been grown in the East only in an experimental way.

OLDENBURG.

REFERENCES. 1. *London Hort. Soc. Cat.*, 1831:No. 341. 2. Kenrick, 1832:64. 3. Manning, 1838:52. 4. Ives, *Mag. Hort.*, 6:125. 1840. 5. Manning, *Ib.*, 7:44. 1841. 6. Downing, 1845:82. 7. Cole, 1849:102. 8. Thomas, 1849:147. 9. Hovey, *Mag. Hort.*, 16:495. 1850. fig. 10. Emmons, *Nat. Hist. N. Y.*, 3:34. 1851. 11. Barry, 1851:283. 12. Waring, 1851:28. 13. Elliott, 1854:131. 14. Hooper, 1857:30. 15. Gregg, 1857:42. 16. *Am. Pom. Soc. Cat.*, 1862. 17. Barry, *Horticulturist*, 22:148. 1867. 18. Warder, 1867:431. 19. Todd, 1871:186. fig. 20. Leroy, 1873:148. fig. 21. *Montreal Hort. Soc. Rpt.*, 1876:6. 22. *Ib.*, 6:97. 1880. 23. *Am. Pom. Soc. Cat.*, 1883:12. 24. Hogg, 1884:64. 25. *Can. Hort.* 11:221. 1888. 26. Hoskins, *Rural N. Y.*, 47:646. 1888. 27. Dunlap, *Ill. Hort. Soc. Rpt.*, 1889:23. 28. *Can. Hort.*, 12:75, 110. 1889. 29. *Montreal Hort. Soc. Rpt.*, 15:26. 1890. 30. Lyon, *Mich. Hort. Soc. Rpt.*, 1890:294. 31. Bailey, *An. Hort.*, 1892:237. 32. *Am. Gard.*, 14:519. 1893. 33. *Can. Hort.*, 17:291. 1894. 34. *Rural N. Y.*, 53:28. 1894. 35. *Am. Gard.*, 17:519. 1896. 36. Bunyard, *Jour. Roy. Hort. Soc.*, 1898:354. 37. Woolverton, *Ont. Fr. Stas. An. Rpt.*, 6:8. 1899. figs. 38. Craig, *Cyc. of Hort.*, 1901:1404. 39. Van Deman, *Rural N. Y.*, 60:248. 1901. 40. Alwood, *Va. Sta. Bul.*, 130:121. 1901. 41. Waugh, *Vt.*

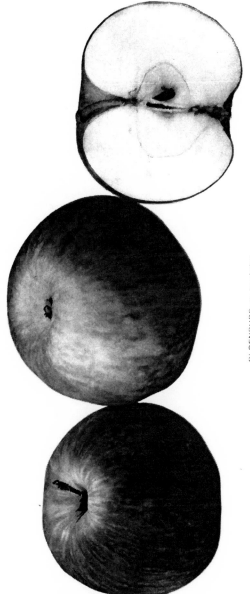

OLDENBURG (Redhead Size)

Sta. An. Rpt., **14**:302. 1901. **42.** Hansen, *S. D. Sta. Bul.*, **76**:46. 1902. **43.** Ib., **76**:79. 1902. *fig.* **44.** Dickens and Greene, *Kan. Sta. Bul.*, **106**:52. 1902. **45.** Bruner, *N. C. Sta. Bul.*, **182**:21. 1903. **46.** Farrand, *Mich. Sta. Bul.*, **205**:45. 1903. **47.** Budd-Hansen, 1903:141. *fig.* **48.** Powell and Fulton, *U. S. B. P. I. Bul.*, **48**:51. 1903. **49.** Beach and Clark, *N. Y. Sta. Bul.*, **248**:136. 1904.

SYNONYMS. *Baroveski* (20). *Barowiski* (20). *Borovitsky* (20, 37, 38). BOROWICKI (20). *Borowitski* (24). *Borowitsky* (43). *Charlamowiski* (24). *Charlamowski d'Automne* (20). *Charlamowskircher Nalleoid* (20). *Charlamowsky* (43). DUCHESS (27, 29, 32, 35, 37, 38, 43). DUCHESS OF OLDENBURG (3, 4, 11, 12, 16, 17, 19, 21, 22, 24, 25, 28, 31, 33, 36, 44). *Duchess of Oldenburg* (23, 41, 48, 49). DUCHESS OF OLDENBURGH (1, 2, 5, 9, 10, 14, 18). *Duchesse d'Oldenbourg* (20). DUTCHESS (13). DUTCHESS OF OLDENBERG (15). DUTCHESS OF OLDENBURGH (6, 7, 8). *Dutchess of Oldenburgh* (13). *New Brunswick* (34). OLDENBURG (23, 26, 39, 45, 48, 49). *Oldenburg* (35, 37). OLDENBURGH (30, 34). OLDENBURG, *Duchess of* (40, 42, 46, 47).

This Russian apple is known throughout the West either by the name Duchess, or by the full name Duchess of Oldenburg; the American Pomological Society has abbreviated the full name to Oldenburg, but this has not been generally accepted by Western fruit growers. In European nurseries it is propagated under the names of Charlamowsky and Borowitsky. It was early imported into the West, coming to this country by the way of England and it was the extreme hardiness of this variety in the early test winters that kept up the hopes of prairie orchardists in time of great discouragement and led to the importations of more varieties from Russia (42).

Oldenburg is one of the most valuable of the Russian apples thus far introduced into this country. It is of good size and attractive appearance. It is generally highly esteemed for home use on account of its excellent culinary qualities and with some fruit growers it has proved a very profitable variety for the commercial orchard. When properly grown and carefully handled it stands shipment pretty well and sells well for a variety of its season. In some few localities in Western New York it is grown in sufficient quantities so that it can be shipped in car lots to distant markets, but in very many places it is produced in greater quantities than the local markets can absorb and yet not in quantities large enough so that it can be economically shipped to distant markets. Since the fruit is quite perishable it does not stand heat well before shipment and goes down rather quickly, particularly if the weather is unfavorable. When sent to distant markets it should be shipped under ice. The fruit ripens in succession so that several pickings are required in order to secure the crop in prime marketable condition. It is in season during late August and September, but it may be used for culinary purposes before it is fully ripe. The tree is highly valued because of its great hardiness. It is vigorous when young but with age it becomes a rather moderate or slow grower. It is only moderately long-lived, but is a reliable cropper, yielding good crops biennially, often with lighter crops alternating. Generally speaking, the trees require good cultivation, thorough fertilizing and careful spraying in order to secure the best commercial results. The fruit hangs fairly well to the tree till it is ripe. It is quite uniform in size and quality, with but a small percentage of loss from unmarketable fruit.

Historical. This is one of the four pioneers among Russian apples in America, the other three being Alexander, Tetofsky and Red Astrachan (38). These four varieties were imported by the Massachusetts Horticultural Society from the London, England, Horticultural Society about 1835. Oldenburg was brought to England from Russia about twenty years prior to that date. It was tested by Robert Manning, Superintendent of the Test Garden of the Massachusetts Horticultural Society at Salem who published the following description in 1838 (3): "A valuable and handsome apple said to be of Russian origin. The size is middling, form round and rather flat; skin of a beautiful yellow, striped with red; flavor very pleasant and good. It bears well and ripens in September and October." In 1850 Hovey wrote, " Mr. Manning, we believe, first proved the Duchess of Oldenburg and gave a brief account of it in his Book of Fruits. Since then it has been considerably disseminated, and though yet far from being common is to be found in many fine collections of fruit" (9). Later it became disseminated throughout the Middle West and Northwest where it proved to be much superior in hardiness to Baldwin, Rhode Island *Greening*, Northern Spy and other varieties which have been commonly cultivated in this state. Its ability to withstand severe climates encouraged the importation of other Russian sorts some of which have proved valuable in the northern portion of the apple belt. Oldenburg is commonly listed by nurserymen (31) and its planting both in home orchards and in commercial orchards is increasing in this state.

TREE.

Tree medium in size. *Form* at first upright spreading but eventually roundish. *Twigs* moderately long, curved, slender; internodes long. *Bark* dark brown, lightly mottled with scarf-skin; slightly pubescent. *Lenticels* scattering, small to medium, oblong, not raised. *Buds* medium size, plump, obtuse, free, slightly pubescent.

Fruit medium to large, averaging above medium, uniform in size and shape. *Form* roundish oblate to oblate, regular, symmetrical. *Stem* short to sometimes medium, moderately slender. *Cavity* acute to acuminate, deep, broad, usually partly covered with greenish-russet. *Calyx* medium to rather large, usually closed; lobes rather broad, acute. *Basin* moderately deep to deep, wide, abrupt, smooth or with small mammiform protuberances.

Skin moderately thick, tender, smooth, pale greenish-yellow or pale yellow, almost covered with irregular splashes and stripes of bright red mottled and shaded with crimson. *Dots* scattering, small, light colored. *Prevailing effect* red striped; attractive.

Calyx tube moderately long, rather wide, funnel-shape with broad truncate cylinder or approaching urn-shape. *Stamens* median.

Core medium to rather large, axile; cells symmetrical, closed or slightly open; core lines clasping. *Carpels* broadly ovate, slightly emarginate. *Seeds* medium to rather large, wide, obtuse to acute, moderately plump, dark brown.

Flesh tinged with yellow, rather firm, moderately fine, crisp, tender, juicy, sprightly subacid, aromatic, good to very good for culinary purposes. It has too much acidity for a good dessert apple.

Season late August and September.

ORANGE.

REFERENCES. 1. M'Mahon, *Am. Gard. Cal.*, 1806:585. 2. Coxe, 1817:139. 3. Emmons, *Nat. Hist. N. Y.*, 3:91. 1851. 4. *Horticulturist*, 8:247. 1853. 5. *Mag. Hort.*, 19:172. 1853. 6. Hooper, 1857:67. 7. Downing, 1857:178. 8. Warder, 1867:728. 9. Downing, 1869:294. 10. Bailey, *An. Hort.*, 1892: 245.

SYNONYMS. None.

Different varieties of the apple have been known under the name Orange. The Fall Orange has already been described on page 60.

Orange has sometimes been used as a synonym for Lowell which is described on page 128.

ORANGE OF NEW JERSEY (1, 2, 3, 6, 7, 8, 9, 10). Coxe (2) gives the following description of this variety: " This is a fine table apple in the fall and early winter months; and is thought to be a good cider fruit; the size is small, the form oblong — the colour a greenish-yellow — the flesh yellow, rich, juicy and sprightly; the tree is of moderate size, the growth upright, and its fruitfulness great. It is much cultivated in several of the middle counties of New-Jersey as a highly estimable apple." Downing (7, 9) states that the tree is vigorous and moderately productive; the fruit pleasant subacid; very good; season September and October.

ORANGE OF PENNSYLVANIA. A variety which originated at Reading, Pa., was brought to notice under the name Orange by the *ad interim* report of the Fruit Committee of the Pennsylvania Horticultural Society in 1853 (4, 5). The fruit is described as medium size, roundish, nearly orange-yellow, sprightly, good (4, 5, 8, 9). We have received no reports concerning this variety from any of our correspondents and so far as we know it is not in cultivation in New York.

ORANGE PIPPIN.

REFERENCES. 1. Forsyth, 1803:54. 2. Ib., 1824:119. 3. Buel, *N. Y. Bd. Agr. Mem.*, 1826:476. 4. *London Hort. Soc. Cat.*, 1831:No. 587. 5. Kenrick, 1832:81. 6. Lindley, 1833:80. 7. Warder, 1867:728. 8. *Am. Pom. Soc. Cat.*, 1869. 9. Downing, 1872:62 app. fig. 10. Leroy, 1873:457. fig. 11. *Am. Pom. Soc. Cat.*, 1873. 12. Hogg, 1884:116. 13. Ib., 1884:164. 14. Thomas, 1885:519. 15. Lyon, *Mich. Hort. Soc. Rpt.*, 1890:296. 16. Bailey, *An. Hort.*, 1892:245.

SYNONYMS. *Englese Orange Appel* (12). ISLE OF WIGHT PIPPIN (4, 12). *Isle of Wight Pippin* (5, 6). *Isle of Wight Orange* (4, 5, 6, 12). MARIGOLD (10). *Marigold* (5). *Marigold Creed's* (10). *Marigold Pippin* (2). *Marygold* (6). ORANGE (7). ORANGE PIPPIN (1, 2, 3, 5, 6, 8, 9, 11, 13, 14, 15, 16). *Orange Pippin* (4, 12). *Pomme d'Orange* (12).

The above references are not all to the same variety and are included only because in many cases it is uncertain which variety the writer had in mind.

At least two varieties have been known in this country under the name Orange Pippin but so far as we can learn neither of them is now considered of superior value by fruit growers and both are going out of cultivation. One, which has been called also the Isle of Wight Pippin, Isle of Wight Orange, Marygold and Marigold, was disseminated from the Isle of Wight where, as some have supposed, it was brought from Normandy (1, 3, 4, 5, 6, 10, 12). Fruit medium size, roundish, skin yellowish, golden gray russeted and highly colored with orange and red on the sunny side; flesh firm, crisp, pleasant acid, suitable for dessert; season October to January (6, 9). This was entered on the list of the American Pomological Society in 1869, dropped in 1871 and re-entered in 1873.

An Orange Pippin grown in some parts of New Jersey is described (8, 9, 11, 14, 15) as a profitable summer market apple of unknown origin. Tree vigorous, at first upright but eventually spreading; a reliable biennial cropper. Fruit medium or above, pale yellow with some orange red in the sun; flesh white, half fine, tender, pleasant subacid; season September and October.

ORANGE SWEET.

REFERENCES. 1. *Mag. Hort.*, 1:396. 1835. 2. Warder, 1867:566. 3. Downing, 1869:295. 4. Thomas, 1885:519.

SYNONYMS. *Orange Russet* (2). ORANGE SWEET (3, 4). ORANGE SWEETING (1, 2).

Several varieties are described under this name by Downing (3): one from Ohio, large, greenish-yellow; flesh whitish, tender, sweet, good; season October and November: one from Massachusetts, the fruit medium, oblate, greenish-yellow; the flesh yellowish-white, rather coarse, rich, sweet; season August and September: and one from Maine; fruit medium, roundish ovate, bright yellow with blush; flesh yellowish, tender, sweet, rich; season September and October.

Warder (2) describes under the name Orange Sweeting or Russet "An eastern variety not much cultivated; fruit large, very round, regular, greenish-yellow, bronzy, orange russeted; flesh rather tough, fine-grained, juicy, good; season December."

The name Orange Sweet has also been used as a synonym for both Munson (p. 146) and Golden Sweet (p. 81).

OSTRAKOFF.

REFERENCES. 1. Gibb, *Montreal Hort. Soc. Rpt.*, **1883**:106. fig. **2.** *Ib.*, *Ia. Hort. Soc. Rpt.*, **1883**:443. **3.** Budd, *Ia. Agr. Coll. Bul.*, **1885**:18. **4.** Schroeder, *Montreal Hort. Soc. Rpt.*, **1886–87**:71. **5.** Craig, *Ib.*, **1886–87**:103. **6.** Budd, *Rural N. Y.*, **47**:692. 1888. **7.** *Ib.*, *Ia. Agr. Coll. Bull.*, **1890**:23. **8.** Bailey, *An. Hort.*, **1892**:246. **9.** Budd, *Ia. Sta. Bul.*, **19**:540. 1892. **10.** Taylor, *Me. Pom. Soc. Rpt.*, **1892**:58. **11.** *Can. Hort.*, **16**:402. 1893. **12.** Beach, *N. Y. Sta. An. Rpt.*, **13**:583. 1894. **13.** Munson, *Me. Sta. Rpt.*, **1896**:75. **14.** Thomas, **1897**:648. **15.** Munson, *Me. Sta. Rpt.*, **1902**:84. **16.** Hansen, *S. D. Sta. Bul.*, **76**:80. 1902. fig. **17.** Beach and Clark, *N. Y. Sta. Bul.*, **248**:136. 1904.

SYNONYMS. *Astravaskoe* (12). OSTRAKOFF (7, 9, 10, 12, 13, 15, 16, 17). OSTRAKOFF GLASS (11). *Ostrakoff Glass* (12). OSTREKOFF (3, 5). *Ostrekoff's Glass* (1, 2). *Ostrekovskaya Steklianka* (3). OSTREKOWSKAJA STEKLIANKA (1, 2). OSTROKOFF (6, 8, 14). OSTROKOFF'S GLASS (4). *No. 4 M* (4, 5, 6, 7, 9, 11, 13, 15, 16). *No. 472* (1, 3).

A Russian variety of good size, greenish-yellow, brisk subacid, fair to good quality. Its keeping qualities vary much in different seasons. As grown at this Station it is commonly in its prime from late September into November but a portion of the fruit may often be kept into the winter in very good condition. It is reported as a promising variety for portions of Northern New England and other regions where superior hardiness is a prime requisite. It is of no value where our common standard varieties succeed.

Historical. Described by Budd in 1885 under the name Ostrakoff's Glass and in 1890 under the name Ostrakoff (3, 7). It was received in 1884 for testing at this Station from Ellwanger and Barry, Rochester, N. Y., under the name Astravaskoe.

TREE.

Tree moderately vigorous. *Form* spreading or roundish, open. *Twigs* short, curved, stout with large terminal buds; internodes medium. *Bark* dark brown tinged with green, heavily streaked with scarf-skin; pubescent near tips. *Lenticels* quite numerous, medium size, round, raised, rather conspicuous. *Buds* prominent, large, long, plump, obtuse, free.

FRUIT.

Fruit medium or above, pretty uniform in size and shape. *Form* roundish to somewhat ovate or oblong, somewhat conical, a little angular. *Stem* characteristically long, often curved, twisted or irregularly enlarged or inserted under a fleshy protuberance. *Cavity* acute or approaching acuminate, shallow to moderately deep, medium in width to narrow, partly covered with light greenish-russet, often lipped. *Calyx* closed or open, rather large, leafy; lobes rather broad, acute to obtuse. *Basin* characteristically irregular, medium in width and depth, abrupt, sharply ridged and wrinkled.

Skin moderately thin, rather tough, smooth, pale waxen-yellow sometimes with a faint reddish shade. *Dots* very numerous, small, submerged, often areolar.

Calyx tube medium to large, rather wide, conical to peculiarly funnel-form, with broad truncate cylinder. *Stamens* basal to median.

Core medium size, axile; cells closed or slightly open; core lines meeting. *Carpels* roundish to broadly ovate, emarginate. *Seeds* medium brown, large, wide, rather flat, obtuse to acute.

Flesh yellowish-white, firm, rather fine, juicy, brisk subacid, fair to good. *Season* late fall and early winter.

PALOUSE.

REFERENCES. **1.** Van Deman, *U. S. Pom. Rpt.*, **1891** :390. **2.** *Rural N. Y.*, **50** :815. 1891. **3.** Hexamer, *Am. Pom. Soc. Rpt.*, **1891** :159. **4.** Williams, *Gard. and For.*, **5** :11. 1892. **5.** Bailey, *An. Hort.*, **1892** :246. **6.** Craig, *Can. Dept. Agr. Rpt.*, **1896** :133. **7.** Macoun, *Ib.*, **1901** :97.

SYNONYMS. None.

Palouse is a comparatively new variety which originated in Washington. In color, texture, flavor and aroma it is so much like Tompkins King that some suppose it to be a seedling of that variety. Its form, however, is quite different from that of Tompkins King, typical fruit being oblong, as described by Craig (6) and others (1, 2), rather than oblate or roundish oblate, as described by Hexamer (3) and Macoun (7). It is hardly as good a keeper as Tompkins King and would probably be classed as a late fall variety, being in season from October to early winter. It is, however, more productive than Tompkins King and is being much planted in commercial orchards in Washington where many regard it as one of the most valuable of the seedling varieties which have originated in that region. It appears to be worthy of testing in New York.

Historical. Palouse originated in Whitman county, Washington, from seed brought from Illinois in 1879. The original tree is located five miles east of Colfax[1]. It was introduced about 1892 by George Ruedy, Colfax, Wash., whose

---

1 Ruedy, Letter and Circular, 1904.

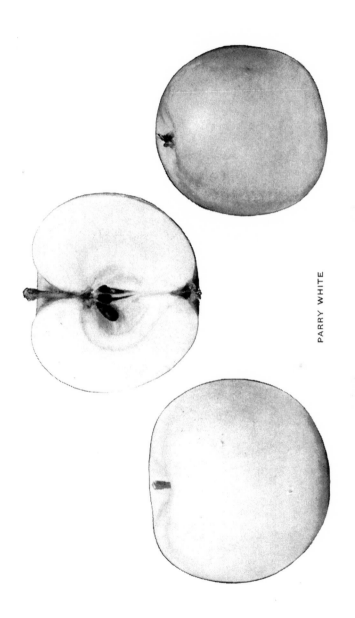

PARRY WHITE

attention was first called to the variety in 1889 when it took first premium as the best seedling apple exhibited at the Whitman County Fair. It is as yet but little grown in the East and so far as we can learn it has as yet been planted in New York to but a limited extent and for trial only.

FRUIT (2, 3).

Fruit large. *Form* oblong conic, ribbed or scalloped. *Stem* long, slender. *Cavity* remarkably deep. *Calyx* closed or partly open. *Basin* rather shallow to deep, distinctly furrowed, the furrows often extending to the cavity.

Skin bright yellow, blushed and more than half covered with crimson, splashed, blotched and dotted with darker red. *Prevailing effect* attractive red and yellow.

Core large.

Flesh yellowish, crisp, firm, tender, juicy, very aromatic, subacid, very good. *Season* October and early winter.

PARRY WHITE.

REFERENCES. 1. Downing, 1872:25 app. 2. Bailey, *An. Hort.*, 1892:246. 3. Beach, *N. Y. Sta. An. Rpt.*, 14:263. 1895. 4. Beach and Clark, *N. Y. Sta. Bul.*, 248:137. 1904.

SYNONYMS. *Imperial White* (1). PARRY WHITE (1, 2, 3, 4). *Superior White* (1). *White Apple* (1).

Fruit pale yellow or whitish, waxen, of medium size; quite attractive in appearance for an apple of its class. The flesh is white, juicy, subacid, good in quality for either dessert or culinary use. It follows Yellow Transparent in season, beginning to ripen late in August or early in September and continuing in use into or through October (4). The tree comes into bearing young and is an annual cropper, yielding good to very heavy crops. In spite of its remarkable productiveness it makes a pretty good growth. It is worthy of trial where an apple of its type is desired.

Historical. Origin unknown. It is supposed to be a Pennsylvania apple. It is occasionally listed by nurserymen (2). It has not yet become known to any considerable extent in New York.

TREE.

Tree of medium size and moderately vigorous. *Form* at first upright spreading but after bearing full crops it becomes roundish and somewhat drooping; dense. *Twigs* short, curved, stout with large terminal buds; internodes short. *Bark* brown tinged with olive-green, lightly streaked with scarf-skin; slightly pubescent near tips. *Lenticels* quite numerous, rather conspicuous, medium size, round, not raised. *Buds* medium to large, plump, obtuse, free, pubescent.

FRUIT.

Fruit usually medium but varies according to the abundance of the crop from below medium to rather large; quite uniform in size and shape. *Form* nearly globular varying to somewhat oblate or slightly inclined to ovate, quite regular. *Stem* above medium to rather short, slender. *Cavity* slightly acuminate, medium to shallow, medium in width, smooth, symmetrical. *Calyx* small, closed; lobes medium in length, narrow, acute. *Basin* very shallow, moderately narrow to rather broad, obtuse, smooth or slightly wrinkled, symmetrical.

Skin moderately thick, rather tough, waxen yellowish-white or greenish, Occasionally blushed. *Dots* medium size to very small, pale or brown, numerous, depressed.

Calyx tube short, narrow, funnel-shape. *Stamens* marginal to median.

Core medium to small, abaxile; cells open; core lines meeting or slightly clasping. *Carpels* round, emarginate. *Seeds* medium or above, acute or inclined to obtuse, light brown.

Flesh white, quite firm, rather fine, tender, juicy, subacid, good.

Season very late August into or through October.

PATTEN.

REFERENCES. 1. Watrous, *Am. Pom. Soc. Rpt.*, **1889** :124. 2. Patten, C. G., *Descriptive Circular*, **1891**. 3. Taylor, *Me. Pom. Soc. Rpt.*, **1892** :60. 4. *Me. Sta. Rpt.*, **1892** :90. 5. Macoun, *Can. Hort.*, **22** :396. 1899. 6. *Am. Pom. Soc. Cat.*, **1899** :19. 7. Macoun, *Can. Dept. Agr. Rpt.*, **1901** :98. 8. Munson, *Me. Sta. An. Rpt.*, 18 :84. 1902. 9. Hansen, *S. D. Sta. Bul.*, 76 :81. 1902. fig. 10. Budd-Hansen, 1903 :145. fig. 11. Ragan, *U. S. B. P. I. Bul.*, 56 :226. 1905.

SYNONYMS. *Duchess No. 3* (2, 9, 10). PATTEN (11). *Patten's Duchess No. 3* (11). PATTEN GREENING (1, 2, 3, 4, 5, 6, 7, 8, 9). *Patten Greening* (11). PATTEN *Greening* (10).

A seedling of Oldenburg which, on account of its hardiness, productiveness and the uniformly large size of its fruit is valuable in the northern portions of the apple-growing regions of the country (1, 5, 6, 8, 9, 10). It is grown as far north as the Red River valley of Minnesota and North Dakota and in other regions where the winters are correspondingly severe. It is attractive in color for a green apple, has a sprightly subacid flavor and good texture and is very good in quality for culinary use. The tree is a somewhat stronger grower than Oldenburg, with limbs strongly shouldered (2, 9, 10). As grown at this Station it comes into bearing moderately young and is an annual cropper, yielding moderate to full crops. It is worthy of trial in the colder regions of the state.

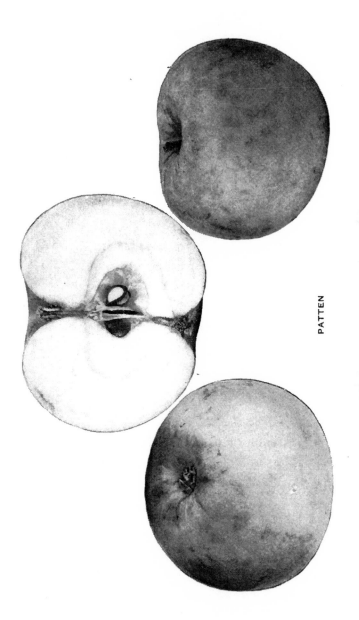

PATTEN

Historical. Originated by C. G. Patten, Charles City, Ia. (2), who states that it is a seedling of the Oldenburg from seed grown near Portage, Wis., and planted by him at Charles City, Ia., in the fall of 1869. It was first illustrated and described in the catalogue of the originator in the autumn of 1885 when stock of this variety was first offered for sale. In 1899 it was entered in the catalogue of the American Pomological Society as a valuable variety for the Upper Mississippi valley (6). It has as yet been but little disseminated in New York.

TREE.

Tree moderately vigorous with moderately long, somewhat stout, curved, drooping branches. *Form* spreading, dense, flat. *Twigs* rather short, somewhat curved, moderately stout or rather slender; internodes medium to long. *Bark* brownish-red with some olive-green, lightly streaked with scarf-skin; slightly pubescent. *Lenticels* scattering, small, roundish, sometimes raised. *Buds* medium size, plump, acute, free, slightly pubescent.

FRUIT.

Fruit medium to large, pretty uniform in size and shape. *Form* oblate or roundish oblate, sometimes inclined to conic, usually regular, pretty symmetrical. *Stem* very short to medium in length, moderately thick. *Cavity* acuminate, deep or sometimes medium in depth, rather broad or compressed, russeted and with outspreading russet rays. *Calyx* large or very large, closed or somewhat open. *Basin* deep to medium in depth, medium in width, often abrupt, usually smooth and symmetrical.

Skin moderately thin, tough, smooth, clear pale greenish-yellow, sometimes blushed and occasionally faintly striped. *Dots* small, numerous, pale and submerged or brownish.

Calyx tube conical to funnel-shape. *Stamens* median to basal.

Core below medium to small, axile or somewhat abaxile; cells sometimes unsymmetrical, closed or partly open; core lines clasping. *Carpels* roundish, irregular. *Seeds* dark brown, medium or above, plump, obtuse.

Flesh tinged with yellow, moderately firm, a little coarse, rather tender, juicy, sprightly subacid, good in quality especially for culinary purposes.

Season October to January.

PEACH (*MONTREAL*).

REFERENCES. 1. *Montreal Hort. Soc. Rpt.*, 1876:7. 2. Raynes, *Ib.*, 1879:26. 3. Budd, *Ia. Hort. Soc. Rpt.*, 1880:524. 4. Lyon, *Mich. Hort. Soc. Rpt.*, 1881:178. 5. *Am. Pom. Soc. Cat.*, 1883:12. 6. Thomas, 1885:520. 7. *Montreal Hort. Soc. Rpt.*, 1885:99. 8. *Ib.*, 1886-87:92. 9. Burnet, *Can. Hort.*, 12:339. 1889. 10. Hamilton, *Montreal Hort. Soc. Rpt.*, 15:26. 1890. 11. Bailey, *An. Hort.*, 1892:246. 12. Munson, *Me. Sta. Rpt.*, 1893:133. 13. Hoskins, *Am. Gard.*, 15:272. 1894. 14. Hansen, *S. D. Sta. Bul.*, 76:82. 1902. 15. Budd-Hansen, 1903:147.

SYNONYMS. *Canada Peach* (14). *Montreal Peach* (3, 14). PEACH (3, 11, 14). PEACH APPLE *of Montreal* (13). PEACH OF MONTREAL (1, 4, 5, 6, 7, 8, 9). PEACH *of Montreal* (2, 10, 12, 15). *Pomme Peche* (1).

Fruit predominantly yellow with some red; in form it somewhat resembles Porter being oval or conical. It is salable in local markets but being easily bruised it does not stand transportation well (2, 3, 6, 13). The tree is hardy, thrifty and very productive.

According to Hoskins it is a very popular fall apple all through Northern New England and Eastern Canada. It has long been the leading market apple of its season, September, in Montreal and the surrounding territory on both sides of the line. Its season does not extend far into October except by extra care but it forms a very good successor to the Yellow Transparent which it resembles except for its blushed cheek (13).

This variety is but little known in New York. It cannot be expected to displace Oldenburg which is of the same season, more productive (10) and much better known.

Historical. Some writers state that this is a variety of French origin (1) but Hoskins considers this doubtful. He states: "Some of its characters would indicate it to be a Russian apple which has reached Canada via France, but this is only a conjecture" (13).

PEACH POND.

REFERENCES. 1. Downing, 1845:91. 2. Thomas, 1849:145. *fig.* 3. Emmons, *Nat. Hist. N. Y.,* 3:36. 1851. 4. Elliott, 1854:151. *fig.* 5. Hooper, 1857:68. 6. Warder, 1867:476. *fig.* 7. *Am. Pom. Soc. Cat.,* 1871:8. 8. Lyon, *Mich. Hort. Soc. Rpt.,* 1890:296. 9. Bailey, *An. Hort.,* 1892:246. 10. Burrill and McCluer, *Ill. Sta. Bul.,* 45:335. 1896.

SYNONYMS. PEACH POND (3, 4, 5, 6, 7, 8, 9). PEACH-POND SWEET (1, 2). PEACH POUND SWEET (10).

A beautiful autumn sweet apple of excellent quality in season from September to November. The tree is vigorous and spreading. It originated in Dutchess county, N. Y. (1). It was entered in the Catalogue of the American Pomological Society in 1871 and dropped in 1899. Although it has long been in cultivation it has failed to establish itself as a commercial variety in New York and is comparatively little grown for home use.

FRUIT (1, 6).

Fruit medium to small. *Form* slightly conic, rather flat, angular and a little one-sided. *Stem* medium to long, slender, green, sometimes knobbed. *Cavity* acute, deep, regular, brown. *Calyx* small, closed. *Basin* narrow, regular, wrinkled.

Skin smooth, pale yellow lightly covered with mixed striped red and beautifully splashed with crimson.

Flesh yellowish, very mellow, fine-grained, moderately juicy, rich, sweet, agreeable, very good or almost best.

Season September to November.

PEARSALL.

References. 1. Downing, 1869:300. 2. Thomas, 1875:508.
Synonyms. Pearsall's Sweet (1, 2).

This variety is supposed to have originated in Queens county, N. Y. According to Downing the fruit is a good keeper and valuable for baking. The tree upright spreading, quite productive. Fruit rather large, yellow, partly covered with light red. Flesh moderately juicy, sweet, good. Season November to January (1).

PEASE.

References. 1. *Rural N. Y.*, 54:776. 1895. fig. 2. Heiges, *U. S. Pom. Rpt.*, 1895:36. 3. *Rural N. Y.*, 56:222. 1897. 4. *Am. Pom. Soc. Cat.*, 1899: 19. 5. *Rural N. Y.*, 61:249. 1902. 6. Budd-Hansen, 1903:147. 7. J. W. Adams and Co., Springfield, Mass., *Cat.*
Synonyms. Pease, *Walter* (4, 6). Walter Pease (1, 2, 3, 5, 7).

A pleasant-flavored apple of good size, attractive appearance and excellent dessert quality, but too mild in flavor to excel for culinary uses. The fruit being rather tender requires careful handling and on this account is better adapted for local than for distant markets. It is worthy of the attention of New York fruit growers where a dessert apple of this type is desired. The crop ripens unevenly. The earliest fruit comes in season the latter part of September or early in October, while a considerable portion of the later ripening fruit may remain sound till midwinter or later. Sometimes there is considerable loss from premature dropping of the fruit during September wind storms. The tree is a good grower, hardy, comes into bearing moderately young and is a pretty reliable cropper, alternating light with heavier crops.

Historical. Originated in the seedling orchard of Walter Pease, Somers, Conn., in the early part of the last century (3). It was at first propagated by the Shakers near the place of its origin and there came to be recognized locally as a valuable variety. Within recent years it has been propagated to a considerable extent by nurserymen and is being more widely disseminated.

Tree.

Tree rather large, moderately vigorous to vigorous. *Form* upright to roundish. *Twigs* moderately long, a little curved, stout; internodes medium to short. *Bark* clear brownish-red, heavily coated with scarf-skin; pubescent. *Lenticels* scattering, below medium to above medium, roundish, slightly raised. *Buds* below medium to above, broad, plump, rather obtuse, free or nearly so, slightly pubescent.

FRUIT.

Fruit large or above medium, somewhat variable in size and shape. *Form* flattened at base, varying from oblate to roundish oblong and often inclined to conic; sides often unequal. *Stem* below medium to long, slender. *Cavity* obtuse to acute, moderately deep to deep, broad, sometimes lipped, often somewhat russeted. *Calyx* usually medium to large, closed or nearly so; lobes leafy. *Basin* moderately deep or sometimes shallow, rather narrow, abrupt, often compressed or furrowed, wrinkled.

Skin thin, tough, smooth, somewhat glossy, with pale green or yellowish ground color which in highly colored specimens is largely covered with bright red, striped with bright carmine and flecked with whitish scarf-skin. *Dots* numerous, often submerged, whitish or russet, sometimes areolar. *Prevailing effect* greenish-yellow more or less striped with red.

Calyx tube small, conical.

Core small to medium, axile; cells partly open or sometimes closed; core lines meeting. *Carpels* small, roundish, somewhat tufted. *Seeds* rather large, narrow, long, somewhat tufted, dark; often some are abortive.

Flesh whitish, slightly tinged with yellow, firm, rather fine, crisp, tender, juicy, aromatic, sprightly, mild pleasant subacid, good to very good for dessert.

Season October to midwinter.

PEASGOOD NONSUCH.

REFERENCES. 1. Downing, 1881:100 app. 2. Hogg, 1884:170. 3. Bailey, *An. Hort.*, 1892:246. 4. *Can. Hort.*, 15:346. 1892. 5. Bunyard, *Jour. Roy. Hort. Soc.*, 1898:356.

SYNONYMS. PEASGOOD'S NONESUCH (1, 2, 5). PEASGOOD NONSUCH (3, 4).

An English culinary apple, very large, green or yellowish, blushed and striped with red, excellent for culinary use. In season during September and October (1). In England it is regarded as one of the valuable varieties introduced in the last fifty years (2, 5). It has been but little tested in this country.

PERRY REDSTREAK.

REFERENCES. 1. *Horticulturist*, 24:157. 1869. 2. Downing, 1876:63 app. 3. Ragan, *U. S. B. P. I. Bul.*, 56:230. 1905.

SYNONYMS. PERRY REDSTREAK (3). PERRY RED STREAK (1, 2). *Perry Red Streak* (3).

A November apple of medium size and mild flavor. It originated at Lowville, N. Y., with Dr. David Perry (1). The tree is hardy, vigorous and a reliable cropper alternating heavy with lighter crops. The fruit is of medium size, yellow, shaded, striped and splashed with light and dark red; flesh whitish, fine, tender, juicy, slightly aromatic, mild subacid (2).

This variety is unknown to us and we have received no report concerning it from any of our correspondents.

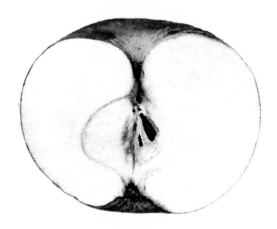

PEASE *WALTER*

PETER.

REFERENCES. 1. *Iowa Hort. Soc. Rpt.*, **1886**:180. 2. *N. Y. Sta. An. Rpt.*, 7:50, 90. 1888. 3. Bailey, *An. Hort.*, **1892**:246. 4. Beach, *N. Y. Sta. An. Rpt.*, **12**:601. 1893. 5. Heiges, *U. S. Pom. Rpt.*, **1895**:31. 6. Munson, *Me. Sta. Rpt.*, **1896**:75. 7. Beach, *W. N. Y. Hort. Soc. Rpt.*, **41**:52. 1896. 8. *Am. Pom. Soc. Cat.*, **1899**:19. 9. Hansen, *S. D. Sta. Bul.*, **76**:84. 1902. 10. Munson, *Me. Sta. An. Rpt.*, **18**:84, 95. 1902. 11. Farrand, *Mich. Sta. Bul.*, **205**:46. 1903. 12. Budd-Hansen, **1903**:149. 13. Powell and Fulton, *U. S. B. P. I. Bul.*, **48**:52. 1903. 14. Beach and Clark, *N. Y. Sta. Bul.*, **248**:137. 1904.

SYNONYMS. None.

This fruit resembles its parent Wealthy so closely that it is very difficult to distinguish between the two. It is similar to Wealthy in season as well as in the appearance and quality of the fruit. In ordinary storage its commercial season is September and October (14). In cold storage it extends to about January 1 (13). Sometimes a portion of the fruit may keep into or through the winter (14). Hansen states that even if really distinct the two varieties are now mixed to a considerable extent. As fruited at this Station the flesh of Peter is not so white as that of Wealthy but somewhat milder and better in quality (4). It has been found that the seeds of Peter are larger, broader, less pointed and a little darker than those of Wealthy. The tree is a moderate grower, comes into bearing young and yields full crops biennially. The fruit does not ripen uniformly and on this account there is apt to be some loss from drops unless more than one picking is made.

Historical. Originated from seed of Wealthy by Peter M. Gideon, Excelsior, Minn. (1), from whom this variety was received in 1888 for testing at this Station.

TREE.

Tree a fairly strong grower in the nursery; in the orchard it makes a moderately vigorous growth and eventually becomes rather large with moderately stout, somewhat drooping branches. *Form* upright spreading to roundish, open. *Twigs* short, straight, slender, with large terminal buds; internodes medium. *Bark* brown tinged with red, lightly streaked with scarf-skin; pubescent near tips. *Lenticels* quite numerous, medium size, oval, not raised. *Buds* medium size, plump, obtuse, free, slightly pubescent.

FRUIT.

Fruit medium or above, uniform in size and shape. *Form* oblate or roundish oblate, a little inclined to conic, regular. *Stem* long to medium, sometimes short, slender. *Cavity* acuminate, deep, medium to rather broad, compressed, lightly russeted or nearly smooth. *Calyx* small, closed; lobes medium in length, rather broad, acute. *Basin* deep to moderately deep, narrow to medium in width, abrupt, gently furrowed, sometimes compressed.

Skin thin, moderately tough, nearly smooth, clear pale yellow washed and mottled with bright red conspicuously striped and splashed with deep carmine. Highly colored specimens are nearly covered with deep red. *Dots* medium size, scattering, brown, mingled with some that are whitish and submerged. *Prevailing effect* red or striped red.

Calyx tube small, funnel-shape. *Stamens* median to marginal.

Core medium to below, usually axile; cells symmetrical, closed or partly *open;* core lines clasping. *Carpels* roundish, emarginate. *Seeds* above medium to large, moderately wide, long, flat, moderately acute.

Flesh slightly tinged with yellow, sometimes stained with red, firm, medium-grained, tender, juicy, with a pleasant, mild subacid, somewhat aromatic flavor, good to very good.

Season September and October or later (14).

PLUMB CIDER.

REFERENCES. 1. *Wis. Hort. Soc. Rpt.,* 1869 (cited by 2). 2. *Horticulturist,* 27:310. 1872. 3. *Ib.,* 28:119. 1873. 4. *Am. Pom. Soc. Cat.,* 1873. 5. Williams, *Horticulturist,* 29:16. 1874. *fig.* 6. Downing, 1876:65 app. 7. Budd, *Ia. Hort. Soc. Rpt.,* 1879:472. 8. Barry, 1883:352. 9. Thomas, 1885:520. 10. Bailey, *An. Hort.,* 1892:246. 11. *Rural N. Y.,* 53:794. 1894. 12. Alwood, *Va. Sta. Bul.,* 130:124. 1901. 13. Hansen, *S. D. Sta. Bul.,* 76: 35. 1902. *fig.* 14. Budd-Hansen, 1903:151. *fig.* 15. Beach and Clark, *N. Y. Sta. Bul.,* 248:138. 1904.

SYNONYMS. PLUMB CIDER (1, 2, 3, 4, 5, 6, 7, 8, 9, 12, 13, 14, 15). PLUM CIDER (10, 11).

This variety has been received with some favor in many parts of the country on account of its hardiness and productiveness. The fruit is of good medium size, fairly attractive in color, yellowish shaded and splashed with red. As grown in New York state it is inferior to standard varieties of its season.

Historical. Origin unknown. It was brought from Ohio in 1844 to Wisconsin by Mr. Plumb, where it proved to be a good grower, hardy and productive (5).

FRUIT (5, 13, 14).

Fruit above medium. *Form* round-ovate, slightly conic in some specimens. *Stem* stout, short. *Cavity* shallow, narrow. *Calyx* very small, closed. *Basin* very narrow and shallow, slightly plaited.

Skin yellowish shaded with pale red and somewhat striped with brighter red. *Dots* few, fine, gray.

Calyx tube long, very narrow, funnel-form. *Stamens* extremely marginal touching the segments, a marked characteristic.

Core little above medium; cells open; core lines clasping. *Carpels* cordate. *Seeds* pale brown, short, plump, pointed.

Flesh of a greenish cast, firm, fine, breaking, juicy, brisk subacid, good.

Season October to January.

POMONA.

REFERENCES. 1. Downing, 1869:135. 2. Leroy, 1873:248. *fig.* 3. Hogg, 1884:55. 4. Bailey, *An. Hort.,* 1892:237. 5. Beach, *N. Y. Sta. An. Rpt.,* 13: 579. 1894. 6. *Ib., Gard. and For.,* 8:428. 1895. 7. *Ib., Can. Hort.,* 20:

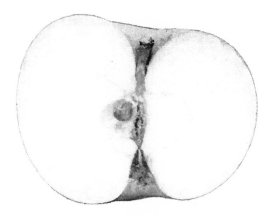

POMONA (Reduced Size)

183. 1897. **8.** Bunyard, *Jour. Roy. Hort. Soc.*, **1898**:356. **9.** Beach and Clark, *N. Y. Sta. Bul.*, **248**:139. 1904.

SYNONYMS. COX'S POMONA (1, 2, 3, 4, 5, 6, 7, 8). *Cox's Pomona* (9). *Dean's Codlin* (2). POMONA (9).

Fruit frequently large and when highly colored rather attractive, being mottled and striped with crimson over a clear pale yellow ground color. The fruit is not very uniform in size, often unsymmetrical, tender, easily bruised and not a very good keeper. In ordinary storage its commercial limit is October (9). The tree is a good grower, comes into bearing young and is an annual cropper, or nearly so, but only moderately productive. It is not recommended for commercial planting in New York.

Historical. Originated by Mr. Cox, Colnbrook Lawn near Slough, Bucks, England, who also originated Cox Orange (3).

TREE.

Tree medium size, moderately vigorous with branches moderately stout, spreading and often drooping. *Form* roundish. *Twigs* straight, stocky, long; internodes medium. *Bark* rather bright reddish-brown mingled with olive-green, thinly overlaid with narrow streaks of gray scarf-skin. *Lenticels* rather numerous, conspicuous, medium to sometimes large, roundish or sometimes elongated. *Buds* medium to large, broad, obtuse, appressed, somewhat pubescent. *Leaves* rather large, broad, dark green; base of petioles red.

FRUIT.

Fruit medium to very large, fairly uniform in size but not in shape. *Form* oblate conic, very irregular, ribbed; sides usually unequal. *Stem* usually short, moderately thick. *Cavity* large, acuminate to acute, deep, broad, rather symmetrical or sometimes compressed, irregularly russeted. *Calyx* medium size, open or nearly closed; lobes separated at base, short, rather broad, obtuse to acute, reflexed. *Basin* deep, medium in width to rather wide, abrupt, smooth or ridged, slightly wrinkled.

Skin thin, rather tender, waxy, smooth, greenish-yellow or pale yellow partly blushed with crimson, and mottled and narrowly striped with carmine. *Dots* scattering, small, inconspicuous, usually whitish and submerged, sometimes gray or russet.

Calyx tube wide, conical, sometimes extending to the core. *Stamens* median to nearly marginal.

Core medium to small, somewhat abaxile; cells open or closed, symmetrical; core lines clasping. *Carpels* ovate to broadly roundish or elliptical, emarginate. *Seeds* medium to small, wide, short, very plump, flat, obtuse, dark brown.

Flesh whitish, not very firm, rather fine, crisp, tender, juicy, subacid, sprightly, good to very good for culinary use.

Season September and October.

PORTER.

REFERENCES.   1. Kenrick, **1832**:27.   2. *Mag. Hort.*, 1:363.   1835.   3. Manning, **1838**:51.   4 *Ib., Mag. Hort.*, 7:48.   1841.   5. Downing, **1845**:92.   fig. 6. Floy-Lindley, **1846**:411 app.   7. *Horticulturist*, 1:196, 256.   1846.   8. Hovey, *Mag. Hort.*, **14**:116.   1848.   fig.   9. Cole, **1849**:107.   fig.   10. Thomas, **1849**:157.   fig.   11. Waring, **1851**:28.   12. Barry, **1851**:285.   13. Emmons, *Nat. Hist. N. Y.*, 3:37.   1851.   col. pl. No. 27 and fig.   14. Hovey, 1:43. 1851.   col. pl. and fig.   15. *Horticulturist*, 7:217.   1852.   16. *Am. Pom. Soc. Cat.*, 1852.   17. Elliott, **1854**:98.   18. Hooper, **1857**:71.   19. Gregg, **1857**:47. fig.   20. Warder, **1867**:673.   fig.   21. Fitz, **1872**:153, 162.   22. Leroy, **1873**: 580.   fig.   23. Downing, **1881**:11, 12 index, app.   24. *Rural N. Y.*, **47**:713. 1888.   25. Wickson, **1889**:243.   26. Lyon, *Mich. Hort. Soc. Rpt.*, **1890**:296. 27. Bailey, *An. Hort.*, **1892**:246.   28. Burrill and McCluer, *Ill. Sta. Bul.*, **45**:336.   1896.   29. Waugh, *Vt. Sta. An. Rpt.*, **14**:303.   1901.   30. Budd-Hansen, **1903**:152.   fig.

SYNONYMS.   *Jennings* (23).   PORTER (1, 2, 3, 4, 5, 6, 7, 8, 9, 10, 11, 12, 13, 14, 15, 16, 17, 18, 19, 20, 21, 22, 23, 24, 25, 26, 27, 28, 29, 30).   *Yellow Summer Pearmain* (23).

This fruit is of very fine dessert quality.   It is also highly esteemed for canning and other culinary uses, because when it is cooked it is not only excellent in quality but it retains its form remarkably well.   The fruit is yellow, faintly marked with red, decidedly attractive for an apple of its class.   It does not stand shipping very well because the skin is rather tender and readily shows marks of handling.   Since it is quite variable in its season of ripening there is apt to be considerable loss from dropping unless more than one picking is made.   It varies in size from large to small, with a considerable percentage of the crop undersized or otherwise unmarketable.   The tree is vigorous, compact, hardy, comes into bearing early and is a pretty reliable biennial cropper. Fifty years ago it was the principal September apple in the Boston market (1, 3, 5, 9, 18, 19), and in spite of the fact that it is not red it continues to sell well in that market (29).   It is also in good demand in many local markets.   It is desirable for planting for home use or for some local markets, but generally it is not regarded as a profitable commercial variety by New York fruit growers.

Historical.   Originated about 1800 with Rev. Samuel Porter, Sherburne, Mass. (1, 3, 5, 14), and up to about 1850 its cultivation was confined principally to the vicinity of its origin.   It gradually became very widely known and has become well disseminated in many of the more important apple-growing regions of the country.   Old trees of it are occasionally found in New York orchards but it is now seldom planted here.

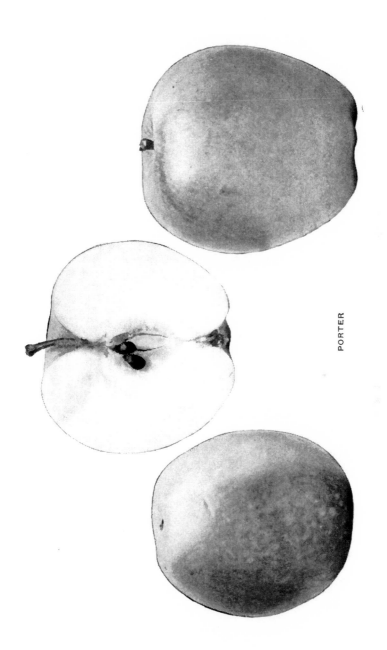

PORTER

TREE.

Tree medium to large, vigorous. *Form* roundish or somewhat spreading. *Twigs* rather slender, very short-jointed, with prominent shoulders (14). *Buds* medium in size.

FRUIT.

Fruit small to large, usually rather large. *Form* oblong inclined to conic, rather truncate at base and with apex oblique and somewhat ribbed. *Stem* medium to rather short, moderately thick to slender, sometimes knobbed, curved. *Cavity* acute to acuminate, medium to deep, medium in width to rather narrow, symmetrical or compressed, sometimes lipped, usually faintly russeted. *Calyx* rather large, closed or partly open; lobes usually separated at base, short, rather narrow, broadly acute. *Basin* moderately deep to shallow, rather narrow, abrupt, broadly furrowed and wrinkled.

Skin moderately thin, smooth, rather glossy, clear bright yellow with a faint blush, usually rather obscurely striped with darker red marked with scattering red dots. *Dots* usually medium to very small, often submerged, green with whitish center, sometimes russet.

Calyx tube rather short, wide, broadly conical. *Stamens* median to basal. *Core* medium to large, axile to somewhat abaxile; cells partly open to wide open; core lines meeting or slightly clasping. *Carpels* broadly ovate to elliptical, mucronate. *Seeds* below medium to rather large, plump, rounded, acute.

Flesh yellow, fine, crisp, tender, juicy, subacid, agreeably aromatic, sprightly, good to very good for either dessert or culinary uses.

Season. It begins to ripen in September and continues in use till November or later.

POUND SWEET.

REFERENCE. 1. Downing, **1869**:311.
SYNONYMS. None.

This name has been applied to several varieties of large sweet apples. Downing mentions one which is large, roundish conic, greenish-yellow with slight red in sun; flesh yellowish, tender, moderately juicy, sweet; season September and October; and another which is large, roundish, red; flesh whitish, moderately juicy, aromatic, sweet (1). Others are described by other authors and some which are known locally by this name have perhaps never been described in any publication.

The variety most commonly known in Central and Western New York under the name Pound Sweet is large, globular, marbled with yellow and green and streaked with whitish scarf-skin. It is described under its correct name Pumpkin Sweet on page 171.

PRIMATE.

REFERENCES. 1. Cowles, *Mag. Hort.*, 16:450. 1850. fig. 2. *Ib.*, 17:506. 1851. 3. *Am. Pom. Soc. Cat.*, **1854**. 4. *Mag. Hort.*, 20:241. 1854. 5. Elliott, **1854**:153. fig. 6. *Mag. Hort.*, 21:62. 1855. 7. Gregg, **1857**:38. 8. Downing, **1857**:93. fig. 9. *Horticulturist*, 14:471. 1859. 10. *Mag. Hort.*,

27:69. 1861. **11.** *Horticulturist,* **17**:103, 150. 1862. **12.** *Mag. Hort.,* **32**:17. 1866. **13.** Warder, **1867**:643. *fig.* **14.** Downing, **1869**:313. **15.** Fitz, **1872**: 161. **16.** Thomas, **1875**:196. **17.** Downing, **1881**:11, 12 index, app. **18.** Barry, **1883**:334. **19.** *Rural N. Y.,* **47**:649. 1888. **20.** Lyon, *Mich. Hort. Soc. Rpt.,* **1890**:296. **21.** Blackwell, *Rural N. Y.,* **50**:447. 1891. **22.** Bailey, *An. Hort.,* **1892**:247. **23.** Hoskins, *Rural N. Y.,* **53**:248. 1894. **24.** *Can. Hort.,* **17**:252. 1894. **25.** Woolverton, *Ont. Fr. Stas. An. Rpt.,* **8**:9. 1901. *figs.* **26.** Budd-Hansen, **1903**:153. *fig.* **27.** *Rural N. Y.,* **62**:740. 1903.

SYNONYMS. *Belle Rose* (17). *Early Baldwin* (17). *Early Tart Harvest* (14). *Harvest* (2). *Highland Pippin* (17). *July Apple* (14). NORTH AMERICAN BEST (9). *North American Best* (14). *Powers* (2, 14). PRIMATE (2, 3, 4, 5, 6, 7, 8, 10, 11, 12, 13, 14, 15, 16, 17, 18, 19, 20, 21, 22, 23, 24, 25, 26, 27). ROUGH AND READY (1). *Rough and Ready* (2, 5, 7, 8, 14). *Scott* (14). *Sour Harvest* (9, 14). *Zour Bough* (9, 14).

A dessert apple, pale yellow or whitish, often slightly blushed; in season in August and September. It is well known throughout the state, but not much grown except for home use. It is commonly considered the best apple of its season for the home orchard because the tree is a pretty good grower and a reliable cropper, and the fruit ripens in succession during a period of several weeks and is of fine flavor and excellent quality particularly for dessert use. Being less attractive than a red apple it is in demand in market only where its fine quality is known. The fruit ripens unevenly and it should be picked from time to time as it matures to prevent loss from the dropping of the fruit. In some localities the tree has proved somewhat tender, not very long-lived and rather susceptible to the attacks of the apple canker, but, generally speaking, as grown throughout Central and Western New York, particularly where it has been topworked upon good thrifty stock, the tree is a pretty good grower, moderately long-lived and reliably productive. Often it yields very heavy crops biennially with lighter crops, or none, on alternate years, but in some localities it is almost an annual bearer.

Historical. This variety was disseminated by traveling grafters in Central and Western New York as much as fifty years ago. In 1850, Charles P. Cowles of Syracuse in a communication to the Magazine of Horticulture stated: "As it is not known in this place, nor state, by the best judges, I safely think it is a seedling. I found a few trees in Onondaga county in a town of the same name which had been circulated by grafts but nothing further could be traced of its origin. * * * I propose to call it 'Rough

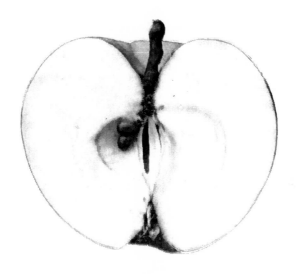

PRIMATE

and Ready' from the fact of its being first tested during that campaign. * * * Messrs. Downing, Barry and Thomas think it a new variety. * * * It is but little known as yet but where it is its qualities are much esteemed " (1). The following year Mr. A. Fahnstock, a nurseryman of Syracuse, showed that this variety had been disseminated in Ontario and Monroe counties as well as in Onondaga county and that it was generally known by the name of Primate. Recently John T. Roberts of Syracuse has taken the trouble to look up the history of this variety and is convinced that the original seedling tree grew in the town of Camillus, Onondaga county, and through his efforts a bronze tablet has been erected to mark the spot. The tablet bears the following inscription: " On this farm Calvin D. Bingham about 1840 produced the marvelous Primate apple, named by Charles P. Cowles. God's earth is full of love to man " (27). In 1854 it was listed by the American Pomological Society (3) as a valuable variety. It is listed by various nurserymen in the region from the Atlantic to the Middle West but apparently is but little known either in the Southwest or the Northwest (22).

TREE.

Tree below medium to rather large, usually moderately vigorous. *Form* upright spreading to roundish, rather dense. *Twigs* short, straight, stout with large terminal buds; internodes short. *Bark* dull brown mingled with green, heavily streaked with scarf-skin, pubescent and rather rough. *Lenticels* scattering, medium size, oblong, raised. *Buds* prominent, large, broad, plump, acute, pubescent.

FRUIT.

Fruit medium or above, sometimes large. *Form* roundish conic to oblate conic, often distinctly ribbed. *Stem* short to medium, thick. *Cavity* acute, deep, broad, distinctly furrowed. *Calyx* medium size, closed; lobes long, narrow. *Basin* moderately shallow to rather deep, medium in width to rather narrow, abrupt, furrowed and wrinkled.

Skin thin, moderately tender, smooth, light green, often changing to whitish, sometimes with faint yellowish tinge, often slightly blushed but not striped. *Dots* scattering, numerous, rather small, submerged or russet.

Calyx tube rather large, rather long, broadly conical to somewhat funnelshape. *Stamens* median. *Core* medium to large, nearly axile to somewhat abaxile with hollow cylinder in the axis; cells symmetrical, open; core lines clasping. *Carpels* cordate. *Seeds* medium to rather large, moderately wide, plump, acute.

Flesh whitish, fine, crisp, very tender, juicy, subacid, aromatic, sprightly, very good to best.

Season August and September.

PROLIFIC SWEETING.

REFERENCES. 1. Webster, *Montreal Hort. Soc. Rpt.*, **1881**:54. 2. Gibb, *Ia. Hort. Soc. Rpt.*, **1883**:439. 3. *Ib.*, *Am. Pom. Soc. Rpt.*, **1887**:46. 4. Van Deman, *U. S. Pom. Rpt.*, **1888**:571. *fig.* 5. Hoskins, *Rural N. Y.*, **47**:646. 1888. 6. *N. Y. Sta. An. Rpt.*, **7**:91. 1888. 7. Bailey, *An. Hort.*, **1892**:247. 8. Beach, *N. Y. Sta. An. Rpt.*, **14**:254. 1895. 9. Munson, *Me. Sta. Rpt.*,

1896:71. **10.** Waugh, *Vt. Sta. An. Rpt.*, **14**:304. 1901. **11.** Munson, *Me. Sta. Rpt.*, **1902**:84, 86, 88. **12.** Hansen, *S. D. Sta. Bul.*, **76**:88. 1902. fig. **13.** Budd-Hansen, **1903**:154.

SYNONYMS. *No. 351* (3, 4, 12). PLODOWITKA CUADKAJA (1). *Plodowitka Cuadkaja* (3). PLODOWITKA CAUDKAJA (2). PROLIFIC SWEET (10). *Prolific Sweet* (1). PROLIFIC SWEETING (3, 4, 5, 6, 7, 8, 9, 11, 12, 13). *Prolific Sweeting* (2).

A Russian variety which in size and color resembles Yellow Transparent but in form is roundish oblate and somewhat irregular. It has proved to be a valuable sweet apple for autumn use in Northern New England (5, 11, 12, 13). Worthy of trial in Northern New York when a variety of this class is desired.

Historical. Imported from Russia by the United States Department of Agriculture in 1870. It was received for testing at this Station from Dr. T. H. Hoskins, Newport, Vt., in 1888 (6). It has thus far been but little disseminated in this state.

TREE.

Tree moderately vigorous. *Form* upright spreading to roundish, open. *Twigs* long, curved, stout; internodes short. *Bark* brown, tinged with green, lightly streaked with scarf-skin; slightly pubescent. *Lenticels* scattering, medium size, round, not raised. *Buds* medium size, broad, flat, obtuse, appressed, pubescent.

FRUIT.

Fruit medium or above. *Form* roundish oblate, somewhat irregular. *Stem* medium size. *Cavity* deep, acute to acuminate, ribbed, russeted and with some outspreading russet rays. *Calyx* closed. *Basin* shallow, wide, wrinkled. *Flesh* white, crisp, fine-grained, mildly sweet, good.
Season late August, September and October.

PUMPKIN RUSSET.

REFERENCES. **1.** Kenrick, **1832**:37. **2.** *Mag. Hort.*, **1**:363. 1835. **3.** Downing, **1845**:93. **4.** Thomas, **1849**:146. **5.** Cole, **1849**:115. **6.** Elliott, **1854**: 152. **7.** Hooper, **1857**:73. **8.** Warder, **1867**:566. **9.** Downing, **1881**:11 index, app. **10.** Bailey, *An. Hort.*, **1892**:247. **11.** Powell and Fulton, *U. S. B. P. I. Bul.*, **48**:53. 1903. **12.** Beach and Clark, *N. Y. Sta. Bul.*, **248**:139. 1904.

SYNONYMS. *Flint Russet* (3, 6). *Kingsbury Russet* (9). PUMPKIN RUSSET (3, 4, 6, 7, 8, 9, 10, 11, 12). *Pumpkin Russet* (5). PUMPKIN SWEET (5). *Pumpkin Sweet* (3). PUMPKIN SWEETING (2). PUMPKIN SWEETING *of New England* (1). *Sweet Russet* (3, 4, 6). *York Russet* (6).

This is a very large, round, yellowish-russet apple, sweet, rich, very good for baking but of little value for other purposes. The tree is a vigorous, rapid grower, hardy, moderately long-lived and yields fair to good crops biennially or in some cases almost annually. It is not a profitable commercial variety and is now seldom cultivated even for home use.

Historical. Pumpkin Russet is an old New England variety. Kenrick (1) in 1832 described it under the name Pumpkin Sweeting of New Eng-

PUMPKIN RUSSET

land. In 1849 Cole (5) described it under the name Pumpkin Sweet giving Pumpkin Russet as a synonym. In 1845 it was described by Downing (3) under the name Pumpkin Russet which is the name now generally accepted for it by pomologists. It is still occasionally listed by nurserymen but is now seldom planted in New York.

TREE.

Tree large, vigorous or very vigorous, at first upright but eventually becoming roundish or spreading, open; branches long, stout, curved. *Twigs* short, curved, stout; internodes long. *Bark* dark reddish-brown tinged with olive-green, lightly streaked with scarf-skin, pubescent. *Lenticels* quite numerous, oblong, slightly raised. *Buds* large, broad, plump, obtuse, free, pubescent.

FRUIT.

Fruit large, fairly uniform in size and shape. *Form* oblate or somewhat inclined to conic, sometimes irregular, faintly ribbed, often compressed. *Stem* medium to short, moderately slender to thick. *Cavity* acute to acuminate, usually deep, moderately broad to rather narrow, nearly smooth, sometimes slightly furrowed. *Calyx* large, closed or slightly open; lobes long, narrow, acute to acuminate. *Basin* small to medium, rather shallow to moderately deep, medium in width, somewhat abrupt, slightly furrowed and wrinkled.

Skin thick, rather tough, greenish or yellowish sometimes with bronze blush on exposed cheek, more or less covered with russet patches or netted veins of russet. *Dots* large and small, scattering, usually russet, irregular.

Calyx tube short, wide, broadly conical to nearly urnshape. *Stamens* median to basal.

Core above medium to below, abaxile; cells usually open, symmetrical but not uniformly developed; core lines slightly clasping. *Carpels* broadly ovate, very slightly emarginate, sometimes tufted. *Seeds* moderately light brown, rather large, wide, flat, acute.

Flesh greenish-white or yellowish, firm, rather coarse, tender, juicy, sweet, good.

Season September and October or in cold storage extending to January 1 (12).

PUMPKIN SWEET.

REFERENCES. 1. *N. E. Farmer*, 1834 (cited by 20). 2. Downing, 1845:89. fig. 3. Emmons, *Nat. Hist. N. Y.*, 3:48. 1851. 4. *Mag. Hort.*, 20:241. 1854. 5. Elliott, 1854:152. 6. Hooper, 1857:56. 7. *Am. Pom. Soc. Cat.*, 1862. 8. *Horticulturist*, 17:150. 1862. 9. Warder, 1867:527. 10. Barry, 1883:339. 11. Thomas, 1885:216. 12. Lyon, *Mich. Hort. Soc. Rpt.*, 1890:296. 13. Bailey, *An. Hort.*, 1892:247. 14. Munson, *Me. Sta. Rpt.*, 1893:133. . 15. Miller, *Rural N. Y.*, 53:278. 1894. 16. Taylor, *Am. Pom. Soc. Rpt.*, 1895:198. 17. Powell and Fulton, *U. S. B. P. I. Bul.*, 48:53. 1903. 18. Budd-Hansen, 1903:155. fig. 19. Beach and Clark, *N. Y. Sta. Bul.*, 248:139. 1904. 20. Ragan, *U. S. B. P. I. Bul.*, 56:244. 1905.

SYNONYMS. *Lyman's Large Yellow* (20). LYMAN'S PUMPKIN SWEET (2, 3, 6, 9, 10, 11). *Lyman's Pumpkin Sweet* (5, 14, 17, 19, 20). *Pound*

Sweet (9, 11, 12, 14, 17, 18, 19). PUMPKIN SWEET (1, 4, 5, 7, 8, 12, 13, 14, 15, 16, 17, 18, 19, 20). *Pumpkin Sweet* (10, 11). *Pumpkin Sweeting* (20). *Rhode Island Sweet* (20). *Round Sweet* (20). *Sweet Lyman's Pumpkin* (20). *Vermont Pumpkin Sweet* (10, 20). *Vermont Sweet* (20). *Yankee Apple* (5, 20).

Fruit large to very large, marbled with light and dark green and streaked over the base with whitish scarf-skin; well colored specimens eventually become quite yellow and sometimes are faintly bronzed on the exposed cheek. It is never marked with red, nor is it russeted except about the cavity. So far as we know all other varieties which have been cultivated under the name Pumpkin Sweet are either russeted or marked with red.

This is the variety generally known in Central and Western New York as Pound Sweet, and it commonly appears under this name in market quotations. By many it is esteemed as one of the best sweet apples of its season for baking and for canning or stewing with quinces, but generally it is not valued for dessert because it is rather coarse and has a peculiar flavor. It often sells well in local or special markets, and there is a limited demand for it in the general trade. Its keeping qualities differ greatly in different localities and in different seasons. As grown in Western New York it comes in season early in October. The rate of loss in ordinary storage is usually high during the fall, and the season closes in December or early January, although in some years a considerable portion of the fruit may remain sound till midwinter or later (19).

The tree is a good strong grower, rather long-lived, fairly hardy and generally healthy, but it sometimes suffers from winter injury, sunscald and canker. It appears to thrive particularly well on well fertilized gravelly or sandy loam, with well drained subsoil. Under right conditions it is a pretty reliable cropper, yielding good crops biennially. The crop ripens somewhat unevenly and often there is a considerable loss from water-cored fruit and from windfalls, but on the other hand there is a small percentage of loss in undersized or deformed apples. In order to lessen the loss from windfalls it is well to plant this variety in a location that is sheltered from prevailing winds.

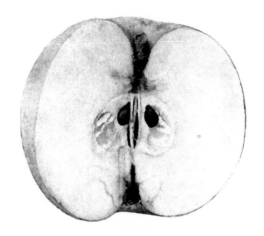

PUMPKIN SWEET

Historical. Originated in the orchard of S. Lyman, Manchester, Conn. (9). It has been distributed throughout this state for more than fifty years, but nowhere has it been largely planted. Generally speaking it is not grown so extensively now as it was formerly, but in a few localities its cultivation for commercial purposes is increasing somewhat.

Tree.

Tree medium to large, vigorous, with long, moderately stout branches. *Form* upright spreading or roundish, open. *Twigs* medium to short, straight or nearly so, stout to moderately slender; internodes short to medium. *Bark* reddish olive-green varying to brownish-red, uniformly mottled with thin scarf-skin, pubescent. *Lenticels* scattering, rather inconspicuous, small, roundish, not raised. *Buds* medium or below, plump, acute, free, slightly pubescent.

Fruit.

Fruit large to very large, pretty uniform in size and shape. *Form* globular to roundish conic, sometimes irregularly elliptical or prominently ribbed. *Stem* very short, stout, often inserted under a lip or having itself a fleshy protuberance. *Cavity* acuminate, moderately shallow to rather deep, narrow to moderately wide, often somewhat furrowed or lipped, sometimes russeted and with outspreading russet. *Calyx* medium to rather large, open; lobes often separated at the base, short, broad, acute. *Basin* small to medium in size, moderately shallow to rather deep, narrow to moderately wide, abrupt to somewhat obtuse, often slightly furrowed or wrinkled.

Skin rather thin, tough, smooth, at first green but eventually clear yellow marbled with greenish-yellow. Stripes of whitish scarf-skin radiate from the cavity. Well colored specimens occasionally show a brownish-red blush but never a distinct red color. *Dots* conspicuous, whitish, often areolar with russet center.

Calyx tube rather wide, conical or elongated cone-shape or sometimes slightly funnel-form. *Stamens* median to basal.

Core medium to rather large, axile; cells symmetrical, closed or somewhat open, not uniformly developed; core lines clasping. *Carpels* thin, broadly roundish, but slightly emarginate if at all, often tufted. *Seeds* medium to rather small, wide, plump, acute, light brown, tufted.

Flesh tinged with yellow firm, medium in texture, crispness and juiciness, decidedly sweet with a peculiar flavor; good for culinary use and especially esteemed for baking.

Season October to January.

McCarty is identical with Pumpkin Sweet in general characters and is sold as Pumpkin Sweet, but it appears to differ enough from the type in certain characteristics to entitle it to recognition as a distinct strain. As compared with typical Pumpkin Sweet the fruit of McCarty averages smaller, is not so yellow and keeps longer. B. J. Case, Sodus, N. Y., who grows McCarty commer-

cially, reports: " The tree does not produce any water-cored fruit
except when the crop is light. It appears to be fully as productive
as Pumpkin Sweet. In common storage it is not unusual to keep
McCarty later than January. In quality it is not so good as Pumpkin Sweet. The origin of this type is unknown."

(I) QUINCE (*of Cole*).

REFERENCES. 1. Cole, 1849:99. *fig.* 2. Downing, 1857:130. 3. Hovey,
Mag. Hort., 27:71. 1861. *fig.* 4. *Am. Pom. Soc. Rpt.,* 1862. 5. Warder,
1867:645. *fig.* 6. Downing, 1869:319. 7. Lyon, *Mich. Sta. Bul.,* 143:201.
1897. 8. Budd-Hansen, 1903:156. *fig.* 9. Powell and Fulton, *U. S. B. P. I.
Bul.,* 48:53. 1903. 10. Ragan, *Ib.,* 56:246. 1905.

SYNONYMS. COLE'S QUINCE (1, 2, 4). *Cole's Quince* (3, 5, 6, 10).
QUINCE (3, 5, 6). QUINCE (Cole) (10). QUINCE *Cole* (7, 8, 9). *Turn Off
Lane* (10).

This is a very good variety for home use and is considered by
some New York fruit growers fairly profitable in commercial
orchards. The fruit is large, angular, yellow with white aromatic
subacid flesh of very good quality; in season in late summer and
early autumn. Commercial limit in cold storage, November
1 (9). The tree is of good medium size, spreading, a good
grower, very hardy, comes into bearing moderately young, and is
a reliable cropper. It is not extensively cultivated in New York.

Historical. Originated at Cornish, Me., from whence it was disseminated
about fifty years ago (1).

FRUIT.

Fruit. Cole gave the following description of this fruit in 1849 (1):
" Fruit large to very large; flattish-conical; ribbed; bright yellow, seldom a
brown cheek, stem short, in a deep cavity; calyx large, in a deep basin;
flesh when first ripe, firm, juicy, pleasant acid, and first-rate for cooking.
When very mellow, remarkably tender, of a mild, rich, high quince flavor
and aroma. When in perfection we have never seen its superior. July to
September."

(II) QUINCE (*of Coxe*).

REFERENCES. 1. M'Mahon, *Am. Gard. Cal.,* 1806:585. 2. Coxe, 1817:138.
fig. 3. Thacher, 1822:132. 4. Cole, 1849:115. 5. Thomas, 1849:158. 6.
Downing, 1857:181. 7. *Horticulturist,* 23:146. 1868. *fig.* 8. Downing,
1869:319. 9. Fitz, 1872:153. 10. Downing, 1872:10 index, app. 11. Ragan,
U. S. B. P. I. Bul., 56:246. 1905.

SYNONYMS. *Pear Apple* (8, 11). QUINCE (1, 2, 3, 5, 6, 8, 9, 10). *Quince
Apple* (11). QUINCE (Coxe) (11). QUINCE OF COXE (4, 7). *Quince of
Coxe* (11). *Seneca Favorite* (10). *Seneca Spice* (11, ?8).

A variety which is distinct from the Quince of Cole was described by Coxe in 1817. According to Downing, it is in appearance much like a large Yellow Newtown, and the young wood is of a different shade of color from that of the Quince of Cole, being dull reddish-brown instead of clear reddish-brown, with buds small, reddish and pointed, instead of short, abrupt and prominent. The following is the description of the fruit given by Coxe (2) : " The size of the apple is large; the shape flat; the skin, when fully ripe, is yellow; the flesh rich, yellow and juicy — in appearance it somewhat resembles a large yellow Newtown Pippin. It came originally from the state of New York; ripens in November."

This variety is unknown to us, and we have received no report concerning it from any of our correspondents.

RAMSDELL SWEET.

REFERENCES. 1. *Mag. Hort.*, 4:47. 1838. 2. Manning and Ives, 1844:41. 3. Downing, 1845:137. 4. *Mag. Hort.*, 12:475. 1846. 5. Thomas, 1849:161. 6. Cole, 1849:118. 7. Emmons, *Nat. Hist. N. Y.*, 3:76. 1851. 8. Elliott. 1854:131. 9. Hooper, 1857:74. 10. *Am. Pom. Soc. Cat.*, 1862. 11. Warder, 1867:664. fig. 12. Downing, 1869:163. 13. Fitz, 1872:121, 145. 14. Leroy, 1873:605. fig. 15. Barry, 1883:352. 16. Lyon, *Mich. Hort. Soc. Rpt.*, 1890:296. 17. Bailey, *An. Hort.*, 1892:247. 18. Burrill and McCluer, *Ill. Sta. Bul.*, 45:337. 1896. 19. Farrand, *Mich. Sta. Bul.*, 205:46. 1903. 20. Budd-Hansen, 1903:159. fig.

SYNONYMS. *Avery Sweet* (12, 14). *Avery Sweeting* (8). ENGLISH SWEET (12, 18). *English Sweet* (14, 15, 16, 20). ENGLISH SWEETING (4, 8). *Hurlbut* (14). *Hurlbut Sweet* (12). RAMSDALE'S SWEETING (9). RAMSDELL (14, 19). RAMSDELL'S RED (11). *Ramsdell Red Sweet* (18). RAMSDELL'S RED SWEETING (1). RAMSDELL SWEET (10, 15, 16, 17, 20). *Ramsdell Sweet* (3, 8, 12). RAMSDELL'S SWEETING (3, 5, 6, 7, 12, 13). *Ramsdell's Sweeting* (8, 14). RAMSDEL'S RED PUMPKIN SWEET (2). *Ramsdel's Red Pumpkin Sweet* (3, 5, 7, 8, 12). *Randall's Red Winter* (12, 14). *Red Pumpkin Sweet* (3, 8, 12). *Red Pumpkin Sweeting* (9). *Reindell's Large* (14).

This is an attractive red apple of good size and very good quality, in season from midautumn to midwinter. The tree is a pretty good grower and an early bearer, yielding some fruit annually or nearly annually, but in many cases it is not satisfactorily productive and the fruit is not very uniform in size and quality, so that there is a considerable loss from unmarketable fruit. Not recommended for commercial planting in New York.

Historical. This variety was first brought to notice by being exhibited before the Massachusetts Horticultural Society by the Rev. H. S. Ramsdell, Thompson, Conn., and was named Ramsdell's Red Sweeting in compliment to him (1). Downing described it in 1845 (3) under the name Ramsdell's Sweeting, but in the 1869 edition (12) it was described under the name English Sweet, the name previously recognized by Elliott (8) but upon what authority we have been unable to learn. In 1862 (10) it was entered on the catalogue of the American Pomological Society under the name Ramsdell Sweet which name has been retained in that catalogue up to the present time. It is also commonly catalogued by nurserymen under the name Ramsdell or Ramsdell Sweet (17).

TREE.

Tree medium size, vigorous or moderately vigorous. *Form* upright, open. *Twigs* long, curved, moderately stout; internodes medium. *Bark* brown, streaked with heavy scarf-skin; slightly pubescent near tips. *Lenticels* scattering, small to medium, oval, raised. *Buds* medium size, plump, obtuse, free, pubescent.

FRUIT.

Fruit above medium, sometimes nearly large, somewhat variable in size, fairly uniform in shape. *Form* oblong conic to roundish conic, often somewhat elliptical and faintly ribbed. *Stem* short to medium in length, moderately slender, often red. *Cavity* acuminate, deep, rather broad, quite symmetrical, often with some stellate russet. *Calyx* small to medium, closed or slightly open; lobes narrow, acute to acuminate. *Basin* rather small, sometimes oblique, medium to rather deep, narrow to medium in width, abrupt, faintly furrowed and wrinkled.

Skin thin, rather tough, smooth, yellow nearly overspread with attractive dark red, or entirely red with obscure splashes and stripes of carmine, overspread with blue bloom. *Dots* many, distinct, conspicuous, small to rather large, pale yellow or grayish, often submerged. *Prevailing effect* red, attractive.

Calyx tube rather large, long, cylindrical to narrow funnel-shape. *Stamens* median.

Core small to medium, axile to somewhat abaxile; cells symmetrical but not uniformly developed, closed or slightly open; core lines clasping. *Carpels* ovate to nearly roundish. *Seeds* below medium, rather narrow, plump, acute.

Flesh tinged with yellow, firm, fine, tender, juicy, very sweet, good to very good.

Season October to February.

RASPBERRY.

REFERENCES. 1. *Ia. Hort. Soc. Rpt.*, 1883:435. 2. *Montreal Hort. Soc. Rpt.*, 1883:90. 3. *Ia. Agr. Coll. Bul.*, 1885:11. 4. Schroeder, *Montreal Hort. Soc. Rpt.*, 1886:77. 5. *U. S. Pom. Rpt.*, 1891:390. 6. Thomas, 1897:252. fig. 7. *Am. Pom. Soc. Cat.*, 1899:19. 8. Hansen, *S. D. Sta. Bul.*, 76:89. 1902. fig. 9. Budd-Hansen, 1903:159. fig.

SYNONYMS. MALINOWSKOE (1, 2). *Malinowskoe* (3). *No. 288* (3, 5, 8). RASPBERRY (3, 4, 5, 6, 7, 8, 9). *Raspberry* (1, 2). *Red Check* (6).

A Russian apple, small, fine dark red, sprightly subacid; season July and August. Hansen states (8, 9) that it is exceedingly productive and a good substitute for Red June where that variety winter-kills.

RED AND GREEN SWEET.

REFERENCES. 1. Coxe, 1817:162. 2. Thacher, 1822:129. 3. Kenrick, 1832: 38. 4. Thomas, 1849:135. 5. Elliott, 1854:176. 6. Downing, 1857:221. 7. Hooper, 1857:78. 8. Warder, 1867:729. 9. Downing, 1872:10 index, app.

SYNONYMS. *Large Red Sweeting* (5). LARGE RED AND GREEN SWEET-ING (2). PRINCE'S LARGE RED AND GREEN SWEETING (1). *Prince's Large Red and Green Sweeting* (3). *Prince's Red and Green Sweet* (5). *Red Bough* (5). RED AND GREEN SWEET (4, 5, 6, 7, 8, 9). RED AND GREEN SWEET-ING (3). *Saille Sweet* (9). *Virginia Sweet* (9).

This is a very large green apple, striped with red, rather attractive when well colored. It does not rank very high in flavor or quality but is suitable for baking. Season August and September. The fruit does not last long after it becomes ripe. The tree is medium to large, moderately vigorous to vigorous, long-lived and a reliable cropper yielding heavy crops annually. Although some find it a profitable apple to grow for local market it is not worthy of being recommended for general planting.

Historical. This is an old variety which was described by Coxe (1). It was formerly grown to a comparatively limited extent in some portions of New York and in adjoining states. Occasionally a tree of it is still found in some of the oldest orchards of the state but it is fast going out of cultivation.

TREE.

Tree large. *Form* upright spreading to roundish, open. *Twigs* short, straight, stout with large terminal buds; internodes short. *Bark* brown mingled with olive-green, heavily coated with gray scarf-skin; pubescent. *Lenticels* scattering, medium size, oval, not raised. *Buds* large, rather prominent, broad, plump, obtuse, free, pubescent.

FRUIT.

Fruit large to very large. *Form* oblong conic, rather strongly ribbed; sides unequal. *Stem* short to medium, moderately slender. *Cavity* nearly acuminate, deep, broad, furrowed, sometimes lipped, sometimes thinly russeted. *Calyx* closed or partly open; lobes moderately long, narrow, acute. *Basin* medium in depth to rather deep, medium in width to rather narrow, wrinkled.

Skin thin, tender, smooth, green changing to yellow, more or less blushed and partly overspread with pinkish-red irregularly striped and splashed with rather bright carmine. *Dots* conspicuous, numerous, large and scattering toward the cavity, small and very numerous toward the calyx.

Calyx tube long, funnel-shape.

Core rather large; cells open; core lines clasping. *Carpels* nearly roundish, tufted. *Seeds* rather small, plump, acute.

Flesh white, fine, very tender, moderately juicy, of pleasant sweet flavor and fair to good quality.

Season August and September.

RED ASTRACHAN.

REFERENCES. **1.** *London Hort. Soc. Trans.*, **4**:522 (cited by **2**). **2.** Forsyth, **1824**:131. **3.** *Pom. Mag.*, **1830**:No. 123, *col. pl.* **4.** *London Hort. Soc. Cat.*, **1831**:No. 31. **5.** Kenrick, **1832**:90. **6.** Floy-Lindley, **1833**:4. **7.** Kenrick, **1835**:58. **8.** *Mag. Hort.*, **1**:391. 1835. **9.** Manning, **1838**:50. **10.** *Ib.*, *Mag. Hort.*, **7**:48. 1841. **11.** Downing, **1845**:75. fig. **12.** *Horticulturist*, **1**:146. 1846. **13.** Hovey, *Mag. Hort.*, **14**:15. 1848. fig. **14.** Cole, **1849**:98. fig. **15.** Goodrich, **1849**:49. **16.** Thomas, **1849**:143. **17.** Waring, **1851**:29. **18.** Barry, **1851**:279. **19.** Emmons, *Nat. Hist. N. Y.*, **3**:14. 1851. *col. pl.* No. 53. **20.** Hovey, **1**:35. 1851. *col. pl.* and fig. **21.** *Mass. Hort. Soc. Trans.*, **1852**:103. *col. pl.* **22.** *Am. Pom. Soc. Cat.*, **1852**. **23.** *Horticulturist*, **7**:437. 1852. **24.** Elliott, **1854**:103. fig. **25.** *Horticulturist*, **10**:443. 1855. fig. **26.** Hooper, **1857**:13, 77. **27.** Gregg, **1857**:38. fig. **28.** *Mag. Hort.*, **30**:162. 1864. **29.** *Ib.*, **32**:17, 51. 1866. **30.** Warder, **1867**:456. fig. **31.** Downing, **1869**:323. fig. **32.** Todd, **1871**:210. fig. **33.** Fitz, **1872**:143, 160, 172. **34.** Leroy, **1873**:82. fig. **35.** Hatch, *Horticulturist*, **29**:51. 1874. **36.** *Montreal Hort. Soc. Rpt.*, **1876**:8. **37.** Hogg, **1884**:185. **38.** Wickson, **1889**: 243. **39.** Lyon, *Mich. Hort. Soc. Rpt.*, **1890**:296. **40.** *Can. Hort.*, **14**:261. 1891. **41.** Bailey, *An. Hort.*, **1892**:234, 247. **42.** *Am. Gard.*, **15**:404. 1894. fig. **43.** Woolverton, *Ont. Fr. Stas. An. Rpt.*, **2**:10. 1895. fig. **44.** Burrill and McCluer, *Ill. Sta. Bul.*, **45**:337. 1896. **45.** Waugh, *Vt. Sta. Bul.*, **61**:31. 1897. **46.** Bunyard, *Jour. Roy. Hort. Soc.*, **1898**:354. **47.** Craig, *Cyc. of Am. Hort.*, **1901**:1404. **48.** Waugh, *Vt. Sta. An. Rpt.*, **14**:305. 1901. **49.** *Can. Hort.*, **25**:305. 1902. figs. **50.** Hansen, *S. D. Sta. Bul.*, **76**:90. 1902. **51.** Bruner, *N. C. Sta. Bul.*, **182**:21. 1903. **52.** Budd-Hansen, **1903**:160. fig.

SYNONYMS. *Abe Lincoln* (31, 32, 34, 48). AMERICAN RED (4, 46). *Anglesea Pippin* (37). ASTRACAN ROUGE (34). ASTRACHAN (23). ASTRACHAN RED (2, 18). *Astrachan Rouge* (31). *Astrakhan Rouge* (32). *Deterding's Early* (31, 32). *Hamper's American* (37). RED ASTRACAN (6, 7, 8, 9, 10, 19). RED ASTRACHAN (1, 3, 5, 11, 12, 13, 14, 15, 16, 17, 20, 21, 22, 24, 25, 26, 27, 28, 29, 30, 31, 33, 35, 36, 37, 39, 40, 41, 42, 43, 44, 45, 47, 48, 49, 50, 51, 52). *Red Astrachan* (34). RED ASTRAKHAN (32). *Rother Astrakhan* (31, 32). *Vermillon d'Ete* (31, 32, 34). *Waterloo* (37).

This is a very beautiful early summer apple of good medium size, yellow, largely covered with light and dark red, presenting a striped appearance, and overspread with bluish bloom. It is generally well known throughout the state, being valued particularly for home use. It is fit for culinary purposes before it becomes fully ripe, so that for home use it is in season from late July to

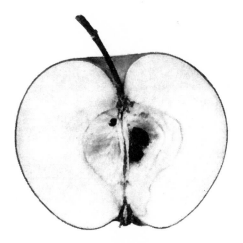

RED ASTRACHAN

September. When fully ripe and mellow it is desirable for dessert
use. The tree is of medium size, a good grower, moderately long-
lived, comes into bearing rather young and is a reliable cropper,
yielding moderate to good crops biennially or sometimes annually.
The fruit hangs to the tree pretty well till it is fully ripe, but as
the crop matures unevenly there is apt to be considerable loss from
the dropping of the fruit unless several pickings are made. It is
not very uniform in size, and a considerable amount of it is small
or otherwise unmarketable. It is very perishable, and on this
account not well adapted for shipping to distant markets. It is
very common in local markets, but often the supply so much ex-
ceeds the demand that prices are consequently low.

Historical. Hogg states that Red Astrachan was imported from Sweden
into England in 1816 but Lindley (6) states that " This very beautiful
apple was imported from Sweden, and first fruited by William Atkinson,
Esq., of Grove End, Paddington, in 1816." It was one of the first of the
Russian apples imported into America. It was received by the Massachusetts Horticultural Society from the London (Eng.) Horticultural Society about 1835 but this was not the first importation for fruit of Red
Astrachan was included in one of the exhibitions of the Massachusetts
Horticultural Society in 1835 (8). It has become generally disseminated
throughout the apple-growing districts of the continent and is commonly
listed from the Atlantic to the Pacific and from Canada to the Gulf states.

TREE.

Tree medium to rather large, moderately vigorous to vigorous. *Form* upright spreading to roundish, rather dense. *Twigs* medium to long, curved,
stout to rather slender; internodes long. *Bark* clear brown, lightly streaked
with scarf-skin, pubescent near the tips. *Lenticels* quite numerous, medium to
small, oblong, slightly raised. *Buds* medium in size, plump, obtuse to acute,
free, pubescent.

FRUIT.

Fruit medium to sometimes large, not very uniform in size or shape.
Form roundish to roundish oblate, inclined to conical, somewhat ribbed;
sides a little unequal. *Stem* medium, rather slender, bracted. *Cavity* acute
to sometimes obtuse, medium to deep, moderately broad, often thinly russeted with greenish russet, usually symmetrical, sometimes lipped. *Calyx*
medium to rather large, open or closed; lobes rather long, moderately broad.
Basin shallow, narrow to medium in width, obtuse, wrinkled.

Skin rather thin, moderately tender, smooth, pale yellow or greenish
often nearly or quite overspread with light and dark red splashed and irregularly striped with deep crimson or carmine and covered with rather heavy
distinct bluish bloom. *Dots* numerous, small, whitish.

Calyx tube long, funnel-form. *Stamens* median to marginal.

Core small, somewhat abaxile; cells closed or somewhat open; core lines clasping or sometimes nearly meeting. *Carpels* broadly ovate or obovate, slightly tufted. *Seeds* small, moderately wide, plump, obtuse.

Flesh white often strongly tinged with red, rather fine, crisp, tender, juicy, brisk subacid, aromatic, sometimes slightly astringent, good to very good.

Season late July to September.

RED GRAVENSTEIN.

REFERENCES. 1. Leroy, **1873**:339. fig. 2. *Can. Hort.*, **16**:362. 1893. **3.** Lucas, Ed., *Ill. Handb. der Obstk.*, **1893**:250.

SYNONYMS. GRAVENSTEIN ROUGE (1). RED GRAVENSTEIN (2, 3). *Rother Gravensteiner* (1).

Bud sports of the Gravenstein have appeared at different times which bear red fruit. For a statement concerning such sports the reader is referred to Gravenstein, page 84. ·

RED HOOK.

This is a large, late summer or early autumn apple which is being grown commercially to a limited extent in the vicinity of Red Hook, Dutchess county, N. Y. W. S. Teator, of Upper Red Hook, who furnished us with the fruit from which the following description was made, states that the variety originated in his locality and has been known under the name of Red Ox or Striped Ox. As the name Striped Ox has been applied to other varieties he proposes the name Red Hook for this apple. The tree is large, low branching and an annual cropper yielding heavy crops. The fruit is firm, smooth, bright, attractive, quite free from the attacks of fungi and good for culinary use but when overripe it becomes dry and worthless. It stands shipment well and is one of the earliest fruits of that locality that can be shipped to Europe.

FRUIT.

Fruit large to very large. *Form* roundish to roundish conic, somewhat elliptical, symmetrical, sometimes faintly ribbed. *Stem* short, thick to rather slender. *Cavity* acuminate, deep, broad, gently furrowed, smooth or partly russeted. *Calyx* medium to rather small, partly closed; lobes broad, obtuse to acute. *Basin* rather small, moderately deep, narrow to medium in width, abrupt.

Skin tough, attractive pale yellow, rather thinly mottled and blushed with lively red, and sparingly striped and splashed with bright carmine. *Dots* rather small, numerous, whitish or with russet center.

Calyx tube elongated funnel-shape approaching conical. *Stamens* median.

Core medium or below, axile or nearly so; cells pretty symmetrical, closed; core lines clasping the cylinder. *Carpels* broadly roundish. *Seeds* rather dark brown, medium size, irregular, obtuse.

Flesh firm, coarse, tender, juicy, sprightly subacid, good.

Season late summer or early autumn.

RED JUNE

RED JUNE.

REFERENCES. 1. Humrickhouse, *Mag. Hort.*, 14:389. 1848. *fig.* 2. Phœnix, *Horticulturist*, 4:472. 1850. 3. Barry, 1851:280. 4. *Horticulturist*, 10:87. 1855. 5. *Am. Pom. Soc. Cat.*, 1856. 6. *Horticulturist*, 12:473. 1857. 7. Downing, 1857:127. 8. Gregg, 1857:35. 9. Hooper, 1857:23. 10. Hovey, *Mag. Hort.*, 27:68. 1861. *fig.* 11. Warder, 1867:666. *fig.* 12. Downing, 1869:118. *fig.* 13. *Ib.*, 1872:10 index, app. 14. Fitz, 1872:151. 15. Thomas, 1875:190. 16. Wickson, 1889:242. 17. Lyon, *Mich. Hort. Soc. Rpt.*, 1890: 206. 18. *Am. Pom. Soc. Cat.*, 1891. 19. Bailey, *An. Hort.*, 1892:236. 20. *Ib.*, 1892:247. 21. Clayton, *Ala. Sta. Bul.*, 47:5. 1893. 22. Hoskins, *Rural N. Y.*, 53:248. 1894. 23. Stinson, *Ark. Sta. Rpt.*, 1894:44. 24. Massey, *N. C. Sta. Bul.*, 149:316. 1898. 25. Budd-Hansen, 1903:162. *fig.* 26. Bruner, *N. C. Sta. Bul.*, 182:21. 1903. 27. Farrand, *Mich. Sta. Bul.*, 205:46. 1903.

SYNONYMS. *Blush June* (12, 15, 23). *Blushed June* (7, 10). CAROLINA JUNE (4, 5, 6). *Carolina Red* (14). CAROLINA RED JUNE (2, 3, 7, 8, 9, 10, 11, 12, 15, 16, 19, 22, 23, 24). *Georgia June* (12). *Jones Early Harvest* (13). JUNE (1). *Knight's Red June* (12). RED JUNE (13, 17, 18, 20, 21, 27). *Red June* (7, 10, 12, 14, 15, 23). RED JUNEATING (14). RED JUNE, *Carolina* (25, 26). *Susy Clark* (13). *Wilson's June* (12).

An attractive little apple, deep red over yellow, tender, brisk subacid, very good. The tree is a moderate grower, a pretty reliable bearer, and commonly yields good crops. Some find it profitable because it is handsome and takes well in some markets. The crop ripens so unevenly that it should have two or three pickings in order to secure the fruit in good condition. The variety is more popular South and West than it is in New York

Historical. This is a southern apple which is supposed to have originated in North Carolina. It has long been known in cultivation and is commonly listed by nurserymen, but it has not been planted to any considerable extent in New York.

TREE.

Tree moderately vigorous with short, moderately stout, curved branches. *Form* at first upright but becoming spreading or roundish. *Twigs* very short, straight, slender; internodes medium size. *Bark* dull brown, lightly mottled with scarf-skin; slightly pubescent. *Lenticels* scattering, small, oblong, not raised. *Buds* small, plump, acute, free, slightly pubescent.

FRUIT.

Fruit small or below medium, uniform in size and shape. *Form* roundish ovate or a little inclined to oblong, rather regular; sides usually unequal. *Stem* variable, usually long, slender. *Cavity* small, acuminate to acute, shallow to medium in depth, narrow, slightly symmetrical, sometimes compressed, russeted but slightly if at all. *Calyx* medium to large, leafy, closed or sometimes a little open; lobes long, rather narrow, acuminate. *Basin* small, shallow, narrow, rather obtuse, smooth or wavy.

Skin thin, tender, smooth, glossy, pale yellow or greenish, nearly overspread with deep purplish-red approaching blackish-purple on the exposed cheek; some specimens are entirely red. *Dots* rather numerous, very small, inconspicuous, light.

Calyx tube short, moderately wide, conical to funnel-form. *Stamens* median to marginal.

Core large, axile to somewhat abaxile; cells symmetrical, open or sometimes closed; core lines slightly clasping or meeting. *Carpels* broadly ovate to elliptical. *Seeds* rather dark brown, numerous, small to medium, plump, acute.

Flesh white, fine, tender, juicy, brisk subacid, good to very good.

Season late July to early winter.

Striped Red June. A variety has found its way into cultivation which appears in all respects identical with the Red June except that the fruit is striped. It is supposed to be either a seedling of the Red June or a sport of that variety (11, 12).

RED TRANSPARENT.

References. **1.** Gibb, *Ia. Hort. Soc. Rpt.*, **1883**:437. **2.** Budd, *Ia. Agr. Coll. Bul.*, **1885**:13. **3.** Van Deman, *U. S. Pom. Rpt.*, **1888**:572. fig. **4.** Budd, *Ia. Agr. Coll. Bul.*, **1890**:18. **5.** Bailey, *An. Hort.*, **1892**:248. **6.** Beach, *N. Y. Sta. An. Rpt.*, 13:584. 1894. **7.** Troop, *Ind. Sta. An. Rpt.*, 12:81. 1899.

Synonyms. *No. 333* (1, 2, 3, 4). Red Transparent (2, 3, 4, 5, 6, 7). *Red Transparent* (1). *Skvosnoi krasnoi* (2). Skwosnoi Krasnoi (1).

A Russian variety of little value where Primate can be grown. Fruit medium size with pale skin nearly covered with red and overspread with delicate bloom. Basin irregularly wrinkled; calyx prominent, closed; flesh greenish-white, not very crisp; water-cores badly; season late July and early August (6).

RED WINE.

References. **1.** Webster, *Montreal Hort. Soc. Rpt.*, 7:54. 1881. **2.** Gibb, *Ib.*, 9:95. 1883. **3.** *Ib.*, *Ia. Hort. Soc. Rpt.*, **1883**:439. **4.** Budd, *Ia. Agr. Coll. Bul.*, **1885**:14. **5.** Bailey, *An. Hort.*, **1892**:248. **6.** Taylor, *Me. Pom. Soc. Rpt.*, **1892**:57. **7.** Hansen, *S. D. Sta. Bul.*, 76:92. 1902. **8.** Budd-Hansen, 1903:163.

Synonyms. *No. 343* (2, 4, 7). Red Wine (4, 5, 6, 7, 8). *Red Wine* (1, 2, 3). *Rother Weinapfel* (7). *Rotherwein appel* (4). *Vinnoe Krasnoe Osennee* (4). Weinapfel Rother (2). Weinapfel rother (3). Weinappel Rother (1).

A Russian apple of the Lowland *Raspberry* type (7, 8). Fruit medium, waxen-white almost completely covered with bright red. Flesh white, tender, subacid, good. Season August and September.

So far as we know this variety has not been tested in New York.

REED.

REFERENCE. 1. Downing, 1869 :329.
SYNONYMS. None.

A local variety which according to Downing originated with George Reed, Leedsville, Dutchess county, N. Y. Fruit medium, whitish shaded and mottled with light and dark red; flesh white, a little stained next the skin, pleasant subacid, good; season November.

We are unacquainted with this variety and have received no report concerning it from any of our correspondents.

REPKA.

REFERENCES. 1. Barry, 1883 :334. 2. Schroeder, *Montreal Hort. Soc. Rpt.,* 1886–87 :79. 3. Gibb, *Am. Pom. Soc. Rpt.,* 1887 :57. 4. Bailey, *An. Hort.,* 1892 :248. 5. Beach, *N. Y. Sta. An. Rpt.,* 13 :584. 1894.
SYNONYMS. *No. 139* (2, 3). REPKA (1, 2, 3, 4, 5). *Riepka* (3).

A medium sized yellow apple of good quality in season in August and early September; inferior to Primate both in appearance and quality. The tree comes into bearing moderately early and is an annual cropper yielding fair to good crops. Not recommended for planting in New York.

This is distinct from either Repka Aport, Repka Sweet or Repka Malenka.

Historical. Origin Russia. Received in 1884 from Ellwanger and Barry, Rochester, N. Y., for testing at this Station. It has been but little disseminated in New York.

TREE.

Tree rather small; not a vigorous grower. *Form* spreading or roundish. *Twigs* short, straight, stout with large terminal buds; internodes short. *Bark* brown or reddish-brown, heavily coated with gray scarf-skin. *Lenticels* scattering, medium to small, round, slightly raised. *Buds* large, prominent, broad, plump, obtuse, free, slightly pubescent.

FRUIT.

Fruit medium or below. *Form* roundish oblate inclined to conic, regular; sides unequal. *Stem* rather short, moderately slender. *Cavity* acute, medium in depth to deep, rather wide, heavily russeted and with outspreading russet rays. *Calyx* rather small, closed. *Basin* moderately deep, wide, somewhat abrupt, usually furrowed or wrinkled.

Skin moderately thin, tough, clear pale yellow or whitish. *Dots* small, white, pale and submerged or russet.

Calyx tube long, narrow, funnel-form.

Core small; cells closed; core lines clasping. *Carpels* broadly roundish. *Seeds* medium size, wide, flat, obtuse.

Flesh white, rather firm, fine, juicy, crisp, rather mild subacid, good.

Season August and September.

RIBSTON.

REFERENCES. 1. Forsyth, 1803:52. 2. Diel, 11:93. 1813. 3. Coxe, 1817:
125. *fig.* 4. Forsyth, 1824:124. 5. Buel, *N. Y. Bd. Agr. Mem.,* 1828:476.
6. Fessenden, 1828:130. 7. *Pom. Mag.,* 3:No. 141. 1830. *col. pl.* 8. *London
Hort. Soc. Cat.,* 1831:32. 9. Ronalds, 1831:54. 10. Kenrick, 1832:52.
11. Floy-Lindley, 1833:59. 12. Manning, 1838:54. 13. Manning, *Mag. Hort.,*
7:49. 1841. 14. Russell, *Ib.,* 10:403. 1844. 15. Downing, 1845:131. 16.
Downing, *Horticulturist,* 2:416. 1847. 17. *Ib.,* 3:421. 1848. 18. Thomas,
1849:152. 19. Cole, 1849:126. 20. *Horticulturist,* 6:16, 292. 1851. 21. Emmons, *Nat. Hist. N. Y.,* 3:75. 1851. 22. Elliott, 1854:155. 23. *Am. Pom.
Soc. Cat.,* 1854. 24. *Mag. Hort.,* 21:62. 1855. 25. Hooper, 1857:80. 26.
Oberdieck, *Ill. Handb. Obst.,* 1:353. 1858. 27. *Mag. Hort.,* 26:116. 1860.
28. Warder, 1867:612. 29. Regel, 1868:463. 30. Berghuis, 1868:No. 3.
col. pl. 31. Mas, *LeVerger,* 1868:99. 32. Leroy, 1873:750. *figs.* 33. Lauche,
1:No. 25. 1882. *col. pl.* 34. Barry, 1883:353. 35. Hogg, 1884:194. 36. Lyon,
Mich. Hort. Soc. Rpt., 1890:296. 37. Hick, *Can. Hort.,* 15:157. 1892. 38.
Bailey, *An. Hort.,* 1892:248. 39. Bredsted, 1893:137. 40. Gaucher, 1894:
No. 19. *col. pl.* 41. Bunyard, *Jour. Roy. Hort. Soc.,* 1898:355. 42. *Can.
Hort.,* 22:510. 1899. 43. Eneroth-Smirnoff, 1901:224. 44. Waugh, *Rural
N. Y.,* 61:285, 286. 1902. *fig.* 45. Budd-Hansen, 1903:165. *fig.* 46. Beach
and Clark, *N. Y. Sta. Bul.,* 248:141. 1904.

SYNONYMS. *Beautiful Pippin* (25). *Englische Granat-Reinette* (40).
Essex Pippin (40). *Formosa* (25). *Formosa Pippin* (7, 10, 15, 22, 32, 40).
Glory of York (10, 15, 22, 25, 32, 35, 40, of some 7). *Granat-Reinette* (40).
Nonpareille (40). *Pepin Ribston* (40). *Reinette Grenade Anglaise* (40).
Reinette de Traver (32). RIBSTON (2, 8, 9, 11, 20, 23, 24, 26, 27, 29, 30, 31,
33, 36, 37, 39, 42, 43, 44, 45). RIBSTON PIPPIN (1, 3, 4, 5, 7, 10, 13, 14, 15,
16, 17, 18, 19, 21, 22, 25, 28, 32, 34, 35, 38, 41, 44). *Ribston Pippin* (45, 46).
RIBSTON PEPPING (40). *Ribston's Pepping* (40). *Ribstone* (32). RIBSTONE
PIPPIN (6, 12). RIDGE (46 by error). *Rockhill's Russet* (32). *Travers*
(15, 22, 25, 32). *Travers Apple* (7, 10, 40). *Travers Peppin* (40). *Travers
Pippin* (35). *Travers Reinette* (40).

Ribston evidently belongs in the same group as Hubbardston.
It is much esteemed for its rich flavor and fine quality and it is
desirable either for dessert or culinary uses. The fruit is pretty
smooth and uniform but often it averages below medium size
and is ordinary in appearance. Heat ripens it quickly and it is
not considered a very good keeper. In cold storage, if properly
handled before storing, it is possibly equal to Tompkins King
or Hubbardston as a keeper (46). Its season in Southern New
York extends from late September to November or December,
and in the northern and more elevated regions from late fall to
early or mid-winter and sometimes a portion of the fruit may be kept

RIBSTON

till spring in ordinary storage. The tree is pretty hardy, vigorous, healthy and long-lived. It comes into bearing rather young and usually bears some fruit every year. Occasionally the crops are heavy but more often they vary from moderate to rather light. Generally speaking, it is hardly satisfactory as a cropper and Hubbardston is much to be preferred for planting in commercial orchards in New York.

Historical. Ribston originated more than two hundred years ago in Yorkshire, England (1, 7). In that country it has long been considered the standard of excellence among dessert apples. It has long been known in cultivation in America but has not gained the standing here that it holds in England. It is not grown to any considerable extent in New York but succeeds better farther north, as in portions of Northern New England and of Canada, where it is of some commercial importance (16, 20, 24, 44).

TREE.

Tree medium in size or sometimes rather large, moderately vigorous to vigorous with rather stout, stocky branches. *Form* rather upright and spreading or roundish, not very regular. *Twigs* medium to rather long, rather slender to moderately stout; internodes medium to long. *Bark* bright dark reddish-brown and olive-green, somewhat mottled with grayish scarf-skin. *Lenticels* conspicuous, scattering, small to medium, elongated or roundish. *Buds* medium to large, broad, plump, obtuse, nearly free, very pubescent. *Foliage* rather dense; leaves broad.

FRUIT.

Fruit medium or above, pretty uniform in shape and size. *Form* roundish, rather broad and flattened at the base, narrowing somewhat toward the basin, occasionally a little inclined to roundish oblong, often broadly and obscurely ribbed. *Stem* pubescent, medium to short, occasionally moderately slender, more often rather thick, sometimes irregularly swollen or inserted under a lip. *Cavity* rather large, acute, moderately shallow to rather deep, wide to moderately narrow, sometimes furrowed or compressed, occasionally smooth and green but often faintly russeted and with some outspreading russet. *Calyx* variable, small to rather large, closed or partly open; lobes sometimes separated at the base, erect or converging, tips usually somewhat reflexed. *Basin* small to medium, shallow to moderately deep, moderately narrow, more or less abrupt or occasionally obtuse, often slightly furrowed and wrinkled.

Skin smooth or slightly roughened with russet, deep yellow or greenish-yellow more or less overspread with rather dull red which in highly colored specimens deepens to a distinct red with some obscure carmine stripes and splashes. *Dots* scattering, conspicuous toward the base, more numerous and smaller toward the basin, pale, sometimes whitish, often areolar with russet center. *Prevailing effect* sometimes rather attractive but more often the colors are rather dull.

Calyx tube rather wide, cone-shape or sometimes funnel-form. *Stamens* basal.

Core below medium to small, axile or with a narrow hollow cylinder at the axis; cells pretty regular, closed; core lines clasping to nearly meeting. *Carpels* roundish to nearly elliptical, emarginate, slightly tufted. *Seeds* variable, some abortive, usually but few are plump, light and dark brown, rather large, moderately narrow to wide, medium to long, obtuse or sometimes approaching acute, sometimes slightly tufted.

Flesh tinged with yellow, firm, very crisp, medium in texture, juicy, pleasantly aromatic, rich, sprightly subacid, very good.

Season late September to December or later.

RICHARD GRAFT.

REFERENCES. 1. *Mag. Hort.*, 18:492. 1852. 2. Downing, 1857:101. fig. 3. Warder, 1867:457. fig. 4. Thomas, 1875:204. 5. *Am. Pom. Soc. Cat.*, 1877:14. 6. Barry, 1883:340. 7. *Mich. Hort. Soc. Rpt.*, 1888. 8. Hendricks, *Rural N. Y.*, 47:759, 811. 1888. 9. Bailey, *An. Hort.*, 1892:248. 10. Budd-Hansen, 1903:166.

SYNONYMS. *Derrick and Ann* (8). *Derrick's Graft* (2, 4). *Red Spitzenberg* (3). *Red Spitzenburgh* (2, 4, 6). RICHARD (1). RICHARD GRAFT (2, 3, 4, 5, 6, 7, 8, 9). *Strawberry* (2, 3). *Wine* (2, 3).

This is a very fine fall apple of superior dessert quality. It begins to ripen during late August or early September; the crop ripens in succession during a period of several weeks, and some portion of the fruit may be kept till late autumn. Several pickings are required in order to secure the fruit in prime condition. The tree is upright, of medium size, moderately vigorous, long-lived and a reliable cropper yielding good crops biennially. It is an excellent variety for home use and is being grown to a limited extent in commercial orchards with profit.

Historical. This variety was originated at Greenport, Columbia county, N. Y., by Richard Delamatter. It was introduced about 1860 by E. G. Studley, a nurseryman of Claverack, Columbia county, N. Y. Its cultivation is being extended somewhat in Columbia county, but as yet it is but little known outside of the Hudson valley.

TREE.

Tree of medium size, moderately vigorous. *Form* upright or roundish, open. *Twigs* moderately long, curved, moderately stout; internodes medium. *Bark* dark brown, lightly streaked with scarf-skin; pubescent. *Lenticels* quite numerous, medium size, round, not raised. *Buds* medium size, broad, acute to obtuse, free, pubescent.

FRUIT (2, 8).

Fruit medium size. *Form* roundish oblate. *Stem* of medium length, slender. *Cavity* large. *Calyx* small, closed. *Basin* medium size.

Skin yellow, nearly covered with stripes and splashes of deep red.

Flesh yellowish, very tender, juicy, aromatic, subacid, very good.

Season September.

ROLFE.

REFERENCES. 1. Downing, **1857**:167. 2. Warder, **1867**:725. 3. Thomas, **1875**:505. 4. *Me. Pom. Soc. Rpt.*, **1876**:149. 5. *Ib.*, **1885**:135, 138. 6. *Ib.*, **1888**:120. fig. 7. Lyon, *Mich. Hort. Soc. Rpt.*, **1890**:294. 8. Bailey, *An. Hort.*, **1892**:248. 9. Munson, *Me. Sta. Rpt.*, **1893**:133. 10. *Ib.*, **1896**:71, 81. 11. *Am. Pom. Soc. Cat.*, **1897**:14. 12. Munson, *Me. Sta. Rpt.*, **1902**:90, 92. 13. *Me. Pom. Soc. Rpt.*, **1902**:49, 50. 14. Budd-Hansen, **1903**:166.

SYNONYMS. MACOMBER (1, 2, 3, 7). *Macomber* (4, 9, 14). ROLFE (4, 5, 6, 8, 9, 10, 11, 12, 13, 14).

Fruit medium to large, of good quality and rather attractive for a yellowish apple. It is in season from late September to December or January. The tree is very hardy, vigorous and a reliable cropper. At the present time it is probably grown more extensively in Maine than in any other section of the country. It is there regarded highly wherever it is known and is gaining in popularity among fruit growers (1, 6, 10, 12). It is worthy of testing in those portions of the state where superior hardiness in a variety is a matter of prime importance.

Historical. Originated in the town of Guilford, Maine, about 1820. Said to be a seedling of the Blue Pearmain. It has, as yet, been disseminated but sparingly in this state and is but little known among New York fruit growers.

TREE.

Tree rather large, vigorous. *Form* roundish to spreading and drooping, rather dense; laterals slender, willowy. *Twigs* rather long, irregularly crooked, slender to moderately stout; internodes long to below medium. *Bark* brown to reddish-brown with an occasional tinge of olive-green, overlaid with scarf-skin, pubescent near tips. *Lenticels* moderately numerous, of a dull color but rather conspicuous, medium or above, roundish, not raised. *Buds* very deeply set in bark, medium in size, broad, flat, obtuse, appressed, pubescent.

FRUIT.

Fruit medium to sometimes large, pretty uniform in shape and size. *Form* roundish to roundish oblate, regular or somewhat angular, symmetrical. *Stem* short to medium and rather slender. *Cavity* acute to slightly acuminate, moderately deep, rather wide, sometimes slightly furrowed or compressed. *Calyx* small to above medium, closed; lobes short to moderately long, rather wide, acute. *Basin* below medium to rather large, pretty regular, shallow to moderately deep, narrow to rather wide, a little abrupt, slightly wrinkled.

Skin moderately thin, rather tough, glossy, clear pale yellow, sometimes faintly blushed or in well colored specimens distinctly shaded and striped with lively red. *Dots* numerous, inconspicuous, small. *Prevailing effect* yellow or yellow and red.

Calyx tube rather narrow, short, funnel-shape. *Stamens* median.

Core variable, below medium to large, abaxile; cells usually symmetrical, wide open; core lines clasping. *Carpels* often markedly concave, broadly ovate, emarginate, tufted. *Seeds* above medium, rather long and narrow, plump, acute or approaching acuminate, light brown.

Flesh whitish with slight tinge of yellow, moderately fine-grained, crisp, tender, juicy, briskly subacid, good.

Season late September to December or January.

ROMAN STEM.

REFERENCES. **1.** Coxe, **1817** :132. *fig.* **2.** Thacher, **1822** :135. **3.** *London Hort. Soc. Cat.,* **1831** :33. **4.** Downing, **1845** :131. **5.** Kirtland, *Horticulturist,* **2** :545. 1848. **6.** Thomas, **1849** :185. **7.** Phœnix, *Horticulturist,* **4** :472. 1850. **8.** Emmons, *Nat. Hist. N. Y.,* **3** :86. 1851. **9.** Elliott, **1854** :155. **10.** *Horticulturist,* **10** :87. 1855. **11.** Hooper, **1857** :81. **12.** *Mag. Hort.,* **24** :110. 1858. **13.** *Am. Pom. Soc. Cat.,* **1862. 14.** Warder, **1867** :579. *fig.* **15.** Barry, **1883** : 354. **16.** Lyon, *Mich. Hort. Soc. Rpt.,* **1890** :296. **17.** Bailey, *An. Hort.,* **1892** :248. **18.** Hansen, *S. D. Sta. Bul.,* **76** :94. 1902. **19.** Budd-Hansen, **1903** :166. **20.** Beach and Clark, *N. Y. Sta. Bul.,* **248** :142. 1904.

SYNONYMS. *French Pippin* of some (9). ROMAN STEM (1, 2, 3, 4, 5, 6, 7, 8, 9, 10, 11, 12, 13, 14, 15, 16, 17, 18, 19, 20).

Fruit about medium size, whitish-yellow, often somewhat blushed. The flesh is juicy, aromatic, subacid and very good in quality, particularly for dessert use. It is in season from midautumn to midwinter. " A good fruit but in a great measure superseded by other sorts " (15). The tree is moderately vigorous, spreading, irregular, very hardy and very productive. In the trying climate of the upper Mississippi valley it has proved hardier than most of the old varieties from the East and has succeeded well where the varieties of the grade of hardiness of Baldwin and Rhode Island *Greening* have failed. It is not well suited for commercial purposes because it is yellow, lacks good size and is not a late keeper.

Historical. Coxe published the following description of Roman Stem in 1817: "This apple was first propagated in the neighbourhood of Burlington, New-Jersey, where the original tree is now standing. It is an excellent early winter fruit, much admired for its tender, mild, juicy and agreeable properties; the size is small, the form round, the stalk of singular appearance, from a fleshy protuberance of the neighboring part, resembling an aquiline nose, whence the apple derives its name — the skin is rough, the color yellow, with black clouds and spots — the tree is of handsome and vigorous growth, with long shoots, and great fruitfulness; it is in every respect deserving of extensive cultivation."

Roman Stem has been pretty widely disseminated and considerably cultivated in various parts of the Southern, Central and Western states but it is now generally superseded by other kinds. It is but little grown in New York.

ROMNA.

REFERENCES. **1.** Budd, *Am. Pom. Soc. Rpt.*, **1883** :73. **2.** *Ib., Ia. Agr. Coll. Bul.*, **1883** :29. **3.** *Ib.*, **1885** :20, 23, 29. **4.** Gibb, *Am. Pom. Soc. Rpt.*, **1887** : 50. **5.** Lyon, *U. S. Pom. Bul.*, **2** :45. 1888. **6.** Budd, *Ia. Agr. Coll. Bul.*, **1890** :24. **7.** *Ib.*, **1892** :7. **8.** *Ib., Ia. Sta. Bul.*, **18** :520. 1892. **9.** *Ib.*, **19** : 541. 1892. **10.** Troop, *Ind. Sta. Bul.*, **53** :124. 1894. **11.** Budd, *Ia. Sta. Bul.*, **31** :333. 1895. **12.** Beach, Paddock and Close, *N. Y. Sta. An. Rpt.*, **15** :275. 1896. **13.** Thomas, **1897** :295. fig. **14.** Waugh, *Vt. Sta. Bul.*, **61** :31. 1897. fig. **15.** Budd, *Ia. Sta. Bul.*, **41** :69, 70, 80. 1899. **16.** Troop, *Ind. Sta. Rpt.*, **1899** :81. **17.** Hansen, *S. D. Sta. Bul.*, **76** :94. 1902. fig. **18.** Budd-Hansen, **1903** :168. **19.** Beach and Clark, *N. Y. Sta. Bul.*, **248** :142. 1904.

SYNONYMS. *No. 11 M* (1, 2, 6, 7, 9). *No. 599 Dept.* (1, 2, 3, 4, 6, 7, 8, 9, 17, 18). *Omensk* (4). ROMENSKOE (2, 4, 5, 8). *Romenskoe* (1, 3, 17, 18). ROMNA (1, 3, 6, 7, 9, 10, 11, 12, 13, 14, 15, 16, 17, 18, 19). *Romnenskoe* (3, 4, 5).

A Russian variety received from Dr. T. H. Hoskins, Newport, Vermont, in 1888 for testing at this Station. It was described in 1896 (12) as being in season that year during the last of August and the first of September. This statement was erroneous because it was incomplete. While the fruit began to come in season during the last of August and the first of September some portion of it was kept in ordinary storage till midwinter. In a subsequent report (19) it was correctly stated that as fruited at this Station the commercial limit of this variety is early October and its season in ordinary storage extends from September to January. It is properly classed as a fall and early winter apple here. The tree is vigorous, hardy, comes into bearing rather young and yields good crops biennially. It does not appear to be worthy of the attention of fruit growers in New York except possibly where superior hardiness is a prime requisite. The fruit corresponds very closely with the illustrated description given by Troop (10, 16) and Waugh (14) but it varies considerably from the descriptions of Budd and Hansen (3, 6, 9, 11, 15, 17, 18) particularly in that it is usually oblate conic and is in season during the autumn and early winter instead of late winter and spring.

The following is one of Budd's descriptions of Romna (9, 11). "This succeeds best on dry soil where its roots run very deep. Fruit medium in size, conical, smooth, handsomely colored. Flesh white, firm, quite acid and best for cooking, but when matured it is much better for dessert use than Willow or Missouri Pippin or other coarse sorts found in our markets. Season, midwinter here, and late winter north of 43d parallel."

TREE.

Tree moderately vigorous to vigorous; branches short, stout, curved, crooked and drooping. *Form* spreading, drooping, flat. *Twigs* short to medium, straight, moderately slender to stout, with large terminal buds; internodes medium to long. *Bark* brown, somewhat tinged with red, streaked with grayish scarf-skin; slightly pubescent near tips. *Lenticels* scattering, small to medium, roundish or oval, slightly raised. *Buds* moderately small to very large and prominent, broad, very plump, acute, free or nearly so, scarcely pubescent.

FRUIT.

Fruit medium or sometimes rather large, not very uniform in shape or size. *Form* usually oblate conic, irregularly elliptical or broadly and obscurely angular, often unsymmetrical with sides unequal. *Stem* medium length to short and stout, pubescent. *Cavity* medium to rather large, acute or sometimes nearly obtuse, medium in depth to rather deep, rather wide to narrow, somewhat furrowed, occasionally lipped, russeted and often with conspicuous outspreading russet. *Calyx* above medium to large, open or partly closed; lobes often separated at the base, medium in length, rather broad, acute. *Basin* medium to large, often oblique, moderately narrow to wide, sometimes compressed, abrupt, furrowed and wrinkled.

Skin thick, tough, smooth or partly roughened with flecks of russet; color greenish becoming yellow more or less blushed and overspread with thin bloom. Well colored specimens are covered to a considerable extent with pinkish-red, blushed and striped with bright carmine. *Dots* small, numerous, pale yellow or grayish, sometimes rather conspicuous.

Calyx tube rather long, wide, funnel-shape. *Stamens* median.

Core medium to small, axile or nearly so; cells closed; core lines meeting or slightly clasping. *Carpels* roundish ovate, somewhat emarginate, slightly tufted. *Seeds* medium to small, rather short, narrow, plump, obtuse to acute, rather dark brown.

Flesh yellowish, firm, moderately coarse, juicy, briskly subacid, slightly astringent, fair to good.

Season September to January (19).

RONK.

REFERENCES. 1. *Rural N. Y.*, 48:279. 1889. *fig.* .2. Lyon, *Mich. Sta. Bul.*, 143:201. 1897. 3. Farrand, *Ib.*, 205:46. 1903. 4. Beach and Clark, *N. Y. Sta. Bul.*, 248:142. 1904.

SYNONYMS. None.

Fruit of the Vandevere type, medium or above, rather dull red, pleasant subacid, good; season October to late winter. Commercial limit in ordinary storage January (4). The tree comes into bearing rather young and is moderately productive. It has not been sufficiently tested to determine its value for this state.

Historical. Originated about 1860 with Mr. Ronk, Boone county, Indiana. It is supposed to be a seedling of Vandevere which it much resembles (1).

ROSE RED.

REFERENCES. 1. *Rural N. Y.*, 1871 (cited by 5). 2. Downing, 1872:30 app. *fig.* 3. Thomas, 1875:511. 4. Lyon, *Mich. Hort. Soc. Rpt.*, 1890:296. 5. Ragan, *U. S. P. B. I. Bul.*, 56:267. 1905.

SYNONYMS. *Autumn Rose* (4). ROSE RED (1, 2, 3, 4, 5).

A variety of unknown origin. It is supposed to have originated in Egypt, Monroe county, N. Y. According to Downing (2) the tree is thrifty, a reliable cropper and very productive; the fruit medium, roundish oblate, whitish, striped and splashed with light and dark red; flesh yellowish, very tender, lively subacid, very good; in season during late September, October and November.

We are unacquainted with this variety and have received no report concerning it from any of our correspondents.

SAFSTAHOLMS.

REFERENCES. 1. Regel, 1868:473. 2. Gibb, *Montreal Hort. Soc. Rpt.,* 1886–87:81. 3. Eneroth-Smirnoff, 1901:46. 4. Hansen, *S. D. Sta. Bul.,* 76:96. 1902.

SYNONYMS. SAFSTAHOLM (2, 4). SÄFSTAHOLMSÄPLE (1). SÄFSTAHOLMS-ÄPPLE (3).

This is an apple of fairly good red color, not particularly bright yet not unattractive. The flesh lacks piquancy and is not very juicy but because of its distinct aroma and rich subacid flavor it is classed among the good dessert apples. It is hardly acid enough for culinary use. The tree is a pretty good grower, comes into bearing young and so far as tested at this Station promises to be productive. It is doubtful whether it has sufficient value for the New York fruit grower to make it worthy of trial in this state.

Historical. Originated in Sweden about 1835. It was received for testing at this Station from the United States Pomologist in 1901.

TREE.

Tree moderately vigorous with rather short, slender branches. *Form* upright spreading or roundish, open. *Twigs* short, rather slender to moderately stout, straight or nearly so; internodes short to medium. *Bark* rather dull brown tinged with red, mottled with heavy scarf-skin, pubescent. *Lenticels* very scattering, small to medium, roundish, not raised. *Buds* often rather deeply set in the bark, medium size or below, plump, obtuse to somewhat acute, free, pubescent.

FRUIT.

Fruit medium to large, pretty uniform in shape and size. *Form* oblong to oblong conic, somewhat elliptical, often indistinctly ribbed; sides often unequal. *Stem* short to medium, moderately slender to rather thick. *Cavity* large, acute to acuminate, moderately shallow to deep, wide, sometimes lipped, often russeted. *Calyx* medium or below, usually partly open; lobes moderately narrow, acute. *Basin* small to medium, obtuse to rather abrupt, shallow to moderately deep, moderately narrow to rather wide, gently furrowed.

Skin thin, smooth or sometimes slightly rough toward the apex, pale yellow mottled and blushed with red, becoming rather dull red over a considerable portion of the fruit, mottled and splashed with carmine and sometimes marked with flecks and irregular lines of russet. *Dots* rather conspicuous, often large, pale gray or with russet center. *Prevailing color* red.

Calyx tube cone-shape. *Stamens* basal.

Core medium to large, abaxile; cells often unsymmetrical, usually somewhat open; core lines meeting. *Carpels* roundish to broadly ovate, mucronate, sometimes emarginate, tufted. *Seeds* numerous, above medium to rather large, wide, usually obtuse, plump.

Flesh yellowish, firm, a little coarse, moderately juicy, peculiarly aromatic, mildly subacid, rich, good for dessert, rather mild for culinary use.

Season late October or November to midwinter; often some portion of the fruit may be kept in ordinary storage to March.

SAILEE RUSSET.

REFERENCE. 1. Waugh, *Vt. Sta. An. Rpt.*, **14**:307. 1901.
SYNONYMS. None.

A local variety grown in the vicinity of Lake Champlain. The following account of it is given by Waugh (1):

"Sailee was a Frenchman who came over from France about a hundred years ago and who had a farm on Cumberland Head, Clinton county, N. Y., just across from Grand Isle. He had a large orchard and grew many varieties of apples, some of which he had brought from France, others of which came from other sources, and some of which he originated himself. From his having given his own name to this variety it is supposed to have originated in his own grounds. It was early distributed to Grand Isle, and may be found in several of the older and more complete collections. It is a good variety, but not superior to Roxbury.

"Fruit oblate, slightly conic, size small to medium, cavity very deep and broad, stem medium long, slender, basin deep, corrugated, calyx small, closed, color dull green with occasional blush and considerable russet, dots russet, skin tough, flesh white, core small, flavor subacid, quality good, season early winter."

SAILLY AUTUMN.

REFERENCES. 1. Downing, **1857**:187. 2. Thomas, **1875**:511.
SYNONYMS. None.

A local variety which originated at Plattsburg, N. Y. Fruit medium, roundish conic, greenish-yellow frequently with a deep red cheek. Stalk short; cavity medium; calyx small, closed; basin small, narrow; flesh very tender, rich, aromatic, subacid, good. September (1, 2).

We are unacquainted with this variety and have received no report concerning it from any of our correspondents.

ST. LAWRENCE.

REFERENCES. 1. *London Hort. Soc. Cat.*, **1831**:No. 1187. 2. Kenrick, **1832**:28. 3. *Mag. Hort.*, **1**:149. 1835. 4. Hovey, *Ib.*, **13**:539. 1847. *fig.* 5. *Mag. Hort.*, **14**:531, 539. 1848. 6. Thomas, *Cultivator*, **5**:246. 1848. 7. Cole, **1849**:104. 8. Thomas, **1849**:152. 9. Barry, **1851**:286. 10. Waring, **1851**:30. 11. Elliott, **1854**:158. 12. Downing, **1857**:193. 13. Hooper,

1857:90. **14.** Gregg, 1857:47. **15.** *Am. Pom. Soc. Cat.*, **1862. 16.** Warder,
1867:731. **17.** Downing, 1872:10 index, app. **18.** Leroy, 1873:799. *fig.* **19.**
Montreal Hort. Soc. Rpt., 1876:11. **20.** *Ib.*, 15:19, 27. 1890. **21.** Lyon,
Mich. Hort. Soc. Rpt., 1890:298. **22.** Taylor, *Me. Pom. Soc. Rpt.*, 1892:57.
23. Bailey, *An. Hort.*, 1892:249. **24.** Woolverton, *Ont. Fr. Stas. An. Rpt.*,
6:9. 1899. *figs.* **25.** Waugh, *Vt. Sta. An. Rpt.*, 14:307. 1901. **26.** Hansen,
S. D. Sta. Bul., 76:96. 1902. **27.** Farrand, *Mich. Sta. Bul.*, 205:46. 1903.
28. Budd-Hansen, 1903:171. *fig.* **29.** *Can. Hort.*, 27:51. 1904. *fig.* **30.**
Beach and Clark, *N. Y. Sta. Bul.*, 248:143. 1904. **31.** Scriver, *Can. Hort.*,
28:277. 1905.

SYNONYMS. *Corse's St. Lawrence* (8). *Montreal* (4, 11, 18). SAINT-
LAURENT (18). ST. LAWRENCE (1, 2, 3, 4, 5, 6, 7, 8, 9, 10, 11, 12, 13, 14, 15, 16,
17, 19, 20, 21, 22, 23, 24, 25, 26, 27, 28, 29, 30, 31). *Saint-Lawrence* (18).
York and Lancaster (17).

When well grown, St. Lawrence is a large, handsome apple.
It is better for dessert than for culinary use but does not excel
standard varieties of its season for either purpose. While it
does very well in some portions of Western New York, generally speaking, it reaches a higher degree of perfection in favorable locations in the St. Lawrence valley and in the Lake Champlain region than in other portions of the state. The crop
ripens somewhat unevenly and should have more than one
picking in order to secure the fruit in prime condition and prevent great loss from dropping. It does not stand heat well
before going into storage and goes down quickly. The fruit
may not remain on the tree till it is well colored, and unless it *is*
well colored it fades in the barrel so much as to render it almost
valueless for market. It varies greatly in keeping qualities in
different seasons but usually October is its commercial limit in
ordinary storage. In cold storage it may be held until December (30). The tree is a moderately strong grower, hardy, generally pretty healthy, moderately long-lived and a reliable
cropper yielding good to rather heavy crops biennially. It is
not a very good grower in the nursery. Some growers hold
that it is desirable to topwork it upon some more vigorous stock
as Northern Spy. Although many fruit growers regard it as
a fairly profitable commercial apple it cannot be recommended
for general cultivation.

Waugh remarks, that in Grand Isle county, Vermont, " It is rather common but not highly prized. It precedes Fameuse in season and is of the same general character " (25). Woolverton (29) states that it is not planted in the commercial orchards of Ontario bordering Lakes Ontario, Erie or Huron, but it is valued in orchards along the St. Lawrence river and parts of the Province between the latitudes 45 and 46. In the Niagara district it is considerably affected by scab and by codling moth.

Historical. As early as 1835 St. Lawrence was recommended as one of the American varieties which was worthy of cultivation in England (3). Its origin does not appear to be definitely known but some credit it to this country (12, 17, 26, 28, 29). In 1848 Thomas (6) described it as a newly introduced variety cultivated in the vicinity of Rochester and originally from Lower Canada. In 1862 it was entered in the catalogue of the American Pomological Society (15). It is frequently listed by nurserymen (23) but is now seldom planted in New York state.

TREE.

Tree medium size, moderately vigorous. *Form* upright spreading. *Twigs* smooth, rather dark reddish-brown.

FRUIT.

Fruit large to medium. *Form* oblate inclined to conic varying to roundish oblate, faintly ribbed. *Stem* short to medium in length, moderately slender. *Cavity* large, acute, deep, regular, greenish-russeted. *Calyx* small, closed. *Basin* rather small, narrow, moderately deep, abrupt, wrinkled.

Skin pale yellow washed and marbled with bright red striped and splashed with bright dark carmine and overspread with thin white bloom. *Dots* numerous, rather obscure, fine, russet.

Calyx tube narrow, cone-shape to funnel-form. *Stamens* median.

Core medium size, somewhat abaxile; cells partly open; core lines clasping. *Carpels* obovate to elliptical, emarginate.

Flesh white, sometimes slightly stained with red, tender, fine-grained, crisp, juicy, mild subacid, good to very good for dessert; rather mild for culinary uses.

Season September and October.

ST. PETER.

REFERENCES. 1. Hoskins, *Ia. Hort. Soc. Rpt.*, 1879:414. 2. Webster, *Am. Pom. Soc. Rpt.*, 1883:113. 3. Gibb, *Ia. Hort. Soc. Rpt.*, 1883:440. 4. Hoskins, *Rural N. Y.*, 45:673. 1886. figs. 5. Schroeder, *Montreal Hort. Soc. Rpt.*, 1886-87:75. 6. *N. Y. Sta. An. Rpt.*, 7:91. 1888. 7. Bailey, *An. Hort.*, 1892:249. 8. Beach, *N. Y. Sta. An. Rpt.*, 13:591. 1894. 9. Ragan, *U. S. B. P. I. Bul.*, 56:231, 273. 1905.

SYNONYMS. *No. 80* (5, 9). *No. 372* (9). PETROVSKOE (5, 9). PETROW-
SKOE (2, 3). *Petrowskoe* (9). ST. PETER (1, 4, 6, 7, 8). *St. Peter* (2, 3, 9).

A small August apple, greenish-yellow streaked and splashed with dull
carmine, mild subacid, fair quality. The tree is a moderately vigorous
grower, rather slow in coming into bearing and not a reliable cropper. Not
valuable for planting in New York.

Historical. A Russian apple imported by the United States Department
of Agriculture in 1870. It was received in 1888 from Dr. T. H. Hoskins,
Newport, Vt., for testing at this Station (6).

SANDY GLASS.

REFERENCES. 1. Budd, *Ia. Agr. Coll. Bul.*, 1885:23, 30. 2. Schroeder, *Montreal Hort. Soc. Rpt.*, 1886:72. 3. Budd, *Ia. Agr. Coll. Bul.*, 1890:22. 4.
Munson, *Me. Sta. Rpt.*, 1896:76. 5. Budd, *Ia. Sta. Bul.*, 19:538. 1896.
6. Stinson, *Ark. Sta. Bul.*, 43:105. 1896. 7. Thomas, 1897:295. fig. 8.
Munson, *Me. Sta. An. Rpt.*, 18:84. 1902. 9. Hansen, *S. D. Sta. Bul.*, 76:96.
1902.

SYNONYMS. *No. 24 M* (1, 2, 3, 5, 8, 9). SANDY GLASS (1, 2, 3, 4, 5, 6, 7,
8, 9). *Steklianka pesotchnaya* (1).

A rather attractive apple of greenish-yellow color and often faintly blushed;
it is of pretty good quality but inferior to Fall Pippin and other standard
varieties of its season. The tree is below medium size, not a strong grower,
comes into bearing rather young and is a reliable cropper yielding pretty good
crops nearly annually. It is not valuable for planting in New York except
possibly in localities where superior hardiness is specially desired.

Historical. Imported from Russia by the Iowa Agricultural College (1),
from which institution it was received in 1890 for testing at this Station.

TREE.

Tree below medium size, moderately vigorous. *Form* rather flat, spreading and somewhat inclined to droop. *Twigs* moderately long, curved, stout;
internodes medium. *Bark* dull brown, heavily coated with rough gray scarf-
skin; slightly pubescent near tips. *Lenticels* very conspicuous, numerous,
large to medium, oval, raised. *Buds* medium size, broad, plump, acute to
obtuse, free, slightly pubescent.

FRUIT.

Fruit above medium to large, quite uniform in size and shape. *Form*
roundish oblate or inclined to ovate, regular, sometimes obscurely ribbed.
Stem short to medium length, rather thick. *Cavity* rather small, acuminate
to acute, moderately deep, narrow to medium in width, usually symmetrical,
more or less russeted and often with outspreading rays of thin russet. *Calyx*
small, closed; lobes medium to short, acute. *Basin* shallow to moderately
deep, medium in width to wide, lightly furrowed, wrinkled.
Skin pale greenish-yellow often becoming clear yellow as it ripens, faintly
blushed and overspread with whitish bloom. *Dots* numerous, light, small,
submerged, mingled with a few that are large and russet.

Calyx tube very long, moderately wide, conical to cylindrical. *Stamens* median to marginal.

Core medium to small, axile; cells symmetrical, closed or slightly open; core lines meeting or clasping. *Carpels* roundish or somewhat ovate, deeply emarginate. *Seeds* large, wide, plump, acute to obtuse, dull dark brown.

Flesh white or with greenish tinge, rather fine, tender, juicy, brisk subacid, fair to good.

Season September to early winter.

SAXTON.

REFERENCES. 1. *Prairie Farmer*, 1860 (cited by 9). 2. *Am. Pom. Soc. Cat.*, 1871:8. 3. Downing, 1872:11 app. 4. Thomas, 1875:511. 5. Gibb, *Montreal Hort. Soc. Rpt.*, 1886–7:94. 6. Bailey, *An. Hort.*, 1892:239. 7. *Ib.*, 1892:249. 8. Burrill and McCluer, *Ill. Sta. Bul.*, 45:321. 1896. 9. Ragan, *U. S. B. P. I. Bul.*, 56:107. 1905. 10. *Ib.*, 56:275. 1905.

SYNONYMS. FALL STRIPE (3, 7, 3, 9). *Fall Stripe* (4, 5, 10). SAXTON (1, 2, 4, 5, 6, 10). *Saxton* (3, 7, 9).

An old New England variety (3). Fruit yellow, shaded and splashed with light and dark red; flesh a little coarse, subacid, good to very good; season September. It was put upon the list of the American Pomological Society in 1871 (2) and dropped from that list in 1897. It is still listed by some nurserymen (6) but so far as we can learn it is practically unknown among New York fruit growers.

SCARLET PIPPIN.

REFERENCES. 1. Jones, *Ont. Fr. Gr. Assn. An. Rpt.*, 27:13. 1895. 2. Craig, *Can. Hort.*, 19:381. 1896. fig. 3. *Ib.*, 19:117. 1896. fig. 4. *Ib.*, *Amer. Gard.*, 20:27. 1899. figs. 5. Waugh, *Vt. Sta. Bul.*, 83:91. 1900. 6. Macoun, *Can. Dept. Agr. Bul.*, 37:41. 1901. 7. Abbott, *Can. Hort.*, 24:18, 123. 1901. 8. Budd-Hansen, 1903:172.

SYNONYMS. CRIMSON BEAUTY (3). *Crimson Pippin* (2). *Crimson Scarlet Pippin* (2). *Leeds Beauty* (4, 5, 6, 8). SCARLET PIPPIN (1, 2, 4, 5, 6, 7, 8).

An apple of the Fameuse group which quite closely resembles McIntosh (2), but is firmer in flesh and slightly more acid. "A very attractive looking apple said to sell better than Fameuse, which it does not equal in quality. Tree a strong, upright grower and said to be a heavy bearer" (6). Season about the same as Wealthy or earlier (1). It appears to be worthy of testing in New York especially in those regions of the state where Fameuse and McIntosh succeed best.

Historical. Originated about 1860 at Lynn, Leeds county, Ontario, near Brockville, where it has been locally grown for some years (4, 7). Mr. Harold Jones, Maitland, Ont., Experimenter for Ontario for apples in the

St. Lawrence river district, has had most to do with bringing this variety to notice as an autumn dessert fruit of value (6), but the report that the variety originated with him is incorrect (7).

TREE.

Tree vigorous. *Form* upright. *Twigs* long, straight, stout; internodes short. *Bark* dark brown or reddish-brown, lightly streaked with scarf-skin, pubescent near tips. *Lenticels* numerous, very conspicuous, medium size, oval, slightly raised. *Buds* medium size, flat, obtuse, appressed, pubescent.

FRUIT (4, 6).

Fruit medium size. *Form* roundish inclined to oblate, regular. *Stem* short, stout to slender. *Cavity* acute, shallow to deep, moderately wide to wide, sometimes lipped. *Calyx* closed or open. *Basin* narrow, shallow, slightly wrinkled or almost wanting.

Core small.

Flesh white, firm, crisp, tender, melting, juicy, mild subacid with a pleasant but not high flavor, very good.

Season fall and early winter.

SCHUYLER SWEET.

REFERENCES. 1. Thomas, *Am. Pom. Soc. Rpt.*, 1871:49. 2. *Rural N. Y.*, 1871:108. 3. Downing, 1872:31 app.

SYNONYMS. None.

This variety is unknown to us. We have received no report concerning it from any of our correspondents. Thomas gave the following description of it in 1871 (1): "A large, showy apple, ripening in October, originated on the lands of Rensselaer Schuyler, Seneca Falls, N. Y. Tree in vigor and form resembles the Baldwin, and is productive.

"Fruit large, roundish, inclining to roundish oblate; pale yellow with a few scattering brown dots; stalk slender, inserted in a large deep cavity; calyx closed; basin large, deep, slightly corrugated; flesh whitish, half fine, tender, moderately juicy, pleasant, sweet; quality good to very good; core small."

SCOLLOP GILLIFLOWER.

REFERENCES. 1. Kenrick, 1835:73. 2. Elliott, 1854:156. fig. 3. Watts, *Horticulturist*, 10:98. 1855. 4. Hooper, 1857:83. 5. Warder, 1867:543. 6. Downing, 1869:348. 7. Downing, *Am. Pom. Soc. Rpt.*, 1875:68. 8. Thomas, 1875:511. 9. Downing, 1876:69, 70, app.

SYNONYMS. *Cornish Gilliflower* (3). *Five-Quartered Gilliflower* (7, 9). *Jellyflower* (7, 9). *Red Gilliflower* (3, 5, of some 7 and 9). *Ribbed Gilliflower* (7, 9). SCALLOPED GILLYFLOWER (5). SCALLOPED GILLIFLOWER (1). SCOLLOP GILLIFLOWER (2, 4, 6, 7, 8, 9). SCOLLOPED GILLIFLOWER (3). *Scolloped Gilliflower* (6).

An old variety of unknown origin which was formerly grown to some extent in this state but is now practically obsolete. It has sometimes been confounded with the Red Gilliflower of Elliott (2) and sometimes with Striped Gilliflower (9). It has been much esteemed in some portions of Ohio (2). Downing describes it as a moderate or poor grower with young shoots much darker colored than those of Striped Gilliflower, the tree more spreading and unproductive and the fruit more ribbed, much darker, rather dull red with broader stripes and splashes, with flesh more yellow, mildly subacid, aromatic, richer in quality and a month or more later in ripening than Striped Gilliflower (9).

Elliott (2) describes the fruit as "medium to large, roundish conical, flattened at base, tapering toward the eye, sometimes angular, always much ribbed or scolloped; light yellow, striped and splashed with shades of light and dark red; stem short, slender; cavity deep, russeted, irregular; calyx with long segments; basin abrupt, deep, ribbed; core large, hollow; seeds ovate, rounded; flesh yellowish, firm, crisp, tender, juicy, slight tinge of sweet. November to February."

SCOTT BEST.

REFERENCE. 1. Downing, 1869:349.
SYNONYMS. None.

We are unacquainted with this variety and have received no report concerning it from any of our correspondents. According to Downing it originated on the farm of Luther Scott, Hinsdale, Cattaraugus county, N. Y. The tree is moderately vigorous, spreading; the fruit medium to large, yellowish, shaded and mottled with light red, striped and splashed with crimson; flesh whitish, fine, tender, subacid, good to very good. Season November and December (1).

SENECA FAVORITE.

REFERENCES. 1. *Mag. Hort.*, 19:165. 1853. 2. Warder, 1867:731.
SYNONYMS. None.

A large, attractive, pale yellow apple. It resembles Swaar, but is earlier and larger, and its texture is more crisp.[1] It is excellent for dessert as well as for culinary uses. The crop begins to ripen in early autumn, and continues ripening in succession through a period of several weeks. The later fruit may be kept into early winter or midwinter. The tree is of medium size, vigorous, round-headed. It is a desirable variety for the home orchard.

Historical. N. S. Page states[2] that the original tree of Seneca Favorite grew upon his father's farm, five miles southwest of Geneva, and was an old tree forty-five years ago. It has been grown to a limited extent as an apple for the home orchard in various localities in Ontario county, particu-

---

1 Wilson, C. S., *Hist. of the Apple in N. Y. State,* unpublished thesis Cornell Univ. 1905.
2 Letter, 1905.

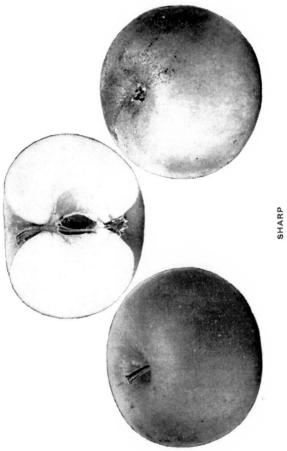

SHARP

larly in the town of Seneca. Downing gives Seneca Favorite as a synonym for Quince[1] but the true Seneca Favorite is surely not identical with Quince. It is now seldom propagated.

FRUIT.

Fruit very large to medium, usually large. *Form* variable, roundish conic to oblong conic, nearly regular but somewhat ribbed and elliptical; axis sometimes oblique; sides usually unequal. *Stem* long to medium, moderately slender. *Cavity* acute, deep, broad, quite strongly furrowed and compressed, usually somewhat russeted. *Calyx* small to above medium, closed or somewhat open; lobes broad, acute to acuminate. *Basin* very small, shallow or very shallow, narrow, obtuse to somewhat abrupt, slightly furrowed and wrinkled.

Skin rather thick, tough, smooth or slightly roughened by russet dots, at first green but becoming attractive pale yellow often with faint blush which sometimes deepens to a moderately bright rather pinkish-red, not striped. *Dots* numerous, irregular, large and small, varying from prominent russet to obscure and submerged, often reddish on blushed cheek.

Calyx tube funnel-form usually with long, narrow cylinder but sometimes short. *Stamens* median to basal.

Core rather large, somewhat abaxile; cells symmetrical, closed or somewhat open; core lines clasping. *Carpels* elliptical, emarginate, smooth. *Seeds* numerous, medium to above, dark brown, plump, obtuse to acute.

Flesh tinged with yellow, moderately coarse, crisp, tender, juicy, agreeably subacid, sprightly, very good.

Season fall and early winter to midwinter.

SHARP.

REFERENCES. 1. Beach, *N. Y. Sta. An. Rpt.*, 11:602. 1893. 2. *Ib., Gard. and For.*, 8:428. 1895. 3. Burrill and McCluer, *Ill. Sta. Bul.*, 45:311. 1896. 4. Powell and Fulton, *U. S. B. P. I. Bul.*, 48:56. 1903. 5. Beach and Clark, *N. Y. Sta. Bul.*, 248:144. 1904.

SYNONYMS. None.

This at its best is an excellent dessert fruit of very attractive appearance and very good quality. It is less suitable for most culinary uses because it is mildly subacid or nearly sweet, and it is not a good market variety because very often it is below medium size and not highly colored. It resembles Maiden Blush somewhat in shape and color. In this region it comes in season early in October or late in September. In ordinary storage it commonly reaches its commercial limit in November, but sometimes a portion of the fruit keeps till March. The tree is not a strong grower, but it comes into bearing young and yields full crops biennially.

1 Downing, **1872**:10 index, app.

It is distinct from both Sharp Greening and Sharp Russet.
Buckman believes that it is the same as the Butler or Butler Sweet
of Pennsylvania.[1]

Historical. Received from Benjamin Buckman, Farmingdale, Illinois, in
1889 for testing at this Station. Mr. Buckman obtained his stock from the
Illinois Experiment Station. That Station secured the variety from A. N.
Lawver, who received it from Halliday and Son, Baltimore, Maryland.

TREE.

Tree below medium size, a slow grower with short, moderately stout
branches. *Form* upright spreading or roundish, open. *Twigs* short to below
medium, stout to rather slender, straight; internodes medium. *Bark* dull
brown or brownish-red with some olive-green, streaked with thin scarf-skin;
slightly pubescent. *Lenticels* quite numerous, medium to small, oblong,
slightly raised. *Buds* medium size or below medium, prominent, plump,
obtuse, free or nearly so, pubescent.

FRUIT.

Fruit often below medium, sometimes above medium, uniform in shape
and size. *Form* roundish oblate to roundish conic, sometimes approaching
oblong conic, regular or very faintly ribbed, symmetrical. *Stem* often very
short and not exserted. *Cavity* usually rather large, acute to acuminate,
moderately deep to deep, moderately wide to wide, sometimes very slightly
furrowed and often russeted. *Calyx* small to medium, closed or partly open;
lobes long. *Basin* moderately shallow to rather deep, moderately wide, abrupt,
smooth or sometimes slightly ridged or wrinkled.

Skin attractive pale yellow partly covered with a bright blush. *Dots*
minute, pale or brown.

Calyx tube funnel-form. *Stamens* median to basal.

Core medium in size, somewhat abaxile; cells open or closed; core lines
clasping. *Carpels* broadly roundish or somewhat elliptical, emarginate. *Seeds*
medium or above, moderately long, rather flat, obtuse, dark.

Flesh whitish, moderately firm, fine-grained, tender, crisp, juicy, mild
subacid, nearly sweet, very good.

Season late September into October.

SHERMAN.

REFERENCES. 1. *Rural N. Y.*, **1870** (cited by **3**). **2.** Downing, **1872**:31 app.
3. Ragan, *U. S. B. P. I. Bul.*, **56**:281. 1905.

SYNONYMS. SHERMAN (3). SHERMAN'S FAVORITE (2). *Sherman's Favorite*
(3). SHERMAN'S SWEET (1). *Sherman's Sweet* (2, 3).

A yellow sweet apple of good medium size and mild, rather rich flavor;
in season from November to January (2). Downing states that it originated on the farm of E. C. Sherman, Wyoming, N. Y. We have received
no report concerning this variety and find no account of its having been
grown outside of the place of its origin.

1 Letter, 1895.

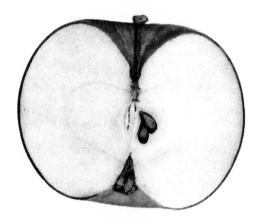

SHIAWASSEE

SHIAWASSEE.

REFERENCES. **1.** Lyon, *Mag. Hort.*, **26** :64. 1860. **2.** Hovey, *Ib.*, **27** :67. 1861. fig. **3.** *Ib.*, **29** :126. 1863. **4.** Warder, **1867** :459. fig. **5.** Downing, **1869** :351. **6.** *Mich. Pom. Soc. Rpt.*, **1872** :459. fig. **7.** Thomas, **1875** :204. **8.** *Am. Pom. Soc. Cat.*, **1875** :12. **9.** Lyon, *Mich. Hort. Soc. Rpt.*, **1881** :220. **10.** Barry, **1883** :354. **11.** Cook, *Rural N. Y.*, **45** :257. 1886. **12.** *Can. Hort.*, **11** :43 1888. **13.** Lyon, *Mich. Hort. Soc. Rpt.*, **1890** :296. **14.** *Ib.*, *Amer. Gard.*, **12** :244. 1891. **15.** *Can. Hort.*, **15** :117. 1892. **16.** Bailey, *An. Hort.*, **1892** :249. **17.** Miller, *Rural N. Y.*, **53** :278. 1894. **18.** Hoskins, *Amer. Gard.*, **15** :299. 1894. **19** Munson, *Me. Sta. Rpt.*, **1896** :72. **20.** Burrill and McClier, *Ill. Sta. Bul.*, **45** :341. 1896. **21.** Van Deman, *Rural N. Y.*, **56** :839. 1897. **22.** Macoun, *Can. Dept. Agr. Rpt.*, **1899** :77. **23.** Waugh, *Vt. Sta. Bul.*, **83** :92. 1900. **24.** *Ib.*, *Vt. Sta. An. Rpt.*, **14** :308. 1901. **25.** Macoun, *Can. Dept. Agr. Bul.*, **37** :41. 1901. **26.** Munson, *Me. Sta. An. Rpt.*, **18** :84, 90, 95. 1902. **27.** Farrand, *Mich. Sta. Bul.*, **205** :46. 1903. **28.** Powell and Fulton, *U. S. B. P. I. Bul.*, **48** :56. 1903. **29.** Budd-Hansen, **1903** :174. **30.** Beach and Clark, *N. Y. Sta. Bul.*, **248** :144. 1904.

SYNONYMS. *Michigan Beauty* (5). SHIAWASSE (21). SHIAWASSE BEAUTY (3, 7, 8, 20). SHIAWASSEE (14, 26). SHIAWASSEE BEAUTY (1, 2, 4, 5, 6, 9, 10, 11, 12, 16, 17, 18, 19, 22, 25). SHIAWASSEL *Beauty* (27). *Shiawassee Beauty* (23, 24, 28, 29, 30). SHIAWASSIE BEAUTY (15).

Fruit of the Fameuse type, of good size, quite attractive appearance and pleasant dessert quality. It has a flavor and aroma somewhat similar to that of McIntosh. Probably McIntosh would be preferred to Shiawassee by most fruit growers. The fruit of Shiawassee is fair, uniform and hangs pretty well to the tree. It ripens in October, and some portion of the fruit may be held till January. The tree is of uniform size, very hardy, vigorous, upright spreading, healthy and long-lived. It does not come into bearing very young, and when mature in some cases it is not a reliable cropper, but it is generally reported as yielding good to heavy crops biennially, or sometimes annually.

Historical. The original tree was planted as an ungrafted seedling in the orchard of Beebe Truesdell, in Vernon, Shiawassee county, Mich., and came into bearing about 1850 (1). The variety is often listed by nurserymen but is seldom planted in this state.

FRUIT.

Fruit medium to nearly large, uniform in shape but not in size. *Form* oblate conic, pretty regular but sometimes elliptical. *Stem* medium in length, slender to moderately thick. *Cavity* acute, varying from nearly acuminate to somewhat obtuse, deep, broad, rather symmetrical, sometimes compressed, often with outspreading russet rays. *Calyx* small to below medium, closed or slightly open; lobes rather short, moderately narrow. *Basin* rather shallow to moderately deep, rather wide, obtuse to somewhat abrupt, somewhat furrowed and wrinkled, often compressed.

Skin rather pale yellow, usually entirely overspread with attractive red, irregularly splashed and striped with carmine. *Dots* small to medium, grayish.

Calyx tube medium size, moderately wide, conical to short funnel-shape. *Stamens* median to nearly basal.

Core below medium size, widely abaxile; cells symmetrical, usually open; core lines meeting or slightly clasping. *Carpels* cordate to broadly ovate. *Seeds* rather dark brown, medium size, rather narrow, plump, acute.

Flesh white, fine, crisp, tender, juicy, pleasant subacid, aromatic, rather sprightly, good to very good.

Season October to January.

SINE-QUA-NON.

REFERENCES. **1.** *London Hort. Soc. Cat.*, **1831**:No. 1220. **2.** Downing, **1845**:76. **3.** Thomas, **1849**:143. **4.** Cole, **1849**:103. **5.** Waring, **1851**:30. **6.** Barry, **1851**:281. **7.** Elliott, **1854**:157. **8.** Hooper, **1857**:84. **9.** Gregg, **1857**:39. **10.** *Horticulturist*, **14**:425. 1859. **11.** *Am. Pom. Soc. Cat.*, **1862**. **12.** Warder, **1867**:732. **13.** Lyon, *Mich. Hort. Soc. Rpt.*, **1890**:296.

SYNONYMS. None.

An August apple of good dessert quality, now seldom found in cultivation. It originated on Long Island and was brought to notice by Wm. Prince (*2*). It was entered on the catalogue of the American Pomological Society in 1862 (*11*) and dropped from that list in 1871. The tree is a rather slow, crooked grower, in some cases an indifferent bearer (*7*), in others productive (*4, 13*). Fruit medium size, roundish ovate, pale greenish-yellow; flesh greenish-white, tender, juicy, mild subacid, sprightly, good; season late August.

SLINGERLAND.

REFERENCES. **1.** *N. Y. Sta. Agr. Soc. Rpt.*, **1849**:594. **2.** Emmons, *Nat. Hist. N. Y.*, **3**:42. 1851. *col. pl.* No. 32. **3.** Downing, **1857**:189. **4.** Warder, **1867**:732. **5.** Thomas, **1875**:512. **6.** Lyon, *Mich. Hort. Soc. Rpt.*, **1890**:296.

SYNONYMS. SLINGERLAND (*6*). SLINGERLAND'S FALL PIPPIN (*2*). SLINGERLAND PIPPIN (*1, 3, 4, 5*).

An excellent flavored apple of the Green Newtown type in season during late fall and early winter. It is not as good a keeper as Green Newtown. Raised from seed of the Newtown about 1830 by a Mr. Slingerland of New Scotland, Albany county, N. Y. (*1, 2*).

FRUIT (1, 2, 3).

Fruit medium to large. *Form* roundish, often oblique. *Stem* exserted but short. *Skin* yellow splashed with reddish-orange over the base. *Dots* minute. *Calyx* small to medium, partly closed. *Core* small. *Flesh* whitish tinged with yellow, firm, tender, juicy, brisk, rather rich subacid, good to very good. *Season* December to February or later.

SOPS OF WINE

SOMERSET (N. Y.).

REFERENCES. 1. Downing, 1869 :356. 2. Downing, *Tilt. Jour. Hort.*, 7 :303. 1870. 3. *Am. Pom. Soc. Cat.*, 1877 :14. 4. Lyon, *Mich. Hort. Soc. Rpt.*, 1881 :318. 5. Hoag, *Am. Pom. Soc. Rpt.*, 1885 :28. 6. Lyon, *Mich. Sta. Bul.*, 129 :40, 43. 1896. 7. *Mich. Sta. Bul.*, 152 :222, 226. 1898.

SYNONYMS. None.

An early apple of high sprightly flavor. A fine family fruit. The tree is an unusually early bearer, upright spreading, vigorous and productive. Season late August to October (4, 6, 7).

There is a distinct variety of Maine origin which is also called Somerset.

Historical. Brought to notice by C. L. Hoag, Lockport, N. Y. Origin unknown but supposed to be Somerset, Niagara county, N. Y. (2). This variety appears to have been but sparingly disseminated.

FRUIT (2, 5).

Fruit below medium. *Form* like Black Gilliflower, roundish conical. *Skin* deep golden-yellow to whitish-yellow with sometimes a few nettings of russet and sparsely sprinkled with brown dots. *Flesh* quite white, tender, juicy, with a rich aromatic flavor; quality very good or best.

SOPS OF WINE.

REFERENCES. 1. Ray, 1688 :No. 21. 2. Knoop, 8 :45. 1758. 3. Kenrick, 1832 :28. 4. *Ib.*, 1835 :98. 5. Floy-Lindley, 1833 :25. 6. Downing, 1845 :77. 7. Cole, 1849 :103. 8. Thomas, 1849 :141. 9. Emmons, *Nat. Hist. N. Y.*, 3 :11, 33. 1851. 10. Barry, 1851 :282. 11. Hovey, *Mag. Hort.*, 18 :545. 1852. fig. 12. Elliott, 1854 :157. 13. Gregg, 1857 :39. 14. Hooper, 1857 :85. 15. *Am. Pom. Soc. Cat.*, 1862. 16. Warder, 1867 :615. fig. 17. Downing, 1869 : 356. 18. *Horticulturist*, 27 :309. 1872. fig. 19. Fitz, 1872 :121, 174. 20. Downing, 1872 :10 index, app. 21. *Montreal Hort. Soc. Rpt.*, 1879 :22. 22. Downing, 1881 :11 index, app. 23. *Ib.*, 1881 :12 index, app. 24. Hogg, 1884 :215. 25. Hoskins, *Rural N. Y.*, 47 :662. 1888. figs. 26. Lyon, *Mich. Hort. Soc. Rpt.*, 1890 :296. 27. Bailey, *An. Hort.*, 1892 :249. 28. Hoskins, *Rural N. Y.*, 53 :248. 1894. 29. Burrill and McCluer, *Ill. Sta. Bul.*, 45 :325. 1896. 30. Waugh, *Vt. Sta. An. Rpt.*, 14 :309. 1901. 31. Budd-Hansen, 1903 :177. fig.

SYNONYMS. *Bell's Early?* (17). *Bell's Favorite* (20). *Bennington* (17, 18). *Dodge's Early Red* (17). *Early Washington* (22). *Hominy* (17, 19). *Horning* (29). *Pie Apple* (10). *Red Shropsavine?* (17). RODE WYN APPEL (2). *Rode Wyn Appel* (5, 6, 9). SAPSON (3). *Sapson* (6, 9, 11, 12, 18). *Sapsonvine* (3). *Shropshirevine* (23). SOPS IN WINE (1, 24). *Sops in Wine* (5, 6, 9, 11, 12, 18). SOPS OF WINE (4, 5, 6, 7, 8, 9, 10, 11, 12, 13, 14, 15, 16, 17, 18, 19, 20, 21, 22, 23, 25, 26, 27, 28, 29, 30, 31). *Sops of Wine* (24). *Strawberry* (30). *Warden's Pie Apple* (17, 18). *Washington* (17, 18).

A dark crimson apple; flesh fine, stained with red; in season in August and September. The tree is a good grower, comes into bearing rather young and is a biennial or nearly annual cropper. Of little value except as a dessert apple for family use.

Historical. "A very ancient English culinary and cider apple" (24). It is frequently listed by nurserymen but is now seldom planted in New York being superseded by other better varieties.

TREE.

Tree medium to large, moderately vigorous to vigorous. *Form* upright or inclined to roundish, rather dense. *Twigs* short to rather long, curved, moderately stout; internodes short. *Bark* dark brown, lightly streaked with scarf-skin; heavily pubescent. *Lenticels* very scattering, small, oblong, not raised. *Buds* medium size, broad, obtuse, free, pubescent.

FRUIT.

Fruit medium to sometimes large, uniform in shape but not in size. *Form* roundish to roundish conic, slightly ribbed; sides unequal. *Stem* short to rather long, moderately slender. *Cavity* acute, moderately deep, medium or sometimes narrow, sometimes slightly furrowed, sometimes with thin, radiating russet rays. *Calyx* medium to rather small, closed or slightly open; lobes rather short. *Basin* shallow, narrow, furrowed, somewhat wrinkled.

Skin moderately thin, moderately tender, slightly roughened, greenish-yellow almost entirely overspread with purplish-red, mottled, irregularly splashed and sometimes indistinctly striped with dark carmine, overspread with thin white bloom. *Dots* small, few, light russet or yellow.

Calyx tube short, wide, cone-shape. *Stamens* marginal to median.

Core medium size, somewhat abaxile; cells usually symmetrical but not uniformly developed, open to nearly closed; core lines meeting. *Carpels* broad ovate, rather concave, mucronate, tufted. *Seeds* rather large or medium size, moderately wide, plump, obtuse.

Flesh yellowish often stained with pink, soft, fine, juicy, aromatic, mild, pleasant, subacid, good.

Season August to October.

SOUR BOUGH.

REFERENCE. 1. Downing, 1869:357.
SYNONYMS. None.

This is an old Westchester county variety which, according to Downing, is of medium size, roundish conic, yellow with whitish, brisk subacid flesh, good for cooking. Season, September. "Often knotty and unprofitable" (1).

The name Sour Bough has also been applied sometimes to the Champlain; see page 30; and also to the Tart Bough; see page 220.

SPECTATOR.

REFERENCE. 1. Downing, 1869:357.
SYNONYMS. None.

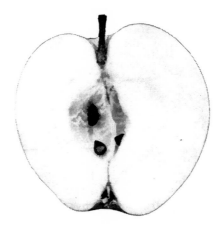

SOUR BOUGH

Originated with J. W. Bailey, Plattsburg, N. Y. According to Downing (1) this is an apple of medium size, ribbed, yellow, shaded with red in the sun; flesh white, subacid, hardly good; season September. The variety is unknown to us.

STARKEY.

REFERENCES. 1. *Am. Pom. Soc. Rpt.*, **1875**:65. 2. Downing, **1876**:69 app. 3. Thomas, **1885**:524. 4. Munson, *Me. Sta. Rpt.*, **1893**:133. 5. *Am. Pom. Soc. Cat.*, **1897**:14. 6. Budd-Hansen, **1903**:179.

SYNONYMS. None.

Fruit of good size, fair, well colored, largely striped and splashed with red, pleasant subacid, excellent for dessert or culinary use. Season, October to midwinter. In Maine, where it originated, it is said to be popular in market. It has not been sufficiently tested to determine its value for this state, but it appears to be worthy of testing. Tree a hardy and vigorous grower in the nursery, becoming rather large and spreading in the orchard; comes into bearing rather young and is a good biennial cropper.

Historical. Originated on the farm of Moses Starkey, North Vassalboro, Kennebec county, Me.

TREE.

Tree medium to rather large, moderately vigorous to vigorous with long, moderately stout, curved branches. *Form* spreading or roundish, open. *Twigs* medium to long, stout, geniculate, often irregularly crooked; internodes long to below medium. *Bark* brownish-red mingled sometimes with olive-green, irregularly mottled with scarf-skin; pubescent near tips. *Lenticels* scattering, inconspicuous, medium size or below, round, raised. *Buds* medium to large, prominent, plump, acute, free, slightly pubescent.

FRUIT.

Fruit medium to rather large. *Form* oblate or oblate conical, regular or faintly ribbed, symmetrical. *Stem* medium length. *Cavity* medium size, rather shallow, partly covered with greenish russet. *Calyx* large, closed or nearly so. *Basin* medium size, shallow, somewhat wrinkled.

Skin pale yellow, washed or deeply blushed with lively red, splashed and striped with carmine. *Dots* pale gray or russet. *Prevailing effect* red.

Calyx tube conical or somewhat funnel-form.

Core rather small.

Flesh whitish, firm, rather fine, juicy, crisp, pleasant, lively subacid, becoming mild subacid, very good.

Season October to January.

STARR.

REFERENCES. 1. Downing, *Tilt. Jour. Hort.*, 6:347. 1869. fig. 2. Downing, 1869:360. 3. Thomas, 1875:512. 4. Hexamer, *Am. Pom. Soc. Rpt.*, 1895:70. 5. *Rural N. Y.*, 54:587. 1895. 6. Parry, Wm., Parry, N. J., *Cat.*, 1896.

SYNONYMS. None.

Fruit large, very attractive for a green or yellowish apple, and very good in quality, especially for dessert use. Season, August and September. The tree is a pretty good grower, comes into bearing young and as tested at this Station gives promise of being an annual bearer. Starr appears to be worthy of testing where a fruit of this type is desired.

Historical. The original tree was found on the grounds of Judge J. M. White, Woodbury, N. J., which property afterward came into the possession of Mrs. Starr. The propagation of the variety was begun by Wm. Parry in 1865 under the name of Starr (6). So far as we can learn it has been but little planted in New York.

TREE.

Tree moderately vigorous with short, moderately stout, curved branches. *Form* upright spreading or roundish, rather dense. *Twigs* long, curved, stout with large terminal buds; internodes long. *Bark* brownish-red, tinged with olive-green, lightly streaked with scarf-skin; pubescent near tips. *Lenticels* quite numerous, medium size, round, not raised. *Buds* prominent, large, long, broad, plump, acute, free, pubescent.

FRUIT.

Fruit very large to large, pretty uniform in size and shape. *Form* distinctly oblate to roundish oblate, regular or faintly ribbed. *Stem* short to medium, moderately thick, sometimes swollen. *Cavity* acute, varying from a little obtuse to somewhat acuminate, shallow to medium, broad, smooth or gently furrowed. *Calyx* medium size, closed, lobes long to medium, rather narrow, acuminate. *Basin* medium in depth, narrow, abrupt, somewhat furrowed.

Skin rather thick, tough, nearly smooth, green becoming yellowish-green, sometimes with indications of a faint blush. *Dots* numerous, small and large, pale or russet.

Calyx tube long, very wide to moderately wide, conical to cylindrical and large, extending to the core. *Stamens* nearly marginal.

Core medium to rather large, abaxile to nearly axile; cells closed or slightly open; core lines clasping. *Carpels* obovate, sometimes tufted. *Seeds* dark brown, medium to large, rather wide, plump, acute to nearly acuminate.

Flesh tinged with yellow, moderately fine, very tender, crisp, very juicy, sprightly subacid, aromatic, very good.

Season August and September.

STILLMAN EARLY.

REFERENCES. **1.** Downing, **1857**:193. **2.** Thomas, **1875**:512. **3.** Lyon, *Mich. Hort. Soc. Rpt.*, **1890**:298.

SYNONYMS. STILLMAN (3) . STILLMAN'S EARLY (1, 2).

This variety originated in Clinton, Oneida county, N. Y. Downing (1) states that the tree is a moderate grower and productive; the fruit small, yellow, sometimes slightly blushed; flesh pleasant subacid, good; season late July and early August. We are unacquainted with this variety and have received no report concerning it from any of our correspondents.

STRAWBERRY.

This name has been applied to a great many different varieties of the apple. Those mentioned in this volume are listed below:

Autumn Strawberry, see Late Strawberry. *Chenango Strawberry*, see Chenango. Early Strawberry. *Fall Strawberry*, see Late Strawberry. Late Strawberry. *St. John's Strawberry*, see Early Strawberry. *Strawberry*, see Chenango, Early Strawberry, Late Strawberry and Richard Graft. Washington Strawberry.

STRIPED GILLIFLOWER.

REFERENCES. **1.** Warder, **1867**:696. fig. **2.** Downing, **1876**:69 app. **3.** Bailey, *An. Hort.*, **1892**:250. **4.** Burrill and McCluer, *Ill. Sta. Bul.*, **45**:342. 1896. **5.** Thomas, **1897**:654. **6.** Budd-Hansen, **1903**:181.

SYNONYMS. *Red Gilliflower* (2). *Scollop Gilliflower*, incorrectly (2). *Striped Bellflower* (2). STRIPED GILLIFLOWER (1, 2, 3, 4, 5, 6).

This variety appears to be practically obsolete in New York. The tree is a vigorous grower and generally productive (2).

FRUIT (1, 2, 6).

Fruit large to very large. *Form* variable roundish conic to oblong conic, often furrowed, angular, but less ribbed than Scollop Gilliflower. *Stem* short, curved. *Cavity* acute, deep, wide, furrowed, brown or russeted. *Calyx* large, closed or partly open; lobes erect. *Basin* shallow, abrupt.

Skin yellowish-white or greenish, partly covered with dull red, striped and splashed with carmine. *Dots* few, indistinct, gray or white.

Calyx tube cone-shape. *Stamens* median.

Core sessile, abaxile, large; cells wide open; core lines meeting or slightly clasping. *Carpels* tufted. *Seeds* few, small, roundish, plump, obtuse, black.

Flesh yellowish-white, breaking, juicy, briskly subacid, fair to good. *Season* September.

STROAT.

REFERENCES. 1. Buel, *N. Y. Bd. Agr. Mem.*, 1826:476. 2. *London Hort. Soc. Cat.*, 1831:No. 1256. 3. Kenrick, 1832:39. 4. Downing, 1845:97. 5. *Horticulturist*, 2:545. 1848. 6. Thomas, 1849:158. 7. Emmons, *Nat. Hist. N. Y.*, 3:38. 1851. 8. Elliott, 1854:158. 9. Hooper, 1857:87.

SYNONYMS. STRAAT (2, 3). *Straat* (4, 8, 9). STROAT (1, 4, 5, 6, 7, 8, 9).

Stroat was formerly much esteemed among the descendants of the Dutch settlers on the North river (4). The fruit is described as above medium, roundish inclined to conic, yellowish-green; flesh yellow, very tender, rich, brisk subacid, good to very good; season September to November or December (4, 6, 8).

We have not seen this fruit nor has it been mentioned by any of our correspondents.

STRODE BIRMINGHAM.

REFERENCES. 1. Downing, 1857:193. 2. Warder, 1867:733. 3. *Pa. Sta. Hort. Assn. Rpt.*, 1886:50. 4. Powell and Fulton, *U. S. P. B. I. Bul.*, 48:57. 1903. 5. Beach and Clark, *N. Y. Sta. Bul.*, 248:145. 1904.

SYNONYMS. *Dumpling* (3). STRODE (4, 5). *Strode's* (1). STRODE'S BIRMINGHAM (1, 2, 3). *Strode's Birmingham* (4, 5).

A medium-sized yellow apple of mild subacid flavor and good quality. Commercial limit September. For home use it is in season in September and October and a few specimens may be kept till January (5). It is reported as a desirable variety for market and general purposes in Pennsylvania (3). The tree comes into bearing rather young and is productive yielding moderate to good crops nearly annually. As compared with standard varieties of its season it does not appear to be worthy of the attention of New York fruit growers.

FRUIT.

Fruit of medium size; uniform in size and shape. *Form* roundish conic or inclined to oblong, regular or faintly ribbed; sides unequal. *Stem* long, slender. *Cavity* acute to almost acuminate, usually rather deep, medium in width, symmetrical, russeted. *Calyx* medium to small, closed or partly open; lobes medium in length and width, acute, reflexed. *Basin* shallow, narrow to medium in width, obtuse, furrowed and wrinkled.

Skin thin, tender, smooth, clear yellow or greenish, often with faint blush and marked with russet flecks. *Dots* scattering, very minute, submerged, inconspicuous, red or russet.

Calyx tube short, wide, urn-shape to broadly conical. *Stamens* nearly basal.

Core medium to small, axile; cells almost closed; core lines meeting. *Carpels* broadly ovate to oblong narrowing toward either end, deeply emarginate. *Seeds* dark dull brown, medium to large, wide, plump, broadly acute, tufted.

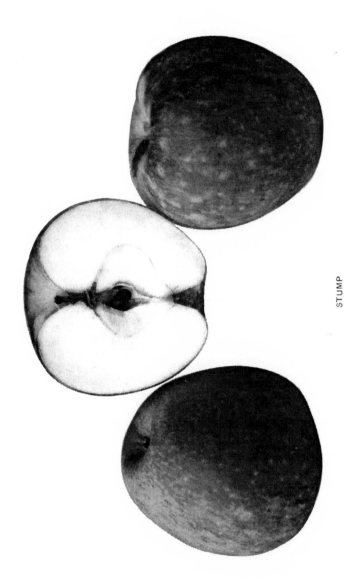

STUMP

Flesh yellowish, rather firm, fine, rather crisp, tender, juicy, brisk subacid becoming mild and pleasant when fully mature, good to very good.

Season September to early winter.

STUMP.

REFERENCES. **1.** Downing, **1881**:110 app. *fig.* **2.** Barry, **1883**:341. **3.** Thomas, **1885**:525. **4.** *Pa. Sta. Hort. Assn. Rpt.,* **1885**:25. **5.** *Can. Hort.,* **11**:8. 1888. **6.** *Rural N. Y.,* **47**:692. 1888. *figs.* **7.** Bailey, *An. Hort.,* **1892**:250. **8.** *N. Y. Sta. An. Rpt.,* **14**:255. 1895. **9.** Beach, *Gard. and For.,* **8**:428. 1895. **10.** *Kan. Sta. Bul.,* **106**:55. 1902. **11.** Beach and Clark, *N. Y. Sta. Bul.,* **248**:145. 1904.

SYNONYMS. None.

This very beautiful apple resembles Chenango in form, size and general appearance. In Western New York it is by some considered a good variety for commercial planting, but others find difficulty in marketing it with profit, since it is esteemed chiefly for dessert purposes and ripens at a season when there is comparatively little demand for apples, and shows bruises so readily that it is not well adapted for barrelling. It may be marketed in local markets or shipped in small packages. The crop ripens unevenly, and on this account should have more than one picking in order to secure the fruit in prime condition. It begins to ripen in late August or early September. Its commercial limit is September or early October, but its season for home use extends to November (11). The trees are upright, compact and stocky, so that they may stand closer together than common varieties in the orchard, or be used for alternating with more spreading trees. They are hardy, long-lived, and reliable croppers, yielding good to heavy crops biennially. The fruit is borne on short spurs close to the limbs. It is recommended for planting in the garden and commercial orchard where a variety of this type is desired.

Historical. Originated as a chance seedling in an old stump on the grounds of John Prue, Chili, N. Y. (1). It appears that it has been planted more in Western New York than in any other section of the state.

TREE.

Tree a slow, stiff, upright grower in the nursery, apt to crack at the collar, not popular with nurserymen; in the orchard it becomes a moderately vigorous or vigorous grower; branches long, moderately stout, curved, filled with fruit spurs. *Form* very upright but eventually somewhat roundish. *Twigs* moderately long, curved, moderately stout; internodes medium. *Bark* brown tinged with green, lightly streaked with scarf-skin; pubescent. *Lenti-cels* numerous, medium size, round, not raised. *Buds* medium size, broad, plump, obtuse, free, slightly pubescent.

FRUIT.

Fruit medium or below, uniform in size and shape. *Form* roundish conic to oblong conic, regular or faintly ribbed; sides sometimes unequal. *Stem* very short, variable in thickness. *Cavity* acute or approaching obtuse, usu-ally rather shallow, medium in width to rather broad, unsymmetrical, fre-quently furrowed, sometimes lipped, partly russeted. *Calyx* medium to small, slightly open or closed; lobes short, rather narrow, acute. *Basin* shallow, narrow, abrupt.

Skin smooth, clear pale yellow largely washed and mottled with bright pinkish-red, becoming deep red in highly-colored specimens, rather indis-tinctly striped and splashed with bright carmine. *Dots* numerous, rather large, areolar with russet point or with whitish point. *Prevailing effect* red and yellow contrasting beautifully.

Calyx tube broadly conical with fleshy pistil point projecting into the base. *Stamens* basal.

Core below medium to rather large, usually abaxile; cells open; core lines meeting or slightly clasping. *Carpels* elongated ovate tapering toward base and apex. *Seeds* rather dark brown, medium to small, usually very wide, short, very plump, obtuse to acute.

Flesh whitish or tinged with yellow, rather fine, tender, juicy, rich, aro-matic, sprightly, pleasant subacid, very good.

Season September and October.

STYMUS.

REFERENCES. **1.** *Am. Pom. Soc. Rpt.*, **1867** (cited by **3**). **2.** Downing, **1869**:365. **3.** Ragan, *U. S. B. P. I. Bul.*, **56**:298. 1905.

SYNONYMS. *Stymer's* (3). STYMUS (1, 2, 3).

This variety was described by Downing in 1869 as a new and really ex-cellent apple which originated on the farm of Jacob Stymus, Dobbs Ferry, N. Y. (2). Fruit medium size, yellowish, shaded, splashed and striped with light and dark crimson; flesh fine, tender, pleasant subacid, very good; season October and November.

We are unacquainted with this variety and have received no report con-cerning it from any of our correspondents.

SUFFOLK BEAUTY.

REFERENCE. **1.** Downing, **1869**:365.

SYNONYMS. None.

Described in 1869 by Downing (1) as a new variety from Deer Park, Long Island. Fruit medium, yellowish-white; flesh subacid; season August and September.

This variety is unknown to us and we have received no report concerning it from any of our correspondents.

SUMMER BELLFLOWER.

REFERENCES. 1. *Horticulturist*, 3:168. 1848. fig. 2. Thomas, **1849**:143. 3. Cole, **1849**:104. 4. Waring, **1851**:31. 5. Elliott, **1854**:159. 6. Downing, **1857**:196. 7. Warder, **1867**:733. 8. *Am. Pom. Soc. Cat.*, **1875**:14.

SYNONYMS. SUMMER BELLEFLEUR (1, 8). *Summer Belle-fleur* (5). SUMMER BELLFLOWER (2, 3, 4, 5, 6, 7). *Summer Bellflower* (1).

This fruit bears considerable resemblance in form and color to Yellow Bellflower. Flesh tender, subacid, good. It is in season from the middle of August to the middle of September. The tree is erect, of medium size, a good grower, hardy and a good cropper. It is not considered a satisfactory variety for commercial planting and so far as we can learn is gradually becoming obsolete in New York. Downing described it in 1848 as a new variety of promise and stated that it was raised by John R. Comstock of Washington, Dutchess county, N. Y., from seed of the Esopus *Spitzenburg* (1, 6). It was entered on the list of the American Pomological Society in 1875 as a variety of value for Nebraska (8). It was dropped from that list in 1897.

A distinct variety of Pennsylvania origin has also been known under the name Summer Bellflower (6, 7).

SUMMER PEARMAIN.

REFERENCES. 1. M'Mahon, *Amer. Gard. Cal.*, **1806**:585. 2. Coxe, **1817**: 104. fig. 3. Cobbett, **1821**:par. 300. 4. Thacher, **1822**:138. 5. Buel, *N. Y. Bd. Agr. Mem.*, **1826**:476. 6. Fessenden, **1828**:129. 7. Kenrick, **1832**:25. 8. *Mag. Hort.*, 1:398. 1835. 9. Manning, **1838**:47. 10. *Ib.*, *Mag. Hort.*, 7: 49. 1841. 11. Downing, **1845**:70. 12. *Horticulturist*, 2:544. 1848. 13. Thomas, **1849**:136. fig. 14. Cole, **1849**:103. 15. Phœnix, *Horticulturist*, 4:472. 1850. 16. Emmons, *Nat. Hist. N. Y.*, 3:11. 1851. fig. 17. Barry, **1851**:279. 18. *Am. Pom. Soc. Cat.*, **1852**. 19. Elliott, **1854**:64. fig. 20. Hooper, **1857**:12, 106, 108. 21. Gregg, **1857**:35. 22. Warder, **1867**:582. fig. 23. Downing, **1869**:78. fig. 24. Fitz, **1872**:143, 160. 25. Hogg, **1884**:7. 25. Lyon, *Mich. Hort. Soc. Rpt.*, **1890**:298. 27. Bailey, *An. Hort.*, **1892**:234. 28. *Ib.*, **1892**:250. 29. Budd-Hansen, **1903**:182. fig.

SYNONYMS. AMERICAN PEARMAIN (19). *American Pearmain* (20). *American Summer* (26). AMERICAN SUMMER PEARMAIN (7, 8, 11, 12, 13, 14, 16, 17, 20, 21, 22, 23, 24, 25, 27). *American Summer Pearmain* (19, 29). EARLY SUMMER PEARMAIN (2, 5, 6). *Early Summer Pearmain* (7, 11, 14, 16, 19, 23, 25, of Coxe 13). SUMMER PEARMAIN (1, 3, 4, 9, 10, 15, 18, 26, 28, 29). *Summer Pearmain* (14). *Watkins Early* (19, 20).

An amateur fruit which when perfect is beautiful and of mild, rich, excellent flavor (26). The tree being of slender, slow growth in the nursery is not a favorite with nurserymen and although it makes a large productive tree in the orchard it is not profitable as a market variety (22). It is desirable for family use because the fruit is suitable both for culinary and dessert purposes and the crop ripens in succession through a period of nearly two months.

There is also another Summer Pearmain or English Summer Pearmain which ripens somewhat later.[1]

Historical. Supposed to be of American origin. It is an old variety; first described in 1817 by Coxe.

FRUIT (11, 14, 22, 23).

Fruit of medium size. *Form* variable, oblong or roundish inclined to conic, sometimes oblate. *Stem* medium to long. *Cavity* deep, acute, regular. *Calyx* large, open or closed. *Basin* medium size, abrupt, slightly wrinkled.

Skin smooth, greenish-yellow, more or less covered with dull purplish-red, marbled, splashed and striped with brighter red. *Dots* minute.

Core medium to small, roundish; cells closed. *Seeds* small, pointed.

Flesh yellowish, very fine, tender, almost melting, juicy, aromatic, crisp, mild subacid, best.

Season August and September.

SUMMER QUEEN.

REFERENCES. **1.** M'Mahon, *Amer. Gard. Cal.*, **1806**:584. **2.** Coxe, **1817**: 102. **3.** Thacher, **1822**:133. **4.** Buel, *N. Y. Bd. Agr. Mem.*, **1826**:476 **5.** Wilson, **1828**:136. **6.** Kenrick, **1832**:28. **7.** Manning, **1838**:46. **8.** Downing, **1845**:77. **9.** Hovey, *Mag. Hort.*, **14**:489. **1848.** fig. **10.** Thomas, **1849**:141. **11.** Cole, **1849**:103. **12.** Barry, **1851**:282. **13.** Waring, **1851**:28. **14.** Emmons, *Nat. Hist. N. Y.*, **3**:14. **1851.** **15.** Elliott, **1854**:158. **16.** Hooper, **1857**:88, 107. **17.** Gregg, **1857**:39. **18.** *Am. Pom. Soc. Cat.*, **1860**:240. **19.** Warder, **1867**:545. fig. **20.** Downing, **1869**:370. fig. **21.** Fitz, **1872**:143, 161. **22.** *Ill. Hort. Soc. Rpt.*, **1874**:295. **23.** Wickson, **1889**:243. **24.** Lyon, *Mich. Hort. Soc. Rpt.*, **1890**:298. **25.** Bailey, *An. Hort.*, **1892**:250. **26.** Budd-Hansen, **1903**:183. fig.

SYNONYMS. *Lancaster Queen* (15, 26). *Polecat* (20). QUEEN (3, 13). *Queen* (6). *Sharpe's Early* (20). SUMMER QUEEN (2, 4, 5, 6, 7, 8, 9, 10, 11, 12, 14, 15, 16, 17, 18, 19, 20, 21, 22, 23, 24, 25, 26). *Summer Queen* (3, 13). SWEET'S HARVEST (1). *Sweet's Harvest* (3, 4, 6). *Swett's Harvest* (2).

A striped red apple of good size and excellent quality for culinary use, in season during late summer. In regions farther west it is a very popular variety for home use and is also considered by some desirable for market. The tree is a moderate grower with rather spreading habit and productive, yielding good crops almost annually.

Historical. This is an old variety which is supposed to have originated in this country (4, 19, 26). It is commonly listed by nurserymen in most parts

1 Ragan, *U. S. B. P. I. Bul.*, **56**:300. 1905.

of the country (25). So far as we have been able to learn it is not often grown in New York and is now seldom planted in this state.

FRUIT (10, 12, 15, 19).

Fruit medium to large. *Form* roundish conical, somewhat angular. *Stem* medium to long, slender. *Cavity* narrow to rather wide, regular, pretty deep. *Calyx* medium to large, open or closed. *Basin* shallow or none, furrowed.

Skin yellow, striped, splashed and shaded with mixed red. *Dots* minute, yellow.

Core medium size; cells open. *Seeds* numerous, acute, brown.

Flesh whitish-yellow, sometimes with tinge of pink, firm, aromatic, juicy, subacid, good to very good for culinary use.

Season August and September.

SUMMER RAMBO.

REFERENCES. **1.** Switzer, **1725** (cited by 7). **2.** Duhamel, 1 :28. 1768. **3.** Forsyth, **1803** :49. **4.** Coxe, **1817** :104. *fig.* **5.** Forsyth, **1824** :123. **6.** Kenrick, **1832** :37. **7.** Floy-Lindley, **1833** :12. **8.** Manning, **1838** :47. **9.** Downing, **1845** :94. **10.** Thomas, **1849** :141. **11.** Elliott, **1854** :178. **12.** *Am. Pom. Soc. Cat.*, **1862.** **13.** Warder, **1867** :733. **14.** *Am. Pom. Soc. Cat.*, **1871** :10. **15.** Leroy, **1873** :598. *fig.* **16.** *Mo. Hort. Soc. Rpt.*, **1883** :76. **17.** Lyon, *Mich. Hort. Soc. Rpt.*, **1890** :298. **18.** Bailey, *An. Hort.*, **1892** :250. **19.** (?) *Revue Horticole*, 66 :202. 1894. **20.** Taylor, *Am. Pom. Soc. Rpt.*, **1895** :199. **21.** Burrill and McCluer, *Ill. Sta. Bul.*, 45 :337. 1896.

SYNONYMS. *Cambour des Lorrains* (15). *Charmant Blanc* (15). *De Lorraine* (15). *De Rambourg* (15). *De Rambure* (15). *De Notre-Dame* (15). FRANK RAMBOUR (1, 7). *Frank Rambour* (9). *Grosh* (16). *Gros-Rambour d'Ete* (15). *Herbstbreitling* (15). *Lothringer Rambour d'Ete* (15). *Pomme de Notre-Dame* (6). RAMBOUR (3). *Rambour* (15, 17). *Rambour Blanc* (15). (RAMBOUR D'AMERIQUE, 19)? RAMBOUR D'ETE (4, 8, 15). *Rambour d'Ete* (6, 9, 10, 11). RAMBOUR FRANC (2, 5, 6, 9, 12). *Rambour Franc* (4, 7, 10, 11, 15, 21). *Rambourg Aigre* (15). *Rambour Gros* (7, of the English 6). *Rambour Raye* (6, 15). *Rambu* (15). *Remboure d'Ete* (15). SUMMER RAMBO (13, 14, 16, 17, 18, 20, 21). *Summer Rambo* (11). SUMMER RAMBOUR (10, 11). *Summer Rambour* (4, 9).

Fruit of the type of Grosh; very attractive in size, form and color; large, oblate, yellowish-green considerably striped and splashed with mixed red, good to very good. Season early autumn. Begins to ripen about a month earlier than Grosh. The tree is a strong grower, comes into bearing young and bears quite regularly yielding moderate to good crops. Although it has long been known in cultivation in this country it has not gained much recognition among New York fruit growers. The fine color and size of this variety combined with its comparatively good quality recommend it for home use or local market. It is an old variety and has been tested in many parts of the United States but its cultivation has never become extensive. These facts would indicate that it has weaknesses not apparent to the casual observer. Possibly it is worthy of further trial in this state.

Historical. This variety is said to have originated in France (15). It has long been known in this country having been described by Coxe in 1817 and Kenrick in 1832 (4, 6). It was listed in the catalogue of the American Pomological Society under the name Rambour Franc from 1862 to 1871 (12, 14, 20). It is still listed by nurserymen (18). It is comparatively little known in New York state but is more often found in cultivation in Ohio and regions farther west.

TREE.

Tree vigorous. *Form* upright spreading to roundish, open. *Twigs* moderately long, curved, moderately stout; internodes medium. *Bark* brown, tinged with green, lightly streaked with scarf-skin; slightly pubescent. *Lenticels* quite numerous, medium size, round, not raised. *Buds* medium size, broad, plump, obtuse, free, slightly pubescent.

FRUIT.

Fruit large to very large, uniform in size and shape. *Form* oblate to roundish oblate, sometimes slightly ovate, sometimes faintly ribbed, pretty regular; sides often unequal. *Stem* short to medium, rather thick. *Cavity* nearly acuminate, deep to medium in depth, rather broad, usually symmetrical, sometimes lipped, sometimes slightly russeted close to the stem. *Calyx* rather large, closed or sometimes slightly open; lobes medium to short, rather narrow, acute to obtuse. *Basin* deep to sometimes medium, wide to medium in width, abrupt, smooth, symmetrical.

Skin thick, tough, smooth, attractive clear bright yellow or greenish, in well colored specimens largely washed and mottled with lively pinkish-red, conspicuously marked with many broken stripes and splashes of bright carmine. *Dots* numerous, usually small and submerged, but some are scattering, large, brown or russet. *Prevailing effect* striped.

Calyx tube medium in length, rather wide, broadly conical. *Stamens* median to marginal.

Core rather small, axile; cells nearly closed; core lines meeting or slightly clasping. *Carpels* roundish to roundish ovate approaching elliptical. *Seeds* frequently abortive, rather large, wide, plump, acute, moderately dark brown.

Flesh yellowish-green, firm, breaking, coarse, tender, very juicy, mildly subacid, somewhat aromatic, good.

Season September to November.

SUMMER REDSTREAK.

REFERENCE. 1. Downing, **1869**:371.
SYNONYMS. None.

A September apple which originated in Columbia county, N. Y. According to Downing (1) the tree is moderately vigorous and productive. The fruit medium, yellowish, shaded, striped and splashed with rich red; flesh white, sometimes a little stained next the skin, brisk subacid, valued for cooking.

We have neither seen this variety nor received any report concerning it.

SUMMER ROSE.

REFERENCES. 1. M'Mahon, *Amer. Gard. Cal.*, 1806:584. 2. Coxe, 1817: 103. *fig.* 3. Buel, *N. Y. Bd. Agr. Mem.*, 1826:476. 4. Wilson, 1828:136. 5. Fessenden, 1828:131. 6. Kenrick, 1832:29. 7. Manning, 1838:47. 8. Downing, 1845:77. 9. *Horticulturist*, 2:483. 1848. 10. *N. Y. Agr. Soc. Trans.*, 1848:277. *fig.* 11. Thomas, 1849:141. *fig.* 12. Cole, 1849:101. *fig.* 13. Waring, 1851:31. 14. Barry, 1851:282. 15. *Am. Pom. Soc. Cat.*, 1852. 16. Elliott, 1854:107. *fig.* 17. Gregg, 1857:39. 18. Hooper, 1857:87. 19. *Horticulturist*, 14:425. 1859. 20. Warder, 1867:616. 21. Fitz, 1872:143, 160. 22. *Ill. Hort. Soc. Rpt.*, 1875:112. 23. Downing, 1881:11 index, app. 24. Van Deman, *U. S. Pom. Rpt.*, 1887:630. *col. pl.* 25. Lyon, *Mich. Hort. Soc. Rpt.*, 1890:298. 26. Bailey, *An. Hort.*, 1892:250. 27. Alwood, *Va. Sta. Bul.*, 130:122. 1901. 28. Waugh, *Vt. Sta. An. Rpt.*, 14:309. 1901. 29. Farrand, *Mich. Sta. Bul.*, 205:46. 1903. 30. Budd-Hansen, 1903:183. *fig.*

SYNONYMS. *French Reinette* (10). *Harvest Apple* (2, 3, 6). *Lippincott* (10, 13, 16). *Lodge's Early* (23). SUMMER ROSE (2, 3, 4, 5, 6, 7, 8, 9, 10, 11, 12, 13, 14, 15, 16, 17, 18, 19, 20, 21, 22, 23, 24, 25, 26, 27, 28, 29, 30). *Wolman's Harvest* (16). *Woolman's Early* (11, 14, 17). WOOLMAN'S HARVEST (1). *Woolman's Harvest* (8, 10, 16). *Woolman's Striped Harvest* (11).

A little dessert apple. Thomas rated it better in quality for the table than Early Harvest but less productive and too small for general value (11). The tree is a moderately vigorous or slow grower but is hardy, comes into bearing young and is productive. Suitable for culinary use in July, ripe in August.

Historical. This is an old New Jersey apple which Coxe described as of singular beauty and excellent for both eating and stewing; the size is moderate, the form flat, the skin smooth, of a beautiful yellow resembling wax, blended with red in streaks and blotches (2). It is still occasionally listed by nurserymen (26) but is now seldom or never planted in New York.

FRUIT (8, 11, 16, 20, 23, 30).

Fruit small to nearly medium. *Form* roundish, somewhat oblate. *Stem* rather short to medium, varying from stout to slender. *Cavity* shallow, acute, regular. *Calyx* small, closed or partly open. *Basin* regular, wide, abrupt, slightly furrowed.

Skin smooth, waxen, very pale yellow, striped and splashed distinctly with bright red and carmine on the exposed cheek. *Dots* minute.

Core medium to large; cells closed; core lines meeting. *Seeds* ovate, numerous, short, plump.

Flesh white, fine-grained, crisp, very tender, sprightly, juicy, subacid, agreeable but not rich, suitable for either culinary or dessert use.

SUMMER SPITZENBURG.

REFERENCE. 1. Downing, 1872:36 app. *fig.*
SYNONYMS. *French Spitzenburgh* (1). SUMMER SPITZENBURGH (1).

This is a September apple of attractive color. It is but little grown in New York. The tree is large, upright or roundish, a good grower, hardy, long-lived and reliably productive yielding good crops biennially. It is not considered valuable for commercial planting because the fruit is apt to be undersized and drops badly. By some it is esteemed for home use.

Historical. Downing states that it originated with Woolsey Ostrander, Plattekill, Ulster county, N. Y. (1).

FRUIT (1).

Fruit medium, whitish almost covered with red and overspread with thin bloom. *Flesh* moderately juicy, a little aromatic, good to very good. *Season* August and September.

SUMMER SWEET.

REFERENCES. **1.** *Mag. Hort.*, **14**:388. 1848. fig. **2.** Cole, **1849**:97. **3.** Hooper, **1857**:87. **4.** Downing, **1869**:372.

SYNONYMS. SUMMER SWEET (2, 3, 4). SUMMER SWEETING (1).

A yellow sweet apple ripe in August and September. The tree is of medium size, moderately vigorous, spreading, productive. Fruit medium size, roundish oblate inclined to conic; flesh whitish, tender, rich, sweet (2, 4).

Historical. An old Connecticut apple (1, 2, 4) now but very seldom found in cultivation in New York.

SWEET BOUGH.

REFERENCES. **1.** (?) *Amer. Gard. Cal.*, **1806**:584. **2.** Coxe, **1817**:101. fig. **3.** (?) Thacher, **1822**:121. **4.** Buel, *N. Y. Bd. Agr. Mem.*, **1826**:477. **5.** Wilson, **1828**:136. **6.** Fessenden, **1828**:131. **7.** Kenrick, **1832**:26. **8.** Floy-Lindley, **1833**:84. **9.** Manning, **1838**:46. **10.** Downing, **1845**:74. **11.** Hovey, *Mag. Hort.*, **14**:486. 1848. fig. **12.** Cole, **1849**:99. **13.** Thomas, **1849**:135. **14.** Phœnix, *Horticulturist*, **4**:472. 1850. **15.** Barry, **1851**:279. **16.** *Am. Pom. Soc. Cat.*, **1852**. **17.** Elliott, **1854**:109. fig. **18.** Hooper, **1857**:20. **19.** *Ib.*, **1857**:107, 111. **20.** Gregg, **1857**:35. **21.** Warder, **1867**:494. fig. **22.** Downing, **1869**:250. **23.** Fitz, **1872**:143. **24.** *Ib.*, **1872**:161. **25.** Leroy, **1873**:154. fig. **26.** Downing, **1881**:11 index, app. **27.** Hogg, **1884**:129. **28.** Wickson, **1889**:243. **29.** Bailey, *An. Hort.*, **1892**:235. **30.** *Ib.*, **1892**:243. **31.** *Ib.*, **1892**:250. **32.** *Amer. Gard.*, **15**:404. 1894. fig. **33.** Taylor, *Am. Pom. Soc. Rpt.*, **1895**:192. **34.** Lyon, *Mich. Sta. Bul.*, **143**:200, 202. 1897. **35.** Woolverton, *Ont. Fr. Stas. An. Rpt.*, **4**:4. 1897. figs. **36.** Beach, *W. N. Y. Hort. Soc. Rpt.*, **1901**:76. **37.** Budd-Hansen, **1903**:55.

SYNONYMS. *August Sweet* (22). *August Sweeting* (12). *Autumn Bough* (11). BOUGH (4, 5, 11, 13, 24, 25, 29, 34). *Bough* (7, 10, 12, 17, 22, 27). BOUGH APPLE (2, 6, 8, 20). BOUGH, *Early Sweet* (18). BOUGH, *Sweet* (37). (BOW APPLE 1, 3)? EARLY BOUGH (7, 9). *Early Bough* (11, 25, 27). *Early French Reinette* (4). *Early Sweet Bough* (10, 11, 13, 17, 22). *Early Sweet-heart* (36). LARGE BOUGH (21). LARGE EARLY BOUGH (28). *Large Early Yellow Bough* (27). LARGE SWEET BOUGH (19, 30). *Large Sweet Bough* (15). LARGE YELLOW BOUGH (10, 16, 22, 23, 26, 27, 33). *Large Yellow*

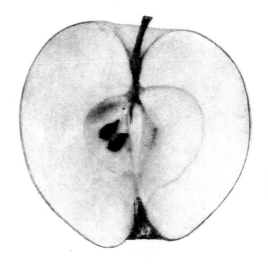

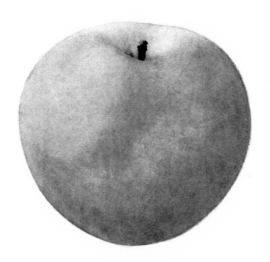

SWEET BOUGH

Bough (11, 13, 15, 17, 20, 21, 25, 30, 31, 34, 35, 37). *Niack Pippin* (17).
Pound's July (26). SWEET BOUGH (12, 14, 17, 31, 32, 35, 36). *Sweet Bough*
(7, 13, 20, 22, 24, 25, 27, 33, 34). *Sweetbough* (28). *Sweet Harvest* (10, 11,
17, 22, 25, 27). *Yellow Bough* (12). *Washington* (17, 25, incorrectly 22).

This variety is a universal favorite throughout the state for the
home orchard. Hovey (11) well says of it: "The Bough is one
of our finest summer apples, having all the good qualities which
should recommend a fruit for general cultivation. The tree is
moderately vigorous, making a handsome head, and bears abundant
crops of large, very fair fruit, which begins to ripen the last of
July, and remains in eating till the first of September. As a table
apple, it will not rank as high as the Early Harvest; but, as a
kitchen fruit, in its honied sweetness and tender flesh, it has no
equal of its season. It should be found in every good collection."

It is handled to a limited extent in local markets, but is too soft
to stand shipping to distant markets. It cannot be ranked among
the profitable commercial varieties. The tree comes into bearing
rather young, and under favorable conditions is long-lived, specimens being found sixty to eighty years old which are still quite productive. In unfavorable locations the tree is sometimes injured by
winter, and the branches are attacked somewhat by the apple
canker.

Historical. This was described by Coxe in 1817 under the name Bough
apple (2) It is evidently of American origin.

TREE.

Tree moderately vigorous. *Form* upright spreading to roundish, dense.
Twigs short, straight, moderately stout with large terminal buds; internodes
short. *Bark* clear brown mingled with olive-green, lightly mottled with
scarf-skin; not pubescent. *Lenticels* scattering, small, round, not raised.
Buds medium in size, plump, acute, free, not pubescent.

FRUIT.

Fruit above medium to large, uniform in size and shape. *Form* roundish
conic or ovate to sometimes slightly oblong conic with broad and rather
flat base, pretty regular; sides often unequal. *Stem* short to medium, moderately thick, usually not exserted. *Cavity* acuminate, deep, rather broad, sometimes furrowed or compressed, usually smooth. *Calyx* small to medium,
closed or partly open; lobes often leafy, sometimes separated at base, long,

narrow, acute. *Basin* rather small, medium to rather shallow, narrow, a little abrupt, smooth or slightly wrinkled.

Skin rather thick, tough, smooth, pale greenish-yellow often changing to yellowish-white, sometimes faintly blushed. *Dots* numerous, small, often light colored and submerged, sometimes russet.

Calyx tube long, wide at top, conical to funnel-shape. *Stamens* median.

Core rather large to medium, abaxile to nearly axile; cells closed or open; core lines clasping. *Carpels* roundish to cordate, slightly emarginate, slightly tufted. *Seeds* light brown, medium to rather small, plump, acute.

Flesh white, moderately firm, fine, somewhat crisp, very tender, juicy, sweet, slightly aromatic, good to very good.

Season August and early September.

SWEET FALL PIPPIN.

REFERENCES. 1. Downing, **1857**:192. 2. Warder, **1867**:733. 3. Thomas, **1875**:513.

SYNONYMS. None.

A large, greenish-yellow apple, good either for dessert or for culinary uses; in season from October to January. The tree is large, spreading, vigorous to very vigorous, hardy and a reliable cropper yielding good crops annually or nearly annually. It is not a good variety for commercial plant-ing. Downing refers to it as being grown in Westchester county (1). It is also occasionally found in Western New York. We do not find it listed by nurserymen and it is gradually going out of cultivation.

SWEET RUSSET.

REFERENCES. 1. Warder, **1867**:528. *fig.* 2. Downing, **1869**:377. 3. Bailey, *An. Hort.*, **1892**:250.

SYNONYMS. *Summer Russet* (2). SWEET RUSSET (1, 2, 3).

A small roundish or oblate apple, yellow, mostly covered with light russet tinged with red in the sun, juicy, sweet, very good; season September and October. Tree large, spreading and drooping, a moderately vigorous grower, hardy, long-lived and usually a reliable cropper yielding good crops bien-nially. Origin unknown. It was at one time disseminated by Parsons and Company, Flushing, N. Y.

The name Sweet Russet has also been applied to the variety described as Pumpkin Russet on page 170.

SWITZER.

REFERENCES. 1. Hoskins, *Montreal Hort. Soc. Rpt.*, **1880**:50. 2. *Ill. Hort. Soc. Rpt.*, **1881**:55. 3. *Montreal Hort. Soc. Rpt.*, **1883**:91. 4. Gibb, *Ia. Hort. Soc. Rpt.*, **1883**:436. 5. *Ia. Agr. Coll. Bul.*, **1885**:12. No. 304. 6. *Montreal Hort. Soc. Rpt.*, **1886-87**:16. 7. *Can. Hort.*, 12:344. 1889. 8. *Am. Pom. Soc. Cat.*, **1889**:14. 9. Budd, *Ia. Agr. Coll. Bul.*, **1890**:18. No. 304. 10.

Can. Hort., **13**:216. 1890. **11.** Van Deman, *U. S. Pom. Rpt.*, **1890**:418.
col. pl. **12.** Bailey, *An. Hort.*, **1892**:251. **13.** *Amer. Gard.*, **13**:639. 1892.
14. *Can. Hort.*, **16**:359. 1893. **15.** Hoskins, *Rural N. Y.*, **53**:279. 1894.
16. *Amer. Gard.*, **16**:332, 412. 1895. fig. **17.** Beach, *N. Y. Sta. An. Rpt.*,
14:255. 1895. **18.** *Can. Hort.*, **20**:183, 412. 1897. **19.** *Amer. Gard.*, **19**:652.
1898. **20.** Macoun, *Can. Dept. Agr. Rpt.*, **1901**:98. **21.** Hansen, *S. D. Sta.
Bul.*, **76**:103. 1902. **22.** Munson, *Me. Sta. An. Rpt.*, **18**:85. 1902. **23.** Budd-
Hansen, **1903**:186. fig. **24.** Thomas, **1903**:303.

SYNONYMS. SUISLEPPER (3, 4). *Suislepper* (5). SWITZER (1, 2, 5, 6, 7, 8,
9, 10, 11, 12, 13, 14, 15, 16, 17, 18, 19, 20, 21, 22, 23, 24). *Switzer* (3, 4).

When well grown this is a very handsome fruit of medium
size or below, nearly white with beautiful blush. It is very
good in flavor and quality either for dessert or culinary uses.
As fruited at this Station the tree comes into bearing rather
early and is a fairly reliable cropper yielding pretty good crops
biennially. As compared with standard varieties of its season
it does not appear to merit the attention of New York fruit
growers.

Historical. A Russian apple imported by the U. S. Department of Agriculture in 1870. It was received in 1888 for testing at this Station from
T. H. Hoskins, Newport, Vt.

TREE.

Tree moderately vigorous with short, moderately stout, curved and crooked
branches. *Form* spreading, rather flat, open. *Twigs* short, curved, stout
with large terminal buds; internodes medium. *Bark* dark brown, streaked
with heavy scarf-skin, slightly pubescent. *Lenticels* scattering, small, round,
not raised. *Buds* large, prominent, broad, plump, obtuse, free, heavily pubescent.

FRUIT.

Fruit below medium to above medium. *Form* roundish or oblate, regular.
Stem medium to rather long, rather slender. *Cavity* acuminate, moderately
shallow, narrow, lightly russeted with thin, greenish-russet. *Calyx* small,
closed; lobes medium in length, narrow, acute. *Basin* shallow or almost none,
narrow to wide, furrowed, often wrinkled.

Skin clear white or becoming yellowish, washed with bright pink which
often deepens to crimson. *Dots* whitish, obscure.

Calyx tube variable, elongated conical to cylindrical or funnel-form.
Stamens median to somewhat basal.

Core large, axile; cells closed or partly open; core lines clasping. *Carpels*
round, deeply emarginate. *Seeds* large, dark brown, medium in width, long.

Flesh white, firm, fine, juicy, mild subacid, good.

Season late August to October.

VOL. II — 10

SYLVESTER.

REFERENCES. 1. *Horticulturist,* 17:150. 1862. 2. Warder, 1867:617. fig.
3. Downing, 1869:379. 4. *Ill. Hort. Soc. Rpt.,* 1871:154. 5. Fitz, 1872:170.
SYNONYMS. None.

A waxen-white fruit with crimson blush and brisk subacid flesh; very
good for culinary uses. Season September and October. The tree is large,
roundish, moderately vigorous, hardy, long-lived and a reliable cropper
yielding good crops biennially. It is not desirable for commercial planting
because the fruit shows bruises very readily.

Historical. Originated at Lyons, N. Y. (3). It is but little grown even
in the locality of its origin.

TART BOUGH.

REFERENCES. 1. Thomas, 1849:142. 2. Elliott, 1854:178. 3. Warder,
1867:734. 4. Downing, 1869:380.
SYNONYMS. *Sour Bough* of some (4). TART BOUGH (1, 2, 3, 4).

An old variety which according to Downing (4) was originated and disseminated by Judge Buel of Albany, N. Y. Elliott (2) states that it resembles
Early Harvest, but it ripens ten days later, has more acid and the trees
are more rapid in growth. He regarded it as unworthy of cultivation.

Downing recognizes another Tart Bough the fruit of which is small and
whitish with white, tender flesh, juicy, sprightly, pleasant subacid, good.
Season August (4).

We do not know either of these varieties.

TETOFSKY.

REFERENCES. 1. *London Hort. Soc. Cat.,* 1831:No. 1291. 2. Manning,
Mag. Hort., 7:50. 1841. 3. Downing, 1845:78. 4. Thomas, 1849:141. 5.
Elliott, 1854:111. fig. 6. Hooper, 1857:93. 7. *Horticulturist,* 14:425. 1859.
8. *Am. Pom. Soc. Cat.,* 1862. 9. *Horticulturist,* 21:294. 1866. fig. 10. Warder,
1867:657. 11. Todd, 1871:120. fig. 12. *Mich. Pom. Soc. Rpt.,* 1872:458.
fig. 13. *Horticulturist,* 29:317. 1874. 14. *Montreal Hort. Soc. Rpt.,* 1876:
18. 15. *Ill. Hort. Soc. Rpt.,* 1876:251. 16. *Montreal Hort. Soc. Rpt.,* 1879:
22. 17. Barry, 1883:335. 18. *Montreal Hort. Soc. Rpt.,* 1886-87:27. 19.
Hoskins, *Rural N. Y.,* 45:593. 1886. 20. Lyon, *Mich. Hort. Soc. Rpt.,*
1890:298. 21. Bailey, *An. Hort.,* 1892:251. 22. *N. Y. Sta. An. Rpt.,* 11:588.
1892. 23. Munson, *Me. Sta. Rpt.,* 1896:76. 24. *Can. Hort.,* 19:358. 1896.
25. Waugh, *Vt. Sta. Bul.,* 61:32. 1897. 26. Troop, *Ind. Sta. An. Rpt.,*
12:81. 1899. 27. Waugh, *Vt. Sta. An. Rpt.,* 14:310. 1901. 28. Craig,
Cyc. of Hort., 1901:1404. 29. Hansen, *S. D. Sta. Bul.,* 76:104, 132. 1902.
fig. 30. Munson, *Me. Sta. Rpt.,* 1902:85. 31. Dickens and Greene, *Kan. Sta.
Bul.,* 106:56. 1902. 32. Budd-Hansen, 1903:188. fig.

SYNONYMS. TETOFFSKY (2). TETOFSKI (10, 12, 27, 29). TETOFSKY (1, 3,
4, 5, 6, 7, 8, 9, 11, 13, 14, 15, 16, 17, 18, 19, 20, 21, 22, 23, 24, 25, 26, 28, 30, 31,
32). *Tetofsky* (29).

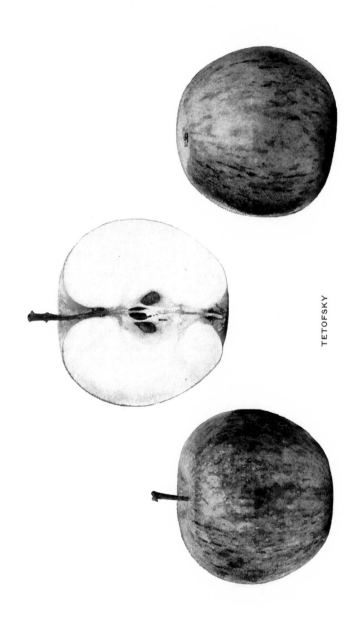

TETOFSKY

A Russian apple below medium size, yellow, striped with crimson, sprightly acid, suitable for culinary use in July, ripe in August. The tree is very hardy, very upright, deep rooted, comes into bearing young and yields full crops biennially or sometimes annually. Desirable for planting in regions where superior hardiness is particularly desired. It is but little earlier than Yellow Transparent which is superior to it in size and dessert qualities. There is a limited demand for the fruit in some local and special markets.

Historical. Tetofsky is one of the pioneers of the Russian varieties in this country having been imported by the Massachusetts Horticultural Society from the London, England, Horticultural Society about 1835 (28). Manning (2) described it as early as 1841 as a new fruit of value. It has been widely disseminated particularly in regions where its superior hardiness renders it peculiarly valuable. It has never been commonly grown in New York state and is now seldom planted here.

TREE.

Tree medium size to dwarfish, moderately vigorous, deep rooted with moderately stout branches filled with small spurs. *Form* very erect, rather dense. *Twigs* short, straight, moderately stout; internodes short. *Bark* dull brown with tinge of red, lightly coated with gray scarf-skin, slightly pubescent. *Lenticels* scattering, small, oblong, not raised. *Buds* small, plump, obtuse, free, slightly pubescent.

FRUIT.

Fruit medium to rather small but usually below medium; uniform in size and fairly uniform in shape. *Form* oblate or roundish, a little inclined to conic, pretty regular. *Stem* medium in length, rather slender. *Cavity* obtuse, medium to rather deep, moderately broad, usually symmetrical, gently furrowed. *Calyx* rather large, closed; lobes long, moderately broad. *Basin* shallow, medium in width, furrowed and wrinkled.

Skin moderately thick, somewhat tough, smooth, waxy, greenish-yellow, more or less striped and splashed with rather attractive bright red, overspread with very faint bloom. Many specimens have little or no red. *Dots* inconspicuous, pale or greenish, submerged.

Calyx tube long, wide, funnel-shape with broad cylinder varying to nearly urn-shape. *Stamens* median to nearly marginal.

Core large, axile or somewhat abaxile; cells open; core lines clasping. *Carpels* broadly roundish, concave. *Seeds* medium size, short, moderately plump, somewhat obtuse.

Flesh white, firm, a little coarse, crisp, tender, juicy, sprightly, slightly aromatic, subacid, fair to good.

Season late July to early September.

THALER.

REFERENCES. 1. Webster, *Montreal Hort. Soc. Rpt.*, **1881** :54. 2. Tuttle, *Ib.*, **8** :135. 1881–82. 3. *Ib.*, **1883** :94. 4. Gibb, *Ia. Hort. Soc. Rpt.*, **1883** : 438. 5. Budd, *Ia. Agr. Coll. Bul.*, **1885** :14. 6. Gibb, *Montreal Hort. Soc. Rpt.*, **1886–87** :14. 7. Schroeder, *Ib.*, **1886–87** :79. 8. Bailey, *An. Hort.*, **1892** : 236. 9. *Ib.*, **1892** :251. 10. Green, *Minn. Sta. Bul.*, **32** :240. 1893. 11. Jack, *Gard. and For.*, **7** :99. 1894. 12. Hoskins, *Ib.*, **7** :138. 1894. 13. *Rural N. Y.*, **54** :539. 1895. 14. Troop, *Ind. Sta. Rpt.*, **1899** :81. 15. Hansen, *S. D. Sta. Bul.*, **76** :38. 1902.

SYNONYMS. CHARLOTTENTHALER (2, 6, 7, 8, 11, 15). *Charlottenthaler* (3, 4). CHARLOTTEN THALER (13). *Charlotten Thaler* (10). *Charlottenthaler Apple* (1). *Charlottelthaler Golba* (5). *No. 147* (7). SCHARLOTTENTHALER GOLBA (1, 3, 4). THALER (5, 9, 10, 12, 14). *Yellow Transparent* (11).

A Russian variety of the Yellow Transparent type. It resembles the Yellow Transparent so closely that some have considered them identical but they are distinct (6, 12). Since Yellow Transparent is superior in health, vigor and productiveness Thaler is not recommended for planting.

THOMPSON.

REFERENCES. 1. Hansen, *S. D. Sta. Bul.*, **76** :104. 1902. 2. Munson, *Me. Sta. Rpt.*, **1902** :85.

SYNONYMS. THOMPSON (1). THOMPSON No. 24 (2). *Thompson's Seedling No. 24* (1).

Fruit of pretty good size, striped red and yellow, rather attractive. Flesh subacid, fair or possibly good in quality. Season late winter. The tree is a pretty good grower, comes into bearing rather young and bears nearly annually yielding moderately good crops. This is a new variety which has gained recognition in the upper Mississippi valley on account of its hardiness in that region. It is also reported as promising in the Northern apple districts of Maine (2). It is not worthy of planting in this state where standard varieties of its season succeed but may be worth testing in those localities where a tree of superior hardiness is desired.

Historical. Originated by J. S. B. Thompson, Grundy county, Ia., and first propagated under the name Thompson Seedling No. 24 (1). In 1892 it was received for testing at this Station from the Jewell Nursery Company, Lake City, Minn., by which the variety was introduced.

TREE.

Tree moderately vigorous with moderately long, slender, curved, drooping branches. *Form* spreading, open, inclined to droop. *Twigs* moderately long, curved, moderately stout; internodes medium. *Bark* brown tinged with red, lightly streaked with scarf-skin; slightly pubescent near tips. *Lenticels* numerous, medium size, oval, raised, conspicuous. *Buds* medium size, broad, obtuse to acute, free, slightly pubescent.

FRUIT.

Fruit below medium to above or rather large. *Form* roundish or roundish oval, pretty regular but somewhat unequal. *Stem* medium in length, slender. *Cavity* acuminate to acute, deep, medium in width to rather narrow, more or less russeted. *Calyx* medium size, open; lobes separated at base. *Basin* deep, narrow to rather wide, abrupt, somewhat furrowed.

Skin pale yellow more or less overspread and mottled with pinkish-red striped and splashed with carmine. *Dots* grayish or brownish, few, small, inconspicuous.

Calyx tube short, conical to funnel-form. *Stamens* basal to median.

Core medium size, abaxile; cells fairly symmetrical, open; core lines nearly meeting. *Carpels* nearly cordate to elliptical. *Seeds* numerous, medium size, flat, moderately acute.

Flesh white, moderately fine, crisp, rather tender, juicy, subacid to mild subacid, fair to good.

Season October to early winter or midwinter.

TINMOUTH.

REFERENCES. 1. Downing, 1857:197. 2. *Am. Pom. Soc. Cat.*, 1862. 3. Downing, *Horticulturist*, 19:145. 1864. figs. 4. Warder, 1867:734. 5. Downing, 1869:383. 6. Thomas, 1875:514. 7. Taylor, *Am. Pom. Soc. Rpt.*, 1895:193. 8. Burrill and McCluer, *Ill. Sta. Bul.*, 45:343. 1896. 9. Waugh, *Vt. Sta. An. Rpt.*, 14:310. 1901.

SYNONYMS. TEIGNMOUTH (3). *Teignmouth* (5, 6). TINMOUTH (1, 2, 4, 5, 6, 7, 8, 9). *Tinmouth Sweet* (8). *Vermont Pippin* (3, 5).

Tinmouth is a fall and early winter apple of good size, good quality and rather attractive appearance. The tree is a good grower, with an upright habit. It is a regular cropper and very productive. It does not seem to be desirable for general commercial planting in New York.

Historical. Downing remarked that this variety originated at Tinmouth, Vt., and was much esteemed in the region of its origin (5). Waugh calls it a good apple and states that it is almost unknown in Grand Isle county but is much more common in other parts of Vermont (9). So far as we have discovered it is but little known in New York.

FRUIT.

Fruit medium to large. *Form* oblate to roundish, regular or obscurely ribbed; sides often distinctly unequal. *Stem* often bracted, short to medium, usually not exserted. *Cavity* large, acute or approaching acuminate, deep, broad, russeted and with outspreading russet rays. *Calyx* small, partly closed or open; lobes often small, sometimes long, acute, recurved. *Basin* rather large, deep, moderately wide, abrupt to moderately abrupt, often somewhat wrinkled.

Skin tender, pale yellow or greenish, often with a bright deep blush and overspread with thin bloom. *Dots* numerous, greenish or russet, giving the surface a somewhat rough appearance. *Prevailing effect* yellow.

Calyx tube rather small, cone-shape or approaching funnel-form. *Stamens* median.

Core rather small, axile or nearly so; cells closed; core lines clasping. *Carpels* roundish to obcordate, emarginate, mucronate. *Seeds* rather large, broad, somewhat obtuse.

Flesh whitish tinged with yellow, moderately fine, tender, rather juicy, mild subacid with a peculiar flavor, sprightly, good in quality.

Season October to early winter or midwinter.

TITOVKA.

REFERENCES. 1. *Montreal Hort. Soc. Rpt.,* **8**:44. 1881–82. fig. **2.** *Ib.,* **8**:74. 1881–82. **3.** *Ia. Hort. Soc. Rpt.,* **1882**:80. **4.** Budd, *Ia. Agr. Coll. Bul.,* **1883**:31. **5.** Gibb, *Ia. Hort. Soc. Rpt.,* **1883**:431. **6.** *Mo. Hort. Soc. Rpt.,* **1883**:173. **7.** Barry, **1883**:335. **8.** Budd, *Ia. Agr. Coll. Bul.,* **1885**:8. **9.** Thomas, **1885**:526. **10.** Gibb, *Montreal Hort. Soc. Rpt.,* **1886–87**:15. **11.** Schroeder, *Ib.,* **1886–87**:78. **12.** Hoskins, *Can. Hort.,* **13**:175. 1890. **13.** Bailey, *An. Hort.,* **1892**:251. **14.** Taylor, *Me. Pom. Soc. Rpt.,* **1892**:58. **15.** Troop, *Ind. Sta. Bul.,* **53**:124. 1894. **16.** Beach, *N. Y. Sta. An. Rpt.,* **13**:584. 1894. **17.** Munson, *Me. Sta. Rpt.,* **1896**:77. **18.** *Mass. Hatch Sta. Bul.,* **44**:4. 1897. **19.** *Am. Pom. Soc. Cat.,* **1897**:15. **20.** Woolverton, *Ont. Fr. Stas. An. Rpt.,* **6**:11. 1899. figs. **21.** Troop, *Ind. Sta. Rpt.,* **1899**:81. **22.** Eneroth-Smirnoff, **1901**:470. **23.** Hansen, *S. D. Sta. Bul.,* **76**:105. 1902. fig. **24.** Munson, *Me. Sta. An. Rpt.,* **18**:85. 1902. **25.** Budd-Hansen, **1903**:188. fig. **26.** Powell and Fulton, *U. S. B. P. I. Bul.,* **48**:58. 1903. **27.** Farrand, *Mich. Sta. Bul.,* **205**:46. 1903.

SYNONYMS. *No. 134* (11). *No. 230 Gov.* (4). TITOVCA (9). TITOVKA (1, 6, 7, 8, 10, 11, 12, 13, 14, 15, 16, 17, 18, 19, 20, 21, 22, 23, 24, 25, 26, 27). TITOWKA (5). TITUS APPLE (2, 3, 4). *Titus Apple* (1, 5, 7). *Titus Riga* (25).

A Russian apple, large, roundish or somewhat oblong, greenish-yellow, handsomely shaded and striped with red and covered with light bloom. When fully mature the ground color is yellow and the red is bright and dark often nearly covering the fruit. Quality good to very good for culinary use. Season August and September. The tree is a vigorous grower, comes into bearing rather young and is moderately productive. It is one of the best Russian apples of its season which we have tested. The crop does not ripen uniformly and more than one picking is required in order to secure the fruit in prime condition for market. Titovka is perhaps worthy of testing for market where fruit of this type and season is desired.

This appears to be the variety which Hansen describes under the name Titovka Department, which name he adopts to distinguish it on the one hand from a variety called Titovka with Titus Riga as a synonym and on the other from a variety called Titovka Speer (23).

Historical. Imported from Russia by the U. S. Department of Agriculture in 1870. It was received in 1883 from Ellwanger and Barry, Rochester, N. Y., for testing at this Station. In 1897 it was entered in the catalogue of the American Pomological Society as a variety of value in the pomological district which includes the Dakotas, Montana and Wyoming (19). It is but little known in New York and so far as we can learn its cultivation is not increasing in this state.

FRUIT.

Fruit large. *Form* roundish or somewhat oblong, a little inclined to conic, nearly regular, pretty symmetrical. *Stem* short, usually not exserted. *Cavity* acuminate, very deep, sometimes slightly russeted. *Calyx* medium size, closed; segments small, convergent. *Basin* moderately shallow to deep, very abrupt, wrinkled.

Skin smooth, pale green becoming yellow, shaded and striped with bright red and overspread with light bloom.

Calyx tube elongated cone-shape or funnel-form. *Stamens* median or below.

Core rather large, somewhat abaxile; cells pretty symmetrical, open; core lines clasping. *Carpels* broadly roundish or somewhat obovate, emarginate. *Seeds*, few, rather small, plump.

Flesh whitish, coarse, crisp, juicy, subacid, good to very good for culinary uses.

Season August and September.

TOM PUTT.

REFERENCES. **1.** *London Hort. Soc. Cat.*, **1831** :No. 1299. **2.** Hogg, **1884** : 229

SYNONYMS. *Coelbrook* (2). *Marrow-bone* (2). TOM PUT (1). TOM PUTT (2).

A rather attractive red apple of good size, moderately coarse, subacid, fair to good for culinary uses. The tree is a moderately vigorous grower, comes into bearing rather early and yields full crops annually or nearly annually. As compared with standard varieties of its season it does not appear to be worthy of the attention of New York fruit growers.

Historical. This is an old English variety (1, 2). In 1892 it was received for testing here from W. and T. Smith, Geneva, N. Y.

TUFTS.

REFERENCES. **1.** *Mag. Hort.*, **14**:519. 1848. **2.** Cole, **1849**:107. **3.** Hovey, *Mag. Hort.*, **16**:496. 1850. fig. **4.** Hovey, **2**:23. 1851. *col. pl.* **5.** Downing, **1857**:198. **6.** Warder, **1867**:734. **7.** Thomas, **1885**:527. **8.** Bailey, *An. Hort.*, **1892**:251. **9.** *Ib.*, **1892**:251. **10.** Beach, *N. Y. Sta. An. Rpt.*, **11**:589, 596. 1892. **11.** Burrill and McCluer, *Ill. Sta. Bul.*, **45**:344. 1896. **12.** Powell and Fulton, *U. S. B. P. I. Bul.*, **48**:58. 1903. **13.** Beach and Clark, *N. Y. Sta. Bul.*, **248**:147. 1904.

SYNONYMS. TUFTS (3, 4, 7, 8, 10, 11, 12, 13). TUFTS BALDWIN (2, 5, 6, 9). *Tufts Baldwin* (7, 10, 12, of some 3 and 5). TUFTS SEEDLING (1).

An apple of the Baldwin group, somewhat like Baldwin in form, color and general appearance, but more mild in flavor and less desirable for market or culinary uses. In ordinary storage it is in season from October to January with October as the commercial limit, but in cold storage it may be held through the winter (13). In some years nearly all of the fruit is discolored at the core. The crop does not ripen evenly, and there is apt to be considerable loss from dropping of the fruit. The tree is large, a pretty good grower, comes into bearing rather early and yields full crops biennially. Not recommended for planting in New York.

Historical. This variety originated in Cambridge, Mass., about 1830. It was first exhibited at the annual show of the Massachusetts Horticultural Society in 1848 (4). It is now rarely listed by nurseymen (8, 9) and is seldom or never planted in this state.

TREE.

Tree large, moderately vigorous. *Form* very spreading, flat, open. *Twigs* moderately long, curved, slender; internodes short. *Bark* brown, heavily coated with gray scarf-skin; pubescent. *Lenticels* scattering, medium size, oblong, not raised. *Buds* medium size, plump, obtuse, free, slightly pubescent.

FRUIT.

Fruit large or nearly so, quite uniform in size and shape. *Form* roundish to roundish oblate, sometimes with a broad protuberance above the cavity on one side, often flattened at apex, broadly ribbed. *Stem* long, rather slender. *Cavity* acute to acuminate, medium in depth to deep, rather broad, often furrowed, usually with outspreading, irregular, greenish-russet. *Calyx* medium to rather small, usually closed. *Basin* rather shallow to moderately deep, medium in width to wide, obtuse to somewhat abrupt, slightly wrinkled, somewhat ridged.

Skin moderately thin, tough, smooth, green or yellowish nearly covered with bright deep red like the Baldwin, not striped or with indistinct stripes of purplish carmine. *Dots* conspicuous, medium to rather small, gray or russet.

Calyx tube medium in length, conical or funnel-shape. *Stamens* median to marginal.

Core large, axile or nearly so; cells closed or partly open; core lines clasping. *Carpels* broadly roundish, often discolored, rather flat, emarginate. *Seeds* often few, not well developed, dark brown, large, long, somewhat acute, slightly tufted.

Flesh tinged with yellow or greenish, firm, moderately coarse, crisp, rather tender, moderately juicy, rather mild subacid, fair to good.

Season October to December or January.

TWENTY OUNCE.

REFERENCES. **1.** *Mag. Hort.,* **10**:210. 1844. **2.** Downing, **1845**:140. **3.** Hovey, *Mag. Hort.,* **13**:70. 1847. fig. **4.** Thomas, **1849**:153. **5.** Cole, **1849**: 120. **6.** Elliott, **1854**:126. **7.** Hooper, **1857**:94. **8.** Downing, **1857**:198. **9.** *Am. Pom. Soc. Cat.,* **1862.** **10.** Warder, **1867**:510. fig. **11.** Downing, **1869**:388. **12.** Fitz, **1872**:168. **13.** Leroy, **1873**:261. fig. **14.** Barry, **1883**: 356. **15.** Wickson, **1889**:245. **16.** Lyon, *Mich. Hort. Soc. Rpt.,* **1890**:298. **17.** Bailey, *An. Hort.,* **1892**:236. **18.** *Ib.,* **1892**:251. **19.** Budd-Hansen, **1903**: 191. **20.** Powell and Fulton, *U. S. B. P. I. Bul.,* **48**:59. 1903. **21.** Beach and Clark, *N. Y. Sta. Bul.,* **248**:147. 1904.

SYNONYMS. *Aurora* (8, 11, 13). *Cabashaw,* incorr. (21). CAYUGA RED STREAK (6, 10, 17). *Cayuga Red Streak* (3, 5, 8, 11, 12, 13, 14, 15, 16, 19, 20, 21, 22). *Coleman* (8, 11, 13). *De Vin du Conn.* (13). DIX-HUIT ONCES (2, 13). *Eighteen Ounce* (4, 6, 13). *Eighteen Ounce Apple* (2, 8, 11). *Gov. Seward's* (3, 6). *Lima* (8, 11, 13). *Morgan's Favorite* (8, 11, 13). TWENTY OUNCE (1, 2, 3, 4, 5, 7, 8, 9, 11, 12, 14, 15, 16, 18, 19, 20, 21). *Twenty Ounce* (6, 10, 13). *Twenty Ounce Apple* (2, 3, 6, 8, 11, 12). *Twenty Ounce Pippin* (3, err. 4 and 6). *Wine* (21, of Conn. 11).

This is one of the most satisfactory of the fall varieties for commercial planting in New York. It is also highly esteemed for home use. The fruit is large, attractive, green becoming yellowish with broad stripes and splashes of red. It is in season from September to early winter. It keeps well for a fall variety and stands shipping well. Usually it should be handled direct to the consumer without going into cold storage. In common storage the fruit goes down rapidly during October and November. In cold storage it may be kept till midwinter (21). It hangs pretty well to the tree for so large an apple, is pretty uniform in size and generally reliable and satisfactory in color and quality. The fruit is in good demand in general market and sells at good prices. It is especially esteemed for culinary uses but it is inferior to other varieties for evaporating. The tree is a rather vigorous grower with main branches erect and laterals rather willowy and more or less drooping. It seems to succeed particularly well in favorable locations in the apple belt south of Lake Ontario. It is especially subject to sunscald and canker on the trunk and larger limbs. For this reason it is desirable to topwork it upon some hardy and thrifty stock such as Tolman *Sweet* or Northern Spy. Careful attention should be given to treating the canker.[1] The top is inclined to grow rather dense and requires constant attention to keep it properly pruned to admit the light to the foliage in all parts of the tree so that the fruit may color properly. The tree when full grown is of medium size or below medium and may be planted closer in the orchard than Baldwin, Rhode Island *Greening* or Northern Spy. It comes into bearing rather young and is almost an annual bearer yielding moderate to good or even heavy crops. The skin of the fruit is apt to be roughened by the application of spray mixtures. In spraying Twenty Ounce after the fruit is set, it is therefore desirable to use an abundance of lime in the bordeaux mixture and make the application uniform and thorough but not excessive.

In different localities in New York Twenty Ounce is known under the various synonyms of Cayuga Redstreak, Wine Apple and Limbertwig. It is quite distinct from Twenty Ounce Pippin; see Volume I, page 349.

Historical. This variety was brought to the notice of pomologists about sixty years ago (1, 3), when fruit of it grown in Cayuga county, N. Y., was exhibited before the Massachusetts Horticultural Society. At that time its cultivation appeared to be mostly confined to Cayuga county and its origin was unknown. In 1857 Downing (8) reported that it originated in Connecticut but upon what authority we are unable to state. Twenty Ounce is well known in most of the apple-growing sections of the state and in certain districts its cultivation for commercial purposes appears to be increasing. It is pretty generally listed by nurserymen (17).

TREE.

Tree moderately vigorous with branches moderately long and moderately stout. *Form* upright becoming roundish, dense; laterals willowy, slender and more or less drooping. *Twigs* short, straight, slender; internodes medium. *Bark* reddish-brown tinged with green, lightly streaked with scarf-skin; slightly pubescent. *Lenticels* quite numerous, medium size, round, not raised. *Buds* medium size, broad, flat, obtuse, appressed, pubescent.

---

1 *N. Y. Sta. An. Rpt.*, **18**:399-418. 1899. *Ib.*, **22**:321-386. 1903.

TWENTY OUNCE

FRUIT.

Fruit very large. *Form* variable, usually roundish or roundish conic, sometimes broadly ribbed. *Stem* deep set, short to medium, moderately thick or rather slender. *Cavity* acuminate, very deep, sometimes lipped, sometimes russeted. *Calyx* below medium size to above, usually closed. *Basin* often oblique, often shallow but occasionally deep, moderately narrow to rather wide, rather abrupt, broadly and deeply furrowed.

Skin thick, tough, greenish becoming rather yellow, washed, mottled and splashed with bright red or deepening to dark or purplish-red with carmine stripes. *Dots* grayish or russet, small to large, often raised, sometimes whitish and submerged.

Calyx tube large, long, wide, conical or funnel-shape extending to the core. *Stamens* usually basal.

Core large, axile or somewhat abaxile; cells symmetrical, usually closed, sometimes wide open; core lines clasping the funnel cylinder. *Carpels* elongated ovate, slightly emarginate, somewhat tufted. *Seeds* medium size, round to narrow, obtuse to acute, variable.

Flesh whitish somewhat tinged with yellow, coarse, moderately tender, juicy, subacid, good for culinary use, second rate for dessert.

Season late September to early winter.

RED TYPE OF TWENTY OUNCE.

A red Twenty Ounce which originated at Hilton, Monroe county, N. Y., is being propagated under the name " Collamer." See page 36.

TYRE BEAUTY.

REFERENCES. **1.** Downing, 1869:388. **2.** *Horticulturist*, 24:52. 1869. fig. SYNONYMS. None.

This was brought to notice about thirty-five years ago as a new seedling apple of value in the locality of its origin, Tyre, Seneca county, N. Y. Fruit medium, pale yellow, splashed, marbled and shaded with crimson. Flesh tender, slightly acid, neither rich nor peculiarly sprightly. Season early September (2).

We are unacquainted with this variety and so far as we know it has not been grown outside of the locality of its origin.

UTTER.

REFERENCES. **1.** *Horticulturist*, 10:528. 1855. **2.** *Ib.*, 23:10. 1868. fig. **3.** Downing, 1869:389. **4.** *Am. Pom. Soc. Cat.*, **1873.** **5.** *Montreal Hort. Soc. Rpt.*, 5:35. 1879. **6.** Budd, *Ia. Hort. Soc. Rpt.*, **1879**:472. **7.** Thomas, **1885**:527. **8.** *Montreal Hort. Soc. Rpt.*, **1886–87**:97. **9.** Bailey, *An. Hort.*, **1892**:251. **10.** Harris, *U. S. Pom. Rpt.*, **1892**:271. **11.** Burrill and McCluer, *Ill. Sta. Bul.*, **45**:311, 344. 1896. **12.** Macoun, *Can. Dept. Agr. Rpt.*, **1901**: 98. **13.** Hansen, *S. D. Sta. Bul.*, 76:108. 1902. fig. **14.** Budd-Hansen, **1903**:193. fig.

SYNONYMS. *English Janneting* (6). *Fameuse* (6). *Seever's Red Streak* (6). UTTER'S (1). UTTER (2, 3, 4, 6, 7, 8, 9, 10, 11, 13, 14). UTTER'S LARGE RED (9). UTTER'S RED (5, 12). *Utter's Red* (13, 14).

Fruit of good size, yellow and red, rather attractive in appearance. The tree is a rather upright regular grower, forming a full rounded head, healthy and productive (11). It is very hardy and on this account has been grown to some extent in regions where standard varieties do not succeed (13, 14).

Historical. Originated in Wisconsin where it was known as early as 1855 (1). It has been much grown in that state and in other parts of the Middle West (13, 14) but it is little known in New York.

FRUIT.

Fruit above medium to large. *Form* usually roundish oblate varying to roundish, sometimes a little inclined to oblong, often somewhat broadly ribbed, pretty regular. *Stem* short to medium, moderately stout. *Cavity* acute to acuminate, deep, medium in width to wide, furrowed gently if at all, sometimes partly russeted. *Calyx* small, closed or partly open; lobes small, short, obtuse. *Basin* rather shallow to moderately deep, medium in width, abrupt, slightly furrowed and wrinkled.

Skin moderately thick, tough, clear, rather pale yellow usually washed with orange-red and narrowly streaked with bright carmine. Some fruits show little or no red but on highly colored specimens the prevailing color is red. *Dots* not conspicuous, numerous, often submerged or whitish or occasionally with russet point.

Calyx tube elongated funnel-form. *Stamens* median or below.

Core sessile, medium size, abaxile; cells symmetrical, open or closed; core lines clasping. *Carpels* broadly roundish or approaching elliptical, but slightly emarginate if at all, smooth or slightly tufted. *Seeds* moderately numerous, medium to rather large, somewhat narrow to rather wide, obtuse or approaching acute, moderately light reddish-brown.

Flesh whitish tinged with yellow, somewhat coarse, crisp, tender, juicy, mild subacid, pleasantly flavored, good.

Season October to December or later.

VANDEVERE.

REFERENCES. 1. *Am. Gard. Cal.*, 1806:585. 2. Coxe, 1817:141. fig. 3. Thacher, 1822:139. 4. Buel, *N. Y. Bd. Agr. Mem.*, 1826:477. 5. Floy-Lindley, 1833:85. 6. Downing, 1845:141. fig. 7. Thomas, 1849:173. 8. Cole, 1849:122. 9. *Horticulturist*, 10:87. 1855. 10. *Ib.*, 11:89. 1856. 11. Warder, 1867:735. 12. Fitz, 1872:121, 149, 153. 13. *Am. Pom. Soc. Cat.*, 1873. 14. Lyon, *Mich. Hort. Soc. Rpt.*, 1890:298. 15. Bailey, *An. Hort.*, 1892:251. 16. Budd-Hansen, 1903:193.

SYNONYMS. *Oxeye* (8, 12). *Staalcubs* (2, 4). *Stalcubs* (3, 6). VANDER-VERE (2, 6, 9, 10, 11). VANDEVEER (4). VANDEVERE (1, 3, 5, 7, 8, 12, 13, 14, 15, 16).

The old variety which is commonly called Vandevere in New York is known to pomologists by the name Newtown Spitzenburg, under which name it is described in Vol. I, page 225. It originated in Newtown, L. I. The true Vandevere which we are here considering is quite distinct from this Newtown Spitzenburg.

When in perfection Vandevere is a beautiful and fine apple, medium in size, marked with light red in indistinct streaks over a yellow background; well colored specimens become deep red; dots numerous, green or light gray; flesh yellowish, crisp and tender with a rich, sprightly, mild subacid flavor, valued especially for culinary purposes; in season from October to January. The tree is of medium size, spreading, moderately vigorous, not very productive (2, 6, 7).

Historical. An old variety native of Wilmington, Del. (2, 6). It is sometimes called the Vandevere of Delaware or the Vandevere of Pennsylvania. It has never been much cultivated in New York and is now seldom or never planted here.

VANDEVERE PIPPIN.

REFERENCES. **1.** Phœnix, *Horticulturist,* 4:471. 1849. **2.** Elliott, **1854**:113. fig. **3.** Downing, **1857**:199. **4.** Hooper, **1857**:94. **5.** Warder, **1867**:462. **6.** Thomas, **1875**:204. **7.** Budd-Hansen, **1903**:193. fig.

SYNONYMS. *Baltimore* of some, incorrectly (2). *Big Vandevere* (3). *Fall Vandevere* (2). *Gibbon's Smathhouse?* (2). *Gibbon's Smokehouse?* (2). *Imperial Vandevere* (2). *Indiana Vandevere* (3, 6). *Large Vandevere* (5). *Millcreek* (2). *Millcreek Vandevere* (2). *Pennsylvania Vandevere* (2). *Red Vandevere* (2). *Smokehouse?* (2). *Spiced Oxeye* (2). *Staalclubs* (2). *Striped Ashmore?* (2). *Striped Vandevere* (2). VANDERVERE (2). *Vandervere* (5). VANDERVERE PIPPIN (1, 5). *Vandervere Pippin* (2). VANDEVERE PIPPIN (3, 6, 7). *Vandevere Pippin* (4). VANDEVERE YELLOW (4). *Watson's Vandervere* (2, 5). *Watson's Vandevere* (3, 6). *Windower* (1). *Yellow Vandervere* (2, 5).

A large, coarse apple, yellow, more or less covered with marbled red and scarlet stripes; flesh of rather sharp acid flavor, excellent for culinary use but not esteemed for dessert (5); in season from September or October to early winter. The tree is vigorous, large, spreading, a reliable cropper and productive. The twigs and leaves much resemble those of Vandevere (5). It appears that it is no longer listed by nurserymen.

Historical. Origin unknown (3, 5, 7). It has been grown to some extent in the West but has never been much cultivated in New York.

VICTORIA.

REFERENCES. **1.** Downing, **1881**:111 app. fig. **2.** Bailey, *An. Hort.,* **1892**: 251. **3.** Powell and Fulton, *U. S. B. P. I. Bul.,* **48**:59. 1903. **4.** Beach and Clark, *N. Y. Sta. Bul.,* **248**:148. 1904.

SYNONYMS. VICTORIA (3, 4). VICTORIA SWEET (1). *Victoria Sweet* (4). VICTORIA SWEETING (2).

This variety belongs in the same group with Mabie. The fruit is of good medium size, dark red, with conspicuous, large dots somewhat like those seen on Westfield *Seek-No-Further* and Blue Pearmain. The flesh is moderately coarse, very tender, rather juicy, sweet, good to very good, for either dessert or culinary uses. In ordinary storage it is in season from October to January, with October as the commercial limit; in cold storage it may be held till January (4). The tree is a pretty good grower, comes into bearing rather young and yields full crops biennially. It is recommended for trial in Central and Eastern New York where a variety of this type is desired either for the home or for the local market.

Historical. Origin uncertain. It is supposed by some to have originated in Chenango county. Probably it is nowhere grown extensively but it is cultivated more in Chenango and adjacent counties than in any other region. It is occasionally listed by nurserymen (2).

TREE.

Tree moderately vigorous with rather short, rather stocky, crooked branches. *Form* spreading. *Twigs* moderately long, rather slender; internodes medium. *Bark* dull reddish-brown or olive-green, slightly mottled with scarf-skin; pubescent. *Lenticels* scattering, usually large and elongated. *Buds* medium size, rather narrow, plump, appressed, acute, pubescent. *Leaves* medium size, rather broad.

FRUIT.

Fruit above medium to medium, fairly uniform in size and shape. *Form* roundish inclined to conic, somewhat flattened at base, faintly and broadly ribbed. *Stem* usually short, moderately thick. *Cavity* moderately deep, medium in width to broad, symmetrical, often lipped, sometimes red and smooth, but often bright yellow russet or greenish-russet overspreads the cavity and radiates irregularly over the base in broken lines and splashes. *Calyx* small to medium, closed or partly open; lobes usually short and not separated at base, acute. *Basin* medium in depth to moderately deep, narrow to wide, somewhat abrupt, slightly wrinkled.

Skin tough, nearly smooth, yellow, blushed and faintly mottled with rather dull red and marked with numerous, narrow stripes of deeper red. Highly colored specimens are purplish-red with obscure stripes. *Dots* or flecks conspicuous, gray or russet, becoming smaller and more numerous toward the cavity.

Calyx tube short, medium size, conical or somewhat funnel-form. *Stamens* median to basal.

Core medium to somewhat distant, usually abaxile; cells closed or partly open; core lines clasping the funnel cylinder. *Carpels* roundish cordate to

VICTORIA SWEET

elliptical, decidedly concave, tufted. *Seeds* numerous, dark, medium size, flat, acute to obtuse.

Flesh tinged with yellow, firm, moderately coarse, very tender, juicy, sweet, good to very good.

Season October to January.

VICTUALS AND DRINK.

REFERENCES. 1. Downing, 1845:141. 2. Thomas, 1849:163. 3. Emmons, *Nat. Hist. N. Y.*, 3:88. 1851. 4. Elliott, 1854:179. 5. Hooper, 1857:94. 6. Warder, 1867:499. fig. 7. *Am. Pom. Soc. Cat.*, 1873. 8. Taylor, *Am. Pom. Soc. Rpt.*, 1895:200.

SYNONYMS. *Big Sweet* (1, 4, 5). *Fall Green Sweet* (6). *Green Sweet* of Indiana (6). *Pompey* (1, 4, 5, 6). VICTUALS AND DRINK (1, 2, 3, 4, 5, 6, 7, 8).

A large, somewhat rough, dull green or yellowish apple often veined with russet. The flesh is sweet, very tender, fine-grained, very good to best in quality; in season from October to January or later. The tree is medium to rather large, upright or roundish, stocky, vigorous, very productive, often carrying so heavy a load of fruit that many of the apples are small. Downing states that it originated in the neighborhood of Newark, N. J., about 1750 (1). In 1873 (7) it was entered in the catalogue of the American Pomological Society but was dropped from that list in 1897. Bailey does not mention it in his Inventory of Apples Offered by American Nurserymen in 1892.[1] It has been popular in some portions of the West but so far as we know has never been much cultivated in New York. It is undoubtedly an excellent variety for the home orchard.

VINEUSE ROUGE.

REFERENCES. 1. Leroy, 1873:230. fig. 2. *Ib.*, 1873:846. fig. 3. Hoskins, *Ia. Hort. Soc. Rpt.*, 1879:414. 4. Gibb, *Ib.*, 1883:442. 5. *N. Y. Sta. An. Rpt.*, 3:20. 1884. 6. Budd. *Ia. Agr. Coll. Bul.*, 1885:16. 7. Craig, *Montreal Hort. Soc. Rpt.*, 12:102. 1886–87. 8. Beach, *N. Y. Sta. An. Rpt.*, 11:587. 1892. 9. Bailey, *An. Hort.*, 1892:240. 10. Beach, *N. Y. Sta. An. Rpt.*, 12: 600. 1893. 11. *Ib.*, 13:581. 1894. 12. Dempsey, *Ont. Fr. Stas. An. Rpt.*, 1:24. 1894. fig. 13. Hansen, *S. D. Sta. Bul.*, 76:110. 1902.

SYNONYMS. *Aromatic Spike No.* 354 (13). COMPTE ORLOFF (1). COUNT ORLOFF (8). *Count Orloff* (13). *De Revel* (2). GRAND SULTAN (3, 7, 9, 10, 12). *Grand Sultan* (2). *Green Transparent* (13). GROSKOE ṢELENKA GRÜNER (5, 11). ORLOFF (6). *Orloff* (4). *Orlovskoe* (6). ORLOWSKOE (4). *Red Transparent* (13). *Revelstone Pippin* (2). TRANSPARENTE JAUNE (2). *Transparente Rouge* (1). *Transparente de Sainte-Léger* (2). *Transparente Verte* (1). VINEUSE ROUGE (13). *Vineuse Rouge* (1).

Hansen gives the following description of this variety (13): "Origin, Russia; as fruited in the Iowa Experiment Station orchard, this variety and Red Transparent, Count Orloff, Grand Sultan, Green Transparent and

---

[1] *An. Hort.*, 1892.

Aromatic Spike No. 354 are identical or very similar. Tree a strong grower, round topped, a heavy annual bearer. Fruit medium to large, round oblate conic, regular; surface greenish-yellow, rarely faintly splashed with red on sunny side, overlaid with white bloom; dots large, white, few; cavity narrow, abrupt, with irregular patch of russet, stem short, stout, often clubbed; basin small, shallow; calyx, small, closed. Core closed or nearly so, clasping: tube long, funnel-shaped; flesh white, firm, juicy, fragrant, subacid, good for table, very good for cooking. Season very early, about one week before Yellow Transparent, but perishable and should be picked early to prevent water-coring and rotting on the tree. Evidently the name is a misnomer as it means Red Wine Colored."

As grown at this Station Count Orloff, Grand Sultan and Groskoe Selenka Grüner are identical or very similar, and none of them is very desirable.

WASHINGTON STRAWBERRY.

REFERENCES. **1.** *N. Y. Agr. Soc. Trans.*, **1849**:117. **2.** *Mag. Hort.*, **23**:26. 1857. **3.** Hovey, *Ib.*, **24**:79. 1858. fig. **4.** *Am. Pom. Soc. Cat.*, **1869**. **5.** Downing, **1869**:396. fig. **6.** Thomas, **1875**:205. **7.** Downing, **1881**:11, 13 index, app. **8.** Barry, **1883**:341. **9.** Wickson, **1889**:244. **10.** Lyon, *Mich. Hort. Soc. Rpt.*, **1890**:298. **11.** Bailey, *An. Hort.*, **1892**:252. **12.** Burnett, *La. Sta. Bul.*, **27**:926. 1894. **13.** Powell and Fulton, *U. S. B. P. I. Bul.*, **48**:60. 1903. **14.** Budd-Hansen, **1903**:197. fig. **15.** Farrand, *Mich. Sta. Bul.*, **205**:47. 1903. **16.** Beach and Clark, *N. Y. Sta. Bul.*, **248**:150. 1904.

SYNONYMS. *Juniata* (7). WASHINGTON (2, 3). *Washington of Maine* (7). *Washington County Seedling* (2). WASHINGTON STRAWBERRY (1, 4, 5, 6, 7, 8, 9, 10, 11, 12, 13, 15, 16). WASHINGTON *Strawberry* (14). *Washington Strawberry* (3).

Fruit smooth, of good size and pretty good color, fairly uniform in shape but somewhat variable in size, desirable for either dessert or culinary uses. It is quite variable in season in different years and in different localities. As fruited at this Station it comes in season in September or October, and some portion of the fruit may be kept in fair condition into the winter or sometimes through the winter. In ordinary storage its commercial limit is October, and in cold storage November (13, 16). The fruit hangs well to the tree. The tree is vigorous, hardy, healthy, moderately long-lived, comes into bearing rather early and is a reliable cropper, yielding good crops biennially or almost annually. It is a good variety for home use, but evidently is not wanted in market. Its season is rather short, and it begins to mature at a time when the markets are filled with other fruits.

Historical. Washington Strawberry was first exhibited at the Fair of the State Agricultural Society in Syracuse in 1849 (1, 3). It originated on the farm of Job Whipple, Union Springs, Washington county, N Y. (1). It was included in the catalogue of the American Pomological Society in 1869 (4). It is still listed by nurserymen and has been disseminated to some extent in various parts of the continent. Although it has been known for a half century it has failed to establish itself in the commercial orchards of this state and is but little known among New York fruit growers.

TREE.

Tree medium to large, vigorous to moderately vigorous. *Form* rather flat, spreading, open. *Twigs* below medium to short, straight or nearly so, rather slender to stout with large terminal buds; internodes medium or below. *Bark* clear brownish-red or with more or less olive-green, lightly streaked with scarf-skin; pubescent. *Lenticels* scattering, small to medium, round or somewhat elongated, slightly raised. *Buds* medium to large, broad, plump, obtuse, free or nearly so, pubescent.

FRUIT.

Fruit medium to large or very large. *Form* globular, usually inclined to conic, base rounding or sometimes flattened, nearly regular; sides often a little unequal. *Stem* short and rather thick or sometimes long. *Cavity* below medium to medium, acute to somewhat acuminate, rather shallow to deep, narrow to moderately broad, occasionally lipped, often somewhat furrowed, usually thinly russeted. *Calyx* below medium to rather large, usually somewhat open; lobes a little separated and broad at the base, narrow above, long, acute to acuminate. *Basin* small to medium, narrow to moderately wide, medium in depth, abrupt, somewhat furrowed, wrinkled.

Skin rather thin, tough, smooth, somewhat waxy, greenish or yellow, washed and mottled with red, conspicuously splashed and striped with bright carmine and overspread with thin bloom. *Dots* numerous, russet or whitish and rather conspicuous, often submerged. *Prevailing effect* striped red.

Calyx tube rather large, wide, cone-shape with core lines meeting, sometimes becoming funnel-form with clasping core lines. *Stamens* basal or nearly so.

Core below medium to above, axile or sometimes abaxile; cells not uniformly developed, usually symmetrical and more or less open, sometimes closed; core lines meeting if the calyx tube is cone-shape, clasping if it is funnel-form. *Carpels* variable, ovate to broadly obcordate, sometimes a little emarginate, often tufted. *Seeds* dark, medium in size, rather long, somewhat acute; often many are abortive.

Flesh whitish tinged with yellow, firm, rather fine to a little coarse, crisp, tender, very juicy, pleasant subacid, sprightly, good to very good.

Season from September or October into early winter.

WATER.

REFERENCES. 1. Downing, *Horticulturist*, 19:172. 1864. *figs.* 2. Warder, 1867:735. 3. Downing, 1869:397. *fig.* 4. Thomas, 1875:315. 5. *Am. Pom. Soc. Cat.*, 1877:16. 6. Lyon, *Mich. Hort. Soc. Rpt.*, 1890:298. 7. Bailey, *An. Hort.*, 1892:252.

SYNONYMS. None.

A mild flavored dessert apple of medium size, pale yellow or greenish with attractive blush of lively red; in season from October to December. The tree is a rather moderate grower, does not come into bearing young and is a biennial bearer yielding from fair to good crops. Not recommended for commercial planting.

Historical. Origin Durham township, Bucks county, Pa. (1, 3). It was entered in the catalogue of the American Pomological Society in 1877 (5) and dropped from that list in 1897. It is but little known in this state.

TREE.

Tree moderately vigorous with short, slender, curved branches. *Form* erect or roundish, rather dense. *Twigs* long, curved, moderately stout; internodes short. *Bark* dark brown, heavily coated with gray scarf skin; pubescent near tips. *Lenticels* scattering, small, round, not raised. *Buds* rather prominent, medium to large, plump, obtuse, free, pubescent.

FRUIT.

Fruit medium size. *Form* broadly ovate to roundish conic varying to oblong conic with flattened ends, nearly regular. *Stem* short to medium, slender. *Cavity* acuminate, rather narrow to moderately broad, moderately shallow to deep, often compressed, sometimes thinly russeted, the russet not extending beyond the cavity. *Calyx* small to medium, closed or open; lobes long, narrow, acute to acuminate. *Basin* varying from shallow to rather deep and abrupt, narrow to medium in width, furrowed and wrinkled.

Skin pale yellow or greenish with very attractive, lively pinkish-red blush, in well colored specimens deepening to dark or purplish-red, not striped, overspread with thin bloom. *Dots* numerous, medium to small, grayish or whitish, often submerged.

Calyx tube short, wide, broadly conical. *Stamens* basal to median.

Core rather small, somewhat abaxile; cells closed or slightly open; core lines slightly clasping. *Carpels* small, slightly obovate to obcordate, emarginate. *Seeds* medium in size, few, dark brown, varying from blunt and flat to acute and rather narrow.

Flesh nearly white, fine, crisp, tender, juicy, pleasant mild subacid, good.

Season October to December or later.

WEALTHY.

REFERENCES. 1. Downing, 1869:398. 2. Foster, *Horticulturist*, 25:362. 1870. 3. *Am. Pom. Soc. Cat.*, 1871:10. 4. Thomas, 1875:515. 5. *Montreal Hort. Soc. Rpt.*, 1876:19. 6. *Ib.*, 1879:33. *fig.* 7. *Ia. Hort. Soc. Rpt.*, 1879:

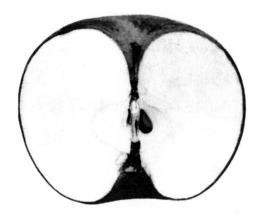

WEALTHY

453. **8.** Sheppard, *Montreal Hort. Soc. Rpt.,* **8**:140. 1881–82. **9.** Foster, *Ia. Hort. Soc. Rpt.,* **1882**:100. **10.** Barry, **1883**:356. **11.** Gideon, *Am. Pom. Soc. Rpt.,* **1885**:114. **12.** *Montreal Hort. Soc. Rpt.,* **1886–87**:17, 27. **13.** *Rural N. Y.,* 46:494, 751. 1887. **14.** *Am. Pom. Soc. Rpt.,* **1887**:92. **15.** *Can. Hort.,* **11**:31. 1888. **16.** *Rural N. Y.,* 48:177. 1889. **17.** Gibb, *Montreal Hort. Soc. Rpt.,* **15**:19. 1890. **18.** Hamilton, *Ib.,* **15**:27. 1890. **19.** Lyon, *Mich. Hort. Soc. Rpt.,* **1890**:298. **20.** *Can. Hort.,* **14**:119, 131, 331. 1891. **21.** Taylor, *Me. Pom. Soc. Rpt.,* **1892**:57. **22.** *Rural N. Y.,* **51**:705. 1892. **23.** *Ont. Fr. Gr. Assn. An. Rpt.,* 26:65. 1894. **24.** *Rural N. Y.,* **54**: 682. 1895. **25.** Woolverton, *Ont. Fr. Stas. An. Rpt,* 3:17. 1896. figs. **26.** Waugh, *Vt. Sta. Bul.,* **61**:32. 1897. **27.** Bunyard, *Jour. Roy. Hort. Soc.,* **1898**:357. **28.** *Am. Gard.,* 20:404. 1899. **29.** Waugh, *Vt. Sta. An. Rpt.,* 14:312. 1901. **30.** Hays, *U. S. Div. of Vegetable Physiology and Pathology Bul.,* 29:13. 1901. **31.** *Can. Hort.,* 25:121. 1902. **32.** Van Deman, *Rural N. Y.,* **61**:249. 1902. **33.** Munson, *Me. Sta. An. Rpt.,* 18:85, 90. 1902. **34.** Hansen, *S. D. Sta. Bul.,* 76:112. 1902. fig. **35.** Dickens and Greene, *Kan. Sta. Bul.,* 106:56. 1902. **36.** *Can. Hort.,* 26:12. 1903. **37.** Budd–Hansen, **1903**:198. fig. **38.** Farrand, *Mich. Sta. Bul.,* 205:47. 1903. **39.** Powell and Fulton, *U. S. B. P. I. Bul.,* 48:60. 1903. **40.** Macoun, *Can. Hort.,* 27:71. 1904. fig. of tree. **41.** Beach and Clark, *N. Y. Sta. Bul.,* 248:150. 1904. **42.** Ragan, *U. S. B. P. I. Bul.,* 56:326. 1905.

SYNONYMS. None.

This variety is particularly valuable for cold climates because the tree is very hardy and the fruit sells well, being bright red and good in quality for either dessert or culinary uses. It is in season from October to early winter or mid-winter. In ordinary storage its commercial limit is October, but in cold storage it may be kept till January or later. It does not stand heat very well before going into storage, and goes down rather quickly (41). Young trees or trees which are making a thrifty growth produce fruit of good size, but mature, slow-growing trees are apt to yield a considerable percentage of undersized fruit, especially when they are overloaded, as is often the case. The crop ripens unevenly, and more than one picking should be made in order to secure the fruit in prime condition. If it is left upon the tree till fully colored there is apt to be considerable loss by dropping. The tree is a good thrifty grower when young, but with maturity it becomes a moderate or rather slow grower, forming a medium-sized or rather dwarfish tree. Wealthy is being planted for commercial purposes in many parts of the state, but in most localities the trees are as yet comparatively young; in some sections of the state it is being planted more than any other apple of its season. Trees that have become old enough to develop the tendency to produce rather small fruit are in some places being grafted over to other sorts. In other places fruit growers, by adopting such treatment as thinning the fruit and keeping the soil fertile, continue to produce apples of good marketable size when the trees are mature.

Historical. Originated by Peter M. Gideon, Excelsior, Minn., from seed of the Cherry Crab, which he obtained about 1860 from Albert Emerson, Bangor, Me. (11, 28). Ragan (42) states that the fruit was first described in the Western Farmer in 1869. It has been extensively disseminated, particularly in those apple-growing districts where a tree of superior hardiness is especially desired. It is generally listed by nurserymen and its cultivation is gradually increasing.

TREE.

Tree somewhat dwarfish to medium size, moderately vigorous with short, moderately stout, curved branches. *Form* upright spreading or roundish, open and somewhat drooping. *Twigs* long, curved, slender; internodes long. *Bark* dark brown, lightly streaked with scarf-skin; pubescent. *Lenticels* quite numerous, medium to small, oblong, not raised, rather conspicuous. *Buds* medium size, broad, plump, obtuse, free, pubescent.

FRUIT.

Fruit above medium to large when well grown but often small on old trees; pretty uniform in shape and quality but more or less uneven in size. *Form* roundish conic, slightly flattened at base, regular, symmetrical. *Stem* usually short to medium, but rather long on small fruit and rather slender. *Cavity* decidedly acuminate, rather deep, moderately narrow to rather broad, russeted. *Calyx* medium size, closed or partly open; lobes broad, obtuse to acute. *Basin* medium in depth to rather shallow, rather narrow, abrupt, smooth, symmetrical.

Skin thin, tough, pale yellow or greenish, blushed and marked with narrow stripes and splashes of red, deepening in highly colored specimens to brilliant red, very attractive. *Dots* numerous, small, inconspicuous, pale or russet. *Prevailing effect* bright red.

Calyx tube conical approaching funnel-form. *Stamens* median.

Core medium to very small, axile or sometimes slightly abaxile; cells symmetrical, slightly open; core lines clasping. *Carpels* medium to rather small, roundish, narrowing toward base and apex, smooth, flat. *Seeds* moderately dark brown, above medium, rather acute.

Flesh whitish sometimes stained with red, moderately fine, crisp, tender, very juicy, agreeable subacid, sprightly, somewhat aromatic, good to very good.

Season October to January.

WESTERN BEAUTY.

REFERENCES. 1. *Gardeners' Monthly*, 1861:124 (cited by 2). 2. Kenrick, *Mag. Hort.*, 29:73. 1863. fig. 3. Warder, 1867:464. fig. 4. Downing, 1869: 89. 5. *Ib.*, 1872:37 app. 6. *Am. Pom. Soc. Cat.*, 1877. 7. Barry, 1883:356. 8. Thomas, 1885:528. 9. Bailey, *An. Hort.*, 1892:252. 10. Burrill and Mc-Cluer, *Ill. Sta. Bul.*, 45:345. 1896.

SYNONYMS. BEAUTY OF THE WEST (4). *Beauty of the West* (10). *Big Rambo* (3, 5). *Musgrove's Cooper* (3, 4, 5). OHIO BEAUTY (1). *Ohio Beauty* (3, 4, 5). WESTERN BEAUTY (2, 3, 5, 6, 7, 8, 9, 10).

The three varieties, Western Beauty, Grosh and Summer Rambo, resemble each other so closely in fruit that it is practically impossible to distinguish the one from the other from the examination of the fruit alone. The Summer Rambo, however, ripens about a month earlier than the other two varieties and it can consequently be readily distinguished in the orchard. Pomologists are in doubt as to whether the Grosh and Western Beauty are two distinct varieties or the same variety under two names. We have been unable to obtain sufficient evidence to determine this point.

For a technical description of the fruit, see Grosh, page 89.

Hyde King was received here for testing under the name Western Beauty and consequently is referred to under that name erroneously in some published accounts of its record at this Station. See Volume I, page 166.

Historical. Origin unknown. First introduced to notice by William F. English of Rhinehart, Auglaize county, Ohio (1, 2).

WHITE ASTRACHAN.

REFERENCES. 1. *Pom. Mag.*, 2:No. 96. 1829. col. pl. 2. *London Hort. Soc. Cat.*, 1831:No. 32. 3. Floy-Lindley, 1833:6. 4. *Mag. Hort.*, 1:391, 392. 1835. 5. Manning, *Ib.*, 7:52. 1841. 6. Downing, 1845:78. 7. Emmons, *Nat. Hist. N. Y.*, 3:17. 1851. 8. Elliott, 1854:179. 9. Warder, 1867:735. 10. Leroy, 1873:79. fig. 11. Thomas, 1875:516. 12. *Montreal Hort. Soc. Rpt.*, 1:9. 1876. 13. *Ib.*, 5:23. 1879. 14. Hogg, 1884:238. 15. Wickson, 1889:243. 16. *Am. Pom. Soc. Cat.*, 1889:14. 17. Hansen, *S. D. Sta. Bul.*, 76:113. 1903.

SYNONYMS. ASTRACAN BLANCHE (10). *Astracan d'Ete* (10). *Astracanischer Sommer* (10). ASTRACHAN WHITE (2). *Blanche Glacee d'Ete* (10). *De Glace d'Ete* (10). *De Glace Hative* (10). *De Moscovie d'Ete* (10). *Gelee d'Ete* (10). *Glace de Zelande* (1, 2, 3, 6, 7, 8, 10). *Glacee d'Ete* (10). *Naliwi Jabloky* (10). *Pomme Astrachan* (3). *Pomme d'Astrachan* (2). *Pyrus Astracanica* (1, 2, 6, 7). *Taffitai* (10). *Transparent Apple* (14). *Transparente de Astracan* (10). *Transparente d'Ete* (10). *Transparente de Zurich* (10). *Transparente de Muscovie d'Ete* (10). *Transparent Muscovie* (7). *Transparent de Muscovie* (1, 2, 3, 6, 8). WHITE ASTRACAN (1, 3, 4, 5, 7, 15). *White Astracan* (10). WHITE ASTRACHAN (6, 8, 9, 11, 12, 13, 14, 16, 17).

A Russian apple of little or no value for this region. Fruit medium size, roundish to roundish oblate, waxen yellow or whitish with faint streaks of red; flesh white, acid, good for culinary use; season August and September (6, 17).

Historical. It has been known in this country for many years (4, 5, 6, 7, 8, 9). It was not entered on the catalogue of the American Pomological Society till 1889 (16) and was dropped from that list in 1891. It is practically unknown in New York.

WHITE JUNEATING.

REFERENCES. 1. *Am. Gard. Cal.*, 1806:584. 2. Coxe, 1817:100. fig. 3. *London Hort. Soc. Cat.*, 1831:No. 612. 4. Floy-Lindley, 1833:3. 5. *Mag. Hort.*, 1:326. 1835. 6. Downing, 1845:78. fig. 7. Thomas, 1849:144. fig. 8. Cole, 1849:97. 9. Emmons, *Nat. Hist. N. Y.*, 3:17. 1851. 10. Elliott, 1854:162. 11. Hooper, 1857:20. 12. *Am. Pom. Soc. Cal.*, 1862. 13. *Horticulturist*, 21:292. 1866. fig. 14. Warder, 1867:417. 15. Fitz, 1872:143, 151, 161. 16. Hogg, 1884:117. 17. Wickson, 1889:242. 18. Bruner, *N. C. Sta. Bul.*, 182:23. 1903. 19. Budd-Hansen, 1903:200.

SYNONYMS. *Bracken* (8, 11, of Ohio 7). *Carolina* (10). *Caroline* (10). *Early Jenneting* (16). *Early May* (10, ?14). *Gennetting* (17). GINETTING (1). *Ginetting* (16). *Jenneting* (2). *Jennetting* (17). JOANETING (16). *Juneateing* (1). JUNEATING (4). *Juneating* (6, 8, 10, 11, 14, 16). JUNETING (2). *Juneting* (16). *Owen's Golden Beauty* (3, 6, 10, 16). *Primiting* (16). WHITE JUNEATING (3, 5, 6, 7, 8, 9, 10, 11, 12, 13, 15, 17, 18, 19). *White Juneating* (16). *Yellow May* (18, 19). *Yellow June* (14).

This apple has little to recommend it except that it ripens very early in the season. It is small, roundish oblate, pale yellow, sometimes faintly blushed and has white, crisp, pleasant subacid flesh which becomes mealy if kept only a few days after it ripens. The tree is not large, only a moderate grower and not a great bearer (6, 8, 16).

Historical. Hogg (16) gives the following interesting account of the history of this apple and the probable derivation of the name Juneating:

"One of our oldest apples, and although generally known and popular, seems to have escaped the notice of Miller, who does not even mention it in any of the editions of his Dictionary. As I have doubts of this being the Geneting of Parkinson — his figure being evidently intended for the Margaret, which in some districts is called Joaneting — the first mention we have of this variety is by Rea, in 1665, who describes it as 'a small, yellow, red-sided apple, upon a wall, ripe in the end of June.'

"'Juneating,' as applied to this apple, is quite a misnomer. Abercrombie was the first who wrote it June-eating, as if in allusion to the period of its maturity, which is, however, not till the end of July. Dr. Johnson, in his Dictionary, writes it Gineting, and says it is a corruption of Janeton (Fr.), signifying Jane or Janet, having been so called from a person of that name. Ray[1] says, 'Pomum Ginettinum, quod unde dictum sit met latet.' Indeed, there does not seem ever to have been a correct definition given of it.

"My definition of the name is this. In the Middle Ages, it was customary to make the festivals of the Church periods on which occurrences were to take place or from which events were to be named. Even in the present day we hear the country people talking of some crop to be sown, or some other

---

1 *Hist. Plant.*, ii. 1447.

to be planted, at Michaelmas, St. Martin's, or St. Andrew's tide. It was also the practice for parents to dedicate their children to some particular saint, as Jean Baptiste, on the recurrence of whose festival all who are so named keep it as a holiday. So it was also in regard to fruits, which were named after the day about which they came to maturity. Thus, we have the Margaret Apple, so called from being ripe about St. Margaret's Day, the 20th of July; the Magdalene, or Maudlin, from St. Magdalene's Day, the 22d of July. And in Curtius[1] we find the *Joannina*, so called, 'Quod circa divi Joannis Baptistæ nativitatem esui sint.' These are also noticed by J. Baptista Porta; he says, 'Est genus alterum quod quia circa festum Divi Joannis maturiscit, vulgus *Melo de San Giovanni* dicitur.' And according to Tragus,[2] 'Quæ apud nos prima maturantur, Sanct Johans Opfell, *Latine*, Præcocia mala dicuntur.'

"We see, therefore, that apples were called Joannina because they ripened about St. John's Day, and we have among the old French pears Amiré Joannet — the 'Wonderful Little John,' which Merlet informs us was so called because it ripened about St. John's Day. If, then, we add to Joannet the termination *ing*, so general among our names of apples, we have *Joannet-ing*. There can be no doubt that this is the correct derivation of the name of this apple."

WHITE SPANISH REINETTE.

REFERENCES. 1. *Pom. Mag.*, 3:No. 110. 1830. col. pl. 2. Floy-Lindley, 1833:61. 3. Downing, 1845:130. 4. Emmons, *Nat. Hist. N. Y.*, 3:88. 1851. 5. Elliott, 1854:162. 6. Downing, 1869:404. 7. Leroy, 1873:069. fig. 8. Thomas, 1875:231. 9. Hogg, 1884:190. 10. Lyon, *Mich. Hort. Soc. Rpt.*, 1890:300.

SYNONYMS. *American Fall Pippin* (9). *Belle Joséphine* (9). *Blanche* (7). *Blanche d'Espagne* (7). *Camuesar* (1, 6, 9). *Camoisas du roi d'Espagne* (7). *Camoise Blanche* (7). *Camoisée Blanche* (7). *Camuezas* (7). *Camuzar* (7). *Cobbett's Fall* (1) err. *Cobbett's Fall Pippin* (2, 3, 6, 7) err. *Concombre Ancien* (1, 2, 5, 7, 9). *De Ratteau* (1, 2, 5, 7, 9). *D'Espagne* (1, 2, 3, 5, 6, 7). *Elgin Pippin?* (6). *Episcopale* (7). *Fall Pippin* (1, 2, 3, 7, err. 6) err. *Joséphine* (9). *Large Fall* (1). *Large Fall Pippin* (2, 3, 6, 7). *Philadelphia Pippin* (7). *Reinette A Gobelet* (7). *Reinette Blanche* (7). REINETTE BLANCHE D'ESPAGNE (3, 9). *Reinette Blanche d'Espagne* (1, 2, 5, 6, 7, 8). REINETTE D'ESPAGNE (7). *Reinette d'Espagne* (1, 6, 9). *Reinette Tendre* (7). *Saint-Germain* (7). WHITE SPANISH REINETTE (1, 2, 4, 5, 6, 8, 10). *White Spanish Reinette* (3, 7, 9). *York Pippin* (7).

This variety belongs in the group with Fall Pippin and Holland Pippin. It resembles Fall Pippin in the growth of the tree as well as in the color and character of the fruit, but is less regular in shape and keeps later (3, 6). Season here October to January or February; Hogg gives its season in

---

1 *Hortorum*, p. 522.
2 *Hist.*, p. 1043.

England as December to April (9). Lyon gives its season in Michigan as October to January (10).

Historical. This is an old European variety which has long been cultivated in Spain, France and England (1, 2, 3, 6, 7, 9). It was early imported into this country and is perhaps the parent of our Fall Pippin and Holland Pippin (6). According to Lyon (10) it is seldom seen under its own name. It appears to be but little cultivated in New York having been superseded by other varieties.

FRUIT.

Fruit very large. *Form* roundish oblate or inclined to oblong, angular, uneven at the crown where it is nearly as broad as at the base (3, 6, 9). *Stem* short. *Cavity* narrow, rather small, regular. *Calyx* large, open. *Basin* deep, broadly angular, irregular, oblique.

Skin smooth, waxy, yellowish-green, with orange tinge and brownish-red blush on the exposed cheek.

Calyx tube conical. *Stamens* marginal. *Cells* open, obovate.

Flesh yellowish-white, crisp, tender, juicy, subacid, very good for either dessert or culinary purposes.

Season October to January or February.

WILLIAMS.

REFERENCES. **1.** Kenrick, **1832**:29. **2.** Manning, **1838**:49. **3.** *Ib.*, *MagHort.*, **7**:51. 1841. **4.** Downing, **1845**:79. **5.** Hovey, *Mag. Hort.*, **14**:118. 1848. fig. **6.** Goodrich, **1849**:51. **7.** Cole, **1849**:100. fig. **8.** Thomas, **1849**: 142. fig. **9.** Waring, **1851**:32. fig. **10.** Barry, **1851**:282. **11.** Emmons, *Nat. Hist. N. Y.*, **3**:12. 1851. **12.** Elliott, **1854**:163. **13.** *Am. Pom. Soc. Cat.*, **1854.** **14.** Hooper, **1857**:100. **15.** Warder, **1867**:618, 736. **16.** Fitz, **1872**:161. **17.** *Montreal Hort. Soc. Rpt.*, **1879**:26. **18.** *Ia. Hort. Soc. Rpt.*, **1883**:507. **19.** Hogg, **1884**:243. **20.** Lyon, *Mich. Hort. Soc. Rpt.*, **1890**:300. **21.** Bailey, *An. Hort.*, **1892**:252. **22.** Hoskins, *Rural N. Y.*, **53**:248. 1894. **23.** Beach, *N. Y. Sta. An. Rpt.*, **14**:255. 1895. **24.** *Gard. and For.*, **8**:248. 1895. **25.** *Can. Hort.*, **20**:183. 1897. **26.** Bunyard, *Jour. Roy. Hort. Soc.*, **1898**:357. **27.** Waugh, *Vt. Sta. An. Rpt.*, **14**:312. 1901. **28.** Budd-Hansen, **1903**:203. fig.

SYNONYMS. *Lady's Apple* (5). *Queen* (5). WILLIAMS (1, 5, 6, 7, 12, 20, 26, 27). *Williams* (7, 8). *Williams Early* (5, 12, 15, 19). *Williams Early Red* (7, 12). WILLIAMS FAVORITE (3, 8, 9, 10, 11, 13, 14, 15, 16, 17, 18, 21, 22, 23, 24, 25). *Williams Favorite* (5, 7, 12, 27). *Williams Favorite Red* (5, 8, 12). WILLIAMS *Favorite* (28). WILLIAMS FAVOURITE RED (2). WILLIAMS FAVOURITE (4, 19). *Williams Red* (8, 12, 19).

Williams is a very beautiful, bright red apple of mild agreeable flavor, good for dessert but not suitable for culinary uses. It is a favorite in Boston and other eastern markets, and is grown to a limited extent for commercial purposes in some portions of Eastern New York. It does not stand shipping very well, the skin being

WILLIAMS.

thin, tender and easily bruised, therefore best handled in small packages. It is in season during late August and early September. Under favorable conditions the fruit becomes rather large, but with very heavy crops it is apt to be rather small unless properly thinned. The crop ripens unevenly, and more than one picking is required to secure the fruit in prime condition. The tree being only moderately vigorous, it is an advantage to topwork it upon some thrifty hardy stock, such as Northern Spy, Rhode Island *Greening*, or Tolman *Sweet*. When topworked in this way the Williams becomes a rather vigorous grower, makes a tree of pretty good size, comes into bearing early and in favorable locations, under good treatment, is a reliable cropper, yielding good crops annually or nearly annually. It can be recommended for commercial planting where fruit of this type and season is desired.

Historical. Williams originated in Roxbury, Mass., more than 150 years ago. It was brought to the notice of the Massachusetts Horticultural Society in 1830 and then named Williams. It had previously been known in market under the name Queen and Lady's Apple (5). It was entered in the catalogue of the American Pomological Society in 1854 and is still retained on that list (13). It has become widely disseminated and is still often listed by nurserymen (21) but is nowhere being planted to any considerable extent.

TREE.

Tree rather small and a slow grower but when topworked on vigorous stock and properly tilled and fertilized it becomes rather large and vigorous. *Form* upright spreading or roundish, somewhat dense. *Twigs* short, curved, moderately stout, with large terminal buds; internodes short. *Bark* dark brown tinged with green, lightly streaked with scarf-skin; slightly pubescent. *Lenticels* quite numerous, small to medium size, oblong, raised. *Buds* medium size, broad, plump, obtuse, free, slightly pubescent.

FRUIT.

Fruit medium or under favorable circumstances rather large, pretty form in size and shape. *Form* oblong conic to roundish conic, broadly ribbed; sides often unequal. *Stem* medium to long, moderately thick. *Cavity* obtuse, shallow, rather broad, furrowed, sometimes russeted. *Calyx* above medium size, usually closed; lobes long. *Basin* medium to rather shallow, rather narrow to moderately broad, a little abrupt, somewhat furrowed.

Skin moderately thick, rather tender, nearly smooth, pale yellow overlaid with bright deep red, indistinctly striped with dark red or crimson. *Dots* numerous, inconspicuous, small, grayish or russet.

Calyx tube long, narrow, funnel-shape or approaching cylindrical, sometimes extending to the core. *Stamens* marginal.

Core medium to rather large, axile; cells closed or slightly open; core lines clasping. *Carpels* ovate to roundish. *Seeds* above medium, rather narrow, long, moderately plump, acute or nearly acuminate, dark brown.

Flesh sometimes tinged with red, firm, a little coarse, moderately crisp, tender, rather juicy, becoming dry when overripe, pleasant mild subacid, aromatic, good.

Season late August and September.

WILLIS SWEET.

REFERENCES. 1. *Mag. Hort.*, 18:491. 1852. 2. ? Elliott, 1854:179. 3. Hicks, *Horticulturist*, 21:361. 1866. fig. 4. Warder, 1867:635. 5. Downing, 1869: 408. fig. 6. *Am. Pom. Soc. Cat.*, 1869. 7. Thomas, 1875:516. 8. Bailey, *An. Hort.*, 1892:252.

SYNONYMS. *Pear Lot* (5). *Pear-Tree Lot* (5). WILLIS SWEET (2, 4, 5, 6, 7, 8). WILLIS SWEETING (1, 3).

A rather large sweet apple in season in late summer and early autumn. According to Downing the tree is a good grower and productive; the fruit whitish with shade of light red washed with crimson; flesh crisp, juicy, tender, rich, sweet, very good; valuable for dessert, for culinary purposes and for market (5).

Historical. A chance seedling that originated at Oyster Bay, Long Island, about 1800, on the farm of Edmond Willis. It first had the local name of Pear-tree Lot or Pear Lot. Later it was named Willis Sweeting by Parsons & Co., of Flushing, N. Y. (3). In 1869 it was entered in the catalogue of the American Pomological Society (6), but was dropped from that list in 1899. It is still occasionally listed by nurserymen (8) but is now seldom planted. It is not generally known in New York.

WINE RUBETS.

REFERENCES. 1. Budd, *Ia. Agr. Coll. Bul.*, 1885:7. 2. Beach, *N. Y. Sta. An. Rpt.*, 12:600. 1893. 3. *Ib.*, 12:603. 1893. 4. Ragan, *U. S. B. P. I. Bul.*, 56:337. 1905.

SYNONYMS. CUT WINE (2). *Cut Wine* (3, 4). *No. 210* (1, 2, 3, 4). *Rubets Vinogradnui* (4). *Rubets vinogradnui* (1). *Rubez vuinogradnui* (4). VINOGRAD (1). *Vinograd* (3). WINE RUBETS (3, 4).

Fruit below medium size, nearly symmetrical, covered with delicate bloom. Skin green, lightly shaded with red and with a crimson cheek. Basin shallow, wrinkled. Stem medium length, slender, set in a deep cavity. Flesh mild subacid, fair to good in quality. Begins to ripen here about the 1st of August. Not recommended for planting in New York.

Historical. A Russian apple imported by the United States Department of Agriculture. It was received here in 1888 from Dr. T. H. Hoskins, Newport, Vt., under the name Cut Wine.

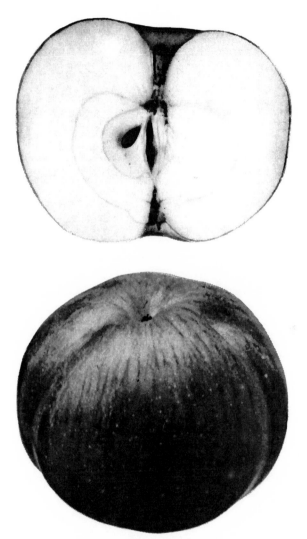

WOLF RIVER

WINTHROP GREENING.

REFERENCES. 1. Hovey, *Mag. Hort.*, 12:475. 1846. 2. Cole, 1849:104. 3. *Am. Pom. Soc. Cat.*, 1854. 4. *Mag. Hort.*, 21:63. 1855. 5. Downing, 1857: 204. 6. Warder, 1867:737. 7. Thomas, 1875:209. 8. Downing, 1881:11 index, app. 9. Lyon, *Mich. Hort. Soc. Rpt.*, 1890:300. 10. Burrill and McCluer, *Ill. Sta. Bul.*, 45:347. 1896.

SYNONYMS. *Howe Apple* (2, 5). *Kennebec Seedling* (8). LINCOLN (1). LINCOLN PIPPIN (4). *Lincoln Pippin* (2, 5). WINTHROP GREENING (2, 3, 5, 6, 7, 8, 9, 10).

Fruit yellow, tinged with red, of good size and good quality; season September to early winter. The flesh is tender, crisp, very juicy, sprightly, mild subacid (2). The tree is a shy bearer.

Historical. Originated in Winthrop, Me., about the year 1800 (1, 2). It was entered in the catalogue of the American Pomological Society in 1854 (3) and dropped from that list in 1897. It is but little known in New York.

WOLF RIVER.

REFERENCES. 1. *Wis. Hort. Soc. Rpt.*, 1875:107. 2. *Ia. Hort. Soc. Rpt.*, 1879:452. 3. Budd, *Ib.*, 1880:524. 4. Downing, 1881:113 app. 5. *Am. Pom. Soc. Cat.*, 1881:16. 6. Barry, 1883:357. 7. *Wis. Hort. Soc. Rpt.*, 1886:148. 8. Van Deman, *U. S. Pom. Rpt.*, 1886:271. fig. 9. *Am. Pom. Soc. Rpt.*, 1887:93. 10. *Can. Hort.*, 11:9. 1888. 11. Bailey, *An. Hort.*, 1892:253. 12. *Can. Hort.*, 16:34. 1893. 13. *Ib.*, 20:34. 1897. 14. Thomas, 1897:286. fig. 15. Waugh, *Vt. Sta. Bul.*, 61:32. 1897. 16. Woolverton, *Ont. Fr. Stas. An. Rpt.*, 6:32. 1899. 17. *Can. Hort.*, 22:121, 437. 1899. figs. 18. Woolverton, *Ont. Fr. Stas. An. Rpt.*, 7:10. 1900. figs. 19. Waugh, *Vt. Sta. An. Rpt.*, 14:313. 1901. 20. Hansen, *S. D. Sta. Bul.*, 76:116. 1902. fig. 21. Dickens and Greene, *Kan. Sta. Bul.*, 106:56. 1902. 22. Budd-Hansen, 1903:207. fig. 23. Powell and Fulton, *U. S. B. P. I. Bul.*, 48:61. 1903. 24. Beach and Clark, *N. Y. Sta. Bul.*, 248:151. 1904.

SYNONYMS. None.

This is a variety of the Aport group. It resembles Alexander very closely in size, form, and color. Hansen states (20) that it is "supposed to be a seedling of the Alexander, which it sometimes resembles, but is more round and less conical, and averages larger, as grown in the West. The Wolf River has largely superseded Alexander in the western states. Tree a strong spreading grower, not an early bearer, but productive in alternate years." As fruited at this Station it is in season from September to December, with October as the commercial limit in ordinary storage. In cold storage it may be held till January. It does not stand heat well, and goes down quickly (24). The tree is very hardy and a good grower, and is a biennial or sometimes annual cropper, yielding moderate to good crops. The fruit, being large, shapely and highly colored, often sells well because of its attractive appearance; some fruit growers are finding it a profitable variety.

Historical. Originated by W. A. Springer, near Wolf River, Fremont county, Wis., hence its name. It was entered in the catalogue of the American Pomological Society in 1881 (5). It is frequently listed by nurserymen (11). Within recent years it has been planted to a limited extent in New York state and at the present time its cultivation is probably increasing somewhat.

TREE.

Tree large, moderately vigorous. *Form* much spreading, open and inclined to droop. *Twigs* short, straight, slender; internodes short. *Bark* brown, tinged with green, lightly streaked with scarf-skin; slightly pubescent. *Lenticels* scattering, small, round, not raised. *Buds* small, plump, obtuse to acute, free, slightly pubescent.

FRUIT.

Fruit large, uniform in size and fairly uniform in shape. *Form* broad and flat at the base and somewhat inclined to conic or roundish, often somewhat irregular. *Stem* short to medium, rather thick, not exserted. *Cavity* acuminate, usually deep, rather wide and very heavily russeted. *Calyx* medium to large, open or closed. *Basin* medium to deep, moderately narrow, abrupt, usually smooth, somewhat broadly furrowed.

Skin rather thick, pale bright yellow or greenish, mottled and blushed with bright deep red and marked with conspicuous splashes and broad stripes of bright carmine. *Dots* numerous, medium to rather large, areolar, depressed, pale or russet.

Calyx tube conical. *Stamens* median to basal.

Core below medium to rather large, somewhat abaxile; cells closed or partly open; core lines clasping. *Carpels* broadly cordate, approaching elliptical, slightly emarginate, somewhat tufted. *Seeds* dark brown, of medium size, rather wide, short, moderately plump, obtuse.

Flesh slightly tinged with yellow, firm, moderately coarse, tender, juicy, subacid, a little aromatic, fair to good.

Season September to December.

WORKAROE.

REFERENCES. 1. *N. Y. Sta. An. Rpt.*, 8:349. 1889. 2. Beach, *Ib.*, 11:588. 1892.

SYNONYMS. None.

A Russian apple of good size, pale yellow, blushed and striped with red and overspread with pinkish bloom. Flesh firm, crisp, tender, juicy, rather

WORKAROE (Reduced Size)

mild subacid with an agreeable but not high flavor and good quality. It is a good apple but hardly equal to other varieties of its season. The tree does not come into bearing very young but is a pretty good grower and eventually a good cropper yielding full crops biennially.

Received in 1884 from Ellwanger and Barry, Rochester, N. Y., for testing at this Station.

YELLOW CALVILLE.

REFERENCES. 1. Budd, *Ia. Agr. Coll. Bul.*, 1885:17. 2. Gibb, *Am. Pom. Soc. Rpt.*, 1887:48. 3. Beach and Paddock, *N. Y. Sta. An. Rpt.*, 13:584. 1894. 4. Beach, *W. N. Y. Hort. Soc. Rpt.*, 41:50. 1896. 5. Ragan, *U. S. B. P. I. Bul.*, 56:345, 353. 1905.

SYNONYMS. *Kalvil jeltui* (2, 5). *Kalville scholti* (1, 2, 5). *No. 442* (1, 2, 3, 5). *Voronesh No. 21* (3). YELLOW CALVILLE (1, 2, 3, 4, 5).

An August apple, medium to rather small, smooth, pale yellow, sometimes with faint blush, oblate to oblate conic. Cavity acute, wide, rather shallow; calyx closed; basin shallow, slightly wrinkled; flesh white, fine-grained, tender, moderately juicy, subacid, fair or sometimes good. The tree comes into bearing moderately young and is nearly an annual cropper. Not recommended for cultivation in this state being much inferior to standard sorts of its season.

Historical. This is a Russian apple, being No. 442 of the importation of the United States Department of Agriculture of 1870 (3, 5). Later it was imported by the Iowa Agricultural College under the designation Voronesh No. 21 (1). In 1888 it was received for testing at this Station from Dr. T. H. Hoskins, Newport, Vt. It is practically unknown in New York.

YELLOW TRANSPARENT.

REFERENCES. 1. Leroy, 1873:846. fig. 2. Budd, *Ia. Hort. Soc. Rpt.*, 1880: 523. 3. Downing, 1881:114 app. fig. 4. *Am. Pom. Soc. Cat.*, 1881:16. 5. Webster, *Montreal Hort. Soc. Rpt.*, 7:54. 1881. 6. Gibb, *Ib.*, 7:154. 1881. 7. *Ib., Ia. Hort. Soc. Rpt.*, 1883:437. 8. Barry, 1883:336. 9. Hoskins, *Rural N. Y.*, 43:651. 1884. fig. 10. Penhollow, *Montreal Hort. Soc. Rpt.*, 10:65. 1884. 11. Thomas, 1885:530. 12. *Rural N. Y.*, 44:185, 200. 1885. 13. Gibb, *Montreal Hort. Soc. Rpt.*, 1886–87:14. 14. *Am. Pom. Soc. Rpt.*, 1887:92. 15. *Rural N. Y.*, 46:107, 201, 382. 1887. fig. 16. *Can. Hort.*, 11:209, 223. 1888. 17. Fisk, *Montreal Hort. Soc. Rpt.*, 14:33. 1889. 18. *Can. Hort.*, 13:121, 132, 216, 272, 301. 1890. 19. Hamilton, *Montreal Hort. Soc. Rpt.*, 15:27. 1890. 20. *Can. Hort.*, 15:281. 1892. 21. Bailey, *An. Hort.*, 1892:253. 22. Budd, *Ia. Sta. Bul.*, 19:535. 1892. 23. *Pa. Sta. Rpt.*, 1892:110. fig. 24. Hoskins, *Gard. and For.*, 7:138. 1894. 25. Woolverton, *Ont. Fr. Stas. An. Rpt.*, 2:11. 1895. figs. 26. Van Deman, *Rural N. Y.*, 55:613. 1896. 27. Hoskins, *Ib.*, 56:156. 1897. 28. Woolverton, *Ont. Fr. Stas. An. Rpt.*, 4:5. 1897. figs. 29. Waugh, *Vt. Sta. Bul.*, 61:32. 1897. 30. Alwood, *Va. Sta. Bul.*, 130:122. 1901. 31. Waugh, *Vt. Sta. An. Rpt.*, 14:313. 1901. 32. Hansen, *S. D. Sta. Bul.*, 76:119. 1902. fig. 33. Dickens and Greene, *Kan. Sta. Bul.*, 106:56. 1902. 34. Munson, *Me. Sta. An. Rpt.*, 18:85, 88. 1902. 35. *Rural N. Y.*, 61:626. 1902. fig. 36. Budd-Hansen,

1903:213. *fig.* **37.** Farrand, *Mich. Sta. Bul.,* **205**:47. 1903. **38.** Bruner, *N. C. Sta. Bul.,* **182**:24. 1903.

SYNONYMS. *De Revel* (1). *Grand-Sultan* (1). *Revelstone* (1). SKWOSNOI SCHOTOI (7). *Skwosnoi Schotoi* (5). *Transparente de Saint-Leger* (1). TRANSPARENTE JAUNE (1). YELLOW TRANSPARENT (2, 3, 4, 5, 6, 8, 9, 10, 11, 12, 13, 14, 15, 16, 17, 18, 19, 20, 21, 22, 23, 24, 25, 26, 27, 28, 29, 30, 31, 32, 33, 34, 35, 36, 37, 38). *Yellow Transparent* (7).

This is one of the best of the extra early apples, being excellent for culinary use and acceptable for dessert. It is not equal in quality to Early Harvest, but it begins to ripen somewhat earlier and is a more reliable cropper, yielding good crops annually or nearly so. Generally speaking, it is grown in New York state for home use only, but in some places it is cultivated to a limited extent for market, particularly for local market. It is desirable for this purpose because it takes on a good clear yellow color before becoming overripe. On account of its delicate color and tender skin it shows bruises readily and must be handled with extra care. The crop ripens continuously through a period of three or four weeks, and two or more pickings are required in order to secure the fruit in prime condition. It begins to ripen in July, and continues in season in some cases till early September. On young or vigorous-growing trees the fruit may grow rather large, but on mature slow-growing trees, especially when they are overloaded, the fruit is apt to be below medium size unless thinned. The tree is a moderately vigorous grower, hardy, healthy and comes into bearing very young. In some portions of the West it suffers from twig blight (fire blight) but it appears to be quite free from this disease in New York.

Historical. Imported from Russia by the United States Department of Agriculture in 1870. Its merits were first brought to notice in this country by Dr. T. H. Hoskins, of Newport, Vt. (9). It has been disseminated throughout the apple-growing regions of the country from the Atlantic to the Pacific and is now commonly listed by nurserymen (21). In New York its cultivation for home use is gradually increasing, and occasionally it is grown to a limited extent for market.

TREE.

Tree of medium size, moderately vigorous, with short, stout, crooked branches filled with short spurs. *Form* upright at first but becoming spreading or roundish and rather dense. *Twigs* short, curved, stout with large

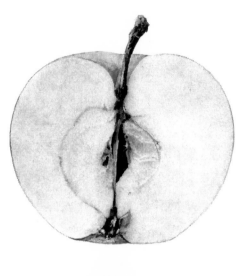

YELLOW TRANSPARENT

terminal buds; internodes medium. *Bark* conspicuously yellow or tawny, lightly streaked with scarf-skin; pubescent. *Lenticels* quite numerous, medium to small, oval or elongated, not raised. *Buds* medium size, broad, plump, obtuse, free, slightly pubescent.

FRUIT.

Fruit medium or above medium, sometimes large, pretty uniform in shape and size. *Form* roundish ovate to roundish conic or oblate conic, slightly ribbed; sides unequal. *Stem* medium to long, rather thick. *Cavity* acute or approaching obtuse, medium to deep, rather narrow, sometimes slightly lipped, sometimes russeted. *Calyx* medium size, closed; lobes medium in length, broad. *Basin* moderately shallow, rather narrow, somewhat abrupt, furrowed and slightly wrinkled.

Skin thin, tender, smooth, waxy, pale greenish-yellow changing to an attractive yellowish-white. *Dots* moderately numerous, greenish and light colored, often submerged.

Calyx tube conical. *Stamens* marginal.

Core medium to small; cells partly open to wide open; core lines clasping. *Carpels* broadly ovate. *Seeds* medium size, rather wide, rather flat, obtuse to slightly acute.

Flesh white, moderately firm, fine-grained, crisp, tender, juicy, sprightly subacid with a pleasant but not high flavor, good or sometimes very good.

Season late July and August.

YOPP.

REFERENCES. 1. Downing, 1857:205. 2. *Horticulturist,* 12:179. 1857. 3. Warder, 1867:737. 4. Fitz, 1872:175. 5. *Am. Pom. Soc. Cat.,* 1873. 6. Leroy, 1873:871. *figs.* 7. Thomas, 1875:517. 8. Bailey, *An. Hort.,* 1892:253. 9. Clayton, *Ala. Sta. Bul.,* 47:7. 1893. 10. Budd-Hansen, 1903:213.

SYNONYMS. YOPP (10). YOPP'S FAVORITE (1, 2, 3, 4, 5, 6, 7, 8, 9).

A southern apple of little value in New York. It originated in Georgia. In 1873 it was entered in the catalogue of the American Pomological Society (5). It is practically unknown in this state.

As grown at this Station the fruit is medium to rather large, oblate conic to roundish conic, somewhat ribbed; stem short, slender; cavity acuminate, moderately wide, rather deep, usually russeted; calyx small, open; basin narrow, moderately deep to deep, abrupt, wrinkled. Skin light yellow usually with a dull red blush; dots numerous, small, russet. Calyx tube conical; stamens median. Core medium to small; cells partly open; core lines clasping. Carpels broadly roundish, emarginate, somewhat tufted. Flesh whitish, somewhat tinged with yellow, moderately fine, tender, juicy, breaking, subacid, fair to good; season October and November.

The tree is below medium size, a rather slow grower with spreading top. It comes into bearing moderately early and yields good crops biennially.

YORK.

A variety which is known to many in Central and Western New York under the name York Pippin is now called by

pomologists Golden Pippin, under which name it is described on
page 78. It is an apple of the Fall Pippin group, large, quite
yellow when fully ripe, often with a brownish blush on the
exposed cheek.

Fall Pippin has also been known to some under the name
York Pippin. It is described on page 61.

Both of these are distinct from the York which is a Massachusetts apple of medium size, pale yellow with shade of red,
good to very good for culinary uses.   Season October and
November.[1]

1 Downing, 1869:420.

SIBERIAN CRABAPPLES AND THEIR HYBRIDS AND OTHER CRABAPPLES.

BAILEY CRIMSON.

REFERENCES. 1. *Am. Pom. Soc. Rpt.*, 1871:50. 2. *Montreal Hort. Soc. Rpt.*, 1879:91. 3. *Ib.*, 1884:38. 4. Bailey, *An. Hort.*, 1892:234.

SYNONYMS. BAILEY'S CRIMSON (2, 4, of New York 3). BAILEY'S CRIMSON CRAB (1).

In 1871 the Committee of the American Pomological Society on Native Fruits made the following report concerning this variety: "Originated with Wm. H. Bailey, Plattsburgh, N. Y. Tree vigorous, upright, very productive and very handsome.

"Fruit medium or large for its class; roundish, inclining to conic; skin yellow, shaded over the whole surface with deep rich crimson; flesh similar to other Siberian crabs."

We have not seen this variety nor have we obtained any report concerning it from our correspondents.

BRIER.

REFERENCES. 1. *Rural N. Y.*, 1870 (cited by 2). 2. *Am. Pom. Soc. Rpt.*, 1871:51. 3. Downing, 1872:39 app. 4. *Wis. Hort. Soc. Rpt.*, 1876:70. 5. Lyon, *Mich. Hort. Soc. Rpt.*, 1881:322. 6. Barry, 1883:358. 7. Gibb, *Montreal Hort. Soc. Rpt.*, 1884:34. 8. Keffer, *S. D. Sta. Bul.*, 23:141. 1891. 9. Bailey, *An. Hort.*, 1892:235. 10. Thomas, 1897:629. 11. Budd-Hansen, 1903:216. fig.

SYNONYMS. BRIAR SWEET (1, 2, 9). BRIER (11). BRIER'S SWEET (4, 5, 6, 7, 8). *Brier Sweet* (11, erroneously 10). BRIER'S SWEET CRAB (3). VAN WYCK (10).

Tree vigorous, hardy, comes into bearing rather young and is productive.

Historical. Originated with B. B. Brier, of Baraboo, Wis., as a result of the fertilization of the Siberian crab with the Bailey apple (3).

FRUIT.

Fruit large. *Form* roundish to conic, ribbed. *Stem* long, slender. *Cavity* narrow, deep, russeted. *Calyx* small, closed or slightly open. *Basin* deep, narrow, abrupt, wrinkled.

Skin pale yellow washed with lively red, striped with carmine, dotted and flecked with yellow and covered with thin, whitish bloom.

Calyx tube conical to funnel-form. *Stamens* median.

Core medium in size, axile or nearly so; cells closed.

Flesh yellowish, rich, fine-grained, moderately juicy, pleasant, sweet, aromatic, not astringent, good in flavor and quality.

Season September and October.

CHERRY.

REFERENCES. 1. Warder, 1867:715. 2. Downing, 1869:422. 3. Barry, 1883:359. 4. *Montreal Hort. Soc. Rpt.*, 1884:39. 5. Thomas, 1897:298. *fig.* 6. Budd-Hansen, 1903:217.

SYNONYMS. CHERRY (2, 5, 6). CHERRY CRAB (1, 3, 4).

Cherry is an old variety of unknown origin. The tree is a pretty good grower, particularly on light soils, attains considerable size and is quite a regular bearer.

TREE.

Tree moderately vigorous with long, slender, curved branches. *Form* upright spreading to roundish, open. *Twigs* moderately long, straight, moderately stout; internodes long. *Bark* clear reddish-brown tinged with olive-green, mottled with scarf-skin especially at the tips; slightly pubescent. *Lenticels* very scattering, small, roundish, not raised. *Buds* prominent, medium to large, plump, acute, free, not pubescent.

FRUIT.

Fruit small. *Form* oblate or roundish, ribbed. *Stem* long to very long, slender, bracted. *Cavity* rather broad, shallow, obtuse to slightly acute, somewhat russeted. *Calyx* medium to large, usually closed or eventually deciduous. *Basin* wide, shallow, obtuse, wrinkled.

Skin pale yellow nearly covered with bright red, often striped with carmine and overspread with a thin bluish bloom. *Dots* distinct, numerous, large, whitish or russet.

Calyx tube funnel-form. *Stamens* marginal.

Core large, axile; cells closed. *Carpels* broadly roundish or elliptical, emarginate, mucronate.

Flesh yellowish, rather coarse, juicy, crisp, mild subacid, somewhat astringent.

Season last of August to October.

CORAL.

REFERENCES. 1. Warder, *Tilt. Jour. Hort.*, 5:208. 1869. 2. Downing, 1869:423. 3. Barry, 1883:359. 4. *N. Y. Sta. An. Rpt.*, 2:35. 1884.

SYNONYMS. None.

Fruit of pretty good size, brilliant color, sprightly subacid flavor, in season from October to February. The tree is a pretty good grower, rather spreading, comes into bearing early and is a reliable cropper yielding good crops annually.

Historical. In 1869 Warder described this as No. 4 of the Marengo Winter Siberian crabapples received from Charles Andrews, Marengo, Ill. (1). It originated in the vicinity of Marengo (2). It is but little cultivated in New York.

FRUIT.

Fruit medium size or above, about an inch and a half in diameter. *Form* roundish to somewhat oblong, regular. *Stem* medium to rather long, slender, bracted. *Cavity* somewhat acute, medium in width and depth, regular, usually russeted. *Calyx* small, closed; lobes reflexed. *Basin* very shallow, broad and obtuse, or none.

Skin smooth, yellow, blushed with scarlet. *Dots* numerous, medium to small, gray or russet.

Calyx tube long, narrow, funnel-form. *Stamens* median.

Core medium to rather small, axile with narrow cylinder in the axis; cells closed or nearly so; core lines clasp the funnel cylinder. *Carpels* roundish ovate. *Seeds* compactly fill the cells; small to above medium, obtuse to somewhat acute, plump, dark.

Flesh yellow, breaking, juicy, crisp, sprightly, mild subacid to nearly sweet.

Season October to February.

CURRANT.

REFERENCES. 1. Downing, 1857:229. 2. Barry, 1883:359. 3. Bailey, *An. Hort.*, 1892:237. 4. Gibb, *Montreal Hort. Soc. Rpt.*, 1884:39.

SYNONYMS. CURRANT (2). CURRANT CRAB (1, 3). CURRENT CRAB (4). *Pomme Groseille* (1).

Fruit small, borne in clusters; said to be hardier than Transcendent. Of no commercial value. The tree is a good grower, comes into bearing young and is productive.

TREE.

Tree moderately vigorous with moderately long, slender, curved branches. *Form* upright spreading or roundish, open. *Twigs* long, curved, slender; internodes short. *Bark* dark brown, lightly mottled with scarf-skin; slightly pubescent near tips. *Lenticels* quite numerous, medium size, roundish, slightly raised. *Buds* medium size, plump, acute, free, slightly pubescent.

FRUIT.

Fruit small or below medium. *Form* somewhat oblate, regular, uniform. *Stem* medium to long, rather slender. *Cavity* obtuse, rather deep, broad, symmetrical, frequently russeted. *Calyx* sometimes deciduous, medium size, closed; lobes rather narrow, acute. *Basin* rather deep, wide, abrupt, obscurely furrowed.

Skin thin, tough, smooth, glossy, yellow, striped with brilliant red, overspread with bluish bloom. *Dots* numerous, small, pale or whitish.

Calyx tube broadly cone-shaped, short. *Stamens* marginal.

Core medium to rather large, axile; cells closed; core lines clasping. *Carpels* roundish to elliptical, emarginate. *Seeds* light brown, medium to large, wide, somewhat obtuse.

Flesh yellowish, firm, moderately fine, tender, dry, subacid, medium to poor. *Season* October and November.

DARTMOUTH.

REFERENCES. 1. Barry, 1883:359. 2. Beach, *N. Y. Sta. An. Rpt.*, 15:277. 1896. 3. Lyon, *Mich. Sta. Bul.*, 143:200. 1897. 4. Farrand, *Ib.*, 205:47. 1903. 5. Ragan, *U. S. B. P. I. Bul.*, 56:363. 1905.

SYNONYMS. None.

Fruit large, brilliantly colored, good in flavor and quality. The tree is not a vigorous grower, comes into bearing rather early and yields full crops in alternate years.

Historical. Origin New Hampshire (1).

TREE.

Tree a moderately vigorous or rather slow grower with moderately long, stout, crooked branches. *Form* upright spreading to roundish, open. *Twigs* short, curved, moderately stout; internodes short. *Bark* clear brown, mingled with olive-green, lightly mottled with scarf-skin; pubescent near tips. *Lenticels* scattering, small, round, slightly raised. *Buds* rather prominent, medium to large, long, narrow, acute, free, slightly pubescent.

FRUIT.

Fruit medium to large. *Form* oblate or roundish oblate, ribbed. *Stem* long and slender, often bracted. *Cavity* acute, broad, deep, russeted. *Calyx* small; lobes long, reflexed. *Basin* rather broad, shallow.

Skin pale yellow, almost entirely overlaid with bright red deepening to a dark red or purple on the exposed side, dotted with yellow and covered with a heavy bluish bloom.

Calyx tube elongated cone-shape approaching funnel-form. *Stamens* marginal.

Core large, abaxile; cells open; core lines clasping.

Flesh yellowish, tinged with red next the skin, fine-grained, juicy, mild subacid, good in quality and flavor.

Season August.

EXCELSIOR.

REFERENCES. 1. *Ill. Hort. Soc. Rpt.,* **1880.** 2. Gideon, *Am. Pom. Soc. Rpt.,* **1885**:26. 3. *Rural N. Y.,* **45**:184. 1886. *figs.* 4. Bailey, *An. Hort.,* **1892**:238. 5. Beach and Paddock, *N. Y. Sta. An. Rpt.,* **13**:580. 1894. 6. Munson, *Me. Sta. An. Rpt.,* **12**:73. 1896. 7. Lyon, *U. S. Pom. Bul.,* **6**:11. 1897. 8. *Am. Pom. Soc. Cat.,* **1897**:11. 9. Munson, *Me. Sta. An. Rpt.,* **18**:83. 1902. 10. Thomas, **1903**:348. 11. Budd-Hansen, **1903**:218. 12. Farrand, *Mich. Sta. Bul.,* **205**:47. 1903. 13. Powell and Fulton, *U. S. B. P. I. Bul.,* **48**:41. 1903.

SYNONYMS. None.

Fruit very large for a crabapple being nearly as large as a medium sized apple. It is very attractive in appearance and excellent in quality for either dessert or culinary uses. As grown at this Station it appears to be one of the most desirable varieties of its class during early September. The tree is a good strong grower, hardy, healthy, comes into bearing rather young and yields full crops in alternate years.

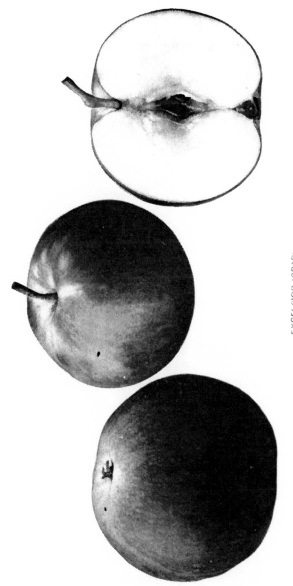

EXCELSIOR (CRAB)

Historical. Originated by Peter M. Gideon, Excelsior, Minn. "It came from seed of Wealthy which had a chance to be crossed with the Cherry Crab and also the Oldenburg" (2).

TREE.

Tree large with long, moderately stout branches. *Form* somewhat flat and spreading, rather dense. *Twigs* short, curved, stout; internodes medium. *Bark* dark brown tinged with red; slightly pubescent. *Lenticels* quite numerous, medium size, oval, slightly raised. *Buds* medium to large, plump, obtuse, free, slightly pubescent.

FRUIT.

Fruit very large. *Form* roundish ovate to roundish oblate, symmetrical. *Stem* rather long and slender, sometimes bracted. *Cavity* small, acute or approaching acuminate, narrow, rather shallow, often slightly russeted. *Calyx* rather large, closed; lobes reflexed. *Basin* shallow, moderately broad, obtuse, furrowed.

Skin smooth, yellow, shaded and splashed with red over much of its surface. *Dots* numerous, russet.

Calyx tube wide, cone-shape. *Stamens* median or above.

Core large, decidedly abaxile; cells unsymmetrical, wide open; core lines clasping. *Carpels* elongated ovate, sometimes tufted. *Seeds* above medium size, long, moderately narrow, acute, tufted.

Flesh whitish, firm, a little coarse, crisp, juicy, subacid, with some Siberian crab flavor yet agreeable for dessert use, good to very good in quality.

Season early September.

FLORENCE.

REFERENCES. 1. Stark, *Mo. Hort. Soc. Rpt.,* **1886**:233. 2. *Am. Pom. Soc. Rpt.,* **1887**:134. 3. Lyon, *Mich. Sta. Bul.,* **118**:59, 60. 1895. 4. Thomas, **1897**:298. 5. Lyon, *Mich. Sta. Bul.,* **152**:219, 224. 1898. 6. Budd-Hansen, **1903**:219.

SYNONYMS. None.

This variety seems to be very desirable for commercial planting because the trees commence bearing very young, are reliable croppers and very prolific and the fruit is of good size, very attractive in appearance and of good quality. Although not superior to Martha in quality, Florence is more beautiful and more prolific.

Historical. Originated by Peter M. Gideon, Excelsior, Minn.

TREE.

Tree moderately vigorous. *Form* at first upright spreading but eventually inclined to droop. *Twigs* long, curved, moderately stout; internodes long.

Bark bright reddish-brown, slightly tinged with olive-green, mottled with scarf-skin; slightly pubescent. *Buds* large, broad, plump, obtuse, free, not pubescent.

FRUIT.

Fruit medium in size, uniform in size and shape. *Form* oblate, faintly ribbed. *Stem* very long, slender. *Cavity* acute, deep, medium in width, symmetrical, sometimes slightly russeted. *Calyx* variable, usually small, closed. *Basin* very shallow, rather wide, obtuse, slightly furrowed.

Skin moderately thin, moderately tough, smooth, yellowish-white mostly overspread with brilliant pinkish-red, sometimes with whitish bands radiating from the cavity, overspread with faint bloom. *Dots* minute, whitish.

Calyx tube moderately long, moderately wide, varying from somewhat urn-shape to funnel-form. *Stamens* marginal.

Core large; cells closed; core lines clasping. *Carpels* broadly obovate, emarginate. *Seeds* medium to rather small, moderately wide, flat, obtuse.

Flesh tinged with yellow, coarse, crisp, rather tender, juicy, very brisk subacid, somewhat astringent, good.

Season late August and early September.

GIBB.

REFERENCES. **1.** *Montreal Hort. Soc. Rpt.*, **1884**:35. fig. **2.** *Am. Pom. Soc. Rpt.*, **1885**:29. **3.** Stark, *Mo. Hort. Soc. Rpt.*, **1886**:233. **4.** *Ill. Hort. Soc. Rpt.*, **1889**:22. **5.** Craig, *Can. Hort.*, **15**:225. 1892. fig. **6.** *Am. Pom. Soc. Cat.*, **1897**:11. **7.** Thomas, **1897**:298. fig. **8.** Farrand, *Mich. Sta. Bul.*, **205**:47. 1903. **9.** Powell and Fulton, *U. S. B. P. I. Bul.*, **48**:42. 1903. **10.** Budd-Hansen, **1903**:219. fig.

SYNONYMS. None.

Fruit large, yellow blushed with dull red. It is thinner skinned and much less astringent than Hyslop with remarkably yellow flesh. It is highly esteemed for canning; season last half of September. It is recommended for the home orchard and is worthy of trial for commercial planting where a crabapple of its season is desired. The tree is a slow, spreading grower, fairly hardy as far north as Montreal, very productive (5).

Historical. Originated with George P. Peffer, Pewaukee. Wis., being a seedling of an oblate Yellow Siberian crab crossed with Fall Greening (5, 10).

FRUIT (5, 7, 10).

Fruit large. *Form* roundish oblate. *Stem* short to medium length, thick. *Cavity* wide, deep, regular. *Calyx* medium size, open. *Basin* very wide, shallow, wrinkled.

Skin thin, yellow, blushed with dull red, attractive. *Dots* white, minute.

Flesh remarkably yellow, firm, crisp, juicy, pleasantly acid, a little astringent, sprightly.

Season early.

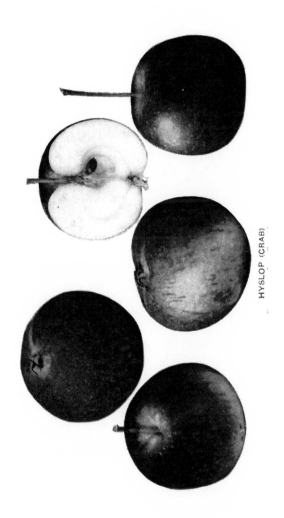

HYSLOP (CRAB)

HYSLOP.

REFERENCES. 1. Warder, *Tilt. Jour. Hort.*, **1869**:206. *figs.* 2. Downing, **1869**:424. 3. Fitz, **1872**:147. 4. Gibb, *Montreal Hort. Soc. Rpt.*, **1876**:21. 5. *Minn. Hort. Soc. Rpt.*, **1876**:110. 6. Barry, **1883**:359. 7. Gibb, *Montreal Hort. Soc. Rpt.*, **1884**:39. 8. Thomas, **1885**:513. 9. Wickson, **1889**:249. 10. Bailey, *An. Hort.*, **1892**:241. 11. Munson, *Me. Sta. Rpt.*, **1893**:134. 12. *La. Sta. Bul.*, **27**:926. 1894. 13. *Can. Hort.*, **26**:489. 1903. *figs.* 14. Budd-Hansen, **1903**:220. *fig.*

SYNONYMS. HISLOP (1). HYSLOP (2, 3, 4, 5, 6, 7, 9, 10, 11, 12, 13, 14). HYSLOP'S CRAB (8).

Fruit large, very brilliantly colored, dark red or purplish overspread with thick blue bloom; borne in clusters. The tree is a good grower, very hardy, and a reliable cropper yielding good crops biennially or in some cases annually. It is desirable both for home use and for market.

Historical. Origin unknown. In 1869 Downing remarked: "This variety has been long and pretty extensively cultivated" (2). It is commonly listed by nurserymen throughout the country (10). It is one of the best known and most widely cultivated of the crabapples.

TREE.

Tree vigorous or moderately vigorous. *Form* upright spreading, rather open. *Twigs* long, curved, slender; internodes long. *Bark* olive-green, tinged with reddish-brown, lightly streaked with scarf-skin; slightly pubescent near tips. *Lenticels* numerous, very conspicuous, greenish-yellow, medium to large, oblong. *Buds* exceptionally large and prominent, very long, narrow, plump, acute, free, slightly pubescent.

FRUIT.

Fruit above medium to large, very uniform in size and shape. *Form* roundish ovate or obovate, sometimes a little inclined to oblong, regular or obscurely ribbed, symmetrical. *Stem* rather short to very long, slender. *Cavity* acuminate, rather small, shallow, narrow to medium in width, sometimes furrowed, often slightly russeted. *Calyx* medium to large, closed; lobes medium to long, narrow, acuminate, reflexed. *Basin* shallow, medium to wide, distinctly furrowed and wrinkled.

Skin clear pale yellow almost completely overspread with lively dark red shading to deep carmine or purplish carmine and covered with thick, blue bloom. *Dots* small, numerous, pale or gray.

Calyx tube short, narrow, cone-shape to urn-shape. *Stamens* median.

Core medium size, axile; cells symmetrical, closed; core lines meeting. *Carpels* elongated ovate, emarginate. *Seeds* small, narrow, short, plump, obtuse to acute, medium brown.

Flesh yellow, sometimes with tinge of red next the skin, very firm, moderately fine, at first juicy but eventually becoming dry and mealy, subacid, astringent, good for culinary purposes.

Season late September and October.

LARGE RED SIBERIAN.

REFERENCES.   1. Downing, **1845**:147.   2. Cole, **1849**:137.   3. Fitz, **1872**:147.
4. Barry, **1883**:359.   5. Wickson, **1889**:249.   6. Bailey, *An. Hort.*, **1892**:243.
SYNONYMS.   None.

This fruit is of medium size for a Siberian crab, being larger than Red Siberian, but smaller than either Transcendent or Hyslop. It is similar to Red Siberian in appearance and quality. The foliage is coarser than that of Red Siberian, and the tree is larger, being medium to rather large, a vigorous grower, erect or roundish, with long, slender twigs. It is very hardy, healthy, moderately long-lived, and a reliable cropper, yielding heavy crops biennially or sometimes annually. It has long been known in cultivation, and is still listed by nurserymen (6), but larger and handsomer varieties of more recent introduction are generally preferred in market.

FRUIT.

Fruit of medium size, uniform in size and shape. *Form* roundish to roundish ovate, regular. *Stem* medium to long, slender. *Cavity* acuminate, shallow, moderately broad, often furrowed, usually russeted. *Calyx* medium size, closed; lobes long, narrow, acuminate. *Basin* shallow or none, obtuse, wrinkled, having mammiform protuberances.

Skin thin, tough, smooth, pale yellow, almost wholly overlaid with bright red and marked with obscure narrow stripes of dark red. *Dots* very small, light, inconspicuous.

Calyx tube short, wide, urn-shape. *Stamens* median to marginal.

Core medium size, axile; cells closed; core lines meeting. *Carpels* ovate to obovate, emarginate. *Seeds* glossy, dark brown, rather small, short, wide, obtuse.

Flesh yellowish, very firm, subacid, astringent, good for culinary uses.

Season September and October.

LARGE YELLOW SIBERIAN.

REFERENCES.   1. Warder, **1867**:732.   2. Downing, **1869**:425.   3. Barry,
1883:360.   4. Bailey, *An. Hort.*, **1892**:243.
SYNONYMS.   None.

Fruit large, similar in size to Large Red Siberian, clear pale yellow with a shade of red in the sun, roundish approaching oblong truncate; season September and October. Tree upright, somewhat irregular in form, of me-

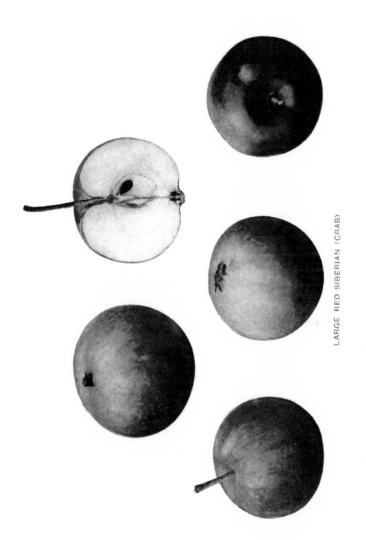

LARGE RED SIBERIAN (CRAB)

dium size, vigorous or moderately vigorous, very hardy, healthy, comes into bearing young and is very productive. It is generally superseded in market by larger varieties.

MARENGO.

REFERENCES. 1. Elliott, *Horticulturist*, 23:136. 1868. *fig.* 2. Warder, *Tilt. Jour. Hort.*, 5:207. 1869. *fig.* 3. Downing, 1869:425. 4. *Horticulturist*, 26:371. 1871. 5. *Ill. Hort. Soc. Rpt.*, 1877:112. 6. *Ib.*, 1879:196. 7. Barry, 1883:360. 8. *Montreal Hort. Soc. Rpt.*, 1884:37. 9. Thomas, 1885:226, 517. 10. Bailey, *An. Hort.*, 1892:244. 11. *Me. Sta. Rpt.*, 1893:134. 12. Budd-Hansen, 1903:222.

SYNONYMS. MARENGO (5, 6). MARENGO CRAB (3, 7, 9, 10, 11, 12). MARENGO No. 1 (2, 8). MARENGO WINTER CRAB (1, 4). *Marengo Winter Crab* (2).

Originated at Marengo, Ill. (3, 6). This is a good variety for home use where a late-keeping crabapple is desired, and some have found it a profitable market variety but other varieties of its season which are more attractive in color are generally preferred for commercial purposes. The tree is of medium size, vigorous, spreading, very hardy, long-lived and a reliable cropper usually yielding heavy crops annually. The limbs are very tough and support heavy loads well. The fruit hangs well to the tree till very late in the season. It agrees well with the following description given by Warder (2): "Fruit globular, truncate, regular, or slightly flattened on the sides, one of the largest of its class; surface smooth, yellow, blushed or covered with crimson; dots minute; basin shallow, folded; eye small, closed; cavity medium, regular; stem long; core large, closed, meeting the eye; seeds few, small, plump, light brown; flesh yellow, firm, rather juicy; flavor subacid, aromatic. Use, kitchen and dessert; quality, good; season, winter, and till spring in the North."

MARTHA.

REFERENCES. 1. ? *Ia. Hort. Soc. Rpt.*, 1879:452. 2. *Ib.*, 1880:68. 3. *Rural N. Y.*, 45:284. 1886. *figs.* 4. *Am. Pom. Soc. Rpt.*, 1887:134. 5. Bailey, *An. Hort.*, 1892:244. 6. Thomas, 1897:299. 7. *Am. Pom. Soc. Cat.*, 1897:11. 8. Budd-Hansen, 1903:222. 9. *Rural N. Y.*, 62:235. 1903. 10. Farrand, *Mich. Sta. Bul.*, 205:47. 1903.

SYNONYMS. None.

Fruit large, very handsome clear yellow more or less overspread with bright red; excellent in flavor and quality; one of the very best of its class for all culinary purposes. The tree is of medium size, moderately vigorous, roundish or spreading, very hardy, comes into bearing young, and is a reliable cropper, yielding good to heavy crops annually or nearly annually. The fruit hangs well to the tree, is uniform, reliable, and satisfactory in appearance and quality. Season, September to late fall. It should be more generally grown in New York.

Historical. Originated with Peter M. Gideon, Excelsior, Minn. It has as yet been grown but little in this state.

Tree.

Tree medium in size, moderately vigorous. *Form* spreading, open and somewhat inclined to droop. *Twigs* long, curved, slender; internodes long. *Bark* reddish-brown tinged with green, lightly streaked with scarf-skin, not pubescent. *Lenticels* quite numerous, small, oblong, not raised. *Buds* very prominent, large, long, acute, free, not pubescent. *Leaves* rather long, somewhat twisted and drooping.

Fruit.

Fruit usually rather large, uniform in size and shape. *Form* roundish or oblate, regular or very faintly ribbed, usually symmetrical; sides sometimes unequal. *Stem* long, slender. *Cavity* acute to somewhat obtuse, medium in depth to rather shallow, rather broad, sometimes furrowed, often thinly russeted. *Calyx* medium to small, closed or partly open, occasionally deciduous. *Basin* shallow, wide, obtuse, smooth.

Skin moderately thin, tough, smooth, clear pale yellow almost entirely covered with an attractive bright light red overspread with bluish bloom; sometimes faint narrow stripes extend from the cavity to calyx. *Dots* rather numerous, light-colored, small to medium size.

Calyx tube short, rather narrow, very small, conical or somewhat funnelform. *Stamens* median to marginal.

Core medium size, axile; cells closed or nearly so. *Carpels* roundish or somewhat obovate, slightly tufted. *Seeds* medium size, rather narrow, acute to acuminate.

Flesh yellowish, firm, moderately coarse, crisp, juicy, rather brisk subacid, good to very good in flavor and quality.

Season September to November.

MINNESOTA.

REFERENCES. **1.** Gideon, *Horticulturist*, **27**:244. 1872. **2.** Gibb, *Am. Pom. Soc. Rpt.*, **1883**:125. **3.** *Ib.*, *Montreal Hort. Soc. Rpt.*, **10**:36. 1884. **4.** Bailey, *An. Hort.*, **1892**:244. **5.** Beach, *N. Y. Sta. An. Rpt.*, **15**:277. 1896. **6.** Budd-Hansen, **1903**:223. **7.** Thomas, **1903**:349.

SYNONYMS. MINNESOTA CRAB (2, 3, 4, 5, 6, 7). MINNESOTA (1).

This variety originated in Minnesota. The fruit is very large for its class, roundish; skin pale yellow blushed or mottled on the sunny side and overspread with thin whitish bloom; flesh white, firm, crisp, juicy, fine-grained, subacid to mild subacid or nearly sweet, slightly astringent, good. Season September and October. As grown at this Station the tree is of spreading form, moderately vigorous and not very productive.

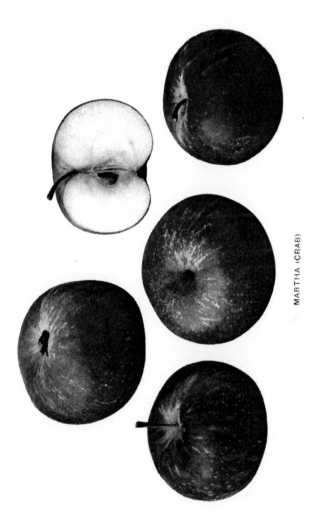

MARTHA (CRAB)

MONTREAL BEAUTY.

REFERENCES. 1. Downing, 1869:425. 2. Gibb, *Montreal Hort. Soc. Rpt.*, 1876:17. 3. *Ill. Hort. Soc. Rpt.*, 1877:112. 4. Barry, 1883:360. 5. *Montreal Hort. Soc. Rpt.*, 1884:39. 6. Wickson, 1889:249. 7. Bailey, *An. Hort.*, 1892:244. 8. *Me. Sta. Rpt.*, 1893:134. 9. Thomas, 1897:299. 10. Budd-Hansen, 1903:223.

SYNONYMS. MONTREAL (10). *Montreal Beauty* (10). MONTREAL BEAUTY CRAB (1, 2, 3, 4, 5, 6, 7, 8, 9).

This very beautiful fruit originated in Quebec and was propagated as early as 1833. Gibb (2, 5) states the tree is less hardy than that of Transcendent, but is strong, vigorous, rather large, at first very close and upright, does not come into bearing early, but bears heavily. The fruit is large for its class, oblong conic to roundish oblong and truncate, yellowish-green, mostly covered with red; flesh yellowish-white, tender, rather juicy, unless overripe, subacid, very slightly astringent; season, late September and October. It is well known in the vicinity of Montreal and other portions of Quebec. In the United States it is quite frequently listed by nurserymen (7), yet it is not generally known.

OBLONG.

REFERENCES. 1. Desportes, *Horticulturist*, 6:507. 1851. fig. 2. Downing, 1869:425. 3. Barry, 1883:360.

SYNONYMS. *Baccata fructa oblonga* (1). OBLONG-FRUITED SIBERIAN CRAB (2). OBLONG SIBERIAN CRAB (1, 3).

Fruit medium size, oblong conic, yellowish-white, partly shaded with crimson, striped with carmine and covered with thin bloom; stem very long, slender, usually bracted. This variety has been sparingly disseminated in New York but is now seldom or never planted here. It is not superior to other varieties of its season.

ORANGE.

REFERENCES. 1. Downing, 1869:425. 2. *Montreal Hort. Soc. Rpt.*, 1884:36. fig. 3. Thomas, 1897:299. fig. 4. Budd-Hansen, 1903:224.

SYNONYMS. None.

A variety of American origin but little grown in New York. Some regard it as a desirable variety for both home use and market. The tree is roundish, spreading, dwarfish, a moderate or rather slow grower, hardy, moderately long-lived and a reliable cropper yielding good to heavy crops annually. It comes into bearing rather young. Season September to November.

FRUIT (1, 4).

Fruit medium size. *Form* roundish, slightly oblate. *Stem* very long, slender. *Cavity* open, deep, acute with trace of russet. *Calyx* closed. *Basin* very shallow or flat, wrinkled.

Skin orange-yellow often netted with russet. *Dots* minute, white, obscure.

Core open.

Flesh light salmon-yellow, a little dry, rather mild subacid with sweet after-taste, good.

Season September to November.

PAUL IMPERIAL.

REFERENCES. 1. Ellwanger and Barry, *Cat.*, 1888:14. 2. Thomas, 1897:299. SYNONYMS. None.

A September variety in season about with Transcendent; somewhat irregular in shape; of very good general appearance but less attractive in size and color than Hyslop and inferior to Martha in quality. The tree is below medium size, comes into bearing rather young and is a reliable annual cropper.

Historical. Introduced by Paul and Son, Cheshunt, England. A cross between the Red Astrachan and Siberian Crab (1).

TREE.

Tree moderately vigorous with short, stout, crooked branches having numerous small spurs. *Form* spreading, flat, open. *Twigs* olive-green tinged with brown, lightly streaked with scarf-skin; slightly pubescent. *Lenticels* scattering, medium to large, oval, slightly raised. *Buds* large, prominent, plump, obtuse, free, pubescent.

FRUIT.

Fruit small to medium, uniform in size but not in shape. *Form* usually oblate, often irregularly elliptical, strongly ribbed; sides unequal. *Stem* long to medium, slender. *Cavity* obtuse to acute, moderately deep, broad, furrowed, not russeted. *Calyx* large, closed, prominent, persistent; lobes long, moderately broad. *Basin* very shallow, wide, obtuse, furrowed and wrinkled and sometimes mammillate.

Skin thin, rather tender, smooth, yellow, often entirely covered with dark bright red or with but little of the yellow ground color exposed, overspread with blue bloom. *Dots* very small, numerous, indistinct, light.

Calyx tube small, short, moderately wide, urn-shape. *Stamens* nearly marginal.

Core rather large, axile or nearly so; cells closed or slightly open; core lines meeting. *Carpels* nearly roundish, narrowing toward apex, tufted. *Seeds* below medium size, moderately wide, acute, light brown.

Flesh yellowish sometimes stained with pink, firm, moderately coarse, crisp, rather tough, juicy, brisk subacid, less astringent than Red Siberian, good.

Season September and October.

MONTREAL BEAUTY (CRAB)

PICTA STRIATA.

REFERENCES. 1. Ellwanger and Barry, *Cat.*, **1888**:14. 2. Beach, *N. Y. Sta. Am. Rpt.*, **12**:601. 1893. 3. Ragan, *U. S. B. P. I. Bul.*, **56**:370. 1905.
SYNONYMS. PICTA STRIATA (1, 2). PIETA (3). *Picta Striata* (3).

Fruit handsome, rather mild in flavor; season late fall and early winter. It is hardly large enough for a good commercial variety. The tree is a good grower, comes into bearing rather late and is an annual cropper yielding moderate to good crops.

Historical. Received from Ellwanger and Barry, Rochester, N. Y., in 1888 for testing at this Station.

TREE.

Tree rather large. *Form* upright spreading to roundish with rather drooping laterals. *Twigs* long, curved, slender; internodes short. *Bark* clear brown, tinged with green, lightly mottled with scarf-skin; slightly pubescent near tips. *Lenticels* quite numerous, rather conspicuous, medium size, oval, not raised. *Buds* medium size, plump, acute, free, not pubescent.

FRUIT.

Fruit medium or above, uniform in size but not in shape. *Form* oblate or roundish oblate, irregularly ribbed. *Stem* long, slender. *Cavity* obtuse, medium to rather deep, medium to broad, compressed, smooth or nearly so. *Calyx* usually small, closed; lobes separated at base, long, medium in width, acute to acuminate. *Basin* shallow to medium in depth, medium in width, obtuse, nearly smooth.

Skin thin, tender, smooth, rather glossy, pale greenish-yellow nearly covered with crimson, blushed and striped with carmine. *Dots* indistinct, small, gray.

Calyx tube moderately short, rather narrow, conical to urn-shape. *Stamens* marginal or nearly so.

Core medium to large, axile; cells slightly open or closed; core lines clasping. *Carpels* roundish to elliptical, concave, deeply emarginate, sometimes tufted. *Seeds* rather dark brown, medium size, wide, short, obtuse.

Flesh tinged with yellow, firm, a little coarse, tender, juicy, somewhat astringent, sprightly subacid, good.

Season October to early winter.

QUAKER.

REFERENCES. 1. *Rural N. Y.*, **1870** (cited by 7). 2. Bailey, *An. Hort.*, **1892**:247. 3. Thomas, **1897**:299. 4. Lyon, *Mich. Sta. Bul.*, **152**:224. 1898. 5. Farrand, *Ib.*, **205**:48. 1903. 6. Budd-Hansen, **1903**:224. 7. Ragan, *U. S. B. P. I. Bul.*, **56**:371. 1905.
SYNONYMS. None.

This variety has been disseminated more in the western states than it has in New York. It is but little grown here. Farrand (5) describes it as a late ripening variety of only fair quality, size medium to large; color yellow with a red cheek; tree handsome, vigorous but not very productive; season October.

QUEEN CHOICE.

REFERENCES. 1. Bailey, *An. Hort.*, 1892:247. 2. Ellwanger and Barry, *Cat.*, 1894:15. 3. Thomas, 1897:299. 4. Budd-Hansen, 1903:224.

SYNONYMS. QUEEN'S CHOICE (1, 2, 3). QUEEN *Choice* (4).

This crab has a fruit which is medium or above, roundish conical, of a beautiful crimson color, showy and attractive; flesh whitish and of pleasant flavor and quality; season October; tree vigorous, very prolific (2, 3, 4).

It is but little known in New York.

RED SIBERIAN.

REFERENCES. 1. Forsyth, 1803:57. 2. Coxe, 1817:106. 3. Fessenden, 1828:129. 4. Kenrick, 1832:57. 5. *Ib.*, 1835:75. 6. Downing, 1845:147. 7. Thomas, 1849:158. 8. Cole, 1849:137. 9. Barry, 1851:287. 10. Elliott, 1854:157. 11. Gregg, 1857:62. fig. 12. Downing, 1869:426. 13. Fitz, 1872:147. 14. Thomas, 1875:208. 15. *Montreal Hort. Soc. Rpt.,* 10:39. 1884. 16. Lyon, *Mich. Hort. Soc. Rpt.,* 1890:300. 17. Bailey, *An. Hort.,* 1892:248. 18. Lyon, *U. S. Pom. Bul.,* 6:11. 1897. 19. Budd-Hansen, 1903:224.

SYNONYMS. RED SIBERIAN (11, 15, 16, 17, 18, 19). RED SIBERIAN CRAB (5, 8, 9, 12). SIBERIAN CRAB (1, 2, 3, 4, 6, 7, 10, 13, 14).

Origin France (19). Fruit small, decidedly ornamental, borne in clusters. It is three-quarters of an inch to an inch in diameter, roundish oblate to somewhat oblong, irregularly elliptical; stem long and slender; cavity acute, medium in width and depth; calyx small to medium, often deciduous; basin but slightly depressed. Skin smooth, pale yellow striped and blushed with lively red and overspread with blue bloom; flesh subacid, astringent, good for culinary uses. Season September and October.

SEPTEMBER.

REFERENCES. 1. *Mich. Hort. Soc. Rpt.,* 1888:319. 2. Beach, *N. Y. Sta. An. Rpt.,* 12:602. 1893.

SYNONYMS. None.

A very handsome fruit of good quality for either dessert or culinary use. It ripens a few days later than Transcendent.

SMALL RED SIBERIAN

The tree is a good grower, comes into bearing young and yields full crops biennially.

This is distinct from the September apple described by Downing.[1]

Historical. Originated with Peter M. Gideon, Excelsior, Minn., from seed of Cherry Crab. In 1888 Mr. Gideon sent stock of this variety to this Station for testing.

TREE.

Tree vigorous, with short, stout, crooked and twisted branches. *Form* rather flat, spreading, open. *Twigs* moderately long, curved, moderately stout with large terminal buds; internodes long. *Bark* clear brown, lightly mottled with scarf-skin; slightly pubescent near tips. *Lenticels* quite numerous, medium size, round, not raised. *Buds* prominent, large, long, plump, acute, free, not pubescent.

FRUIT.

Fruit medium to large for a crab, uniform in size but not in shape. *Form* roundish oblate to somewhat oblong, inclined to conic, frequently ribbed; sides usually unequal. *Stem* usually long and slender. *Cavity* somewhat obtuse, rather shallow to medium in depth, medium to broad, occasionally furrowed, sometimes russeted. *Calyx* medium to rather large, closed or partly open. *Basin* mammillate, very shallow to moderately deep, medium in width, slightly obtuse.

Skin thin, tender, smooth, pale yellow or greenish, striped with red, in well colored specimens becoming nearly covered with dark red, overspread with bluish bloom. *Dots* small, scattering, inconspicuous, gray or brownish.

Calyx tube rather short, medium in width, broadly funnel-form; pistil point persistent. *Stamens* median to nearly marginal.

Core medium size, axile or slightly abaxile; cells closed or wide open; core lines clasping. *Carpels* roundish, elongated. *Seeds* variable in shape, medium size, moderately wide, rather short, acute to broadly acute, rather light dull brown.

Flesh tinged with yellow, medium in grain, moderately tender, juicy, subacid, not astringent but with an agreeable crabapple flavor, good to very good in quality.

Season September.

SOULARD.

REFERENCES. 1. Soulard, *Gard. Monthly*, **10**:199. 1868 (cited by **13**). 2. *Ib.*, *Ill. Hort. Soc. Rpt.*, **1869**:195, 260. 3. Downing, **1869**:426. 4. *Am. Pom. Soc. Cat.*, **1871**:8. 5. Soulard, *Ill. Hort. Soc. Rpt.*, **1873**:291. 6. *Montreal Hort. Soc. Rpt.*, **5**:91. 1879. 7. *Ib.*, **10**:37. 1884. 8. Thomas, **1885**:524. 9. Lyon, *Mich. Hort. Soc. Rpt.*, **1890**:300. 10. Bailey, *An. Hort.*, **1892**:249. 11. Budd, *Amer. Gard.*, **14**:244. 1893. 12. Thomas, **1897**:264. fig. 13. Bailey, *Evol. Native Fruits*, **1898**:261. fig. 14. Craig, *Ia. Acad. Sci.*, **7**:130. 1899. *pl.* 15. Budd-Hansen, **1903**:225. fig.

SYNONYMS. None.

---

1 Downing, **1869**:350.

This is regarded by Bailey as a hybrid between the native prairie crab, *Pyrus Ioensis*, and the common apple, *Pyrus malus* (13), in which opinion he is supported by Craig (14). It is distinct from the Soulard apple. According to Soulard's account (13) "it originated on a farm about twelve miles from St. Louis, Mo., where stood an American crab thicket not inclosed, near the farmhouse, about twenty-five years since. The thicket was cut down and the ground cultivated some two or three years; culture being discontinued, another crab thicket sprang up, and when bearing, one tree (the identical kind now called Soulard crab) was discovered. The fruit astonished me by its remarkably large size, being sent to me by a friend whose widowed mother, Mrs. Freeman Delauriere, occupied the farm. I immediately propagated it by grafting upon crab stock and upon our common seedlings. Upon both stocks producing the same fruit and thriving admirably, I disseminated it among my friends as a very desirable fruit, having nothing of the Siberian type. It is to me conclusive that this crab is the offspring of an accidental hybridization of the wild crab by our common apple. The tree, its foliage, habit, increased size of fruit and tree, and decreased acerbity, convince me it is a hybrid, and as far as I know, the first instance of such cross.

"I consider it the most desirable of all crabs that I have seen. Adding sweetness, it is delicious baked. It makes most excellent preserves, being large enough to be quartered, and unsurpassed by any crab for jams, jellies, etc., imparting its delicate taste and rich crab aroma. The largest have measured over seven inches around. In form, color and smell it is like the common crab, and it hangs on the tree until destroyed by frost. It will keep two years, with common care, in a cellar, and will stand repeated freezing and thawing in a dark place. It is agreeable to many palates in the spring.

"The tree is an immense grower in the nursery, coming early into fruit and making but little growth afterward, and is an immense and regular bearer. I have made some cider as clear as wine, with sugar or a quarter part of sweet apples. It will make delicious strong cider. Tree perfectly hardy, having stood the severest winters here and at St. Paul, Minn., for twenty-five years."

After giving the testimony of several observers with regard to the value of this hybrid for the Upper Mississippi valley Bailey concludes: "It is probable that too much was expected of the Soulard crab when it was first introduced, and that it afterward, suffered from the partial collapse. Such an array of apples has now been introduced into the cold Northwest — from the East, from Russia, offspring of the Siberian crab, and local seedlings of the common apple — that the Soulard crab and its kin have been obscured" (13).

The variety is still listed by some nurserymen (10). It is practically unknown in New York and has no value for this state.

TRANSCENDENT.

REFERENCES. 1. *Horticulturist*, 22:125. 1867. 2. Warder, *Tilt. Jour. Hort.*, 5:205. 1869. fig. 3. Downing, 1869:426. 4. Todd, 1871:83. fig. 5. Fitz,

1872:147. **6.** Gibb, *Montreal Hort. Soc. Rpt.*, 1:21. 1876. **7.** Barry, **1883**: 360. **8.** Gibb, *Montreal Hort. Soc. Rpt.*, 10:39. 1884. **9.** Wickson, **1889**:249. 10. Bailey, *An. Hort.*, **1892**:251. **11.** Thomas, **1897**:300. **12.** *U. S. Pom. Bul.*, 6:11. 1897. **13.** *Can. Hort.*, 26:489. 1903. figs. **14.** Budd-Hansen, 1903:226. fig.

SYNONYMS. TRANSCENDANT (5, 9, 10, 13). TRANSCENDENT (1, 2, 3, 4, 6, 7, 8, 11, 12, 14).

This beautiful fruit has for many years been one of the most popular of the crabapples cultivated in this state. The tree is a good grower, roundish, spreading, hardy and usually very productive yielding good to very heavy crops nearly annually. It is in season from late August to the middle of September or a little later.

Historical. The history of Transcendent seems to be unknown. Although our first reference to this variety is 1867, William Prince had it listed in his nursery catalogue as early as 1844.[1] It seems to have been in the hands of nurserymen for years before it came to the attention of pomological writers, hence the obscurity in regard to its origin.

TREE.

Tree large with stout, curved and drooping branches. *Form* very spreading, drooping, rather dense. *Twigs* moderately long, curved, slender, with large terminal buds; internodes long. *Bark* brown, tinged with green, lightly streaked with scarf-skin; slightly pubescent near tips. *Lenticels* quite numerous, medium to large, oval, raised, conspicuous. *Buds* medium to large, rather prominent, plump, obtuse or slightly acute, free, slightly pubescent.

FRUIT.

Fruit medium to rather large. *Form* roundish or roundish oblong, flattened at the ends, somewhat ribbed. *Stem* medium to long, rather stout, bracted. *Cavity* narrow, shallow, obtuse. *Calyx* large, closed; lobes long, leafy, reflexed. *Basin* shallow, wrinkled.

Skin thin, clear bright yellow with bright red cheek, overspread with bloom. Highly colored specimens are nearly covered with bright red.

Calyx tube conical. *Stamens* marginal.

Core medium size; cells closed.

Flesh yellow, crisp, juicy, moderately fine, somewhat astringent, subacid, very good for culinary uses.

Season late August to the middle of September.

VAN WYCK.

REFERENCES. **1.** Downing, **1872**:39 app. **2.** Barry, **1883**:360. **3.** *Montreal Hort. Soc. Rpt.*, 10:37. 1884. **4.** Bailey, *An. Hort.*, **1892**:251. **5.** *Am. Pom. Soc. Cat.*, **1897**:11. **6.** Thomas, **1897**:300. fig. **7.** Budd-Hansen, 1903:227.

---

1 Ragan, *U. S. P. B. I. Bul.*, **56**:373. 1905.

SYNONYMS. *Brier Sweet* (6). VAN WYCK CRAB (2, 4, 5, 6, 7). VAN WYCK SIBERIAN (1). VAN WYCK SWEET (3, 4).

A sweet crabapple which according to Downing (1) originated as a chance seedling in Fishkill, Dutchess county, N. Y. Fruit large for a Siberian crabapple, whitish shaded with bright red, covered with bloom; flesh whitish, tender, moderately juicy, sweet, rich; it sometimes water-cores; core small, closed; season August and September (1, 2). This variety is occasionally listed by nurserymen (4). It is not generally known in New York and it appears that its cultivation in this state is not increasing.

WHITNEY.

REFERENCES. 1. Warder, *Tilt. Jour. Hort.*, 5:206. 1869. fig. 2. *Minn. Hort. Soc. Rpt.*, 1876:109. 3. *Am. Pom. Soc. Cat.*, 1881:16. 4. Barry, 1883:360. 5. Gibb, *Montreal Hort. Soc. Rpt.*, 1884:34. fig. 6. *Ib., Am. Pom. Soc. Rpt.*, 1885:29. 7. Thomas, 1885:529. 8. *Can. Hort.*, 11:42. 1888. 9. Wickson, 1889:249. 10. Lyon, *Mich. Hort. Soc. Rpt.*, 1890:300. 11. Bailey, *An. Hort.*, 1892:252. 12. Beach, *N. Y. Sta. An. Rpt.*, 13:584. 1894. 13. Burrill and McCluer, *Ill. Sta. Bul.*, 45:346. 1896. 14. Farrand, *Mich. Sta. Bul.*, 205:48. 1903. 15. *Can. Hort.*, 26:489. 1903. figs. 16. Budd-Hansen, 1903:228.

SYNONYMS. WHITNEY (3, 10, 11, 14, 15, 16). WHITNEY CRAB (4, 7, 9). WHITNEY NO. 20 (1, 2, 5, 6, 8, 11, 12, 13). *Whitney No. 20* (15, 16).

One of the most popular of the large crabapples particularly in the West and North. The fruit is attractive, yellow, striped with lively red, subacid, good for dessert and very good for culinary uses. It is in season in August and early September. The tree is a thrifty, upright grower, comes into bearing young and is very productive.

Historical. This variety originated with A. R. Whitney, Franklin Grove, Ill. (1). It was at first disseminated under the name Whitney No. 20, under which name it was described by Warder as early as 1869 (1). It has not been much planted in New York but in regions farther north and west its cultivation is gradually increasing.

TREE.

Tree below medium with moderately stout, moderately long, curved branches. *Form* upright becoming somewhat spreading after fruiting heavily. *Twigs* short, straight, stout with large terminal buds; internodes medium size. *Bark* bright brown tinged with green, lightly streaked with scarf-skin; slightly pubescent near tips. *Lenticels* numerous, small, oval, not raised. *Buds* medium to large, broad, obtuse, free, pubescent.

FRUIT.

Fruit large, pretty uniform in size and shape. *Form* roundish inclined to conic or to ovate. *Stem* slender. *Cavity* narrow to moderately wide, rather deep, obtuse. *Calyx* medium to large, closed or partly open. *Basin* broad, shallow, wrinkled.

Skin light yellow largely shaded and striped with red.

Flesh yellowish, crisp, juicy, mild subacid or nearly sweet with slight crab-apple flavor, good to very good.

Season late August and early September.

YELLOW SIBERIAN.

REFERENCES. 1. Buel, *N. Y. Bd. Agr. Mem.*, 1826:477. 2. Kenrick, 1832:58 3. Downing, 1845:147. 4. Cole, 1849:137. 5. Thomas, 1849:158. 6. Waring, 1851:30. 7. Barry, 1851:287. 8. Gregg, 1857:62. 9. Warder, 1867:732. 10. Budd-Hansen, 1903:228.

SYNONYMS. *Amber Crab* (3). *Golden Beauty.* SIBERIAN CRAB (6). YELLOW SIBERIAN (1, 2, 3, 4, 5, 7, 8, 9, 10).

This is sometimes called Golden Beauty. It is similar to Red Siberian except in the color and size of the fruit, it being rather large and of a clear golden-yellow color. Season September. Tree medium size or below, a good grower, upright becoming roundish, and somewhat drooping, very hardy and healthy except that under certain circumstances it suffers from blight. It comes into bearing rather young and is a reliable cropper, yielding heavy to very heavy crops annually or nearly annually. It is grown principally for home use but sometimes a portion of the fruit is disposed of in local markets.

ERRATA — VOL. I.

Page 24. Under Rhode Island Greening group, "Northwestern Greening" should be omitted.

25. Under Alexander group, "Bismark" should be "Bismarck."

71. Under Different Types of Ben Davis, in the last paragraph omit Rutledge.

76. Under Black Annette, second line, "1886" should be "1866."

95. First line of text, under Carlough, (2) should be (3).

141. Under Golden Medal, fourth line, reference "U. S. B. P. I. bulletin 56:124" should be "U. S. B. P. I. bulletin 56:125."

168, Colored plate facing. Legend "Jacob Sweet" should be "Jacobs Sweet."

196. McAfee, first line of second paragraph, insert (7). between Indian and Wyandotte; Wyandotte (7). should precede Zeeke on p. 197.

270, Colored plate facing. "Genet," in italic should be omitted.

333. Under Sweet Russet all of the second line, including the words "Synonym" and "Summer Russet (1)," should be omitted.

392. Twenty-sixth line, second column, "Bismark" should be "Bismarck."

403. "Pomme Grise," first column, fifteenth line, should be roman instead of italic.

409. Eighth line from bottom of left column, ' Winter Sweet Paradise" should be roman capitals and small capitals instead of italic.

ERRATA — VOL. II.

Page 222. Under Thompson, paragraph 3, line 2, "Season late winter" should be "Season early winter."

245. Eighth line from bottom, last word, "sometimes" should be "somewhat."

281. Second paragraph, insert "to 981 inclusive," so that the sentence will read: "The following numbers to 981 inclusive are those given the varieties included in the Department of Agriculture importations of 1870."

282. "Number 21 Veronesh" should be "No. 21 Voronesh."

INDEX TO VARIETIES.

(Accepted names appear wholly or in part in roman type; synonyms in italic.)

	PAGE.
Abe Lincoln	178
ADIRONDACK	1
ADMIRABLE	1
ALBION	2
Albertin	3
ALEXANDER	3
Alexander the First	3
Alexandre	3
American	110
American Fall	62
American Fall Pippin	241
American Gloria Mundi	77
American Golden	83
American Golden Pippin	83
American Mammoth	77
American Mother	143
American Pearmain	211
American Red	178
American Red Juneating	55
American Summer	211
American Summer Pearmain	211
AMSTERDAM	5
Amsterdam Sweet	5
Anglesea Pippin	178
ANISIM	5
Anisim of Peterson	5
Antenovka	6
Antonowka	6
ANTONOVKA	6
Antony	6
APORT	6
Aport (synonym of Aport Orient)	7
Aporta	3
Aporta Nalivia	3

	PAGE.
APORT ORIENT	7
Aport Oriental	7
Arabka	32
ARCTIC	7
Arcad Krasivui	14
Arkad Krasivui	14
Arkad Krasivui	14
Aromatic Spike No. 354	233
Astracan Blanch	239
Astracan d'Ete	239
Astracanischer Sommer	239
Astracan Rouge	178
Astrachan	178
Astrachan Red	178
Astrachan Rouge	178
Astrachan White	239
Astrakhan Rouge	178
Astravaskoe	155
Auberlin	3
AUGUST	9
August (synonym of July)	112
August Apple	53
AUGUSTINE	10
August Sweet	216
August Sweeting	216
Aunt Ginnie	75
Aurora	227
Autumnal Bough	10
Autumnal Swaar (synonym of Autumn Swaar)	11
Autumnal Swaar (synonym of Autumn Sweet Swaar)	12
Autumnal Sweet	12
Autumnal Sweet Swaar	12
AUTUMN BOUGH	10

PAGE.

Autumn Bough 10
Autumn Bough (synonym of
   Sweet Bough) 216
Autumn Pearmain 124
Autumn Pippin 62
Autumn Rose 190
Autumn Seek-No-Further 88
Autumn Strawberry 120
AUTUMN STREAKED 10
AUTUMN SWAAR 11, 12
Autumn Swaar (synonym of
   Autumn Sweet Swaar) 12
Autumn Sweet 12
Autumn Sweet Bough 10
AUTUMN SWEET SWAAR 12
Avery Sweet 175

Babouskino 83
Babuscheno 83
Babuschkino 83
Babushkino 83
BAILEY SPICE 13
Bailey's Spice 13
BAKER SWEET 13
Baker's Sweet 13
Baltimore (synonym of Gloria
   Mundi) 77
Baltimore (synonym of Vande-
   vere Pippin) 231
Baltimore Pippin 77
BANKS 14
Banks Gravenstein 14
Banks Red Gravenstein 14
Bard Apple 49
Baroveski 151
Barowiski 151
Beard Burden 49
Beaute de Kent 15
BEAUTIFUL ARCAD 14
Beautiful Arcade 14
Beautiful Pippin 184
BEAUTY OF KENT 15
Beauty of Queen 3
Beauty of the West (synonym of
   Western Beauty) 230
Beauty of the West (synonym of
   Grosh) 89
Beauty Red 40

PAGE.

Beel Solotofskaja 82
Beitigheimer 17
BELBORODOOSKOE 15
Belle d'Angers 21
Belle de Boscoop 25
Belle de Boskoop 25
Belle d'Orleans 3
Belle Dubois 77
Belle Josephine (synonym of
   Gloria Mundi) 77
Belle Josephine (synonym of
   White Spanish Reinette) 241
Belle of Boskoop 25
Bellerdovskoe 15
Belle Rose 168
Bellflower of the West 148
Bell's Early 203
Bell's Favorite 203
BEN FORD 45
Benniger 15
BENNINGER 15
Bennington 203
BENONI 16
Bergamot 6
Berry Apple 39
Bielborodovskæ 15
BIETIGHEIMER 17
Big Rambo (synonym of West-
   ern Beauty) 239
Big Rambo (synonym of Grosh) 89
Big Sweet 233
Big Vandevere 231
BIRTH 18
BISMARCK 19
Bismark 19
BLACK ANNETTE 20
Black Apple 46
Black Detroit 46
Blanche 241
Blanche d'Espagne 241
Blanche Glacee d'Ete 239
BLENHEIM 20
Blenheim Orange 21
Blenheim Pippin 21
Blenheimsrenett 21
BLOOM 69
Blooming Orange 21
Blumen Calvill 85

PAGE.

Blushed Calville 22
Blushed June 181
Blush June 181
Bogdanoff (synonym of Grand-
mother) 83
Bogdanoff Steklianka 83
Bohannon 118
Bonum 23
Borovinka 24
Borovinka Angluskaia 24
Borovitsky (synonym of Boro-
vinka) 24
Borovitsky (synonym of Olden-
burg) 151
Borowicki 151
Borowitski 151
Borowitsky 151
Borsdorfer 5
Boskoop 25
Bough 216
Bough Apple 216
Bough, Early Sweet 216
Bough Sweet 216
Bow Apple 216
Bracken 240
Bracy's Seek-No-Further 88
Breskovka 26
Brilliant 69
Buckley 33
Buckram 97
Buchanan 149
Bullripe 49
Bunker Hill 27
Butter 27
Butter Pippin 78

Cabane du Chien 98
Cabashaw 227
Cabashea 28
Cabashie 28
Calkin's Pippin 30
Calville de Gravenstein 85
Calville Grafensteiner 85
Calville Krasmui 22
Cambour des Lorrains 213
Camoisas du roi d'Espagne 241
Camoise Blanche 241
Camoisee Blanche 241

PAGE.

Camuesar 241
Camuezas 241
Camuzar 241
Canada Baldwin 69
Canada Peach 159
Canada Reinette (synonym of
Cheeseboro) 33
Carolina 240
Carolina June 181
Carolina Red 181
Carolina Red June 181
Caroline 240
Cathead 29
Cathead (synonym of Cheese-
boro) 33
Cathead (synonym of Fall Pip-
pin) 62
Cathead Greening 29
Catshead 29
Catshead Greening 29
Cattell Apple 148
Cayuga Red Streak 227
Celestia 29
Champlain 30
Chandler 31
Chandler's Red 31
Charlamoff 32
Charlamoski 32
Charlamovskœ 32
Charlamowciski 151
Charlamowski d'Automne 151
Charlamowskircher Nalleoid ... 151
Charlamowskœ 32
Charlamowsky 151
Charlottenthaler 222
Charlottenthaler Apple 222
Charlottenthaler Golba 222
Charmant Blanc 213
Cheesborough 33
Cheeseboro 33
Cheesboro's Russet 33
Cheeseborough 33
Cheeseborough Russet 33
Chenango 33
Chenango Strawberry 33
Chimney Apple 65
Christ Birth 18
Christ Birth Apple 18

PAGE.

Christmas 18
Cinnamon 6
CLAPPER FLAT 34
CLARKE 35
Clarke Beauty 35
CLYDE 36
Clyde Beauty 36
Coalbrook 225
Cobbett's Fall (synonym of Fall
  Pippin) 62
Cobbett's Fall (synonym of
  White Spanish Reinette) 241
Cobbett's Fall Pippin (synonym
  of Fall Pippin) 62
Cobbett's Fall Pippin (synonym
  of White Spanish Reinette) .. 241
CODLING 117
Codlin, Keswick 117
Coe's Spice 49
Coleman 227
Cole's Quince 174
COLLAMER 36
Collamer Twenty Ounce 36
COLTON 37
Colton Early 37
COLVERT 38
Compte Orloff 233
Comte Woronzoff 3
Concombre Ancien (synonym of
  Fall Pippin) 62
Concombre Ancien (synonym of
  White Spanish Reinette) 241
Conic June 118
CONSTANTINE 39
COOPER 40
Copp's Mammoth 77
Corail 3
CORNELL 40
Cornell Fancy 41
Cornell's Favorite 41
CORNER 41
Cornish Gilliflower 197
Corse's St. Lawrence 193
Cos Orange 42
Costard 29
Costard Ray 29
Count Orloff 233
Coustard 29

PAGE.

COX ORANGE 42
Cox's Orange 42
Cox's Orange Pippin 42
Cox's Pomona 165
CRANBERRY PIPPIN 43
Crandall Seedling 107
CREAM 44
Crimson Beauty 196
Crimson Pippin (synonym of
  Scarlet Pippin) 196
Crimson Pippin (synonym of
  Detroit Red) 46
Crimson Scarlet Pippin 196
CROW EGG 44
Crow's Egg 44
Cumming's Rambo 89
Cut Wine 244
Czarskui Schip 45
CZAR THORN 45

DEADERICK 45
Dean's Codlin 165
De Glace D'Ete 239
De Glace Hative.............. 239
De La Madeleine Rouge........ 55
De Lorraine 213
Demary 73
De Moscovie d'Ete........... 239
De Neige 65
De Notre Dame 213
De Rambourg 213
De Rambure 213
De Rateau 62
De Ratteau 241
De Revel (synonym of Yellow
  Transparent) 248
De Revel (synonym of Vineuse
  Rouge) 233
Derrick and Ann.............. 186
Derrick's Graft 186
De Seigneur d'Automne........ 29
D'Espagne (synonym of White
  Spanish Reinette) 241
D'Espagne (synonym of Fall
  Pippin) 62
Deterding's Early 178
Detroit 46
Detroit Black 46

PAGE.

Detroit Red 46
D'Eve 141
De Vin du Conn............... 227
Diels Sommerkönig 85
Dix-huit Onces 227
Dodge's Early Red............ 203
Douse 95
Dows 95
Dowse 95
Dredge's Fame 21
Duchess 151
Duchesse d'Oldenbourg......... 151
Duchess No. 3................. 158
Duchess of Oldenburg.......48, 151
Duchess of Oldenburgh......... 151
Dudley 48
Dudley Winter 48
Dudley's Winter 48
Du Marechal 65
Dumpling 208
Dutchess 151
Dutchess of Oldenberg......... 151
Dutchess of Oldenburgh....... 151
Dutch Mignonne (synonym of
    Blenheim) 21
Duverson's June 141
Dyer 49

Early Baldwin 168
Early Bough 216
Early Colton 37
Early Congress 85
Early French Reinette (synonym
    of Early Harvest).......... 51
Early French Reinette (synonym
    of Sweet Bough)............ 216
Early Golden Sweet............ 81
Early Harvest................. 50
Early Jack.................... 106
Early Jennetting.............. 240
Early Joe.................... 52
Early July Pippin............. 51
Early June (synonym of Early
    Harvest) 51
Early June (synonym of Egg
    Top) 56
Early June of South........... 141
Early Margaret 141

PAGE.

Early May 240
Early Pennock 53
Early Red 141
Early Red Juneating........... 141
Early Red Margaret............ 141
Early Red Pippin.............. 93
Early Redstreak............... 93
Early Red Streak.............. 93
Early Ripe.................... 54
Early Strawberry.............. 54
Early Striped Juneating........ 141
Early Summer Pearmain........ 211
Early Sweet................... 98
Early Sweet Bough............. 216
Early Sweetheart 216
Early Tart Harvest............ 168
Early Washington 203
Egg Job 44
Egg Top 56
Eighteen Ounce 227
Eighteen Ounce Apple.......... 227
Elgin Pippin 56
Elgin Pippin (synonym of White
    Spanish Reinette) 241
Empereur Alexandre I......... 3
Empereur Alexandre de Russie. 3
Empereur de Russie............ 3
Emperor Alexander 3
Englese Orange Appel.......... 154
Englische Granat-Reinette...... 184
Englischer Pepping............ 57
English Borovinka 24
English Codling............... 117
English Jannetting 230
English King 3
English Pearmain 125
English Pippin 57
English Pippin (synonym of
    Longfield) 123
English Rambo 89
English Sweet (synonym of
    Ramsdell Sweet) 58, 175
English Sweeting 175
Episcopal 62
Episcopale 241
Ernst's Apple 149
Ernst's Pippin 149
Essex Pippin 184

PAGE.

Eve 56
Eve Apple (synonym of Egg
  Top) 56
Eve Apple (synonym of Mar-
  garet) 141
Everbearing 108

Fall Bough 10
Fall Geneting 59
Fall Gennetting 59
FALL GREENING 58
Fall Green Sweet.............. 233
FALL HARVEY................... 58
Fall Jenetting 59
FALL JENNETING 59
Fall Jennetting 59
Fall Orange 12, 60
FALL PIPPIN................... 61
Fall Pippin (synonym of Fall
  Harvey) 58
Fall Pippin (synonym of Holland
  Pippin) 101
Fall Pippin (synonym of White
  Spanish Reinette) 241
Fall Queen 91
Fall Strawberry 120
Fall Stripe 196
Fall Swaar 11
Fall Swaar of the West........ 11
Fall Vandervere 231
FALL WINE 63
FAMEUSE 65
Fameuse (synonym of Utter)... 230
Fameuse Baldwin 98
FAMEUSE GREEN................. 69
FAMEUSE GROUP................. 68
FAMEUSE NOIRE................. 69
FAMEUSE SUCRE................. 69
FANNY 69
Fin d'Automne 3
FISHKILL 70
Fishkill Beauty 70
Five-Quartered Gilliflower ... 197
Flat 34
Flint Russet 170
Flower (of Genesee).......... 73
Flushing Seek-No-Further 88
FORD 71

PAGE.

Forever Pippin 33
Formosa 184
Formosa Pippin 184
Fourth of July................ 112
Fraise 55
FRANCHOT 71
Frank 33
Frank Rambour 213
French Pippin (synonym of Hol-
  land Pippin)................ 101
French Pippin (synonym of
  Roman Stem) 188
French Rambo 89
French Reinette 215
French Spitzenburgh (synonym
  of Summer Spitzenburg)..... 215
FULLERTON SWEET............... 71

GARDEN ROYAL.................. 72
Gardiner's Apple 143
GARDNER SWEET PEARMAIN....... 73
Gelee d'Ete 239
General Chandler 31
GENESEE FLOWER 73
Geneva Pearmain 30
Gennetting 240
German Calville 6
German Calville 324........... 6
Georgia June 181
Gibbon's Smathhouse 231
Gibbon's Smokehouse 231
GIDEON 74
Gideon White 74
Ginetting 240
GINNIE 75
Glace de Zelande.............. 239
Glacie d'Ete.................. 239
GLADSTONE 75
Glazenwood 77
Glazenwood Gloria Mundi...... 77
GLORIA MUNDI 76
Glory of York................. 184
Gloucester Pippin 21
Golden Apple 83
GOLDEN PIPPIN (I)............. 78
GOLDEN PIPPIN (II)............ 79
Golden Pippin (synonym of Fall
  Pippin) 62

PAGE.

Golden Pippin (synonym of Golding) 83
GOLDEN PIPPINS 78
GOLDEN REINETTE 79
Golden Spice 49
GOLDEN SWEET 81
Golden Sweet (synonym of Northern Sweet) 147
Golden Sweeting 81
GOLDEN WHITE 82
GOLDING 82
Goldreinette von Blenheim 21
Good Peasant (synonym of Longfield) 123
Good Peasant (synonym of Anisim) 5
Gov. Seward's 227
Grafen Apfel 85
Grafensteiner 85
Granat-Reinette 184
Grand Alexander 3
Grand Alexandre 3
Grand Duc Constantin 39
Grand Duke Constantine 39
GRANDMOTHER 83
Grand Mother 83
Grand Sultan (synonym of Vineuse Rouge) 233
Grand Sultan (synonym of Yellow Transparent) 248
Grantham 108
GRAVENSTEIN 84
Gravensteiner 85
Gravenstein Rouge 180
Gravenstine 85
Grave Slige 85
Grave Slije 85
Greasy Pippin 128
GREAT MOGUL 87
GREEN SEEK-NO-FURTHER 88
Green Sweet (synonym of Victuals and Drink) 233
Green Transparent 233
Gros-Alexandre 3
GROSH 89
Grosh (synonym of Summer Rambo) 213
Grosh's Mammoth 89
    VOL. II — 23

PAGE.

Groskoe Selenka Grüner 233
Gros Pomier 91
Gros Pommier 91
Gros-Rambour d'Ete 213
Grosser Mogul 87
Grosse-Schafnasé 29
GRUNDY 90

HAAS 91
HAGLOE 92
Hagloe Crab 92
Hampers American 178
Harmony 53
Harvest (synonym of Early Harvest) 51
Harvest (synonym of Primate) . 168
Harvest Apple 215
HARVEST REDSTREAK 93
Harvest Red Streak 93
Harvey 58
HASKELL 93
Haskell Sweet 94
Hass 91
Haverstraw Pippin 30
Hawkins Pippin 73
HAWLEY 94
Hawley (synonym of Hawthornden) 96
Hawthorndean 96
HAWTHORNDEN 96
Heickes Summer Queen 53
Herbstbreitling 213
Herbst Strefling 10
Herbst Streifling 10
Herr's June 141
HIBERNAL 96
HICKS 97
Highland Pippin 168
HIGHTOP SWEET 97
High Top Sweet 98
High Top Sweet (synonym of Amsterdam) 5
High Top Sweeting 98
HILAIRE 98
HILTON 99
Himbeerapfel Lievlander 129
Himbeerapfel Livlander 129
HOADLEY 99

PAGE.

Hog Island Sweet.............. 100
Hogpen 60
Holden 60
Holden Pippin 60
Holland Pippin................ 101
Holland Pippin (synonym of
  Fall Pippin)................ 62
Hollow Crown Pearmain....... 124
Hominy 203
Hook 103
Horning 203
Horse 91
Hoss 91
House 64
Howard Best.................. 103
Howard Russet 33
Howard's Best 103
Howard's Best Russian........ 103
Howe Apple 245
Hower 64
Hoypen 60
Hudson Red Streak............ 125
Hunter Pippin................ 104
Hurlburt 105
Hurlbut 104
Hurlbut (synonym of Ramsdell
  Sweet) 175
Hurlbut Stripe 105
Hurlbut Sweet 175
Hurlbutt 105

Imperial Vandervere 231
Imperial White 157
Imperatrice Eugenie 21
Imperatrice Josephine 77
Indian Queen 53
Indiana Vandevere 231
Isham 106
Isham Sweet 106
Isle of Wight Orange.......... 154
Isle of Wight Pippin.......... 154

Jack 106
Jack Apple 106
Jackson 33
Jarvis 107
Jefferies 108
Jefferis 108

PAGE.

Jefferson County 109
Jeffries 108
Jellyflower 197
Jenneting 240
Jennetting 109
Jennetting (synonym of White
  Juneating) 240
Jennings 166
Jersey Sweet 110
Jersey Sweeting 110
Joaneting 240
Joe Precoce 52
Jolly Gentleman 3
Jonathan of the North 5
Jones Early Harvest 181
Jones Pippin 60
Josephine (synonym of Gloria
  Mundi) 77
Josephine (synonym of White
  Spanish Reinette) 241
Judson 111
July 112
July Apple 168
July Early Pippin 51
July, Fourth of 112
July Pippin 51
June (synonym of Margaret) .. 141
June (synonym of Red June) .. 181
Juneateing 240
Juneating 109
Juneating (synonym of White
  Juneating) 240
Juneting 240
Juniata 234

Kaighn 113
Kaighn's Spitzemburg 113
Kaighn's Spitzenberg 113
Kaighn's Spitzenbergh 113
Kaighn's Spitzenburg (synonym
  of Kaighn) 113
Kaighn's Spitzenburg (synonym
  of Long Red Pearmain) 125
Kaighn's Spitzenburgh 113
Kaign's Spitzenburg 113
Kaiser Alexander 3
Kajabowka 114
Kalkidon 114

PAGE.

Kalkidonskæ 114
Kalkidouskæ 114
Kalkidovskæ 114
Kalvil jeltui 247
Kalville scholti 247
Karaboff 114
KARABOVKA 114
Karabowka 115
Kempster's Pippin 21
Kennebec Seedling 245
Kent Beauty 15
Kent Fillbasket 115
Kentish Filbasket 115
KENTISH FILLBASKET 115
Kentish Pippin 15
Kentucky Bellflower 125
Kentucky Gilliflower 125
KESWICK 116
Keswick Codlin 117
Keswick Codling 117
Khalkidonskæ 114
Kinderhook Pippin 77
Kingsbury Russet (synonym of
    Cheeseboro) 33
Kingsbury Russet (synonym of
    Pumpkin Russet) 170
KIRKBRIDGE 118
Kirkbridge White 118
Knight's Red June 181
Korallen Apfel 3

La Belle Fameuse 65
Lady Blush 139
Lady de Grey's 115
LADY FINGER 118
Lady Finger (synonym of
    Kaighn) 113
Lady Finger (synonym of Long
    Red Pearmain) 125
Lady's Apple 242
Lady Suffield 126
Lady Sutherland 126
Lady Washington 40
La Fameuse 65
Lammas 142
Lancaster Queen 212
LANDSBERG 119
Landsberger Reinette 119

PAGE.

Landsburg 119
Langerfeldskæ 123
Lansberger Reinette 119
Large Bough 216
Large Early 51
Large Early Bough 216
Large Early Harvest 51
Large Early Yellow Bough 216
Large Fall 241
Large Fall Pippin 241
Large Golden Pippin (synonym
    of Champlain) 30
Large Golden Pippin (synonym
    of Golden Pippin I) 78
Large Rambo 89
Large Red and Green Sweeting 177
Large Red Sweeting 177
Large Summer Rambo 89
Large Sweet Bough 216
Large Vandervere 231
Large White Juneating 51
Large Yellow Bough 216
Late Bough 10
Late Chandler 31
Late Golden Sweet 13
LATE STRAWBERRY 120
LATHAM 121
LA VICTOIRE 69
LEAD 121
Lead Apple 121
Leeds Beauty 196
Lievland Raspberry 129
Lima 227
Lincoln 245
LINCOLN PIPPIN 122
Lincoln Pippin (synonym of
    Winthrop Greening) 245
Lincolnshire Pippin 96
LINDENWALD 122
Lippincott 215
Liveland Raspberry 129
Livesley's Imperial 126
Livland Raspberry 129
Lodge's Early 215
LONGFIELD 122
Longfield's Apple 123
Long Island 60
Long Island Graft 60

PAGE.

Long Island Pearmain 124
Long John (synonym of Kaighn) 113
Long John (synonym of Long
   Red Pearmain) 125
Long Pearmain (synonym of
   Kaighn) 113
Long Pearmain (synonym of
   Long Red Pearmain) 125
LONG RED PEARMAIN 125
LONG STEM 125
Long Stem Sweet 13
LONGWORTH 125
Longworth Red Winter 125
Lord Kingston 96
Lord Nelson (synonym of Blen-
   heim) 21
LORD SUFFIELD 126
Lothringer Rambour 89
Lothringer Rambour d'Ete 213
LOU 126
Louis XVIII 55
LOUISE 69, 126
Louise, Princess 127
LOWELL 128
Lowell Pippin 128
LOWLAND RASPBERRY 129
LUBSK QUEEN 129
Lubsk Reinette 130
Lucius Apfel 21
Lyman's Large Yellow 171
Lyman's Pumpkin Sweet 171
LYSCOM 130

MABIE 131
McAdow's June 112
McCARTY 132, 173
McClellan 135
MACDONOUGH 132
McINTOSH 69, 132
McIntosh Red 133
Mackie's Clyde Beauty 36
McLELLAN 134
McLelan 135
McMahan 136
McMahan White 136
McMAHON 136
McMahon White 136
Macomber 187

PAGE.

Magdalene 142
Magnum Bonum 23
MAGOG 138
Magog Red Streak 138
MAIDEN BLUSH 139
MAIDEN FAVORITE 141
Maiden's Apple 141
Maiden's Blush (synonym of
   Hawthornden) 96
Malinowskæ 177
Mammoth (synonym of Gloria
   Mundi) 77
Mammoth (synonym of Golden
   Pippin) 78
Mammoth Pippin 77
Mammoth Rambo 89
Maralandica 51
MARGARET 141
Margaret Early 142
Margaret, Early Red 142
Margaretha Apfel 142
Marget Apple 142
Marguerite 142
Marigold 154
Marigold, Creed's........... 154
Marigold Pippin 154
Marrow-bone 225
Martin 135
Marygold 154
Matthews Stripe 131
Maudlin 142
Meachem Sweet 146
Melon (synonym of Gloria Mun-
   di) 77
Michigan Beauty 201
Millcreek 231
Millcreek Vandervere 231
MILLER 142
Miller Seedling 142
MILLIGEN 142
Mississippi 77
Mr. Gladstone 75
Montgomery Sweet 10
Monstreuse Pippin 77
Monstrous Pippin 77
Monstrous Rambo 89
Montreal 193
Montreal Peach 159

PAGE.

Moose 145
Morgan's Favorite 227
Mosher 143
Mosher Sweet 143
Mother 143
Mother Apple 143
Mother of America 143
Mountaineer 145
Mountain Flora 77
Mountain Sweet 145
Mouse 145
Mudhole 125
Munson 146
Munson Sweet 146
Munson Sweeting 146
Musgrove 89
Musgrove's Cooper (synonym of
Grosh) 89
Musgrove's Cooper (synonym of
Western Beauty) 239
Mushroom 24
Musk Spice 64
Mygatt's Bergamot 49
Myer's Nonpareil 148

Naliwi Jabloky 239
Naylor Rambo 89
Neige 65
Neige-Framboise de Gielen 65
New Brunswick 151
N. J. Red Streak 53
Newtown Greening 83
N. Y. Bellflower 60
N. Y. Gloria Mundi 77
N. Y. Greening 83
Niack Pippin (synonym of
Sweet Bough) 217
Nonpareil 148
Nonpareille 184
North American Best 168
Northampton 21
Northern Golden Sweet 147
Northern Golden Sweeting 147
Northern Sweet 147
Northern Sweeting (synonym of
Munson) 146
Northern Sweeting (synonym of
Northern Sweet) 147

PAGE.

North Star 48
Northwick Pippin 21

The following numbers are those
given by Schroeder in his shipment
to the Iowa Experiment Station in
1870:
No. 3 M 121
No. 4 M 155
No. 6 M 83
No. 9 M 24
No. 11 M 189
No. 14 M 5
No. 18 M 5
No. 21 M 115
No. 22 M 22
No. 23 M 7
No. 24 M 195
No. 26 M 6
No. 54 M 87
No. 56 M 123
No. 57 M 123
No. 80 M 195
No. 94 M 114
No. 105 M 32
No. 134 M 224
No. 139 M 183
No. 140 M 45
No. 147 M 222
No. 152 M 27
No. 161 M 18

The following numbers are those
given to varieties included in the De-
partment of Agriculture importation
of 1870:
No. 161 123
No. 205 115
No. 206 45
No. 210 244
No. 224 6
No. 230 224
No. 236 6
No. 245 24
No. 252 7
No. 262 32
No. 288 177
No. 333 182

PAGE.

No. 340 129
No. 343 182
No. 351 170
No. 372 195
No. 442 247
No. 444 130
No. 453 14
No. 457 39
No. 469 83
No. 472 155
No. 477 18
No. 540 114
No. 587 57
No. 599 189
No. 964 ....·..................... 10
No. 978 82
No. 979 82
No. 981 82
No. 12 Orel 7
No. 21 Veronesh 247
No. 51 Vor. 79
No. 84 Vor. 83
Nyack 30
Nyack Pippin 30

Oats 51
OGDENSBURG 147
Ohio Beauty (synonym of West-
  ern Beauty).................. 239
Ohio Beauty (synonym of Grosh) 89
OHIO NONPAREIL................ 148
Ohio Nonpareil (synonym of
  Gravenstein) 85
Ohio Nonpariel 148
OHIO PIPPIN.................... 149
Ohio Wine (synonym of Fall
  Wine) 64
Ohio Wine (synonym of
  Kaighn) 113
OKABENA 150
Okobena 150
OLDENBURG 150
Oldenburg, Duchess of.......... 151
Oldenburgh 151
Old Hawthorndean 96
Omensk 189
Oporto 7
ORANGE 153

PAGE.

Orange (synonym of Fall
  Orange) 60
Orange (synonym of Lowell).. 128
Orange (synonym of Orange
  Pippin) 154
Orange Blenheim 21
Orange de Cox................. 42
ORANGE (OF NEW JERSEY)....... 153
ORANGE (OF PENNSYLVANIA).... 153
ORANGE PIPPIN................. 154
Orange Pippin (synonym of
  Blenheim) 21
Orange Russet 154
ORANGE SWEET.................. 154
Orange Sweet (synonym of
  Golden Sweet)............... 81
Orange Sweet (synonym of
  Munson) 146
Orange Sweeting (synonym of
  Golden Sweet)............... 81
Orange Sweeting (synonym of
  Orange Sweet)............... 154
Orloff 233
Orlovskoe 233
Orlowskoe 233
Orsimui 97
Osgood's Favorite 131
Osimoe 97
Oskaloosa 106
OSTRAKOFF 155
Ostrakoff Glass................ 155
Ostrekoff 155
Ostrekoff's Glass.............. 155
Ostrekovskaya Steklianka....... 155
Ostrekowskaja Steklianka 155
Ostrokoff 155
Ostrokoff's Glass.............. 155
Ox Apple....................... 77
Oxeye 230
Oxheart 33
Owen's Golden Beauty.......... 240
Ozark Pippin 45

PALOUSE 156
Paper 30
Paper-skin 30
Paradies Apfel 85
Park 125

PAGE.

PARRY WHITE.................... 157
PATTEN 158
Patten's Duchess No. 3......... 158
Patten Greening 158
PEACH (Montreal)............... 159
Peach Apple of Montreal....... 159
Peach of Montreal.............. 159
PEACH POND.................... 160
Peach Pond Sweet.............. 160
Peach Pound Sweet............. 160
Pear Apple 174
Pear Lot 244
Pearmain 125
PEARSALL 161
Pearsall's Sweet 161
Pear Tree Lot.................. 244
PEASE 161
Pease, Walter 161
PEASGOOD NONSUCH 162
Peasgood's Nonesuch 162
Pennsylvania Vandevere........ 231
Pepin de Kent................. 15
Pepin Ribston 184
Pepping Englishcher 57
Perle d'Angleterre 21
PERRY REDSTREAK............... 162
Perry Red Streak.............. 162
PETER 163
Peterson's Charlamoff 32
Petrovskoe 195
Petrowskoe 195
Philadelphia Pippin (synonym of
    Fall Pippin)................ 62
Philadelphia Pippin (synonym of
    White Spanish Reinette)...... 241
Philadelphia Sweet 10
Phœnix 3
Phönix 3
Pickaway Rambo 89
Pie Apple (synonym of Holland
    Pippin) 101
Pie Apple (synonym of Sops of
    Wine) 203
Pippin Kent 15
Pittstown Pippin 79
Plodowitka Cuadkaja 170
Plodowitka Caudkaja 170
PLUMB CIDER................... 164

PAGE.

Plum Cider 164
Pointed Pipka 32
Polecat 212
Pomme Astrachan............... 239
Pomme d'Astrachan 239
Pomme de Blenheim............. 21
Pomme de Fameuse.............. 65
Pomme de Hawthornden......... 96
Pomme de Neige................ 65
Pomme de Notre-Dame.......... 213
Pomme d'Ete (of Canada)...... 51
Pomme d'Orange............... 154
Pomme Fameuse 65
Pomme Graefenstein........... 85
Pomme Peche 159
Pomme Royal.................. 49
Pomme Royale................. 49
Pomme Roye.................. 49
Pomme Water.................. 49
Pommewater (in Illinois)...... 49
POMONA 164
Pomona Brittannica........... 3
Pompey 233
PORTER 166
Possaris Naliva.............. 6
Potter's Large............... 116
Potter's Large Grey Seedling... 116
Potter's Large Seedling....... 116
Pound 77
Pound Pippin................. 62
Pound Royal (synonym of Fall
    Pippin) 62
Pound Royal (synonym of
    Golden Pippin I.)........... 78
Pound Royal (synonym of
    Lowell) 128
Pound Royal (synonym of Long
    Island Pearmain)............ 125
Pound's July................. 217
POUND SWEET.................. 167
Pound Sweet (synonym of
    Pumpkin Sweet).............. 171
Powers....................... 168
President Napoleon........... 3
Pride of Genesee............. 73
PRIMATE 167
Primiting 240
Prince Bismark 19

PAGE.   PAGE.

Prince of Wales................ 21
Prince's Early Harvest......... 51
Prince's Harvest............... 51
Prince's Large Pippin of N. Y.. 62
Prince's Large Red and Green
   Sweeting 177
Prince's Red and Green Sweet.. 177
Prince's Yellow Harvest........ 51
Princess Louise 127
Prinzessin Apfel 85
Prolific Sweet 170
PROLIFIC SWEETING 169
Prussian 38
PUMPKIN RUSSET 170
PUMPKIN SWEET 171
Pumpkin Sweet (synonym of
   Cheeseboro) 33
Pumpkin Sweet (synonym of
   Pumpkin Russet)............. 170
Pumpkin Sweeting (synonym of
   Pumpkin Sweet)............. 172
Pumpkin Sweeting (synonym of
   Pumpkin Russet)............. 170
Pyrus Astracanica............. 239

Queen (synonym of Summer
   Queen) 212
Queen (synonym of Williams). 242
Queen Anne (synonym of Low-
   ell) 128
Queen Anne (synonym of
   Mother) 143
QUINCE (of Cole)............. 174
QUINCE (of Coxe)............. 174
Quince Apple.................. 174

Rag Apple..................... 146
Rambour 213
Rambour Aigre................. 213
Rambour Blanc................. 213
Rambour d'Amerique........... 213
Rambour d'Ete................. 213
Rambour Franc................. 213
Rambour Gros.................. 213
Rambour Lorraine............. 89
Rambour Raye.................. 213
Rambu 213
Ramsdale's Sweeting........... 175

Ramsdell 175
Ramsdell Red Sweet........... 175
Ramsdell's Red................. 175
Ramsdell's Red Pumpkin Sweet. 175
Ramsdell's Red Sweeting....... 175
RAMSDELL SWEET.............. 175
Ramsdell's Sweeting........... 175
Randall's Red Winter.......... 175
RASPBERRY 176
Ray Apple..................... 146
RED AND GREEN SWEET........ 177
Red and Green Sweeting....... 177
Red Astracan 178
RED ASTRACHAN 178
Red Astrakhan................. 178
Red Beitigheimer.............. 17
Red Bellflower (synonym of Ohio
   Nonpareil) 148
Red Bellflower (synonym of
   Long Red Pearmain)......... 125
Red Bietigheimer.............. 19
Red Bough..................... 177
Red Cheek (synonym of Rasp-
   berry) 177
Red Cheek (synonym of Maiden
   Blush) 139
Red Cheek (synonym of Fall
   Orange) 60
Red Gilliflower (synonym of
   Scollop Gilliflower)........... 197
Red Gilliflower (synonym of
   Striped Gilliflower) 207
RED GRAVENSTEIN.............. 180
Red Gravenstein (synonym of
   Banks) 14
Red Hawthornden.............. 96
RED HOOK...................... 180
Red Joaneting................. 142
RED JUNE...................... 181
Red Juneating (synonym of
   Margaret) 142
Red Juneating (synonym of Red
   June) 181
Red Juneating (synonym of
   Early Strawberry)............ 55
Red June, Carolina............ 181
Red June of South............. 142
Red Juneting.................. 142

PAGE.

Red Pearmain (synonym of
  Kaighn) 113
Red Pearmain (synonym of
  Long Red Pearmain) 125
Red Phoenix (synonym of
  Kaighn) 113
Red Phoenix (synonym of Long
  Red Pearmain) 125
Red Pippin (synonym of
  Kaighn) 113
Red Pippin (synonym of Long
  Red Pearmain) 125
Red Pumpkin Sweet 175
Red Pumpkin Sweeting 175
Red Reinette 83
Red Shropsavine 203
Red Spitzenberg (synonym of
  Kaighn) 113
Red Spitzenberg (synonym of
  Long Red Pearmain) 125
Red Spitzenberg (synonym of
  Richard Graft) 186
Red Spitzenburg 113
Red Transparent 182
Red Transparent (synonym of
  Vineuse Rouge) 233
Red Type of Twenty Ounce... 229
Red Vandervere 231
Red Wine 182
Red Winter Pearmain (synonym
  of Kaighn) 113
Red Winter Pearmain (synonym
  of Long Read Pearmain) 125
Reed 183
Reindell's Large 175
Reinette A Gobelet 241
Reinette Belle de Boskoop 25
Reinette Blanche 241
Reinette Blanche d'Espagne
  (synonym of White Spanish
  Reinette) 241
Reinette Blanche d'Espagne
  (synonym of Fall Pippin).... 62
Reinette de Blenheim 21
Reinette d'Espagne 241
Reinette d'Holland 101
Reinette d'Hollande 101
Reinette de Landsberg 119

Reinette de Traver 184
Reinette Grenade Anglaise 184
Reinette Landsberger 119
Reinette Liubski 130
Reinette Monstrueuse 25
Reinette Orange de Cox 42
Reinette Quarrendon 142
Reinette Tendre 241
Reinette von Montfort 25
Renet Liubskui 130
Repka 183
Remboure d'Ete 213
Reschestwenskoe 19
Revelstone 248
Revelstone Pippin 233
Rhode Island Sweet 172
Riabinouka 39
Ribbed Gilliflower 197
Ribbed Pippin 83
Ribston 184
Ribstone 184
Ribstone Pippin 184
Ribstone Pepping 184
Ribston Pippin 184
Richard 186
Richard Graft 186
Ridge (synonym of Ribston)... 184
Riepka 183
Ripp Apfel 85
Rockhill's Russet 184
Rode Wyn Appel 203
Rolfe 187
Roman Stem 188
Romenskoe 189
Romna 189
Romna (synonym of Hibernal). 97
Romnenskoe 189
Ronk 190
Roschdestwenskoe 19
Roschdestwenskoe 19
Rose Red 190
Roshdestrenskoe 19
Rother Astrakhan 178
Rother Gravensteiner 180
Rother Jacobs 142
Rother Jacobs Apfel 142
Rother Weinapfel 182
Rotherwein Appel 182

PAGE.

Rough and Ready.............. 168
Round Catshead................ 29
Round Sweet 172
Round Top..................... 56
Rubets Vinogradnui............ 244
Rubez Vuinogradnui............ 244
Russam (synonym of Kaighn).. 113
Russam (synonym of Long Red
    Pearmain) 125
Russian Emperor............... 3
Russian Gravenstein............ 6
Rusty Core.................... 148

Sabine 85
Sabine of the Flemmings 85
Safstaholm 191
SAFSTAHOLMS 191
Säfstaholmsäple 191
Säfstaholmsäpple 191
SAILEE RUSSET 192
Saille Sweet 177
SAILLY AUTUMN 192
Saint-Germain 241
St. Hilaire 98
St. John Strawberry 55
ST. LAWRENCE 192
Saint-Lawrence 193
Saint Laurent 193
ST. PETER 194
SANDY GLASS 195
Sanguineus 65
Sapson 203
Sapsonvine 203
Sassafras Sweet 94
SAXTON 196
Scalloped Gilliflower 197
Scalloped Gillyflower 197
Scarlet Pearmain (synonym of
    Kaighn) 113
Scarlet Pearmain (synonym of
    Long Red Pearmain) 125
SCARLET PIPPIN 196
Schafnasé 29
Scharlottenthaler Golba 222
Schoone van Boskoop 25
Schoone von Boskoop 25
SCHUYLER SWEET 197

PAGE.

SCOLLOP GILLIFLOWER 197
Scollop Gilliflower (synonym of
    Striped Gilliflower) 207
Scolloped Gilliflower 197
Scott 168
SCOTT BEST 198
Seek-No-Further (synonym of
    Cooper) 40
Seek-No-Further (synonym of
    Green Seek-no-Further)..... 88
Seever's Red Streak 230
SENECA FAVORITE 198
Seneca Favorite (synonym of
    Quince [of Coxe]) 174
Seneca Spice 174
Shaker's Yellow 53
Shannon 149
SHARP 199
Sharpe's Early 212
Sharpe's Spice 64
Sheepnose (synonym of Egg
    Top) 56
Sheepnose (synonym of Long
    Red Pearmain) 125
SHERMAN 200
Sherman's Favorite 200
Sherman's Sweet 200
Sherwood's Favorite 33
Shiawasse Beauty 201
SHIAWASSEE 69, 201
Shiawassee Beauty 201
Shiawassie Beauty 201
Shoreditch White 96
Shropshirevine 203
Siberian August 112
SINE-QUA-NON 202
Skvosnoi krasnoi 182
Skwosnoi Krasnoi 182
Skwosnoi Schotoi 248
Sleeper's Yellow 53
SLINGERLAND 202
Slingerland's Fall Pippin 202
Slingerland Pippin 202
Small Admirable 1
Small's Admirable 1
Smithfield Spice 49
Smokehouse (synonym of Van-
    devere Pippin) 231

PAGE.

Smyrna 33
Snow 65
Solotoc Renet 79
SOMERSET (N. Y.) 203
Sops in Wine 203
SOPS OF WINE 203
Sourbough (synonym of Cham-
    plain) 30
SOUR BOUGH 204
Sour Bough (synonym of Cham-
    plain) 30
Sour Bough (synonym of Tart
    Bough) 220
Sour Harvest 168
Speckled 60
SPECTATOR 204
Spiced Oxeye 231
Staalclubs 231
Staalcubs 230
Stalcubs 230
STARKEY 205
STARR 206
Steklianka pesotchnaya 195
Stewart's Nonpareil 112
Stillman 207
STILLMAN EARLY 207
Stillman's Early 207
Stoke Tulip 3
Straat 208
Strawberry (synonym of Sops of
    Wine) 203
Strawberry (synonym of Che-
    nango) 33
Strawberry (synonym of Late
    Strawberry) 120
Strawberry (synonym of Richard
    Graft) 186
Strawberry 207
Striped Ashmore 231
Striped Bellflower 207
STRIPED FAMEUSE 68
STRIPED GILLIFLOWER 207
Striped Harvest 93
Striped Juneating 142
Striped Pearmain 125
Striped Quarrendon 142
STRIPED RED JUNE 182
Striped Shropshire 55

PAGE.

Striped Vandervere 231
STROAT 208
Strode 208
STRODE BIRMINGHAM 208
Strode's 208
Strode's Birmingham 208
Strohmer 85
Stromling 85
STUMP 209
Stymer's 210
STYMUS 210
SUFFOLK BEAUTY 210
Suislepper 219
Summer Bellefleur 211
SUMMER BELLFLOWER 211
Summer Bellflower (synonym of
    Autumn Bough) 10
Summer Hagloe 92
SUMMER PEARMAIN 211
Summer Pippin (synonym of
    Champlain) 30
Summer Pippin (synonym of
    Fall Pippin) 62
Summer Pippin (synonym of
    Holland Pippin) 101
SUMMER QUEEN 212
SUMMER RAMBO 213
Summer Rambo (synonym of....
    Grosh) 89
Summer Rambour 213
SUMMER REDSTREAK 214
SUMMER ROSE 215
Summer Russet 218
SUMMER SPITZENBURG 215
Summer Spitzenburgh 215
SUMMER SWEET 216
Summer Sweet (synonym of
    Hightop Sweet) 98
Summer Sweeting (synonym of
    Summer Sweet) 216
Summer Sweeting (synonym of
    Hightop Sweet) 98
Summer Traveller 142
Superior White 157
Susy Clark 181
Svinsovka 121
Swedish Borsdorf of Patten 5
SWEET BOUGH 216

PAGE.

SWEET FALL PIPPIN 218
Sweet Golden Pippin 12
Sweet Harvest 217
Sweet June 98
Sweet Lyman's Pumpkin 172
Sweet Pippin 100
Sweet Rambo 89
SWEET RUSSET 218
Sweet Russet (synonym of
    Pumpkin Russet) 170
Sweet Russet (synonym of
    Cheeseboro) 33
Sweet's Harvest 212
Sweet Swaar 12
Sweet Wine 64
Swett's Harvest 212
Swinez 121
Swinzovska 121
SWITZER 218
SYLVESTER 220

Taffitai 239
Tallow 128
Tallow Apple 128
Tallow Pippin 128
Tars Thorn 45
TART BOUGH 220
Tart Bough (synonym of Early
    Harvest) 51
Tart Bough (synonym of Cham-
    plain) 30
Teignmouth 223
Tennessee Early Red 55
Tete d'Ange 29
Tete de Chat 29
Tetoffsky 220
Tetofski (synonym of July).... 112
Tetofski (synonym of Tetofsky). 220
TETOFSKY 220
Tetofsky (synonym of July).... 112
THALER 222
THOMPSON 222
Thompson Seedling No. 24..... 222
Thompson No. 24 222
Thompson's Seedling No. 29.... 111
Thompson's Seedling No. 38.... 90
TINMOUTH 223

PAGE.

Tinmouth Sweet 223
Titovca 224
TITOVKA 224
Titowka 224
Titus Apple 224
Titus Riga 224
Tom Harryman 85
Tompkins 49
Tom Put 225
TOM PUTT 225
Transparente de Astracan...... 239
Transparente d'Ete 239
Transparent de Muscovie 239
Transparente de Muscovie d'Ete. 239
Transparente de Saint-Leger
    (synonym of Vineuse Rouge). 233
Transparente de Saint-Leger
    (synonym of Yellow Trans-
    parent) 248
Transparente de Zurich 239
Transparente Jaune (synonym of
    Vineuse Rouge) 233
Transparente Jaune (synonym of
    Yellow Transparent) 248
Transparente Rouge 233
Transparente Verte 233
Transparent Muscovie 239
Travers 184
Travers Apple 184
Travers Peppin 184
Travers Pippin 184
Travers Reinette 184
Trenton Early 81
Tsarskui Schip 45
TUFTS 226
Tufts Baldwin 226
Tufts Seedling 226
Turn Off Lane 174
TWENTY OUNCE 227
Twenty Ounce Pippin 227
TYRE BEAUTY 229

Uncle Sam's Best 64
Underdunk 30
UTTER 229
Utter's Large Red 230
Utter's Red 230

PAGE.

Vandervere (synonym of Van-
devere) 230
Vandervere (synonym of Van-
devere Pippin) 231
Vandervere Pippin 231
Vandeveer 230
VANDEVERE 230
VANDEVERE PIPPIN 231
Vandevere Yellow 231
Van Duym's Pippin 62
Van Dyne Apple 77
Van Dyn's Pippin 62
Van Kleek's Sweet 100
Vargul 6
Vermillon d'Ete 178
Vermont 30
Vermont Pippin 223
Vermont Pumpkin Sweet 172
Vermont Sweet 172
VICTORIA 231
Victoria Sweet 231
Victoria Sweeting 231
VICTUALS AND DRINK 233
Vilikui Mogul 87
VINEUSE ROUGE 233
Vinnoe Krasnoe Osennee 182
Vinograd 244
Virginia June 142
Virginia Sweet 177
Voronesh No. 21 247

Wabash Bellflower 125
Walter Pease 161
Walworth 30
Warden's Pie Apple 203
Ward's Pippin 21
Warren Pennock 53
Washington (synonym of Sops
of Wine) 203
Washington (synonym of Wash-
ington Strawberry) 234
Washington (synonym of Sweet
Bough) 217
Washington Co. Seedling 234
Washington of Maine 234
WASHINGTON STRAWBERRY 234
WATER 236
Waterloo 178

PAGE.

Watkins Early 211
Watson's Vandervere 231
Watson's Vandevere 231
WEALTHY 236
Weinapfel Rother 182
Weinappel Rother 182
Weiser Hawthornden 96
Wells 148
Westbrook 60
WESTERN BEAUTY 239
Western Beauty (synonym of
Grosh) 89
Western Beauty (synonym of
Ohio Nonpareil) 148
Wheelers Kernel 96
White Apple (synonym of Haw-
thornden) 96
White Apple (synonym of Parry
White) 157
White Astracan 239
WHITE ASTRACHAN 239
White Borodovka 15
White Graft of Wisconsin 60
White Hawthorndean 96
White Hawthornden 96
White June 118
WHITE JUNEATING 240
White Newell 60
White Seek-No-Further 88
WHITE SPANISH REINETTE 241
White Spice 49
WILLIAMS 242
Williams Early 242
Williams Early Red 242
Williams Favorite 242
Williams Favorite Red 242
Williams Red 242
Willis Sweet 244
Willis Sweeting 244
Wilsons June 181
Windower 231
Wine (synonym of Egg Top) . . . 56
Wine (synonym of Fall Wine) . . 64
Wine (synonym of Richard
Graft) 186
Wine (synonym of Twenty
Ounce) 227
Wine of Cole 64

PAGE.

WINE RUBETS 244
Winter Chandler 31
Winter Golden Sweet 13
Winter Pearmain (synonym of
   Long Island Pearmain)....... 124
Winter Pearmain (synonym of
   Long Red Pearmain)........ 125
Winter Seek-No-Further 88
WINTHROP GREENING 245
WOLF RIVER 245
Wolf River (synonym of Alex-
   der) 3
Wolman's Harvest 215
Woodstock (synonym of Blen-
   heim) 21
Woodstock (synonym of Dyer). 49
Woodstock Pippin 21
Woolman's Early 215
Woolman's Harvest 215
Woolman's Striped Harvest 215
Woolverton 127
WORKAROE 246
Wunderapfel 3

Yankee Apple 172
Yellow Bough 217
YELLOW CALVILLE 247
Yellow Flat 118
Yellow Harvest 51
Yellow June (synonym of White
   Juneating) 240

Yellow June (synonym of Kirk-
   bridge) 118
Yellow Juneating 51
Yellow May 240
Yellow Summer Pearmain 166
Yellow Sweeting 81
YELLOW TRANSPARENT 247
Yellow Transparent (synonym
   of Thaler) 222
Yellow Vandervere 231
YOPP 249
Yopp's Favorite 249
YORK 249
York and Lancaster 193
York Pippin (synonym of Fall
   Pippin) 62
York Pippin (synonym of Golden
   Pippin I).................. 78
York Pippin (synonym of White
   Spanish Reinette) 241
York Russet (synonym of
   Cheeseboro) 33
York Russet (synonym of
   Pumpkin Russet) 170
York Russeting 33

Zarskischip 45
Zarski Schip 45
Zarski Zars 45
Zolotoi Renet 79
Zour Bough 168
Zuzoff of Tuttle 5

CRABAPPLES.

Amber Crab 269

Baccata fructa oblonga......... 261
BAILEY CRIMSON 251
Bailey's Crimson 251
Briar Sweet 251
BRIER 251
Brier's Sweet 251
Brier Sweet (synonym of Brier) 251
Brier Sweet (synonym of Van
   Wyck) 268
CHERRY 252

CORAL 252
CURRANT 253
Current Crab 253

DARTMOUTH 253

EXCELSIOR 254

FLORENCE 255

GIBB 256
Golden Beauty 269

PAGE.

Hislop 257
HYSLOP 257

LARGE RED SIBERIAN........... 258
LARGE YELLOW SIBERIAN....... 258

MARENGO 259
Marengo No. 1 259
Marengo Winter Crab 259
MARTHA 259
MINNESOTA 260
Montreal 261
MONTREAL BEAUTY 261

OBLONG 261
Oblong-Fruited Siberian Crab.. 261
Oblong Siberian Crab 261
ORANGE 261

PAUL IMPERIAL 262
PICTA STRIATA 263
Picta 263
Picta Striata 263
Pomme Groseille 253

PAGE.

QUAKER 263
QUEEN CHOICE 264
Queen's Choice 264

RED SIBERIAN 264

SEPTEMBER 264
Siberian Crab (synonym of Red
  Siberian) 264
Siberian Crab (synonym of Yel-
  low Siberian) 269
SOULARD 265

TRANSCENDENT 266
Transcendant 267

VAN WYCK 267
Van Wyck (synonym of Brier). 251
Van Wyck Siberian 268
Van Wyck Sweet 268

WHITNEY 268
Whitney No. 20 268

YELLOW SIBERIAN 269

COMBINED INDEX TO VARIETIES.

Volumes 1 and 2.

(Accepted names appear wholly or in part in roman type; synonyms in italic.)

	VOL. I. PAGE.	VOL. II. PAGE.
Abe Lincoln		178
Aberdeen	227	
Accidental	227	
Acuba-leaf Reinette	52	
Acuba-leaved Reinette	52	
ADIRONDACK		1
ADMIRABLE		1
Æsopus Spitzemberg	120	
Æsopus Spitzenberg	120	
Æsopus Spitzenburg	120	
Æsopus Spitzenburgh	120	
Aiken	41	
Aikens Winter (of Downing)	41	
Aikin's Red	41	
Aken	41	
AKIN	41	
Akin Red	41	
Akin Seedling	41	
Akin's Red	41	
Albemarle	146	
Albemarle Pippin	18, 146	
Albertin		3
ALBION		2
ALEXANDER	17, 18, 20, 25	3
ALEXANDER GROUP	25	
Alexander the First		3
Alexandre		3
Alleghany	227	
ALLINGTON	42	
Allington Pippin	42	
ALLISON	43	
Almindelig	181	
AMASSIA	44	
Amber Crab		269

	VOL. I. PAGE.	VOL. II. PAGE.
American		110
American Beauty (synonym of Sterling).............	45, 319	
American Beauty (synonym of Sheriff)..................	308	
American Blush	45	
American Blush (synonym of Hubbardston).............	161	
American Fall		62
American Fall Pippin		241
American Gloria Mundi.............................		77
American Golden		83
American Golden Pippin.............................		83
American Golden Russet...............................	89	
American Golden Russet (of New England).............	164	
American Mammoth		77
American Mother		143
American Newtown Pippin............................	146	
American Nonparcille	161	
American Pearmain		211
American Pippin	45	
American Red		178
American Red Juneating		55
American Seek-No-Further	273	
American Summer		211
American Summer Pearmain		211
Amos	46	
Amos Jackson	46	
Amsterdam		5
Amsterdam Sweet		5
Andrews	46	
Andrews Winter	46	
Anglesea Pippin		178
Anis	26	
Anisim		5
Anisim (of Peterson)		5
Antenovka		6
Antonowka		6
Antonovka		6
Antony		6
Api	181	
Api eller	181	
Api Fin	181	
Api Ordinaire	181	
Api Petit	181	
Api Rose	181	
Api Rouge	181	
Aport		6
Aport Group	20, 25	
Aport (synonym of Aport Orient)......................		7
Aporta		3

	VOL. I. PAGE.	VOL. II. PAGE.
Aporta Nalivia		3
APORT ORIENT		7
Aport Oriental		7
Apple of Commerce	66	
Apple of the Well	363	
Apy Rouge	181	
Arabka		32
ARCTIC	24	7
Arkad Krasiwui		14
Arkad Krasivui		14
Arcad Krasivui		14
ARKANSAS	24, 47	
Arkansas Baptist	140	
ARKANSAS BEAUTY	49	
ARKANSAS BLACK	24, 49	
Arkansas Black (synonym of Arkansas)	47	
Arkansas Black Twig	47, 50	
Arkansaw	47	
ARNOLD	50	
Arnold's Beauty	50	
Aromatic Spike No. 354		233
Arsapple	116	
ARTHUR	51	
Astracan Blanch		239
Astracan d'Ete		239
Astracanischer Sommer		239
Astracan Rouge		178
Astrachan		178
Astrachan Red		178
Astrakhan Rouge		178
Astrachan White		239
Astrachan Rouge		178
Astravaskoe		155
Aubertin		3
AUCUBA	52	
Acubæfolia	52	
AUGUST		9
August (synonym of July)		112
August Apple		53
AUGUSTINE		10
August Sweet		216
August Sweeting		216
Aunt Dorcas	145	
Aunt Ginnie		75
Aurora		227
Austin	236	
Autumnal Bough		10
Autumnal Swaar (synonym of Autumn Swaar)		11

	VOL. I. PAGE.	VOL. II. PAGE.
Autumnal Swaar (synonym of Autumn Sweet Swaar)....		12
Autumnal Sweet		12
Autumnal Sweet Swaar		12
AUTUMN BOUGH	15	10
Autumn Bough (synonym of Sweet Bough).............		216
Autumn Pearmain (synonym of Winter Pearmain).......	378	
Autumn Pearmain (synonym of Long Island Pearmain)..		124
Autumn Pippin		62
Autumn Rose		190
Autumn Seeknofurther		88
Autumn Strawberry		120
AUTUMN STREAKED		10
AUTUMN SWAAR		11, 12
Autumn Swaar (synonym of Autumn Sweet Swaar)....		12
Autumn Sweet		12
Autumn Sweet Bough		10
AUTUMN SWEET SWAAR		12
Avery Sweet		175
BABBITT	53	
Babouskino		83
Babuscheno		83
Babuschkino		83
Babushkino		83
Baccata fructa oblonga		261
Bachelor	88	
Back Creek	146	
Baer	158	
BAILEY CRIMSON (Crab)		251
Bailey's Golden Sweet...............................	54	
BAILEY SPICE..		13
Bailey's Spice		13
BAILEY SWEET	54	
Bailey Sweet (synonym of Sweet Winesap).............	333	
BAKER	55	
BAKER SWEET		13
Baker's Sweet		13
BALDWIN............................12, 15, 17, 18, 19, 24, 32,	56	
Baldwin Rosenapfel	56	
Baldwin's Rother Pippin.............................	56	
Ball Apple	250	
Baltimore (synonym of Roseau)	292	
Baltimore (synonym of Gloria Mundi).................		77
Baltimore (synonym of Vandevere Pippin).............		231
Baltimore Pippin (synonym of Ben Davis).............	69	
Baltimore Pippin (synonym of Gloria Mundi)...........		77
Baltimore Red	69	
Baltimore Red Streak................................	69	
Banana	377	

	VOL. I. PAGE.	VOL. II. PAGE.
Banana Sweet	60, 377	
Banks		14
Banks Gravenstein		14
Banks Red Gravenstein		14
Baptist	61	
Barbel	61	
Bard Apple		49
Baroveski		151
Barowiski		151
Barretts Spitzenburgh	225	
Barringer	62	
Barry	63	
Batchellor	88	
Batullen	64	
Baxter	64	
Baxter's Red	64	
Beach	66	
Beard Burden		49
Beaute de Kent		15
Beautiful Arcad		14
Beautiful Arcade		14
Beautiful Pippin		184
Beauty	324	
Beauty of America	45, 319	
Beauty of Kent		15
Beauty of Queen		3
Beauty of the West (synonym of Western Beauty)		239
Beauty of the West (synonym of Grosh)		89
Beauty Red		40
Bec de Lievre	264	
Beel Solotofskaja		82
Beitigheimer		17
Belborodooskoe		15
Belle Bonde	75	
Belle Bonne	75	
Belle d'Angers		21
Belle de Boscoop		25
Belle de Boskoop		25
Belle d'Orleans		3
Belle de Rome	290	
Belle Dubois		77
Belle et Bonne	67	
Belle Fille	264	
Belle Flavoise	381	
Belle-fleur	381	
Belle-fleur jaune	381	
Belle-Flower	381	
Belleflower Improved	204	

	VOL. I. PAGE.	VOL. II. PAGE.
Belle Josephine (synonym of Gloria Mundi).............		77
Belle Josephine (synonym of White Spanish Reinette)....		241
Belle of Boskoop		25
Bellerdovskoe		15
Belle Rose		168
Bell-Flower	381	
Bellflower	381	
Bellflower of the West.................................		148
Bell's Early		203
Bell's Favorite		203
Bellyband	67	
BELMONT	67	
Belmont Late	.67	
Belpre Russet.....	293	
BEN DAVIS 17, 18, 19, 21, 24,	68	
Ben Ford...		45
Benniger		15
BENNINGER		15
Bennington		203
BENONI		16
BENTLEY	71	
Bentley's Sweet..	71	
Bergamot		6
BERGEN	72	
Berry	227	
Berry Apple..		39
Bersford	269	
BESS POOL..	72	
Best Pool	72	
BETHEL 19, 24, 72,	321	
BETHLEHEMITE	74	
Bethlemite	74	
Bielborodovska		15
BIETIGHEIMER		17
Big Hill (synonym of Nickajack).......................	227	
Big Hill (synonym of Pryor)...........................	269	
Big Rambo (synonym of Western Beauty)................		239
Big Rambo (synonym of Grosh)........................		89
Big Romanite (synonym of Greyhouse).................	153	
Big Romanite (synonym of Pennock)....................	255	
Big Sweet..		233
Big Vandevere..		231
BILLY BOND..	75	
BIRTH		18
Bishop's Pippin of Nova Scotia.........................	381	
BISMARCK	25	19
Bismark		19
Black American	79	

	VOL. I. PAGE.	VOL. II. PAGE.
BLACK ANNETTE	76	20
Black Apple (synonym of Black *Jersey*)	79	
Black Apple (synonym of Detroit Red)		46
Black Baldwin	60	
BLACK BEN DAVIS	76	
Black Ben Davis (synonym of Gano)	135	
Blackburn	88	
Black Detroit		46
BLACK GILLIFLOWER	12, 16, 17, 18, 32, 77	
Black Jack	153	
BLACK JERSEY	79	
BLACK LADY APPLE	182	
Black Pennock	153	
Black Spitz	77	
Black Spitzenberg	132	
Black Spy	189	
Black Sweet	219	
Black Twig	247	
Black Vandervere	153	
Black Vandevere	153	
Blair	208	
Blanche		241
Blanche d'Espagne		241
Blanche Glacee d'Ete		239
BLENHEIM		20
Blenheim Orange		21
Blenheim Pippin		21
Blenheimsrenett		21
BLOOM		69
Blooming Orange		21
Blue Baldwin	60	
BLUE PEARMAIN	17, 18, 19, 24, 80	
BLUE PEARMAIN GROUP	24	
Blumen Calvill		85
BLUSHED CALVILLE		22
Blushed June		181
Blush June		181
Boatman's Seedling	359	
Bogdanoff (synonym of Bogdanoff Glass)	81	
Bogdanoff (synonym of Grandmother)		83
BOGDANOFF GLASS	81	
Bogdanoff Steklianka		83
Bohannon		118
BOIKEN	82	
Boiken Apfel	82	
Bonford	269	
BONUM		23
BOROVINKA		24

	VOL. I. PAGE.	VOL. II. PAGE.
Borovinka Angluskaia		24
Borovitsky (synonym of Oldenburg)	25	151
Borovitsky (synonym of Borovinka)		24
Borowicki		151
Borowitski		151
Borowitsky		151
BORSDORF	83	
Borsdorfer (synonym of Borsdorf)	84	
Borsdorfer (synonym of Anisim)		5
BOSKOOP		25
BOSTON RUSSET	85	
Boston Russet (synonym of Roxbury)	293	
BOTTLE GREENING	24, 85	
BOUCKEN	86	
Bough		216
Bough, Early Sweet		216
Bough Sweet		26, 216
Bow Apple		216
Bowers Apple	329	
BOYS DELIGHT	86	
Bracken		240
Bracy's Seck-No-Further		88
Brandywine	213	
Bread and Cheese	273	
BRESKOVKA		26
Briar Sweet		251
BRIER (Crab)		251
Brier Sweet (synonym of Brier)		251
Brier Sweet (synonym of Van Wyck)		268
BRILLIANT		69
BRISTOL	86	
Bristol (synonym of Red Canada)	276	
Broad River	289	
Brooke Pippin	146	
Brown' Golden Sweet	343	
BROWNLEES	86	
Brownlees Russet	86	
Brownlees Seedling Russet	86	
BROWN SWEET	87	
BUCKINGHAM	18, 88	
Buckley		33
Buckram		97
Buchanan		149
Buler	174	
BULLOCK	15, 89	
Bullock (synonym of Hunt Russet)	164	
Bullock's Pippin (synonym of Bullock)	89	
Bullock's Pippin (synonym of Ewalt)	124	

	VOL. I. PAGE.	VOL. II. PAGE.
Bullripe		49
Bunker Hill		27
Burlington	225	
Burlington Greening	282	
Burlington Spitzenberg	225	
Butter		27
Butter Pippin		78
Byers	88	
Byers Red	88	
Cabane du Chien		98
Cabashaw		227
Cabashea (*Winter*)	91, 176	
Cabashea		28
Cabashea (synonym of Twenty Ounce Pippin)	349	
Cabashie		28
Calkin's Pippin		30
Calville Butter	56	
Calville de Gravenstein		85
Calville Grafensteiner	85	
Calville Krasmui		22
Cambour des Lorrains		213
Camoisas du roi d'Espagne		241
Camoise Blanche		241
Camoisee Blanche		241
Campfield	91	
Camuesar		241
Camuezas		241
Camuzar		241
Canada Baldwin	25, 92	69
Canada Peach		159
Canada Pippin (synonym of Canada Reinette)	93	
Canada Pippin (synonym of White Pippin)	368	
Canada Red (synonym of Red Canada)	276	
Canada Red (synonym of Roseau)	292	
Canada Redstreak	276	
Canada Reinette	32, 93	
Canada Reinette (synonym of Cheeseboro)		33
Canadian Reinette	93	
Canadisk Reinet	93	
Canfield	91	
Cannon Pearmain	95	
Capp Mammoth	206	
Cardinale	181	
Carlough	95	
Carnation Apple	96	
Carolina (synonym of Nickajack)	227	
Carolina (synonym of White Juneating)		240
Carolina June		181

	VOL. I. PAGE.	VOL. II. PAGE.
Carolina Red		181
Carolina Red June		181
Carolina Red Streak	69	
Carolina Spice	227	
Caroline (synonym of Nickajack)	227	
Caroline (synonym of White Juneating)		240
CARPENTIN	96	
Carpentin Reinette	96	
Carthouse	138	
CATHEAD		29
Cathead (synonym of Cheeseboro)		33
Cathead (synonym of Fall Pippin)		62
Cathead Greening		29
Catshead		29
Catshead Greening		29
Cattell Apple		148
Caux	114	
Cayuga Red Streak		227
CAYWOOD	96	
CELESTIA		29
Chaltram Pippin	227	
Champion	99	
Champion Red	99	
CHAMPLAIN		30
CHANDLER		31
Chandler's Red		31
CHARLAMOFF		32
Charlamoski		32
Charlamovskoe		32
Charlamowiski		151
Charlamowski d'Automne		151
Charlamowskircher Nalleoid		151
Charlamowskoe		32
Charlamowsky		151
Charles Apple	199	
Charlottenthaler		222
Charlottenthaler Apple		222
Charlottenthaler Golba		222
Charmant Blanc		213
Chase	166	
Chatham Pippin	227	
Cheat (synonym of Domine)	109	
Cheat (synonym of Wells)	363	
Cheatan Pippin	227	
Cheataw	227	
Cheesborough		33
CHEESEBORO		33
Cheeseboro's Russet		33

	VOL. I. PAGE.	VOL. II. PAGE.
Cheeseborough		33
Cheeseborough Russet		33
CHENANGO		33
Chenango Strawberry		33
CHERRY (Crab)		252
Chimney Apple		65
Christ Birth		18
Christ Birth Apple		18
Christmas		18
Christmas Apple	181	
Christ's Golden Reinette	114	
Choice Kentuck	311	
Cider	311	
Cider Apple	311	
Cinnamon		6
CLAPPER FLAT		34
CLARKE		35
Clarke Beauty		35
CLAYTON	96	
Cling Tight	109	
Clothes-yard Apple	145	
CLYDE		36
Clyde Beauty		36
Coalbrook		225
Cobbett's Fall (synonym of Fall Pippin)		62
Cobbett's Fall (synonym of White Spanish Reinette)		241
Cobbett's Fall Pippin (synonym of Fall Pippin)		62
Cobbett's Fall Pippin (synonym of White Spanish Reinette)		241
CODLING		117
Codlin, Keswick		117
Coe's Spice		49
COFFELT	97	
Coffelt Beauty	97	
Coggeswell	98	
COGSWELL	98	
Cogswell Pearmain	98	
Coleman		227
Cole's Quince		174
COLLAMER		36
Collamer Twenty Ounce		36
COLLINS	99	
Collins' Red	99	
COLTON		37
Colton Early		37
COLVERT		38
Combermere Apple	206	
Compound	329	

	VOL. I. PAGE.	VOL. II. PAGE.
Compte Orloff		233
Comte Woronzoff		3
Concombre Ancien (synonym of Fall Pippin)		62
Concombre Ancien (synonym of White Spanish Reinette)		241
Conford	269	
Conic June		118
Connecticut Seek-No-Further	364	
CONSTANTINE		39
Coon	107	
Coon Red	107	
COOPER	16	40
COOPER MARKET	100	
Cooper's Red (synonym of Cooper Market)	101	
Cooper's Red (synonym of Etowah)	123	
Cooper's Redling	101	
Copmanthorpe Crab	114	
Copp's Mammoth		77
Corail		3
CORAL (Crab)		252
CORNELL		40
Cornell Fancy		41
Cornell's Favorite		41
Cornell's Savewell	299	
CORNER		41
CORNISH GILLIFLOWER	138	
Cornish Gilliflower (synonym of Scollop Gilliflower)		197
Corse's St. Lawrence		193
Cos Orange		42
Coss Champion	99	
Costard		29
Costard Ray		29
Count Orloff		233
Coustard		29
COX ORANGE		42
Cox's Orange Pippin		42
Cox's Pomona		165
CRANBERRY PIPPIN	300	43
Crandall Seedling		107
Crane's Pippin	244	
CREAM		44
Crimson Beauty		196
Crimson Pippin (synonym of Scarlet Pippin)		196
Crimson Pippin (synonym of Detroit Red)		46
Crimson Scarlet Pippin		196
CROTTS	102	
CROW EGG		44
CROWNS	102	
Cuir, De	264	

	VOL. I. PAGE.	VOL. II. PAGE.
Cumming's Rambo		89
CURRANT (Crab)	3	253
Current (Crab)		253
Curtis Greening	331	
Cut Wine		244
Czarskui Schip		45
CZAR THORN		45
Dahlonega	227	
Dame de Menage	206	
DANVERS *Sweet*	103	
Danvers Winter	103	
Danvers Winter Sweet	15, 103	
Dark Baldwin	60	
DARTMOUTH (Crab)		253
DEACON JONES	104	
DEADERICK		45
Dean's Codlin		165
De Bretagne	93	
De Cuir	264	
De Glace d'Ete		239
De Glace Hative		239
Deiltz	201	
De La Madeleine Rouge		55
Delaware	273	
Delaware Red Winter	189	
Delaware Winter	189	
De Lorraine		213
Demary		73
DEMOCRAT	105	
De Muscovie d'Ete		239
De Neige		65
De Notre-Dame		213
De Rambourg		213
De Rambure		213
De Rateau		62
De Ratteau		241
Der Carpentin	96	
De Revel (synonym of Yellow Transparent)...............		248
De Revel (synonym of Vineuse Rouge)		233
Derrick and Ann..		186
Derrick's Graft		186
Der Schwere Apfel.......................................	326	
De Seigneur d'Automne...................................		29
D'Espagne (synonym of Fall Pippin).....................		62
D'Espagne (synonym of White Spanish Reinette).......		241
Deterding's Early		178
Detroit (synonym of Ortley)............................	244	
Detroit (synonym of Detroit Red).......................		46

	VOL. I. PAGE.	VOL. II. PAGE.
Detroit Black		46
DETROIT RED	12	46
Detroit of the West	244	
D'Eve		141
De Vin du Conn		227
Dewit Apple	107	
De Witt	107	
Dickenson	106	
DICKINSON	106	
Die Haarlemer Reinette	93	
Diels Sommerkönig		85
Die Weiberreinette	93	
DISHAROON	107	
Dix-huit Onces		227
DOCTOR	17, 107	
Doctor Dewitt	107	
DOCTOR WALKER	108	
Dodge's Black	79	
Dodge's Early Red		203
DOMINE	17, 109	
Domine (synonym of Wells?)	363	
Dominie	109	
Doppelte Casselar Reinette	114	
D'Or d'Angleterre	141	
DOUBLE ROSE	110	
Douse		95
Downing's Winter Maiden Blush	152	
Dows		95
Dowse		95
Dredge's Fame		21
DU BOIS	111	
Duchess		151
Duchesse d'Oldenbourg		151
Duchess No. 3		158
Duchess of Oldenburg		48, 151
Duchess of Oldenburgh		151
Ducks Bill	378	
DUDLEY		48
Dudley Winter		48
Duitsch Mignonne	114	
DUKE OF DEVONSHIRE	111	
Duke of Wellington	112	
Du Marechal		65
DUMELOW	112	
Dumelow's Crab	112	
Dumelow's Pippin	112	
Dumelow's Seedling	112	
Dumpling		208

	VOL. I. PAGE.	VOL. II. PAGE.
DUNCAN	113	
Durable Trois ans	116	
Dutchess		151
Dutchess of Oldenberg		151
Dutch Greening	253	
DUTCH MIGNONNE	32, 114	
Dutch Mignonne (synonym of Blenheim)		21
Dutch Minion	114	
Duverson's June		141
DUZENBURY	115	
DYER		49
Early Baldwin		168
Early Bough		216
EARLY CHANDLER	16	
Early Colton		37
Early Congress		85
Early French Reinette (synonym of Early Harvest)		51
Early French Reinette (synonym of Sweet Bough)		216
Early Golden Sweet		81
EARLY HARVEST	15, 17, 18	50
Early Jack		106
Early Jennetting		240
EARLY JOE		52
Early July Pippin		51
Early June (synonym of Early Harvest)		51
Early June (synonym of Egg Top)		56
Early June of South		141
Early Margaret		141
Early May		240
EARLY PENNOCK		53
Early Red		141
Early Red Juneating		141
Early Red Margaret		141
Early Red Pippin		93
Early Redstreak		93
Early Red Streak		93
EARLY RIPE		54
EARLY STRAWBERRY	15, 17	54
Early Striped Juneating		141
Early Summer Pearmain		211
Early Sweet		98
Early Sweet Bough		216
Early Sweetheart		216
Early Tart Harvest		168
Early Washington		203
Edelborsdorfer	84	
Edgar County Red Streak	357	
Edgar Red Streak	357	

	VOL. I. PAGE.	VOL. II. PAGE.
Edgerly Sweet	54	
EDWARDS	115	
Edwards (synonym of Nickajack)	227	
Edwards Favorite	115	
Edward Shantee	227	
Egg Jop		44
EGG TOP		56
Eighteen Ounce		227
Eighteen Ounce Apple		227
EISER	116	
Eiser Rouge	116	
ELGIN PIPPIN		56
Elgin Pippin (synonym of White Spanish Reinette)		241
ELLSWORTH	117	
Empereur Alexandre I		3
Empereur Alexandre de Russie		3
Empereur de Russie		3
Emperor Alexander		3
Englese Orange Appel		154
Englische Granat-Reinette		184
Englischer Pepping		57
English Beauty of Pennsylvania	109	
English Borovinka		24
ENGLISH CODLING		117
English Golden	143	
English Golden Pippin	141	
English Golden Russet	143	
English Jannetting		230
English King		3
ENGLISH PEARMAIN	16	
English Pearmain (synonym of Long Red Pearmain)		125
ENGLISH PIPPIN		57
English Pippin (synonym of Longfield)		123
English Pippin (synonym of Golden Reinette)	142	
English Rambo (synonym of Grosh)		89
English Rambo (synonym of Domine)	109	
English Rambo (synonym of Wells)	363	
English Red Streak (synonym of Domine)	109	
English Red Streak (synonym of Redstreak)	278	
English Red Streak (synonym of Wells)	363	
English Redstreak	278	
ENGLISH RUSSET	118	
English Russet (synonym of Long Island Russet I)	194	
English Spitzemberg	225	
English Spitzenberg	225	
English Sweet		58, 175
English Sweeting		175
English Vandevere	312	

	VOL. I. PAGE.	VOL. II. PAGE.
English Winter Red Streak (synonym of Domine)	109	
English Winter Red Streak (synonym of Wells)	363	
Episcopal		62
Episcopale		241
Eppes Sweet	103	
Epse's Sweet	103	
Equinetely	88	
Ernst's Apple		149
Ernst's Pippin		149
Esopus	120	
Esopus Spitzenberg	121	
Esopus Spitzenberg	121	
Esopus Spitzenberg (New)	172	
ESOPUS *Spitzenburg* 12, 15, 16, 17, 18, 19, 24,	120	
Esopus Spitzenburgh	121	
Essex Pippin		184
ETOWAH	123	
Etowah (synonym of Cooper Market)...............	101	
ETRIS	123	
Eve		56
Eve Apple (synonym of Egg Top)...............		56
Eve Apple (synonym of Margaret)...............		141
Everbearing		108
EVENING PARTY	123	
EWALT	124	
EXCELSIOR (Crab)		254
Faldwalder	125	
FALIX	125	
FALLAWATER 18, 32,	125	
Fall Bough		10
Fall de Waldes	125	
Fallenwalder	125	
Fall Geneting		59
Fall Gennetting		59
FALL GREENING		58
Fall Green Sweet		233
FALL HARVEY		58
Fall Jenetting		59
FALL JENNETING		59
Fall Jennetting		59
FALL ORANGE		12, 60
FALL PIPPIN 12, 15, 16, 17, 18,	24	61
FALL PIPPIN GROUP	24	
Fall Pippin (synonym of Fall Harvey)		58
Fall Pippin (synonym of Holland Pippin)		101
Fall Pippin (synonym of White Spanish Reinette)		241
Fall Queen (synonym of Buckingham)	88	
Fall Queen (synonym of Haas)		91

	VOL. I. PAGE.	VOL. II. PAGE.
Fall Queen of Kentucky	88	
Fall Romanite	273	
Fall Strawberry		120
Fall Stripe		196
Fall Swaar		11
Fall Swaar of the West		11
Fall Vandervere		231
FALL WINE		63
Fall Winesap	89	
FAMEUSE	15, 16, 17, 18, 19, 23, 25	65
Fameuse (synonym of Utter)		230
Fameuse Baldwin		98
FAMEUSE, GREEN		69
FAMEUSE GROUP	20, 25	68
FAMEUSE NOIRE		69
FAMEUSE SUCRE		69
FAMILY	127	
FANNY		69
FARRIS	128	
Faust's Rome Beauty	290	
Fay's Russet	164	
Felch	56	
Femme de Menage	206	
FERDINAND	129	
FERRIS	130	
Feuilles D'Aucuba	52	
Filliken	153	
Fin d'Automne		3
Fine Winter	373	
Fink	336	
Fink's Seedling	336	
FISHKILL	32	70
Fishkill Beauty		70
Five-Quartered Gilliflower		197
Flanders Pippin	206	
Flat		34
Flat Spitzenburg	345	
Flint Russet		170
FLORENCE	130	
FLORENCE (Crab)		255
FLORY	131	
Flory Bellflower	131	
Flower (of Genesee)		73
Flushing (synonym of Flushing *Spitzenburg*)	132	
Flushing (synonym of Newtown Spitzenburg)	225	
Flushing Seek-No-Further		88
Flushing Spitzenberg	132	
FLUSHING *Spitzenburg*	132	

	VOL. I. PAGE.	VOL. II. PAGE.
Flushing Spitzenburg	132	
Flushing Spitzenburg (synonym of Roseau)	292	
Flushing Spitzenburgh	132	
Ford		71
Forest	133	
Forever Pippin		33
Formosa		184
Formosa Pippin		184
Fornwalder	125	
Forsythe's Seedling	227	
Fourth of July		112
Fowler	311	
Fraise		55
Fraker	133	
Fraker's Seedling	133	
Franchot		71
Frank		33
Frankfort Queen	88	
Frank Rambour		213
French Pippin	24, 134	
French Pippin (synonym of Holland Pippin)		101
French Pippin (synonym of Roman Stem)		188
French Pippin (synonym of Newark Pippin)	223	
French Rambo		89
French Reinette		215
French Russet	264	
French Spitzenburgh		215
French Spitzenburg of Vermont	292	
Fuller	311	
Fullerton Sweet		71
Funkhouser	69	
Gait	67	
Gano	21, 135	
Garden Royal		72
Gardener's Apple		143
Gardner Sweet Pearmain		73
Gate	67	
Gay's Romanite	255	
Gelber Bellefleur	381	
Gelber Englischer Schönbluhender	381	
Gelee d'Ete		239
General Chandler		31
Genesee Flower		73
Genet	271	
Geneton	271	
Geneva Pearmain		30
Geneva Pippin	136	
Geniton	271	

	VOL. I. PAGE.	VOL. II. PAGE.
Gennetin	271	
Genneting	271	
Gennetting (synonym of Ralls)	271	
Gennetting (synonym of White Juneating)		240
Germaine	378	
German Calville		6
German Calville 324		6
German Green	93	
German Spitzenberg	153	
Georgia June		181
GIBB (Crab)		256
Gibbon's Smokehouse (synonym of Vandevere Pippin)		231
Gibbons Smokehouse (synonym of Smokehouse)	312	
GIDEON		74
GIDEON SWEET	24, 137	
Gideon White		74
Gillet's Seedling	290	
GILLIFLOWER	16	
Gilliflower	77, 138	
GILPIN	17, 32, 138	
Ginet	271	
Ginetting		240
GINNIE		75
GIVENS	140	
Glace de Zelande		239
Glacie d'Ete	239	
GLADSTONE	25	75
Glazenwood		77
Glazenwood Gloria Mundi		77
GLENLOCH	140	
GLORIA MUNDI		76
Glory of York		184
Gloucester Pippin		21
Golden Apple		83
Golden Beauty		269
Golden Gray	328	
GOLDEN MEDAL	141	
GOLDEN PIPPIN	16, 141	
GOLDEN PIPPIN (I)		78
GOLDEN PIPPIN (II)		79
Golden Pippin (synonym of Fall Pippin)		62
Golden Pippin (synonym of Golding)		83
Golden Pippin (synonym of Belmont)	67	
Golden Pippin (synonym of Ortley)	244	
GOLDEN PIPPINS		78
GOLDEN RED	142	
GOLDEN REINETTE	142	79
Golden Rennet	142	

	VOL. I. PAGE.	VOL. II. PAGE.
GOLDEN RUSSET	17, 18, 143, 295	
Golden Russet (synonym of Bullock)	89	
Golden Russet (synonym of Perry Russet)	257	
Golden Russet, American	89	
Golden Russet (not of New York)	164	
Golden Russet of Massachusetts	164	
Golden Russet of New England	164	
Golden Russet of New York	143	
Golden Russet of Western New York	143	
Golden Spice		49
GOLDEN SWEET		81
Golden Sweet (synonym of Northern Sweet)		147
Golden Sweeting		81
GOLDEN WHITE		82
GOLDING		82
Gold Medal	141	
Goldreinette von Blenheim		21
Good Peasant (synonym of Longfield)		123
Good Peasant (synonym of Anisim)		5
Gov. Seward's		227
Gowden	227	
Gowdie	227	
Grafen-Apfel		85
Grafensteiner		85
Graham's Red Warrior	227	
Granat-Reinette		184
Grand Alexander		3
Grand Alexandre		3
Grand Duc Constantin		39
Grand Duke Constantine	25	39
GRANDMOTHER		83
Grand Mother		83
Grandmother's Apple	145	
Grand Sultan (synonym of Vineuse Rouge)		233
Grand Sultan (synonym of Yellow Transparent)		248
GRANITE BEAUTY	145	
Grantham		108
GRAVENSTEIN	12, 15, 17, 18	84
Gravensteiner		85
Gravenstein Rouge		180
Gravenstine		85
Grave Slige		85
Grave Slije		85
Gray Apple (synonym of McAfee)	196	
Gray Apple (synonym of Pomme Grise)	264	
Gray Baldwin	60	
Grayhouse	153	
Gray Romanite (synonym of Greyhouse)	153	
Gray Romanite (synonym of Rambo)	273	

	VOL. I. PAGE.	VOL. II. PAGE.
Gray's Keeper	196	
Greasy Pippin (synonym of Ortley)	244	
Greasy Pippin (synonym of Lowell)		128
GREAT BARBE	145	
GREAT MOGUL		87
Great Pearmain	378	
Green Bellflower	244	
Greening	145, 282	
Green Mountain Pippin (synonym of Fallawater)	125	
Green Mountain Pippin (synonym of Virginia Greening)	352	
GREEN NEWTOWN	17, 18, 24, 145, 149	
Green Newtown Pippin	146	
Green Newton Pippen (synonym of Rhode Island *Greening*)	282	
GREEN PIPPIN	16	
GREEN SEEK-NO-FURTHER		88
GREEN SWEET	150	
Green Sweet (synonym of Repka Malenka)	282	
Green Sweet (synonym of Victuals and Drink)		233
GREEN SWEETING	151	
Green Sweeting (synonym of Green Sweet)	151	
Green Transparent		233
GREENVILLE	152	
Green Winter Pearmain	378	
Green Winter Pippin	146	
GREYHOUSE	153	
GRIMES	18, 19. 23, 153	
Grimes Golden	154	
Grimes Golden Pippin	154	
Grindstone	45	
Grise	264	
Gros-Alexandre		3
Gros Api Rouge	181	
GROSH		89
Grosh (synonym of Summer Rambo)		213
Grosh's Mammoth		89
Groskoe Selenka Grüner		233
Gros Pomier		91
Gros Pommier		91
Gros-Rambour d'Ete		213
Gros Rambour d'Hiver	206	
Grosse Casselar Reinette	114	
Grosse Reinette d'Angleterre	93	
Grosser Mogul		87
Grosse-Schafnasé		29
GRUNDY		90
Gul. Bellefleur	381	
HAAS		91

	VOL. I. PAGE.	VOL. II. PAGE.
Hagloe		92
Hagloe Crab		92
Hampers American		178
Hampshire Greening	282	
Hang-On	339	
Hard Red	153	
Hardwick	326	
Hargrove	155	
Harmony		53
Harrigan	208	
Harvest (synonym of Early Harvest)		51
Harvest (synonym of Primate)		168
Harvest Apple		215
Harvest Redstreak		93
Harvey		58
Haskell		93
Haskell Sweet		94
Hass		91
Haus Mütterchen	206	
Haverstraw Pippin		30
Hawkins Pippin		73
Hawley	15, 24	94
Hawley (synonym of Hawthornden)		96
Hawthorndean		96
Hawthornden		96
Hays	373	
Hays Apple	373	
Hays Wine	373	
Hays Winter	373	
Hays Winter Wine	373	
Haywood	155	
Hazen	156	
Heaster	158	
Heicke's Summer Queen		53
Heister	158	
Helen	183	
Hempstead	321	
Hendrick	333	
Hendrick Sweet	333	
Henniker	156	
Henrick	333	
Henrick Sweet	333	
Henry Sweet	333	
Henshaw	88	
Herbstbreitling		213
Herbst Strefling		10
Herbst Streifling		10
Herefordshire	157	

	VOL. I. PAGE.	VOL. II. PAGE.
Herefordshire Beefing	157	
Herefordshire Pearmain	378	
Herefordshire Redstreak	278	
Herr's June		141
Hertfordshire Pearmain	378	
Hibernal	26	96
Hicks		97
Hiester	158	
Highland Beauty 159, 183		
Highland Pippin		168
Hightop Sweet		97
High Top Sweet		98
High Top Sweet (synonym of Amsterdam)		5
High Top Sweeting		98
Hilaire		69, 98
Hilton		99
Himbeerapfel Lievlander		129
Himbeerapfel Livlander		129
Hislop		257
Hoadley		99
Hogan	109	
Hog Island Sweet		100
Hogpen		60
Holden		60
Holden Pippin		60
Holland Pippin		101
Holland Pippin (synonym of Fall Pippin).............		62
Holland Pippin (synonym of Domine) 24, 109		
Holland Pippin (synonym of Holland Winter)........	159	
Holland's Red Winter	375	
Holland Winter	159	
Hollow Cored Pippin	244	
Hollow Core Pippin	244	
Hollow Crown Pearmain (synonym of Wine)........	373	
Hollow Crown Pearmain (synonym of Long Island Pearmain)		124
Holmes	161	
Holmes Sweet	161	
Hominy		203
Honey Greening 16, 151		
Honey Sweet	380	
Hook		103
Hoop	153	
Hoopes	153	
Hoopes Pearmain	153	
Hoops	153	
Hopscy	153	
Hopson	153	

	VOL. I. PAGE.	VOL. II. PAGE.
Horning		203
Horse		91
Hoss		91
House (synonym of Greyhouse)	153	
House (synonym of Fall Wine)		64
Howard	227	
HOWARD BEST		103
Howard Russet		33
Howard's Best		103
Howard's Best Russian		103
Howard's Sweet	54	
Howe Apple		245
Hower		64
Hoypen		60
Hubbard	227	
HUBBARDSTON	17, 18, 161	
Hubbardston Nonsuch (synonym of Hubbardston)	161	
Hubbardston Nonsuch (synonym of Sutton)	324	
Hudson Red Streak		125
HUNTER PIPPIN		104
HUNT RUSSET	164	
Hunt's Fine Green Pippin	146	
Hunt's Green Newtown Pippin	146	
HUNTSMAN	18, 165	
Huntsman's Favorite	165	
Hurlburt		105
HURLBUT		104
Hurlbut (synonym of Ramsdell Sweet)		175
Hurlbut Stripe		105
Hurlbut Sweet		175
Hurlbutt		105
HYDE KING	166	
Hyde's King (of the West)	166	
HYSLOP (Crab)		257
Illinois Greening	331	
Imperial Vandervere		231
Imperial White		157
Imperatrice Eugenie		21
Imperatrice Josephine		77
Indian	196	
Indiana Jannetting	271	
Indiana Vandevere		231
Indion Queen		53
Ingraham	167	
INGRAM	24, 167	
Ingram Seedling	167	
Inman	244	
ISHAM		106

	VOL. I. PAGE.	VOL. II. PAGE.
Isham Sweet		106
Isle of Wight Orange (synonym of Marigold)	202	
Isle of Wight Orange (synonym of Orange Pippin).....		154
Isle of Wight Pippin (synonym of Marigold)............	202	
Isle of Wight Pippin (synonym of Orange Pippin).......		154
JACK		106
Jack Apple		106
JACKSON	168	
Jackson (synonym of Amos)............................	46	
Jackson (synonym of Chenango).......................		33
Jackson Red	227	
Jackson Seedling	168	
Jackson Winesap	311	
Jacks Red	135	
Jacobs	169	
JACOBS SWEET	169	
Jacobs Winter Sweet	169	
James River (synonym of Limbertwig).................	193	
James River (synonym of Willow)......................	370	
Janet	271	
Janetting	271	
Januarea	93	
JARVIS		107
Jefferies		108
JEFFERIS		108
JEFFERSON COUNTY		109
Jefferson Pippin	271	
Jeffries		108
Jellyflower		197
Jeniton	271	
Jenneting		240
Jennett	271	
Jennette	271	
Jennetting		109
Jennetting (synonym of White Juneating)...............		240
Jennings		166
Jenniton	271	
Jersey Black	79	
Jersey Greening (synonym of Ortley)...................	244	
Jersey Greening (synonym of Rhode Island *Greening*)....	282	
JERSEY SWEET	12	110
Jersey Sweeting		110
JEWETT *Red*	19, 170	
Jewett's Fine Red	170	
Jewett's Red	170	
Joaneting		240
Joe Berry	225	
Joe Précoce		52

	VOL. I. PAGE.	VOL. II. PAGE.
Johnathan	172	
John May	161	
Johnson	278	
Johnson's Fine Winter	385	
Jolly Gentleman		3
JONATHAN	17, 18, 24, 32, 172	
JONATHAN BULER	174	
Jonathan of Buler	174	
Jonathan of the North		5
Jones Early Harvest		181
Jones Pippin		60
Jones Seedling	43	
Josephine (synonym of Gloria Mundi)		77
Josephine (synonym of White Spanish Reinette)		241
Josie Moore	219	
JUDSON		111
JULY		112
July Apple		168
July Early Pippin		51
July, Fourth of		112
July Pippin		51
June (synonym of Margaret)		141
June (synonym of Red June)		181
Juneateing		240
Juneating		109
Juneating (synonym of White Juneating)		240
Juneting		240
Juniata		234
KAIGHN	183	113
Kaighn's Spitzemburg		113
Kaighn's Spitzenberg		113
Kaighn's Spitzenbergh		113
Kaighn's Spitzenburg (synonym of Kaighn)		113
Kaighn's Spitzenburg (synonym of Long Red Pearmain)		125
Kaighn's Spitzenburgh		113
Kaign's Spitzenburg		113
Kaiser Alexander		3
Kajabowka		114
KALKIDON		114
Kalkidonskoe		114
Kalkidouskoe		114
Kalkidovskoe		114
Kalvil jeltui		247
Kalvil scholti		247
Kanada Reinette	94	
Kanada-renett	93	
Kansas	175	
KANSAS GREENING	175	

	VOL. I. PAGE.	VOL. II. PAGE.
Kansas Keeper	175	
Karaboff		114
Karabovka		114
Karabowka		115
Kelley's Sweet	219	
Kelly White	67	
Kempster's Pippin		21
Kennebec Seedling		245
Kent Beauty		15
Kent Fillbasket		115
Kentish Filbasket		115
Kentish Fillbasket		115
Kentish Pippin		15
Kent Pippin	16	
Kentucky Beliflower		125
Kentucky Gilliflower		125
Kentucky Pippin	69	
Kentucky Queen	88	
Kentucky Red Streak	357	
Kentucky Streak	69	
Keswick		116
Keswick Codlin		117
Keswick Codling		117
Kettageska	178	
Keystone	153	
Khalkidonskoe		114
Kinderhook Pippin		77
King (synonym of Buckingham)	88	
King (synonym of Tompkins King)	176, 345	
King (synonym of Twenty Ounce Pippin)	349	
King Apple	345	
King George the Third	84	
King of Tompkins County	345	
King Philip	172	
Kingsbury Russet (synonym of Cheeseboro)		33
Kingsbury Russet (synonym of Pumpkin Russet)		170
Kinnaird	18, 176	
Kinnaird's Choice	176	
Kinnaird's Favorite	176	
Kinnard	176	
Kinnard's Choice	176	
Kirkbridge		118
Kirkbridge White		118
Kirkes Golden Reinette	142	
Kirkland	177	
Kittageskee	18, 178	
Kleine Graue Reinette	96	
Kleiner Api	181	

	VOL. I. PAGE.	VOL. II. PAGE.
Knight's Red June		181
Korallen Apfel		3
Kountz	225	
La Belle Fameuse		65
LACKER	179	
Lacquier	179	
Ladies Favorite of Tennessee	88	
Ladies Sweet (synonym of Lady Sweet)	184	
Ladies Sweet (synonym of Sweet Winesap)	333	
Ladies Sweeting	184	
LADY 15, 17, 32,	180	
Lady Apple	181	
Lady Blush		139
Lady de Grey's		115
LADY FINGER	183	118
Lady Finger (synonym of Kaighn)	183	113
Lady Finger (synonym of Long Red Pearmain)..........		125
Lady Finger Pippin	183	
LADY GROUP	182	
Lady Henniker	156	
Lady Pippin	66	
Lady's Apple		242
LADY SEEDLINGS	183	
Lady Suffield		126
Lady Sutherland		126
Lady's Sweet	184	
Lady's Sweeting	184	
LADY SWEET	184	
Lady Sweet (synonym of Sweet Winesap)..............	333	
Lady Sweeting	333	
Lady Washington (synonym of Yellow Bellflower)......	381	
Lady Washington (synonym of Cooper).................		40
La Fameuse		65
Lambertwig	193	
Lammas		142
Lancaster Queen		212
LANDON	185	
LANDSBERG		119
Landsberger Reinette		119
Landsburg		119
Landsburger Reinette		119
Lane Albert	268	
Lane's Prince Albert	268	
Langerfeldskoe		123
Langford	186	
LANKFORD 18,	186	
Lankford's Seedling	186	
Lansberger Reinette		119

	VOL. I. PAGE.	VOL. II. PAGE.
Lansinburg	188	
LANSINGBURG	187	
Lansingburgh	188	
Lansingburg Pippin	188	
Laquier	179	
Large Bough		216
Large Early		51
Large Early Bough		216
Large Early Harvest		51
Large Early Yellow Bough		216
Large Fall		241
Large Fall Pippin		241
Large Golden Pippin (synonym of Champlain)		30
Large Golden Pippin (synonym of Golden Pippin)		78
LARGE LADY APPLE	182	
Large Newtown Pippin	146	
Large Rambo (synonym of Rambo)	273	
Large Rambo (synonym of Grosh)		89
Large Red and Green Sweeting		177
LARGE RED SIBERIAN (Crab)		258
Large Red Sweeting		177
Large Romanite	255	
Large Striped Pearmain	196	
Large Striped Winter Pearmain	196	
Large Summer Rambo		89
Large Sweet Bough		216
Large Vandervere		231
Large White Juneating		51
Large Winter Red	373	
Large Yellow Bough		216
Large Yellow Newton Pippin	146	
Large Yellow Newtown Pippin	146	
LARGE YELLOW SIBERIAN (Crab)		258
La Rue	64	
Late Baldwin	56	
Late Bough		10
Late Chandler		31
LATE DUCHESS	25	
Late Golden Sweet		13
LATE STRAWBERRY		120
LATHAM		121
LA VICTOIRE	188	69
La Victoria Seedling	188	
LAWVER	18, 189	
LEAD		121
Lead Apple		121
Leanham	227	
Leather Apple of Turic	264	

	VOL. I. PAGE.	VOL. II. PAGE.
Lecker	179	
Leder	264	
Leeds Beauty		196
Lee Sweet	191	
Lehigh *Greening*	134, 192	
Lexington Queen	88	
Lievland Raspberry		129
Lille Api	181	
Lilly of Kent	193	
Lily of Kent	193	
Lima		227
Limber Twig	193	
Limbertwig	193	
Limbertwig (small or red)	193	
Limbertwig (large or green)	194	
Lincoln		245
Lincoln Pippin		122
Lincoln Pippin (synonym of Yellow Bellflower)	381	
Lincoln Pippin (synonym of Winthrop Greening)		245
Lincolnshire Pippin		96
Lindenwald		122
Lineous Pippin	381	
Linnoeus Pippin	381	
Lippincott		215
Litsey	108	
Little Pearmain	89	
Little Red Romanite (synonym of Gilpin)	138	
Little Red Romanite (synonym of Romanite)	289	
Little Repka	282	
Little Seedling	282	
Liveland Raspberry		129
Livesley's Imperial		126
Livland Raspberry		129
Livre	206	
Lock's Favorite	361	
Lodge's Early		215
Logan's Northern Pippin	213	
Long Bois	181	
Longfield	26	122
Longfield's Apple		123
Long Island		60
Long Island Graft		60
Long Island Pearmain		124
Long Island Pippin	16	
Long Island Russet (I)	17, 194	
Long Island Russet (II)	195	
Long Island Seek-No-Further	130	
Long John (synonym of Kaighn)		113

	VOL. I. PAGE.	VOL. II. PAGE.
Long John (synonym of Long Red Pearmain)...........		125
Long Pearmain (synonym of Kaighn)....................		113
Long Pearmain (synonym of Long Red Pearmain).......		125
Long Pippin	183	
LONG RED PEARMAIN		125
LONG STEM OF PENNSYLVANIA	196	
LONG STEM		125
Long Stem Sweet		13
LONGWORTH		125
Longworth Red Winter...............................		125
Lopside	153	
Lop-sided Pearmain	153	
Lop-side Pearmain	153	
Lord Kingston		96
Lord Nelson		21
LORD SUFFIELD		126
Lothringer Rambour		89
Lothringer Rambour d'Ete............................		213
LOU		126
Louis XVIII		55
LOUISE 20,	25	69, 126
Louise, Princess		127
LOWELL 16,	24	128
Lowell Pippin		128
LOWLAND RASPBERRY		129
LUBSK QUEEN		129
Lubsk Reinette		130
Lucius Apfel		21
Lyman's Large Yellow		171
Lyman's Pumpkin Sweet		171
LYSCOM		130
MABIE	24	131
McAdow's June		112
McAFEE	196	
McAfee Red	196	
McAfee's Nonesuch	196	
McAfee's Nonsuch	196	
McAfee's Red	196	
McAffee	197	
McAffee's Nonesuch	197	
McCARTY		132, 173
McClellan		135
McLouds Family	127	
MACDONOUGH		132
McINTOSH 17, 18, 20,	25	69,132
McIntosh Red		133
Mackie's Clyde Beauty		36
Mackinlav	197	

	VOL. I. PAGE.	VOL. II. PAGE.
McKinley	197	
McKinney	198	
McLellan		134
McLelan		135
McLouds Family	127	
McMahan		136
McMahan White		136
McMahon		136
McMahon White		136
Macomber		187
Magdalene		142
Magenta	198	
Magnum Bonum		23
Magog		138
Magog Red Streak		138
Maiden Blush	17, 18	139
Maiden Favorite		141
Maiden's Apple		141
Maiden's Blush (synonym of Hawthornden)		96
Makefield	312	
Mala Carle	199	
Malcarle	199	
Mal Carle	199	
Male Carle	199	
Malinda	199	
Malinowskoe		177
Mamma Beam	67	
Mamma Bean	67	
Mammoth (synonym of Gloria Mundi)		77
Mammoth (synonym of Golden Pippin)		78
Mammoth Black Twig (synonym of Arkansas)	47	
Mammoth Black Twig (synonym of Arkansas Black)	50	
Mammoth Black Twig (synonym of Paragon)	247	
Mammoth Pippin		77
Mammoth Rambo		89
Manchester	200	
Manks Codling	379	
Mann	201	
Maralandica		51
Marengo (Crab)		259
Marengo No. 1		259
Marengo Winter Crab		259
Margaret		141
Margaret Early		142
Margaret Early Red		142
Margaretha Apfel		142
Marget Apple		142

	VOL. I. PAGE.	VOL. II. PAGE.
Marguerite		142
Marietta Russet	293	
Marietta Seek-No-Further	364	
MARIGOLD	202	
Marigold (synonym of Orange Pippin).................		154
Marigold Creed's		154
Marigold Pippin (synonym of Marigold)...............	202	
Marigold Pippin (synonym of Orange Pippin)...........		154
Marle Carle	199	
Maroquin	264	
Marrow-bone		225
MARTHA (Crab)	3	259
Martin		135
Marygold (synonym of Marigold)	202	
Marygold (synonym of Orange Pippin).................		154
MASON ORANGE	204	
Mason's Improved	204	
Mason's Orange	204	
Massachusetts Golden Russett	164	
MASTEN	204	
Masten's Seedling	204	
Matchless	225	
Matthews Stripe		131
Maudlin		142
May	153	
May Apple	153	
May Seek-No-Farther	153	
May Seek-No-Further	153	
Meachem Sweet		146
Mela Carla	199	
Mela de Carlo	199	
Mela di Carlo	199	
Mela Januera	94	
Melinda	199	
MELON	15, 24, 204	
Melon (synonym of Gloria Mundi).......................		77
Melon Apple	204	
Melon de Norton	204	
Melon, Norton	204	
Melting Pippin	244	
Menage	206	
MÉNAGÈRE	206	
Menagerie	206	
Mere de Menage...	206	
Merit	88	
MERRILL	207	
Merrill's	207	

	VOL. I. PAGE.	VOL. II. PAGE.
Merrill's Apple	207	
Metzgerapfel	381	
Metzger's Calvill	381	
Michel Miller	158	
Michigan Beauty		201
MIDDLE	207	
MILAM	208	
MILDEN	209	
Milding	209	
Millcreek (synonym of Smokehouse)	312	
Millcreek (synonym of Vandevere Pippin)		231
Millcreek Vandevere	312	
Millcreek Vandevere		231
MILLER		142
Miller (synonym of Hiester)	158	
Miller Seedling		142
MILLIGEN		142
MILWAUKEE	25, 211	
MINISTER	212	
Minister Apple	212	
MINKLER	18, 213	
MINNESOTA (Crab)		260
MISSING LINK	214	
Mississippi		77
Missouri	215	
Missouri Janet	271	
Missouri Keeper	215	
Missouri Orange	215	
MISSOURI *Pippin*	18, 215	
Missouri Pippin (synonym of Nickajack)	227	
Missouri Red	227	
Missouri Superior	197	
Mr. Gladstone		75
Mittle	207	
Mobbs	227	
MONMOUTH	216	
Monmouth Pippin	217	
MONROE SWEET	24	
Montgomery Sweet		10
Monstreuse Pippin		77
Monstrous Pippin		77
Monstrous Rambo		89
Montreal (synonym of Montreal Beauty)		260
Montreal (synonym of St. Lawrence)		193
MONTREAL BEAUTY (Crab)		261
Montreal Peach		159
MOON	218	
Moore's Late Sweet	219	

	VOL. I. PAGE.	VOL. II. PAGE.
Moore's Shanty	219	
Moore's Sweet	219	
Moore's Sweeting	219	
MOORE SWEET	219	
Moor's Sweeting	219	
Moose		145
Morgan's Favorite		227
Morris Red	324	
MOSHER		143
Mosher Sweet		143
MOTHER	15, 24	143
Mother Apple		143
Mother of America		143
Mountaineer		145
Mountain Flora		77
Mountain Pippin (synonym of Fallawater)	125	
Mountain Pippin (synonym of Newtown Pippin)	146	
MOUNTAIN SWEET		145
MOUSE		145
MOYER	220	
Moyer Prize	220	
Mudhole		125
Mumper Vandevere	213	
MUNSON		146
Munson Sweet		146
Munson Sweeting		146
Musgrove		89
Musgrove's Cooper (synonym of Grosh)		89
Musgrove's Cooper (synonym of Western Beauty)		239
Mushroom		24
Musk Spice		64
Mygatt's Bergamot		49
Myer's Nonpareil		148
Naliwi Jabloky		239
Naylor Rambo		89
Neige		65
Neige-Framboise de Gielen		65
Neisley's Winter	255	
Neisley's Winter Penick	255	
NELSON	221	
Nelson Sweet	221	
Ne Plus Ultra	88	
NERO	222	
Neustadt's gelber Pepping	146	
Never Fail	271	
Neverfail	271	
NEWARK PIPPIN	223	
Newark Sweeting	91	

	VOL. I. PAGE.	VOL. II. PAGE.
New Brunswick		151
Newby	107	
New England Golden Russet	164	
New England Russet	164	
New England Seeknofurther	364	
New Greening	331	
N. J. Red Streak		53
NEWMAN	24, 224	
Newman Seedling	224	
New Missouri	197	
New Rhode Island Greening	331	
Newton's Pippin	146	
Newton Spitzemberg	225	
Newton Spitzenburgh	225	
Newton Yellow Pippin	146	
Newtown Greening		83
NEWTOWN PIPPIN	11, 15, 16, 19, 146	
Newtown Spitzemberg	225	
Newtown Spitzenbergh	225	
NEWTOWN SPITZENBURG	15, 17, 225	
Newtown Spitzenburgh	225	
NEW WATER	226	
New York Bellflower		60
New York Gloria Mundi		77
New York Greening	146	
New York Greening (synonym of Golding)		83
New York Pippin (synonym of Ben Davis)	69	
New York Pippin (synonym of Newtown Pippin)	146	
Niack Pippin (synonym of Sweet Bough)		217
NICKAJACK	18, 227	
Nickejack	227	
Nodhead	170	
Nonesuch (synonym of Red Canada)	276	
Nonesuch (synonym of Hubbardston)	161	
Nonpareil		148
Nonpareille		184
Nonpareille de Hubbardston	161	
Nonsuch (synonym of Hubbardston)	161	
Nonsuch (synonym of McAfee)	197	
Nonsuch (synonym of Red Canada)	276	
Normanton Wonder	112	
North American Best		168
Northampton		21
North Carolina	227	
Northern Golden Sweet		147
Northern Golden Sweeting		147
NORTHERN SPY	12, 15, 17, 18, 21, 24, 37, 229	
NORTHERN SPY GROUP	24	

	VOL. I. PAGE.	VOL. II. PAGE.
NORTHERN SWEET		147
Northern Sweeting (synonym of Munson)		146
Northern Sweeting (synonym of Northern Sweet)		147
North Star		48
NORTHWESTERN *Greening* 24, 233		
North West Greening 233		
Northwick Pippin		21
Norton's Melon 204		
Norton Watermelon 204		
No. 3 M		121
No. 4 M		155
No. 6 M		83
No. 9 M		24
No. 11 M		189
No. 14 M		5
No. 18 M		5
No. 21 M		115
No. 22 M		22
No. 23 M		7
No. 24 M		195
No. 26 M		6
No. 54 M		87
No. 56 M		123
No. 57 M		123
No. 80 M		195
No. 94 M		114
No. 105 M		32
No. 131 M		224
No. 139 M		183
No. 140 M		45
No. 147 M		222
No. 152 M		27
No. 161 M		18
No. 161		123
No. 205		115
No. 206		45
No. 210		244
No. 224		6
No. 230		224
No. 236		6
No. 245		24
No. 252		7
No. 262		32
No. 288		177
No. 333		182
No. 340		129
No. 343		182
No. 351		170

	VOL. I. PAGE.	VOL. II. PAGE.
No. 372		195
No. 410	282	
No. 418	282	
No. 442		247
No. 444		130
No. 453		14
No. 457		39
No. 467	61	
No. 469		83
No. 472		155
No. 477		18
No. 540		114
No. 587		57
No. 599		189
No. 964		10
No. 978		82
No. 979		82
No. 981		82
No. 12 Orel		7
No. 21 Veronesh		247
No. 51 Vor.		79
No. 84 Vor.		83
Nyack		30
Nyack Pippin		30
Oakland	234	
Oakland County Seek-No-Further	234	
Oats		51
Oblong (Crab)		261
Oblong-Fruited Siberian Crab		261
Oblong Siberian Crab		261
Occident	24, 235	
Oel	236	
Oel Austin	24, 236	
Ogdensburg		147
Ohio Beauty (synonym of Western Beauty)		239
Ohio Beauty (synonym of Grosh)		89
Ohio Favorite	244	
Ohio Nonpareil		148
Ohio Nonpareil (synonym of Gravenstein)		85
Ohio Nonpariel		148
Ohio Pippin		149
Ohio Wine (synonym of Fall Wine)		64
Ohio Wine (synonym of Kaighn)		113
Okabena		150
Okobena		150
Oldenburg	17, 18, 25, 26	150
Oldenburg, Duchess of		151
Oldenburg Group	25	

	VOL. I. PAGE.	VOL. II. PAGE.
Oldenburgh		151
Old English Pearmain	378	
Old Golden Pippin	141	
Old Hawthorndean		96
Old Nonsuch	276	
Old Pearmain	378	
OLIVE	237	
OLIVER	238	
Oliver's Red	238	
OLYMPIA	24, 60, 239	
Olympia Baldwin	239	
Omensk		189
ONTARIO	21, 24, 240	
OPALESCENT	242	
Oporto		7
ORANGE		153
ORANGE (Crab)		261
Orange (synonym of Fall Orange)		60
Orange (synonym of Lowell)		128
Orange (synonym of Orange Pippin)		154
Orange Blenheim		21
Orange de Cox		42
ORANGE OF NEW JERSEY		153
ORANGE OF PENNSYLVANIA		153
ORANGE PIPPIN		154
Orange Pippin (synonym of Marigold)	202	
Orange Pippin (synonym of Blenheim)		21
Orange Russet		154
ORANGE SWEET		154
Orange Sweet (synonym of Munson)		146
Orange Sweet (synonym of Golden Sweet)		81
Orange Sweeting (synonym of Golden Sweet)		81
Orange Sweeting (synonym of Orange Sweet)		154
Orleans	161	
Orloff		233
Orlovskoe		233
Orlowskoe		233
ORNAMENT	243	
Ornament de Table	243	
Ornement de Table	243	
Orsimui		97
ORTLEY	244	
Ortley Apple	244	
Ortley Pippin	244	
Osgood's Favourite		131
Osimoe		97
Oskaloosa		106
OSTRAKOFF		155

	VOL. I. PAGE.	VOL. II. PAGE.
Ostrakoff Glass		155
Ostrekoff		155
Ostrekoff's Glass		155
Ostrekovskaya Steklianka		155
Ostrekowskaja Steklianka		155
Ostrokoff		155
Ostrokoff's Glass		155
Ox Apple		77
Ox-Eye (synonym of Buckingham)	88	
Ox Eye (synonym of Newtown Spitzenburg)	225	
Oxeye (synonym of Vandevere)		230
Oxheart (synonym of Cheeseboro)		33
Oxheart (synonym of Twenty Ounce Pippin)	349	
Owen's Golden Beauty		240
Ozark	135	
Ozark Pippin		45
Palouse		156
Palmer	246	
Palmer Greening	361	
Palmer of N. Z.	246	
Paper		30
Paper-skin		30
Paradies Apfel		85
Paradise Winter	380	
Paradise Winter Sweet	380	
Paragon	24, 246	
Paragon (synonym of Arkansas)	47	
Pariser Rambour Reinette	94	
Park (synonym of McAfee)	197	
Park (synonym of Park Spice)	248	
Park (synonym of Long Red Pearmain)		125
Park Apple	248	
Parks Keeper	197	
Park Spice	248	
Parlin	248	
Parlin's Beauty	248	
Parmain d'Angleterre	378	
Parmain d'Hiver	378	
Parmain-Pepping	378	
Parry White		157
Parson	249	
Parson's Sweet	249	
Paternoster Apple	114	
Paterson's Sweet	54	
Patten		158
Patten's Duchess No. 3		158
Patten Greening		158
Patterson's Sweet	54	

	VOL. I. PAGE.	VOL. II. PAGE.
Paul Imperial (Crab)		262
Pawpaw	250	
Pawpaw Seedling	250	
Payne	250	
Payne Late Keeper	250	
Payne's Keeper	250	
Payton	135	
Peach	251	
Peach (Montreal)		159
Peach Apple of Montreal		159
Peach of Kentucky	251	
Peach of Montreal		159
Peach Pond		160
Peach Pond Sweet		160
Peach Pound Sweet		160
Pear Apple		174
Pear Lot		244
Pearmain	252	
Pearmain (synonym of Winter Pearmain)	378	
Pearmain (synonym of Long Red Pearmain)		125
Pearmain d'Hiver	378	
Pearmain Herefordshire	378	
Pearsall		161
Pearsall's Sweet		161
Pear-Tree Lot		244
Pease		161
Pease, Walter		161
Peasgood Nonsuch		162
Peasgood's Nonesuch		162
Peau	264	
Peck	253	
Pecker	56	
Peck Pleasant	12, 24, 32, 253	
Peck's Pleasant	253	
Peewaukee	258	
Pelican	255	
Penick	255	
Pennick	255	
Pennock	17, 255	
Pennock's Red Winter	255	
Pennsylvania Cider	311	
Pennsylvania Red-Streak	373	
Pennsylvania Vandevere		231
Pipin de Kent		15
Pepin de New-York	69	
Pepin d'Or	141	
Pepin Parmain d'Angleterre	378	
Pepin Parmain d'Hiver	378	

	VOL. I. PAGE.	VOL. II. PAGE.
Pepin Ribston		184
Pepping Englischer		57
Peremenes	379	
Perle d'Angleterre		21
Permaine	379	
Permein	379	
Perry Redstreak		162
Perry Red Streak		162
Perry Russet	256	
Peter	25	163
Petersburgh Pippin	146	
Peterson's Charlamoff		32
Petit Api	181	
Petit Api Rose	181	
Petit Api Rouge	181	
Petit Apis	181	
Petite Reinette Grise	96	
Petrovskoe		195
Petrowskoe		195
Pewaukee	25, 258	
Pfeifer	262	
Pfeiffer	262	
Pfund	206	
Philadelphia Pippin (syonym of Fall Pippin)		62
Philadelphia Pippin (synonym of White Spanish Reinette)		241
Philadelphia Sweet		10
Philip Rick	172	
Phoenix (synonym of Pennock)	255	
Phoenix (synonym of Rome)	290	
Phœnix		3
Phönix		3
Picard	260	
Picard's Reserve	260	
Pichard	260	
Pickard Reserve	260	
Pickard's Reserve	260	
Pickaway Rambo		89
Picta Striata (Crab)		263
Pie Apple (synonym of Holland Pippin)		101
Pie Apple (synonym of Sops of Wine)		203
Pieta		263
Pieta Striata		263
Pifer	262	
Pilliken	153	
Pim's Beauty of the West	125	
Pineapple	257	
Pineapple Russet	257	
Pine's Beauty of the West	125	

	VOL. I. PAGE.	VOL. II. PAGE.
PINE STUMP	263	
Piper	262	
PIPPIN	263	
Pippin (synonym of Newtown Pippin)	146	
Pippin, Bullock	89	
Pippin Kent		15
Pittstown Pippin		79
Pitzer Hill	269	
Platarchium	379	
Plodowitka Caudkaja		170
Plodowitka Cuadkaja		170
PLUMB CIDER		164
Plum Cider		164
Pointed Pipka		32
Polecat		212
Polhemus	219	
Pomme Astrachan		239
Pomme d'Api	181	
Pomme d'Api Rouge	181	
Pomme d'Apis	181	
Pomme d'Astrachan		239
Pomme de Blenheim		21
Pomme de Caen	94	
Pomme de Charles	199	
Pomme de Cuir	269	
Pomme d'Ete of Canada		51
Pomme de Fameuse		65
Pomme de Fer	292	
Pomme de Hawthornden		96
Pomme de Laak	114	
Pomme de Neige		65
Pomme de Notre-Dame		213
Pomme d'Orange		154
Pomme de Transylvania	64	
Pomme Fameuse		65
Pomme Finale	199	
Pomme Graefenstein		85
Pomme Gree	264	
Pomme Gris	264	
POMME GRISE	264	
Pomme Grise d'Or	328	
Pomme Groseille		253
Pomme Peche		159
Pomme Rose	181	
Pommeroy	184	
Pomme Royal		49
Pomme Royale		49
Pomme Roye (synonym of Pennock)	255	

	VOL. I. PAGE.	VOL. II. PAGE.
Pomme Roye (synonym of Dyer)		49
Pomme Water		49
Pommewater in Illinois		49
POMONA		164
Pomona Brittannica		3
Pomone d'Apis	181	
Pompey		233
Poplar Bluff	311	
Popular Bluff	311	
PORTER	12, 15	166
Portugal	94	
Possaris Nalivia		6
Potter's Large		116
Potter's Large Grey Seedling		116
Potter's Large Seedling		116
Poughkeepsie Russet (synonym of English Russet)	118	
Poughkeepsie Russet (synonym of Perry Russet)	257	
Pound (synonym of Fallawater)	125	
Pound (synonym of Nickajack)	227	
Pound (synonym of Gloria Mundi)		77
Pound Pippin		62
Pound Royal (synonym of Fall Pippin)		62
Pound Royal (synonym of Golden Pippin)		78
Pound Royal (synonym of Lowell)		128
Pound Royal (synonym of Long Red Pearmain)		125
Pound's July		217
POUND SWEET	266	167
Pound Sweet (synonym of Moore Sweet)	219	
Pound Sweet (synonym of Pumpkin Sweet)		171
Powers		168
Prager Reinette Franche de Grandville	264	
Pratt	266	
PRATT SWEET	266	
President Napoleon		3
Pride of Genesee		73
Pride of Hudson	62	
Pride of Texas	337	
Pride of the Hudson	62	
PRIESTLY	267	
Priestley	267	
Priestley's American	267	
PRIMATE		167
Primiting		240
PRINCE ALBERT	268	
Prince Albert (Lane)	268	
Prince Bismark		19
Princesse Noble	142	
Prince of Wales		21

	VOL. I. PAGE.	VOL. II. PAGE.
Prince's Early Harvest		51
Prince's Harvest		51
Prince's Large Pippin of New York		62
Prince's Large Red and Green Sweeting		177
Prince's Red and Green Sweet		177
Prince's Yellow Harvest		51
Princess Louise		127
Prinzessin-Apfel		85
Prior's Late Red	269	
Prior's Red	269	
PROLIFIC BEAUTY	16	
Prolific Beauty (synonym of Pennock)	255	
Prolific Beauty (synonym of Blue Pearmain)	80	
Prolific Sweet		170
PROLIFIC SWEETING		169
Prussian		38
PRYOR	269	
Pryor Red	269	
Pryor's Pearmain	269	
Pryor's Red	269	
PUMPKIN RUSSET		· 170
PUMPKIN SWEET 16, 17,	18	171
Pumpkin Sweet (synonym of Cheeseboro)		33
Pumpkin Sweet (synonym of Pumpkin Russet)		170
Pumpkin Sweeting (synonym of Pumpkin Sweet)		172
Pumpkin Sweeting (synonym of Pumpkin Russet)		170
Putman's Russet	293	
Putnam Russet	293	
Putnam's Savewell	299	
Pyrus Astracanica		239
QUAKER (Crab)		263
Quaker (synonym of Streaked Pippin)	321	
Queen (synonym of Buckingham)	88	
Queen (synonym of Summer Queen)		212
Queen (synonym of Williams)		242
Queen Anne (synonym of Lowell)		128
Queen Anne (synonym of Mother).......................		143
QUEEN CHOICE (Crab)		264
Queen of Haywood	155	
Queens	84	
Queen's Choice		263
QUINCE (of Cole)		174
QUINCE (of Coxe)	17	174
Quince Apple		174
Rag Apple		146
RALLS 18, 24,	270	
RALLS GROUP	24	
Ralls Genet	271	

	VOL. I. PAGE.	VOL. II. PAGE.
Ralls Janet	271	
Rambo	17, 18, 32, 273	
Rambouillet	273	
Ramboulette	273	
Ramboulrette	109	
Rambour		213
Rambour Barre	379	
Rambour Blanc		213
Rambour d'Amerique		213
Rambour d'Ete		213
Rambour Franc		213
Rambourg Aigre		213
Rambour Gros		213
Rambour Lorraine		89
Rambour Raye		213
Rambu		213
Ramsdale's Sweeting		175
Ramsdell		175
Ramsdell Red Sweet		175
Ramsdell's Red		175
Ramsdell's Red Sweeting		175
Ramsdell Sweet		175
Ramsdell's Red Pumpkin Sweet		175
Randall's Red Winter		175
Raspberry		176
Raule Jannet	271	
Raule's Genet	271	
Raule's Janet	271	
Raule's Janette	271	
Raule's Jannetting	271	
Raule's Jennetting	271	
Raul's Gennetting	271	
Rawle's Genet	271	
Rawle's Janet	271	
Rawle's Jennet	271	
Rawle's Jenneting	271	
Rawle's Jennette	271	
Ray Apple		146
Reagan	135	
Red and Green Sweet		177
Red and Green Sweeting		177
Red Astracan		178
Red Astrachan	15, 17, 18, 25, 26	178
Red Astrakhan		178
Red Baldwin Pippin	56	
Red Beitigheimer		17
Red Bellflower (synonym of Ohio Nonpareil)		148
Red Bellflower (synonym of Long Red Pearmain)		125

	VOL. I. PAGE.	VOL. II. PAGE.
Red Ben Davis	135	
Red Bietigheimer		19
Red Bough		177
RED CANADA	15, 24, 37, 275	
Red Canada of Ontario	292	
Red Cathead	267	
Red Cheek (synonym of Monmouth)	217	
Red Cheek (synonym of Raspberry)		177
Red Cheek (synonym of Maiden Blush)		139
Red Cheek (synonym of Fall Orange)		60
Red Cheeked Pippin	217	
Red Cheek Pippin	217	
Red Codlin	132	
Red Doctor	107	
Red Eiser	116	
Red Everlasting	153	
Red Gilliflower (synonym of Black Gilliflower)	77	
Red Gilliflower (synonym of Scollop Gilliflower)		197
Red Gilliflower (synonym of Striped Gilliflower)		207
Red Gloria Mundi	88	
RED GRAVENSTEIN		180
Red Gravenstein (synonym of Banks)		14
Red Hawthornden		96
Red Hazel	227	
RED HOOK		180
Red Horse	88	
Red Joaneting		142
RED JUNE		181
Red Juneating (synonym of Margaret)		142
Red Juneating (synonym of Red June)		181
Red Juneating (synonym of Early Strawberry)		55
Red June, Carolina		181
Red June of South		142
Red Juneting		142
Red Lady Finger	183	
Red Limbertwig	193	
Redling	101	
Red Neverfail	271	
Red Ox	255	
Red Pearmain (synonym of Kaighn)		113
Red Pearmain (synonym of Long Red Pearmain)		125
Red Pennock	255	
Red Phœnix (synonym of Kaighn)		113
Red Phœnix (synonym of Long Red Pearmain)		125
Red Pippin (synonym of Ben Davis)	69	
Red Pippin (synonym of Nickajack)	227	
Red Pippin (synonym of Streaked Pippin)	321	
Red Pippin (synonym of Kaighn)		113

	VOL. I. PAGE.	VOL. II. PAGE.
Red Pippin (synonym of Long Red Pearmain)		125
Red Pound	64	
Red Pumpkin Sweet		175
Red Pumpkin Sweeting		175
Red Reinette		83
Red Rock	188	
Red Romanite	289	
Red Romanite of Ohio	138	
RED RUSSET	278	
Red Russet (synonym of Pryor)	269	
Red Shropsavine		203
RED SIBERIAN (Crab)		264
Red Spitzenberg (synonym of Kaighn)		113
Red Spitzenberg (synonym of Long Red Pearmain)		125
Red Spitzenberg (synonym of Richard Graft)		186
Red Spitzenburg		113
REDSTREAK	278	
Red Streak	278	
Red Sweet Pippin	219	
Red Sweet Winesap	333	
RED TRANSPARENT		182
Red Transparent (synonym of Vineuse Rouge)		233
RED TYPE OF TWENTY OUNCE..............................		229
RED TYPE OF WESTFIELD Seek-No-Further.................	366	
Red Vandervere		231
Red Vandevere	312	
Red Warrior	227	
RED WINE		182
Red Winter	276	
RED WINTER PEARMAIN	183	
Red Winter Pearmain	279	
Red Winter Pearmain (synonym of Westfield Seek-No-Further)	364	
Red Winter Pearmain (synonym of Kaighn)		113
Red Winter Pearmain (synonym of Long Red Pearmain)..		125
RED WINTER PIPPIN	183	
Red Winter Sweet	219	
REED		183
Reindell's Large		175
REINETTE	279	
Reinette a feuille d'Acuba	52	
Reinette A Gobelet		241
Reinette Belle de Boskoop		25
Reinette Blanche		241
Reinette Blanche d'Espagne (synonym of White Spanish Reinette)		241
Reinette Blanche d'Espagne (synonym of Fall Pippin)....		62
Reinette Canada	94	

	VOL. I. PAGE.	VOL. II. PAGE.
Reinette Carpentin	96	
Reinette de Blenheim		21
Reinette de Caen	94	
Reinette de Canada	94	
Reinette de Canada a'Cotes	94	
Reinette de Caux	114	
Reinette de Darnetal	264	
Reinette d'Espagne		241
Reinette d'Holland		161
Reinette de Landsberg		119
Reinette de New York	146	
Reinette d'Or	114	
Reinette de Traver		184
Reinette Doree	114	
Reinette du Canada	94	
Reinette du Canada a'Cortes	94	
Reinette du Canada Blanche	94	
Reinette Grenade Anglaise		184
Reinette Grise	264	
Reinette Grise Brownlees	86	
Reinette Grise de Darnetal	264	
Reinette Grise Double	265	
Reinette Grise de Grandville	265	
Reinette Grise d'Hiver	265	
Reinette Grise Extra	265	
Reinette Grise Franchaise	264	
Reinette Grosse de Angleterre	94	
Reinette Landsberger		119
Reinette Liubski		130
Reinette Monstrueuse		25
Reinette Monstreuse de Canada	94	
Reinette Orange de Cox		42
Reinette Pepin	280	
Reinette Pippin	280	
Reinette Quarrendon		142
Reinette Tendre		241
Reinette toute Grise	265	
Reinette von Canada	94	
Reinette von Montfort		25
Reipka Melenkaya	282	
Renet Liubskui		130
Repka		183
Repka Malenka	281	
Remboure d'Ete		213
Reschestwenskoe		19
Revelstone		248
Revelstone Pippin		233
Rhode Island	282	

	VOL. I. PAGE.	VOL. II. PAGE.
Rhode Island *Greening* 12, 15, 16, 17, 18, 19, 24, 282		
Rhode Island *Greening* Group........................... 24		
Rhode Island Russet.................................... 257		
Rhode Island Seek-No-Further......................... 130		
Rhode Island Sweet.....................................		172
Riabinouka		39
Ribbed Gilliflower		197
Ribbed Pippin		83
Ribston 17		184
Ribstone		184
Ribstone Pippin		184
Ribston Pepping		184
Ribston Pippin		184
Richard		186
Richard Graft		186
Richardson's Red 66		
Richfield Nonsuch 276		
Rickman's Red 227		
Ridge 287		
Ridge (synonym of Ribston)............................		184
Ridge Pippin 287		
Riepka		183
Ripp Apfel		85
Roa Yon 184		
Robinson 316		
Rock 289		
Rock Apple 188		
Rockhill's Russet		184
Rock Pippin 288		
Rock Remain 271		
Rock Rimmon 271		
Rode Wyn Appel.......................................		203
Rolfe		187
Rolland 67		
Roman Beauty 290		
Romanite 289		
Romanite (synonym of Gilpin).......................... 138		
Romanite (synonym of Greyhouse)...................... 153		
Romanite (synonym of Pennock)....................... 255		
Romanite (synonym of Rambo)......................... 273		
Romanite of the South................................. 289		
Romanite of the West.................................. 138		
Romanite, South 289		
Roman Knight 255		
Roman Stem 17, 18		188
Rome 32, 290		
Rome Beauty 290		
Romenskoe		189

	VOL. I. PAGE.	VOL. II. PAGE.
ROMNA		189
Romna (synonym of Hibernal)		97
Romnenskoe		189
RONK		190
Roschdestvenskoe		19
Roschdestwenskoe		19
ROSEAU	292	
ROSE-COLORED LADY APPLE	182	
ROSE RED		190
Rose Sweet	333	
Roshdestrenskoe		19
Rosseau	292	
Ross Greening	352	
Rother Astrakhan		178
Rother Eiser	116	
Rother Eiser Apfel	116	
Rother Gravensteiner		180
Rother Jacobs		142
Rother Jacobs Apfel		142
Rother Weinapfel		182
Rotherwein Appel		182
Rouge de Pryor	269	
Rouge Rayee (synonym of Eiser)	116	
Rouge Rayee (synonym of Redstreak)	278	
Rough and Ready		168
Round Catshead		29
Round Sweet		172
Round Top		56
Rox	294	
ROXBURY	15, 16, 17, 18, 23, 293	
Roxbury Russet	293	
Roxbury Russeting	293	
Rox Russet	294	
Royal Janette	271	
Royal Red of Kentucky	375	
Rubets Vinogradnui		244
Rubez Vuinogradnui		244
Rubicon	250	
Ruckman	227	
Ruckman's Red	227	
Russam (synonym of Kaighn)		113
Russam (synonym of Long Red Pearmain)		125
Russet	294	
RUSSET BALDWIN	59	
Russet, Boston or Roxbury	294	
Russet, Golden	143	
Russet Pearmain	164	
Russet Seek-No-Further	364	

	VOL. I. PAGE.	VOL. II. PAGE.
RUSSIAN BALDWIN	295	
Russian Emperor		3
Russian Gravenstein		6
Rusty Core		148
RUTLEDGE	296	
Sabine		85
Safstaholm		191
SAFSTAHOLMS		191
Säfstaholmsäple		191
SAILEE RUSSET		192
Saille Sweet		177
SAILLY AUTUMN		192
Saint-Germaine		241
St. Helena Russet	94	
St. Hilaire		98
St. John's Strawberry		55
ST. LAWRENCE	17, 18	192
Saint-Lawrence		193
Saint Laurent		193
ST. PETER		194
SALISBURY	297	
Salisbury Pippin	297	
Salisbury Winter	297	
SALOME	24, 297	
SANDY GLASS		195
Sanguineus		65
Sapson		203
Sapsonvine		203
Sassafras Sweet		94
SAVEWELL	299	
SAXTON		196
Scalloped Gilliflower		197
Scalloped Gillyflower		197
SCARLET BEAUTY	24	
SCARLET CRANBERRY	299	
Scarlet Pearmain (synonym of Kaighn)		113
Scarlet Pearmain (synonym of Long Red Pearmain)		125
SCARLET PIPPIN	25	196
Schafnasé		29
Scharlottenthaler Golba		222
SCHODACK	300	
Schöner von Boskoop		25
Schoolmocker	301	
Schoone van Boskoop		25
SCHOONMAKER	301	
SCHUYLER SWEET		197
Schwere Apfel	326	
SCOLLOP GILLIFLOWER		197

	VOL. I. PAGE.	VOL. II. PAGE.
Scollop Gilliflower (synonym of Striped Gilliflower)......		207
Scolloped Gilliflower		197
SCOTT	301	
Scott (synonym of Baker)..............................	55	
Scott (synonym of Primate)...........................		168
SCOTT BEST		198
Scott's Red Winter	302	
Scott's Winter	302	
SCRIBNER	303	
Scribner's Spitzenberg	303	
Scribner's Spitzenburgh	303	
Scudamore's Crab	278	
Scudamous Crab	278	
Seek-No-Farther	273	
Seeknofurther	364	
Seek-No-Further (synonym of Rambo)...................	273	
Seek-No-Further	303	
Seek-No-Further of Del., N. J., and Penn.............	273	
Seek-No-Further (synonym of Cooper)..................		40
Seek-No-Further (synonym of Green Seek-No-Further).		86
Seever's Red Streak		230
Senator	238	
SENECA FAVORITE		198
Seneca Favorite (synonym of Quince [of Coxe])........		174
Seneca Spice		174
SEPTEMBER (Crab)		264
SHACKLEFORD	304	
Shackleford's Best	304	
Shaker's Yellow		53
SHANNON (I)	305	
SHANNON (II)	306	
Shannon (synonym of Ohio Pippin).....................		149
Shannon Pippin	305	
SHARP		199
Sharpe's Early		212
Sharpe's Spice		64
SHEDDAN	306	
Sheepnose (synonym of Bullock).......................	89	
Sheepnose (synonym of Lady Finger)...................	183	
Sheepnose	307	
Sheepnose (synonym of Egg Top).......................		56
Sheepnose (synonym of Long Red Pearmain)............		125
Sheep Shire	131	
Sheep's Nose	89	
Sheep's Snout	89	
SHERRIFF	308	
SHERMAN		200
Sherman's Favorite		200

	VOL. I. PAGE.	VOL. II. PAGE.
Sherman's Sweet		200
Sherwood's Favorite		33
Shiawasse Beauty		201
SHIAWASSEE	25	69, 201
Shiawassee Beauty		201
Shiawassie Beauty		201
Shippens Russet	294	
SHIRLEY	308	
Shoreditch White		96
Shropshirevine		203
Siberian August		112
Siberian Crab	17	
Siberian Crab (synonym of Red Siberian)		264
Siberian Crab (synonym of Yellow Siberian)		269
SINE-QUA-NON		202
SKANK	309	
Sklanka	81	
Sklanka Bogdanoff	81	
Skunk	321	
Skvosnoi Krasnoi		182
Skwosnoi Krasnoi		182
Skwosnoi Schotoi		248
Sleeper's Yellow		53
SLEIGHT	310	
Sleight's Lady Apple	310	
Slight's Lady Apple	310	
SLINGERLAND		202
Slingerland's Fall Pippin		202
Slingerland's Pippin		202
Small Admirable		1
Small's Admirable		1
SMITH CIDER	18, 310	
Smithfield Spice		49
Smith's	311	
Smith's Cider	311	
SMOKEHOUSE	15, 312	
Smoke House	312	
Smokehouse (synonym of Vandevere Pippin)		231
Smyrna		33
Snorter	197	
Snow		65
Sol Carter	88	
Solotoc Renet		79
SOMERSET (N. Y.)		203
Sondergleichen von Hubbardston	161	
Sops in Wine		203
SOPS OF WINE		203
SOULARD (Crab)		265

	VOL. I. PAGE.	VOL. II. PAGE.
Sourbough (synonym of Champlain)		30
SOUR BOUGH		204
Sour Bough (synonym of Champlain)		30
Sour Bough (synonym of Tart Bough)		220
Sour Harvest		168
Southern Romanite	289	
Speckled		60
SPECTATOR		204
Spiced Oxeye		231
Spiced Ox Eye	225	
SPICE SWEET	12	
Spitzenberg	121	
Spitzenberg Newtown	225	
Spitzenburg	314	
Spitzenburgh (synonym of Esopus *Spitzenburg*)........	121	
Spitzenburgh (synonym of Newtown Spitzenburg)	225	
Spitzenburgh Newtown	225	
SPRING PIPPIN	314	
Springport	314	
Springport Pippin	314	
Spy 229,	315	
Staalclubs (synonym of Newtown Spitzenburg)	225	
Staalclubs (synonym of Vandevere Pippin)		231
Staalcubs		230
Stalcubs		230
STANARD	315	
Stanard's Seedling	315	
Stannard	315	
Stannard's Seedling	315	
STARK	316	
STARKEY		205
Starke Apple	316	
STAR LADY APPLE	182	
STARR		206
Stayman	318	
Stayman's Winesap	318	
STAYMAN WINESAP	318	
Steele's Red	324	
Steele's Red Winter (synonym of Baldwin).............	56	
Steele's Red Winter (synonym of Red Canada)..........	276	
Steele's Red Winter (synonym of Sutton)..............	324	
Steel's Red	276	
Stehly	158	
Steklianka Bogdanoff	81	
Steklianka pesotchnaya		195
STERLING	319	
Sterling Beauty 45,	319	
Stettin Pippin	114	

	VOL. I. PAGE.	VOL. II. PAGE.
Stevenson Pippin	197	
Stewart's Nonpareil		112
Stillman		207
STILLMAN EARLY		207
Stillman's Early		207
Stine	197	
Stoke Tulip		3
STONE	24, 320	
Stone (synonym of American Pippin)	45	
Stor Casseler Reinet	114	
Stor Kasselrenett	114	
Storr's Wine	197	
STOWE	321	
Stowe's Winter	321	
Straat		208
Strawberry (synonym of Sops of Wine)		203
Strawberry (synonym of Chenango)		33
Strawberry (synonym of Late Strawberry)		120
Strawberry (synonym of Richard Graft)		186
Strawberry		207
STREAKED PIPPIN	321	
Striped Ashmore		231
Striped Bellflower		207
STRIPED FAMEUSE		68
STRIPED GILLIFLOWER	16	207
Striped Harvest		93
Striped Juneating		142
Striped Pearmain (synonym of McAfee)	197	
Striped Pearmain (synonym of Long Red Pearmain)		125
Striped Quarrendon		142
Striped Rambo	273	
Striped Red June		182
Striped Rhode Island Greening (synonym of Domine)	109	
Striped Rhode Island Greening (synonym of Wells)	363	
Striped Shropshire		55
STRIPED SWEETING	16	
Striped Sweet Pippin	197	
Striped Vandervere		231
Striped Winter Pearmain	197	
STROAT		208
Strode		208
STRODE BIRMINGHAM		208
Strode's		208
Strode's Birmingham		208
Strohmer		85
Stromling		85
Stuart	323	
STUART GOLDEN	323	

	VOL. I. PAGE.	VOL. II. PAGE.
Stuart's Golden	323	
STUMP		209
Stump (synonym of Stuart Golden)	323	
Stymer's		210
STYMUS		210
SUFFOLK BEAUTY		210
Sugar Barbel	61	
Suislepper		219
Summer Belllefleur		211
SUMMER BELLFLOWER		211
Summer Bellflower (synonym of Autumn Bough)		10
Summer Hagloe		92
Summerour	227	
SUMMER PEARMAIN	15	211
SUMMER PIPPIN	11	
Summer Pippin (synonym of Champlain)		30
Summer Pippin (synonym of Fall Pippin)		62
Summer Pippin (synonym of Holland Pippin)		101
SUMMER QUEEN	16	212
SUMMER RAMBO		213
Summer Rambo (synonym of Grosh)		89
Summer Rambour		213
SUMMER REDSTREAK		214
SUMMER ROSE	15	215
Summer Russet		218
SUMMER SPITZENBURG		215
Summer Spitzenburgh		215
SUMMER SWEET		216
Summer Sweet (synonym of Hightop Sweet)		98
Summer Sweeting (synonym of Summer Sweet)		216
Summer Sweeting (synonym of Hightop Sweet)		98
Summer Traveller		142
Superior White		157
Sussex Scarlet Pearmain	379	
Susy Clark		181
SUTTON	32, 324	
Sutton Beauty (synonym of Dumelow)	112	
Sutton Beauty (synonym of Sutton)	324	
Svinsovka		121
SWAAR	15, 16, 17, 18, 326	
Swaar Apple	326	
Swaysie Pomme Gris	328	
Swaysie	328	
Swaysie Pomme Grise	328	
SWAZIE	328	
Swazie Pomme Grise	328	
Swazie's Pomme Gris	328	
Swasy	328	

	VOL. I. PAGE.	VOL. II. PAGE.
Swazy Pomme Gris	328	
Swedish Borsdorf of Patten		5
Sweet and Sour	329	
Sweet Bough	12, 15, 16	216
Sweet Fall Pippin		218
Sweet Golden Pippin		12
Sweet Greening	151, 331	
Sweet Harvest		217
Sweet June		98
Sweet King	333	
Sweet Lyman's Pumpkin		172
Sweet Maiden's Blush	91	
Sweet Pearmain	333	
Sweet Pippin (synonym of Moore Sweet)	219	
Sweet Pippin (synonym of Hog Island Sweet)		100
Sweet Rambo		89
Sweet Rhode Island Greening	331	
Sweet Russet	333	
Sweet Russet		218
Sweet Russet (synonym of Pumpkin Russet)		170
Sweet Russet (synonym of Cheeseboro)		33
Sweet's Harvest		212
Sweet Swaar		12
Sweet Wine		64
Sweet Winesap	333	
Sweet Wine Sap	333	
Swenker	335	
Swett's Harvest		212
Swines		121
Swinzovska		121
Switzer		218
Sylvan Russet	294	
Sylvester		220
Taffitai		239
Tallman's Sweet	343	
Tallman Sweet	343	
Tallman Sweeting	343	
Tallow		128
Tallow Apple		128
Tallow Pippin		128
Talman's Sweet	343	
Talman Sweet	343	
Talman's Sweeting	343	
Talman Sweeting	343	
Tars Thorn		45
Tart Bough (synonym of Early Harvest)		51
Tart Bough (synonym of Champlain)		30
Tart Bough		220

	VOL. I. PAGE.	VOL. II. PAGE.
Teignmouth		223
Teller	206	
Tennessee Early Red		55
Tenon Hills	67	
Terry's Redstreak	273	
Tete d'Ange		29
Tete de Chat		29
Tetoffsky		220
Tetofski (synonym of July)		112
Tetofski (synonym of Tetofsky)		220
TETOFSKY	25, 26	220
Tetofsky (synonym of July)		112
Tewkesbury Blush	336	
Tewkesbury Winter Blush	336	
Tewksberry Winter Blush	336	
TEWKSBURY	336	
Tewksbury Blush	336	
Tewksbury Winter Blush	336	
Texan Red	375	
TEXAS	337	
THALER		222
Thomas	208	
THOMPSON		222
Thompson No. 24.		222
Thompson's Seedling No. 24.		222
Thompson's Seedling No. 29.		111
Thompson's Seedling No. 38.		90
Timothy	339	
Timothy Titus Sort	339	
TINMOUTH		223
Tinmouth Sweet		223
Titovca		224
TITOVKA		224
Titowka		224
TITUS	339	
Titus (synonym of Titus Pippin)	339	
Titus Apple		224
TITUS PIPPIN	338	
Titus Riga		224
TOBIAS	340	
Tobias Apple	340	
TOBIAS BLACK	341	
TOBIAS PIPPIN	342	
Tolman	343	
TOLMAN *Sweet*	16, 17, 18, 343	
Tolman's Sweeting	343	
Toma Red	345	
Tom Harryman		85

	VOL. I. PAGE.	VOL. II. PAGE.
Tommy Red	345	
Tompkins		49
Tompkins County King	345	
Tompkins King	17, 18, 19, 345	
Tom Put		225
Tom Putt		225
Tom's Red	345	
Tom Woodward Pippin	244	
Transcendant (Crab)		267
Transcendent (Crab)		266
Transparente de Astracan		239
Transparente d'Ete		239
Transparent de Muscovie		239
Transparente de Muscovie d'Ete		239
Transparente de Saint-Leger (syn. of Vineuse Rouge)		233
Transparente de Saint-Leger (syn. of Yellow Transparent).		248
Transparente de Zurich		239
Transparente Jaune (synonym of Vineuse Rouge)		233
Transparente Jaune (synonym of Yellow Transparent)		248
Transparente Rouge		233
Transparente Verte		233
Transparent Muscovie		239
Travers'		184
Travers Apple		184
Travers Peppin		184
Travers Pippin		184
Travers Reinette		184
Treanham	227	
Trenham	227	
Trenton Early		81
True Spitzenburgh	121	
Trumpington	273	
Tsarskui Schip		45
Tufts	24	226
Tufts Baldwin		226
Tufts Seedling		226
Tulpahocken	125	
Tulpehocken	125	
Turn Off Lane		174
Twenty Ounce	17, 18, 193	227
Twenty Ounce Pippin	349	
Twenty Ounce Pippin (synonym of Twenty Ounce)		227
Twitty's Paragon	247	
Tyre Beauty		229
Ulster Seedling	172	
Uncle Sam's Best		64
Underdunk		30
Utter		229

	VOL. I. PAGE.	VOL. II. PAGE.
Utter's Large Red		230
Utter's Red		230
Valandingham	197	
Vandervere (synonym of Newtown Spitzenburg)	225	
Vandervere (synonym of Smokehouse)	312	
Vandervere of New York	225	
Vandervere (synonym of Vandevere)		230
Vandervere (synonym of Vandevere Pippin)		231
Vandervere Pippin		231
Vandeveer		230
VANDEVERE	18	230
Vandevere (synonym of Newtown Spitzenburg)	225	
Vandevere, English	312	
Vandevere of New York	225	
VANDEVERE PIPPIN		231
Vandevere Yellow		231
Van Duym's Pippin		62
Van Dyne	244	
Van Dyne	244	
Van Dyne Apple		77
Van Dyn's Pippin		62
VANHOY	351	
Van Hoy	351	
Van Hoy No Core	351	
Van Kleek's Sweet		100
Van Vleet	161	
VAN WYCK (Crab)		267
Van Wyck (synonym of Brier)		251
Van Wyck Siberian		268
Van Wyck Sweet		268
Vargul		6
Varick	105	
Vermillon d'Ete		178
Vermont		30
Vermont Pippin		223
Vermont Pumpkin Sweet		172
Vermont Sweet		172
Verte de l'Ile de Rhodes	283	
Verte de Rhode Island	283	
Vickers	186	
Victoire, La.	188	
VICTORIA	24	231
Victoria Pippin	69	
Victoria Red	69	
Victoria Sweet		231
Victoria Sweeting		231
VICTUALS AND DRINK		233
Vilikui Mogul		87

	VOL. I. PAGE.	VOL. II. PAGE.
Vineuse Rouge		233
Vinnoe Krasnoe Oseinee		182
Vinograd		244
Virginia Greening	352	
Virginia June		142
Virginia Pippin (synonym of Newtown Pippin)	146	
Virginia Pippin (synonym of Virginia Greening)	352	
Virginia Sweet		177
Voronesh No. 21		247
Wabash	353	
Wabash Bellflower (synonym of Long Red Pearmain)		125
Wabash Bellflower (synonym of Wabash)	353	
Wabash Red	353	
Wabash Red Winter	353	
Wagener	21, 24, 354	
Wahr Reinette	94	
Walb	227	
Walbridge	356	
Walker	358	
Walker Beauty	358	
Walker's Winter	358	
Walker Yellow	358	
Wall	227	
Wallace Howard	359	
Wallbridge	357	
Walter Pease		161
Waltz Apple	253	
Walworth		30
Wander	227	
Wandering Spy	360	
Warden's Pie Apple		203
Ward's Pippin		21
Warren Pennock		53
Warren Pippin (synonym of Ortley)	244	
Warren Pippin (synonym of Yellow Bellflower)	381	
Washington (synonym of Sops of Wine)		203
Washington (synonym of Washington Strawberry)		234
Washington (synonym of Sweet Bough)		217
Washington County Seedling		234
Washington of Maine		234
Washington Royal	361	
Washington Strawberry		234
Water		236
Waterloo		178
Watermelon	204	
Watkins Early		211
Watson's Vandervere		231
Watson's Vandevere		231

	VOL. I. PAGE.	VOL. II. PAGE.
Watts Apple	253	
Watwood	362	
Waxen	67	
Waxen Apple	67	
Wealthy 17, 19,	25	236
Wealthy Group	25	
Weinapfel Rother		182
Weinappel Rother		182
Weiser Hawthornden		96
Weisser Metzgerapfel	381	
Well Apple (synonym of Domine)	109	
Well Apple (synonym of Titus Pippin)	339	
Wellington	112	
Wellington's Reinette	112	
Wells	363	
Wells (synonym of Domine)	109	
Wells (synonym of Ohio Nonpareil)		148
Wells Apple	363	
Wesse Antillische Winterreinette	94	
Westbrook		60
Westchester Seek-No-Further	130	
Western Baldwin (synonym of Babbitt)	53	
Western Baldwin (synonym of Pawpaw)	250	
Western Beauty		239
Western Beauty (synonym of Hyde King)	166	
Western Beauty (synonym of Grosh)		89
Western Beauty (synonym of Ohio Nonpareil)		148
Westfield	364	
Westfield Seek-No-Farther	364	
Westfield Seek-No-Further 12, 16, 17, 18, 32,	364	
Westfield *Seek-No-Further; Red type*	366	
Wheelers Kernel		96
White	67	
White Apple (synonym of Hawthornden)		96
White Apple (synonym of Parry White)		157
White Astracan		239
White Astrachan	25	239
White Bellefleur	244	
White Bellflower	244	
White Borodovka		15
White Crow	197	
White Detroit	244	
White Graft of Wisconsin		60
White Hawthorndean		96
White Hawthornden		96
White June		118
White Juneating		240
White Newell		60

	VOL. I. PAGE.	VOL. II. PAGE.
WHITE PEARMAIN	367	
WHITE PIPPIN	24, 368	
White Pippin (synonym of Canada Reinette)	94	
White Pippin (synonym of Ortley·)	244	
White Robinson	380	
WHITE SEEK-NO-FURTHER	15	
White Seek-No-Further (synonym of Green Seek-No-Further)		88
WHITE SPANISH REINETTE		241
White Spice		49
White Winter Pearmain	367	
White Zurdel	387	
WHITNEY (Crab)		268
Whitney No. 20		268
Wilcox's Winter	302	
Wild Apple	384	
WILLIAMS		242
Williams Early		242
Williams Early Red		242
Williams Favorite		242
Williams Favorite Red		242
Williamson	109	
Williams Red		242
WILLIS SWEET		244
Willis Sweeting		244
WILLOW	18, 370	
Willow Leaf	370	
Willow Leaf Pippin	244	
Willow Twig	370	
WILLSBORO	372	
Wilsons June		181
Windower		231
WINDSOR	372	
Windsor Chief	372	
WINE	15, 373	
Wine (synonym of Jonathan)	172	
Wine (synonym of Newtown Spitzenburg)	225	
Wine (synonym of Egg Top)		56
Wine (synonym of Fall Wine)		64
Wine (synonym of Richard Graft)		186
Wine (synonym of Twenty Ounce)		227
Wine Apple	373	
Wine of Cole		64
WINE RUSSETS		244
WINESAP	17, 24, 374	
WINESAP GROUP	24	
Winesap (synonym of Jonathan)	172	
Winesap (synonym of Roseau)	292	

VOL. II — 28

	VOL. I. PAGE.	VOL. II. PAGE.
Wine Sop	375	
Wine Sweet	380	
WINTER BANANA	377	
Winter Belle Bonne	67	
Winter Blush (synonym of Fallawater)	125	
Winter Blush (synonym of Rock Pippin of Eastern New York)	288	
Winter Chandler		31
Winter Genneting	271	
Winter Golden Sweet		13
WINTER HOG ISLAND SWEET	378	
Winter Horse	227	
Winter Jonnetting	271	
Winter King	345	
Winter Nonsuch	276	
Winter Peach	251	
WINTER PEARMAIN	378	
Winter Pearmain (synonym of McAfee)	197	
Winter Pearmain (synonym of Milam)	208	
Winter Pearmain (synonym of Long Island Pearmain)		124
Winter Pearmain (synonym of Long Red Pearmain)		125
Winter Pippin	197	
Winter Pippin of Geneva	136	
Winter Queen	88	
Winter Queening	88	
Winter Rose	227	
Winter Russet (synonym of English Russet)	118	
Winter Russet (synonym of Perry Russet)	257	
WINTER ST. LAWRENCE	379	
Winter Seek-No-Further		88
Winter Sweet Paradise	380	
Winter Wine	373	
WINTHROP GREENING		245
WISMER	380	
Wismer's Dessert	380	
Wisner's Dessert	380	
WOLF RIVER	20, 25	245
Wolf River (synonym of Alexander)		3
Wolman's Harvest		215
Wonder	227	
Woodman's Song	244	
Woodpecker	56	
Woodstock (synonym of Blenheim)		21
Woodstock (synonym of Dyer)		49
Woodstock Pippin		21
Woodward's Pippin	244	
Woolman's Early		215
Woolman's Harvest		215

	VOL. I. PAGE.	VOL. II. PAGE.
Woolman's Long	244	
Woolman's Long Pippin	244	
Woolman's Striped Harvest		215
Woolnary Long	244	
Woolverton		127
WORKAROE		246
World's Wonder	227	
Wunderapfel		3
Wyandotte	196	
Yankee Apple		172
Yeats	316	
Yellow Bellefleur	381	
Yellow Belleflower	381	
YELLOW BELLFLOWER	15, 16, 17, 18, 19, 23, 381	
YELLOW BELLFLOWER GROUP	383	
Yellow Bough		217
YELLOW CALVILLE		247
Yellow Flat		118
YELLOW FOREST	384	
Yellow German Reinette	142	
YELLOW HARVEST	12	
Yellow Harvest (synonym of Early Harvest)		51
Yellow Janett	271	
Yellow June (synonym of White Juneating)		240
Yellow June (synonym of Kirkbridge)		118
Yellow Juneating		51
Yellow May		240
Yellow Newton's Pippin	146	
YELLOW NEWTOWN	17, 18, 24, 145, 150, 385	
Yellow Newtown (synonym of Canada Reinette)	94	
Yellow Newtown Pippin	146	
Yellow Pippin (synonym of Newark Pippin)	223	
Yellow Pippin (synonym of Ortley)	244	
YELLOW SIBERIAN (Crab)		269
Yellow Summer Pearmain		166
Yellow Sweeting		81
YELLOW TRANSPARENT	17, 25	247
Yellow Transparent (synonym of Thaler)		222
Yellow Vandervere		231
YOPP	18	249
Yopp's Favorite (Synonym of Yopp)		249
Yopp's Favorite (synonym of Yellow Newtown)	146	
YORK		249
York and Lancaster		193
YORK IMPERIAL	18, 19, 32, 385	
YORK PIPPIN	24	
York Pippin (synonym of Fall Pippin)		62
York Pippin (synonym of Golden Pippin I)		78

	VOL. I. PAGE.	VOL. II. PAGE.
York Pippin (synonym of White Spanish Reinette)		241
York Russet (synonym of Cheeseboro)		33
York Russet (synonym of Pumpkin Russet)		170
York Russeting		33
Zarskischip		45
Zarski Schip		45
Zarski Zars		45
Zeeke	197	
Zolotoi Renet		79
Zour Bough		168
ZURDEL	387	
Zuzoff of Tuttle		5

CPSIA information can be obtained at www.ICGtesting.com
Printed in the USA
BVOW07*2325141214

379393BV00003B/36/P